D0084937

The New Simonides

The New Simonides

Contexts of Praise and Desire

EDITED BY

DEBORAH BOEDEKER

AND

DAVID SIDER

UNIVERSITY PRESS

2001

OXFORD
UNIVERSITY PRESS

Oxford   New York
Athens   Auckland   Bangkok   Bogotá   Buenos Aires   Cape Town
Chennai   Dar es Salaam   Delhi   Florence   Hong Kong   Istanbul   Karachi
Kolkata   Kuala Lumpur   Madrid   Melbourne   Mexico City   Mumbai   Nairobi
Paris   São Paulo   Shanghai   Singapore   Taipei   Tokyo   Toronto   Warsaw

and associated companies in
Berlin   Ibadan

Published by Oxford University Press, Inc.
198 Madison Avenue, New York, New York 10016

Oxford is a registered trademark of Oxford University Press

Library of Congress Cataloging-in-Publication Data
The new Simonides: contexts of praise and desire /
edited by Deborah Boedeker and David Sider
     p.   cm.
Includes bibliographical references and index.
ISBN 0-19-513767-1
1. Simonides, ca. 556–467 B.C.—Criticism and interpretation.
2. Simonides, ca. 556–467 B.C.—Manuscripts.   3. Manuscripts,
Greek (Papyri).   4. Praise in literature.   5. Desire in literature.
I. Boedeker, Deborah Dickmann.   II. Sider, David.
PA4411 .N49   2000
884'.01—dc21   00-022462

9 8 7 6 5 4 3 2 1

Printed in the United States of America
on acid-free paper

Contents

Contributors   vii

Abbreviations   xi

Part I

Introduction   3
   DEBORAH BOEDEKER AND DAVID SIDER

Photographs of POxy 2327 and 3965   7

Fragments 1–22 W²: Text, Apparatus Criticus, and Translation   13
   DAVID SIDER

Part II

1. *The New Simonides: Toward a Commentary*   33
   IAN RUTHERFORD

2. *"These Fragments We Have Shored against Our Ruin"*   55
   PETER PARSONS

3. *The Genre of* Plataea: *Generic Unity in the New Simonides*   65
   DIRK OBBINK

4. *The Proem of Simonides' Plataea Elegy and the Circumstances
   of Its Performance*   86
   ANTONIO ALONI

5. *A Bard of the Iron Age and His Auxiliary Muse*   106
   EVA STEHLE

6. *Heroic Historiography: Simonides and Herodotus on Plataea*   120
   DEBORAH BOEDEKER

7. *Epic and Epiphanies: Herodotus and the "New Simonides"*   135
   SIMON HORNBLOWER

8. *Paths to Heroization at Plataea*   148
    DEBORAH BOEDEKER

9. *Lords of Hellas, Old Men of the Sea: The Occasion of Simonides'*
    Elegy on Plataea   164
    P.-J. SHAW

10. *The New Simonides and Homer's* Hemitheoi   182
    JENNY STRAUSS CLAY

11. *Utopian and Erotic Fusion in a New Elegy by Simonides*   185
    SARAH MACE

12. *To Sing or to Mourn? A Reappraisal of Simonides 22 W²*   208
    DIMITRIOS YATROMANOLAKIS

13. *"New Simonides" or Old Semonides? Second Thoughts*
    on POxy 3965 fr. 26   226
    THOMAS K. HUBBARD

14. *Heroes, Descendants of* Hemitheoi: *The Proemium of Theocritus 17*
    and Simonides 11 W²   232
    MARCO FANTUZZI

15. *The Poet Unleaved: Simonides and Callimachus*   242
    RICHARD HUNTER

16. *Simonides and Horace on the Death of Achilles*   255
    ALESSANDRO BARCHIESI

17. *Simonides and Horace*   261
    STEPHEN HARRISON

18. *"As Is the Generation of Leaves" in Homer, Simonides, Horace,*
    and Stobaeus   272
    DAVID SIDER

Bibliography   289
Index Locorum   307
General Index   310

Contributors

Antonio Aloni is professor of Greek literature at the University of Torino (Italy). His main interests are archaic poetry, both epic and lyric. At present, he is studying the interaction between performance and writing in sixth- and fifth-century Athens. His recent publications include a text, translation, and commentary on Sappho (1997) and *Cantare glorie di eroi* (1997).

Alessandro Barchiesi works especially on Roman poetry of the classical age, with a specific interest in Greek influence on Latin literature and in the dialogue between Classics and literary theory. He has published books on Vergil (*La traccia del modello*, 1984) and Ovid (*The Poet and the Prince*, 1997), and papers on Horace and other Roman authors. He is professor of Latin literature at Stanford University and the University of Verona.

Deborah Boedeker is professor of Classics at Brown University. She writes on archaic poetry, tragedy, and historiography, and has edited or co-edited volumes on *Herodotus and the Invention of History* (1987), *The New Simonides* (1996), and *Democracy, Empire, and the Arts in Fifth-Century Athens* (1998). From 1992 to 2000 she was co-Director of the Center for Hellenic Studies.

Jenny Strauss Clay is professor of Classics at the University of Virginia. She is the author of *The Wrath of Athena* (1983) and *The Politics of Olympus* (1989) as well as numerous articles on Greek and Latin poetry. She is currently completing a book entitled *Hesiod's Cosmos*.

Marco Fantuzzi teaches ancient Greek literature at the University of Florence. He has a special interest in Hellenistic poetry. His publications include a commentary on Bion of Smyrna, *Adonidis epitaphium* (1985), and *Ricerche su Apollonio Rodio: diacronie della dizione epica* (1988). A book on Hellenistic poetry, written jointly with R. Hunter, is forthcoming.

STEPHEN HARRISON is Reader in Classical Languages and Literature at Corpus Christi College, Oxford. He is author of a commentary on Vergil, *Aeneid* 10 (1991) and of *Apuleius: A Latin Sophist* (2000), and editor of multi-authored volumes on the *Aeneid* (1990), Horace (1995), and the Roman novel (1999). His current research includes projects on poetic genre in Augustan poetry and on cooperation between traditional scholarship and literary theory.

SIMON HORNBLOWER is professor of Classics and Ancient History at University College London. He edited and contributed to *Greek Historiography* (1994), and co-edited the third edition of the *Oxford Classical Dictionary*. At present he is working on the third and final volume of a commentary on Thucydides.

THOMAS K. HUBBARD is professor of Classics at the University of Texas, Austin. His books include *The Pindaric Mind* (1985), *The Mask of Comedy* (1991), and *The Pipes of Pan: Intertextuality and Literary Filiation in the Pastoral Tradition from Theocritus to Milton* (1998). He is currently assembling a sourcebook on homosexuality in the ancient world.

RICHARD HUNTER is Regius Professor elect of Greek and Latin literature at the University of Cambridge and a fellow of Pembroke College. His principal research interests are post-classical Greek literature and the Roman reception of Greek culture. His books include studies and editions of Apollonius of Rhodes, Longus, and Theocritus.

SARAH MACE is assistant professor of Classics at Union College and author of articles on Greek lyric and the *Oresteia*. She is currently working on *Epic Nights: Form, Function and Significance of Night Scenes in Homer and Virgil*.

DIRK OBBINK is University Lecturer in Papyrology and Greek Literature, and Student and Tutor in Greek at Christ Church, Oxford. He has published widely in papyrology, as well as in Greek religion and philosophy. Among his books are *Magika Hiera: Ancient Greek Magic and Religion* (co-edited and co-authored, 1991), and *Philodemus on Piety: Critical Text with Commentary* (1996).

PETER PARSONS is Regius Professor of Greek at Oxford University. His research focuses on unpublished papyri of Greek literature, and he is a frequent contributor to the series *Oxyrhynchus Papyri*, in which he produced the *editio princeps* of the 'new Simonides' fragments (1992). He is the author, with Hugh Lloyd-Jones, of *Supplementum Hellenisticum* (1983).

IAN RUTHERFORD teaches at the University of Reading where he is Professor and Head of the Department of Classics. His academic interests include Greek lyric poetry, papyrology, pilgrimage in the ancient world, the demotic literature of Greek and Roman Egypt, and ancient Anatolia. He has recently completed a book on the paean.

P.-J. SHAW read archaeology and anthropology at Cambridge and taught Classical studies at Monmouth School for Girls. Her publications include a reconstruction of Pheidippides' route to Sparta, and a reappraisal of Olympiad chronography and "early" Peloponnesian history, the subject of her recently completed doctoral thesis at Cardiff.

DAVID SIDER, whose scholarly interests lie mainly in Greek poetry and philosophy, is professor of Classics at Fordham University. Publications include *The Fragments of Anaxagoras* (1981), *The New Simonides* (co-edited and co-authored, 1996), and *The Epigrams of Philodemos* (1997). He is currently working on an edition with commentary of Pseudo-Theophrastus, *On Weather Signs*.

EVA STEHLE teaches Classics at the University of Maryland, College Park. Her research interests have focussed on Greek lyric poetry and gender studies. Recent publications include *Performance and Gender in Ancient Greece: Nondramatic Poetry in Its Setting* (1997) and an essay on Erinna. She is currently working on Athenian religion and performance.

DIMITRIOS YATROMANOLAKIS is a Junior Fellow at Harvard University's Society of Fellows. He has published articles on archaic Greek poetry and Greek vase paintings, and has completed a book on *Sappho in the Making*. Currently he is working on a new book on the institution of musical contests in the archaic, classical, and Hellenistic periods.

Abbreviations

AP	*Anthologia Palatina*
C	D. A. Campbell, ed. *Greek Lyric.* Vol 3. Cambridge, Mass., 1991.
CAH²	*Cambridge Ancient History*, 2d ed.
CEG	P. A. Hansen, ed. *Carmina Epigraphica Graeca.* 2 vols. Berlin 1983, 1989.
CIA	*Corpus Inscriptionum Atticarum*
CIG	A. Boeckh, ed. *Corpus Inscriptionum Graecarum.* Berlin 1828–77.
DK	H. Diels and W. Kranz, eds. *Die Fragmente der Vorsokratiker.* 3 vols. Berlin 1951–52 (6th ed.).
FGE	D. L. Page, ed. *Further Greek Epigrams.* Cambridge 1981.
FGrH	F. A. Jacoby, ed. *Die Fragmente der griechischen Historiker.* Many vols. Berlin, then Leiden, 1923–.
HE	A. S. F. Gow and D. L. Page, eds. *The Greek Anthology: Hellenistic Epigrams.* 2 vols. Cambridge 1965.
IEG	*see* W
IG	*Inscriptiones Graecae*
KA	R. Kassel and C. Austin, eds. *Poetae Comici Graeci.* Berlin 1983–.
LfgrE	*Lexikon des frühgriechischen Epos.* Göttingen 1955–.
LP	E. Lobel and D. L. Page, eds. *Poetarum Lesbiorum Fragmenta.* Oxford 1955.
LGPN	P. M. Fraser and E. Matthews, eds., *A Lexicon of Greek Personal Names.* Oxford 1987–.
LSJ	H. G. Liddell, R. Scott, and H. S. Jones. *A Greek-English Lexicon⁹.* Oxford 1940.
ML	R. Meiggs and D. Lewis, eds. *A Selection of Greek Historical Inscriptions to the End of the Fifth Century* B.C. Oxford 1969.
OGIS	W. Dittenberger, ed. *Orientis Graeci Inscriptiones Selectae.* 2 vols. Leipzig 1903, 1905.
OLD	P. G. W. Glare, ed. *Oxford Latin Dictionary.* Oxford 1982.

PEG   A. Bernabé, ed. *Poetae Epici Graeci Testimonia et Fragmenta*, Pt. I. Leipzig 1987.

PMG   D. L. Page, ed. *Poetae Melici Graeci*. Oxford 1962.

PMGF   M. Davies, ed. *Poetarum Melicorum Graecorum Fragmenta*. Vol. 1. Oxford 1991.

PW   H. W. Parke and D. E. W. Wormell, *The Delphic Oracle*. Vol. 2, *The Oracular Responses*. Oxford 1956.

RE   Pauly-Wissowa, eds. 1893–1980. *Real-Encyclopädie der klassischen Altertumswissenschaft*. Stuttgart.

SEG   *Supplementum Epigraphicum Graecum*.

SH   H. Lloyd-Jones and P. Parsons, eds. *Supplementum Hellenisticum*. Berlin 1983.

SIG   W. Dittenberger, ed. *Sylloge Inscriptionum Graecarum*³. 4 vols. Leipzig 1915–24.

SLG   D. L. Page, ed. *Supplementum Lyricis Graecis*. Oxford 1974.

TLL   *Thesaurus Linguae Latinae*. 1900–.

TrGF   B. Snell, R. Kannicht, and S. Radt, eds. *Tragicorum Graecorum Fragmenta*. Vols. 1– . Göttingen 1971– .

W   M. L. West, ed. *Iambi et Elegi Graeci ante Alexandrum Cantati*, 2 vols. Oxford 1971, 1972 (1st ed.) and 1991, 1992 (2d ed.). [= *IEG*]

W¹   M. L. West, ed. *Iambi et Elegi Graeci ante Alexandrum Cantati*. 2 vols. Oxford 1971, 1972.

W²   M. L. West, ed. *Iambi et Elegi Graeci ante Alexandrum Cantati*, 2d ed. 2 vols. Oxford 1991, 1992.

PART I

DEBORAH BOEDEKER AND DAVID SIDER

Introduction

The publication in 1992 of *POxy* 3965, edited by P. J. Parsons, gave to the world of classical scholarship a significant fragment of something it had had only an inkling of before: a long elegiac poem dealing with an important recent event. Although the papyrus did not expressly identify the author, two passages overlapped with literary quotations credited to Simonides by Plutarch and Stobaeus.[1] Since, moreover, the new papyrus also overlapped in two places with *POxy* 2327, hitherto anonymous (although its perspicacious editor Edgar Lobel raised the possibility of Simonidean authorship),[2] this earlier papyrus could now be added to the corpus of new Simonidean elegy; the two papyri were brought together for the first time under Simonides' name in the second edition of Martin West's *Iambi et Elegi Graeci*, vol. 2, which was published soon after Parsons' *editio princeps* of 3965.[3]

Where four and a half pages sufficed for Simonides in West's first edition, this poet now occupies more than twenty-four pages, and West's original seventeen fragments are now ninety-two (many admittedly quite scrappy). Both *POxy* 2327 and 3965 would seem to be copies of an Alexandrian book which contained all or some part of Simonides' elegiac poetry (Parsons 1992a: 5). At first glance this original book appears to contain more than one poem (but see Obbink and Sider in this volume) on topics both military and erotic, which would seem to suggest that all of Simonides' elegies could be contained in one book. See Rutherford in this volume for further discussion of the papyri.

---

1. On the latter passage (Simon. fr. 20 W[2]), doubt had often been expressed earlier as to whether Stobaeus was quoting from Simonides of Ceos or Semonides of Amorgos; see in this volume Hubbard (who marshals the arguments for Semonides) and Sider (who believes that the papyrus established Simonides as the author).

2. Lobel 1954: 67. Later, Lobel 1981: 23 alerted the public to the existence of another papyrus (the then unnumbered 3965) which established Simonides as the author of 2327.

3. West had printed *POxy* 2327 as Adespota Elegiaca 28–60 in *IEG* 2[1], but by and large, with the notable exceptions of Barigazzi 1963 and Podlecki 1968, it was neglected. On the relationship between *POxy* vol. 59 and *IEG* 2[2], see Parsons, this volume.

What can we say about the contents of the New Simonides, as the union of the two Oxyrhynchus papyri has come to be known? It is easy to see from West's text (largely reprinted in this volume) that much of it describes one or more (probably recently fought) historical battles, a topic of elegiac poetry for which we had some secondhand evidence and to which we could assign a few literary fragments, but of which we did not possess many continuous lines. We could not, therefore, form a picture of the overall structure of such a poem. The historical subject matter which so piques our interest now would have been omitted by later excerptors such as Stobaeus, who plucked for their anthologies only passages of a more general nature.

Now, however, we have substantial portions of a battle narrative with a hymnlike proem (if not to the poem as a whole, at least to an important segment) making mention of Homer, his heroes, and his Muses—all suggesting that just as the Greek warriors of the fifth century are comparable to those of the Trojan War, so too is the contemporary poet Simonides to be likened to Homer. That the death of Achilles described here was not in fact in Homer does not weaken this simile, nor is it without its own significance; see Barchiesi, Shaw, and Boedeker ("Heroization") below.

Simonides was known to have dealt with current and recent events in inscriptional epigrams and in longer poems. Literary testimonia, not without some confusion, credit him with both elegy and lyrics on Artemisium, with lyrics on Salamis and Thermopylae, and with an elegy on Plataea. To these perhaps we can add an elegy on the battle of Marathon which was chosen in a public competition over entries by others, including Aeschylus.[4]

Some of the new fragments clearly belong, if only on the basis of subject matter, to this group. As the proem shows, however, and as we should not be surprised to discover of a Greek poem, the Plataea poem goes beyond mere reporting of events. What little we knew previously of elegy suggests that individual poems of a political nature could range widely from mythical origins and wars down to current matters before the state, and then, with the past as template, look ahead to the immediate future.[5] A rapid and partial survey of elegies by Aeschylus (?), Callinus, Mimnermus, Panyassis, Semonides, Solon, Tyrtaeus, and Xenophanes suggests several possible parallels to the new Simonides. Tyrtaeus 2 and 4, for example, to say nothing of most if not all "*ktisis*

---

4. The chief doubt here lies in the use of the word ἐλεγεῖον, which in the singular usually refers either to a single distich or to its pentameter line, but there are some few passages that apply the term to two or three distichs (two: Diod. Sic. 10.24.3, 11.14.4; *V.Hom.* 2.77, etc.; three: Constantine Porphyr. *De sent.* 13). There are, moreover, three extracts where the passage quoted as an ἐλεγεῖον seems to refer to a longer narrative elegy: Athenaeus 699c quoting 10 vv. of Alex. Aetol. fr. 5 Powell; Dion. Hal. 1.49.2 quoting two distichs of Agathyllus Arcas fr. 15 SH; Ion of Samos 1 D = *CEG* 2.189.9–13. (LSJ are mistaken to include Diod. Sic. 11.14 and Plut. *Them.* 8; West 1974: 4 would count Strabo 14.6.3 and Paus. 7.18.1. But these four passages all seem to quote, in full or in part, short—in some cases inscriptional—epigrams.) Since, moreover, Aeschylus is credited with the composition of elegies (Suda at 357 Adler = T 2 *TrGF*), one of which seems to have been on Marathon (T 12 and [?]13), there may indeed have been a contest for the best elegy; so Scheidewin 1835 (fr. 58), Barigazzi 1963: 61f., Cameron 1995: 331; cf. Molyneux 1992: 151f.

5. Bowie 1986: 28f. is particularly acute in pointing out the evidence that some elegies must have dealt with both the distant and the recent past. Bowie's important article will be cited many times in this volume for the ways its arguments on the nature of historical elegy are borne out or refined by the evidence of the new Simonides.

poetry" on the foundations of cities, have the gods play a major initiating role. In his *Ionika*, Panyassis begins his historical account with the Ionian migrations and Codrus and Neleus. Mimnermus, too, links present and past.[6] Solon clearly uses the recent past to urge his fellow Athenians to act as he thinks best. Did Simonides' poem, very likely composed soon after Plataea, also contain advice on how Greeks might best prepare for the return of the Persians? And Callinus intriguingly, though in what context we cannot tell, not only wrote of the early (mythical) battle for Thebes but found occasion to allude to Homer as the author of the *Thebaid* (Paus. 9.9.3 = Call. fr. 6 W). Is this too a parallel to Simonides?

We are far from claiming that every historical-political elegy of each of these poets contained every element we have mentioned. We merely wish to keep open the question of the nature of these longer poems before we assign to them, and to Simonides' poem in particular, what may turn out to be overly rigid genre categories, especially since we do not know which of the new fragments can be surely excluded from the poem that contained the battle narrative. Few scholars, for example, are willing to include fr. 21 W^2, with its obviously erotic thighs, but the death of Patroclus[7] in battle allowed Aeschylus in the *Myrmidons* to mention σέβας δὲ μηρῶν ἁγνόν.

Nor are we all in agreement as to the circumstances of the poem's first performance, which must surely have shaped Simonides' telling of the story of Plataea. For various possibilities, see Aloni, Boedeker "Heroization," Shaw, and Yatromanolakis. And for all the similarities with his predecessors (and successors) noted above, the particular hymnic elements (see Obbink) came as a surprise. Are they part of the literary trimmings and so to be interpreted along purely formal lines? Or do they suggest the heroization of the recent dead just as the Greek heroes were regarded as heroes (see Boedeker, "Heroization," Clay, and Shaw)?

It was long known that Simonides frequently, explicitly, and usually critically alluded to his predecessors, but the elaborate comparison between himself and Homer (all the more elaborate if frr. 19–20 are part of the Plataea poem: see Sider) is something new (see Stehle on how Simonides both likens himself to and distinguishes himself from Homer). What comes as even more of a surprise is how many echoes of this one poem had long lain hidden in later literature: not only Herodotus (see Boedeker, "Historiography," and Hornblower) but also, in the allusive manner now the object of much study, the poets Pindar (Mace; cf. Barchiesi 1996), Aeschylus (Rutherford), Callimachus (Hunter), Theocritus (Fantuzzi and Hunter), and Horace (Barchiesi, Harrison, and Sider).

The papers collected in this volume have a varied history. Several chapters were first presented at a panel on "The New Simonides" presented in Atlanta, Georgia, at the 1994 meeting of the American Philological Association (Boedeker, Obbink, Sider,

---

6. μνησθεὶς τῆς Σμύρνης ὅτι περιμάχητος ἀεί, Strabo 14.1.4, introducing fr. 9 W; cf. frr. 10, 13, 13a, 14.

7. Or is it Achilles? Cf. Snell *ad* Aesch. fr. 135 *TrGF*. Since Plutarch *Amat.* 751b quotes both Aeschylus and Solon fr. 25 W (μηρῶν ἱμείρων) in the same context, it is just barely possible that the latter, too, appeared in a military context where the loss of a companion was portrayed in erotic terms. (Plutarch's comments here and at 751e = fr. 26 suggest that he was ignorant of the lines' original context.)

Stehle, with Rutherford as commentator). When it was decided to present these papers in printed form, Rutherford contributed a commentary; Barchiesi allowed us to publish his paper, originally printed in Italian in *ZPE;* and both Clay and Hubbard contributed original articles—all of which appeared as a special issue of *Arethusa,* edited by Boedeker and Sider. When another panel on the new material was presented in Oxford in November 1997, it became clear that Simonides' new text continues to fascinate students of fifth-century history, cult practices, performance theory, and literary history and intertextuality. Joining the Oxford panel (Parsons, Harrison, Hornblower, Hunter; E. Bowie had already committed his paper for publication elsewhere) to the first panel, the editors were fortunate to obtain permission to reprint, with revisions, some articles that appeared after the publication of the *Arethusa* volume (Aloni, Fantuzzi [originally in Italian], Mace, Yatromanolakis) as well as the unpublished paper of Shaw. To a greater or lesser extent, all the *Arethusa* papers have been revised for publication here.

In addition to all our contributors, we would like to thank research assistants Suzanne Abrams, Carol King, Heath Martin, and Malcolm Hyman, who helped us at various stages of the editing process. We also thank the Johns Hopkins University Press for permission to reprint the revised contents of the *Arethusa* issue, as well as the chapter by Aloni. The Egypt Exploration Society has granted permission to publish photographs of the papyri, the editors of *Zeitschrift für Papylorogie und Epigraphik* have allowed us to reprint articles by Mace and Yatromanolakis, and the University Press of Wales has granted permission to publish material in Boedeker's "Heroization" essay. Finally, it is a pleasure to acknowledge gratefully the superb contributions of our skilled and tactful copyeditor, Angela Blackburn.

Photographs of *POxy* 2327 and 3965

The papyrus fragments are identified by both *POxy* fragment numbers (here a bare number) and W(est²) numbers. The photographs are published here with the kind permission of the Egypt Exploration Society, London.

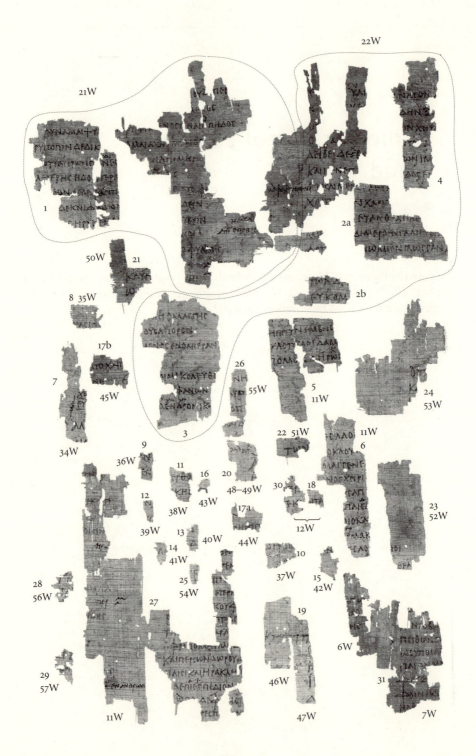

POxy 2327

POxy 3965 frr. 1–11

POxy 3965 frr. 12–25

POxy 3965 frr. 26–47

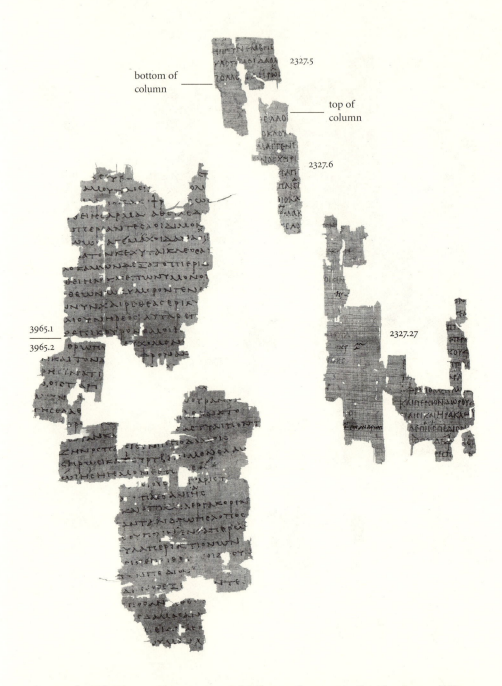

bottom of column — 2327.5

top of column — 2327.6

3965.1
3965.2

2327.27

Frr. 11 and 13 W². *POxy* 2327 frr. 5 + 6 + 27 and *POxy* 3965 frr. 1 + 2 are placed as they would have been when their respective papyri were whole. The two papyri are also aligned with each other along their overlapping lines (to the extent possible). The overlap occurs at fr. 11.9–13 (using West's text for easy reference): υσαπ. | υ παισί | οιο κακ | τες ἀοί. Note that fr. 5, which ends one column, has been placed by West to precede fr. 6, which begins another column; and that there is no overlap of letters between 2327.27 and 3965.

Fragments 1–22 W²

Text, Apparatus Criticus, and Translation

Sigla: B = Burzacchini, C-C = Capra & Curti, L = Luppe, Lo = Lobel, P = Parsons, Pa = Pavese, W = West, Y = Yatromanolakis

1 = 635 PMG Schol. ad Apollonium Rhodium 1.583–4a, «εἰναλίη Σκίαθος»

ἡ παραθαλασσία. νῆσος γὰρ ἡ Σκίαθος ἐγγὺς Εὐβοίας, ἧς καὶ Σιμωνίδης μέμνηται.

"The (island) alongside the [sc. shore of the] sea. For Skiathos is an island near Euboia which Simonides mentions."

---

2 *POxy* 3965 fr. 13

]καυχ. .[

]εμαχ[

].οτεσ[

]βίας α[

]μεγαλαφ[5

]εχει.[

]. .[ ].[

3]. : κ, χ, π, σ   **4** εὐρυ]βίας ἁ[νέμους e.g. W   **5** φ[ρονέοντες e.g. W   **6** χειμ[ερι- e.g. W

(with West's suggestions) "vaunt . . . battled . . . [winds of wide] force . . . [thinking] great [thoughts] . . . [stormy] . . ."

13

3 Ibid. fr. 20

                              ]ρ[

                   ]νεριων[

                      ]ν· ἀνδρ.[

          ἀθανάτων] ἰότητι· τ[

             Ζήτην καὶ] Κάλαϊ[ν   5

                   ]σὲλθε[ ]χ[

                   ]ι ἐξ ἐρέβεος κ[

                   ]ε δῶρο[ν

                   ]εων δ[

             ]αφοισι θ[10

             ]ιητ' ἠΰ[κόμοιο] κόρ[ης

          θάλ]ασσαν ὐ[πὸ] τ[ρ]υγός· α[

                ἀγ]λαόφημον ἁλός [

             ]ων· τίνα δ.[.].λωπ[

                      ]ωτεχ[   ]ενον[15

                      ] . . [

3 "fort. ανδρ.[cum sscr. ανδρων," West   5 vel Ζήτης καὶ] Κάλαϊ[ς B   7 ερεβευς sscr. ο
Π   10 ἐλ]άφοισι θ[οοῖς ἴσα e.g. W   12–15 ὤριναν δὲ θάλ]ασσαν ὐ[πὸ] τ[ρ]υγός· ἂν δὲ
γέροντα | ἤγειραν, ταμίην ἀγ]λαόφημον ἁλός. | [εἶπε δὲ θεσπίζ]ων· τίνα δὴ [τ]ηλωπ[ὸν
ἀκούω | δοῦπον ἄθ' ὑσμίνης] ὤτε χ[ροΐζόμ]ενον; e.g. W   15 ον sscr. ·ω·

(West's translation, incorporating his suggestions) "by the immortals' will
... Zetes and Kalais ... [They came as swif]t as dee[r, the sons of Boreas and
Oreithyia,] maid with lovely hair. [They stirred the] sea up from its murky
bed, [and roused the Old Man, b]right-famed [guardian] of the deep, [who
spoke in prophecy:] 'What is this distant [din I hear] b[rush]ing my ears, [as
of a battle?']"

Schol. ad Apollonium Rhodium 1.211–15c, «Ζήτης καὶ Κάλαϊς»

τὴν δὲ Ὠρείθυιαν Σιμωνίδης ἀπὸ Βριλησσοῦ φησιν ἀρπαγεῖσαν ἐπὶ τὴν
Σαρπηδονίαν πέτραν τῆς Θράκης ἐνεχθῆναι ... ἡ δὲ Ὠρείθυια Ἐρεχθέως
θυγάτηρ, ἣν ἐξ Ἀττικῆς ἁρπάσας ὁ Βορέας ἤγαγεν εἰς Θράκην, κἀκεῖσε
συνελθὼν ἔτεκε Ζήτην καὶ Κάλαϊν, ὡς Σιμωνίδης ἐν τῇ Ναυμαχίᾳ.

Two scholia to Apollonios Rhodios 1.211–215c ("Zetes and Kalais"): "Simonides says
that Oreithyia was snatched from Mt. Brilessos [in Attika] and taken to the
Sarpedonian rock in Thrace." ... "She was the daughter of [king] Erechtheus whom
Boreas [the north wind] took from Attica to Thrace, where he lay with her and
fathered Zetes and Kalais, as Simonides says in his *Sea-battle*."

4 Ibid. fr. 12 (ex eadem columna)

```
                              ] . [
                              ] . [
                        ]. πανθυμω[ι]σ[
                      ]ξ ἄνθρωπον[
                       ] . [ ]εφορμηθ[              5
                       ]χέρσον διέπω[ν
                         ]. ἔχθεος ασ[
              ] . . α[   ]κον β(.)[ ]ρέ[
              ]..κε[. . . .].νον[   ] . [
                         ]ηα δολ[              10
                           ]ὅρμον ε[
                          ]εινομ[
```

3 -παν (vel πᾶν) θυμῶ[ι] σ- B   **4** "an Θρήιξ ἄνθρωπος (sc. Scyllias, Hdt. 8.8)?" W   **5**
μησ[sscr. ·θ[·] ἐφορμήθ[η W ap. P   ἐφορμηθ[είς vel -θ[έν B   **6** κύματα (vel πόντον) καὶ]
χέρσον e.g. W   **7** ἀθ[ανάτων tent. W   **8** βαρέ[vel B[ο]ρέ[W   **12** ὀρ]εινομ[
(ὀρινομεν-) tent. W

"very courageously(?) . . . man . . . attack(ed?) . . . (over sea and?) dry land
conducting (the battles?) . . . hatred . . . wreath . . ."

Vita Pindari Ambros. i.2.21 Drachmann

ἐπέβαλλε δὲ τοῖς χρόνοις Σιμωνίδη νεώτερος πρεσβυτέρῳ· τῶν γοῦν αὐτῶν
μέμνηνται ἀμφότεροι πράξεων· καὶ γὰρ Σιμωνίδης τὴν ἐν Σαλαμῖνι ναυμαχίαν
γέγραφε, καὶ Πίνδαρος μέμνηται τῆς Κάδμου βασιλείας (fr. 272 Snell-Maehler)

Life of Pindar: "Pindar's lifetime overlapped with that of his elder, Simonides. At any
rate, they both mention the same events; thus, to give but one example, Simonides
has written on the sea-battle at Salamis, and Pindar mentions the reign of Cadmus"
(the ruler of Cos; cf. Hdt. 7.163f.).

---

5 Plut. *Them.* 15.4

οἱ δὲ ἄλλοι τοῖς βαρβάροις ἐξισούμενοι τὸ πλῆθος ἐν στενῷ κατὰ μέρος προσ-
φερομένους καὶ περιπίπτοντας ἀλλήλοις ἐτρέψαντο, μέχρι δείλης ἀντισχόντας,
ὥσπερ εἴρηκε Σιμωνίδης, τὴν καλὴν ἐκείνην καὶ περιβόητον ἀράμενοι νίκην, ἧς οὔθ'
Ἕλλησιν οὔτε βαρβάροις ἐνάλιον ἔργον εἴργασται λαμπρότερον.

Plutarch, *Life of Themistocles* 15.4: "And as the Persians fought in a narrow arm of the
sea, and could bring but part of their fleet to fight, and fell foul of one another, the
Greeks thus equalled them in strength, and fought with them till the evening forced

them back, and obtained, as says Simonides, that noble and famous victory, than which neither amongst the Greeks nor the barbarians was ever known more glorious exploit on the seas" (tr. Dryden).

---

6 *POxy* 2327 fr. 31 col. i

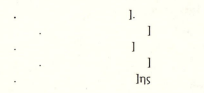

              ].
                  ]
                ]
                  ]
               ]ης   5

marginalia: **1** λ[**2** χ[**3** Ἀ]πίων μα.[**4**]χη.

---

7 Ibid. fr. 31 col. ii

      .]ω. . . [
∩ ποντοβοα[
× πειθωντα[
   ὡς ὑπὸ σάλ[πιγγος
   παισὶν μη[5
   Φρυξί τ[ε
   Φοινίκω[ν
   ἦλθ[

5 Μη[δείων vel Μη[δείης e.g. W (coll. 13.9–10)

"acclaimed on the sea(?) . . . obey . . . as by the trump[et(s)] . . . to/for sons (of Medes?), to Phrygians, and . . . of Phoenicians . . . came . . ."

---

8 = 625 PMG *Et. Gen.* (Miller, *Mélanges* 256; codicis A textus in *IEG* imprimitur); *Et. Magn.*, p. 692.25; Zonaras p. 1581

κυανοπρῴραν

"Πρώ(ε)ιρα (*prora*): Some spell this with an iota (πρῴρα), others with the epsilon-iota diphthong (πρώειρα). . . . It is found separate, with diaeresis, as in Homer's κυανοπρώιρους [cf. *Od.* 3.299 κυανοπρῳείους; so Campbell and Haslam] and in Simonides' κυανοπρώιραν,

blue-prowed."

---

9 Schol. ad Hom. *Il.* 7.76 in *POxy* 1087.22 sqq., «ἐπὶ μάρτυρος ἔστω»

τὸ δὲ μάρτυρος παρώνυμον [τῆι γ]ενικῆ[ι] τοῦ πρωτοτύπου συμ[πέ]πτωκεν, ὡς τὸ Τροίζηνος, ἔνθεν [Τρο]ιζήνοιο (*Il.* 2.847) . . . (39) τὸ λᾶος, ἀφ' οὗ φησι Σιμωνίδης

ξύλα καὶ λάους ἐπιβάλλων.

Scholium to Homer *Iliad* 7.76 ("let a witness be present"): "The word *marturos* [witness in the nominative case] happens to be a paronym of the genitive of the primary form [i.e., it equals the genitive of μάρτυς, the more usual word for *witness*], like *Troizenos* [a nominative whose form equals the genitive of *Troizen*] and its genitive *Troizenoio*. . . . The word *laos* [stone, a nominative = the genitive of the more common word *laas*], from which Simonides says:

hurling logs and stones."

---

10 *POxy* 3965 fr. 22

> .   ]υχν[
> . . . . . . ₍.₎ πατὴ]ρ προπάτω[ρ τε
> . . . . ₍.₎].θωνην σ[
> . . . . μελε]τῶν ὑπὲρ ἡμ[ετέρων
> κούρης εἰν]αλίης ἀγλαόφη[με πάϊ   5
> . . . . ₍.₎]ησι[

"*ex prooemio ad Achillem, cf. fr.* 11" W   **3** Μ]ηθώνην vel -θων ἦν σ[◡◡ e.g. W   **5** ησ sscr. ·α·

"(lamp[s]?) . . . (fathe)r and forefather . . . (Methone?) . . . in behalf of our composition [? = this poem; cf. Emp. B 131.2] . . . (O son of) the sea-(nymph), glorious in your fame . . ."

---

11 *POxy* 2327 fr. 5 + 6 + 27 col. i + 3965 fr. 1 + 2

παι[. .]σ.[
ἢ πίτυν ἐν βήσ[σαις

ὑλοτόμοι τάμ[νωσι
   πολλὸν δ᾽ †ἥρῶσ[
         ]ος λαὸν[5
.   Πατρ[όκλου σα[
.   σ᾽ ἐδ]άμασσεν ἐφ[
ἀλλ᾽ ὑπ᾽ Ἀπόλλ]ωνος χειρὶ [
.   ]σεουσαπ.[. . . . . . .(.)]στ[
— � — Πρ]ιάμου παισὶ χ[. . . .]ομ[10
— ⏑ Ἀλεξά]νδροιο κακόφρ[ονο]ς, ὡς . . . [
   — ⏕ —]. θείης ἄρμα καθεῖλε δίκ[ης.
— ⏕ —]ν πέρσαντες ἀοίδιμον [— ⏑ ἵ]κοντο
   — ⏕ —]ωων ἀγέμαχοι Δαναοί[
οἷσιν ἐπ᾽ ἀθά]νατον κέχυται κλέος ἀν[δρὸς] ἕκητι   15
   ὅς παρ᾽ ἰοπ]λοκάμων δέξατο Πιερίδ[ων
— ⏕ —]θείην καὶ ἐπώνυμον ὁπ[λοτέρ]οισιν
   — ⏕ ἡμ]ιθέων ὠκύμορον γενεή[ν.
ἀλλὰ σὺ μὲ]ν νῦν χαῖρε, θεᾶς ἐρικυ[δέος υἱέ
   κούρης εἰν]αλίου Νηρέος· αὐτὰρ ἐγώ [20
κικλήισκω] σ᾽ ἐπίκουρον ἐμοί, π[⏕ — ⏑]ε Μοῦσα,
   εἴ περ γ᾽ ἀν]θρώπων εὐχομένω[ν μέλεαι·
ἔντυνο]ν καὶ τόνδ[ε μελ]ίφρονα κ[όσμον ἀο]ιδῆς
   ἡμετ]έρης, ἵνα τις [μνή]σεται ὑ[⏑⏑ —
ἀνδρῶ]ν, οἵ Σπάρτ[ηι ⏕ — ⏕ δούλιον ἦμ]αρ   25
.   ] ἄμυν[ ]..[   ]ω[
οὐδ᾽ ἀρε]τῆς ἐλάθ[οντο ⏑ — ⏕]ν οὐρανομ[ήκ]ης
   καὶ κλέος ἀ]νθρώπων [ἔσσετ]αι ἀθάνατο‹ν›.
— ⏕ Εὐ]ρώταν κα[ὶ Σπάρτη]ς ἄστυ λιπόντ[ες
   — ⏕ —] Ζηνὸς παισὶ σὺν ἱπποδάμοις   30
Τυνδαρίδα]ις ἥρωσι καὶ εὐρυβίηι Μενελάω[ι
   — ⏕ πατ]ρώιης ἡγεμόνες π[ό]λεος,
τοὺς δ᾽ υἱὸς θείοιο Κλεο]μβ[ρ]ότου ἐξ[α]γ᾽ ἄριστ[ος
.   ]αγ. Παυσανίας.
— ⏕ — ⏕ —]. καὶ ἐπικλέα ἔργα Κορίν[θ]ου   35
   — ⏕ — ⏕ —] Τανταλίδεω Πέλοπος
   — ⏕ — ⏕ — Ν]ίσου πόλιν, ἔνθα περ ὤ[λλοι
   — ⏕ — ⏕ —] φῦλα περικτιόνων
— ⏕ — ⏕ —]οσσι πεποιθότες, οἱ δὲ συν[
   — ⏕ — ⏕ — ‖ — ⏑]ρατὸν πεδίον   40
— ⏕ — ⏕ — Παν]δίονος ἐξε[λάσα]ντες

— ‿‿ — ‿‿ — Κέκρ]οπος ἀντιθέου[
.   ].ς δαμάσαντ[
.   ].ι εἴδομεν[
.   -ώ]νυμον α.[45

Unattributed restorations are West's. Unidentified quotation marks are used to identify some of West's longer remarks in the app. crit. to *IEG²*. Restorations have been kept to a minimum in the text given above. For West's many suggestions (not all of which are recorded here) as to how the text ran, see the appendix below, pp. 27–29, along with his translation.

"1–9 mors Achillis. 1–4 (2327 fr. 5 ex ima columna) ante 5 sqq. (2327 fr. 6 ex summa columna) locavi" 2 οὔρεος e.g. Lo ἐν βήσ[ησ᾽ ὀρέων Gentili-Prato 3 δαμ[sscr. τ τάμ[νωσι W τάμ[νουσι B fin. e.g. ταναήκεῖ χαλκῷ Danielewicz (coll. Ψ 118 s.) 4 ὦ sscr. η ἡρώησ[(ε) Danielewicz (sc. αἷμα; cf. Α 303) 5 vel]ως ἢ μέγα πένθ]ος λαὸν [ἐπέλλαβε W ἢ μέγα δή ποτ᾽ ἄχ]ος λαὸν [λαβέ Pa 6 "oder Πατρ[όκλους" L fin.: vel σχ[vel σλ[7 οἰστῷ Ἀλεξάν]δροιο tent. Merkelbach 8 "vel δαμεὶς ἔπεσες, sim." δαμεὶς ἔθανες Pa (coll. *CEG* 572,5) 9]σεουσπ, α scripto supra σπ, Παλλὰς δ᾽ ἐγγὺς ἐοῦσα πε[ρικλεὲς ἄ]στ[υ καθεῖλεν W πε[ρικλυτὸν ἄ]στ[υ Pa 10 Τρωσί τε καὶ Πρ]ιάμου C-C "παισι 2327 in textu, 3965: (παι)δ(ι) sscr. 2327" χ[αριζ]ομ[εν- tent. P, χ[αριζ]όμ[ενος] L (sc. Apollo), χ[αλεπτ]όμ[εναι] W 11 init.: εἴκεκ᾽ (approb. W) vel ὕβριν vel θάρσος P αἶψα vel ῥίμφα Pa οἰστῷ Merkelbach ap. C-C ἀλλὰ (vel αὐτάρ) γ᾽ Ἀλεξά]νδροιο L fin.: "fort. ωστε. vel ὡς το" ὡς τ(ε)ί[νοι ὕβριν L 12 init.: ιθείης vel ε]ὐθείης P ἀλλὰ χρόνω]ι θείης W τούτους ε[ὐθείης L τούς μὲν ἄ[ρ᾽ ε]ὐθείης Pa α]ρμα sscr. τερ 2327 (sc. τέρμα), αρμα 3965 "(ἐ)κίχανε malim; puta καθεῖλε ex 9 irrepsisse" 13 οἱ δὲ πόλι]ν P τοὶ δὲ πόλι]ν W καὶ Τροίη]ν L 14 Τρ]ώων vel (φέρτατοι) ἡρ]ώων P ἔ[ξοχοι ἡρ]ώων C-C αγεμάχοι 3965 a.c., αγέμαχοι p.c. 15 init. Lo τοῖσιν δ᾽ ἀθά]νατον L ἀν[δρός] P 17 init. vel γῆρυν ‿— ὁπλοτέρ]οισιν Hutchinson 18 init.: ποίησ᾽ vel ἤνυσεν W ἄεισ᾽ C-C ἡμ]ιθέων Lo α]ν P 19 init.: μὲν νῦν P μὲν νυν L ἐρικυ[δέος υἱέ Lo 20 suppl. Lo 21 init.: κικλήσκω] P 22 init. εἴ τι ποτ᾽ tent. P "marg. περ αᵘ 2327, sc. 'per (pro περι?) legunt ἀμφότεροι (Apio et Nicanor)'; et in 3965 spatium ad περι quadrat. Ad sensum cf. Emp. B 131" 23 "vel δα]ΐφρονα" κ[όλλοπα χο]ρδῆς C-C 24 [μνήσ]ετ᾽ ἐ[ν ὀψιγόνοις] vel ἐσσομένοις P μνήσεται ὕ[στερον αὖ e.g. W 27 οὐδ᾽ ἀρε]τῆς ἐλάθ[οντο, φάτις δ᾽ P ἔχεν W κλέος δ᾽ ἦ]ν (pro φάτις δ᾽ ἔχε]ν) Pa οὐρανομ[ήκ]ης I. C. Rutherford 28 marg. αν(τι του) εν ανθρωπ[οις 2327 καὶ κλέος ἀ]νθρώπων ἔ[σσεται ἀθάνατο‹ν› W καὶ φάτις ἀ]νθρώπων ἔσσεται ἀθάνατο‹ς› Pa 29 οἱ μὲν ἄρ᾽ Εὐ]ρώταν W βῆσαν δ᾽ Εὐ]ρώταν L ("vgl. Ζ 281") κα[ὶ Σπάρτη]ς Lo (sed contra legem Naekianam) κα[ὶ εὐκλεὲ]ς Fowler 30 ἐξῆλθον (Fowler) vel ἐξέλασαν vel (W) ὥρμησαν P 31 init.: Τυνδαρίδα]ις W ἀγνοτάτο]ις vel σύν τ᾽ ἄλλο]ις P και, κατ a.c. 32 init.: ἐσλοί W, approb. L, qui tent. et πολλοί πόλεως Apio 34 γε, τι, sim. η sscr. ·α· (i.e. Παυσανίας) 35 αἶψα δ᾽ ἵκοντ᾽ Ἰσθμὸ]ν W 36 init.: νῆσον δ᾽ ἐχέλιπον] P ἔνθα πύλαι νήσου] vel νήσου τ᾽ ἐσχατίην] W 37 ὡ] Π ὥ]λλοι | ἤντησαν μαχίμοι P 39 σύν[οπλοι P σὺν αὐτοῖς W συν[όντες Lehnus ap. Aloni (p. 87) 40 ἦλθον Ἐλευσῖνος — ‿]ατον P ἶκον Ἐλευσῖνος γῆς ἐ]ρατόν W ἦλθον Ἐλευσῖνος ῥίμφ᾽ ἐρατόν Pa 41 P 42 Κέκρ]οπος P μάν]τιος W

"pine in (the) glade(s) . . . (which) woodcutters cut . . . Much . . . (of) Patroclus . . . overcame . . . by the hand of (Apoll)o . . . to/for the sons of

(Pr)iam . . . evil-mi(nded Alexa)nder . . . chariot of divine/straight(?) Justice . . . destroyed . . . having destroyed they came to famous . . . Danaan battle chiefs . . . (on whom imm)ortal glory has been poured thanks to a man (who) received from the (violet-wr)eathed Muses of Pieria . . . truth/divine(?) and (made) the short-lived race of (dem)igods a famous name for later men. (But you) now rejoice, o (son) of the glorious daughter of Nereus of the sea. But I (invoke) you, Muse, as my ally, (if you care for) the prayers of men, (help me) so that someone l(ater re)call (the me)n who for Sparta . . . (Nor did they for)get their (vir)tue . . . (fame) reaching the heavens (and glory) of men (will) be immortal. . . . leaving the Eurotas and Sparta . . . with the horse-taming sons of Zeus, the (Tyndarid) heroes and mighty Menelaus, the leaders of their (ances)tral city. (But these men [of our day]) the very best son of (Cleo)mbrotus led out . . . Pausanias. . . . famous deeds of Corinth . . . Tantalid Pelops . . . city of Nisus, the very place where the others . . . tribes of neighboring men . . . trusting in, they who with . . . plain . . . of (Pan)dion having d(riv)en out . . . of divine (Cecr)ops . . . having conquered . . ."

---

12 *POxy* 2327 fr. 30 + 18

```
          ] . [
         ]δερ.[
         ]τεκ.[            ]ντα[
            ] . [
```

"fort. in eadem columna stetit ac fr. 13" W

---

13 Ibid. fr. 27 col. ii

```
    .              ]θεα[
            .          ]ρεμ[
      .            ]πτο[
        .              ]ετερη[
    .              ]κουφ[                5
        θ[         ]πτολε[μ-
   τα.[          ]αρα[
       ὄφρ' ἀπὸ μὲν Μήδ[ων
   καὶ Περσῶν, Δώρου δ[ὲ
       παισὶ καὶ Ἡρακλέος [            10
   οἳ] δ' ἐπεὶ ἐς πεδίον [
```

εἰ]ϲωποὶ δ' ἔφ[α]νεν[
                    ]ρεϲτε[.]οντ[

6 μενε]πτομε[μ- Gentili-Prato   **7** "fort. ται.[" W   **8** λαὸν ἄπαντ' ἐλάϲαι e.g. W   **9**
Περϲέων Lo   **10** οϲ sscr. υ (sc. -εουϲ)   **11** οἳ] Lo   επιεϲ a.c. επιειϲ p.c.   fin.: [Βοιώτιον
εὐρὺ κατῆλθον e.g. W (coll. "Sim." 16.7 *FGE*)   **12**].ὠποιδέφ[.]ν[θ]ν[(sscr. ε) *Π*, vel fort.
φ[.]ν[θ]η[**13** ἵ[ζ]οντ[ο tent. W

> "in order to . . . [drive] away [the army] of the Medes and Persians; and . . .
> [to/for?] the sons of Doros and Herakles, [who], when they [came] into the
> plain and [the Medes?] came into view, . . ."

---

14 *POxy* 3965 fr. 21

                    ].[ ] . . .[ ]. . . .[
                    ]αδον βαλλομε[ν
              λ]έγω ποταμοῦ λα[
                    ]ρψαι πρῶτα β[ι]η[
δεινὸν ἀμαι]μάκετόν τε κακ[όν ‿‿ — ‿‿ — —   5
        — ‿‿ — μνή]μην ἤματα πάντ[α ◡ —
— ‿‿ ἐξ 'Α]ϲί[η]ϲ ἐλάϲει νεύϲαντο[ϲ ◡ — —
        — ‿‿ — ‿‿]νην ϲυμμα[χ]ίην φιλέω[ν
        ].νωι γάρ [ὑ]πὸ κ]ρηπῖδα τ[
              ]επα[. . . . . . ⟨.⟩]ορίην β[10
        ]ν δε[   ]ει ποτεφ[
                          ]πολω[
                          ]ωϲτ[
                    ]   [
                          ]λυων[15
                          ]χεκ[
                          ]ιν[

"Tisameni vaticinium" W (coll. Hdt. 9.36)   **2** ὅμ]αδον βαλλομέ[νων ϲακέων tent. W
3–4 προλ[έγω ποταμοῦ λα[οῖϲ ἐθέλουϲιν | ὅττι πέρην μά]ρψαι πρῶτα β[ι]η[ϲαμένοιϲ e.g. W
β[ ]η sscr. ·α[·   **7** ἦ ϲφε καὶ ἐξ e.g. W   **8** init.: Ζηνόϲ e.g. W   και]νήν e.g. W   ]ινην sscr.
·α·   φι sscr. ·τε· (sc. τελέων)   **9** init.: Ἄρηϲ e.g. W   fin.: τ[ανύϲϲει e.g. W   **10** ἐπά[γων
εὐπ]ορίην β[ιότου e.g. W   **16** Ἐ]χεκ[ρατιδ- e.g. W (coll. 22.9)

(West's translation, which understands this to be Teisamenos' prediction; see app.
crit.):

> "[. . . c]lash of blows on [shields . . . I de]clare that, should the army pr]ess
> [across] the river first . . . a great disaster will [be theirs; but if they wait, a

victory that] ne'er shall be for[got. And . . .] will drive them [out of A]si[a too with Zeus'] approval, favouring a n[ew] alliance; for [. . . will la]y a firm base . . ."

---

15 Plut. *De Herod. malign.* 42 p. 872d

ἀλλὰ Κορινθίους γε καὶ τάξιν ἣν ⟨ἔχοντες⟩ ἐμάχοντο τοῖς βαρβάροις καὶ τέλος ἡλίκον ὑπῆρξεν αὐτοῖς ἀπὸ τους Πλαταιᾶσιν ἀγῶνος ἔξεστι Σιμωνίδου πυθέσθαι γράφοντος ἐν τούτοις·

> μέσσοις δ' οἵ τ' Ἐφύρην πολυπίδακα ναιετάοντες,
>
> παντοίης ἀρετῆς ἴδριες ἐν πολέμωι
>
> οἵ τε πόλιν Γλαύκοιο Κορίνθιον ἄστυ νέμνονται·

1 μέσσοις W   μέσσοισι codd.   μέσσοι Turnebus   μεσσόθι Polterra   τ' Ἔφυραν Reiske (-ρην Schneidewin)   γέφυραν vel γ' Ἔφυραν codd.   **3** νέμονται codd.   νέμοντες Ald. (approb. W)   post h.v. lacunam II versuum stat L (cum verbo "kämpften")

"From Simonides we can learn about the Corinthians, their battle formation against the barbarians, and the consequences for them after the battle of Plataea. He writes:

and in the center both the inhabitants of Ephyra with its many springs, well acquainted with all sorts of virtue in battle, and those who rule Glaucus' town, the Corinthian citadel . . ."

---

16 Plut. pergens + *POxy* 3965 fr. 5

οἳ

> — ⏝⏝ κάλλιστον μάρτυν ἔθεντο πόνων
>
> χρυσοῦ τιμήεντος ἐͺν αἰθέριͺ· καί σφιν ἀέξει
>
> αὐτῶν τ' εὐρεῖαν κλιͺηδόνιͺα καὶ πατέρων
>
>]πολυͺ[

ταῦτα γὰρ οὐ χορὸν ἐν Κορίνθωι διδάσκων, οὐδ' ᾆσμα ποιῶν εἰς τὴν πόλιν, ἄλλως δὲ τὰς πράξεις ἐκείνας ἐλεγεῖα γράφων ἱστόρηκεν.

"οἳ Plutarchi est excerpta consuentis" (W), sed, ut frr. 15 et 16 W² sint excerptum unum continuum, edd. coniecerunt, ut verba Simonidis, οἳ καὶ (Ursinus), οἶον (Hermann), οἵπερ (Hiller), οἶον Bamberger ap. Bergk (approb. Pa); et, post κάλλιστον, ἑῶν L 1994, qui (approb. Pa) ita dividit totum in IV excerpta: 15.1-2 et 15.3 + 16.1 + 16.2 sqq.   **1** καλλίστων Bamberger post h.v. lacunam II versuum stat L: (i) hex. ("mit γάρ eingeletet?") + (ii) — ⏝⏝ — ⏝⏝ — ǀ ἔντεα (vel τεύχεα) λαμπομένα (-ομένου); cf. Simon. fr. 87 W²

(continued, in Plutarch if not also in Simonides, from fr. 15)

"[who] served as the finest witnesses of their toils, the precious gold in the sky; this to their benefit will increase their own and their fathers' broad fame."

Simonides has recorded this, neither for a choral production in Corinth nor for a song in honor of the city, but simply writing up these events in elegiacs.

---

17 *POxy* 3965 fr. 19

Δημητ[		ο[ὐ]κ ἴσχε[	
χ[ρ]ῆμα δ[		ἀλλ᾽ ετε[	
φῆ δὲ δυ[		ησπαι[	15
ἄγρετο σε[		φρικωθ[	
δηρὸν [	5	σπευδον[	
τοὺς α[		ἐν λεκτ[	
ῥύσιον [		ξείνου δ[	
καὶ μ[		ἐρχομε[	20
καὶ μ[		φηδε.[	
δαι.. [	10	χρ[	
θηευμη[		.]. φ[	
η[.]εου α[		αλλ[	

1 Δημητ[ρι- e.g. W (coll. Hdt. 9.57: τὸ Δημήτριον) vel Δημήτηρ   8 καὶ μ[ιν e.g. W   12
ἡ[λ]εοῦ e.g. P   14 vel επ   15 ἤσπαι[ρ vel ἧς παι[18 φρεικ Π φρικωθ[είς vel sim. P
19 vel α[22 sscr. κ[, i.e. fort. χρ[ημ- sscr. κ[τ(ημ-)   **post 24** litterae quas Lo vidit non
nunc legi possunt: (25)]θυ.α[, (26)]ασ[

"the sacred area of Demeter. . . a thing . . . and he says . . . a long time . . . the . . . reprisal. . .(10) regard (or a marvel) . . . (crazed?) . . . does not hold(?) . . . but (it is true?) . . . (they?) struggled(?) . . . in fear . . . hasten(ed?) . . . among (those gathered?) . . . foreigner . . . arriving . . . thing . . ."

---

18 Ibid. fr. 10

]ει[	
] ἐλπιδ[	
]ντισ[	
]ιμαχη[	
]λων καλο[	5

                              ] οὐδεμε[

                    ]. ἐκυδα[ιν

"hope ... battle ... no- ... gloried ..."

---

19 Stobaeus 4.34.28 (cod. S) Σιμωνίδου

ἓν δὲ τὸ κάλλιστον Χῖος ἔειπεν ἀνήρ·
«οἵη περ φύλλων γενεή, τοίη δὲ καὶ ἀνδρῶν»
παῦροί μιν θνητῶν οὔασι δεξάμενοι
στέρνοις ἐγκατέθεντο· πάρεστι γὰρ ἐλπὶς ἑκάστῳ
ἀνδρῶν ἥ τε νέων στήθεσιν ἐμφύεται.   5

1 τι Hecker   2 = *Il.* 6.146 (τοιήδε S)   3 μήν Hermann

"The man from Chios said one thing best: 'As is the generation of leaves, so
is the generation of men.' Few men hearing this take it to heart, for in each
man there is a hope which grows in his heart when he is young."

---

20 *POxy* 3965 fr. 26 + Stobaeus ibid. (codd. SMA)

            .]ειθο[
            .]ντ[. . .].[
          . τυτ]θὸν ἐπὶ χρό[νον
     . . . . . .]ρλ[. . . . .]ω παρμενο[
θνητῶͺν δ' ὄͺφρα τιςͺ ἄνθος ἔχει πολυήρατον ἥβης,   5
   κοῦφοͺν ἔχωͺν θυμὸͺν πόλλ' ἀτέλεσͺτα νοεῖ·
οὔͺτε γὰρ ἐλπιͺδ' ἔχͺει γηρασέμεν ͺοὔτε θανεῖσθαι,
   οὐδ' ὑγιὴς ὅταͺν ἦͺι, φͺροντίδ' ἔχει κͺαμάτου.
νήͺπιοι, οἷς ταύͺτηͺι κεῖται νόος, οὐͺδὲ ἴσασιν
   ὡς χρόͺνος ἔͺσθ' ἥβηͺις καὶ βιότοͺι· ὀλίγος   10
θνηͺτοῖς. ἀλλὰ ͺσὺͺ ταῦτα μαθὼν ͺβιότου ποτὶ τέρμα
   ψυχῆι τῶͺνͺ ἀγαθῶν τλῆθι χαιριζόμενος.
— ∪∪ —]φράζεο δὲ παλα[
   — ∪∪ —] γλώσσης ἔκφυγ' Ὁμηρ[
. . . . . . (.)]πα.δαμα[15
   . . . . . (.)]ω ψυδρῆις ε[
   . . . . . (.)] ἐν θαλίηισι[

. . .]ι ἐϋστρέπτων [

. . . .]ων, ἔνθα καὶ [

.   ]. .[20

---

1 vel]ευ ?ὀπίσω P   **4** ο[vel ε[**5** εχε[ι P ἔχῃ Stob.   **9** νηπίοισι Stob. (correxerat Camerarius)   **10** βιοτοι· Π (coniecerat Camerarius) βιότου Stob.   **13** φραζευ Π corr. W παλα[ιτέρων P   **13–14** παλα[ιοτέρου (vel παλα]ιγενέος) λόγον ἀνδρός | ἢ λήθην] W   **14** ἔκφυγ· Ὅμηρ[ος vel ῥῆμα δὲ πᾶν] γλώσσης ἔκφυγ· ὃ μὴ ν[όμιμον P Ὅμηρος ἑῆς e.g. W   **15** ὕ]παρ e.g. P πανδαμά[τωρ W (contra, Haslam)   **15–16** κού μιν] πανδαμά[τωρ αἱρεῖ χρόνος οὐδ᾿ ἀπαμαυροῖ, | οὐδέ ἕ π]ω ψυδρῆις ε[ἶλεν ἐπ᾿ ἀγγελίηις e.g. W   **17** εἶπεν δ᾿] e.g. W   **18** ων sscr. ·οι[, "fort. igitur . . . λόγοι | ἀνδρ]ῶν" W

"for a short time . . . abide . . . As long as a mortal has the lovely bloom of youth, with a light spirit he plans many deeds that will go unfulfilled. For he does not expect to grow old or die; nor when healthy does he think about illness. Fools are they whose thoughts are thus! Nor do they know that the time of youth and life is short for mortals. But you, learning this at the end of your life, endure, delighting in good things in your soul . . . Consider [the account of the man of] old. Homer escaped [(men's) forgetting his words] . . . false . . . in feasts . . . well-plaited . . . here and [there] . . ."

---

21 *POxy* 2327 fr. 1 + 2(a) col. i

.   ].οὐδ᾿ ὑπερ[

.   ]. .[. . . .]μενος

ο]ὺ δύναμαι, ψυχ[ή,] πεφυλαγμένος ε[ἶ]ναι ὀπηδός·

χρυσῶπιν δὲ Δίκ[ην —]ομαι ἀχνύμενος,

ἐ]ξ οὗ τὰ πρώτιστα νεο[τρεφέ]ων ἀπὸ μηρῶ[ν   5

ἡ]μετέρης εἶδον τέρμ[ατα πα]ιδείης,

κ]υά[ν]εον δ᾿ ἐλεφαντίνεόν [τ᾿ ἀνεμί]σγετο φέ[γγος,

— ⏑⏑] δ᾿ ἐκ νιφάδων [— ⏑⏑ — ⏑⏑ ἰ]δεῖν.

ἀλλ᾿ αἰδ]ὼς ἤρυκε, νέου δ.[. .].ι[   ] ὕβριν

.   ] ἐπέβη[   ]νοι·   10

.   ]οφύλλοις

.   ←? ἀκροπόλοις]

.   ]ιηι

---

3 pro h.v. "⊗?" W, sed cf. Obbink in hoc vol. ψυχή W (approb. Obbink) ψυχ[ῆι] W (1993a: 11) ψυχῶν Barigazzi ψυχήν Danielewicz ap. Bartol 1999 (quae approbat)   **4** ἄζομαι vel αἴδομαι Peek   **5** suppl. W νε sscr. ·δι·   **6** suppl. W   **7** ελεφαντι[textu, marg. ελεφαντίνεον Π κ]υά[ν]εον δ᾿ ελαφαντι[νέωι cum v.l. [κυανέωι δ᾿] ἐλεφαντίνεον Merkelbach, qui et tent. κ]υά[ν]εον δ᾿ ἐλέφαντι νέον [συνεμί]σγετο φέ[γγος   **8** καλῶν] (vel ποίην) δ᾿ ἐκ

νιφάδων [ἦν ζοφοειδὲς (vel νεοθηλε’) ἰ]δεῖν e.g. W   **9**].σηρυκε, νο.[textu, marg. νεουδ’ .[ ].ι·
Π   **10** ἐπέβη non exstat in textu; id verbum "intuli nota marginali fretus, Ἀπίων επεβη" W,
sed cf. Obbink in hoc vol.   **11** ἀκριτ]οφύλλοις Lo   **12** marg. ακροποροις α[et infra rur-
sus α.[ακ[ροπολοις Lo

"O my soul, I am unable to be your faithful attendant. But grieved I . . . glorious
Dikê, from the moment I saw from . . . thighs the end of my youth, when an ivory
gleam was sprinkled with black, and from . . . snows . . . to see. But [sha]me kept me
back . . . violence . . . entered onto . . . high-ranging (mountains?) with (countless?)
leaves . . ."

---

22 *POxy* 2327 fr. 3 + 2(a) col. ii + 4 + 3965 fr. 27

    .   ].οιο θαλάσσης
    .   ].ουσα πόρον·
    .   ]μενος ἔνθα περανα[
       [   ]
    .   ]οιμι κελευθο[5
                   ]ν κόσμ[ο]ν ἰο[στ]εφάνων
    .   ] ἕδος πολύδενδρον ἰκο[
        ε.[. . . .] εὐαγ[έ]α νῆσον, ἄγαλμα .[
    κα[ί κεν] Ἐχεκ[ρατί]δην ξανθότρ[ιχα
    ο.[. . . . .].ν χεῖρα λάβοι.[10
    ὄφρα νέο[ν] χ[αρίε]ντος ἀπὸ χροὸς ἄν[θος
    λείβοι δ’ ἐκ βλ[εφάρ]ων ἱμερόεντα [πόθον
    καί κεν ἐγ[ώ(ν)   ].δος ἐν ἄνθε[σι(ν)
    κεκλιμένος λευκ[.]. . φαρκίδας ἐκ.[
    χαίτη[ισι]ν χαρίε[ντ]α νεοβλαστ[15
    .[. . . . . .] εὐανθέα πλε[
    μο[. . . . .] δ’ ἱμερόεντα λιγὺν .[
    ἀρτι[επέα] νωμῶν γλῶσσαν α[
       [   ]
       τῶνδε.[20
    εὐκομπ[

1].οισι sscr. ·ο·   **2** "navis? fort. φέ]ρουσα" W (contra Y)   **3** περάνα[ς (Lo) vel περάνα[ι
W   **5** v. Y infra, p. 214   ἐθέλ]οιμι κέλευθο[ν Hunter (-[ν iam P)   πρήσσ]οιμι κ. W   ἀνύ]οιμι
e.g. Mace   τύχ]οιμι κελεύθο[υ e.g. Y   **6** init. φόρτον ἄγων Μουσέω]ν e.g. W   fin. suppl.
Lo   **7** init. εὐαγέων δ’ ἀνδρῶν ἐς] e.g. W   πολυδε[3965   ]δενδρον sscr. ·υμν· (i.e. lg.
πολύυμνον) 2327   ἰκο[ίμην W   ἵκο[ιτο Hunter   **8**]ευ sscr.].ν 2327   εὐαγ[έα W ap. P   εὐαέα
W   β[ίου W   **9** suppl. P   fin.: τοῖσδε γεραιοῖς e.g. W   κεῖνον ἰδοῦσα Y   **10**]ον vel]ων

P ὀφ[θαλμοῖσιν ἰδ]ών W φίλ]ον Y λάβοιμ[ι vel λάβοι [P fin.: φίλην vel πάλιν e.g. W
11 suppl. W (ὄφρα iam P) fin.: ἀείη vel ἕλοι με W **12** λείβοι W λείβει sscr. ·π· (i.e. lg.
λείπει) 2327 βλ[εφάρων W fin.: P **13** εγ] vel επ] ἐγ[ώ(ν) P ἐγ[ὼ μετὰ πα]ιδός W
ἔπ]ειτα e.g. Y ἄσπο]υδος vel ὁ φρο]ῦδος P ἐν ἄνθε[σι vel ἐν ἄνθε[ι P ἐν ἄνθε[σιν ἁβρὰ πάθοιμι W ἐν ἄνθε[σι τηλεθάεσσι tent. Mace ἐν ἄνθε[σι ἡδέσιν εἴη Y **14** λευκάς W
λευκ[ο]ῖς P π[vel τ[vel γ[P ἐκπ[ροφυγών tent. P ἐκτ[ὸς ἑλών W ἐκτ[ανύσας Bernsdorff
et Y ἐκπ[υριῶν e.g. Hunter ἐκ π[άλι δύς vel ἐκ τ[ότε δύς Koenen **15** suppl. W fin.:
νεοβλάστ[οισιν ἔλαια P νεοβλάστ[οιο κυπείρου vel -οι' ἐλιχρύσου W **16** π[οικίλον] e.g.
W πλε[ξάμενος στέφανον W πλε[κτόν P **17** μο[λπῆς P Μο[ύσαις vel μο[λπαῖς vel
μο[λπῆι W fin.: π[ροχέοιμί κεν οἶμον e.g. W **18** ἀρτι[επέα] W ἀ[πὸ στόματος W **21**
ἐυ·κ·ομπ sscr. π (i.e. lg. ευπομπ)

"(of the) ... sea ... (ship's?) passage ... arrangement of violet-crowned ...
(come/came to a/the) thickly-wooded site ... island conspicuous from afar
[or airy island], ... adornment ... and ... auburn-haired Echecratidas ...
take him by the hand, so that the young bloom from his l[ovel]y (might) ...
and he might drop delightful [desire on me] ... Reclining, white wrinkles(?)
[wiping away] ... I'll weave a fresh charming [wreath] for [my] hair ... and
[I will sing] a lovely clear [song], plying an eloquent tongue ..."

APPENDIX

The Text and Translation of fr. 11 as Restored by M. L. West

11 *POxy* 2327 fr. 5 + 6 + 27 col. i + 3965 fr. 1 + 2

παῖ[σέ] ο.[σὺ δ' ἤριπες, ὡς ὅτε πεύκην
    ἤ] πίτυν ἐν βήσ[σαι' οὔρεος οἰοπόλου
ὑλοτόμοι τάμ[νωσι
    πολλὸν δ' †ἥρωσ[
ἤ μέγα πένθ]ος λαὸν [ἐπέλλαβε· πολλὰ δ' ἐτίμων,   5
    καὶ μετὰ Πατρ[όκλου σ' ἄ[γγεϊ κρύψαν ἐνί.
οὐ δή τίς σ' ἐδ]άμασσεν ἐφ[ημέριος βροτὸς αὐτός,
    ἀλλ' ὑπ' Ἀπόλλ]ωνος χειρὶ [τυπεὶς ἐδάμης.
Παλλὰς δ' ἐγγὺ]ς ἐοῦσα πε[ρικλεὲς ἄ]στ[υ καθεῖλεν
    σὺν δ' Ἥρη, Πρ]ιάμου παισὶ χ[αλεπτ]όμ[εναι   10
εἵνεκ' Ἀλεξά]νδροιο κακόφρ[ονο]ς, ὡς τὸν [ἀλιτρόν
    ἀλλὰ χρόνω]ι θείης ἄρμα καθεῖλε δίκ[ης.
τοὶ δὲ πόλι]ν πέρσαντες ἀοίδιμον [οἴκαδ' ἵ]κοντο
    φέρτατοι ἡρ]ώων ἀγέμαχοι Δαναοί[,
οἷσιν ἐπ' ἀθά]νατον κέχυται κλέος ἀν[δρὸς] ἕκητι   15

ὃς παρ' ἰοπ]λοκάμων δέξατο Πιερίδ[ων
πᾶσαν ἀλη]θείην, καὶ ἐπώνυμον ὁπ[λοτέρ]οισιν
ποίησ' ἡμ]ιθέων ὠκύμορον γενεή[ν.
ἀλλὰ σὺ μὲ]ν νῦν χαῖρε, θεᾶς ἐρικυ[δέος υἱέ
    κούρης εἰν]αλίου Νηρέος· αὐτὰρ ἐγώ[20
κικλήισκω] σ' ἐπίκουρον ἐμοί, π[ολυώνυμ]ε Μοῦσα,
    εἴ περ γ' ἀν]θρώπων εὐχομένω[ν μέλεαι·
ἔντυνο]ν καὶ τόνδ[ε μελ]ίφρονα κ[όσμον ἀο]ιδῆς
    ἡμετ]έρης, ἵνα τις [μνή]σεται ὕ[στερον αὖ
ἀνδρῶ]ν, οἳ Σπάρτ[ηι τε καὶ Ἑλλάδι δούλιον ἦμ]αρ   25
    ἔσχον] ἀμυνόμ[ενοι μή τιν' ἰδεῖν φανερ]ῶ[ς
οὐδ' ἀρε]τῆς ἐλάθ[οντο, φάτις δ' ἔχε]ν οὐρανομ[ήκ]ης
    καὶ κλέος ἀ]νθρώπων [ἔσσετ]αι ἀθάνατο⟨ν⟩.
οἳ μὲν ἄρ' Εὐ]ρώταν καὶ Σπάρτη]ς ἄστυ λιπόντ[ες
    ὥρμησαν] Ζηνὸς παισὶ σὺν ἱπποδάμοις   30
Τυνδαρίδα]ις ἥρωσι καὶ εὐρυβίηι Μενελάω[ι
    ἐσθλοὶ πατ]ρώιης ἡγεμόνες π[ό]λεος,
τοὺς δ' υἱὸς θείοιο Κλεο]μβ[ρ]ότου ἔξ[α]γ' ἄριστ[ος
                    ]αγ. Παυσανίης.
αἶψα δ' ἵκοντ' Ἰσθμὸ]ν καὶ ἐπικλέα ἔργα Κορίν[θ]ου   35
    νήσου τ' ἐσχατιὴν] Τανταλίδεῳ Πέλοπος
καὶ Μέγαρ' ἀρχαίην Ν]ίσου πόλιν, ἔνθά περ ὤ[λλοι
                 ] φῦλα περικτιόνων
—͞ω θεῶν τεράε]σσι πεποιθότες, οἳ δὲ συν[
Ἶκον Ἐλευσῖνος γῆς ἐ]ρατὸν πεδίον   40
Μηδείους γαίης Παν]δίονος ἐξε[λάσα]ντες
    Ἰαμίδεῳ τέχναις μάν]τιος ἀντιθέου[
               ].ς δαμάσαντ[
               ].ι εἰδομεν[
       -ώ]νυμον α.[45

West's Translation

str[uck you . . . and you fell, as when a larch]
    or pine-tree in the [lonely mountain] glades
is felled by woodcutters . . .
    and much . . .
[A great grief seized] the war-host; [much they honoured you,]   5
    [and with Patr]oclus' [ashes mingled yours.]
[It was no ordinary mortal] laid you low,

['twas by Apoll]o's [hand that you were struck.]
[Athena] was at [hand, and smote the famous t]ow[n]
   [with Hera; they were wro]th with Priam's sons
[because of P]aris' wickedness. The car of God's
   Justice o'ertakes [the sinner in the end.]   10
[And so] the valiant Danaans, [best of warr]iors,
   sacked the much-sung-of city, and came [home;]
[and they] are bathed in fame that cannot die, by grace   15
   [of one who from the dark-]tressed Muses had
the tru[th entire,] and made the heroes' short-lived race
   a theme familiar to younger men.
[But] now farewell, [thou son] of goddess glorious,
   [daughter] of Nereus of the sea, while I   20
[now summon] thee, i[llustriou]s Muse, to support,
   [if thou hast any thought] for men who pray:
[fit ou]t, as is thy wont, this [grat]eful song-a[rray]
   [of mi]ne, so that rem[embrance is preserved]
of those who held the line for Spart[a and for Greece,]   25
   [that none should see] the da[y of slavery.]
They kept their co[urage, and their fame rose] heaven-high;
   [their glory in] the world [will] never die.
[From the Eu]rotas and from [Sparta's] town they [marched,]
   accompanied by Zeus' horsemaster sons,   30
[the Tyndarid] Heroes, and by Menelaus' strength,
   [those doughty] captains of [their fath]ers' folk,
led forth by [great Cleo]mbrotus' most noble [son,]
                  . . . Pausanias.
[They quickly reached the Isthmus] and the famous land   35
   of Corinth, [furthest bounds] of Pelops' [isle,]
[and Megara, N]isus' [ancient] city, where the r[est]
   [then joined the army from] the country round.
[Again they marched, the ome]ns giving confidence,
   [and soon they reached Eleusis'] lovely plain,   40
driving [the Persians from Pan]dion's [land, by help]
   of that most godlike se[er, the Iamid.]
. . . overcame . . .

Postscript, January 2001. Note Philodemus *On Poems* I col. 187.1–2 ed. Janko "[κα]κ[ό]ποτμον" τὴ[ν] Θέτι[ν . . (.)]νιδο[.], where Hausrath supplements [Σιμω]νίδο[υ]. Janko 2000: 411 n. 1 thinks that "if Simonides' name could be read, which would require a very long line one, it might be quoted from his famous elegy on the battle of Plataea (. . . with, I suggest, *PMG* fr. 557)." I thank Richard Janko for calling this passage to my attention before publication of this book.

PART II

1

IAN RUTHERFORD

The New Simonides

Toward a Commentary

The Text

The main sources are two papyri from Oxyrhynchus in the Fayyum, both probably to be dated to the second century C.E. These are *POxy* 2327 and *POxy* 3965, which overlap with each other in two places. Simonidean authorship is established by two coincidences with passages of poetry otherwise attributed to Simonides by Plutarch and Stobaeus. The scribe of *POxy* 2327 is the same as that of *POxy* 2430, a collection of fragments of the Simonidean paeans and epinicia and perhaps other genres in lyric meters.[1]

The papyri contained elegiac poems, some apparently military or historical in theme, others sympotic. It looks as if *POxy* 3965 represents a roll entirely devoted to elegiacs; the roll from which *POxy* 2327 comes may also have been all elegiacs, but if *POxy* 2327 is not wholly distinct from *POxy* 2430, it contained lyric poems as well. In the Hellenistic edition of Simonides, the principle of classification must have been in part by perceived genre, with sections for. *threnoi*, dithyrambs, encomia, epinicia, and paeans, perhaps *kateukhai* (537 *PMG*), and a miscellaneous category of *summikta* (540 *PMG*).[2] The arrangement might have been one genre per book-roll, though that would depend on the number of poems assigned to each genre.[3] Suda also says that there were epigrams, perhaps the so-called *Sylloge Simonidea*.[4] How the elegiac poems were arranged is unclear. Suda refers only to titles—the *Xerxou Naumachia*

An earlier version of this paper appeared in Deborah Boedeker and David Sider (eds.), *The New Simonides*, *Arethusa* 29.2 (1996): 167–92, and is used here by kind permission of the Johns Hopkins University Press. I would like to thank the organizer, panelists, and members of the audience at the 1994 APA meeting, as well as people who attended an informal talk I gave on this subject at Harvard in March of 1995, particularly C. P. Jones and C. Watkins.

1. Overlaps: in 11 W^2/13 W^2 and in 22 W^2; coincidences with Simonides: in 15 W^2 and 20 W^2; scribe of *POxy* 2327 and 2430: Lobel 1981.

2. Poltera 1998 has now argued that the textual evidence for a category *summikta* is flawed.

3. See Rutherford 1990: 201–2.

4. *Sylloge Simonidea*: see Page 1981: 122–23; also Cameron 1993: 1–2.

and the *Ep' Artemisioi Naumachia*. These and other poems might have been long enough to fill a whole book-roll on their own, but it seems more likely that they were at most a couple of hundred lines long, and that they were grouped in a book, or books, of elegies. Perhaps there were separate book-rolls for, say, historical and sympotic elegies. The epigrams, if they were included, perhaps formed a short appendix of a few hundred lines at the end of one of the books of elegies.[5] The arrangement in the edition(s) represented in the papyri does not necessarily correspond to the arrangement in the Hellenistic edition, since a large papyrus, with tall columns of forty lines, might have absorbed several Hellenistic books. One such large roll perhaps contained longer elegiac fragments, one contained lyrics.

Should we think of an anthology? That might be suggested by the fact that the overlaps between the two papyri are so great. It might be thought that the odds of this sort of coincidence are reduced if we postulate that the texts come from anthologies; there would be fewer poems in circulation, and the chance of more than one papyrus contributing to the same poem increases. However, the same result can be obtained if we postulate merely that some sections of the full editions were more popular than others; the elegies of Simonides might have been more popular than, say, his lyric *Threnoi*.[6]

The papyrus is furnished with short scholia supplying variant readings (*diorthoses*), some from the commentators Apion and Nicanor (both Roman period).[7] There are no signs of longer scholia. No beginnings or endings of poems are preserved, with the exception of *POxy* 2327, fr. 7 = 34 W², a small fragment with a marginal coronis and (perhaps) the last letter of a marginal title;[8] otherwise, we have no information about employment of titles in either papyrus. Sigla in *POxy* 2327 include χ (marking points in the text deemed to be of special interest) and an inverted υ sign (of indeterminate meaning).[9]

As Peter Parsons points out (at n. 4), to the inconvenience of the scholar, the fragments of Simonides are divided among a number of modern collections. For the elegiac fragments, we have West, *IEG* II² (= W²); for the lyric fragments (paeans, epinicia, hymns, *threnoi*, dithyrambs, etc.), the standard text is *Poetici Melici Graeci*; and for the epigrams, Simonidean and pseudo-Simonidean, we have Page's *Further Greek Epigrams*. In some cases, the same testimony appears in both *Poetici Melici Graeci* and *Further Greek Epigrams*. Campbell's Loeb follows the enumeration of *Poetici Melici Graeci* and *Further Greek Epigrams*, but for the elegiac fragments, its model is West's first edition, having been completed just before the publication of the new fragments. Campbell also includes a collection of useful testimonia. A compre-

---

5. No fragment in either papyrus seem to correspond to epigrams, but the possibility should be borne in mind.

6. Parsons 1992a.

7. *POxy* 2327: fr. 2a, 10 (21 W²) (Apion); fr. 19 (46 W²) (Apion; also Nicanor?); fr. 31 (6 W²) (Apion); *POxy* 3635: fr. (11 W²) (α^π N = Apion and Nicanor); fr. 18 (64 W²) (Apion).

8. There seems to be a slightly increased space between the two lines, so perhaps there could have been an interlinear title.

9. For the latter, see McNamee 1992: 46, with 14, 32; is it a form of antisigma, which introduces textual revisions?

hensive survey of Simonides is a desideratum; it was last attempted by Schneidewin, whose book is still in some respects useful after 160 years.

Military Fragments

The Naumachia

The situation is still not resolved beyond doubt. There are five pieces of information.

a. A list of Simonidean works in Suda (printed in West 1992: 114; 532, 536 *PMG*) includes ἡ Καμβύσου καὶ Δαρείου βασιλεία and (ἡ) Ξέρξου ναυμαχία and ἡ ἐπ᾽ Ἀρτεμισίῳ ναυμαχία, said to be δι᾽ ἐλεγείας, and ἡ ἐν Σαλαμῖνι (ναυμαχία), said to be μελικῶς. West (1992: 114) suggests that ἡ Καμβύσου καὶ Δαρείου βασιλεία and (ἡ) Ξέρξου ναυμαχία are corrupt, and that the original text specified Simonides' lifetime as having covered the reigns of Cambyses and Darius and the sea-battle(s) of Xerxes.

b. The story of Oreithyia, Boreas, and the birth of Zetes and Kalais is attributed to "The Naumachia" by Σ Ap. Rhod. 1.211–15, who claims that the story of the rape of Oreithyia from Brilessus was narrated there (reprinted under 3 W^2; 534 *PMG*).[10] It is assumed that this must be the poem on the battle of Artemisium, since the Athenians were supposed to have invoked Boreas and Oreithyia before the Persian shipwreck (Hdt. 7.189); but it might also have been (ἡ) Ξέρξου ναυμαχία, which could have included descriptions of both battles.

c. Two lyric fragments from the ἐπ᾽ Ἀρτεμισίῳ ναυμαχία are cited by Priscian, 533 *PMG* (not in West).

d. Fragment 3 W^2 (= *POxy* 3965, fr. 20) has been interpreted to show that Kalais, the brother of Zetes and son of Boreas and Oreithyia, was mentioned in an elegiac poem by Simonides (see below).

e. Fragment 7 W^2 (= *POxy* 2327, fr. 6) seems to be an elegiac fragment describing a sea-battle, and it has been thought that it suits Salamis better than Artemisium (see below).

Before the discovery of (d), it was common to trust (c) and hence disbelieve (a), which could be emended, for example, so that the Artemisium poem was in lyric and the Salamis poem in elegiacs (was it the same as (ἡ) Ξέρξου ναυμαχία?), or in some other way. And this hypothesis suited (e).[11] Now that we have (d), it looks as if Suda might be right after all.

In that case, what do we make of (c)? Were there two such poems on Artemisium, one elegiac, one lyric, perhaps performed in different contexts? Even that does not fully solve the problem that the Suda and Priscian seem to know poems in different meters as "the" Artemisium poem. Is Priscian mistaken? Alternatively, maybe Suda is

---

10. For the tradition, see Simon 1967.
11. Cf., e.g., Molyneux 1992: 160.

wrong, and the Artemisium poem was in lyric. In that case, perhaps the Salamis poem was after all in elegiacs, and 3 W² may come from there. Maybe Simonides described the battle of Artemisium again before proceeding to Salamis. Or perhaps he described a sea-battle in the Plataea poem (perhaps the battle of Mycale after the description of the land-battle). Or (c) may have belonged to a poem on a nonmilitary subject in which the battle was only mentioned incidentally.

Another possibility is that in the Hellenistic edition the title (ἡ) Ἀρτεμισίῳ ναυμαχία was applied to a sequence of at least two compositions in different meters. Some inscriptions contain texts in different meters, for example, an inscription of Isyllus from Epidauros, which contains several poems, one in trochaics (A), two in hexameters (B, F), one in prose (D), one section in elegiacs (C1–2), and one in lyric meter (E).[12] Simonides may well have composed poems in different forms to commemorate the same victory.[13] Perhaps they were grouped together.[14] Yet another possibility is that the composition as a whole was called (ἡ) Ξέρξου ναυμαχία, and that it had two sections, one on Artemisium (in elegiacs?), one on Salamis (in lyrics?), and that Priscian misapplies to the whole of it the title of part of it.

I see no way of resolving this issue. The publication of the new papyrus has increased the probability that the Artemisium poem was in elegiacs, but there is still room for doubt.

Fragments Attributed to the Artemisium Poem by West

1 W² (Σ Ap. Rhod. 1.583–84). It may have been in this poem that Simonides mentioned Skiathos, which featured in the events leading up to the battle of Artemisium (cf. Hdt. *Hist.* 7.176, 179, etc.), but plenty of other contexts are possible also (e.g., Simonides might have written a paean for a Skiathian theoria visiting Delphi: Sokolowski 1962, n. 16).

2 W² (*POxy* 3965, fr. 13). μαχ[makes it likely this is from a battle description, but it is not certain that the fragment comes from the Artemisium poem.

3 W² (*POxy* 3965, fr. 20). In line 5, the name Kalais (as in Καλαΐς) is reconstructed on the basis of]ΚΑ΄ΛΛ . . [, where the dot over the letter before the bracket could be from a diaeresis over an iota, marking that it belongs to an independent syllable. In line 11, the κόρη could be Oreithyia, as West says, if Kalais was mentioned earlier on; otherwise Thetis, or another Nereid. In lines 12ff., West 1992: 3 argues for the presence of the old man of the sea, presumably prophesying.

4 W² (*POxy* 3965, fr. 12). This could well come from a description of a sea-battle: we catch a reference to dry land, something about a harbor, and perhaps Boreas (?). In line 4, West suggests there might be a reference to the diver Skyllias of Skione, mentioned by Herodotus (8.8), but this is a long shot.

12. Powell 1925.

13. He may have written "Simon." 24 *FGE*, which commemorates the battle of Artemisium.

14. David Sider suggests that the classification *summikta* (see above) might have referred to mixed groups of poems of this sort.

A side issue is that Himerius in two passages connects the wind with Simonides, suggesting that the wind as invoked by Simonides might accompany the procession at the Athenian Panathenaia (47.14 [Panathenaia] and 12.32–33; 535 *PMG*). The natural interpretation is that these references come from the Artemisium-poem, the battle in which Boreas played a major part.[15] Bowra objected that the wind mentioned by Himerius was gentle, and took it to refer to Zephyrus and Salamis (cf. Hdt. 8.96.2); Podlecki 1968: 265–66, following other scholars, reasserted the case for the Artemisium poem.[16] Whichever the battle, it could still be inferred from Himerius *Or.* 47 that Simonides invoked the wind in the context of the Panathenaia, and that the poem was a prosodion accompanying the sacred ship, perhaps in lyric meter. But such an inference would be a mistake: the context of Himerius' speech is the Panathenaia, and the speaker links with it the wind that he knows has an Athenian connection.

Fragments Attributed by West to the Salamis Poem

8 W² (= 625 *PMG, Eleg.* 2 C) and **9 W²** (= *Eleg.* 3 C). These could come from anywhere, not necessarily a poem on a sea-battle.[17] Fragment 5 W² (= *Eleg.* 1 C) and *Vita Pindari Ambros.*, i.2.21 Dr. (= 536 *PMG* [note] = Pindar, fr. 272) show that Simonides mentioned the battle of Salamis, but tell us nothing of the form.[18] Fragments 6–7 W² (= *POxy* 2327, fr. 31) are taken by Barigazzi 1963: 64 and (tentatively) Podlecki 1968: 268 as referring to Salamis, partly because of the trumpet (line 4), which has a parallel in Aeschylus' account of the battle (*Pers.* 395ff.). But there are other possibilities; for example, it could come from an account of Mycale in the Plataea poem.

Podlecki believes in a Salamis elegy, and suggested that it included the following two texts. First, the "Democritus Epigram" ("Simon." 19 *FGE* = 65 D = Plutarch, *De Herod. malign.* 36 p. 869c), in which a certain Democritus is praised for having been the third to attack the Persians at Salamis.[19] However, this text could equally well be a self-contained epigram (Page attributes it to an anonymous Naxian); the detail that Democritus was "third" might seem to fit better in the context of a longer narrative, but the explicit reference to Salamis seems to suit an epigram better (why would such a reference be necessary in a longer narrative, where the location of the victory would have been obvious from the context?).[20] Second, an epigram concerning Athens, 86 W² = *Eleg.* 9 C:[21] (. . . . εἰκός . . . .) εἰ δ' ἄρα τιμῆσαι, θύγατερ Διός, ὅστις ἄριστος |

---

15. Wilamowitz-Moellendorff 1913: 206–8; Molyneux 1992: 162.

16. Bowra 1961: 343–44; passages discussed in Cuffari 1983: 80ff.

17. West in his text thinks both were in elegiacs; in his article (1993a: 2–3), he changes his mind, and concludes that the Salamis poem was probably in lyrics.

18. According to *Vita Pindari Ambros.*, i.2.21 Dr., it is an indication that Simonides and Pindar were of the same generation that Simonides described the battle of Salamis and Pindar the kingdom of Cadmus; can τῆς Κάδμου βασιλείας be right here? Some think this is a fifth-century Cadmus (Hdt. 7.165); I suspect rather τῆς Καμβύσου βασιλείας (Boeckh).

19. Podlecki 1968: 268, not mentioned by West: also discussed by Gentili 1968: 44.

20. Molyneux 1992: 189–90.

21. ἐξετέλεσσε is Hartung's emendation for ἐξετέλεσα.

δῆμος Ἀθηναίων ἐξετέλεσσε μόνος ("But if [it is right] to honor the best, daughter of Zeus, the people of Athens performed it alone"), according to Σ to Aristophanes *Peace* 736ff. derived ἐκ τῶν ἐλεγείων, and positioned by West 1992 as fr. 86, grouping under "Incertum an ex epigrammatis."[22] This might have come from an elegy in which the Athenians are singled out for praise. The "daughter of Zeus" is probably the Muse, as Podlecki 1968: 270–71 points out, and hence it seems likely that these were the first lines of a poem. Salamis is obviously a possibility. Could it perhaps have been the Artemisium poem? Or was it some entirely unrelated poem, something like the Eion elegy ("Simon." 40 [c] *FGE*)? Other scholars have taken the lines as referring to the Athenian victory at Marathon.[23]

If the Salamis poem was lyric rather than elegiac, it may be worth reviving Schneidewin's suggestion (1835: 9) that it is the source of 571 *PMG*, a line in which a group of women complain about being imprisoned by an island (ἴσχει δέ με πορφυρέας ἁλὸς ἀμφιταρασσομένας ὀρυμαγδός "I am restrained by the crash of the dark sea raging around").

The Plataea Poem (10 W²–18 W²)

Structure and scope.   Apparently a hymn to Achilles followed by a narrative. Can we think of this as analogous to a citharodic proem preceding a recital of Homer, or perhaps like a proemium introducing a *nomos*?[24] Perhaps the narrative was followed by a *sphragis*, as we find one in the analogous *Persai* of Timotheus. The most reasonable interpretation is that the narrative was concerned only with the battle of Plataea, although there is no independent attestation of a Simonidean poem on this theme. We cannot rule out the possibility that the sea-battle at Mycale, which was supposed to have happened on the same day, was mentioned also, perhaps as a sort of coda. In theory, the Achilles section might have been preceded by an account of earlier events, such as the battle of Artemisium (a second treatment, presumably, in addition to the independent poem). Carlo Pavese has suggested that the earlier and main theme of this poem was the battle of Thermopylae, arguing from the fact that Achilles is a more appropriate paradigm for Leonidas than for Pausanias insofar as Leonidas, like Achilles, was killed in battle.[25] But surely the point of the Achilles paradigm is not so much the fact that he died (although of course many Greeks died at Plataea), but rather the fact that his war was a panhellenic effort, like the Plataea campaign, and that his exploits were immortalized in song, just as Simonides promises to immortalize the Plataiomachoi.

Origin of the poem.   There are two issues. (A) Does it show bias in favor of some one state or states? Herodotus presents the battle as a panhellenic effort. He begins his

---

22. The terms ἐπίγραμμα and ἐλεγεῖον were clearly confusable: cf. West 1974: 3–4; *Life of Aeschylus* on the Marathon *elegeion* = Test. 15 C.
23. Barigazzi 1963: 74; Molyneux 1992: 150.
24. *Prooimion* followed by *nomos*: Koller 1956; Nagy 1990: 355; *prooimion* followed by recitation of Homer: Pindar *Nem.* 2; Kranz 1961: 1ff. (= 1967: 32ff.)
25. Pavese 1995: 22.

narrative with Athenian messengers coming to request Spartan help, and he describes how the Athenians cross over from Salamis to join the expedition, and how they take a major part in the battle. Contrast this with Aeschylus, *Persae* 817, where Darius describes blood shed at Plataea Δωρίδος λόγχης ὕπο ("by Dorian spear"); so too Pindar in *Pyth.* 1.77 imagines himself describing the "victory before Cithaeron" in Sparta, implying that Plataea was a battle the Spartans had the major role in. Prima facie, the Simonidean version seems to stress the Spartan contribution as well. Central to this issue is the apparent reference to Attica in 11.41 (see below, after n. 67): I tend to believe, as Aloni does, that it is mentioned as a place liberated by the Spartans, and not because the Athenians joined the expedition at this point. Other features pointing towards Sparta are the stress on the punishment of Paris in lines 11–12,[26] and the Doric form ἀγεμάχοι in line 14.[27] Notice also the ancient tradition that links Simonides and Pausanias.[28] The existence of the catalog (fr. 15–16 W²), which included Corinth, shows that Sparta was not the sole focus (a special Corinthian interest seems to be ruled out by Plutarch's statement that the poem was not performed in Corinth).

There are several ways of interpreting the data. (a) The poem is an accurate record of the dominant Spartan role in the conflict (Herodotus exaggerates the Athenian role); as such, it may been angled toward the interests (a.i) of Sparta, or (a.ii) of Pausanias himself, as a self-encomium; or (a.iii) it may have reflected the point of view of the Greek states as a whole, generously recognizing Sparta's contribution. (b) Reflecting the point of view of (b.i) Sparta or (b.ii) Pausanias, the poem exaggerated the Spartan role in the conflict; in that case Herodotus' account would perhaps be more balanced. (c) Our fragments are not representative of the poem as a whole, and the Athenians played a greater role elsewhere (perhaps even in hypothetical parts of the poem concerned with the sea-battles).

By definition, (c) is unprovable. Most scholars have argued that Simonides faithfully records the major role played by Sparta in the conflict (a): a more panhellenic version of this is argued for forcefully by Boedeker (1995b: 224–25 and this volume, "Historiography"); a more Spartan-oriented version has been maintained by Aloni (this volume), followed now by Schachter (1998). Option (b) has not been popular, but we should perhaps not ignore the possibility that, as a hired poet, Simonides saw his task as to magnify the role of his patrons at the expense of the rest of the Greek forces.

(B) Was it commissioned, or was it the winning entry in a competition? Aloni asserts that the poem was commissioned by the Spartans. Bearzot has recently sug-

26. Suggested by C. P. Jones.

27. Cf. ἀγχεμάχων in "Simon." 14 *FGE*. We should at least consider the possibility that, e.g., μνάσεται might be the true supplement in line 24. Cf. also the variation Παυσανίης/Παυσανίας in line 34; and a similar one in 14.4 W². For Doric form suggesting Spartan context, see now Burzacchini 1997: 194; on dialect, Pavese 1995: 12. However, Poltera 1997: 409, 535 regards ἀχέμαχοι as a hyperdoricism and restores ἠχέμαχοι. (All students of Simonides benefit from Poltera's excellent study, to which I make frequent reference.)

28. "Simon." 17 (a) *FGE*; Molyneux 1992: 198 and 209 n. 103, citing Plato *Epist.* 2.311a (Test. 17 C); Plut. *Consol.* 6 (105a); Aelian *VH* 9.41. The link between Pausanias and Achilles is explored further by Shaw in this volume.

gested a commission by the Athenian Themistocles during the period after the war when the medism of the Thessalians was an issue, and Themistoclean policy was to draw them back; is the poem perhaps rehabilitating Thessaly by praising Achilles?[29] Boedeker suggests first that the poem might have been commissioned by a group of states organizing the festival, or second that it may have been the result of a competition, basing this on the tradition that Aeschylus and Simonides competed to write an ἐλεγεῖον (elegy? or epigram?) in honor of those who died at Marathon, as well as on the well-established practice of having poetic competitions at funeral games.[30] But the hypothesis of a poetry competition might equally account for a Spartan bias, since the poem may have been the winning Spartan entry in a poetry competition. A further refinement is suggested by the fact that a feature of the later Eleutheria was a ritualized debate between the Spartans and the Athenians about who had the right to lead the procession.[31] If the later Eleutheria continued features of the earlier festival, the possibility arises that the Spartans had won such a debate, and then had the poem commissioned.

Place of performance.   I start from the following principles. First, the poem was performed (and not published as a text). Second, it was intended for some particular venue and for an original performance there. Third, the original performance took place on a major occasion, a major political or religious event, not a mere *sumposion*, although reperformance at a *sumposion* would be a possibility (see the next point).[32] Fourth, there might have been reperformances of various sorts (at the original venue, at other festivals); and secondary performances in other contexts, for example, in the context of the *sumposion* (like the performances of Simonidean μέλη referred to at Aristophanes, *Clouds* 1357–58). Fifth, the poem may also have circulated in written form, and a significant proportion of its "audience" will have become acquainted with it through writing.

The likeliest venue is Plataea itself, and particularly the Eleutheria festival, where the battle was commemorated every fourth year with great pomp, as Plutarch describes, and as it is attested in a number of inscriptions; however, many authorities think that the Eleutheria festival dates only from the late fourth century.[33] On the other hand, we cannot prove that there was not a primitive Eleutheria in the years

---

29. Bearzot 1997: 71ff.; see Plut. *Them.* 21–22; Frost 1980: 178–79; Bengston 1951: 85–92. We should not overestimate the extent to which Achilles is identified with Thessaly in this period. Less successful is Bearzot's attempt to correlate this with the role of Achilles in Aeschylus *Myrmidoneans*, since that play is probably from the 490s: see Boardman 1976: 14.

30. See Boedeker 1995b; *Vita Aeschyli* 8 (*TrGF* 3.33f.); cited by West before 86 W², p. 136. Cf. the Introduction to this volume, n. 6.

31. See Robertson 1986.

32. West 1993a: 5 supports the *sumposion*. Timokreon, *PMG* 727, is probably an example of an encomiastic (or anti-encomiastic?) poem performed at a *sumposion* in this period, but notice that it is only twelve lines long, a tiny fraction of the length of the Plataea poem.

33. The *locus classicus* is Plut. *Arist.* 21; also Thucydides 3.58.4. See Parsons 1992a: 6; Haslam 1993: 135; Boedeker 1995b; Aloni, this volume, at n. 62. Skeptical: Raaflaub 1985: 126–27; Étienne and Piérart 1975, referring to an important inscription honoring Glaucon at the Eleutheria; Robertson 1986, referring to *IG* II² 2086, *IG* II² 2788, and other inscriptions; W. C. West 1977.

immediately after the battle. And at the very least, we know that there was some sort of dedication immediately after the battle.[34]

Other venues are possible also. One is Sparta (cf. Pindar, *Pyth.* 1.77), particularly the temple of Achilles at which ephebes sacrificed.[35] Those who choose to stress the link to Pausanias above anything else might sympathize with Albert Schachter's recent suggestion that the poem was performed at the Achilleion near Sigeum which Pausanias may be presumed to have visited in the course of his journey from Cyprus to Byzantium in 478/477.[36] In one way this theory is appealing—nowhere else in the Greek world would a hymn to Achilles be more appropriate—but how likely is it that Simonides remained in the retinue of Pausanias through the winter of 478/477?

Equally possible is a panhellenic venue: a meeting of the Delphic Amphictyony was suggested by Bearzot.[37] If we imagine performance at Olympia, that might have the advantage that there is a cult of Achilles right there; the Isthmus is not out of the question (Shaw, this volume); but a strong candidate for the first performance must be Delphi, where the Greeks dedicated the famous Serpent Column, a thirty-foot-high column surmounted by a golden tripod, surrounded by three snakes' heads, with the names of the Greek states that took part written on the coils (ML 27).[38] According to a tradition reported by Thucydides (1.132), Pausanias originally inscribed an arrogant epigram on the monument ("Simon." 17a *FGE*; cf. *AP* 6.147; Paus. 3.8.2), which was subsequently erased by the Spartans when they inscribed the names of the cities. The link to Pausanias suggests that the event being celebrated was the battle of Plataea, not the war as a whole.[39] There must have been a general celebration on the occasion when the column was dedicated. It seems possible that the ceremony of the dedication of the Serpent Column would have accommodated the original performance of the elegy.[40]

Genre. Few poems in commemoration of military victories survive, but we do have Pindar, *Paean* 2, which celebrates a victory won by Abderites over a local Thracian enemy; this is a triadic lyric poem, probably performed in procession. Another poem comparable in some respects is Timotheus' *Persai*, which describes the battle at Salamis in astrophic lyric style. This was a *nomos*, apparently a solo form.

Simonides used the elegiac meter for the Plataea poem as well as the Artemisium poem (see above) and perhaps even an elegy on Marathon (cf. 86 W², quoted above).

---

34. See Thuc. 2.71.2; 3.58.4.

35. Paus. 3.20.8; see Parsons 1992a: 32.

36. Schachter 1998; Thuc. 1.94–96.

37. Bearzot 1997 (see above, n. 29).

38. I hope to argue elsewhere for Delphi as a performance-scenario. For the Serpent Column, see most recently Laroche 1989: 184ff. Shaw, this volume, suggests the Isthmus.

39. Meiggs and Lewis 1969: 59: "It is clear that the list does not refer exclusively to the battle of Plataea, though the monument was dedicated from the booty there captured, for the island states took no part in the battle."

40. Schachter 1998 thinks the theme of Achilles would have been inappropriate at Delphi, in view of the myth of Neoptolemus' ill-fated visit to Delphi; but if anything the presence of a hero cult for Achilles' son at Delphi would seem to make Achilles an appropriate choice for a hymn there.

There were antecedents: the *Smyrneis* of Mimnermus was in elegiacs (and, unlike the poems of Simonides, was composed many years after the victory it celebrated), as were Tyrtaeus' *Politeia Eunomia*, Semonides of Amorgos' *Arkhaiologia Samiôn*, Xenophanes' poem on the foundation of Colophon, and Ion's on the foundation of Chios. There may have been Hellenistic imitations, for example, 969, 958 SH.[41]

It is difficult to say what the implications of choosing elegiac meter were. The proem shows that Simonides takes the heroic narrative of Homer as his ultimate model; Stehle in this volume suggests that the choice of meter was a way of expressing a difference from Homeric epic.[42] If the elegy had an association with mourning early on, that would be relevant to the choice of this form for composition of a poem one of whose functions was to commemorate the war dead; unfortunately, it is by no means certain that this association predates the late fifth century.[43] Even if an association with lamentation is anachronistic, there may be a link with commemorative epigrams in elegiac meter, at least some of which are known to have been composed by Simonides.[44] A text which bridges the two forms is the pseudo-Simonidean "Eion epigram" (40 *FGE*), commemorating the Athenian expedition to Eion in Thrace in 475 B.C.E., a poem of fourteen lines which was divided into three sections and distributed between the bases of three statues, almost as if it were three independent epigrams.[45]

Section 1: Introduction

From χαῖρε in line 19, it seems that Achilles is probably the addressee of the first part of the poem, and furthermore that he is addressed as an immortal, since it would be used only of someone who attained special status after death, as indeed Achilles was usually deemed to have done.[46] How does Simonides envisage Achilles? In one fragment, he seems to think of him living on the Islands of the Blessed with Medea (558 *PMG*), but Simonides' presentation of him may have varied from one poem to another.

---

41. Narrative poems: Bowie 1986: 27ff.; Aloni 1994: 12. Deborah Boedeker suggests to me that the two generations of Muses (the first daughters of Ouranos, the second daughters of Zeus) attested for the *Smyrneis* of Mimnermus (fr. 13 W) might reflect a two-part structure similar to that of the Plataea poem (see below), with the older generation controlling mythical time, and the younger generation presiding over the accomplishments of mortal men. Hellenistic imitations: see Barbantani 1997, and add the recently discovered poem from the Letoon of Xanthos in honor of Arbinas of Lycia: Bousquet 1992: 157–58.

42. Pigres, *IEG* II²: 95 (Suda 4.127.24), is supposed to have attempted to rewrite Homer, inserting a pentameter after every hexameter.

43. See West 1974: 6–8; that association is challenged by Bowie 1986: 22ff., who thinks that it is based on a pseudo-etymology from ἐλέγω which became current in the period 415–408 B.C.E.

44. Some of the parallels in phraseology between pseudo-Simonidean epigrams and the Plataea elegy are striking, e.g., δούλιον ἦμαρ in 11.25 W2 with "Simon." 20(a).4, 16.1 *FGE*. But such argumentation is to some extent circular, since the epigrams have been used in reconstructing and supplementing the elegy.

45. Aeschines 3.187, who cites it, in fact seems to put the three parts together in the wrong order. For the text and further discussion, see Boedeker, "Historiography," this volume, at n. 26.

46. See Sourvinou-Inwood 1995: 199ff., Boedeker, "Heroization," this volume.

How the poem began we do not know. The poet could have told of the early career of Achilles; or, looking further back, the marriage of Peleus and Thetis, or even the genealogy of the Aiakidai.

10 W². This is an address to Achilles. West puts it before 11 W², but perhaps the poet returned to Achilles at the end, as Pindar begins and ends *Paean* 2 with references to Abderus. The rest is obscure. In line 2, the poet is less likely concerned with the father and forefather of Achilles than with Achilles as the father and forefather, so that the starting point might have been someone who was a descendant of Achilles. In line 3, West suggests that some form of Μηθώνη should be read, but the relationship between Achilles and any of the places that had this name is mysterious. In line 4, "our labors" could be the labors of the poet, or perhaps the performers.[47]

11 W². This fragment is assembled from *POxy* 3965, fr. 1 (= lines 9–23) and fr. 2 (lines 22–45), along with *POxy* 2327, fr. 5 (lines 1–4? [bottom of a column]), fr. 6 (line 5–14 [top of a column]), and fr. 27 (right ends of lines 13–29). The successes of editors in supplementing the text should not blind the reader to the fact that less than half of the total width of the column survives. The basic thought is: "Achilles, you were killed by Apollo. But (Athena and Hera caused the downfall of Troy?) because of Paris, so that the chariot of justice overtook him. The Greeks returned home, to be immortalized in song by Homer. Farewell, Achilles."

Lines 1–4 = *POxy* 2327, fr. 5, were placed here by West. If the reference is to the death of Achilles, the narrative is curiously circular, with the description of the death in lines 1–4 and the identification of the killer in lines 7–8. Lloyd-Jones 1994: 1 doubts this arrangement, suggesting from the account of the death of Mardonius or Masistius that the fragment might have come later on. Barchiesi (this volume) tries to corroborate West's hypothesis, arguing from the fact the Achilles is compared to a pine in other sources, though one should bear in mind, as Barchiesi notes, how readily this imagery would have suggested itself, whatever the background.

If lines 1–4 describe the death of Achilles, lines 5–6 presumably describe his burial. Otherwise, they might describe the events preceding the death, perhaps giving his motivation (e.g., fighting on behalf of Patroclus).

In line 5, Simonides perhaps said that pain (ἄχ]ος: Pavese) or sorrow (πένθ]ος: West) seized the army (λαός) of the Greeks, perhaps alluding to the perceived etymology of the name Achilles.[48]

At or before line 11, the focus shifts from Apollo's killing of Achilles to divine and/or human vengeance on Paris. It is not clear which section lines 9–10 belong to. West thinks they point forward, describing Athena and Hera destroying Troy "angered at the sons of Priam, because of wicked Alexander."[49] Luppe 1993 thinks they point back, resuming Apollo's action against Achilles, "gratifying the sons (son?) of Priam" (χ[αριζ]όμ[εν—proposed by Parsons), and suggesting that a new thought

---

47. There is a parallel for μελέτη in this sense at Empedocles B131.2 (an invocation of the Muse). See Obbink 1993: 64–70, Pavese 1995: 8.

48. Palmer 1963: 79; Nagy 1976: 209–37; Pavese 1995: 9.

49. For the epithet κακόφρονος Poltera 1997: 379 compares Zenodotus' reading Ἀντιμάχοιο κακόφρονος at *Iliad* 11.123 and 138, suggesting that Zenodotus might have imitated Simonides here.

starts asyndetically with line 11 (ὕβριν or θάρσος). The second alternative has the difficulty of being highly abrupt.

In line 12, ἄρμα has the unexpected variant τέρμα superscribed in *POxy* 2327. The reconstruction θείης (ἰθείης?) ἄρμα (τέρμα) . . . δίκης is attractive (e.g., "the chariot [supremacy?][50] of justice brings down Paris"), but we cannot be certain that δίκ[η] was not the subject (e.g., "justice smashes the chariot [supremacy?] of arrogance"). The "chariot of justice" is a unique image in Greek,[51] though it has Indo-European antecedents.[52] For the verb καθεῖλε a good parallel is provided by Aeschylus, *Ag.* 398: φῶτ᾽ ἄδικον καθαιρεῖ (θεός) . . .. Since the following lines show that the chorus is thinking of Paris, it seems likely that there is a reminiscence of the Plataea poem here.[53] West (apparatus) boldly suggests that the true verb was something like (ἐ)κίχανε (with καθεῖλε perhaps intruding from line 9), a hypothesis that allows for both variants (i.e., "The chariot of justice finds Paris" or "Paris finds the limit of justice").

There are some spectacular redeployments of epic language in these lines. In line 13, ἀοίδιμον is a literary adjective, and also a self-referential one, insofar as it is poems like that of Simonides that make Troy "singable."[54] In lines 17ff., Homer is said to have made the short-lived race of heroes famous to future generations.[55] Simonides applies the adjective ὠκύμορον to the race of heroes, redeploying the epithet that Homer had used of Achilles.[56] The long-lasting fame provided by epic poetry compensates for the brevity of their lives.

In line 19, χαῖρε represents a hymnic close, followed by the formula of closure or transition: αὐτὰρ ἐγώ (see further Obbink, this volume, at nn. 25–32). The use of χαῖρε for Achilles may also recall its use to address the dead Patroclus in Homer, *Il.* 23, 19–20, and 179–80. The indirect way of referring to Achilles ("son of the daughter of Nereus") is very unusual (cf. Euripides, *IT* 217), but Achilles is identified as "son of the Nereid" in Bacchylides 13.122 (from 485 B.C.E.), and reasonably commonly as "son of Thetis."[57]

50. The sense would presumably be "supreme justice" (cf. LSJ s.v. τέρμα II 4).

51. In a satyr-drama (Aesch. *TrGF* 281a.12–13), Zeus sends off justice to travel round the world, but there is no reference to a vehicle. The slightly different image of a ruler driving the chariot of justice is found in a late epigram, *AP* 9.779.4: Δίκης θρόνον ἡνιοχεύων ("driving the chariot of the throne of justice") used of the Roman emperor; also Himerius *Or.* 36.11: πέμψωμεν αὐτὸν τὸν μέγαν τῆς δίκης ἡνίοχον ("Let us send him, the great charioteer of justice"); these are cited by Robert 1948: 98, a reference for which I am grateful to C. P. Jones. Poltera 1997: 112–13 finds a parallel for the "chariot of justice" in Aesch. *Cho.* 935ff.

52. The theme of the "chariot of justice" is Indo-European; in the *Rg Veda* the concept *rta* is symbolized by a chariot, e.g., at 2.33.3: see Lüders 1959: 457–61, Wagner 1970: 14. It also occurs in the Old Irish *Audacht Morainn*: Kelly 1976: 33–34, Watkins 1979, 1995: 16. I am indebted to Calvert Watkins for these references.

53. Calvert Watkins brilliantly points to an emendation by Blomfield, who suggested φῶτα δίκα instead of φῶτ᾽ ἄδικον, supplying a subject for καθαιρεῖ. In view of the likely restoration of the Plataea poem, it seems that this could well be right.

54. Lloyd-Jones 1994: 1 refers to *Il.* 6.357–58; see also Stehle and Clay, this volume; also Poltera 1997: 199–200.

55. For ἐπώνυμος in the sense of "famous," Lloyd-Jones 1994: 2 compares the hypothetical ὤνυμοι at Quintus Smyrnaeus 8.452 and 12.220; the sense "famous" is endorsed by Poltera 1997: 344.

56. On the epithet, see Poltera 1997: 354–55.

57. Arianna Trail drew my attention to the parallel at Eur. *IT* 217 (τῷ τᾶς Νηρέως κούρας) for "son of Thetis." See *Il.* 4.512, 16.860; Pindar *Pa.* 6.83–84 (for Schachter 1998, this passage is reason to think that Pindar imitates Simonides), *Ol.* 9.76; Eur. *El.* 438, 450, 454 (i.e., thrice in the "Achilles Ode").

There is a close parallel with sections of Theocritus, *Id.* 16. In this poem, Theocritus justifies the practice of writing praise poetry on commission by citing the example of the relationship between Simonides and his Thessalian patrons,[58] and in lines 44ff. he says that Simonides' Thessalian patrons would never have been remembered εἰ μὴ θεῖος ἀοιδὸς ὁ Κήιος αἰόλα φωνέων | βάρβιτον ἐς πολύχορδον ἐν ἀνδράσι θῆκ' ὀνομαστούς | ὁπλοτέροις ("if the divine Cean singer, sounding varied notes on the many-stringed lyre, had not made them famous among younger men"). The key parallel is ὁπλοτέροις, noticed by Hutchinson, and these lines can be thought of as an allusion to the Plataea poem. The structure of Theocritus, *Id.* 16 as a whole resembles that of the Plataea poem, with an earlier section discussing earlier praise-poetry (Simonides and the Thessalians), and a later hinting at the possibilities of contemporary praise (the military exploits of Hiero), thus replicating what Simonides does for himself vis-à-vis Homer.[59]

Section 2: Narration

11 W², continued. "Help me, Muse, preserve the memory of the Spartans who defended freedom, who left Sparta with Castor and Pollux, led by Pausanias. They reached Corinth and Megara" (and Eleusis, where the Athenians joined them?). Fragment 13 W²: "the two sides faced each other in battle formation." Fragment 14 W² is a prophecy about the battle.

In line 21, κικλήσκω could begin a poem without a preceding proem. The speaking subject is presumably primarily the poet.[60] ἐπίκουρον is a military metaphor; Simonides imagines his situation as a poet as analogous to that of a fighter in a battle, and he calls on the Muse to assist him. The Muse is thus a mercenary in the military sense (contrast with the traditional view that Simonides' Muse was mercenary in the sense that she sold herself for money, an ἐργάτις [Pindar, *Isth.* 2.6]).[61] Simonides

---

58. See Merkelbach 1952; Parsons 1992b.

59. There may be another allusion to it shortly afterwards in lines 64–66, where Theocritus dismisses a covetous man and described the generous patron he wants: χαιρέτω ὅστις τοῖος, ἀνήριθμος δέ οἱ εἴη | ἄργυρος, αἰεὶ δὲ πλεόνων ἔχοι ἵμερος αὐτόν· | αὐτὰρ ἐγώ τίμην τε καὶ ἀνθρώπων φιλότητα | πολλῶν ἡμιόνων τε καὶ ἵππων πρόσθεν ἑλοίμαν ("Farewell to such as he; and countless silver may he have, and desire of more be ever possessed. But I would prefer fame and friendship of men to wealth in mules and horses"). Simonides had applied the formulas χαῖρε and αὐτὰρ ἐγώ to older and newer forms of praise poetry; Theocritus reapplies them to two types of patrons, a neat adaptation considering Simonides' reputation for venality. The redeployment reminds us that the concerns of Theocritus are very different from those of Simonides. Perhaps one can go further and argue that *Id.* 16 is a highly critical reading of Simonides' self-aggrandizing self-presentation in the Plataea poem, offering a more realistic description of the mechanism of poetic patronage. To put it another way, the implication of the Simonides poem is that great exploits need the poet, whereas Theocritus turns it round and presents himself as an indigent praise-poet in need of great exploits to eulogize. Similar allusions to the Plataea poem in Theocritus 17 are explored by Fantuzzi, this volume.

60. Cf. the late epigram in Cougny 1890: 4.54: υἷα πάλαι φθίμενον, πάλιν ἄμβροτον, Ἀπόλλωνος, | κικλήσκω λοιβαῖσι μολεῖν ἐπίκουρον ἐμαῖσιν·

61. For passages, see Test. 22 C; this pattern is reversed in Pindar *Ol.* 13.96–97: Μοίσαις γὰρ ἀγλαοθρόνοις ἑκὼν Ὀλιγαίθιδαισίν τ' ἔβαν ἐπίκουρος ("I have come willingly as a helper for the Muses with their glorious thrones and for the Oligaithidai"). Cf. Stehle, this volume, at nn. 11ff.

thus makes some contribution himelf, and is superior to Homer, who relied entirely on the Muses.

Just as Simonides invokes the Muse as ἐπίκουρος, so in the *Persai* Timotheus invoking Apollo called him ἐπίκουρος (202ff.). Like the invocation in Simonides, that in Timotheus comes at a point of transition, in this case the transition from the main narrative part of the song to the *sphragis*. Just as Simonides invokes the Muse to help him in his song, so Timotheus calls on Apollo as inspirer of his song to help him because he has been abused by the Spartans who disapprove of his new music, unfairly, since he is the continuer of an ancient tradition of music; Timotheus follows Simonides in invoking the Muse as poetic helper, but the help he wants is in respect of his status as a poet, not in respect of the theme or organization of the song. There is a further allusion in Lucretius 1.24 where the poet invokes Venus to help him in his song as *sociam*, a translation of ἐπίκουρος. As O'Hara points out, in this passage Lucretius surely uses this allusion as a way of referring to the philosopher Epicurus.[62]

In line 23, ἔντυνο]ν is the word used in the introduction of the Sirens' song at Homer, *Od.* 12.183 (also noted by Stehle in this volume at n. 25; unfortunately, the supplement is less than certain). κ[όσμον ἀο]ιδῆς (if right)[63] seems at first sight unremarkable, but it is thrown into relief when set against κόσμον . . . ἐπέων at Parmenides B8.52 (cf. διάκοσμον at 60), used of the part of Parmenides' poem that covers the deceptive world of mortals, and contrasted with the truthful presentation of the real world of being, which precedes. The relationship between the two parts of Simonides' poem is in some respects analogous, and perhaps one poem has influenced the other in the use of the expression κόσμον; which might have influenced which could be determined only if we knew when Parmenides published his poem. In line 24, the idea that someone will remember is reminiscent of the eulogy for those who fell at Thermopylae (531 *PMG*). Compare also the reflections on the durability of Homeric poetry in 21 W². In an epigram or elegy (89 W²), Simonides is supposed to have praised himself for his excellence in respect of μνήμη (see below on the *sphragis*).[64]

After the invocation, the main part of the narrative starts in line 25 with a relative clause. The word Σπάρτ[ηι is a key reason for thinking that the Spartans had a special interest in the composition or performance of the poem. In line 29, the Spartans leave with the Tyndaridai and Menelaus (Castor and Pollux are also mentioned in 70 W²).[65] As Parsons 1992a: 35 notes, the practice here is different from that implied in Herodotus 5.75, according to which only one king and one Tyndarid accompanied the army. The primary concern of Simonides was perhaps not so much to articulate Spartan military practices as to produce a narrative which would be impressive at the panhellenic level. Is it a coincidence that Menelaus and the

62. O'Hara 1998, referring to Gale 1994: 137. For Timotheus and Simonides, see Rutherford (forthcoming).

63. This supplement is now endorsed by Poltera 1997: 350. Capra and Curti 1995: 31 argue for]ρδῆς and suggest κ[όλλοπα χο]ρδῆς, allowing that fr. 1 and fr. 2 (line beginning and line end) need not have been correctly aligned at this point.

64. See Goldhill 1988; for memory, cf. also 646 *PMG*.

65. The same collocation in Oenomaus, fr. 10.13 Hammerstaedt (Lloyd-Jones 1994: 3).

Tyndaridai are three deities who would have a particular interest in recovering Helen? On the significance of the Tyndarids, see Hornblower (this volume).

In line 36, the Spartan army reaches the Isthmus,[66] and in line 37, Megara.[67] In line 41, it seems to have reached the borders of Attica, since Pandion is prima facie the Attic hero (though Schachter 1998 has recently suggested that he might be the Megarian hero of the same name). Thus in line 40, it probably reached the area of Eleusis, an important way-station, especially in view of the role that Demeter plays in the Herodotean narrative (cf. fr. 17 W^2). What happens in line 41 has become a point of contention. Parsons thought that this might be where the Athenians join the Spartans, as in Herodotus. But it is difficult to find a supplement that suits the idea that they came over from Salamis. ἐξε[λαθέν]τες is inappropriate, because the Athenians were not driven out of Salamis, but came over voluntarily. Perhaps the intransitive ἐξε[λάσαν]τες ("sallying forth") could describe the Athenian contingent, but this would be an odd way to refer to a sea-crossing. More likely, as West believes, ἐξε[λάσαν]τες is transitive, and describes the Spartans driving the Medes out of the land of Pandion (used of the Greeks driving the Persians out in "Simon." 15.3 *FGE*). But this hypothesis removes the evidence for the Athenians joining the expedition here, and thus for one point of contact between Herodotus and Simonides.

In line 42, the two readings proposed are Κέκρ]οπος (Parsons) and μάν]τιος (West).[68] If the former, Attica is still the subject; if the latter (which seems preferable paleographically), we may have a reference to the Iamid Teisamenos, who figures prominently in Herodotus' narrative. Simonidean interest in prophets is independently indicated by the epigram in honor of Megistias ("Simon." 6 *FGE* = Hdt. 7.228.3). And cf. 13 W^2 below. In line 43, West thinks we might have a reference to the early skirmish described between Masistius and the Greeks (Hdt. 9.22–23)

12 W^2 (*POxy* 2327 fr. 30 + fr. 18). A small fragment tentatively assigned to the same column as 13 W^2.

13 W^2 (*POxy* 2327, fr. 27 col. ii). This was in the column immediately following 11 W^2, and therefore about ten lines on from line 45. The sequence of hexameter/pentameter is not certain, since the papyrus does not indent or otherwise distinguish the pentameter lines.

One side "becomes visible"; εἰσωποὶ δ' ἐγένοντο νεῶν is used by Homer, *Il.* 15. 653, at the point where the retreating Greek catch sight of their own ships. Barigazzi 1963: 74 takes this as referring to the moment when the Spartans viewed the battlefield at Marathon (Hdt. 6.108); for the existence of a Simonidean elegy in honor of Marathon, he depended on 86 W^2 (see above), which can be interpreted in different ways. West 1993a: 7 more reasonably takes the fragment to refer to the Greek descent to the Asopus plain described in Herodotus 9.19.3. But the fragment might just as easily come from later on in the battle.

---

66. West 1993a: 14 suggests that the line should be supplemented on the assumption that the Isthmus is the location of the gates of the Peloponnese, following Bacchylides 1.13ff.

67. With the city of Nisus; cf. "Simon." 16 *FGE*, in honor of the Megarians: ὀμφάλῳ ἀμφίς | Νισαίων.

68. For the text, see the on-line images at Obbink 1998b (cited July 10, 1999). The traces are not easy to reconcile with the first omicron of Κεκρ]οπος.

Section 3: The Prophecy

14 W^2 (*POxy* 3965, fr. 21). West 1993a: 8 restores like this: (a) he connects lines 3–6 with the prophecy of Teisamenos in Herodotus 9.36 that if the Greeks crossed the river Asopus they would fail, whereas if they stayed on this side of it they would win a great victory; (b) in lines 7–8 he finds an extension of the prophecy: someone, perhaps Ares, will drive the Medes out of Asia (which he understands as Ionia), with the permission of Zeus; (c) in lines 9–10, Ares stretches a foundation under Delos, providing a symbolic basis for the Athenian Empire.

Of these, (c) is a long shot; κρηπῖδα might be metaphorical, as in κρηπῖδ᾽ ἐλευθερίας in Pindar, fr. 77.[69] Conjecture (b) is more reasonable, though far from certain.[70] Point (a) must be right. It is also worth pointing out that even if the prophecy itself is the same as the one in Herodotus, the prophet may be different; a divine speaker (like Nereus in 3.12 W^2) would seem more appropriate in a poem. Interestingly, the one direct speech in Pindar *Paean* 2 is a prophecy delivered by Hecate. It would be reasonable to conclude that prophecy was a standard and expected feature of poems describing battles.

Section 4: Catalog

15–16 W^2 (= *Eleg.* 10–11 C). These two fragments are cited by Plutarch in *On the Malice of Herodotus*; 16 W overlaps with *POxy* 3965, fr. 5.[71] Plutarch quotes these lines as evidence that Herodotus has by contrast maligned the Corinthians. Simonides' praise of the Corinthians here would contrast with another fragment in which he is said to have angered them by stating that Troy was not angry with Corinth, referring to the Corinthian ancestry of Glaucus, son of Hippolochus (572 *PMG*). The epigram, "Simon." 11 *FGE*, in honor of the Corinthians who died at Salamis (in local dialect), is probably not Simonidean.[72]

These lines probably come from a general catalog of the forces comparable to the one in Herodotus. By including a catalog, Simonides was following Homeric practice; poems such as the *Smyrneis* of Mimnermus may also have contained catalogs.

In 15 W^2, Simonides distinguishes Ephyre and Corinth. What is the significance of the two names? On one level, Ephyre is perceived as the older name, just as Ephyre, daughter of Oceanus, occupies an early point in the mythological history of the city, whereas Korinthos, son of Marathon, occupies a comparatively late stage, as does

---

69. Rea, cited in Parsons 1992a: 42. We find κακῶν κρηπίς in Aeschylus' description of the battle at *Persae* 814–15, though the reading is disputed. Poltera 1997: 271–72 observes that Stella 1946: 21 had already suggested that "Pindar fr. 77" might in fact be from Simonides' Artemisium poem.

70. West finds a problem in the fact that Asia is where the Persians originate from in "Simon." 24 *FGE*, so that if the Persians are being driven out of Asia here, they are being driven from their own home. But perhaps the prophecy ends with a fantasy of panhellenic hegemony stretching to the ends of the known world (see Flower 1999: 67 n. 12, whose criticism of my earlier view I appreciate).

71. Luppe 1994: 22ff. considers and rejects the possibility that]πολυ[in 16.4 W^2 might correspond to πολυπίδακα in 15.1 W^2, implying that Plutarch has inverted the order of the fragments.

72. On this, see Boegehold 1965.

Glaucus, son of Sisyphus. On another level, the difference may be geographical: Ephyre "with its many fountains" seems to be the citadel (the epithet πολύπιδαξ is the one that Homer had used of Ida [*Il*. 8.47 etc.]), whereas the Κορίνθιον ἄστυ may be the city as a whole.[73] Elsewhere Simonides may have provided a genealogy for Ephyre (596 *PMG*).[74]

In 16 W^2, prima facie the sun in the sky is represented as witness of the valor of the combatants, and it is referred to by the kenning "esteemed gold in the sky."[75] Similar is 87 W^2 (= *Eleg*. 12 C): ξεινοδόκων δ' ἄριστος ὁ χρυσὸς ἐν αἰθέρι λάμπων where ξεινοδόκος is supposed to have the unusual sense of "witness," though it is not clear whether the witness is the sun or gold. For the sun to be a witness is a common idea,[76] for it to be a witness of a battle is rarer (though cf. Sophocles, *Ant*. 100ff.). Perhaps it is relevant that Helios played an important part in Corinthian genealogical traditions and had a cult there.[77] However, although sense can be made of the fragments, it must be admitted that the thought is awkward.[78] On these grounds, Luppe 1994 suggests that at least two lines may be lost between πόνων and χρυσοῦ, and that χρυσοῦ τιμήεντος ἐν αἰθέρι is an attribute of something literally made of gold, such as golden weapons taken from the Persians.

Unassigned

17 W^2. Demeter (?) is important in the narrative of Herodotus, figuring in the battle of Plataea and that of Mycale, as West 1993a: 9 suggests (Hdt. 9.57, 62, 65, 69, 101); Boedeker ("Historiography," this volume, at nn. 37–41) finds this the most explicit indication of Simonidean influence on Herodotus' account. In line 3, φῆ also seems to occur as first word in line 21. This pattern is also found in "Simon." 74 *FGE*, which begins φῆ ποτε Πρωτόμαχος, where Protomachus laments his father slain in battle. The sense may have been: "(someone) said that two . . .."[79] We have no idea who is speaking; it might be a prophet. The dramatic use of speeches in a description of a battle is illustrated by the *Persai* of Timotheus. In line 7, ῥύσιον could perhaps refer to reprisals taken by Demeter for violations committed by the Persians round the temple of Demeter at Eleusis.

18 W^2. ἐκυδα[ιν- is a word that suggests a military context; cf. "Simon." 9 *FGE* (virtue glorifies and immortalizes the fallen), 64 *FGE* ("glorified her city").

---

73. Schneidewin 1835: 83. On the two terms, see Σ *Il*. 6.152; Steph. Byz. *Ethn*. 290.9ff., 300.20ff., 374.1. Huxley 1969: 61–62, believes that it was only Eumelus who applied the obscure Homeric name Ephyre to Corinth.

74. The testimony is uncertain; Bernabé 1987: 108 (on Eumelus fr. 1) and Davies 1988: 97 (on Eumelus fr. 1B) doubt it.

75. See Waern 1951: 84, 123; a different kenning for the sun is found at Aesch. *Suppl*. 212.

76. It also occurs in the Homeric formula ὃς πάντ' ἐφορᾷς καὶ πάντ' ἐπακούεις (*Il*. 3.277, *Od*. 11.109); also Aesch. *Cho*. 986–97, *Prom*. 91; and a few times in Euripides.

77. Helios was awarded the city over Poseidon by Briareus (Paus. 2.1.6), and he was the father of Aloeus and Aietes (Eumelus, fr. 3 Bernabé = fr. 2 Davies). Cult of Helios at Corinth: Paus. 2.4.6.

78. Schneidewin 1835: 83 suggested that Simonides called the sun "esteemed gold" in order to defuse the criticism of people who accused him of making money, but that seems far-fetched.

79. Cf. Ap. Rhod. 3.495: φῆ δὲ δύω πεδίον τὸ Ἀρήιον ἀμφινέμεσθαι | ταύρω χαλκόποδε.

Section 5: *Sphragis* (?)

The poem may well have had a final *sphragis* section, in which the poet discusses his art, like the *Persai* of Timotheus, which is concerned with poetry.[80] Could the "Leaves" fragment have come here (the idea of mourning the dead would lead into a meditation on the mutability of life, especially the warrior's life, since the Homeric "leaves" fragment evokes the idea of death in war: see Obbink, this volume, at nn. 71–75); or perhaps the epigram or elegiac fragment 89 W[2], in which Simonides praises himself for skill at "memory"? He claims to be 80 years old in this fragment; if he was born in about 556, he would have been 77 when the battle of Plataea took place, and perhaps 80, or almost 80, by the time the poem was commissioned or otherwise composed.

Sympotic Fragments

Several passages of poetry to which the two papyri contribute seem to have been sympotic in character. The sympotic poems from which these come are generally regarded as distinct from the military/historical elegies, and different in character; but these distinctions may be in part bogus, especially if any of the military/historical elegies were performed at *sumposia*.[81]

The Leaves (frr. 19–20 W²).

The two fragments are transmitted by Stobaeus as one unit; *POxy* 3965, fr. 26 overlaps with the second half of Stobaeus' passage, also supplying scraps of four preceding lines and of seven following ones. The thought is:

19 W²: Homer said that men are like leaves, and men should heed the message
20 W²: While men are young, they do not think they will grow old. Learning this, enjoy life. But consider the word of Homer, which outlasts time, and contrast it with the ephemeral words people utter every day.[82]

West considers reversing the transmitted order of 19–20 W², but, as Sider (this volume) shows, there is no reason to do this: Homer is cited at the start for what he says about mutability, and at the end as an example of something that defies it. The fragments are attributed to "Simonides" by Stobaeus, but had sometimes been assigned to Semonides of Amorgos (by Bergk and others). West's conclusion that

---

80. I thank Jenny Strauss Clay for a discussion of this fragment.
81. For the possibility that 19–20 W² come from the *sphragis* of the Plataea poem, see immediately above. So there is a faint chance that 21 W² could come from a similar context (perhaps the theme of justice there (l. 4) echoes 11.12 W²).
82. For the restoration of lines 17–19, see West 1993a.

Simonides was the author was nicely confirmed by the fragment.[83] Hubbard (this volume, at nn. 4–5) points out that even now we cannot be sure that confusion between Simonides and Semonides had not taken place by the Hellenistic period. However, other sections of the poem now lost to us might have contained clear signs of authorship.

Fragment 20 W² is parallel to 531 *PMG*, the eulogy for those who died at Themopylae (οὔθ' ὁ πανδαμάτωρ ἀμαυρώσει χρόνος). A contrast can be drawn with the poem on the statue on the tomb of Midas and the epigram of Cleoboulus (581 *PMG*), where Simonides mocked the idea that anything could last forever.[84] In spirit it seems to represent the opposite point of view, though it is not strictly inconsistent with 19–20 W², since the poem of Homer is not a physical object, like a stone, or an inscription.

A Wish to Be Somewhere Else (21–22 W²)

21 W² (*POxy* 2327, fr. 1 + 2[a] col. i). West tentatively posits the start of a poem at line 3; the only evidence for this is the sense, though the asyndeton supports this somewhat.[85] Barigazzi 1963: 65 thought the context was military, and saw it as a *recusatio* to list all the names of the fallen, reading ψυχῶν; this was challenged already by Podlecki 1968, and West 1993a rightly interprets the fragment as erotic. The poet announces that he can no longer be a faithful companion to his soul,[86] and that he has respected justice, though with pain, since the end of his boyhood and the onset of adolescence. "Justice" here might mean either chastity, or, as Bartol (1999a, 1999b: 341–46) has recently suggested, the principle that the *eromenos* (which he has been) must respect the *erastes* (which he has now become). The sexual awakening that took place at this time is symbolized by colorful imagery: ivory skin is darkened by burgeoning hair, and it is as if white snow melts away, revealing verdant grass (an image that, as West suggests, may have inspired Horace, *Odes* 4.7). West points out that one of the three poems in the *Theognidea* (1345–50) that address a "Simonides," attributed on that ground to Euenos of Paros (fr. 8c; cf. fr. 8 and fr. 8a), has the similar theme of "I am in love, but reluctantly." In view of this parallel, should we infer that Euenos— an older poet of that name if the better-known Euenos is too young—was addressing our Simonides (cf. Bowra 1934)? [87]

22 W² (*POxy* 2327, fr. 3 + fr. 2[a] col. ii + [b] + fr. 4 + *POxy* 3965, fr. 27). The singer describes a journey, apparently to an island (1–8), where he meets Echecratidas, probably to be identified with the late Thessalian ruler, father of Antiochus and husband

---

83. Cf. West 1974: 180.

84. This "philosophical" aspect of the program of Simonides is brought out by Austin 1967.

85. There is no sign of a gap between the lines in the papyrus here, as there is in *POxy* 2327 fr. 7.

86. In his article, West favors ψυχῇ, whereas his text has the vocative ψυχή, but the vocative is too short for the space. We should also consider Danielewicz's ψυχήν, an accusative of respect.

87. For allusions in Horace, see also Barchiesi, this volume and 1996, and Harrison, this volume. For Simonides in the *Theognidea*, cf. Bowra 1934.

of Dyseris (9–10). (Simonides wrote a *threnos* for the son: 528 *PMG*).[88] He imagines himself being rejuvenated (11–12), having sex with a male, reclining as if in a *sumposion*,[89] and singing, so that the situation described mirrors the performance context of the poem. West may be right in his suggestion that the lines immediately preceding the description of the island (1–3) are part of a propemptic frame; perhaps he began with the well-established image of the *sumposion* as a ship at sea he then imagined setting sail.[90]

Parsons 1992a: 46 reasons that the journey might be (a) real, (b) escapist, or (c) post mortem. Richard Hunter has argued for a version of (a), similar to that of the *Propemptikon* in Theocritus, *Id.* 7.61ff., where the singer imagines his beloved traveling to an island, and himself celebrating independently.[91] The beloved might be featured in lines 1–8 (ἵκοιτο) and the singer in 9ff., or the beloved might be featured in lines 1–12 (λάβοι) and the singer in 13ff. The problem with (a) is the word φαρκίδας in line 14, which means "wrinkles" and implies rejuvenation (Hunter tries to deal with φαρκίδας by suggesting that the word might have the unattested sense of some sort of food),[92] so the context is probably one of rejuvenation, and the hypothesis of a real-life journey seems ruled out.

The possibility of a post-mortem journey (c) seems likely enough, if the Echecratidas mentioned was the father of Antiochus; perhaps Simonides imagines himself making a voyage to join him in the Islands of the Blessed.[93] Either Echecratidas or Simonides or both would be rejuvenated. It is worth considering the possibility that it draws on a traditional belief that the poet is someone who can contact the dead, rather as Pindar represents himself as sending songs to the underworld, or as the Hellenistic poet Poseidippus described himself following a mystical path to Hades.[94]

A variation of the post-mortem hypothesis is argued for by Dimitrios Yatromanolakis. He suggests that the speaking subject is not male, but a woman, Dyseris, the wife of Echecratidas, mourning her husband. This elegiac lament would be parallel to the lyric *threnos* of Simonides in which Dyseris mourned for her son Antiochus.[95]

---

88. See Molyneux 1992: 127ff. West also suggests that the name Echecratidas could be restored in 14.16 W². Early on, before the name Echecratidas was restored (i.e., before *POxy* 2327, fr. 27 was added at the left), it seemed that these might actually be the Islands of the Blessed, and]δην might be Peleides, which would suit the emphasis on Achilles in the other fragments very well. However, the position of fr. 27 seems certain.

89. κεκλιμένος recalls Archilochus, fr. 2 W; cf. Bowie 1986: 18.

90. Slater 1976; Bowie 1986: 17.

91. Hunter 1993a.

92. The sense "wrinkles" is now endorsed by Poltera 1997: 272–73.

93. This is basically the conclusion reached by West. I would add that there exists a parallel for song in the Islands of the Blessed in Philostratus' description of Achilles and Helen playing music there (*Heroicus* c.54; 72.7ff. de Lannoy).

94. Segal 1985; Poseidippus 704.21–25 SH.

95. Yatromanolakis, this volume.

The remaining possibility is (b), that the poem was an escapist fantasy. Parsons compared the "imagery of elsewhere" odes in Greek tragedy,[96] in particular Euripides, *Hippolytus* 732ff., where the chorus wish they could fly away to the island of the Hesperides, or *Bacchae* 403ff., where the chorus want to fly off to Cyprus where they will consort with Eros. Not much different is the mood of Horace, *Epode* 16, where the poet imagines leaving contemporary Rome and sailing to the islands to the west. Rejuvenation could perhaps have been mentioned in such "escapist" texts. A persuasive version of the escapist fantasy hypothesis is argued for by Sarah Mace; for her, the singer imagines himself journeying to a utopian island where he will take part in an erotic fantasy. Crucial to this reconstruction is the assumption that the Echecratidas in the poem is not the father of Antiochus, but an otherwise unattested son, a young man, the object of the singer's sexual desire.[97]

Can 21 W^2 be connected with 22 W^2, which came in the next column? West argues that the fragments are from distinct poems, though consecutive ones. Parsons, however, suggested that there might be a connection, arguing that the poet might have passed from a description of his sexual awakening to expressing the desire for rejuvenation and continued sexual activity in the Islands of the Blessed.[98] Mace's interpretation of 22 W^2 points in the same direction.

Other Fragments

The remaining fragments classified by West as sympotic tell us little. Fragments 23–26 W^2 are fragments transmitted by manuscript paradosis. Number 25 W^2 is a strange fragment about snow; 26 W^2, from Chamaeleon, seems to be drawn from a poem about a *lagoon*. 27–33 W^2 are papyrus fragments. Number 27 W^2, from the top of a column, may make reference to stomachs; 31 W^2, a negligible fragment, is the subject of an extremely ambitious reconstruction by West in his apparatus; 33W^2 is a mess: we catch a trace of a paean (line 1); a donkey (line 6); baskets (line 9); Kypris (line 15; cf. 72 W^2); but it seems impossible to put these elements together into any sort of whole.

Numbers 34–85 W^2 are papyrus fragments too small or obscure to be definitely classed as either military or sympotic. Numbers 86–92 W^2 are literary fragments, which West judges could derive from epigrams or elegies. Numbers 34–57 W^2 are the remaining fragments of *POxy* 2327; 58–85 W^2 the remaining fragments of *POxy* 3965. Number 34 W^2 is a small fragment, apparently from the end of one poem and the beginning of another, with a marginal coronis and (probably) title. Reference to

---

96. See Padel 1974.

97. Mace, this volume. A sort of poetic precedent to this would be Sappho fr. 58, where the singer considers the possibility of achieving immortality in a distant land like Tithonus, but rejects it because Tithonus still grew old. Might 22 W^2 have ended with a similar rejection of the possibility sketched?

98. Parsons 1992: 49: "I can never be a cautious wallflower. Even now, in old age, I long for love and wine. Hasten the day, when I recover my youth in the symposium of the Blest." Mace and Yatromanolakis both treat 22 W^2 as a separate poem.

horses in 35 W^2 might justify putting it with the Plataea poem. If 59.5 W^2 can be sup-plemented φόρμιγξ, as Parsons 1992a: 39, suggests, that might indicate it should be placed with the sympotic fragments. Number 70 W^2 refers to Castor and Pollux, which can be compared with 11.31 W^2, but sympotic contexts should be imagined for them also; one thinks in particular of the tradition that the Tyndaridai saved Simonides from death at a banquet in Crannon (510 *PMG*).

2

PETER PARSONS

"These Fragments We Have Shored against Our Ruin"

In September 1819, the poet Wordsworth fell to comparing the autumn birdsong with his own now elderly Muse. His thoughts turned to the fresh inspiration of the Greek poets; most of their work was lost, but perhaps scholarship might recover more:

> O ye who patiently explore
> The wreck of Herculanean lore,
>   What rapture, could ye seize
> Some Theban fragment, or unroll
> One precious tender-hearted scroll
>   Of pure Simonides.[1]

He was of course to be disappointed. The buried library of Herculaneum has not been good to Greek poets—at least, not so far. Egypt did better, at least for Pindar, once systematic digging for papyri began in the late nineteenth century; but even there Simonides, a poet whom longevity and productivity had made a classic in his lifetime and a legend thereafter, remained unrepresented until quite recently.

Until 1959, indeed, all that survived was a scatter of quotations to contrast with the solid reputation. The miserable remains were last comprehensively collected and commented by Schneidewin in 1835.[2] After that, much scholarship accrued but no more evidence. What Diehl could offer in his *Anthologia Lyrica* of 1925 was the same;[3] but at least it offered all, indeed more than all, of what could reasonably be attributed to this poet. It was, in this respect, a backward step that the Oxford editions, which did now have new material to add, separated the lyric Simonides in Page from the elegiac Simonides in West, and both from the epigrams which had by then been judged to be pseudepigraphic.[4] It is a great merit of the Loeb by David Campbell[5] that it

---

1. Wordsworth (ed. Ketcham) 1989: 286, ll. 49–54; de Selincourt and Darbishire 1947: 99–101.
2. Schneidewin 1835.
3. Diehl 1925: 61–118.
4. 186–302 *FGE*.
5. Campbell 1991: 330–591.

reunites the scattered limbs; and we must hope that the commentary in preparation by O. Poltera will do the same.[6] This is not just a matter of tidiness. In Simonides, we have a supreme example of the jobbing poet who is also a celebrity: a wider range of genres and correspondingly of styles and perhaps correspondingly of occasions than any Greek poet we know—and it is the juxtaposition of his fragments that highlights his activity.

Images

We inherit small fragments of a great name; time has largely destroyed the words of Simonides, but his image has remained various and powerful.

Of the historical Simonides we know, as usual, very little.[7] He celebrated the athletic victories of Eualcidas of Eretria, who was killed in 498 B.C.E.;[8] he celebrated the battle of Plataea, fought in 479.[9] Anecdote (known already to Aristotle) has him working at the court of Hipparchus, before 514;[10] later tradition makes him live to be 90.[11] The absolute chronology remains disputable;[12] but on any analysis Simonides began his career in the age of the tyrants, and finished it in the age of democracy. The list of his patrons shows panhellenic activity, overlapping that of a younger competitor, Pindar. One patron was Hiero of Syracuse; and a tomb of Simonides was shown at Acragas.[13] Clearly Simonides was famous in his time, at least with the rich and princely. Anacreon, another member of Hipparchus' court, made a deeper impression in Athens; from his appearance on the "booner" vases,[14] he seems to have struck the popular imagination like the young Mick Jagger. Vase painters also depict Sappho and Alcaeus; they do not depict Simonides or indeed Pindar[15]—it is the pop singers (alive or dead) who concern the public, not the composers of cantatas. Nonetheless, Simonides left a name and a complex of overlapping images, as poet, sage, inventor, and money-grabber.

In our sources, the money comes first. It was Xenophanes, according to the gossip-collecting Chamaeleon, who called Simonides "stingy"; Pindar's reference to the greedy working-girl Muse was certainly interpreted by Callimachus as pointing the finger at Simonides.[16] It is easy enough to explain this as the envy of a senior and a

6. There is at present no up-to-date commentary on Simonides. For bibliographic surveys see Gerber 1991 (elegy) and 1994 (lyric); Poltera 1997.

7. Campbell offers a most useful collection of testimonia. Lefkowitz 1981: 49–56, takes a scalpel to the legend. Molyneux 1992 takes the historicist line.

8. 518 *PMG*.

9. See below.

10. Arist. *Ath. Pol.* 18.1

11. T 8–9 Campbell.

12. Scholars have traditionally set his birth ca. 556; others ca. 532. For arguments against the low chronology, see Molyneux 1992.

13. Call. fr. 64.

14. Kurtz and Boardman 1986.

15. Richter 1965: 1. 69–78, 142–44.

16. Xenoph. fr. 21 W (Chamaeleon fr. 33 Wehrli). Pind. *Isthm.* 2.6 with Call. fr. 222.

junior at Simonides' ability to market his skills; and it may indeed be that Simonides was the first great commercial success of Greek poetry, exploiting an age when princes and poleis were prepared to pay for poetry and immortality. Aristophanes continues the line: Simonides had been a man who, even as a senile wreck, would go to sea on a doormat if there were money to be made.[17] That, perhaps, seemed all the more incongruous in a classic poet who by now counted as old fashioned:[18] so young Pheidippides rejects Simonides and Aeschylus in favor of the new-fangled immoralities of Euripides.[19] Tightwad, genius—and, before long, sage as well. Plato lists him with Bias and Pittacus; Aristotle records crisp (and cynical) apophthegms.[20]

The legend, and the text, passed on to Alexandria. Callimachus classified the victory poems;[21] at some stage, someone installed Simonides among the Nine Lyric Poets.[22] We assume that his works were collected and edited; and that, as usual, the biographical entry in the Suda reproduces the outline of this collection. But the entry is garbled,[23] incomplete, and now further complicated by our new information. Part of it conforms to our expectation that Alexandrian scholars would have organized Simonides in books by genre, as they did with Pindar, each book with a generic title or (as in the case of Sappho) a number. "Laments, encomia, epigrams, paeans" suit this pattern; from other sources we could add epinicians,[24] dithyrambs,[25] partheneia, prosodia.[26] What is unusual is the note on elegy, where two subjects are described explicitly.[27]

Typically, the object of scholarship is also the exemplar of poetry. In Theocritus 16, the poet addresses Hiero II; and, in the familiar argument that only poetry can save the patron from oblivion, cites Simonides and his Thessalian clients.[28] We now know, from the new elegiac fragments, that Theocritus looked back to the Plataea poem: he quotes five words of it, out of context[29]—and implies that he can do for the new Hiero what Simonides did for his own heroes, just as Simonides proposes to do for the Persian War what Homer did for the Trojan War. Simonides, like Pindar, suits the new poets of the new monarchies: their examples make patronage more glamorous to the patron, and more respectable for the poet; if Simonides preferred cash to gratitude, why should not Theocritus (who begins his poem with a virtuoso fantasy on this famous anecdote)? In *Aetia* 3, Callimachus makes the dead Simonides narrate the fate

17. *Peace* 698f.
18. Eupolis fr.148 KA (with Stesichorus and Alcman).
19. Aristoph. *Clouds* 1355ff.
20. Plato *Rep.* 335e. Arist. *Rhet.* 1391a; fr. 92 Rose.
21. Call. fr. 441.
22. Pfeiffer 1968: 205.
23. For a critical text, see W²: 114. On the question of how many poems Simonides wrote on the battle of Artemisium, see Rutherford, this volume, at n. 10.
24. 506 *PMG*.
25. 539 *PMG*, cf *AP* 6.213 (241 *FGE*).
26. [Plut.] *De musica* 17; cf. Aristoph. *Birds* 919.
27. See Obbink, this volume, at nn. 36–38.
28. Theocr. 16.34ff. See Fantuzzi, this volume.
29. Theocr. 16.45–6, cf. Simon. 11.17–18 W². See this volume, Rutherford at n. 58 and Fantuzzi. Capra and Curti 1995 try to dilute the allusion.

of his tomb in Sicily; thus the poet of short epitaphs expands his own into a short elegy.[30] Here the emphasis is not on the poet, but on the inventor: the man who "contrived memory."[31] That introduces the most famous of anecdotes, how the Dioscuri saved Simonides when the palace fell in on the Scopadae; Simonides (the Callimachean text breaks off, but we can guess the rest from later versions) was able to name the mutilated dead by remembering their place at table. Thus he invented mnemonics.[32]

The Romans inherited a more limited Simonides. As mnemonist, he plays his part in anecdote. As poet, he has become the exemplar of pathos,[33] and so he appears in Quintilian's Reader's Digest summary of the Canon.[34] The complete works (we presume) still exist; but not for long. With the Dark Ages, Simonides turns finally from text to paradigm. Wordsworth, as we have seen, looks for the tender-hearted; Leopardi, about the same time, recalled the patriot poet of national resistance to the oppressor.[35] But in the Renaissance, Simonides had another importance: in the dizzy expansion of Memory in hermetic systems, Simonides figures as the founding father of the art; if you spin the Memory Wheel of Giordano Bruno (illustrated in the famous book of Frances Yates),[36] you find Simonides occupying the final place.

Fragments

Simonides, then, survived the Middle Ages in quotation and anecdote; that was enough to inspire much scholarship, and eventually a real novel (Mary Renault's *The*

---

30. Call. fr. 64. On the detail, see Lehnus 1989: 87; Bing 1988a: 67–70.

31. ὃc τὰ περιccά | [. . . .] μνήμην πρῶτοc ὃc ἐφραcάμην (9–10). There remains no clear solution to the difficulty at the beginning of the line. Pfeiffer proposed ἤδη καὶ "I was extraordinarily wise," but there are doubts about the contracted form, even if the space allows it. It is tempting, as many editors have done, to look for a reference to another Simonidean discovery, "the long vowels and double consonants" (see Suda); but the lacuna remains intractable.

32. Cic. *De oratore* 2.86.351–53; Quint. 11.2.11–16. These versions add another element: the patron had refused to pay half the fee, because the poet had devoted half the poem to the Dioscuri and not to himself; it was the Dioscuri who saved the pious poet when the impious patron met his death. This simply turns into biography a late critical misunderstanding of the nature and structure of Greek praise-poetry. There are those who would like to explain the rest on the same lines: the poet's art of making his clients remembered was misunderstood as the invention of a mnemonic system. Against this is the fact that the system works: the mnemonist S., described by A. R. Luria, converted words into images and arranged these images in spatial sequence. "Frequently he would take a mental walk along . . . Gorky Street in Moscow, beginning at Mayakovsky Square, and slowly make his way down, 'distributing' his images at houses, gates and storewindows"; he would then repeat the walk when he needed to recall the items (Luria 1975: 30–31). On this "method of loci" see further Rubin 1995: 46–48.

33. Dion. Hal. *Imit.* 2.420. Cat. 38.8; Hor. *Carm.* 2.1.38.

34. *Inst.* 10.1.64.

35. *Canti* I ("All' Italia").

36. Yates 1966: 221f. The tradition continues: a society devoted to remembering past wars carries SIMONIDES on its escutcheon.

Praise-Singer). From the late nineteenth century, Greek literature in general experienced a new, if lesser, renaissance; the excavation of Greek settlements in Egypt opened a door, here and there, on the well-stocked libraries of the Roman Empire. Of all the settlements, Oxyrhynchus proved to have been a paradise of the bookish bourgeoisie, and in 1959, *POxy* 2430 contributed 166 tatters of epinicians and paeans, of which one fragment overlapped—with a little judicious tampering—a line quoted elsewhere as by Simonides. In 1967, there followed *POxy* 2623, another collection of lyric scraps; two at least looked like epinicians, but there was then no clear indication of authorship (Pindar, Bacchylides, and Simonides were all considered). The editor of these pieces was E. Lobel, to whose austere genius so much Greek poetry owes its second life. In his later years (and he was 93 when he died in 1982), his eyes failed; but he occupied himself in the laborious task of looking for overlaps. Finally, in 1981, he was able to show that one fragment of 2623 overlapped two lines quoted from Simonides by Plutarch; and that three other fragments overlapped three fragments of 2430.[37] We seem, then, to have acquired two fragmentary copies of choral lyric by Simonides.

In 1954, Lobel had published a papyrus of elegiac verse, *POxy* 2327, written by the same scribe as the lyric of 2430, which showed overlaps with an unpublished papyrus of elegy, also from Oxyrhynchus; and that unpublished papyrus overlapped an elegiac couplet quoted, again by Plutarch, as from Simonides. Lobel did not live to publish the unpublished; but it finally appeared as *POxy* 3965 in 1992. The two together (it is likely, though not provable, that these are two copies of one and the same collection) contribute perhaps a hundred lines—mostly incomplete—from elegiac poetry of Simonides.

These new acquisitions, however fragmentary, quadruple the Simonidean text. The first group takes us into the choral world, compositions for private and public occasions; they exemplify paeans and notably a genre of which Ibycus and Simonides are the first known practitioners, the epinician. We glimpse that glamorous world in which athletes competed for victory, and poets for commissions. Such were the Corinthian Oligaithidai, whose family won victories wholesale at the four great games and at others all over the Hellenic world. Pindar celebrated a double Olympic victory in *Olympian* 13 (464); we now know that Simonides had done the same for (perhaps) a second cousin.[38] The second group, the elegies, brings generic surprises: alongside moral and convivial themes (both destined for the symposium?), we find historical subjects—the battle of Artemisium to which the Suda alludes, and a complete novelty, the battle of Plataea.

The papers that follow are concerned above all with the new elegies, and what they show about Simonides and Greek poetry in general. The material carries particular problems, and it may be useful to make some (commonsense) points about method.

37. Lobel 1981: 21–23.
38. Barrett 1978: 1–20.

Fragments, Texts, Styles

1. *Fragments.*   As the recent essays edited by Glenn Most show,[39] there are particular problems about handling a fragmentary author. At first sight, you might think that the quotation fragments correspond to the random decorative instincts of those who quote, and the papyrus fragments to the chances of survival in an Egyptian waste-paper dump. The second is true, within limits; the first needs to be severely qualified. Anthologies may skew the sample; we have Stobaeus, and so we have a slew of moral excerpts. Even in detail, they are not to be trusted: the new papyrus has shown that the thirteen lines quoted by Stobaeus 4.34.28, printed as a unit in all editions until 1992, conflate two passages that were originally separate (now frr. 19 and 20).[40] Beyond the ravages of time, and the dangers of transmission, the larger problem of reconstructing a picture from glimpses.

2. *Texts.*   Most of this volume is concerned with the two new papyri of Simonides' elegiacs; of the texts here printed for reference, one is based on that in Martin West's *Iambi et Elegi Graeci*, vol. 2, second edition (1992).[41] All editors, of course, have to tread a line between rectitude and usability; and most readers will find a reproduction of the papyrus, all doubtful letters and lacunas, unusable. However, there are commonsense (and pessimistic) precautions to be taken in handling such texts on papyrus.

   (i) "The papyrus" is a collection of scraps. We assume that each group of fragments comes from one and the same roll; and that these two rolls represent originally two copies of one and the same text. These are working assumptions. Neither proposition can be guaranteed; in particular, the fragments in each case have been collected from the rubbish tip on the basis of the handwriting, and we do not know absolutely that the same scribe did not copy two different rolls or indeed two different authors. What we do know is that certain verses occurred in both papyri. Still, let us take the optimistic line: fate has given us two different sets of the same jigsaw puzzle; in each set at least 90 percent of the pieces are missing—but not the same 90 percent. There is therefore the chance that any one fragment of one papyrus contains lines of which further remains appear on a fragment of the other papyrus; and a much greater chance that it does not.

   (ii) Juxtapositions. If scraps do not join physically, they may be ranged on the basis of the fiber patterns; conjoined by a perceived continuity of text; juxtaposed by a perceived thematic relation. Thus 11.1–4 W^2 stands on a scrap from the foot of a col-

---

39. Most 1997a.

40. See Sider, this volume.

41. The *editio princeps* of the newer papyrus is *Oxyrhynchus Papyri* vol. 59. The typescript of this edition was shown to M. L. West, who was then preparing the second edition of his *Iambi et Elegi Graeci* vol. 2. He contributed many corrections and suggestions, which were gratefully incorporated before the typescript went to press; in turn, he was able to use the new text in *IEG*. In the event, *IEG* II^2 (= W^2) was published before *Oxyrhynchus Papyri* vol. 59, but the textual priority is the reverse (and so the supplement in 11.27 W^2 is attributed to R. B. Rutherford, instead of I. C. Rutherford, an error of the typescript).

umn, 5ff. on a separate piece with the top of the column; they may be consecutive, but there is no physical proof of this.

(iii) Readings. Decipherment is only in part an objective business. Shadows deceive; legibility is in the eye of the beholder. In a broken text, one half-letter may determine a word, which may determine a clause, which may help create a context. The black and white of a printed page often gives a misleading impression of certainty. Thus in 11.42 W² reads and prints μάν]τιος; the *editio princeps* had proposed Κέκρο]ποϲ. There is a paleographic question. The dotted letters represent damaged traces, and in principle a comparison with other examples of the letters concerned might allow a decision (at the time of this writing, enlarged pictures can be seen on the Oxyrhynchus web page). There is a larger question of thematic context. The *editio princeps* had assumed that, at this point, on the Eleusinian plain, the Athenians arrived to join the allied army; after the Athenian Pandion, the Athenian Kekrops would emphasize the antique credentials of the newcomers. In West's text, Pandion is incidental; μάν]τιος brings in the seer Teisamenos. Of course, the Athenians may have appeared later in the text; if they did not (and here we come to the political issue), we could accuse Simonides of decided tendenz.

(iv) Supplements. Most printed texts incorporate supplements—fillings of the lacunas to complete the sense. Some supplements will be virtually certain—short lacunas in highly predictable poets, for example, or at places where we have intertextual evidence (so at fr. 11.17 ὀπ[λοτέρ]οιϲιν is guaranteed by the quotation at Theocr. 16.46; at 22.14 φαρκίδαϲ ἐκτ[ανύϲαϲ by the reminiscence in Lucillius, *AP* 11.408.2).⁴² Others serve only to show that the sense intuited by the editor could be expressed within the confines of grammar, meter, and space: it is private poetry, *exempli gratia*. The text of W² contains a great many supplements, and many of them are highly speculative. Once supplements are printed, it is very difficult to think them away; as Lobel briskly observed, "a fool can throw a stone into the sea of Spain and all the wise men in the world not manage to get it out."⁴³ What is more, the process tends to become circular: if you judge (say) that your poet writes a conventional Homerizing language, you may propose a supplement that conforms to this style; and once that is made, it may serve to justify another in the same manner—and so on. So: to any one who wants to take these texts seriously, I would recommend retiring for twenty-four hours with a diplomatic transcript of the papyrus only, and a supply of nourishing sandwiches, and trying to work out from scratch how the surviving morsels might be constructed into continuous sense. Better still, begin with photographs of the papyri themselves.

3. *Styles.* It has been observed that the first reaction of classical scholars, when a papyrological novelty appears, is often to wish it away. When the Cologne Archilochus appeared, several scholars argued that it was a Hellenistic invention, since the vocabulary contained unexpected items—as if enough Archilochus sur-

---

42. Bernsdorff 1996: 24–26. D. Yatromanolakis had made the same suggestion in his unpublished doctoral thesis.

43. Lobel 1925: Preface.

vived to prove anything about his vocabulary. When the epigrams of Cornelius Gallus were published, it was held by some that they were a late pastiche, or indeed a forgery, because they seemed so unlike the Gallus we know—the Gallus we know, that is, from one quoted line and the sycophantic tributes of his fellow poets: what evidence is that? And so again, in a lesser degree, with the new Simonides. Alongside the elegy on the battle of Plataea, which I think no one doubts to be by Simonides of Ceos, stands a famous passage already known from Stobaeus, on the theme *carpe diem*. It had for long been argued by some that the ascription in Stobaeus, Cιμωνίδου, might refer to Semonides of Amorgos, known otherwise for his iambs; it was thought that the style and subject—recalling Mimnermus—pointed to a date earlier than the sophisticated Simonides of Ceos. Now it seems that the question is settled—or is it?[44] You can wriggle: perhaps these papyri represent an anthology of elegy, not the elegies of Simonides; failing that, perhaps the Alexandrian editors mixed up the two Simonides. Well, yes, perhaps and perhaps. But why struggle? The evidence of fact, however weak, should carry more weight than the evidence of style, however strong. Here, it seems to me, two factors come into play. One is the dead hand of the past. The nineteenth century created the science of antiquity; what survived of Greek literature was built into that towering positivist structure. Genres were defined, allusions recognized, literary movements constructed—all on the basis of a few flyspecks. Now, in that general crumbling of certainties which began in 1914, we have questioned many of those categories. And yet there remains a certain attachment to the *fable convenue*, the painful squeezing of maximum certainty from minimum evidence. A second factor forms part of that inheritance: the romantic belief that a poet is an individual, and an individual is a style. Once again, we think in general that we know better: not style, but manner; and manner relates to genre, genre to performance, performance to occasion. But it seems to me that there continues to be an underlying assumption of unity. Now Simonides should stand as the counter-example: not one manner, but several, according to circumstance. Why should one of those manners not be a nice old-fashioned bow to Mimnermus?

Old Problems and New Texts

The new fragments impinge on the old, and raise new questions about old problems.

First, Simonides and his patrons. We have no complete list, of course; we hear about dynasts—Hipparchos of Athens and Anaxilas of Rhegium and the Thessalian princes and Hiero of Syracuse—but also about the Corinthian family of the Oligaithidai. Anecdotes note contacts between Simonides and Themistocles, Simonides and Pausanias; hostile contacts with other poets—Timocreon and Aeschylus and Pindar, who attacked his nephew Bacchylides. The older tendency was to build a political-biographical structure from this: whose side was Simonides on? And whose side were his enemies on? J. H. Molyneux has given a detailed and ingenious exploration of the poet's working life in these terms. The new elegies raise the

---

44. See Hubbard and Sider, this volume.

question again: if Simonides begins his narrative of the Great Patriotic War with Pausanias the Spartan, and praises the Corinthians whom Herodotus maligned, does that show something about his personal politics, or about the terms of his commission?[45] In general, do these universal providers pick and choose their employers on ideological grounds? and on what ideological grounds? Simonides' working life began under the tyrants, and ended under the Athenian democracy. In 542 *PMG*, a poem for the dynast Scopas, Hermann Fränkel saw the manifesto of a new ideology: the reference to ὀνηϲίπολιϲ δίκα, the praise of all those who do no wrong of their own free will, would replace aristocratic ambition with bourgeois pragmatism.[46] Now, this relates in part to a general debate: we moderns think that the only reason for explicit moralizing is to put a new or controversial point of view; did Greek poets think the same? For myself, I don't believe so; and I don't visualize Scopas paying for such mealy-mouthed stuff. Put this alongside the poet's sympotic elegies, which so visibly continue the aristocratic world of wine, flowers, and beautiful boys.

Next, and related, Simonides and his fees. The stories of Simonides' greed go back to his own lifetime (see above). By the time of Aristotle, anecdote had connected greed and artistic integrity: when Anaxilas of Rhegium won the mule race, it was said, he offered Simonides a small fee to celebrate the victory, but the poet felt distaste at the idea of writing about mules; but when Anaxilas produced an adequate fee, he wrote, "All hail, you daughters of storm-footed horses."[47] Was Simonides the first Greek poet to sell poems retail? Probably not, if Ibycus had already written epinicians. Was he simply successful enough to attract envy? And to balance profit with self-respect, on the ground that (as Ibycus had already told Polycrates) patron gives money, but poet assures immortality? Certainly, the theme *vixere fortes* is explicitly set out in the new Plataea poem. Near the beginning of that poem, when Simonides turns from the Trojan War to the Persian campaign of which he will be the Homer, he summons the Muse to help him. The word is ἐπίκουροϲ. Is that simply a military metaphor, chosen for the context? Or does it imply a new confidence? The Homeric poet would represent himself simply as the Muse's mouthpiece: the new panhellenic stars claim a more equal partnership.[48]

Thirdly, the poet and the occasion. Simonides writes for individual patrons, sometimes for the symposium, sometimes for religious ceremonies, sometimes for semi-public occasions like the celebration of victories in the games; he also takes part in competitions—fifty-seven prizes for the dithyramb, according to a later epigram.[49] We may also guess that, like Pindar, he handled communal commissions for a variety of occasions. Fragment 531 *PMG*, the praises of those who died at Thermopylae, might be such a piece; and I certainly find myself tempted by the idea that it was performed in Sparta, where the memorial to those dead and the cenotaph of Leonidas

45. See Boedeker, "Historiography," and Hornblower, this volume.
46. Fränkel 1973: 307ff. Recent treatments by Carson 1992: 110–30, Most 1994: 127–52.
47. Arist. *Rhet.* 1405b24 (Simon. 515 *PMG*).
48. See Stehle, this volume. For a similar debate around Ap. Rhod. 1.22, the Muses as ὑποφήτορεϲ, see Hunter 1993b: 125.
49. *AP* 6.213 (241 *FGE*).

existed side by side (or did so by the time of Pausanias).[50] We can then go on to ask who if anyone commissioned, and for what if any occasion, the elegy on the battle of Plataea.[51]

Finally, to return to the poet and his styles. The older fragments already suggest a wide range. That on the dead of Thermopylae (531 *PMG*) exemplifies Dionysius of Halicarnassus' verdict that Simonides was notable for his choice of words and care (ἀκρίβεια) in combining them:[52]

> εὐκλεὴς μὲν ἁ τύχα, καλὸς δ' ὁ πότμος,
>
> βωμὸς δ' ὁ τάφος, πρὸ γόων δὲ μνᾶστις, ὁ δ' οἶκτος ἔπαινος

—an intellectual exercise in the revaluation of terms, a rhetorical exercise in the carefully varied parallelism between its two-word phrases. That to Scopas (542 *PMG*), whose moment of glory must have been limited to the one section of the first stanza that is now lost (exemplifying the anecdote about the Dioscuri), weaves a devious gnomic texture. And then Danae (543)—what genre did that belong to? The metrical structure and often the text remain uncertain: but we seem to see a monody crowded with adjectives, rich with colors, and fully dramatic in portraying a mounting hysteria. Simple paratactic sentences rise in 21 to a triple appeal for peace; at this climax she reproaches Zeus, only to fall back into apology. It could be the model for a tragic heroine. Now the new elegies show two other faces of Simonides. The sympotic elegist dwells on dark hair and ivory skin (fr. 21), on love, song, and youth restored on the Island of the Blessed (fr. 22).[53] The historical elegist proclaims himself the Homer of the Persian War, but not in the form and only partly in the language of Homer: a generic experiment, at least as we see it, which transfuses epic hymn and epic narrative into the smaller compass of elegy.[54] We have yet to find more of Wordsworth's Simonides; but we have gone some way to recovering Leopardi's.

50. 531 *PMG*. Paus. 3.14.1.
51. See Aloni, Boedeker, "Historiography," and Shaw, this volume.
52. Dion. Hal. *Imit.* 2.420.
53. See Hunter, Mace, and Yatromanolakis, this volume.
54. See Aloni, Obbink, and Barchiesi, this volume. Howie 1998: 76f. notes Pindaric analogues.

3

DIRK OBBINK

The Genre of *Plataea*

Generic Unity in the New Simonides

Among recent papyrological finds, a portion of identifiably Simonidean elegy preserved on papyrus from Oxyrhynchus[1] is almost without parallel in its potential for reorienting our thinking about early Greek poetry. The tale is a familiar one: a fragmentary ancient manuscript overlaps with another, previously known, but unidentified, and with two quotations in ancient authors. Out of the composite, a new poem can almost be said to exist. The cost for us is that difficulties are "raised in places where there were none."[2] Plutarch, who quotes several distichs, supplies an author and subject. The two papyrus manuscripts (*POxy* 3965 and 2327) provide us with two different copies of the poem,[3] in all over one hundred completely or partially preserved lines of elegy that uniquely combine features of Pindaric encomion, Homeric phraseology, sub-epic narrative technique, and Tyrtaean battle themes to recount and memorialize a historical event of considerable military and political importance.

For this reason, the new fragments of Simonides' poem on the battle at Plataea augment in an unexpected way our corpus of early Greek celebratory poetry. Some ten years ago, E. L. Bowie posited the existence of just such a class of early Greek elegy as distinct from sympotic elegy.[4] I argue that the new fragment confirms Bowie's suspicions, with a new twist: the epic elegy turns out to be introduced by a proemial hymn to a divinity. On the other hand, such a structure (*prooimion* + *nomos* +

An earlier version of this paper appeared in Deborah Boedeker and David Sider (eds.), *The New Simonides*, *Arethusa* 29.2 (1996): 193–203, and is used here by kind permission of the Johns Hopkins University Press.

1. Parsons 1992a: 4–50 = Simonides frr. 2–85 W². More extensive restorations with interesting discussion are in West 1993a. See also Haslam's review of *IEG* 2² (Haslam 1993). For high-quality color digital images of the papyrus MSS, see Obbink 1998a (for images of *POxy* 3965, see under vol. 59; for images of 2327, see Coles and Obbink 1998 s.v. "Scribes and Scholars").

2. Lobel 1948: 68.

3. As a result we know there were no less than two different copies of this book of Simonides' poetry at Oxyrhynchus. Whether these poems were all of a single genre (e.g., elegies) or a selection from various types organized according to some other criterion remains to be determined.

4. Bowie 1986.

sphragis), which smacks of later Hellenistic genre-crossing,[5] turns out not to be so very alien to early Greek rhapsodic poetry, as I will try to show. An exploration of the genre of the fragment on the battle of Plataea leads to new considerations regarding the relation of the new fragments to one another. In what follows, I try to set out a cumulative case for how the new fragments situate themselves in a reconstruction of Simonides' works.

We now know there were no fewer than six copies of Simonides at Oxyrhynchus alone: *POxy* 2431 (epinicia), 2430 (paeans), 2623 and 2624 (paeans and/or epinicia), 2327, 3965 (elegies).[6] These are professionally edited and professionally produced books, which have been provided with annotations recording the names, opinions, and variant readings of known Alexandrian scholars who supervised the paradosis. An additional, seventh papyrus manuscript of Simonides at Oxyrhynchus may be posited, the one to which was once attached *POxy* 2433, a sillybos or "title-tag" of a commentary, ὑπ(όμνημα) on a book entitled *Simonidea*.[7] The adespotum *POxy* 2432 (541 *PMG*), if Simonidean,[8] would bring the number to eight. *POxy* 2434 may be a commentary on Simonidean lyrics. While on papyri Simonides is dwarfed by comparison with Pindar, it is still a striking number for any lyric poet, even if one accepts the recent arguments of Funghi and Messeri that the annotated, critical texts of certain classical authors at Oxyrhynchus are due to the presence there of a municipal library.[9] Oxyrhynchus is in any case miles ahead of the other great source of literary books, Hermopolis, which by contrast has so far produced not a single scroll of tender-hearted Simonides.[10] On the other hand the new fragments are a startling acquisition to our corpus of early Greek poetry. They raise new questions about the genera and performance of archaic poetry and its reception by later ages. In many cases, where before the νεώτεροι were thought to be innovating, they can now be seen to be taking Simonides as a point of departure.

The question of genre cannot be divorced from the question of performance, addressee, and praise. Since performance is generally taken nowadays to be an integral if not defining feature of generic form, any conclusions about the genre of the poem can only be tentative in light of the unsettled question of the original circumstances of composition. Did Simonides compose *Plataea* in praise of a single individual or city, for performance in a specific venue? Or was he, as Plutarch says, simply putting panhellenic exploits into elegiacs? Or did he praise them all, perhaps up-

---

5. But it is not certain that a "*Kreuzung* of genres" is the appropriate model of explanation for Hellenistic experimentation with generic form.

6. MSS 2430 and 2327 are by the same scribe and in the same format, and both contain scholia. The same roll, however, is unlikely to have contained both lyric poems in the Doric dialect and elegies in Ionic. Perhaps they formed part of a multivolume collected works edition of Simonides' poems.

7. Photo in Turner 1987: no. 7, p. 35, with correction p. 148 n. 8. Lobel (ap. *POxy* 2433) suggested that "Simonidea" might be taken to mean various poems of or passages from Simonides. But the normal title for a commentary on these would be *Hypomnema on Poems of Simonides* (Σιμωνίδου μελῶν ὑπόμνημα). Pfeiffer 1968: 222 argued for "a popular exposition of his famous sayings," for which see Campbell 1991: test. 47a–k, and cf. Simonides' appeal to (and rejection of) the sayings of the wise men Pittacus in 542.11 *PMG* and Cleobulus in 581.

8. Henry 1998: 303–4 adduces additional evidence favoring Simonides.

9. Funghi and Messeri Savorelli 1992. See further Obbink 1999.

10. Minnen and Worp 1993.

staging now this one and now that, varying his encomium by venue, and vacillating, in the manner of a Theocritus or an Elton John, between the tycoons of days gone by and the current media darlings?

Performance is not the only indicator of the poem's genre, however. I will argue that there are other cues present in the text that enable us to specify the genre η̃ τῖ the new fragments, an exercise which may in turn help clarify the range of options for a possible context of performance.

It hardly needs to be said, for example, that meter could have been taken as the defining feature of genre, and that the unvaried presence of the elegiac couplet in the two independent papyrus manuscripts (2327 and 3965) points directly to elegy. But were the poem on Plataea agreed uniformly to be an elegy, we should still have to address the question of what kind of elegy. Martial elegy à la Tyrtaeus seems to fit the subject of the Plataea poem well. But there is no exhortation to battle; for that had already been won. What we read is a celebration or commemoration, and praise of a number of persons and groups for an effort of heroic proportions, combined with reflections on death and mortality. For just how many of the new fragments does this description hold true?

Thus we are reminded that addressee, combined with registers of praise and blame and seriousness, can help to pinpoint genre. But here too difficulties may arise, even within the new fragments that derive indubitably from one and the same poem. In what follows, I first set forth the basic structure of the poem, beginning with fr. 11 W², which provides both proem and narrative of the march out from Sparta to Plataea. After a digression on the place of the poem which contained fr. 11 W² in the Hellenistic edition of Simonides' poetry, I then turn to fr. 16 W² (on the Corinthians calling the sun to witness) which is also quoted by Plutarch, on which there is general agreement that it came from the same poem about the battle and that they came in that order. I shall go a step further, however, in proposing that other fragments from the new papyrus—the comparison of men's lives to leaves, for example, with its parallel Homeric reference—may come from the poem on Plataea as well. Consensus on this point remains to emerge.

The Hymnic Structure of *Plataea*

The structure of fr. 11 W² provides ambivalent but not contradictory indications of its genre. A highly mythologizing opening at first masks, and then pivots to, the poem's ultimate subject in our largest fragment of the poem (*POxy* 2327 fr. 5 + 6 + 27 col. 1 + 3965 fr. 1 + 2). This fundamental transition was perceived by the Oxyrhynchus editors and informed their reconstruction at every stage. At the very point at which this fragment first begins, under discussion is the funeral of Achilles: lines 2–3 ἢ πίτυν ἐν βῆσ[σαις and ὑλοτόμοι τάμ[νωσιν. Patroclus is mentioned (line 7), and Achilles is being addressed; this much is certain from the parting salutation to the son of Thetis at line 19, giving rise to West's restorations of 7–8:

> οὐ δή τίς σ' ἐδ]άμασσεν ἐφ[ημέριος βροτὸς αὐτός,
> ἀλλ' ὑπ' Ἀπόλλ]ωνος χειρὶ [τυπεὶς ἐδάμης.

It is unclear whether this refers to the death of Achilles, or rather that of Patroclus. In addition to the parallels cited by Parsons (1992a: 29), cf. *Il.* 16.849 (the dying Patroclus to Hector): ἀλλά με μοῖρ' ὀλοὴ καὶ Λητοῦς ἔκτανεν υἱός | ἀνδρῶν δ' Εὔφορβος· σὺ δέ με τρίτος ἐξεναρίζεις. But West argues on the basis of the prominence of Achilles in this section that Apollo should figure here for the death of Achilles himself (Parsons compares *Il.* 19.416f., 22.359, noting that Achilles' death is certainly alluded to in line 18).

In lines 10–12, Priam is named, and Paris too, as a result of whose actions the "chariot of divine justice" (θείης ἄρμα . . . δίκ[ης) reaches its destined goal: the ἀγέμαχοι Δαναοί sack the city (13–14). At this point the poet assures us of of the fame that their poet conferred on these short-lived heroes (15–18), bids a fond farewell to his subject Achilles (19), and employs a transitional formula familiar from the Homeric hymns to invoke his "Muse of many names" and lead over to a new theme (20–24): the engagement at Plataea (25ff.). When the time comes there will be on the battlefield (at least in the preserved fragments) no killing and stabbing, no sacking of cities, no chariot of divine justice pursuing her allotted course: but there is no dearth of praise for heroized mortals and no lack of connection implied between the heroic death immortalized by Homer and those fallen at Plataea whom the poem memorializes.

Fragment 11 W²

τοὶ δὲ πόλι]ν πέρσαντες ἀοίδιμον [οἴκαδ' ἵ]κοντο
   φέρτατοι ἡρ]ώων ἀγέμαχοι Δαναοί[,
οἷσιν ἐπ' ἀθά]νατον κέχυται κλέος ἀν[δρὸς] ἕκητι   15
   ὃς παρ' ἰοπ]λοκάμων δέξατο Πιερίδ[ων
πᾶσαν ἀλη]θείην, καὶ ἐπώνυμον ὁπ[λοτέρ]οισιν
   ποίησ' ἡμ]ιθέων ὠκύμορον γενεή[ν.
ἀλλὰ σὺ μὲ]ν νῦν χαῖρε, θεᾶς ἐρικυ[δέος υἱέ
   κούρης εἰν]αλίου Νηρέος· αὐτὰρ ἐγὼ   20
κικλήισκω] σ' ἐπίκουρον ἐμοί, π[ολυώνυμ]ε μοῦσα,
   εἴ πέρ γ' ἀν]θρώπων εὐχομένω[ν μέλεαι·
ἔντυνο]ν καὶ τόνδ[ε μελ]ίφρονα κ[όσμον ἀοι]δῆς
   ἡμετ]έρης, ἵνα τις [μνή]σεται ὕ[στερον αὖ
ἀνδρῶ]ν, οἳ Σπάρτ[ηι   25

And after they sacked the city into infamy, for home
   did the illustrious leading Greek heroes set forth.
On their heads is shed undying fame by the power of a man   15
   who received from the violet-tressed Pierides
all truthfulness, who made a lasting name, among those to come,
   for the generation of demigods, swift to its doom.
But fare ye well now, brave son of goddess,
   daughter of sea-deep Nereus. And I   20
implore you as my ally, O Muse of many names:
   If ever indeed you heeded mortals at their prayers,
furnish too this pleasing arrangement for a song
   of mine, that one might recollect more recent
men, who at Sparta . . .   25

First, the structure of the ode. The new fragment is remarkable for the extent to which it reveals within a fairly brief compass the organization of the elegy and its articulation of forms of address:

1. An opening mythological hymn (or *prooimion*) in which a divinity or hero is apostrophized and directly addressed gives way, in the course of:
2. a traditional hymnic conclusion and medial address to a divinity to:
3. discursive reflection upon and narration of contemporary events and persons, including:

   3a. a listing or catalog of participants by city.[11]

This organization appears to be unique among the surviving corpus of archaic elegy, though (1) and (2) are well exampled in early hymn, encomium, paean, and epinician (e.g., Pindar), and (3) might have been expected from some strands of archaic elegy (e.g., Tyrtaeus), while the encomiastic catalog-style of (3) probably borrows from or imitates (if those are the right words) epic.[12]

Still, the resulting effect is reminiscent of nothing so much as archaic hymnody, in particular the transitional lines 10–21: αὐτὰρ ἐγώ, for instance, exampled at *Hymn. Hom. Apoll.* 545f., exactly at the transition from the "Delian" to the "Pythian" part of the hymn: καὶ σὺ μὲν οὕτω χαῖρε, Διὸς καὶ Λητοῦς υἱέ· / αὐτὰρ ἐγὼ καὶ σεῖο καὶ ἄλλης μνήσομ' ἀοιδῆς. W. Kranz maintained that this formula represented the rhapsode's transition from hymn to epic recitation,[13] a thesis that seems to fit the present elegy even better than the *Hymn to Apollo*. As Parsons notes, in later poetry, the opening hymnic "proem" could be omitted and the formula αὐτὰρ ἐγώ made to serve as the beginning of a poem (Xenoph. 7 W), or, with the following recitation truncated, it could signal the end of a book (Call. fr. 112.8 Pf.) or of a poem (cf. Poseidippos 705.21 SH).[14] For Simonides, however, in Parson's words (1992a: 32), "the formula of closing leads on to a formula of beginning, the invocation of the Muse. But there is no clear divide: the formulae are integrated, both in syntax and in line-structure."

What exactly, then, preceded this transition in Simonides' elegy? How did the poem begin? *POxy* 2327 fr. 6, which overlaps with the new and more extensive 3965 fr. 1 + 2, is the top of a column, while 2327 fr. 5 (i.e., lines 1–4 in West's edition), dealing identifiably with a heroic death, is a column's foot. Therefore lines 5ff. were preceded in the poem by at least one column, consisting of at least twenty-four and perhaps as many as thirty-six lines (by Parson's careful estimates, 1992a: 33). Though certainty is impossible here, it would be apt to see the poem as having a brief proemium of, say, twenty to forty lines (of which the last eighteen are preserved), in which Achilles, or Achilles and Thetis (named in 19), perhaps together with the Muses (who are perhaps reinvoked rather than introduced at lines 20–24), were addressed in suitably hymnic

---

11. It is unclear whether this is meant to be a static catalogue or a narration of an action, i.e., the march to Plataea. Boedeker 1995b discusses the passage.

12. Compare reminiscences of epic theme and diction in Mimnermus frr. 13–13a W. Like Simonides' Plataea poem, the *Iliad*'s Catalog of Ships similarly requires a mid-poem reinvocation of the Muse.

13. Kranz 1961: 11f.

14. And see Lloyd-Jones 1963: 185f. Additional correspondences between the new Simonides fragments and Poseidippos are enumerated by Gigante 1994.

or threnodic manner. Achilles was certainly central in this section. That would explain, as Parsons notes, why "Simonides gave Patroclus a substantial niche even in this short-order view of the Trojan War." Yet the action is telescoped, the transition sudden: lines 11–12 sum up the cause of the war, 13–14 its conclusion. However this may be, the fact that the poet also addresses his Muse directly in line 21 is not at odds with this hypothesis; and the parting salutation to Achilles as Thetis' son in 19 implies that they have been the main subjects of the poet's attentions in the preceding section, a mortal and an immortal foil each of the poet's subjects in the following section: poetic immortality conferred on martial valor.

The appeal to a succession of addressees is in fact fairly consonant with what we know about early didactic, encomiastic, and paraenetic forms of rhapsodic composition.[15] It is well exampled in archaic hymnody, in which even addresses or admonitions to the poet's mortal hearers may appear among a succession of invocations of divinities.[16] Hesiod's *Works and Days*, for instance, begins by addressing the Muses, names Perses at line 10, and addresses him by name in the second person at line 27 and frequently thereafter. So also Pindar in *Pythian* 1: Hieron is named at line 32 and addressed directly from 85 to 100, but the poem also invokes by direct address Zeus (29, 67), Apollo (39), and the Muse (58). Also instructive is a comparison with Empedocles, who (apart from all controversy about the status of his poems as individual works) moved in the same poem from address to his mortal apprentice Pausanias (B1 DK) to a formal invocation of his personal rhapsodic Muse Kalliopeia (B131 DK):[17]

> εἰ γὰρ ἐφημερίων ἕνεκέν τινος, ἄμβροτε Μοῦσα,
> ἡμετέρας μελέτας ⟨ἅδε τοι⟩ διὰ φροντίδος ἐλθεῖν,
> εὐχομένῳ νῦν αὖτε παρίστασο, Καλλιόπεια,
> ἀμφὶ θεῶν μακάρων ἀγαθὸν λόγον ἐμφαίνοντι.

> If for the sake of any one of mortal men, immortal Muse,
> it pleased you that our cares came to your attention,

---

15. The hymnic parody of the rhapsodic theogony at Aristoph. *Birds* 676–736, for example, has a "first proem" (676–84) in glyconics that exhorts the Nightingale to introduce the theogony proper, followed by an anapaestic prelude (685–92) beginning ἄγε δή and addressed directly to "feeble mortals" (ἄνδρες ἀμαυρόβιοι). Hesiod in the *Theogony* begins "from the Muses" (who themselves address ποιμένες ἄγραυλοι at 26–28), exhorts himself at 36 (τύνη), and directly addresses the Muses only at 104–15, imploring them to sing the theogony proper that follows. On addresses to gods in the middle of poems, see also Miller 1986: 57–65.

16. According to Bundy 1972: 83, the compositors of the *Homeric Hymns* "do not in general display awareness of auditors other than the god," adding "although such hymnal announcements as ᾄσομαι are addressed not to the god but to an audience waiting to hear his name, and such concluding prayers . . . doubtless express concern for the pleasure of a critical audience as well as for that of the god." So also at *Hymn. Hom. Apoll.* 3.172f. the rhapsode reveals in his address to the Delian maidens his concern for critical reputation among humans; in *Hymn.* 6 the singer's prayer to the god for victory in the contest presumes a critical audience of human judges (cf. *Hymn.* 30.18; 31.17; 11.5; 2.494; Call. *Hymn. Apoll.* 4 and 17; *Hymn. Iov.* 5–9).

17. Cf. Hesiod, *Theogony* 68–79, with the etymology ὀπὶ καλῇ. On Empedocles' addressees: Obbink 1993.

18. Transl. Wright 1981.

now once more, Kalliopeia, answer my prayer and stand by
as a worthy account of the blessed gods is being unfolded.[18]

A comparison with Lucretius' imitation of Empedocles' procedure is also instructive:[19] in *De rerum natura*, Lucretius' addressee Memmius is named eleven times in the poem, but the first forty-nine lines of book 1 are addressed directly to Venus. While book 3 opens with an address to Epicurus, in book 6 an invocation of the Muses appears at lines 92–95.

We know that Empedocles' invocation of the Muses did not fall at the beginning of its poem (εἰ γάρ in B131 line 1 cannot be inceptive).[20] It is a similar structure of invocation that we find in the new Simonides fragment, where the Muse is invoked in the middle of the poem. Further comparison is revealing. In a recent article, Mark Edwards concludes from the tense of ἐμφαίνοντι in line 4 that Empedocles is already in the process of revealing this λόγος and must also therefore be "the sole composer of the poem." On these grounds he concludes further that Empedocles' invocations of the Muse cannot therefore "describe 'Pierian inspiration'."[21]

In the same way, Simonides might seem at first sight to invoke his Muse in the middle of his poem, only to demote her to the position of mere helper, ἐπίκουρος (21), rather than speaker of his poem, at the conclusion of the opening mythological hymn.[22] As will become clear, I do not think this interpretation can be sustained (either for Empedocles or Simonides). Edwards, for instance, ignores the evidence of Empedocles B4 in which the Muse has already been asked to validate the persuasive elements of the poem, and B131 (see below) in which she is asked to send a pure stream of discourse through the poet's mouth. Rutherford captures the nuance best when he says "Simonides thus makes some contribution himself and is superior to Homer, who relied entirely on the Muses."[23] But the assistance of the Muse does seem to be required in order to go on and complete the poem.[24] For the new Simonides fragment, Empedocles B4 at any rate confirms that the assistance of the Muse may be required even in the middle of a poem. The delayed request for the Muse to ἀστέρας εἰπεῖν at Aratus *Phaen.* 16–18 may be usefully compared. As in the introduction to the catalogue of ships at *Il.* 2.484–93, internal reinvocations of the Muse such as these feign *aporia* and *adunaton* in order to mark the transition to a different type of poetry/discourse.

If we are correct in suspecting that the first section of our fragment (perhaps the first in the elegy) began with a direct address to Thetis (or Thetis and Achilles), it would be interesting to know what suggested to the poet the theme (or name?) of Achilles in the first place, and in particular the topic of Achilles' death, for the com-

19. Sedley 1989 argues further that, like Lucretius' poem, Empedocles' Περὶ φύσεως began with a hymn invoking Aphrodite.

20. Desperately emending to εἰκ ἄρ in order to effect such a beginning is Gallavotti 1973–74.

21. Edwards 1991: 288 n. 20.

22. This possibility was first suggested to me by Eva Stehle (though I should not hold her to it now). Cf. further her contribution to this volume. The same view is also advanced by Parsons in this volume.

23. This volume, at n. 61.

24. Perhaps giving the impression, as Rutherford suggests (this volume, at n. 61) that Simonides' Muse was a mercenary ἐργάτις, who sold herself at will for money (cf. Pind. *Isth.* 2.6).

position of this particular elegy: whether, for example, because Achilles is the arche-typal mortal divinity/divinized mortal, or because he has a special relationship to the laudandus or commissioner of the poem (e.g., Pausanias, as Shaw suggests), or because the real or imagined context for the composition or its performance was a festival or other celebration at one of several cult centers devoted to Achilles in Sparta, or as Parsons suggests, in Thessaly. Or was it rather the kind of cultic honors offered to divinized heroes in sub-Homeric epic and tragedy that suggested to the poet a con-nection between the death of Achilles and an encomiastic occasion memorializing those brave individuals who participated and perished in a famous battle of recent memory?

Still more remarkable may be the almost inescapable reference to Homer him-self (15–18) as responsible, as a result of his direct link with the divine patronesses of poetry, for shedding the *kleos* of immortality on those heroes of a lost age, invoked in the proem, who were fated to know a swift doom and young death. In the case of Achilles, the immortality conferred by that *kleos* is even assimilated to something like the status enjoyed by his divine and paradigmatically youthful Nereid mother Thetis (19–20). Simonides immediately turns, in the familiar form of the cletic prayer with historical exemplum,[25] to invoke his own Muse (21 π[ολυώνυμ]ε Μοῦσα). He thereby agonistically distances himself from Homer, at the same time as he implies an ana-logy between

1. What the Greeks of epic did in rites of burial and funeral cult for Achilles;
2. What Homer did in his divinely inspired poems for the heroes of the *Iliad*; and
3. What Simonides himself does in the present elegy for the near-contem-porary subjects of the section which follows.

In fact the connection between these three is drawn so close in the comparison as almost to be equated outright.

To sum up, the fulcrum of fr. 11 W² thus resides in the transition, introduced by the transitional formula αὐτὰρ ἐγώ, between the hymnic, mythological *prooimion* with its Homeric themes and reminiscences, on the one hand, and the historical sec-tion (from a very different opera indeed). The identical formula αὐτὰρ ἐγώ also occurs at the opening of Empedocles B35 (I quote only the first half of the fragment):

αὐτὰρ ἐγὼ παλίνορσος ἐλεύσομαι ἐς πόρον ὕμνων,
τὸν πρότερον κατέλεξα, λόγου λόγον ἐξοχετεύων
κεῖνον· ἐπεὶ νεῖκος μὲν ἐνέρτατον ἵκετο βένθος
δίνης, ἐν δὲ μέσῃ φιλότης στροφάλιγγι γένηται,

---

25. As also exampled in Empedocles B131 (quoted above), where Diels thought that ἐλθεῖν in line 2 referred to the Muse's prior assistance to the poet on a known historical occasion. This occasion, he concluded, must have been the performance of Empedocles' Περὶ φύσεως, and accordingly he placed B131 among the frag-ments he thought were called Καθαρμοί. But line 11 of the new Simonides fragment εἴ πέρ γ' ἀν]θρώπων εὐχομένω[ν μέλεαι shows this clearly to be a conventional device of rhapsodic invocation: a performative utterance referring to no specific prior event; rather the idea is that the validity of the poet's vow and claim will be born out and tested in the course of his current poetic production.

ἐν τῇ δὲ τάδε πάντα συνέρχεται ἓν μόνον εἶναι,   25
οὐκ ἄφαρ, ἀλλὰ θελημὰ συνιστάμεν' ἄλλοθεν ἄλλα.
τῶν δέ τε μισγομένων χεῖτ' ἔθνεα μυρία θνητῶν·

But I shall return again to the course of my songs
that I previously described, channeling that account
from another. When strife reached the lowest depth
of the eddy, and love is in the middle of the whirl,
in her[26] all these come together to be one alone,   25
not suddenly, but each combining from a different place.
And as they coupled, innumerable tribes of mortals poured forth.

Although the fragment as quoted by Simplicius contains no direct address, we may assume that the formula αὐτὰρ ἐγώ indicates, just as in the new Simonides fragment, the rhapsode's transition from one section of his poem to another. We may conclude further that the type of discourse and the form of address contained in the preceding passage were distinctly different, more mythological, and less specifically didactic.[27] The transitional formula αὐτὰρ ἐγώ thus marks the movement between an introductory section of the poem and the narrative of the poet's subject matter proper.

When Empedocles identifies the source of his previous discourse as ὕμνοι (line 1), he clearly harks back to what must have been an introductory hymnic address to a divinity[28] or to the address in the preserved invocation of the Muse in B3 and/or B131. So also in the case of Simonides: the transition αὐτὰρ ἐγώ is preceded by the invocation of the poet's personal rhapsodic Muse, thereby specifying the generic affinities of the poet's opening discourse. This would yield for lyric and elegy the pattern *prooimion: nomos,*[29] a structure that Koller and Nagy think underlies the Homeric Hymn form.[30] The epic *prooimion* was only one of a number of types differentiated by genre. It was always addressed to a divinity, as far as we can tell. In this way it seems to have served to contextualize the performance within a public festival. In lyric, the functions of the *prooimion* were more diverse;[31] but they centered on relating the occasion of the poem's praise to the figure of the poet. In Simonides' Plataea poem, the form of the proemial hymn appears to have been closest to that of epic, while its function approximates the *prooimion* of lyric.[32]

---

26. Or "there" (Inwood), since ἐν τῇ can mean either.

27. I.e., from a hymnic *prooimion*, in which B115, B6, and B26 might be included as containing introductory material. B26 apparently contains the λόγος from which Empedocles "draws off" this new one (so Wright 1981, ad loc.).

28. Aphrodite/Philotês, if Sedley 1989 is right, probably with some mention of her contrasting principle Neikos. πόρος ὕμνων means not "path" of song, as it is sometimes rendered, but "source" in the sense of "watercourse," as shown by Becker 1937: 148ff.

29. For αὐτὰρ ἐγώ introducing a *nomos*, cf. the last line of Callimachus' *Aitia* (though it must be read paroxytone with Kapsomenos). I owe this point, together with the observations on the *nomos* part of Simonides' poem and other advice, to Ian Rutherford.

30. Koller 1956: 159–206; Nagy 1990: 355f.

31. See, for example, Pindar *Ol.* 10; cf. Aloni in this volume.

32. See Aloni 1990 (1992), or other versions of this article.

Simonides' Book

In addition to the pattern *prooimion: nomos*, we have reason, based on the emulation and allusion in Timotheus' *Persai*,[33] to suppose that the structure of Simonides' hymnic Plataea-poem included a third section (*sphragis*) at the end. We are entitled to ask whether any of the other fragments preserved in *POxy* 3965 and 2327 come from that. This introduces the question of whether the papyri contain the text of a single poem or present a collection of them. We have seen that the appeal to a succession of addressees may appear within the scope of a single elegy (as it certainly did in the poem which contains fr. 11 W^2), based on a comparison of early didactic, encomiastic, and paraenetic forms of rhapsodic composition. This structure is particularly well exampled in archaic hymnody: personal reflection, even addresses or admonitions to the poet's mortal hearers, may appear among a succession of invocations of divinities.

But it seems fairly clear that the poem taken as a whole was not a hymn: for otherwise we would hardly need a special formula of transition to distinguish the hymnic part from the non-hymnic, narrative part, nor a clever comparison of the hymning of an era of demigods with the all-too-mortal fighters at Plataea. The prominent positioning of the Spartan general Pausanias, who heads the catalog of the march out of the city, have suggested to many an encomium or eulogistic elegy. The presence of Athenians[34] in Simonides' narrative hardly lends credence to just such a one-sided picture. If so, we would expect the addressee or, in Bundy's term, laudandus, to play a defining role for the genre of *Plataea*. Let us see if this is so among the surviving fragments.[35]

The exact genre of some of Simonides' most famous fragments remains unascertained.[36] But we have some ground along which to proceed. Only a brief overview of Simonides' oeuvre is needed to show that his poems were in fact differentiated (when they were so differentiated) by addressee or laudandus. The Suda entry, however garbled, "should preserve the outlines of an Alexandrian edition" (Parsons). And that there existed an Alexandrian edition is beyond doubt. We know, for example, that our copy of the poem on Plataea, replete as it is with Alexandria-sourced scholia and variants, derives from it.[37] The Suda entry, in addition to recording such nonsense as that

---

33. Discussed by Rutherford, this volume.

34. For digital analyses of the readings in question, see Obbink 1998b. They support Parsons' supplement [Κέκρ]οπος at fr. 11.42 W^2 over West's [μάν]τιος (sc. Teisamenos).

35. The laudandus could but need not be Pausanias himself, on this scenario: it could have been, e.g., a contemporary descendant, or even an earlier ancestor or some similarly suitable Spartan hero, as a match for the proemial address to Achilles.

36. Most prominently the ode about Scopas, 542 *PMG*. Among the papyri, *POxy* 2431; 2623 and 2624 are variously claimed for paeans or epinicians. The genre of *Danae* (543 *PMG*) in particular poses a puzzle, but Dionysius, who quotes it, does at least say that it is lyric and contained strophe, antistrophe, and epode.

37. Interlinear and marginal corrections and variants in readings and accents occur throughout both papyrus copies, but the relevant ascriptions of these are as follows: at fr. 11.32 W^2, Ap(ion) and Ni(canor), both in the abbreviated forms of their names standard in papyrus scholia and commentaries (McNamee 1981: 5, 63; 1992), are cited for the variant πόλεως over the papyrus's πόλεος (the former read by Apion and

Simonides invented not only the art of memory, but also long vowels and diphthongs, tells us that he wrote dirges, encomia, paeans, and epigrammata (covering here for elegy as well?), in addition to the individually titled sea-battle poems, at least one of which was known to be in elegiacs.[38] It omits epinicians. Yet the one certain thing about the organization of the Alexandrian edition is that it had books containing epinicia. This is known in particular from the fact that they had a grouping unusual for Hellenistic editions of the lyric poets, one that made them stand out as different from those of Pindar, whose epinicians had been ordered (it can still be seen in the medieval manuscripts) by panhellenic festival-site.[39] By contrast, Simonides' were grouped according to athletic event,[40] one book for each. Within each book grouped by event, the poems were individually differentiated and titled by victor, or again, in Bundy's terminology, by laudandus. That editions of Simonides exhibited this pattern of organization is borne out by the surviving citations of his epinician odes.

---

accepted by Parsons in the Oxy. ed., the latter apparently read by Nicanor and printed by West and in *Arethusa* 29.2 p. 160). Both scholars are similarly credited in *POxy* 2327 fr. 19, Apion alone at fr. 31 col. i 3 and fr. 2(a) col. i 10 (= fr. 21.10 W², see below). At *POxy* 2327 fr. 27 col. i 10 (= fr. 11.22 W²) the scholium reads at line end · περ αμ, i.e., ἀμ(φότεροι), no doubt referring to these same two scholars. Note that περ (the reading of their texts) gives rise to and attests in part West's supplement at the beginning of the line εἴ πέρ γ'; but the variant presupposes that the papyrus text itself did not read this. Possibly it read εἴ τι ποτ', suggested by Parsons (implausible is the explanation of Parsons and West that the papyrus text read περί, i.e., a mechanical error that yields nonsense, remediable by a simple stroke of deletion, and hardly requiring the opinions of famous scholars). Likewise in fr. 21.10 W² (*POxy* 2327 fr. 2[a] col. i 10), the marginal variant ἐπέβη(ν) credited to Apio(n) is placed in the text by West, but the variant shows that the papyrus text at least had something else. A pupil of Didymus, Apion worked at Alexandria in the first century C.E., where he succeeded Theon as head of the museum. Nicanor worked in the second century C.E. at Alexandria, where he distinguished himself in particular in his work on punctuation. I note that this means that the scholia of 2327 (and likewise of its sister 2430) were written in at the earliest in the late second century C.E., whereas the hand of the main text could be late first century C.E. (Lobel on 2430, revising the dating originally assigned to 2327).

38. I presume in what follows that in accordance with usual practice the Suda lists titles of whole books, though of course in some cases (as, e.g., with the partheneia and epinicia of Pindar) there may have been more than one book of each type. For discussion of the Pindaric lists, see Hiller 1886; Race 1987.

39. In Pindar's case, however, the classification by athletic event can be seen as a cross- or subclassification, in which poems are ordered within each book by type of event, in decreasing importance/expense (e.g., chariot-race first, and so on). Upon this system is mapped another, differentiating each poem by name of the victor/laudandus (again in decreasing importance: Hieron first, and so on). The books that contained Simonides' epinicians, by contrast, must have followed the latter system as a primary not a subclassification. This can be seen from the fact (first noted by Lobel on *POxy* 2431 fr. 1) that in the titles of Simonides' epinicians, the name of the event always precedes the name of the victor, whereas in Pindar's and Bacchylides' it regularly follows (e.g., Pind. *Ol.* 1 Ἱέρων Συρακοσίων κέλητι, Bacchyl. 3 Ἱ. Σ. ἵπποις Ὀλύμπια.

40. The evidence was set out by Lobel with remarkable precision and lucidity in his extended discussion on *POxy* 2431 fr. 1. For a possible ancient testimony to this principle of organization in Simonides' corpus, see Sider, this volume at n. 29, who (following a suggestion of A. Barchiesi) notes that Horace, immediately after several allusions to Simonides' poetry in the *Ars poetica*, categorizes epinicia by contest in his survey of poetic genres (84): "et pugilem victorem et equum certamine primum." No doubt the answer to the problem posed (but unsolved) by Lobel, as to why the titles/editions of the epinicians of Simonides did not contain notice (as Pindar's and Bacchylides' did) of the festival site of the victory, is that Simonides did not regularly mention in his epinicia (as Pindar and Bacchylides did) the site of the competition, and thus his epinicians were, as far as this differentia was concerned, transparent to Hellenistic editors.

Fragment 506 *PMG* is known to have come from a book which bore the title *Epinicia for Runners.*[41] Note, however, that Photius (who quotes the fragment from it) distinguishes the poem by noting that it praised the famous athlete Astylus from Croton.[42] Lobel (on *POxy* 2431) notes that Δρομεῦσι covers for all kinds of foot-race, though we can infer that the book contained subheadings for winners in each type of contest. This is further suggested by the following testimony.

Fragment 508 *PMG* is cited[43] as having been said by "Simonides in his *Pentathletes*," again attested as a title of a book, that is, epinicians for winners in the pentathlon.

For 511 *PMG* the title itself is recorded initially in the manuscript (*POxy* 2431 fr. 1.1–2) Κέλητι· τοῖς Αἰατίου παισίν· *For the horse-race, for the sons of Aeatius.* It gives the event first, then differentiates by noting the victor(s). The plural is roughly comparable to the plurals in the titles of paeans and prosodia which designate the plurality of competitors in the chorus for whom the poet composed the ode. So also in the case of the epinicians, with the difference (as noted by Lobel 1959a on *POxy* 2431 fr. 1) that here the plural indicates joint ownership of the horse (and not that both boys rode it).

In 519 *PMG* (*POxy* 2430 fr. 120[b].3), the title is likewise recorded in the manuscript: [Κέλη]τι Ἀθηναίωι λ[, *For the horse-race, for Athenaeus* (probably Ἀθήναιος Περικλείδα Λάκων, last quarter of the fifth century B.C.E., Thuc. 4.19, Σ Aristoph. *Knights* 691). Lobel notes (on *POxy* 2431 fr. 1) that in Simonides' epinicians "the signification of the contest preceded the name of the victor."

In 512 *PMG*, the title is supplied by the scholiast (Σ Aristoph. *Eq.* 405f.) as ἐκ τῶν Σιμωνίδου δὲ τοῦτο Τεθρίππων· "From Simonides' *Four-horse Chariots*" or "*Chariot-races.*" Here again we have an attested, not reconstructed title, whose force is "epinicians for winners in the four-horse chariot-race." As Lobel notes (on *POxy* 2431), Τεθρίππων refers to one of a number of different types of horse-race, which would have appeared in Simonides' book under the general heading ἐπίνικοι ἵπποις or the like.

For 513 *PMG*, the scholiast (Σ Pind. *Isthm.* 2 arg.) attests both that the poem was for victory in a horse-race (νενίκηκεν ἵπποις), and that it focussed on the victor: Σιμωνίδης δὲ ἐπαινῶν αὐτὸν (sc. Ξενοκράτην). Page reconstructs the (sub)title accordingly: Ξενοκράτει Ἀκραγαντίνῳ, *For Xenocrates of Acragas.* But the title of the book in which it appeared was undoubtedly *For the Horse-race.*

41. Callim. fr. 441 (An. Ox. Cramer iii 254.23) Σιμωνίδης ἐπέγραψεν "Ἐπινίκοι δρομέσι"; Choerob. *In Theodos.* i 139.60 Δρομέσι παρὰ Καλλιμάχῳ. Cf. Lobel on *POxy* XXV 2431 fr. 1; Pfeiffer 1968: 130.
42. Phot. *Lex.* s.v. περιαγειρόμενοι (ii 77 Naber): Σιμωνίδης περὶ Ἀστύλου φησὶν οὕτως.
43. Phot. *Lex.* A 981 (i 105 Theodoridis) Σιμωνίδης γὰρ ἐν Πεντάθλοις.

In attesting 514 *PMG*, the paroemiographer[44] obligingly gives us the title: Σιμωνίδης δ' αὐτοῦ μνημονεύει ἐν τῷ εἰς Ὄριλλαν ἐπινικίῳ· i.e. Ἡνιόχῳ Ὀρίλλᾳ, "*For Orillas the charioteer, that is, in the chariot-race*."

In quoting 515 *PMG*, Aristotle (*Rhet*. 3.2 1405b) records the famous anecdote about how vigorously Simonides saluted the mules of a mule-cart-race when offered a sufficient fee:

> χαίρετ' ἀελλοπόδων θύγατρες ἵππων.
>
> Hail, daughters of storm-footed horses!

χαίρετ' is usually understood as a greeting in the ode, but much more likely it was a parting salutation, suitably contrasting the praise of the mules as foil with the praise of the boy-victor that no doubt followed. Heraclides of Pontus could supply his name, and the title has been reconstructed to suit: Ἀναξίλᾳ Ῥηγίνῳ. But once again the primary organization of the poems by athletic event is reflected: the anecdote turns on the knowledge of the commentator that the event was a mule cart-race (i.e. for a boy-victor), not a horse- or chariot-race. Discernible to the organizers of the ancient edition was also the name of the victor, in whose honor the poem was composed.

For the remaining epinicians, in every case prominent mention is made either of the victor as laudandus: 507 (Crius of Aegina), 509 (Glaucus of Carystus), 510 (Scopas of Thessaly),[45] 518 (Eualcides of Eretria); or of the event: 516, 517 (both chariot-races).[46] The pattern is sufficiently clear to show that these poems were known from editions in which the poems were collected into books grouped by athletic event, with individual poems subtitled by victor as laudandus in the familiar form of the dative or (alternatively) εἰς plus accusative.[47] In this category of poem, at any rate, we could expect that the person in whose honor the poem was composed was obvious to ancient editors and readers alike.

Identification of the addressee or laudandus is possible in other Simonidean fragments of related genres as well. In fact, in most cases either we are fairly well informed about the addressee/laudandus, or, when we are not, we are dealing with poems that have none. Paeans, as generally (though not exclusively) in honor of Apollo, were grouped together in at least one book,[48] as were θρῆνοι, being obviously differentiated by the departed individual lamented. The same is true of the ἐγκώμια (presumably in lyric meters) also listed by the Suda, many of them (like Pindar's) odes

---

44. [Diogenian.] *Praef. paroem.* (i 179 Leutsch-Schneidewin).

45. An epinician for boxing, according to Quintilian *Inst.* 11.2.11–16, who also notes that the identity of the laudandus was disputed: according to some authorities it was composed for Glaucus of Carystus, in which case it could come from the same poem as 509 (see above).

46. I exempt from consideration here the fragmentary 519 and 519A–B in Campbell (*POxy* 2623 and 2624) which contain fragments of paeans as well as epinicians.

47. This form of title is also used to designate collectivities like choruses as objects of the poet's praise in such genres as prosodia and partheneia: see Rutherford 1997.

48. Rutherford 1990.

to boy-lovers of Simonides' patrons. Though not included in the Suda's list, there was probably a book of Παρθένεια: it is mentioned by [Plut.] *De mus.* 17; Aristoph. *Birds* 919 καὶ παρθένεια καὶ κατὰ τὰ Σιμωνίδου. These might have been differentiated individually by the chorus who competed with them and for whom they were composed, as we know that Simonides' paeans were: 519 *PMG* (*POxy* 2430 fr. 35[b].12), where the papyrus gives the title: Ἀνδρίοις εἰς Πυθώ, *For the Andrians for Pytho (A Paean)*.

Dithyrambs, on the other hand, having no obvious recipient in whose honor they were written, seem to have been designated according to standard practice by the names of the subjects they treated. Strabo refers to Simonides' dithyramb *Memnon*,[49] which went around in a collection called the *Deliaca*, a collection of poems, it has been suggested, composed for and perhaps preserved in Delos. Other such collections of Simonidean poetry may be the Sylloge of epigrams, and the once attested Σύμμικτα,[50] perhaps a collection of poems in meters not fitting any of the standard categories.[51] A Κατευχαί is twice attested,[52] obscure to us. It could have been something like the later collections of *Dirae*. But one also thinks of Danae's prayer, and the ubiquity of the formal request in the hymn form: perhaps they were excerpts from poems in a variety of genres. The exact relation of the epigrams (at least those few deemed genuine) to the elegies is uncertain. But the theory of A. E. Raubitschek that they were excerpted from elegies performed to commemorate the events in question may be noted.[53] The Suda entry itself records epigrams, and lists separately battle-poems, with which the Plataea poem may be plausibly grouped. The difference is that the elegies were longer and more varied in their treatment. Like the dithyrambs, they clearly had no obvious recipient, but rather bore their own separate titles, styled after a specific historical event, as the following testimony for them shows.

a. 532 *PMG* (Sud. Σ 439) καὶ γέγραπται αὐτῷ Δωρίδι διαλέκτῳ ἡ Καμβύσου καὶ Δαρείου βασιλεία καὶ Ξέρξου ναυμαχία καὶ ἡ ἐπ' Ἀρτεμισίῳ ναυμαχία δι' ἐλεγείας, ἡ δ' ἐν Σαλαμῖνι μελικῶς. "He composed in the Doric dialect *The Reign of Cambyses and Darius, The Sea-battle against Xerxes,* and *The Sea-battle at Artemisium* in elegiacs, *The Sea-battle at Salamis* in lyric meter."

b. 533 *PMG* (Prisc. *De metr. Ter.* 24) "Simonides in ἐπ' Ἀρτεμισίῳ ναυμαχίᾳ in dimetro catalectico ἐβόμβησεν θαλάσσας." "Simonides in *The Sea-battle at Artemisium* in catalectic dimeters (says) 'the sea's (wave) roared'."

c. 534 *PMG* = fr. 3 W² (Σ Ap. Rhod. 1.211–15c) ὡς Σιμωνίδης ἐν τῇ ναυμαχίᾳ· "As Simonides says in *The Sea-battle*."[54]

---

49. Fr. 539 *PMG*. The titles of Bacchylides' dithyrambs may be compared.

50. Fr. 540 *PMG*.

51. There is evidence for the classification of Simonides' poems by meter: see (a)–(b) below. The genera of the attested books allow for obvious cross-classification: dactylo-epitrite for epinicia, strophic lyric for paean, partheneia, and dithyramb. Elegiacs will have covered for both epigram and narrative elegy.

52. Fr. 537 *PMG*. J. R. Rea notes (ap. *POxy* 3865) in this connection fr 64.11 W² κατευ[χ-.

53. Raubitschek 1968 = 1991, developed at length by Day 1989 and 2000. Further discussion and bibliography on the subject in Sider 1997: 25–28, who notes (25 n. 5) that this "dissolves somewhat the barrier set up between epigraphic texts and elegies, but the general point [that epigrams are short poems] remains valid."

54. The battle in question must be the battle of Artemisium: see Rutherford, this volume at n. 10.

d. *Vita Aeschyli* 8 ἐν τῷ εἰς τοὺς ἐν Μαραθῶνι τεθνηκότας ἐλεγείῳ· "In the *elegeion* for those who died at Marathon."

In (a)–(c) the titles take the form ναυμαχία, place (ἐν or ἐπί plus dative), with further optional specification by meter. If the texts are sound, (a) attests a sea-battle poem on Artemisium in elegiacs, (b) one in a lyric meter. Simonides probably treated the battle prominently in more than one poem. But the poem on Plataea, since it concerned a land-battle, cannot have followed this pattern, nor can it plausibly have been treated in the course of any of the attested poems on sea-battles. Nowhere is there attested a poem by Simonides in any meter specifically on the battle of Plataea. We do, however, know that Solon wrote one on an earlier struggle over Salamis, entitled simply Σαλαμίς.[55] I suggest that Simonides' elegy had a title similarly phrased after the site of the conflict, that is, Πλαταῖα,[56] though certainty on the matter is unattainable. Example (d) is usually treated as a dubium,[57] since it is uncertain whether ἐλεγεῖον refers to an epigram or an elegy (according to one theory they could have been one and the same).[58] For our purposes, however, it is sufficient to note that it attests a poem designated after those who died in a famous battle, featuring them as honorands. The designation of the poem in (d) may have been due in part to the exceptional treatment of the dead at Marathon as at no other battle, their burial on the spot; we may wonder if the Plataea poem was in fact similarly so designated.

Judged from the citation of these poems by their individual titles, the sea-battle poems and the elegy on Plataea may have circulated separately and individually, each in its own book-roll. Otherwise we should expect the Suda's notice collectively to say that Simonides wrote Ναυμαχίαι.[59] It is also clear that all of them (with the exception of [d]) belong to that group of poems undifferentiated in their titles by addressee, recipient, or honorand. Otherwise we would (as in the case of the other Simonidean poems) expect the addressee or honorand to be named as part of their titles. In the poem on Plataea, Achilles is addressed directly in the parting salutation at fr. 11.19 W². Whether these elegies also had historical addressees or laudandi is unknown. One would have thought that some must have had human addressees, as Theognis' did.[60] But if any of these poems had been clearly written for or in praise of particular individuals or cities, or if the performance context were clearly revealed in the poem, we might have expected some designation of it in the titles, as we find for example in (d), as also in the case of the epinicians discussed above. Rather, it seems that it was for their events of general panhellenic import that they stood out to later

---

55. Solon fr. 1 W (Plut. *Sol.* 1–2). τοῦτο τὸ ποίημα Σαλαμὶς ἐπιγέγραπται, καὶ στίχων ἑκατόν ἐστι.

56. The supposition is supported by similarly phrased titles for elegies on land-battles like Mimnermus' *Smyrneis*.

57. West prints it *sine numero*, before frr. 86–92, a section headed "Incertum an ex epigrammatis," T15 Campbell. See above, Introduction, n. 4.

58. See Raubitschek 1968 = 1991.

59. I have wondered whether the titles in question are cited by the Suda primarily for purposes of anchoring Simonides' dates, since the book-list, beginning with the sea-battle poems, follows immediately upon alternative versions for his birth and death dates.

60. Practice in this respect may have differed in (at least) one of the sea-battle poems that was a lyric poem (cf. 533 *PMG*, [b] above). I consider the matter of human addressees further below.

ages. This seems not only to cohere with what little we know about the other battle-poems, but also with the testimony of Plutarch about the poem on Plataea (Simonides fr. 15–16 W² [Plut. *De Herod. malign.* 42 p. 872d + *POxy* 3865 fr. 5]):

ἀλλὰ Κορινθίους γε καὶ τάξιν ἣν ⟨ἔχοντες⟩ ἐμάχοντο τοῖς βαρβάροις καὶ τέλος ἡλίκον ὑπῆρξεν αὐτοῖς ἀπὸ τοῦ Πλαταιᾶσιν ἀγῶνος ἔξεστι Σιμωνίδου πυθέσθαι γράφοντος ἐν τούτοις·

μέσσοις δ᾽ οἵ τ᾽ Ἐφύρην πολυπίδακα ναιετάοντες,   15
    παντοίης ἀρετῆς ἴδριες ἐν πολέμῳ,
οἵ τε πόλιν Γλαύκοιο Κορίνθιον ἄστυ νέμοντες·

οἳ

        κάλλιστον μάρτυν ἔθεντο πόνων,   16
χρυσοῦ τιμήεντος ἐ₁ν αἰθέρι₁· καί σφιν ἀέξει   [*POxy* 3865 fr. 5]
    αὐτῶν τ᾽ εὐρεῖαν κλ₁ηδόν₁α καὶ πατέρων
        ]πολυ[

ταῦτα γὰρ οὐ χορὸν ἐν Κορίνθῳ διδάσκων, οὐδ᾽ ᾆσμα ποιῶν εἰς τὴν πόλιν, ἄλλως δὲ τὰς πράξεις ἐκείνας ἐλεγεῖα γράφων ἱστόρηκεν.

As for the Corinthians, the position they occupied while fighting among the barbarians and the consequences the battle of Plataea had for them, we may learn all this from Simonides, who writes: "and in the center the men who dwell in Ephyra with its many springs, skilled in all manner of excellence in war, and those who inhabit the Corinthian city of Glaucus"—who "established for themselves the finest witness of their struggle, a witness of precious gold in the sky, which increases the wide glory of both them and their fathers." He gave this account not when training a chorus in Corinth, nor when composing an ode for the city, but simply when putting those exploits into elegiacs.

According to Plutarch, unlike Herodotus, Simonides in his elegy recorded the participation of the Corinthians, in spite of the fact that he was not "training a chorus in Corinth, nor when composing an ode for the city." Unless we take Plutarch to be denying the obvious, this seems to entail not only that the poem was not performed at Corinth for the Corinthians, as has been observed by others, but also that it was not obviously composed as an encomium of any particular city or individual.[61] As it is, he plainly insists that Simonides was "simply putting those exploits into elegiacs." Will anyone believe that Plutarch could have written that the Corinthians were so prominently mentioned (though the poem was not written in their honor), if in another part of the poem their contribution had been entirely overshadowed by the exclusive praise of Spartans or Athenians[62] or indeed Pausanias or the Scopadae or Leonidas?[63]

61. Suggested also by Boedeker 1995b: 225. I add that if the poem was in fact an encomium of some other particular person or city, it might even be thought to have been for him even better (though not absolutely necessary) to have said so explicitly, so as to emphasize that Simonides had given the Corinthians their due nonetheless.

62. Obbink 1998b.

63. It might be objected that Plutarch did not know the poem in its entirety, but only, e.g., in the form of an epigram quoted from the original elegy. But this is unlikely, since such an epigram or quotation can only have been honorific, whereas Plutarch expressly says that the lines were not written εἰς τὴν πόλιν.

Rather it was the collective effort of heroic proportions praised in an elegy that contained a "pocket-book epic" on the subject. On the other hand, the poem also contained an opening hymn, moralizing about the realities of war and justice, young death and poetic fame, after narrating the disposition of the forces at Plataea, in the process no doubt paying compliments to any number of the actors present. What else did the poem relate?

One Poem or Many?

Apart from fragments of *POxy* 2327 and 3965 specifically identifiable as dealing with the narrative of the battle proper,[64] or claimed for one of the attested sea-battle poems,[65] it is certainly possible on papyrological grounds that other or even all the remaining fragments of these two papyri fell within the compass of this single elegy.

An objection to the one-poem hypothesis is that one[66] fragment of one of the two surviving papyrus MSS of Simonides' elegies contains a division between two poems (*POxy* 2327 fr. 7 = Simonides fr. 34 W[2]):

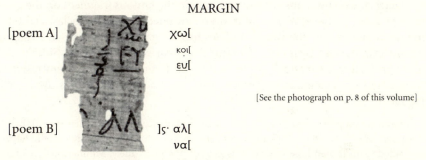

MARGIN

[poem A]   χω[
          κοι[
          ευ[

[See the photograph on p. 8 of this volume]

[poem B]   ]ϛ· αλ[
          να[

Beyond any doubt we have the end of one poem (marked by a coronis, paragraphos, and space of one line), and the beginning of another. The lines begin at the same point, not with every other line indented as in a modern edition. But this does not necessarily mean that the fragment is not from an elegiac poem: such is the standard format for elegy on papyrus.[67] West (app. crit.) conjectures that the final line of poem

---

64. Frr. 10–17 W[2], possibly 18.

65. Frr. 1–9 W[2]; but see Rutherford's commentary in this volume. The claim that these two papyrus rolls contained other elegies as well depends solely on the alleged identification of a fragment from the ἡ ἐπ' Ἀρτεμισίῳ ναυμαχία δι' ἐλεγείας (Suda, s.v. Σιμωνίδης), namely Simonides 3 W[2] where the restoration in line 5 of the names Ζήτην καὶ] Κάλαϊ[ν and their connection with Hdt. 7.189 seems to rest on the flimsiest of evidence.

66. West also marks a possible poem-beginning before line 3 of fr. 21 W[2] (*POxy* 2327 fr. 1 + 2(a) col. i), assuming [ο]ὐ δύναμαι to be in asyndedon with what precedes. But this is ruled out since, as Rutherford points out (this volume, n. 85), there is no space between lines 2 and 3, as there is in *POxy* 2327 fr. 7 (fr. 34 W[2]), and there is no reason for thinking that [ο]ὐ δύναμαι in line 3 begins a new sentence, rather than simply continuing on the masc. sing. participle]μενος that ends line 2.

67. Exceptions that prove the rule: *P. Lit. Lond.* 62 = Page, *Select Literary Papyri* 113 = 982 SH (epigram on Octavian); in Latin: the elegiacs by Gallus, ed. Anderson, Parsons, Nisbet 1979.

A begins with a word in εὑ[ν-, and that this word was glossed above the line with a synonym or variant beginning κοι[τ-. Poem B began with αλ[, which in itself is not very revealing. The sigma to its left, however, is the remains not of the end of a line of the preceding column, but of the title of poem B penned in the margin at the beginning of the poem.[68] As the title of a Simonidean elegy, we might have entertained here, for example,

$$[\Sigma\alpha\lambda\alpha\mu\acute{\iota}]\varsigma.^{69}$$

But it is difficult to accommodate for poem B a title concerning Plataea under the analysis given above. We would of course be free to consider that poem A might be any of the other known Simonidean elegies (including the poem on Plataea), and that it ended with a euphemistic allusion to the pleasures of sex at the symposium. Such is certainly the subject of fr. 22 W^2 under any of the interpretations advanced so far. Therefore fr. 34 W^2 in no way rules out the hypothesis that the remaining fragments of *POxy* 2327 and 3965 derive from one and the same poem on Plataea. At best it shows that *POxy* 2327 contained at least two poems, one of which (poem B) was not the poem on Plataea.[70]

If we ask which of the fragments has the best case for forming part of the poem on Plataea, the obvious answer will be found in the famous fragment on the generation of leaves (frr. 19–20 W^2). As in fr. 11 W^2, the poet there similarly lays claim to his unique authorship of the poem, and secures it against tampering and rhapsodic expansion at the end, by means of a ranked comparison with Homer. Sider in a cautious appraisal of the matter[71] argues that in this fragment Homer is contrasted with Mimnermus by glancing at the latter's earlier treatment of the "leaves" topos, allowing that

> a long poem performed either in private or in public could praise warriors and their poets, and then (after who knows what else) pass on to criticism of poets who have failed to understand the value of this kind of poetry (namely, Mimnermos). And if

---

68. I note that the initial title was in the hand of the main scribe at the time of writing, not later by the second hand as part of the scholia. On initial titles in the margin at the beginning of individual poems, see Rutherford 1997.

69. As an alternative for the Suda's ἡ ναυμαχία ἐν Σαλαμῖνι (532 *PMG*), on analogy with Solon's Σαλαμίς (fr. 1 W). Such a title would describe the main subject of the poem in short-order form, as in the titles of dithyrambs generally, and Simonides' *Memnon* (539 *PMG*).

70. It is not even entirely certain that *POxy* 2327 fr. 7 = 34 W^2 derives from an elegy: all the fragments of 2327 are in the same hand and format as 2430 (Simonides 519 *PMG*), which contains lyric poems in the Doric dialect, and is likewise equipped with similarly sourced and written scholia and poem divisions marked by paragraphoi and coronides as in 2327. The papyri are in fact so similar that, if it were not for the different genres represented (lyric vs. elegy), we would have certainly considered them as part of the same book-roll. Edgar Lobel grouped the fragments first on the basis of their hands, then separated out the ones with Doric forms and lyric cola, as against the ones with Ionic forms and hexameter sequences and line endings. The only reason for thinking that 2327 fr. 7 is from the elegies as opposed to the lyrics is that two of the lyric poems (fr. 35b, a paean for a chorus of Andrians, and fr. 120, an epinician for Athenaeus the Spartan in the horse-race) had initial titles penned by the main scribe not in the margin (as in 2327 fr. 7) but centered in the line of writing at the head of the poem.

71. Sider, this volume at n. 30.

Homer could insert the leaves simile into a battle narrative, so too . . . could Simonides, who clearly puts himself forward as Homer *redivivus.*

Rutherford, independently, concurs, suggesting further that the fragment might have formed a *sphragis* to the poem on Plataea in which the poet discusses his art:[72] "The idea of mourning the dead would lead into a meditation on the mutability of life, especially the warrior's life, since the Homeric 'leaves' fragment evokes the idea of death in war." The meditation on the generation of leaves would in this way provide closure to the poem, or at least one part of it, by employing another mythological paradigm that emphasizes mutability of life and fortune, then immediately reversing the point by giving a famous example of something that defies the paradigm.[73] This seesaw move also figures prominently in fr. 11 W^2, and indeed there may be other examples in Simonides that suggest that it was fairly habitual.[74] The difference is that in frr. 11 + 19–20 W^2 the contrast of an early death of a heroic figure of myth with the immortality of Homer's poetic fame, which the poet will not only emulate but surpass (perhaps, as Sider argues, as Mimnermus failed to do), followed (in third place) by a celebratory, encomiastic narrative, is duplicated more or less exactly, which might well suggest the original design of the poet. It is reasonable to suppose further that Simonides has returned to the original contrast before moving on to a final celebration in a description of a symposium (fr. 22 W^2).[75]

In addition, there are internal indications. A relevant consideration to the coherence of frr. 19–20 W^2 to fr. 11 W^2 is raised by fr. 20.11 W^2, in which the poet directly addresses another:

ὡς χρόνος ἔσθ᾽ ἥβης καὶ βιότοι᾽ ὀλίγος   10
θνητοῖς· ἀλλὰ σὺ ταῦτα μαθὼν βιότου ποτὶ τέρμα
ψυχῇ τῶν ἀγαθῶν τλῆθι χαριζόμενος

Whom does the poet address in the second person singular, who has lived to the end of his life,[76] yet might still be exhorted to take delight in goods as he admonished to persevere? Sider argues that the addressee is Mimnermus himself, who (he argues) must have been invoked by name before the reworking of Homer's (also

---

72. Rutherford, this volume at n. 80. The notion is supported by the fact that the passage is reflected in the *sphragis* of Timotheus' *Persai*, which seems to imitate Simonides' poem on Plataea.

73. This argument depends on accepting the transmitted order (with some textual dislocation), as against West's reversal: so Sider, this volume, accepted by Rutherford, this volume at n. 83.

74. See the brilliant treatment by Carson 1988 of Simonides' repeated rhetorical emphasis through the employment of the negative and double negative. (Ignore her bizarre attempt to make Simonides a member of the Sophistic movement). I note that the effect is primarily one of pathos, and that it could be achieved well (as here) through larger poetic structures as individual expressions. On Simonides' style, see also Orlando Poltera's 700–page study (Poltera 1997).

75. If this fragment with its erotic and celebratory touches does not at first sight appear to cohere with the eulogy of young heroic death (Homeric and Plataean), it certainly does so more after a comparison with Ibycus' Ode to Polycrates (151 *SLG* = 262 *PMGF*).

76. τέρμα recalls var. lect. at fr. 11.12 W^2 τέρμα . . . δίκ[ης].

Mimnermus') image of the generation of leaves. This seems unlikely.[77] The fragment is much more in keeping with the stylized self-address in fr. 21.3 W²:[78]

[ο]ὐ δύναμαι, ψυχ[ή,] πεφυλαγμένος ε[ἶ]ναι ὀπηδός.

The poet can no longer be entirely faithful to the yearnings of his soul:[79] he has respected justice, though with difficulty, throughout the end of boyhood and the awakening of sexuality that comes with adolescence. The description of stages in colorful imagery makes clear that we have a progression of ages of human life described: this series is first extended and then recapitulated in frr. 19–20 W². It will also be recalled from the discussion above that there is a succession of second person addressees in fr. 11 W². First Achilles (and possibly Thetis, recipient of the opening hymn?) is saluted and politely dismissed (19–20); then the Muse (21–22), who is kept on retainer for the narrative of the battle. Finally and in conclusion, the poet reverts to self-address, now completely in contrast to Homer, who relied entirely on the Muses. The self-address neatly suits the dour, reflective mood of the fragment on the generation of leaves, as well as the dream-like quality of the symposiastic pleasures of fr. 22 W².

Other fragments that arguably derive from the poem on Plataea are the epigram or elegiac fr. 89 W², in which the poet receives self-praise for his skill at memory,[80] and fr. 21 W²,[81] where the theme of justice (line 4) plausibly echoes fr. 11.12 W². It is unlikely that we know all of the topoi on which Simonides touched in short compass. We may assume that this poem ranged widely over a range of themes appropriate to its genre of praise and circumstances of performance.[82] Already αὐτὰρ ἐγώ in fr. 11 W² invites the reader to think that the poem will end and a new (kind of) poem begin–but in fact it does not.[83]

In Simonides' Plataea poem, the transitional formula αὐτὰρ ἐγώ in fr. 11 W² heralds a new discourse, one in which "the old heroes move into the hymn, new heroes occupy the narrative" (Parsons 1994: 122). The whole effort is cast in elegiacs, perhaps in as little as two hundred lines. A hymn in elegiacs is certainly no surprise.[84] But

---

77. The decisive counter-argument is that Simonides clearly envisages that the addressee is alive (fr. 20.12), which rules out Mimnermus. Like Ibycus and Anacreon, Simonides seems to have habitually represented himself as old (e.g., fr. 20.11 W²), on which theme see Mace and Hunter, this volume.

78. This seems preferable to assuming that Echecratidas, Dyseris (so Yatromanolakis, this volume), or someone else present in fr. 22 is already being addressed in 19–20.

79. West 1993a favors ψυχῇ, to be construed with πεφυλαγμένος, though fr. 21 W² prints the vocative ψυχή. A rereading of the papyrus shows there to be exactly space for one letter. This rules out the dative, since the scribe of *POxy* 2327 normally writes iota adscript when required.

80. Suggested by Rutherford, this volume after n. 80.

81. Also suggested by Rutherford, this volume, n. 81.

82. By context of performance I refer not to the question, endlessly debated, of where the poem was (first) performed—as if that could be known or would be (finally) determinative if it could be—but to the cultural environment that occasioned the composition and original and all secondary performances and rewritings of the ode: namely, an event of momentous proportions as it was recognized, rhetorically celebrated, and transmitted through fifth-century audiences.

83. Pointed out to me by L. Koenen.

84. Crates' *Hymn to Parsimony* antedates Callimachus. For other Callimachean antecedents see Cameron 1995: 147–50. Early on: Xenophanes' and Theognis' sympotic invocations.

"miniaturization, crossing of genres—wouldn't we be tempted to call that Hellenistic" (Parsons 1994: 122) if the poem had not been securely identified[85] by an ancient author as Simonidean? We are once again struck by the recovery of primitive models where later poets would have seemed to be innovating. One wonders how many generic boundaries (if we could be sure they then existed) Simonides might have been prepared to cross in the same poem. As Michael Haslam noted (1993: 134, confessing that he would "still rather have had a dirge"): "If this does not tell us how we would have guessed Simonidean elegy would look, all the more valuable to know how it does look."

---

85. I.e., by Plutarch, *De Herod. malign.* 42 872d = Simonides fr. 15 W².

4

ANTONIO ALONI

The Proem of Simonides' Plataea Elegy and the Circumstances of Its Performance

Introductory Comments on the Text

This chapter offers a literary-historical rather than a philological interpretation of the proem of the new Simonidean elegy on the battle of Plataea (11 W²), the longest and best-preserved part of the poem.[1]

The text is a largely hypothetical text, the fruit of the editors' interpretation of the material available to them and of stopgaps proposed *exempli gratia* by West and by Parsons. However, while it appears impossible to reconstruct Simonides' actual words with any degree of certainty, one can outline the contents of the piece with some confidence (and, even more important, outline the structure of the elegy as a whole). So, while any aesthetic evaluation of the work is out of the question (apart, that is, from an appreciation of the high quality of the proem), one can discuss the reasons behind the composition, the way in which—and the audience for which—the elegy was composed. I offer some comments on a number of passages in fr. 11.[2]

Line 2. One can recognize a parallel in Homer, usually employed to highlight the death of a warrior (*Il.* 13.389–91 and 16.482–84); cf. Barchiesi, this volume.

Line 6. At the end of the *Odyssey*, Agamemnon in Hades makes a long speech to Achilles in which he recalls the hero's funeral celebrations (*Od.* 24.36–97) and mentions that the bones of Achilles and Patroclus were put in the same urn. This is a reference to the traditional theme of "the funeral of Achilles," at which the Muses were present. Obviously the connection would be very evocative if the performance of the

An earlier version of this paper appeared in Lowell Edmunds and Robert W. Wallace (eds.), *Poet, Public, and Performance in Ancient Greece* (Baltimore 1997): 8–28 (notes pp. 130–36), and is used here by kind permission of the Johns Hopkins University Press.

1. On the same argument, see Aloni 1994.
2. For the text with full apparatus, see above, pp. oo. See also Rutherford at nn. 1–9 and 48ff.

elegy were a part of the commemoration of the warriors who had died at Plataea; cf. Boedeker 1995b and this volume ("Heroization"); and Obbink, this volume, after n. 24.

Line 8. In Homer, there is no explicit account of the death of Achilles, which is often alluded to, or forecast as the result of the joint action of Apollo and Paris (cf. *Il.* 19.416–17, 22.358–60). See Obbink, this volume, after n. 10. Precise reference to the death being the work of Apollo alone is to be found in the tragedies (cf. Aesch. fr. 350, and Soph. *Philoc.* 334–35), which are integral to the Athenian tradition.

Lines 9–12. These can be reconstructed in various ways, but West's seems to fit in with the rhythm of the narrative (the introduction of the principal gods opposed to Troy and the contraposition of Achilles' death and the fall of the city). In fact, the "chariot of justice" is an unusual image; Dike, the goddess of justice, is usually represented with a rod or a pair of scales, but never seated in a chariot. But see Rutherford's commentary above, at nn. 50–53.

Line 15. Obviously the reference is to Homer; what we have here is a veritable exaltation of the role of poetry and the poet as the only means for guaranteeing the continuing fame of men and deeds. Certain key words in early Greek poetry appear here (some clear in the text itself, others very likely suppositions made by the editors): κλέος is the glory conferred by poetry; ἀληθείη is not only the "truth" of the account, it is also the negation of oblivion, the only hope for guaranteeing the survival in time of the transient race of heroes (and the even more transient race of common mortals).

Lines 17–18. The passage is skillfully echoed in Theocritus' *Hymn to the Charites* (16.44–46). The echo is almost a quotation because the Greek poet places it in a passage in which the poetry of Simonides is described as being able to preserve the fame and memory of contemporaries (just as Homer did for the heroes of the past); cf. in this volume Hunter, Rutherford at nn. 58f., and particularly Parsons at nn. 28f.

Lines 25–26. These lines are reconstructed on the basis of two of Simonides' epigrams: "Simon." 16.1 *FGE* and 20a.304 *FGE*; cf. below, the section on "Occasion and Commission."

Line 39. I prefer to supplement συν[όντες], a reading I owe to Luigi Lehnus in a very fruitful discussion of the text with him and E. Cingano.

Line 40. Simonides' account of the Spartans' departure, their march to the Isthmus, rendezvous with the other Peloponnesian forces, and subsequent march to Eleusis is rather cursory and vague (and the present state of the text offers no help in filling in the details). Unlike the other sources, there is no mention here of conflicts and quarrels preceding the Spartan departure (this could be taken as evidence that the elegy is a Spartan commission). And, in contrast to what Herodotus says (9.19), it seems that the rendezvous with the other Peloponnesian forces did not take place at the Isthmus but at Megara, a Dorian city that was a member of the Peloponnesian League. The extant text makes no mention of the arrival of the Athenians, which according to Herodotus took place at Eleusis.[3] Plutarch says the Athenians went straight to Plataea, and Diodorus places their rendezvous with the other Greek forces at some point between the Isthmus and Boeotia. See also Rutherford at n. 67.

Line 42. Another completely conjectural line: Teisamenos was a seer of Elis, a descendant of Iamos, a son of Apollo and nephew of Poseidon, who had been priest and seer at Olympia at the time the games were founded. Teisamenos was hired by the Spartans as official seer for the expedition and, in return, obtained for himself and his brother the much-sought-after and rarely conceded right to Spartan citizenship (cf. Hdt. 9.33–35).

One should again point out that the papyrus' pitiful state of preservation means that any argument based on it risks circularity. Once it is established that Simonides' poem refers to the battle of Plataea, scholars necessarily have to fall back on Herodotus' account of the same event to understand the references in the poem, and (as I indicate below) those references are often fragmentary—the name of a person or a place, the context of a possible action—which means that they can only be clarified by appeal to the fuller account.[4] For example, the reference to Corinth (fr. 11.35) inevitably leads one to fall back on Herodotus (9.19.1) and decide that Simonides is describing the arrival of the Spartans and other Peloponnesians at the Isthmus. Similarly, the probable (but not certain) mention of a seer (fr. 11.42) leads West to identify him as Teisamenos (Hdt. 9.33–36), and to recognize in fragment 14 Teisamenos' prophecy as recorded by Herodotus (9.36).

Introductory Remarks on the Elegy

The unusual content and structure of this elegy make it possible to offer a further contribution to the recent debate as to the occasions on which elegiac poetry was performed.[5] Nowadays nearly everyone is of the opinion that almost all the elegies that have come down to us were originally intended for symposia. Usually sung to the accompaniment of an aulos,[6] the elegy was the means by which the symposium group identified itself; it was a means of reflection and self-preparation as well as an incitement to action.

The contents of an elegy might thus vary a great deal. Sometimes the elegy could be an almost abstract reflection on the values that govern the lives and behavior of

---

3. But see Parsons 1992a: 37–38; Boedeker 1995b and this volume, "Historiography," at nn. 32–33; Obbink 1998b and this volume at n. 34.
4. For the reference of the poem to the battle of Plataea, see Parsons 1992a: 6 and West 1993a: 2–3.
5. See, above all, West 1974: 10–21; Bowie 1986, 1990: 221–29; Vetta 1983, 1992: 177–218; Rösler 1990: 230–37.
6. This was a wind instrument, usually with two pipes (closer to the oboe than to the flute). The verb "sing" as used here is to be understood in the widest sense to include *recitarcantando* and *recitativo*.

men; at other times it might be the exemplary narration of past events—be they part of the remote past or contemporary events that were well known to the audience. With regard to the Ionian elegy of the seventh and sixth centuries, Vetta has drawn up a schema showing how the different types of elegies essentially reflect the spread and evolution of the institution of the symposium.

1. Callinus' elegies go together with symposia that were practically councils held by military commanders—still fairly similar to the sort of assemblies described in the *Iliad*. The Callinus elegy is "poetry of exhortation, outside a narrative context, freed from the intrusion of myths and without the intrusion of personal themes."

2. In the symposia of Archilochus and his companions in colonial military adventures, the fundamental point is the shared experience of the poet and his audience; it is that which becomes the subject of the narrative and the subsequent reflection upon it.

3. Finally there is the Mimnermus symposium, which is less directed toward action and more inclined to generalization and reflection. This is a more intimate form of symposium, from which the themes of public life, of politics, and of war, seem to be excluded. And if they are present, they are filtered through an attitude that is pensive, sometimes even sorrowful.[7]

This schema of symposium types could, with a few variations (different emphasis on the elements of political and philosophical reflection), cover all the symposia that we know to have been the destined audience for other types of elegy that have come down to us (from Solon to Theognis and Xenophanes).

Not all elegiac poetry was, however, destined for a symposium public. There are fragments in which the first-person voice of the poem seems to affirm a function for the elegy outside the context of a symposium.[8] Quite apart from that, there is the sizable group of historical/narrative elegies: Mimnermus composed a *Smyrneis* celebrating the foundation of that city; Tyrtaeus composed a *Politeia* (or *Eunomia*) that was, in part, dedicated to the deeds of Sparta during the Messenian wars; Semonides told the story of his native country in an *Archaeology of the Samians*. In the fifth century there were also elegies composed by Simonides—one dedicated to the battle of Artemisium (frr. 1–4 W^2) and the one now under discussion on the battle of Plataea.[9] Later, Panyassis wrote a *History of Ionia*, which started from the mythical figures of Codrus and Neleus to then recount the foundation of the various Ionic cities on the Anatolian coast (this work—more than 7,000 lines—may have been in stichic pentameters or, more probably, elegiac distichs). Again in the fifth century, Ion of Chios

7. Cf. Vetta 1992: 188–91.

8. This is the case with Solon's *Salamis* (cf. West 1974: 12; contra Bowie 1990: 18–21) and with Archilochus fr. 1 W (cf. Aloni 1981: 32–48).

9. Sources (Suda Σ 439; *Vit. Pind.* [Ambros.] pp. 2.21ff. Drachmann; Plut. *Them.* 15.4) speak of another poem on the battle of Salamis—but this is more likely to have been a lyric rather than an elegy; cf. West 1993a, in particular 2–3.

wrote a *Foundation of Chios*, which there is good reason to believe was an elegiac poem.[10]

Poems of hundreds or thousands of lines, which give an unbroken narrative of historical events, are ill suited to the atmosphere of a symposium (which might be characterized as both dialogic and agonal). In the strictly sympotic elegy—for example, that composed by Theognis—brevity was an essential feature, a result of the egalitarian nature of the gathering and of the fact that the speaker and audience of the poem were continually alternating roles.[11]

What is more, while there is almost no trace of the mourning that numerous sources give as one of the most ancient characteristics of the elegy,[12] there can be no doubt that there was once a functional link between elegiac compositions and threnody. Proof of this is to be had from Page's work on the Doric elegy,[13] and also from Andromache's lament in Euripides' tragedy (ll. 103–16), a piece not only recognized as a *threnos* by ancient scholars[14] but also referred to as such within the tragedy itself.[15] In effect, there is no reason why a symposium could not have been an occasion for the sorrowful and consolatory meditation upon the passing of family, friends, or companions in arms and political allies. There is, in fact, internal evidence that the lament of which Archilochus fr. 13 W² is a part was destined for a symposium in which Pericles participated (particularly significant here is the address to Pericles himself). The symposium, however, was essentially a private occasion; threnody and the consolation of elegy were there exercised on a private scale. As the tradition of the Doric elegy shows, there was also a very important public role for such threnody.

In other words, along with the more strictly sympotic form of elegy one has also to consider two elegiac forms that could be destined for a wider public: the historical elegy (which is much longer than the sympotic elegy) and the threnodic elegy. The dominant function of the latter was consolatory; its forms (length, diction, etc.) and content are still largely unknown to us, but we do know they varied according to occasion—from symposia to public ceremonies of mourning.

According to Bowie, the large-scale elegy recounting historical events would have been performed in public competition—above all at civic or panhellenic celebrations.[16] This means that in civic celebrations from the seventh century onward (and, doubtless, well into the fifth century), the recital of an elegy was an alternative to the *epos*. Instead of dealing with the Age of Heroes, the work would have dealt with the more recent history of the city and its territories. Between the two poetic forms there was a temporal difference. At times, however, more or less sizable parts of these his-

---

10. Perhaps Xenophanes' *The Founding of Colophon* should be added to this list of historical elegies; again this seems to have been an enormous poem of more than 2,000 lines. On the historical elegy see Bowie 1986: 27–34, and Rutherford, this volume, at n. 41.

11. Cf. Vetta 1992: 196–99.

12. Harvey 1955, in particular 170–71; Gentili 1968, in particular 50–53.

13. Page 1936.

14. Cf. schol. ad Eur. *Andr.* 103.

15. Eur. *Andr.* 91–93: ἡμεῖς δ' οἵσπερ ἐγκείμεθ' ἀεὶ | θρήνοισι καὶ γόοισι καὶ δακρύμασι | πρὸς αἰθέρ' ἐκτενοῦμεν· κ.τ.λ.

16. Cf. Bowie 1986, particularly 27–34. See Ps.-Plut. *De musica* 1134a.

torical elegies might be used in symposia; single episodes abstracted from a longer poem might be freely recomposed and presented by an individual singer at a symposium.[17]

To be consistent with his theory of a public elegy of historical narrative, Bowie rules out the existence of elegiac threnodies to express mourning and offer consolation. However, here I think his otherwise excellent analysis falls into excessive formalism: a particular type of subject matter is associated with occasions and functions that, for a given poetic form, are predetermined by the subject matter itself.[18] A historical narrative elegy lies halfway between the performance of an epic and the *apodexis* associated with Herodotus' work.[19] All three have certain features in common: they are directed to a large public and are intended to reinforce the collective memory. However, there was nothing to prevent historical narrative elegy being used in public or private ceremonies of mourning and compensation[20]—through song and remembering—for the deaths of individuals and the misfortunes of the community. And this, quite apart from formal considerations, was the essential role of the *threnos.*[21] It is significant that such a role was the main purpose of a particular form of elegy—the tombstone inscription.[22] While non-oral and not designed for collective consumption (in theory, at least, the reader of an inscription is always alone), a tombstone inscription both is intended for the public (anyone who is literate can read it) and serves to console the living and celebrate the memory of the dead. That these inscriptions, intended for public use, tend to be written in elegiac distichs is an indication that it was traditional to use elegiac meter for such purposes.

The new Simonidean elegy dedicated to the battle of Plataea seems to show that historical narrative elegy and threnody were not necessarily mutually exclusive. The historical narrative was used for largely threnodic purposes to mourn the dead of the battle and to glorify their memory.

Simonides' Elegy

To understand how content and form go together to give us a "pragmatic" definition of Simonides' elegy—that is, to enable us to identify the communicative space for which it was composed—it is best to start from the features that Bowie says are characteristic of the narrative elegy destined for public performance.[23] These features are

---

17. Cf. Vetta 1992: 191–92.

18. Obviously it is an easy criticism to make, after the publication of this previously unknown elegy by Simonides.

19. Nagy 1990: 217–24.

20. On the subject of "compensation," see Nagy 1990: 118–22, 139–43.

21. To a greater or lesser extent historical narrative remains an essential part of the *logos epitaphios* which in fifth-century Athens replaces and renders "democratic" the previous performances of funeral poetry. Cf. Loraux 1986: 3–4 and 132–71.

22. Gentili 1968: 44–46, 54–56.

23. Cf. Bowie 1986: 29.

all to be found in Simonides' poem, but the particular ways in which they are employed give us a clear indication of the function and intended audience of the elegy.

Apart from length, the essential features seem to be the presence of a proem and the use of direct speech. The latter seems the flimsier of the defining characteristics: while it is true that there is no direct speech in the sympotic elegies known to us (see, e.g., Theognis' elegy),[24] it is also true that in other works that were definitely intended for symposia (e.g., Archilochus' epodes) direct speech was used regularly.

However, the explicit testimony of firsthand witnesses and also the material that has come down to us do seem to confirm that it was only historical narrative elegy that made allowance for characters (apart from the narrative "I") to speak in the first person. This is the case with the "king" who is supposed to have talked to the main characters in fr. 13a W^2 of Mimnermus and also of fr. 2 W^2 from Tyrtaeus' Eunomia.[25] As far as the proem is concerned, Bowie's source is Pausanias (9.29.4), who refers to a proem at the beginning of Mimnermus' elegy ἐς τὴν μάχην . . . τὴν Σμυρναίων πρὸς Γύγην τε καὶ Λυδούς.[26]

This outline seems to be borne out by Simonides' elegy, where there is no dialogue between narrator and addressee but there is an ample proem—the twenty final lines of which are in fragment 11 W^2. What is more, in West's reconstruction of the poem, fragment 14 W^2—Teisamenos' supposed prophecy—is in direct speech.

Of the features of narrative elegy, however, the proem is most significant and interesting; it is that which enables us to investigate and understand the function and intended audience of the whole poem.

The Epic and the Lyrical Proem

The term proem is used to refer to a song or part of a song that introduces the poem—be it epic or lyrical—and puts it in context.

The so-called Homeric Hymns are independent proems, probably hypertrophic with respect to their original function, within the context of a festival dedicated to a specific god, to introduce a poem whose content may not have been strictly linked to the theme of the festival.[27] In the performance of epic poetry, the recital passed from a proem dedicated to the god celebrated to a traditional hexametrical tale (usually on a heroic subject)—in other words, to a section (whose length varied according to circumstances) taken from individual poems or cycles of poems, such as the Iliad or the Thebaid.

24. The sole exception (vv. 22–23) is in an exceptional context (the sphragis), and is not dialogic at all.
25. Cf. Bowie 1986: 31.
26. Under the definition used here it would be difficult to consider the brief invocation at the beginning of Solon fr. 13 W (cf. Bowie 1986: 29 n. 85) or those at the beginning of the two books of Theognis (ll. 1–8 and 1231–34; cf. West 1974: 42) as proems.
27. For a discussion of proems and a bibliography on the subject (above all with regard to lyric poetry), see Aloni 1990 (1992).

The proem to lyric poetry served other purposes. In some cases it made it possible to use, within one festival, songs that had been, or could be, performed on other occasions; in other cases—above all, with the epinicia—the proem was an opportunity for the poet to talk about himself, about the victor of the games or about the actual festival taking place.

The typical features of the epic proem, which vary only slightly in the lyrical proem, are:

1. A double opening invocation of both the god celebrated and of the Muses, to whom the poet acknowledges his subjection and appeals for inspiration.
2. An explicit—and, for the epos, exceptional—first-person presence of the poet, with possible references to the occasion for his poetic performance.
3. A fairly fixed procedure for moving on to the main body of the poem. In its full form, this includes:
   a. a farewell to the god(s) (normally χαῖρε is used);
   b. a prayer for the victory for the song;
   c. reference to the passage to another song (usually introduced with an expression such as αὐτὰρ ἐγώ).

Between the initial invocation of and the final farewell to the god, the epic proem contains a section that describes the god's attributes, or narrates the mythical events associated with his or her birth or mythical deeds.[28] The extension of this section made it possible for the epic proem to evolve from an introductory section subordinate to the song that followed it to an almost independent poetic form in its own right. In fact, apart from those cases where the mythical section is missing or else reduced to a mere list of the god's names (*Hymn. Hom.* 21–25), the length of the narrative section can vary a great deal. Hymn 18, for example, which is dedicated to Hermes, takes only five lines to tell the story of the union of Zeus and Maia from which the god was born, while the longer *Hymn to Hermes* (4) takes 570 lines to narrate the birth and early adventures of the god.

The Proem to Simonides' Elegy

The elegiac proem shows significant differences from, as well as similarities to, the epic proem, particularly in the final section. First, as in epic, the addressee of the proem, Achilles, is invoked with the second person (l. 19 χαῖρε). The proem narrative deals with the fundamental point of Achilles' existence, of his status as a hero—the Trojan War and the warrior's death at the hands of Apollo. The Muses are invoked at the end of the proem to assist the poet—present in the first person—in this song dedicated to the men who saved Greece from the barbarian. We do not know if the Muses had already been invoked at the beginning of the proem, but it seems likely.

Diction and theme are other areas in which the conclusion of Simonides' proem is extraordinarily similar to the corresponding section in an epic proem: the

---

28. For a discussion of the structure of the epic proem, see Janko 1981; Obbink, this volume.

addressee is bidden farewell (l. 19 ἀλλὰ σὺ μὲ]ν νῦν χαῖρε, θεᾶς ἐρικυ[δέος υἱέ), in terms that follow the usual wording of the farewells in the *Homeric Hymns* (e.g., *Hymn. Apoll.* 545 καὶ σὺ μὲν οὕτω χαῖρε, Διὸς καὶ Λητοῦς υἱέ). The farewell is followed immediately by an invocation of the Muses and the announcement of the poet's undertaking in the following song (ll. 20–24); this "open" ending to the proem is introduced by the formula αὐτὰρ ἐγώ. Exactly the same transition is to be found at the end of no fewer than thirteen *Homeric Hymns.*[29]

So much for the similarities. The differences consist mainly in the fact that the addressee is not a god but a hero, a demigod who could not avoid the common fate of mortals.[30]

What is more, the invocation of the Muses is complicated by the fact that they are mentioned as the source of the words of the poet who guaranteed the *kleos* of Achilles and the Greeks—that is, they revealed πᾶσαν ἀληθείην to Homer (cf. the very probable reconstruction of l. 17)—and thus are called upon (precisely because of that previous role) to assist the present poet in his endeavors.

So the usual model—in which the proem proceeds from an invocation of a god to the recognition that it is the Muses who guarantee *kleos* by inspiring the poet's song—is slightly modified by the introduction of a mortal in place of a god, and by the reference to the prestigious, exemplary figure of Homer. For the reading I am attempting to outline here, these are decisive differences.

The allusion to the poet of the *Iliad* and the *Odyssey* is important for many reasons. First, it reveals how, by the time of Simonides, the epic tradition concerning the Trojan War had become centered on the work of one author, behind whom there was only the divine, omniscient voice of the Muses. Simonides does not consider Homer as merely the author of two poems (which even then were already known by the names of the *Iliad* and the *Odyssey*), but as the origin of the most prestigious tradition relating the events of the Trojan War. In fact, Simonides' text seems to dwell upon two events, the death of Achilles and the fall of Troy, that are certainly not at the center of the Homeric poems.[31]

The naming of the author of the epic stories of Achilles and the Greeks is central to the affirmation of the epos as panhellenic poetry, which is not subject to the constant recomposition and modifications essential to local and family traditions.[32]

---

29 See also Obbink, this volume, at nn. 12 and 27–28, with reference to Emped. B35.

30. West 1993a: 5–6, too, points out the exceptional nature of the address to Achilles, a mortal demigod in a context normally reserved for gods, and thence puts forward the theory that the poem was written for some festival or ritual dedicated to Achilles. The unusual nature of this apostrophe to Achilles also raises another point. In proems the poet, present in the first person, traditionally apostrophizes the addressee in the second person (l. 19 ἀλλὰ σὺ μὲ]ν νῦν χαῖρε, θεᾶς ἐρικυ[δέος υἱέ); there is, therefore, a copresence of poet and addressee. The proem to Simonides' elegy shows that the addressee need not be a god: depending on the occasion he can also be a hero. Could not these direct apostrophes to the hero/addressee be the model for those rare second-person apostrophes that are addressed to heroes in epic poetry (where the norm is for the poet to refer to heroes in the third person)? See also this volume, Boedeker "Heroization" at nn. 43–55, Fantuzzi at n. 3. On Achilles see also Shaw, and Stehle at nn. 28–36. On moving from invocation to addressee, see Obbink at nn. 15ff.

31. See Clay, this volume, at n. 4.

32. This concept of panhellenic poetry is developed in Nagy 1990, in particular 414–37, and also in Nagy 1989, in particular 29–35.

Here one might compare Simonides' panhellenic tendency with Pindar's (in a poetic, not political, sense) and his inclination to attribute to contemporary victors in games or military exploits a glory similar to that which the heroes of the past earned through their deeds.

The mention of Homer, however, serves not only to identify the function of the two poets (Homer and Simonides); in the specific case of this poem, the two are distinguished by their different relationships with the Muses (as Eva Stehle discusses in this volume). Even allowing for the uncertainty of the text we have, there is no doubt that Homer παρ' ἰοπ]λοκάμων δέξατο Πιερίδ[ων | πᾶσαν ἀλη]θείην ("received all truth from the violet-tressed Pierids"), or, in any case, the revelation of the song (ll. 16–17). Simonides, on the other hand, limits himself to calling upon the Muse for help (l. 21 κικλήισκω] σ' ἐπίκουρον ἐμοί, π[ολυώνυμ]ε Μοῦσα).[33]

The reason for the difference between these two positions is to be found in the subject matter of the poems. Homer could not have been a witness to the events at Troy and therefore relied entirely on the Muses for the truth of his account; Simonides, on the other hand, did witness the Greek war against the Persians and so needs the Muse's help only to guarantee the ability of his poetry to render the truth and thus confer lasting fame on those who took part in the events narrated.[34]

We can see a similar attitude in an Archilochus elegy (fr. 1 W[2]): while proudly affirming his own "recognition" of the sweet gift of the Muses, the poet distinguishes between such recognition and total dependency. (The latter is, however, his position with regard to the God of War.)[35]

Proem and Occasion

From the foregoing it is perhaps possible to define the occasion for which Simonides' elegy was composed.[36] The stylistic and structural similarities between its proem and that of an epic poem indicate that this work was for public performance at some solemn occasion. This hypothesis is also borne out by the length of the poem and by the panhellenic characteristics (exemplified by the reference to the figure of Homer) of the task the poet sets himself. This panhellenism consists mainly in rejecting any local or biased use of the glory achieved by the Greeks who won the battle of Plataea—hence the reference to the supreme example of poetry glorifying the united operation of various Greek powers against a common foe.[37]

---

33. See also this volume, Rutherford at nn. 60–62, Parsons at n. 48, and Clay's conclusion.
34. On Muses as *epikouroi* see this volume, Stehle at nn. 7–23 and Obbink at nn. 22–23.
35. Cf. Aloni 1981: 34–37. For the role of the poet see also Boedeker, this volume, "Heroization," at nn. 38–39.
36. On this point West 1993a: 5 is fairly cautious: "We may guess that these elegiac epyllia were designed to be performed, as entertainment, in that setting in which elegy was usually performed, with aulos accompaniment."
37. As far as I can see, apart from the Trojan epic only three early Greek mythical narratives have a martial theme and involve a conflict between a Greek alliance and an external enemy: those dealing with the Titans, the Centaurs, and the Amazons. During the course of the fifth century these enemies of the Greek heroes were increasingly portrayed as "barbarians." Cf. Hall 1989: 101–59. But see Boedeker, this volume, "Heroization," at nn. 70–73.

Further light is thrown on the function (and thus the intended occasion) of the elegy by the "pragmatic" orientation of the proem. Unlike an epic proem, this one addresses not the Muses and a god but the Muses and a mortal, Achilles (and with him Patroclus), who appears as the addressee of the song, which records the glories of the Trojan adventure. But Achilles, the most valiant of the heroes, was not among those who took Troy; his mortal span came to an end before the heroes leapt from the horse to color the Trojan night with fire and blood. So the poet's song counterbalances the end of Achilles' existence with the event—the fall of Troy—that was made possible by his death (and which made the hero all the more worthy of glory and remembrance). There is an unbroken circularity between the *kleos* of the hero sacrificed to his own destiny, the *kleos* of the undertaking that Achilles and the other heroes brought to fruition at the cost of their own lives, and the *kleos* that the poet's song renews and projects forward through the course of time. The song and the *kleos* to which it bears witness are compensation for the terrible events that put an end to the lives of Achilles, Patroclus, and the other heroes who perished before the walls of Troy.[38] This same mechanism can be seen in Pindar's epinicia, which often narrate the events leading up to the foundation of the Panhellenic Games. The poet's song not only compensates the victorious athlete for his labors, it also renews the fame of the games, which in their turn are compensation and reparation for the original mournful event that was the *aition* of the games themselves.[39] The cyclical repetition of the games is the expression of a culture that saw athletic competitions, the contests of ancient heroes and contemporaries, as playing a central role in the "working out" of collective mourning—and of the sense of guilt that accompanies mourning. The games were above all essential in the struggle between the human desire for eternity (survival) and the inevitable caesura of physical death.[40]

The models for this signification of the funeral games can be found in epinicia and even more in epic poetry. In Homer's poems, there is a ritual continuation to the funerals of Achilles and Patroclus: the games held in honor of the dead. However brief, the account of Achilles' funeral given at the end of the *Odyssey* (24.36–94) brings out the clear link between the funeral rites, the athletic games, and the continuance through time of the dead man's *kleos*. After having mentioned the magnificent gifts Thetis offers to the victors of the games held in honor of her son, Agamemnon concludes with a statement that makes the link clear (ll. 93–94): ὡς σὺ μὲν οὐδὲ θανὼν ὄνομ' ὤλεσας, ἀλλά τοι αἰεὶ | πάντας ἐπ' ἀνθρώπους κλέος ἔσσεται ἐσθλόν, Ἀχιλλεῦ ("Thus not even in death, Achilles, has your name perished, but forever, among all men you will have a noble fame").

In short, in ancient Greece the games were a fundamental occasion for affirming the survival of the dead beyond the moment of their death. So the games are a sort of nonverbal communication, fulfilling the same role as is fulfilled verbally by the epinicia and the *threnos*. Obviously, athletic competition and celebratory song went

---

38. See also this volume, Rutherford at n. 25 and, differently, Stehle at nn. 42–59.
39. Nagy 1990: 118–21; Burkert 1985: 105–7.
40. On κλέος ἀθάνατον, see Boedeker, this volume, "Heroization," at nn. 31–32.

together, as is clear from Hesiod's account of his journey to Calchis to take part in the *aethla* in honor of the hero Amphidamas (*WD* 654–59).

If we move from athletic competitions to war, we can see the same ideological presuppositions behind the attribution and communication of a warrior's *kleos*. The song is the compensation, the *lutron* for the *ponos*, the combatant's labors. Such *ponos* achieves its highest expression when it culminates in the warrior's death, which is a glorious sacrifice that makes victory possible. It is significant that, in both war and athletic games, defeat is not communicated. Just as the games had no second prizes or any other form of consolation for defeat (if anything, subsequent victory was the only consolation for a past defeat), so the voice of the poet does not sing the virtues and valorous deeds of the defeated—which must have existed.[41]

In the song that accompanies the ritual, the dead warrior's *kleos* is nothing other than a present-day expression of the *kleos* of the great warriors (the heroes and ancestors) of the past.[42] This is the cultural context within which one has to read threnodic poetry, whose function was the exaltation of the dead man's *kleos*.

However, such identification of a contemporary's worth with the worth of an ancient hero was soon in conflict with the isonomy practiced in late archaic Greek cities; later, it appeared especially at odds with legislation that was, to some extent, democratic.[43] Public forms of mourning (and the performance of commemorative poetry connected with them) were either banned or rigorously controlled in a number of Greek cities. In democratic Athens, all those who had died in war were commemorated together in the *logos epitaphios*; while in Sparta, a hero's funeral (with the appropriate poetic performances) was the exclusive privilege of kings.[44]

In the specific—and better-documented—case of Athens, we know that this contradiction had already generated a series of laws in the sixth century. Traditionally attributed to Solon (Plut. *Sol.* 12 and 21), these laws were intended to put a stop to the excesses funeral ceremonies might give rise to—and privately commissioned threnodic poetry in honor of individuals was one such "excess." The aim was not to limit private display of wealth per se, but to clamp down on poetic performances that could have political consequences and that gave rise to competitiveness between different groups and clans—all determined to outdo each other in this particular form of public communication.[45]

It is in this context that we have to understand the spread of tombstone inscriptions.[46] Once opulent ceremonies in commemoration of an individual were forbidden (for political reasons), private citizens had to look for another way of publicly announcing and maintaining the glory of the deceased. The new medium was the tomb itself—in particular, the funeral monument and the inscription upon it (which

---

41. The Thermopylae texts are a special case: the sacrifice of Leonidas and his men is not considered in itself but rather as the premise for the subsequent victory of Salamis.

42. Nagy 1990: 152–53.

43. Alexiou 1974: 16–23.

44. Loraux 1986: 42–56.

45. Cf. also Alexiou 1974: 18.

46. Nagy 1990: 18 and 152–153 with bibliography.

"preserved" the dead man's name and worth). The fact that these inscriptions are almost all in dactylic meter (hexametric and, above all, elegiac) is further confirmation of the ideological purpose behind the emergence and spread of this practice, which was intended to proclaim and preserved the dead man's *kleos*.

The fact that Achilles is given as the addressee of the proem makes it possible to outline the main purpose of the elegy. An account of the battle of Plataea, the poem emphasizes a parallel between it and the Trojan War (and, in particular, focuses on Achilles as a symbol of those who took part in both undertakings). The main function of the elegy, therefore, is threnodic; its purpose is compensation and atonement with regard to those who died at Plataea, warriors whose death raises them to the level of heroes. I will look at the question of who might have commissioned the elegy, but first I want to stress how the risks of partiality (which were inherent in threnody and all forms of *epainos*)[47] are avoided here by the clearly panhellenic nature of both the mythical and contemporary events referred to. Achilles does not serve as the heroic paradigm for a particular warrior;[48] he is the model for all those who are mourned and praised—those whose death made victory over the Persians possible.

These elements combine to suggest that the original occasion of Simonides' elegy was an event commemorating the battle of Plataea itself, one of those ceremonies that, according to our sources, were organized to celebrate the memory of those who fell in battle.

The course of the battle of Plataea was rather odd; yet, though hardly a model of military tactics, the event did result in the death of the supreme commander of the Persian forces in Greece (who had been left in charge after Xerxes' retreat), and the numerous solemn celebrations held afterward show that the Greeks realized that, with the death of Mardonius, the threat of a permanent Persian presence on Greek soil had passed forever.[49] According to our sources, Simonides composed various contributions to these celebrations: the two epigrams that, according to Pausanias (9.2.5), were inscribed on the tombs of the Athenian and Spartan dead are attributed to him, though with some reservations.[50]

The first inscription for the Athenians, says ("Simon." 8 *FGE = AP* 7.253):

εἰ τὸ καλῶς θνῄσκειν ἀρετῆς μέρος ἐστὶ μέγιστον,
    ἡμῖν ἐκ πάντων τοῦτ' ἀπένειμε τύχη·
Ἑλλάδι γὰρ σπεύδοντες ἐλευθερίην περιθεῖναι
    κείμεθ' ἀγηράντῳ χρώμενοι εὐλογίῃ.

---

47. Nagy 1990: 152 and 193 with specific reference to the victory of Plataea. Personally I do not see the contradiction—so much emphasized by Loraux 1986: 49–50—between *threnos* (a type of performance) and *epainos* (primarily a definition of a function of song). I would suggest that all future discussions of early Greek literary genres be preceded by an accurate distinction between actual occasions (marriages, funerals, symposia, etc.), modes (song or recital; soloist or chorus), and types of performance (epinicia, *threnos*, etc.), functions (ἔπαινος, ψόγος, etc.), and metrical forms.

48. As Parsons 1992a: 32 suspects. See also this volume, Boedeker, "Heroization," at nn. 57–59; differently, Shaw, n. 79f.

49. See also Hornblower, this volume, at nn. 16–21.

50. Cf. Page 1981: 197–200, which favors attribution to Simonides.

> If a valiant death is the greatest part of virtue,
> > Fate has granted us that above all others;
> Fighting to gain liberty for Greece,
> > we lie here enveloped in a fame that cannot grow old.

The Spartan inscription reads ("Simon." 9 *FGE* = *AP* 7.251):

> ἄσβεστον κλέος οἵδε φίλῃ περὶ πατρίδι θέντες
> > κυάνεον θανάτου ἀμφεβάλοντο νέφος·
> οὐδὲ τεθνᾶσι θανόντες, ἐπεί σφ' ἀρετὴ καθύπερθε
> > κυδαίνουσ' ἀνάγει δώματος ἐξ Ἀίδεω.

> Undying fame these men gave to their beloved fatherland.
> > They put on the dark cloud of death.
> Yet dead, they are not dead; their valor
> > Gives them glory and brings them back from Hades.

What is noteworthy about the two inscriptions is that neither explicitly names the fatherland of the dead warriors: in one case there is a reference to Greece, in the other to the "beloved fatherland" (which could be the city-state or all of Greece). In other words, the inscriptions (in all probability composed soon after the war) reveal none of the conflicts and jealousies that marked nearly every moment of the alliance between Athens and Sparta.

The same can be seen in other inscriptions which, even if not by Simonides, reveal what must have been a common point of view in the period just after the battle. One of these inscriptions is that which the Athenians and Spartans together had raised on the altar of Zeus Eleutherios at Plataea ("Simon." 15 *FGE* = *AP* 6.50).[51] The other ("Simon." 17a *FGE* = *AP* 6.197)[52] is that which the Spartan commander Pausanias had inscribed on the tripod the Greeks dedicated at Delphi after their victory. This latter inscription was subsequently erased by order of the Spartans; in it Pausanias is described as "commander of the Greeks" and, without any reference to Sparta or its allies, is said to have destroyed "the armies of the Persians."[53]

---

51.   Τόνδε ποθ' Ἕλληνες ῥώμῃ χερὸς ἔργῳ Ἄρηος
         [εὐτόλμῳ ψυχῆς λήματι πειθόμενοι.]
         Πέρσας ἐξελάσαντες, ἐλεύθερον Ἑλλάδι κόσμον
         ἱδρύσαντο Διὸς βωμὸν Ἐλευθερίου.

   This altar, the Greeks who by strength of arms and the courage of Ares,
         [obeying the audacious desires of their soul,]
   Having driven off the Persians and freed Hellas,
         by common will, raised to Zeus Eleutherios.

52.   Ἑλλάνων ἀρχαγὸς ἐπεὶ στρατὸν ὤλεσε Μήδων
         Παυσανίας. Φοίβῳ μνᾶμ' ἀνέθηκε τόδε.
   Commander of the Greeks, after destroying the Medes,
         Pausanias dedicated this *mnêma* to Phoebus.

53. At the very least, Simonides' authorship of these two epigrams is unlikely (cf. Page 1981: 211–13 and 216–17). However, they are almost certainly contemporary with the events they refer to and reveal that at the time there was a feeling or, if one prefers, a dominant ideology of panhellenism.

In short, it seems that for once the Greek cities—Athens and Sparta in particular—had abandoned their strong sense of civic identity, of city rivalry. The frequent references to Hellas or the "fatherland"—or even the "common fatherland"—seems to reflect unusual political harmony. This is not contradicted by the Spartan commander's inclination to take all the credit for the Greek victory for himself, without any reference to his city-state.

However, our historical sources would seem to deny that there was any such political idyll in relations between the Greek allies: Herodotus, Diodorus (who bases his account on Ephorus), and Plutarch all paint a picture of sour relations.[54] The allies seem to have been continually exchanging accusations of double-dealing, opportunism, fence-sitting, or even worse. Plutarch (*Arist.* 20) tells us that after the battle there was almost a brawl as a result of a discussion as to which of the allies had fought most valiantly. Plutarch (*De Herod. malign.* 42 p. 872d–e) also explicitly accuses Herodotus (and thus Athens) of having given a distorted account of the battle, diminishing or totally denying the contributions made by cities other than Athens and Sparta.[55]

One has, therefore, to reassess the political panhellenism that is supposed to have reigned at the time of Plataea. Immediately after the battle, each of the allies—and, above all, men such as Pausanias, Themistocles, and Aristides, who had played a leading part in events—tried to use the victory (and the unity that had made it possible) for his own ends.[56] The references to Hellas and "the beloved fatherland" turn out to be nothing but a cover for the scheming of military leaders (and of Themistocles and Pausanias in particular), who do not always seem to have had the interests of even their own city-states close to heart. In fact, as a result of their scheming, both Themistocles and Pausanias would, within a few short years, lose all their power and be condemned as traitors by their respective cities. Even the alliance between Athens and Sparta—solemnly sworn in 481 B.C.E. (Hdt. 7.145)—soon revealed its limits; for each of the two cities, or at least for Athens, the war against the Persians became an opportunity and pretext for trying to assert hegemony over the entire Greek world. Just two years after Plataea, Athens was pushing for the establishment of the Delian League, a maritime alliance that served anti-Spartan ends; in a very short time the league was less a weapon to be used against the Persians than an Athenian tool for imposing hegemony on the other Greek city-states.

It is in this context of political ambiguity and tension that we have to understand who commissioned Simonides' elegy and what occasion it was intended for. The dates in our possession may be of some help here.

---

54. The main source is Herodotus (books 8 and 9): to differing degrees both Diodorus (*Bibliotheca* 11) and Plutarch (*Arist.* and the treatise *De Herod. malign.*) draw upon him. A clear and balanced account of the events connected with the second Persian War along with a careful evaluation of all the sources is to be found in Calabi Limentani 1964, in particular pp. xxxi–xxxiv and liii–lix. The fairly extensive bibliography on the subject of Plataea is taken account of in Prandi 1988, in particular 47–77 and 161–73.
55. See Boedeker, this volume, "Historiography," at nn. 46–47, who gives reason to Plutarch.
56. See Boedeker, "Historiography," at nn. 54–55, for the differences between Herodotus and Simonides with regard to the battle.

Plutarch quotes the lines describing the courage of the Corinthians (*De Herod. malign.* 42 p. 872d–873) and then makes certain specific points:[57] the elegy was not commissioned by the Corinthians, nor does it narrate only the deeds of the Corinthian soldiers. This means, among other things, that the Corinthians were not the central characters of the elegiac narrative but only appeared as one among several other allied contingents (probably in a sort of list given before the battle). What is more, Plutarch emphasizes that he considers the elegy totally trustworthy, a veritable piece of history writing. So, on the one hand, the elegy appeared to Plutarch at least[58] as impartial and free of interference for those who had commissioned it; on the other, there is no doubt that it must have been commissioned (B. Gentili has shown the fundamental role of commissions in early and classical Greek poetry; public performances and the profession of poet depended on them). However flimsy a lead, this clue is a starting point from which to identify who commissioned the elegy, who paid the poet. It is probable that Plutarch himself did not know; but his ignorance can be explained by reasons of chronology. It is more interesting that Herodotus appears not to know of the poem[59] (or, as Plutarch insinuates, chose to ignore it); nor does he appear to have been familiar with a number of events that took place after the battle (and which are referred to by Plutarch). It is always very difficult to give the reasons why facts are passed over in silence; sometimes this can simply be a question of which sources were available to a historian. In Herodotus' case the sources were mainly oral,[60] and there is no doubt that they placed little or no importance on Simonides' elegy (or perhaps they had simply forgotten about it). All of which means, as we shall see, that it is fairly unlikely that the poem was commissioned by Athens.[61]

Some of the characteristics of the proem that have already been outlined go together very well with the apparent panhellenic feeling that (at least according to Plut. *Arist.* 21) marked the celebrations held immediately after the battle. The construction of tumuli to commemorate the fallen, and the erection by the victorious Greeks of a common altar to Zeus Eleutherios, could have been the occasion for the elegy, given the magnificence of the celebrations, which involved the establishment of the Eleutheria, a quadrennial festival that included athletic competitions.[62]

The celebrations were also an occasion for reconfirming the anti-Persian alliance—this time as an offensive rather than defensive pact. There are many open questions as to the actual contents of these celebrations, with regard not only to the festival and competitions, but also to the political decisions that may have accom-

---

57. ταῦτα γὰρ οὐ χορὸν ἐν Κορίνθῳ διδάσκων οὐδ' ᾆσμα ποιῶν εἰς τὴν πόλιν. ἄλλως δὲ τὰς πράξεις ἐκείνας ἐν ἐλεγείᾳ γράφων ἱστόρηκεν.

58. One should anyway bear in mind that Plutarch would have been much more willing to pick up on evidence that suggested the commission came from Athens rather than elsewhere.

59. See this volume, Boedeker, "Historiography," for a different assessment, and also Rutherford at nn. 30–31.

60. The marked pro-Athenian bias in Herodotus' sources is pointed out in Wardman 1959.

61. For a different view see Bearzot 1997.

62. For the honors paid to the Greeks who fell at Plataea, see this volume, Rutherford at n. 33; also Boedeker, "Heroization," at nn. 7–15, and for Eleutheria at nn. 16–26.

panied them.[63] However, some of the clauses in the decree establishing the festival (sacrifice to Zeus Eleutherios, honors paid to the tombs of the fallen, the inviolability of Plataea), which Plutarch ascribes to Aristides (*Arist.* 21), are also implicit in some cursory comments in Thucydides (2.71.2; 3.58.4–5; 3.68.1)—with one small but very important difference: the place of Aristides is taken by the Spartan Pausanias. And, in effect, the dominance of Pausanias and the Spartans would seem to fit better with what we know of the situation: in 472, Aeschylus (*Pers.* 817) was still describing the victory of Plataea as Δωρίδος λόγχης ὕπο "by Dorian spear." In short, it is highly probable that the tumuli and tombs erected immediately after the battle, as attested by Herodotus (9.85), were consecrated in a solemn ceremony presided over by the commander of the victorious army—a ceremony that would have been the perfect setting for the performance of an elegy.[64]

The occasion combined both the celebration of victory and mourning for the dead, and fits perfectly well with the subject matter and addressee of the proem: the conquest of Troy figures not merely as a great military victory but also as the altar on which the greatest of the Greek heroes sacrificed themselves (with Achilles and Patroclus the greatest of them all). The narrative of the proem would act as the *aition* for the ceremony, and the song would, at one and the same time, be a compensation for the death of the ancient heroes and of those who had just fallen in battle. What is more, each city—or, at least, Athens and Sparta—offered specific homage to its own dead through the inscriptions on the tumuli.

Occasion and Commission

The state of the text that has come down to us makes it difficult to offer any more precise suggestions as to who might have commissioned the work. However, there is no doubt that the beginning of the narrative proper (fr. 11.25ff. W²) is happy to dwell on the march of the Spartan army from the Isthmus. The mention of its departure (fr. 11.29 οἱ μὲν ἄρ' Εὐ]ρώταν κα[ὶ Σπάρτη]ς ἄστυ λιπόντ[ες) is followed by a precise reference to the divine or heroic figures charged with protecting the expedition; and the names of the Dioscuri and Menelaus call to mind the most noble and ancient glories of the city.[65] Immediately afterward two entire lines are dedicated to the genealogy and virtues of the Spartan commander Pausanias (fr. 11.33–34 τοὺς δ' υἱὸς θείοιο Κλεο]μβ[ρ]ότου ἔξ[α]γ' ἄριστ[ος | . . .]αγ. Παυσανίης). The other allies from the Peloponnese must have been dealt with rather summarily (fr. 11.37–38 ἔνθά περ ὤ[λλοι | . . .] φῦλα περικτιόνων). And while the present state of the text means we have no knowledge of how the Athenians are introduced onto the scene, it is probable that they are already present by line 41 (the mention of Pandion bears out this supposition: Παν]δίονος ἐξε[λάσα]ντες); their appearance, therefore, is given much less emphasis than that of the Spartan army.

---

63. On this point see the predominantly negative views expressed in Prandi 1988: 161–73.
64. See Rutherford, this volume, at nn. 25–34.
65. See also Hornblower at nn. 22–33 for the Dioscuri, and for Menelaus at nn. 43–50.

Given this Spartan bias, it is worth looking at the reconstruction West proposes for lines 25–26, which would make the argument for a Spartan commission unavoidable: the reconstruction would, in fact, have the soldiers at Plataea saving "Sparta and Hellas" from barbarian slavery (οἳ Σπάρτ[ηι τε καὶ Ἑλλάδι δούλιον ἦμ]αρ | ἔσχον] ἀμυνόμενοι κ.τ.λ.). Obviously this reading of the lines is only hypothetical and any argument based on it must be treated with caution. However, it does fit in perfectly with the text we have and also echoes a connection (Ἑλλάδι καὶ Μεγαρεῦσιν ἐλεύθερον ἆμαρ ἀέξειν | ἱέμενοι κ.τ.λ.) to be found in an epigram—naturally attributed to Simonides (16.1–2 *FGE* = *IG* 7.53)[66]—commissioned by the city of Megara to commemorate those of its citizens who fell in the Persian wars. Placed immediately after the invocation of the Muse (l. 23 ἔντυνο]ν καὶ τόνδ[ε μελ]ίφρονα κ[όσμον ἀο]ιδῆς) and the declaration of the purpose of the song (ll. 24–25 ἵνα τις [μνή]σεται ὕ[στερον αὖ | ἀνδρῶν), the reference to the defenders of "Sparta and Hellas" makes that one city the central figure of the poem, the recipient of the glory and fame conferred by the elegy.

Fragment 13 W[2] lends further support to the possibility of a Spartan commission (even if the evidence is partially concealed by the state of the text: of its thirteen lines, only the left halves of lines 8–12 are legible, and even then with difficulty).[67] While an overall interpretation of the text is impossible, it is significant that in lines 8–10[68] a contrast is drawn between the Persians and Medes on the one hand and the sons of Dorus and Herakles (that is, the Spartans and Peloponnesians in general) on the other. In other words, here again the elegy puts special emphasis on the Spartans and their allies in the Peloponnesian League.[69]

It is difficult at this point not to try to give a precise interpretation of what those who commissioned the elegy expected of it.

While commissioning Simonides to write the inscription for the monument at Plataea and for the tripod at Delphi, the Spartans and/or Pausanias also commissioned an elegy that commemorated the dead and celebrated their victory *in situ*—a work that transformed the battle into an episode in the history of the "Greek people,"

66. Once again attribution to Simonides is likely to be wrong (cf. Page 1981: 213–15); but scholars are agreed in dating the epigram around 479 B.C.E. or shortly after.

67. *POxy* 2327 fr. 27 col. ii, originally edited by West among the Adespota elegiaca (fr. 58).

68. Simonides fr. 13.8–10 W[2]: ὄφρ' ἀπὸ μὲν Μήδ[ων . . . | καὶ Περσῶν, Δώρου δ[ὲ . . . παισὶ καὶ Ἡρακλέος [.

69. Thus it is difficult to accept West's hypothesis (1993a: 8–9) that the above-mentioned lines 8–9 of fr. 14 W[2] are an allusion to the foundation of the Delian League. It would indeed be odd for the Spartan soothsayer to be forecasting the establishment of the union that was to be one of the main weapons in the Athenians' anti-Sparta campaign. Even setting that aside, there are problems with making the reading fit the extant text: line 8 can be read]νὴν συμμ[ ].ην φιλεω[, with traces of corrections (.α..γε. over the group ην φιλε). This enables us to recognize with near certainty a reference to a συμμαχίη (Parsons however does not exclude a συμμορίη). All the rest is uncertain. The alliance Teisamenos is referring to could well be that sworn in 481 B.C.E. (Hdt. 7.145) which might well have been renewed during the commemorative rites, which, I am arguing, were the occasion for Simonides' elegy. Plutarch points out that on that occasion an undertaking was given to raise a body of men annually in order to continue the war against the barbarians (*Arist.* 21). This would fit with the references (l. 7, ἢ σφε καὶ ἐξ Ἀ]σί[η]ς ἐλάσει) to the driving of the barbarians out of Asia—that is, from the Greek-settled coast of Anatolia. See also Boedeker, this volume, "Historiography," at nn. 33–36.

made it into an event comparable with the victory achieved over Troy by the heroes of old.[70]

In all probability, neither his decades of experience as a professional poet nor his "octopus" *mêtis* could prevent Simonides from showing bias in favor of those who had commissioned the elegy.[71] This may have had something to do with the fact that only a couple of years later—even after yet another victory for one of his dithyrambs at the Dionysia[72]—the poet chose to end his career a long way from Athens. At this point it seems fairly safe to conclude that Pausanias was directly involved in the commissioning of the elegy. In this case there is a curious parallel between the subsequent fates of poet and patron.[73] Pausanias was declared an enemy of Sparta, hounded to death, and even then subject to a sort of *damnatio memoriae* (the Athenians themselves had never been particularly fond of him); Simonides thought it best to take himself off to Sicily (or perhaps he was "helped" to reach that conclusion). Of the elegy itself there is not a trace in what is our main source of information on the battle of Plataea—the work of Herodotus. The explanation seems clear enough: with the waning of Pausanias' star, the oral narratives of the events connected with the battle of Plataea (whether pro-Athenian or pro-Spartan) would have drastically reduced the importance attached to the disgraced general—and it was those oral narratives that were Herodotus' main source material. The deliberate slighting of Pausanias would also have meant that nonessential facts and events that were too closely connected with his name were "blacked out"—and one such event was the commissioning and performance of Simonides' elegy.

Conclusion

If the interpretation I have put forward is well founded, then one has to add that the new Simonides elegy makes a substantial contribution to our knowledge of archaic elegy, though it does not resolve all the problems raised. In a certain sense one might say that the situation now is even more complicated than before. In fact, what we have here is a narrative elegy on a historical subject, destined to serve as a threnody for public performance.

The variations in the proem—the epic schema of poetic "I" versus the "you" of a divine addressee plus the Muse(s) being complicated by the presence of a hero addressee (Achilles) and the evocation of Homer (source of the song of the Trojan War)—are decisive in regard to the conclusions reached. Both variations have a paradigmatic value and function. Homer symbolizes the truth of his account of the Trojan

---

70. On Spartan commission, see this volume, Stehle at nn. 52–67 and Rutherford at nn. 27–31.
71. Cf. Gentili 1985: 174–75.
72. At the Dionysian Games of Spring 476 B.C.E.; cf. "Simon." 28 *FGE* and the observations in Page 1981: 241–43. On the end of his residence in Athens, his move to Sicily, and subsequent death, see Molyneux 1992: 211–36.
73. See also Obbink, this volume, after n. 9.

War, the model of truth against which the poetic "I" measures himself. Achilles—and with him Patroclus and all the other heroes who died at Troy—is the model for those referred to in the poem; his eternal glory gives a meaning to the sacrifice of those who died at Plataea (they will share in the common fate of all heroes: courage and death). The essence of elegy's threnodic function is the celebration of the fallen soldiers' heroic glory and fame.

I therefore believe that Simonides' elegy makes clear, once and for all, that links between elegy and the religious practices, of which numerous sources tell, were involved in the mourning for and celebration of the dead.

However, the elegy does not enable us to trace a continuous, unambiguous line linking compositions such as Archilochus fr. 13 W with Andromache's threnodic lament in Euripides' tragedy. And then, of course, there are the other poems—the elegies of Echembrotus, Sacadas, and Olympus—of which we have no direct knowledge and about which, therefore, it is best to offer no theories. It is possible, however, to outline a framework that embraces different forms of elegy, with the metrical form and the function of mourning giving rise to various types of "performance" (determined by nothing other than the nature of the specific occasion and the combined intentions of both poet and patron). Within this framework, the elegy as a form can be recognized as supplying the function of the *threnos* (whose means and methods of performance it also takes over). Nevertheless, one should not forget that the elegy and elegiac performance were not the only means of expressing *threnos*.

In other words, we have no firm evidence for claiming that there was no choral threnodic elegy (or elegy *tout court*). Nor, as a consequence, can we be certain that the elegy under discussion was not choral;[74] no evidence in the text enables us to decide one way or the other. However, the comparison established in the proem between the first-person voice and Homer would seem to suggest that the introductory section at least was monodic. We have no evidence with regard to the presence—or, more important, the significance—of the first-person voice in the historical narrative.

Finally, the recent controversy over the forms of performance of the Pindaric epinician should make us very wary of any conclusion that tends to establish a cast-iron link between poetic meter, occasion of composition, and forms of performance. Created as tools for the rather abstract—though worthy—task of library classification, the categories of "genre" are on this occasion rather misleading, ignoring as they do that the ways in which the songs were performed were determined mainly by practical considerations, on the basis of flexible and pragmatic criteria.

74. Harvey 1955: 170.

5

EVA STEHLE

A Bard of the Iron Age and
His Auxiliary Muse

Recovery of the fragments of Simonides' elegy on the battle of Plataea gives us an example of a genre, historical elegy, that we had not had.[1] But even within that newly recognized category the Plataea elegy is unique, for it does not treat the affairs of a single city and the more distant past.[2] The poem is an anomaly, so performance of it also would not have fit into any of the cultural frameworks that connected occasion, subject matter, and type of performance. It must have been meant for a special occasion. Scholars have made various suggestions about the time and place of its unveiling; I find performance at Plataea, perhaps in connection with the tombs set up on the battlefield, an attractive suggestion (one that I return to at the end), but other locations are possible.[3]

One consequence of the poem's special status is that the poet had to inscribe authority for the performer into the text itself. Most poetic performance in archaic and classical Greece was a kind of public speaking (an aspect of performance too often ignored by scholars), so any poet/performer not speaking within established frameworks of subject matter and occasion, where the speaking roles were given by the context, had to establish an authoritative role and an ideological frame of reference for his words.[4] If poet and performer were different (as was probably the case here), the performer had to fill the role composed for him or her by the poet, since it was the performer who appeared as speaker.

An earlier version of this paper appeared in Deborah Boedeker and David Sider (eds.), *The New Simonides*, *Arethusa* 29.2 (1996): 205–22, and is used here by kind permission of the Johns Hopkins University Press.

1. Simonides frr. 10–17 W². When I give line numbers without a fragment number preceding I am referring to 11, the longest fragment. See Rutherford, this volume, for description of the restorations.

2. Bowie 1986 argues for an established genre of historical narrative in elegy, but the only certain precedent for Simonides is Mimnermus' *Smyrneis*, a poem on struggles with the Lydians in the seventh century. Semonides and Xenophanes may have composed such poems, but that either was elegiac is not firm. Archilochus wrote elegy on military themes, but not demonstrably narrative.

3. See Aloni and Shaw, this volume, and Boedeker 1995b.

4. Stehle 1997 treats these issues.

In this essay, therefore, I will look at how the performer of Simonides' elegy projects a role for himself, one justifying his claim on public attention, and incorporates the system of values that anchors his praise. My thesis is that, as Simonides created the role, the performer sets up a series of parallels between Homer and himself, within which he systematically deviates from the Homeric model. These deviations do two things: they reveal a different relationship between the speaker and his material from Homer's, thus producing a different role for the speaker, and they point to an ideological referent for the speaker's praise in the poetry of Tyrtaeus and the Spartan community. The combination of quasi-Homeric stance and Tyrtaean values as paradigm for the speaker creates a novel persona adapted to the novel subject matter and context for this poem. The essay has two parts, devoted in turn to the speaker's role and the frame of reference for his praise.

The Speaker's Role

The performer begins with a proem in a manner reminiscent of a bard or rhapsode, as though he meant to present himself as a singer in the Homeric tradition. M. L. West observes, "The initial hymn to Achilles struck an epic note for the composition and set the conflict against Mardonios upon a heroic plane. It is full of elevated language, Homeric and para-Homeric epithets, and there is even an epic simile (fr. 11.1–3)."[5] Yet there are two significant deviations from Homer in the proem that show us how the performer is reconfiguring the bardic position: he invokes Achilles rather than a divinity, and he asks the Muse to be "auxiliary," *epikouros* (21), though a moment before he had asserted that Homer got the "whole truth" from the Muses (17).

Each deviation has been explained: as to the first, Achilles is the model for the dead at Plataea, who will be remembered as he is; and as to the second, the performer only needs some help from the Muse because he can supply the content for himself, having been present at the battle. Thus Antonio Aloni says of the latter,

> The reason for the difference between these two positions is to be found in the subject matter of the poems. Homer could not have been a witness to the events at Troy and therefore relied entirely on the Muses for the truth of his account; Simonides, on the other hand, did witness the Greek war against the Persians and so needs the Muse's help only to guarantee the ability of his poetry to render the truth and thus confer lasting fame on those who took part in the events narrated.[6]

These are important observations, but not a full explanation. To invoke Achilles implies that he is more than a model. Nor is the relevant issue, rhetorically, whether Simonides witnessed the battle of Plataea; rather, he must persuade the audience, many of whose members surely participated in the battle, to assent to his account. As Deborah Boedeker has brought out, this poem is the first attempt at a canonical

---

5. West 1993a: 9. See also Obbink, this volume, at nn. 11–32.
6. Aloni, this volume, at n. 34. Pindar asks the Muses to sing of recent events, so the poet's personal knowledge was not inherently in opposition to the Muses' song.

account of the Greek victory and, if successful, will define how the episode will be remembered.[7] Furthermore, these two deviations are juxtaposed in the text: the performer bids farewell to Achilles (*chaire*, 19) and turns forthwith to call the Muse as *epikouros* (20–21). Each cancels the rationale given for the other: if Achilles is the model for the fallen soldiers at Plataea, why would the speaker emphasize that his song about the fallen at Plataea will *not* come from the Muses, unlike the song about Achilles? If the performer wishes to stress his own ability to create heroizing song, why does he begin with an un-Homeric invocation to Achilles? It seems that these two features together mark the performer in his self-presentation as not-quite-a-bard and the poem as something only *similar* to epic.

Let us begin with the second deviation and investigate exactly how the performer contrasts the Muses' contribution to Homer's narrative and to his own. Speaking of the Danaans and Homer he says (13–17):

> τοὶ δὲ πόλι]ν πέρσαντες ἀοίδιμον [οἴκαδ' ἵ]κοντο
>]ώων ἀγέμαχοι Δαναοί[.
> οἷσιν ἐπ' ἀθά]νατον κέχυται κλέος ἀν[δρὸς] ἕκητι   15
> ὃς παρ' ἰοπ]λοκάμων δέξατο Πιερίδ[ων
> πᾶσαν ἀλη]θείην

Homer receives the story (whether wholly true or "divine") from the Muses.[8] The Trojan War has been entirely transposed into song, while song, thanks to the Muses and Homer, is full enough to encompass it. There is no other source of information.

Simonides' use of the adjective *aoidimos* in line 13 (quoted above) confirms that the Trojan War and Homeric song are one. The adjective is well chosen to recall the Trojan War, for it appears only once in the *Iliad*, in the same position in the line, when Helen says that she and Paris will be *aoidimoi* to future generations (6.358).[9] But what lies in the future in Homer's narrative, the transposition of the Trojan War into song, has already occurred in this version, in which the Danaans came home from a "sung-of city."[10]

Of himself, on the other hand, the performer says (20–22):

> αὐτὰρ ἐγώ   20
> κικλήισκω] σ' ἐπίκουρον ἐμοί, π[ολυώνυμ]ε μοῦσα,
> εἴ πέρ γ' ἀν]θρώπων εὐχομένω[ν μέλεαι·

To see just how he envisages the division of labor between himself and the Muse we must look more closely at what the term *epikouros* implies.[11] The word is common in

---

7. Boedeker, "Historiography," this volume.

8. "Divine song," [γῆρυν ‿ –] θείην, is an alternative reported by West in his app. crit. But the text given is better; cf. the same phrase in *Od.* 11.507 at line beginning.

9. As Lloyd-Jones 1994: 1 remarks. It is rare outside the *Iliad* in early hexameter, according to *LfgrE* s.v., being found only at *Homeric Hymn to Apollo* 299, to describe Apollo's temple.

10. The adjective is proleptic but creates the rhetorical effect of collapsing the two stages. Note also that the relationship of the aorist ἵκοντο (13) to the perfect κέχυται (15) is indeterminable.

11. It is possible (as Obbink remarks, this volume, before n. 15) that Simonides invoked the Muse at the beginning of the poem, while the segment to and about Achilles was inset. But even so the Muse is to be *epikouros* for the main narrative.

the plural in Homer (especially the *Iliad*) and later to mean "foreign military auxil-iaries." In the *Iliad*, it designates the non-Trojans, such as Sarpedon and his Lycians, who fight alongside the men from Troy. Later it often means "mercenary." Archilochus 15 W is pithy on the subject: Γλαῦκ', ἐπίκουρος ἀνὴρ τόσσον φίλος ἔσκε μάχηται.[12] Herodotus uses the word frequently to designate auxiliaries or mercenaries.[13]

The singular could be generalized to nonmilitary contexts. The performers of Pindar's *Olympian* 13 (for a victory in 464) use the term in connection with the Muses (96–97): Μοίσαις γὰρ ἀγλαοθρόνοις ἑκὼν Ὀλιγαιθίδαισίν τ' ἔβαν ἐπίκουρος. We have not really abandoned the primary meaning, however, for the line is part of a mil-itary metaphor: the speaker has just allegorized his need to speak truth as a duty to hit the mark with his javelin-throws, and the line quoted explains why. This example is similar to Simonides' in that both concern effective speech, so we might think of a military metaphor in Simonides' case also. But, equally important, Pindar's use shows us the reverse of the terms found in the Plataea elegy: in Pindar the *speaker* is *epi-kouros* to the important figures, the house of the victor and the Muses.

A single auxiliary who effectively aids overwhelmed principals can qualify as a rescuer, and use of *epikouros* in Attic drama shows the word shading into that mean-ing. Euripides exploits the tension between the new connotation "rescuer" and the old meaning "subordinate helper" in his *Ion*. Kreousa, whose husband Xouthos is identi-fied as an *epikouros* to the Athenians, believes that a son of his who inherited would be a usurper of the Athenian royal house; an *epikouros*, she says (1299), "could not be a householder of the land." Ion counters that Xouthos saved Attica with weapons, not words.[14] Elsewhere in Euripides, who favors the word, it ceases to designate an out-sider.[15]

Most uses of the word refer to humans. But it could describe a god, usually a god who aids another. In a line from the *Theogony* (815), the Hundred-handed (who are "foreigners" living at the roots of Oceanus) are the *epikouroi* (clearly, "military auxil-iaries") of Zeus. The Erinyes are *epikouroi* of Dike, according to Heraclitus (B 94 DK).[16] But given its meaning "auxiliary" it is not surprising that early on the word is little used of divinity in relation to humans.[17] I have found one instance originating earlier than the late fifth century B.C.E., apart from Simonides', in which a god is

---

12. Cf. Archilochus 216 W, which refers to a Carian *epikouros* (mercenary, as the context of the quotation makes clear).

13. Powell 1938 s.v. records twenty uses of the word and notes that the meaning "mercenaries" is the more usual. Herodotus' only exceptional use of the word is discussed below.

14. Cf. also Sophocles *OT* 487ff. where the word still means "auxiliary," but it governs the genitive, taking on the syntax of a word meaning "avenger," as Jebb notes ad loc.

15. Cf., e.g., *Or.* 211, *El.* 138, *IA* 1027, where it takes a genitive; *IA* 1241 and *Ba.* 1367, where a family member is an inadequate "aid." The military force of the metaphor seems to have faded.

16. Cf. also *Il.* 21.431; *Hom. Hymn Herm.* 97.

17. In Euripides' plays, in keeping with other shifts in meaning found there, humans call on a god to be *epikouros*, usually for special effect, e.g., *Herakleidai* 921; *Orestes* 1299–1300; fr. 351.2 N. By the fourth cen-tury it was unremarkable to call a god *epikouros* in the sense of "rescuer," sometimes in a medical context. Apollo Epikourios received a temple at Bassai after ending a plague (Paus. 8.41.8). Plato's Aristophanes (*Symp.* 189d) calls Eros an *epikouros* to humans and a doctor.

epikouros to humans.[18] Herodotus reports that the Athenians had received an oracle telling them to take their son-in-law as *epikouros* (7.189). When, therefore, they saw a storm coming up at Artemisium (or before), they sacrificed to Boreas, the North Wind, who had snatched the Erechthid Oreithyia away to be his wife. In this case the oracle appears, misleadingly, to refer to a human auxiliary from outside, although, rightly interpreted, it turns out to name a divine helper.[19]

In the 470s, the speaker's appeal to the Muse to be *epikouros* must have been arresting. The basic meaning must still be "foreign auxiliary."[20] Certainly, given her supplementary status, she is not the guarantor of truth that Aloni (quoted above) suggests. Rather, the battle of Plataea must be alien territory to her. Whereas the war at Troy has been totally transposed into epic, the battle of Plataea does not exist in poetic form; the Muse does not have a version. In other words, there is no master narrative, only a welter of vivid experiences on which no overall perspective exists, although without doubt innumerable stories are already circulating.[21] In requesting that she join him on this ground, the performer attributes to humans the primary struggle to produce the song.[22] The sharp break marked by *autar ego* (20) underlines this difference between Homer's tale and the Simonidean performer's. At the same time, the Muse's help may "rescue" the performer.[23] By calling for aid, the performer also alludes to the magnitude of his task.

Lines 23f., if correctly restored (a very fragile assumption!), tell us more about the nature of the Muse's aid:

ἔντυνο]ν καὶ τόνδ[ε μελ]ίφρονα κ[όσμον ἀο]ιδῆς
 ἡμετ]έρης[24]

I would translate, "prepare this orderly array (which all are about to hear) of our song also." The expression is a variant of *Od.* 12.183 λιγυρὴν δ' ἔντυνον ἀοιδήν ("they began to prepare the clear song"), where the point must be that the Sirens got ready a song specifically for Odysseus.[25] In the elegy, however, the Muse's share is the *kosmos* of the

---

18. Based on a search of the *Thesaurus Linguae Graecae* using Pandora. I thank the Classics Department of the University of Toronto for making the *TLG* disk available to me. One could compare another unusual request, Sappho's prayer to Aphrodite in 1.28 V to be her *symmachos*.

19. On this episode, which Simonides referred to in his poem "The sea-battle at Artemision," see Molyneux 1992: 158–66 and West 1993a: 3–4. The name Kalais (son of Boreas and Oreithyia) may appear in the new papyrus at Simon. 3.5 W², attributed to this poem.

20. Conceivably Simonides chose the word in part to recall the oracle about Boreas (if the story was already circulating at that time), but his orientation toward the Spartans perhaps makes it less likely.

21. If the setting for the original performance was panhellenic, the variety of individual impressions would have been amplified by the perspective of different cities on the events of the battle.

22. Cf. Bowie 1986: 29 on the possibility that Mimnermus 14 W belongs to the *Smyrneis*; it shows the performer giving information as his own and making evaluations.

23. Note, however, that the reference in the following line to humans praying does not seem to specify the performer; contrast Empedocles B 131 DK, cited by Obbink, this volume at n. 17. The noun ἐπικουρία meant "help" or "defense" by the fifth century, e.g., Aeschylus *Pers.* 731, in a military context (and cf. Broadhead 1960 ad loc.). The verb ἐπικουρέω is uncommon before the late fifth century.

24. The words are not at all secure. See Parsons 1992a: 34 for problems and possibilities.

25. The *Odyssey* passage is usually translated "they broke into clear song," but that ignores their need to devise a song enticing to their audience—in Odysseus' case, a tale of the Trojan War. This is the only place

performer's song, which is thus split between content and "ornament." The *Odyssey* gives us guidance as to what *kosmos* adds to a song. Odysseus praises Demodocus for telling the fate of the Achaeans λίην . . . κατὰ κόσμον (*Od.* 8.489), all too clearly. *Kosmos* can be both clarity, plausibility, truth in narrative and tact or positive attitude.[26] Solon, moreover, speaks of his song as κόσμος ἐπέων substituted for prose speech in his Salamis elegy (1 W).[27] Content is again separated from form, for prose would do as well to convey the point, but *kosmos* makes the words more apt to win assent. *Kosmos* is what our performer needs: techniques for making his account clear and generous enough to embrace many perceptions and satisfy the audience.

The difference from Homer so clearly marked in lines 15–22 turns out to be a difference in the shape or condition of the speaker's subject matter. This difference entails a further one. The Homeric performer sets himself above his audience by virtue of his access to the Muses. The Simonidean performer refuses to present himself as tapping a pre-existing, divine source of knowledge. Quite possibly, making such a claim before audience members who were conscious of having their own firsthand knowledge would have aroused resentment. Instead, he presents his own performance as an effort to join segregated realms of experienced event and heroizing poetry.

Investigating lines 21–22 has shown us that the performer separates his material from that of epic and eschews the epic performer's authorizing claim to divine knowledge. We have yet to determine how he does present himself. To pursue that question we can turn to the other major deviation of the proem, the address to Achilles, modeled on rhapsodes' habit of prefacing their performances of epic with an address to a god. The shorter *Homeric Hymns* are examples of such preludes; typically, one begins, "I sing X" (where X is the name of an Olympian god), then offers praise or brief narrative. The rhapsode breaks off with *chaire*, addressed to the deity, "but I (*autar ego*) will remember both you and another song."[28] With this transition the rhapsode presumably turns to his main narrative by calling on the Muse and naming his subject, just as the *Iliad* opens.[29]

---

in Homer where the verb ἐντύνω is used with song. Cf. *Hom. Hymn* 6.20: ἐμὴν δ' ἔντυνον ἀοιδήν directly after the singer asks for victory in "this contest." The clause, now an injunction, must mean "prepare/equip *my* song." Both of these are at line end.

26. Adkins 1972: 13–17 argues that *kosmos* used of speech in epic refers in the first instance to speaking in such a way as not to impugn the *arete* of the *agathoi*, then, that criterion met, to the truth of statements. He observes (15): "Speech or behavior which the ἀγαθοί as a group regard as unbeautiful, unpleasing, disorderly, will be stigmatized as οὐ κατὰ κόσμον; and where ἀρετή is affected, its being οὐ κατὰ κόσμον will override the question of its truth."

27. West, app. crit. ad loc., thinks that ᾠδήν in the text is a gloss on κόσμον ἐπέων, but the latter is in any case contrasted with ἀγορῆς, which must mean speaking in prose (so Photios *lex.* α 221, quoted by West ad loc.). Parmenides B 8.50–52 DK contrasts his πιστὸν λόγον about truth with κόσμον ἐμῶν ἐπέων ἀπατηλόν on human opinions; cf. Democritus B 6 DK for a similar phrase. In *Hom. Hymn* 7.59 the performer cannot κοσμῆσαι ἀοιδήν without Dionysus.

28. E.g., Hymns 6, 10, 25, 27, 28, 30. Others begin by asking the Muse to sing.

29. See the discussion by Obbink in this volume, at n. 25, on αὐτὰρ ἐγώ as "fulcrum on which the poem turns."

Our performer follows this pattern in good bardic fashion, so far as we can tell without the actual opening lines, but instead of an Olympian deity he calls on Achilles. This is more than an idiosyncratic choice: by invoking an epic hero, the performer attributes to him the status of cult hero, and such a move decisively separates him (the performer) from Homer.[30] Homer may indirectly reveal knowledge of the hero cult his characters receive, but he never openly acknowledges it.[31] In the *Odyssey*, Achilles hears about his own death and funeral as he does here (24.36–97), but he learns about it from another of the dead in Hades, where his status seems to be no different from that of the throng of suitors who arrive directly afterward. By thus acknowledging the cult that Homer suppresses, Simonides sets his poem firmly in the iron-age world, when lesser men honor the *hemitheoi* with cult.[32] Just as the Muse is foreign to the territory of poetry about Plataea, so the participants in that battle belong to a different age from Homer's.

The Simonidean performer must expect specific benefits from invoking Achilles as well. That Achilles will provide the model for the dead at Plataea is clear from the aspects of his story that seem to appear: his loyalty to Patroclus and death, the ultimate victory by the others, and their glory.[33] Yet Achilles as a cult hero must be meant to aid the speaker in an active way to succeed as well. In various *Homeric Hymns*, rhapsodes call on Aphrodite, Dionysus, or the Muses and Apollo, all gods of beauty and joy, for help with the song. What does Achilles grant the speaker by way of help?

Heroes like Achilles foster battle spirit.[34] What the Simonidean performer seeks, therefore, is military inspiration.[35] He is like a military leader, publicly calling on divine help at the outset. When at the beginning of the narrative proper he says that the Spartans, led by Pausanias, marched out "with the horse-taming sons of Zeus, the [Tyndarid] heroes, and with Menelaus of wide power" (30–31), he provides the military analogue for his relationship with Achilles. And the following scene (35–41) appears to present contingents gathering from various cities, a marshaling of forces

---

30. Simonides elsewhere vividly depicted Achilles appearing above his tomb as the Greeks were leaving Troy (557 *PMG*). See Shaw, this volume, on cults of Achilles; on the status of Achilles in this poem see Rutherford, this volume, at n. 46, and Boedeker, "Heroization," at nn. 42–59.

31. Nagy 1979: 114–21 and 342–43 shows that a cult of Achilles is a submerged motif in the *Iliad*. Van Wees 1992: 6–8 argues that Homer thought of his heroes as the *hemitheoi* of later tradition; Homer does not show their cult because it was practiced only by later, lesser people.

32. Simonides' use of the word for the Trojan heroes in 18 also calls attention to his difference from Homer. See Clay, this volume.

33. On these lines see Rutherford, this volume; Barchiesi, this volume.

34. Cf. Pritchett 1979: 11–46 on epiphanies in war, 23–26 on those attested for the Persian wars; he comments (41–42) that they were especially numerous during the Persian wars and cites (15) Hdt. 8.109 and Xen. *Cyr.* 1.17 on the importance of the heroes in fighting the "barbarian." Kearns 1989: 44–46 discusses heroes appearing in battle. On epiphanies in the Plataea poem, see Hornblower, this volume. I do not agree with Hornblower that the Tyndarids and Menelaus appeared in an epiphany because, first, an epiphany is an event, one that produces an effect or demands interpretation, and no event is described here; and second, Simonides' purpose is not to document actual procedure but to paint a grand portrait of a force going into motion. The participial phrase seems to be suggesting that an (unspecified) efficacious ritual has taken place rather than an unanticipated manifestation.

35. That Achilles is a singer of κλέα ἀνδρῶν (*Il.* 9.189) as well as a fighter helps the persona that Simonides is creating.

in the poem, as on the ground. The speaker's calling on the Muse to be *epikouros* fits perfectly with this persona. As he marshals troops, the poet calls in an auxiliary force. As I noted above, Pindar's use of *epikouros* in *Ol.* 13.96–97 is part of a military metaphor, which strengthens the idea that the audience would hear one here. *Kosmos* too is a military term, as well as a literary one.[36] The performer therefore presents himself as marshaling stories in good order, finding a pattern within which to set them, and drawing on poetic techniques of amplification.

In keeping with his un-Homeric stance as a leader deploying troops, the speaker adopts a different narrative point of view from Homer's. Homer's Muse provides an Olympian view; the whole panorama and the perceptions of both sides in the war, Greeks and Trojans, constitute the range of Homer's interest. Simonides' narrative could be described as recapitulating the actions and decisions of the Greek (especially the Spartan) commanders. He begins with the Spartans leaving their city and follows their progress. If West is right to argue that fragment 14 included the prophecy of the Spartan diviner Teisamenos, then the narrative must have recaptured a dramatic moment of revelation and decision.[37] In 14.3]εγω points to direct discourse, with its vividness.[38] Unfortunately, we cannot tell how the Persians were described, but nothing in the extant fragments suggests that the performer ever switched to their view of the battle.[39]

Furthermore, the performer moralizes: history is intepreted as judgment. His attitude is visible in the description of the fall of Troy in the proem, where it dictates alterations of Homeric language. Paris is *kakophron* (11), a word not found in epic. The "chariot of divine justice overtook [someone]" (12); chariots are not driven by abstractions in Homer, and the adjective *theios* is not found with *dike*.[40] This set of non-Homeric formulations allows the performer to adopt a partisan attitude foreign to the *Iliad* but one that assimilates the Trojan expedition to the Greek defense against the Persians.

In sum, Simonides marks out his speaker by differentiating him from Homer, making him a combatant who seeks to direct the formation of a master narrative. Focused on recent reality instead of the mythic or distant past, he marshals experiences into a coherent account. He re-enacts in his narrative, as it were, the action on

---

36. Cf. Aesch. *Pers.* 399–400 (with the note in Broadhead 1960 ad loc.: *kosmos* is the preservation of good order during an advance); Hdt. 8.86, 9.66.3. I owe this point and the stimulus to recognize the military stance of the performer to Alessando Barchiesi.

37. Cf. Hdt. 9.33–36. But see Obbink, this volume, n. 34.

38. So West 1993a: 8. He suggests (8–9) that the prophecy ranged over victory and founding of the Delian League. Barchiesi, this volume, n. 22, suggests that the performer may imply an analogy between the prophet who predicts future fame (14.6 with West's restorations) and himself as the preserver of that fame.

39. Fr. 13 contains the section (8–10):

ὄφρ' ἀπὸ μὲν Μήδ[ων
καὶ Περσῶν, Δώρου δ[ὲ
παισὶ καὶ Ἡρακλέος [

which looks as though it represented a Spartan point of view, with its evocation of heroic ancestry. Fr. 17 contains (probably) Demeter's name. Frr. 15 and 16 come from Plutarch and concern the Corinthians, and 12 and 18 are exiguous.

40. See Parsons 1992a: 29 and Rutherford's commentary on this line.

the ground, effecting the transposition to poetry by his generalship, with Achilles providing the energy and the Muse order and amplitude.[41] The performer does not, then, simply eschew the claim to have the whole truth, but constructs his authority on the ground of a different persona, one committed to reliving Greek *arete*.

The Praise-Poet's Frame of Reference

However much he pleased the audience by revivifying their experience, Simonides also had to build a speaking position that incorporated a recognized ideological basis for the honor he bestows, one that would undergird his authority and validate the praise in the eyes of the audience. The performer himself explicitly connects the glory that Homer's heroes received with Homer's access to the Muses (15–18). We must therefore ask how our performer's presentation of his praise supports the stated goal (24–25) of the poem to honor the soldiers of Plataea. Since he creates his persona through marked deviations from Homer, I begin here too by comparing his treatment of glory to Homer's, using the two instances in the fragments in which Simonides mentions glory resulting from the battle of Plataea. In each case, Homeric adjectives or adjective-noun combinations are used in a non-Homeric way.

The first passage is the summary of Simonides' subject that follows the address to the Muse. She should bring him aid (24–28)

ἵνα τις [μνή]σεται ὕ[στερον αὖ
ἀνδρῶ]ν, οἳ Σπάρτ[ηι δούλιον ἦμ]αρ   25
 ] ἀμυν[ ] . . [   ]ω[
οὐδ' ἀρε]τῆς ἐλάθ[οντο   ]ν οὐρανομ[ήκ]ης,
καὶ κλέος ἀ]νθρώπων [ἔσσετ]αι ἀθάνατο⟨ν⟩.[42]

The adjective *ouranomekes* modifies what must have been a word for fame or report. West supplements the preceding lacuna, *exempli gratia*, [φάτις δ' ἔχε]ν. *Ouranomekes* is found once in Homer (*Od.* 5.239) of a tree that will provide wood for Odysseus's raft.[43] Whether or not the audience recalled this line, to their mind's eye fame would tower like a tree.

In the next line, *kleos* is plausibly restored, along with the verb in the future; together they predict an alteration from immediate fame to lasting glory.[44] The adjec-

---

41. Herodotus gives us a line that interestingly, if coincidentally, combines the concepts of cult-hero and *epikouros* in a military context (5.80): the Thebans ask the Aiginetans for help against Athens, οἱ δὲ . . . ἐπικουρίην τοὺς Αἰακίδας συμπέμπειν ἔφασαν.

42. For the tenuous reconstruction of this section of the poem, see Rutherford's commentary and Parsons 1992a: 32–34 and esp. 34 for this line.

43. Herodotus 2.138 uses it of trees as well. In LSJ the first attested "metaphorical" use, i.e., use with a noun not denoting a physical object, is in Aristophanes' *Clouds*, where it occurs twice, at 357 and 459; in the latter line it modifies *kleos*.

44. A scholion in *POxy* 2327 explains ἀ[νθρώπων as equivalent to ἐν ἀνθρώποις. Three syllables are therefore available for a connective plus something that will be undying among humans. Thus *kleos* seems plausible.

tive with *kleos* is *athanatos*, the collocation forming a variant of Homeric κλέος ἄφθι-τον. *Athanatos* is not found with *kleos* in extant hexameter poetry, however, for in Homer the word is used only in its literal sense of living beings. In applying it to the word "glory," Simonides makes glory a living thing. The performer, it should be noted, does not say that his poem will create the *kleos*, though the audience was perhaps encouraged to think that it would help.[45]

The second passage is the praise of the Corinthians quoted by Plutarch (16.1–3 W). The Corinthians

κάλλιστον μάρτυν ἔθεντο πόνων,
χρυσοῦ τιμήεντος ἐν αἰθέρι· καί σφιν ἀέξει
αὐτῶν τ' εὐρεῖαν κληδόνα καὶ πατέρων.

The phrase "honorable gold" must mean the sun.[46] Like the Spartans' *ouranomekes* glory, the witness to the Corinthians' deeds is material and found in the heavens. This golden sun will make increase the "broad notice" won by the Corinthians. Perhaps we should see a metaphor of a plant growing in the sunshine (or perhaps money laid down as a pledge producing return). These phrases seem to suggest that the glory won at Plataea has a materiality or life independent of poets, just as Achilles has a living cult apart from his Homeric instantiation. Its physicality contrasts with the glory of Homeric heroes, which the performer says is "poured" (15) over them by Homer—and also contrasts with the way glory is portrayed within Homeric epic. There, fame is carried by voice in song or speech.[47] Contrast Odysseus's boast in *Od.* 9.19–20 that his glory "comes to" heaven with the Spartans' glory "as tall as heaven."

The "broad notice" that the Corinthians earn does travel via voices, but here there is a different kind of significant deviation from Homer. The phrase is a variation on the Homeric "broad *kleos*." Instead of *kleos*, the performer uses *kledon*; in Homer *kledon* means "a chance remark that is significant as an omen" or, more generally, "report" or "rumor." The crucial point is this: *kledon* is not linked to heroic poetry as *kleos* is. It rather implies prepoetic fame by hearsay in the mouths of people at large. The fame of the soldiers at Plataea exists outside poetry; it is inscribed in the natural world, as it were, and in daily speech.[48] Material and prepoetic—this image of glory in Simonides' poem is in keeping with his other deviations from Homer. Simonides' subject is an iron-age battle that took place in the world inhabited by his audience; to this reality his speaking character as participant and his portrayal of the palpable "presence" of Achilles and of glory are adapted. Chance preserves from the narrative

45. The subject changes to the singular in the lacuna of 27, so the relative clause cannot continue; therefore, 28 cannot be taken as parallel to 24 and part of the ἵνα clause. Furthermore, if Goodwin's categorical statement (1890: 115) that a future indicative never stands after ἵνα holds good, then [μνή]σεται (24) must be a short-vowel subjunctive and line 28 an independent assertion.

46. This is one of the noun-epithet phrases found in epic, but there its meaning is always literal (Cunliffe 1963 s.v.). On the image see Rutherford, this volume, at nn. 75–78.

47. Epic acknowledges the tomb as a source of memory also, but downplays it. Hector's fantasy in *Il.* 7.87–91, the most significant evocation of the tomb as preserver of glory, is an empty hope.

48. For an appreciation of Simonides' filling in "absent presences," see Carson 1988.

section of the poem only the praise of the Corinthians, but other states, and especially the Spartans, must have come in for their share of the meed.

Still, I think there is a more specific source of authority for the Simonidean speaker's predictions of everlasting glory for the Greek fighters at Plataea. As I noted earlier, he does not say that this poem creates their glory. To see what ideological system underwrites their glory we must return to the word *athanatos*. The performer (probably) says that Homer created "undying glory" for his heroes (15: the "man" is Homer). The Danaans returned home:

οἶσιν ἐπ᾽ ἀθά]νατον κέχυται κλέος ἀν[δρὸς] ἕκητι

The performer's recipients of praise have the same (28):

καὶ κλέος ἀ]νθρώπων [ἔσσετ]αι ἀθάνατο⟨ν⟩.

The speaker certainly implies a flattering parallelism, but there are significant differences. In the line about Homer, the adjective is attributive, for Homer's song, coming from the Muses, has staying power *ex hypothesi*.[49] In the line about the men of Plataea, the adjective is predicative. Word-placement supports the disparity. In the line on Homer, *kleos* is in the fourth foot, its usual *sedes* in early hexameter verse.[50] In the second instance, *kleos* (if rightly restored) appears in the first foot, a position it holds only once in extant early hexameter.[51] Finally, Homer's line is a hexameter, appropriately, but the glory recorded by our performer appears in the pentameter, the line that deviates from epic. The pentameter is made to stand for the difference from epic—and it points us to the other important model for the performer's self-presentation and the referent for his praise.

In an elegy (12 W) that was well known, for Plato paraphrases a long section of it, Tyrtaeus pronounces that any Spartan warrior who dies in battle will be mourned by the whole city and have a prominent tomb and honored descendants thereafter.[52] Moreover (31–32),

οὐδέ ποτε κλέος ἐσθλὸν ἀπόλλυται οὐδ᾽ ὄνομ᾽ αὐτοῦ,

ἀλλ᾽ ὑπὸ γῆς περ ἐὼν γίγνεται ἀθάνατος

Tyrtaeus promises that each soldier will become "undying," that is, become a hero in the extra-Homeric sense, one who receives cult.[53] Tyrtaeus' poetry continued to be performed at the king's tent during military campaigns, according to the Athenian

---

49. For the restoration of line 15 and comment on the balance of immortal and mortal, see Parsons 1992a: 30.

50. See the statistics in *LfgrE* s.v.

51. *Il.* 5.172; see *LfgrE*.

52. Plato, *Laws* 629a–630b. For defense of its authenticity, which has been questioned, see Jaeger 1966: 112–26, Prato 1968: 15–19, and Snell 1969: 28–36. It is now accepted as Tyrtaeus'.

53. Fuqua 1981: 221–25 brings this out very well. He points out (216) that it goes beyond anything else in Tyrtaeus. Snell 1969: 33 contrasts *Od.* 24.43–44, in which Agamemnon tells Achilles that he will have good *kleos* forever. In the circularity department, it is to be noted that this line probably influenced the reconstruction of Simonides' line 28; see Parsons 1992a: 34.

orator Lykourgos.[54] Now, Simonides' elegy gives special attention to Sparta, and it is the courage of each *Spartan* warrior that will win undying *kleos* (25). It has even been suggested that Pausanias or the Spartans commissioned the poem.[55] Making good on one of the ideological avowals that grounded their militaristic system would be a priority for Spartan leaders. So I propose that Simonides' poem was meant to fulfill Tyrtaeus' promise for the Spartan soldiers who died at Plataea.

Simonides' poem could not create actual cult observance for each warrior, for that would be a matter of local Spartan practice (and the Spartans did not go that far for ordinary soldiers; for kings, see below).[56] But Simonides has taken the adjective indicating the soldier's continued life and applied it to his *kleos* instead, so that his glory becomes the living thing that represents him.[57] Simonides is also careful to place the word so that it echoes Tyrtaeus. The line predicting "undying fame" for the men of Plataea is pentameter, like Tyrtaeus' line containing the same word "undying." The adjective falls at the end of the line, as it does in Tyrtaeus' poem, a position that it cannot take in a hexameter line. In both, the adjective is predicative and follows the verb. Tyrtaeus promises in the previous line that *kleos* will never perish. It is easy to think that Spartans would hear an echo of Tyrtaeus in the Plataea elegy.

If this is so, we can understand the performer's view of glory more fully. For Tyrtaeus, *kleos* is perpetuated within the community (12.27–30 W):

> τὸν δ' ὀλοφύρονται μὲν ὁμῶς νέοι ἠδὲ γέροντες
> ἀργαλέῳ δὲ πόθῳ πᾶσα κέκηδε πόλις,
> καὶ τύμβος καὶ παῖδες ἐν ἀνθρώποις ἀρίσημοι
> καὶ παίδων παῖδες καὶ γένος ἐξοπίσω·

The *paides* and the tomb are both reminders of the soldier, and the community will feel longing for him. Our performer speaks of *kleos* that exists outside the poem because it is bound up with the community-based remembrance. We can see, too, a further reason for his not claiming special access to the truth, beyond the reaction that the audience might have: the true story is in the keeping of the Spartan state, the guarantor of *kleos* in Tyrtaeus' model.[58] The performer's stance of combatant also suits his appeal to Tyrtaeus: Tyrtaeus adopted the speaking role of military leader to

---

54. *In Leocr.* 107, quoted at Tyrtaeus 10 W. On the styles of performance see Bowie 1990, esp. 225–27. Cf. Athenaeus 14, 630F where it is said that the Spartans kept their movement rhythmical in war by reciting Tyrtaeus' poems.

55. Aloni, this volume, makes this argument at greatest length. See also Pavese 1995.

56. Plutarch *Lyk.* 27.2 does record that the Spartans permitted only warriors who had died in battle (and women who had died while holding sacred office) to have their names recorded on their graves. For possible implied heroization or quasi-heroization, see below and Boedeker, "Heroization," this volume.

57. Cf. two less daring epigrams from the Persian War period: *CEG* 2.11 (= 20a *FGE*) has κλέ]ος ἄφθι[τον] αἰεί, and 9 *FGE* has ἄσβεστον κλέος. The latter epigram contains the same paradox of life and death as Tyrtaeus 12 W. The adjective ἀθάνατος became popular in the fifth-century milieu of conflated war dead and heroic dead. *CEG* 6, a public monument from 447(?), has ἀθάνατον μνῆμ' ἀρετῆς. Cf. *CEG* 10. For ἀθάνατος in Attic funeral orations see Jaeger 1966: 137, who traces it to Tyrtaeus.

58. Jaeger 1959: 138: "The new thing here is that the country, the community of the polis, takes over, as it were, the function of the Homeric singer who praises the virtue of his heroes."

exhort Spartan troops to fight, while our performer as the other side of the Tyrtaean persona celebrates their victory. Perhaps the role of the Spartan community was explicit in a lost part of the poem.[59]

But the Plataea elegy is not only Spartan. Other states are included in the narrative and must have been praised in turn. Simonides' poem on Thermopylae (531 *PMG*), which exhibits the marks of a local song for cult performance, shows up the ecumenical character of the Plataea elegy by contrast.[60] Reference to the Spartans' intracommunal discourse, it seems, was only part of the poetic task. The other part was to create a battle narrative that would recall the victory to all Greeks and spread panhellenic fame of a Homeric type. Glory that reaches the sky, as both the Spartans' and the Corinthians' does, is an image of universal recognition. So Simonides' elegy is Homeric as well as Tyrtaean. The idea of extended battle narrative and the style, along with the Muse, come from Homer. But the performer's affinity with a hero like Achilles, like his adoption of a military stance, point to Tyrtaeus. The doubleness of elegy—hexameter and pentameter—is turned into an expression of the two sources of inspiration by linking each metrical pattern with a different poet.[61] That the poem *is* elegy rather than hexameter or lyric adds to the composite message. The Spartans may have asked for elegy (rather than lyric, say) precisely in order to recall Tyrtaeus. In addition, the poem may have been thought of as lament.[62] The Athenians a few years earlier may have called for an elegy on Marathon, narrative or threnodic, to which this poem would provide a Spartan parallel.[63] In the Plataea elegy, these qualities are superimposed on epic so as to speak to two audiences, Spartan and panhellenic. In other words, the poem would both function in its original ceremonial context and circulate everywhere thereafter.

No poem can create cult heroization by itself, since that depends on practice, as remarked above. But *if* the elegy was performed at Plataea before the tombs of the war dead, then the reference to Tyrtaeus would be even more suggestive.[64] Combined with a ceremony focused on a tomb and with (no doubt) rich sacrifices, this poem evoking a cultic-heroic Achilles and recalling Tyrtaeus would powerfully imply a cult for the dead of Plataea at their tomb.[65] In other words, the Spartan tomb at Plataea would

59. Tarkow 1983: 52–56 emphasizes the collectivity of the new hoplite warfare and of Tyrtaeus' poems.

60. See Boedeker, "Historiography," this volume, n. 47. Podlecki 1968 discusses Simonides' various poetic projects in the year 480.

61. Tyrtaeus' language is largely epic, as Snell 1969 demonstrates.

62. So Aloni, this volume, who suggests a combination of historical narrative and *threnos*. Elegiac verse became identified with lament, although the two were not originally connected.

63. See Molyneux 1992: 148–52 on *Vita Aesch.* 332.5–10 Page. If we throw out the remarks about Aeschylus' state of mind and about competition with Simonides (or think of it as competition for the commission?), we are still left with the possibility that one or the other composed an elegy. See Obbink, this volume, at n. 53 on elegy and epigram; Introduction, n. 4, on the Marathon elegy.

64. For rituals at the tombs at Plataea, see Thuc. 3.58.4 and Plutarch *Aristides* 21. Performance at the Eleutheria, the games established at Plataea, has been suggested by Parsons 1992a: 6 and others; see Boedeker 1995b: 222 for discussion.

65. If West's speculation that the common burial urn of Achilles and Patroclus is the subject of line 6 is correct (1993a: 6; W² app. crit. ad loc.), then the parallel to the common grave at Plataea is brought closer. Xenophon, *Resp. Lac.* 15.9, says that Lycurgan laws provide for honoring Spartan kings not as men but as

create a visual link connecting Spartan worship of Achilles with Tyrtaeus's promise to each Spartan soldier, and would also connect Simonides' proem with the body of his praise poem.[66] (It is entirely possible, of course, that the link was also made explicit somewhere in the poem.) As to genre, then, *if* the poem was performed initially at Plataea, we could describe its character as "panhellenic *epitaphios*": it melds the disparate functions of communal cultic-heroic honoring of war dead at their tomb with panhellenic narrative of Greek epic-heroic courage against a common enemy.[67]

I have been discussing the political and ideological aspects of the Plataea elegy. Finally let me say a word about the poetic effect. By not mythicizing the event but locating it in the iron age and contrasting it with epic, Simonides gave his account immediacy and surely excitement. Possibly the anti-bardic stance created for the performer and the valorization of iron-age heroism, together with use of Homer as a model, are among the things that he bequeathed to Herodotus.[68] Contrast the situation of Choerilus, who composed an epic on the same subject, the *Persika*, later in the fifth century. A quotation from it has been preserved in a commentary on Aristotle's rhetoric (2 *PEG*, SH 317):

> O blessed, whoever was skillful in song at that time, a servant of the Muses when the meadow was still unshorn. Now when all has been handed out and the arts have reached their limits, we are left behind, as if the last in a race, nor is there anywhere, though one peer in all directions, to direct a new-yoked chariot.

Choerilus found no way (or so he says) to revivify epic style for fresh-sounding praise of modern men. That problem faced Simonides as well, and we now know something about how skillfully he solved it.

---

heroes; cf. Fuqua 1981: 224f. on tombs and offerings for kings and others—which would reinforce the connection. Bowra 1961: 346 gives other evidence for Spartan heroization. Farnell 1921: 362f. discusses the heroization of historical figures after death, including the dead at Marathon and Plataea.

66. For evidence that Achilles was honored as a hero in Lacedaemon, see Pausanias 3.20.8 and 3.24.5, Wide 1893: 232–36. Farnell 1921: 285–89 and 409 discusses worship of Achilles as a hero, pointing out that it is well attested in Laconia. Schol. Ap. Rhod. 4.814 cites Anaxagoras as saying that Achilles was honored as a god there (cf. DK 2.420 fin). Shaw, this volume, surveys the areas where his cult was popular. Cf. also Parsons 1992a: 32 for literary evidence.

67. Cf. Loraux 1982a on the difference between epic glorification of the fallen warrior and that of the Athenian *epitaphios*, the yearly oration in honor of all those who died in battle that year. Simonides' poem is closer to Homer than to Athenian practice, but the idea of state-produced "immortal fame" is common to Simonides and the latter. Boedeker, "Heroization," this volume, suggests a broad-based conceptual heroization of the Plataiomachoi outside Sparta.

68. Pindar's mythicizing treatment of athletic victors shows that Simonides' strategy was not necessarily an obvious one for commemorative poetry at that time. We know little about Mimnermus' approach in the *Smyrneis*, though see West 1993a: 5 for parallels with Simonides.

6

DEBORAH BOEDEKER

Heroic Historiography

Simonides and Herodotus on Plataea

POxy 3965 offers a tantalizing glimpse of a kind of poetry virtually unknown to us before: encomiastic narrative elegy that celebrates contemporary historical events. In revealing this genre, Simonides' "Plataea elegy" raises new questions about the relationships among epic, elegy, and historiography in the fifth century. In this poem, the heroic, epic past—including the death of Achilles and sack of Troy—evidently provides a paradigm for recent events.[1] So, too, the poet who conferred undying *kleos* upon the Greeks at Troy serves as a model (or rival) for the present poet, who aspires to glorify the participants in the battle just fought (fr. 11.15–28).

Full of surprises as it is, Simonides' elegy has close connections to several familiar genres. Epic poetry obviously provides an important point of reference, helping to define both what the poem is and what it is not (cf. West 1993a; Clay, Aloni, and Stehle in this volume). So too does hymnic poetry (Obbink, this volume), epinician with its analogies between the contemporary athlete and heroic predecessors (cf. Harrison, this volume, and Aloni at n. 32), and earlier historical elegies. Texts such as the Plataea poem belong to those crowd-pleasing accounts of the past—including epic poetry, public funeral speeches, and Herodotus' *Histories*—that Thucydides rejects in favor of a non-mythodic κτῆμα ἐς αἰεί (1.21–22).[2]

On chronological grounds, the Plataea poem could have been among Herodotus' sources for the great battle that took place two generations earlier;[3] indeed, the

An earlier version of this paper appeared in Deborah Boedeker and David Sider (eds.), *The New Simonides*, *Arethusa* 29.2 (1996): 223–242, and is used here by kind permission of the Johns Hopkins University Press. This paper has profited from discussions with Gregory Nagy, David Sider, Eva Stehle, Mark Toher, and Kurt Raaflaub.

1. Parsons 1992a: 32; Lloyd-Jones 1994: 1. All references to the new Simonides fragments are to W[2].
2. Cf. Thuc. 1.21–22, where encomiastic narratives oriented toward public approval are called ἀγωνίσματα. Such poems and speeches might be so called even if not performed in actual contests, but it is possible that the Plataea elegy was composed for a contest in honor of those who died in that battle. Cf. Boedeker 1995b.
3. On the date of the Plataea elegy, cf. West 1993a: 9, who places the composition of the poem "sometime after the establishment of the Delian League, whose aspirations or achievements are here summarized"

account of Plataea in the *Histories* proved to be the most fruitful resource for both Parsons and West in reconstructing and ordering the fragments of the new elegy. Still, the Plataea elegy's direct influence on the *Histories* is not immediately apparent.[4] Is the connection between them then merely circular and illusory? This essay, together with Simon Hornblower's, takes a step toward a systematic examination of that relationship. My goal is not only further delineation of Herodotus' varied sources, but also better understanding of how public memory of the great events of the Persian War was shaped and transmitted during the fifth century.[5] I first consider how plausible it is that Herodotus knew and used a poetic account of the battle; next, I look at possible convergences between the Simonidean elegy and Herodotus' narrative; finally, I consider some important distinctions between the two versions, especially in the performative function they fulfill.

Herodotus' Poetic Sources

As other essays in this volume amply demonstrate, the Plataea elegy was well known through the Alexandrian period and beyond. Its fame began early: Rutherford notes (at nn. 53 and 57) that two extant Athenian tragedies (*Agamemnon* 398, *Iphigenia in Tauris* 216) seem to echo phrases in the elegy, when referring respectively to Paris and Achilles. If fifth-century poets could allude to the Plataea elegy's elided account of the *Trojan* War, the poem might be expected to resonate even more in works on the Persian Wars. Rutherford (after n. 61) shows that this was the case with Timotheus in his late fifth-century nome *Persians*, where the poet adopts an unusual relationship to his divine patron Apollo, similar to the one Simonides establishes with his Muse in fr. 11.21. It seems generally plausible then that the Plataea elegy, alluded to by a number of his contemporaries, was familiar to Herodotus as well.[6]

Poetic sources have richly influenced Herodotus' text, particularly in narrative passages.[7] In battle narratives, such influence takes several forms. Sometimes Herodotus explicitly cites verses that pertain to the events being recorded, such as

---

(i.e., in West's reconstruction of fr. 14). More likely is a date even closer to the battle of Plataea, for reasons given in Aloni, this volume, and Boedeker 1995b.

4. Cf. esp. Aloni, this volume at n. 48.

5. The problem of how Herodotus' narrative of the Persian Wars relates to poetic sources is not limited to his account of Plataea, for Simonides is also credited with elegies about Marathon (possibly) and Artemisium, and lyric poems about Thermopylae, Artemisium, and Salamis, as well as epigrams; other sources would include Aeschylus' *Persians* and possibly even a *Persika* by Empedocles (attested in Diog. Laert. 8.57; cf. Sider 1982). See this volume, the editors' Introduction and Rutherford's section "Military Fragments."

6. Marincola 1996: xviii says of historical elegies: "it can hardly be doubted that their contents were familiar to [Herodotus]." In his prescient study of earlier historical elegies, on the other hand, Bowie 1986: 35 imagined a quite different fate for such poems, "whose length and subject-matter fitted them only for their place of first performance."

7. Cf. Hornblower 1994: 65–69, Calame 1995, Herington 1991, Rosenmeyer 1982, Verdin 1977 for discussions of poetic influences on Herodotus. Klos 1947 offers a bald but useful summary of the influence of archaic poetic style and structure on the *Histories*.

oracles in hexameters (e.g., 7.140–41, 9.43) and epitaphs in elegiacs (7.228, on those who died at Thermopylae). Elsewhere poetic influence is more diffuse. At least since pseudo-Longinus,[8] readers of Herodotus have been conscious of the impact of Homeric epic on the whole conception of the *Histories* (insofar as the work is the story of a great war between Hellenes and others), as well as epic coloring in many specific passages. The goal expressed in Herodotus' proemium—to preserve the *kleos* of the great deeds performed by Greeks and foreigners—is no doubt the most famous of these passages;[9] but "Homeric influence," ranging from diction and phrasing to the construction of whole scenes, colors many Herodotean accounts. In the Plataea account, specific examples include: [10]

> 9.20.3: The double name of Masistios "whom the Greeks name Makistios"; there may further be a reflection here of the heroic epic epithet μήκιστος "tallest" as in *Il.* 7.155: τὸν δὴ μήκιστον καὶ κάρτιστον κτάνον ἄνδρα.[11]
>
> 9.20: Calling one's enemies women is attested in epic, cf. *Il.* 2.235: Ἀχαιΐδες, οὐκέτ' Ἀχαιοί, as also in fifth-century tragedy and comedy. Related insults occur elsewhere in Herodotus (e.g., 2.102.5, 8.88.3, 9.107.1).
>
> 9.23–25: The battle over Masistios' corpse recalls several Iliadic episodes, most of all the fight for Patroklos' body in *Iliad* 17–18; the Greeks then display the corpse for public viewing as Achilles did that of Hector in *Il.* 22.369ff. (Masaracchia 1978: 162–63.)
>
> 9.41: Mardonios' impatience with the omens advising him not to start battle is reminiscent of Hektor's famous dictum in a similar situation, "One bird-omen is best, to defend your fatherland" (*Il.* 12.243: Masaracchia 1978: 173).
>
> 9.76: Soon after the Greek victory, the Coan concubine of a Persian comes forward with attendants and beautiful attire, to implore Pausanias for mercy and freedom. This supplication would have reminded Herodotus' audience of the appearance of Helen before Menelaus after the sack of Troy, a scene that does not occur in *Iliad* or *Odyssey*, but was a famous motif in the Trojan cycle and a popular subject on Athenian vase-paintings.

Even if all the actions and speeches cited here really took place as described (which few readers would accept), the influence of epic diction and narrative patterns on Herodotus' text could not be discounted: of everything that occurred in the campaign, these are the actions that "registered" with his sources, were given a narrative

---

8. *On the Sublime* 13.3 μόνος Ἡρόδοτος Ὁμηρικώτατος ἐγένετο; See now the new second-century B.C.E. inscription from Halicarnassus, proclaiming Herodotus "the prose Homer of historiography." Cf. Isager 1999.

9. For recent discussions of the prooemium in relation to Homeric epic, cf. Krischer 1965, Nagy 1987, Calame 1995: 78–80 and passim.

10. In this summary (far from comprehensive), I rely largely on commentators on book 9, esp. Masaracchia 1978, whose comments give abundant if not systematic attention to epic influence.

11. On this passage cf. Mararacchia 1978: 161: "L'elaborazione dell'episodio, con la grecizzazione del nome, può resalire a un poeta (Simonide? Cherilo?) o a un prosatore (Dionisio di Mileto?) o, più semplicemente, può ascriversi al gusto delle fonti ateniesi di Erodoto e di chi visse gli avvenimenti."

shape, and subsequently were selected (and reshaped) by Herodotus.[12] Certainly eye-witnesses such as Thersander of Orchomenos (9.16) were available as sources for dis-crete parts of the story; even so, the epic narrative patterns familiar to Herodotus and his sources undoubtedly served as templates for the rendering of later "heroic" events as memorable stories. If poets such as Simonides gave intelligible, repeatable narra-tive shape to certain events, it is altogether likely that their versions influenced pop-ular "memory" and understanding of those events.[13]

Poetic genres other than epic have influenced Herodotus' battle descriptions as well. Echoes of Aeschylus' *Persians* can be detected in the Salamis *logos*,[14] and a high incidence of poetic words suggests that other poems may be reflected there as well.[15] In the Plataea story, moreover, Masaracchia points out that the sad Persian's fore-bodings at the Theban dinner party (9.16) reflect a view of mortality similar to that of the famous "lives like leaves" elegy.[16]

Along with epic *topoi* or language, and verses explicitly cited, the text of Herodotus contains a number of unmarked hexameters or near-hexameters. One such line occurs in the prelude to the sea-battle of Artemisium, when the Delphians unexpectedly receive an oracle to pray to the winds, which will become great allies of Greece. The Delphians pass along this information to the Greek allies, and receive their everlasting gratitude, as expressed in the hexametric clause ἐξαγγείλαντες χάριν ἀθάνατον κατέθεντο (7.178.2).[17] A little later (7.189), we learn that the Athenians were also directed to pray to a wind god, this time by a more cryptic ora-cle that told them to ask for help from their son-in-law (i.e., Boreas, whose wife Oreithyia was the daughter of the Athenian king Erechtheus). Herodotus reports in this connection that a sudden windstorm arose and destroyed many Persian ships (7.188), so that a more equal battle could be fought at Artemisium. Simonides, we know, was credited with a poem on the sea-battle. A fragment of the newly published papyrus preserves the letters καλαι[(fr. 3.5 W²; see Rutherford ad loc.); West ventures to restore here a reference to the sons of Boreas, Zetes and Kalais, and attributes the fragment to the Artemisium elegy. Conceivably, the buried hexameter could be a con-scious or unconscious "quotation" by Herodotus of the same Simonidean poem,[18]

---

12. Cf. Herington 1991 for an eloquent but perhaps too sweeping appreciation of the general relationship of Herodotus to epic narrative.

13. For a succinct introduction to the mythologizing of history, see Flashar 1996 and Boehringer 1996: 48.

14. Cf. Broadhead 1960: 118–33 passim for verbal and semantic parallels in the description of the battle: e.g., δρασμῷ *Pers.* 360, δρησμόν Hdt. 8.75.2; *Pers.* 399–401 and Hdt. 8.86 on Greek τάξις at the start of battle. (Surprisingly, Klos 1947 does not discuss the influence of the *Persians* on Herodotus' narrative of Salamis.) Lazenby 1988 finds numerous close correlations with Aeschylus' account in Herodotus; I would not argue, however, as Lazenby does, that this correlation guarantees general historical accuracy.

15. Cf. How and Wells 1928: vol. 2.257, ad Hdt. 8.65.2.

16. Masaracchia 1978: 162–63. See this volume, Parsons at n. 44, Hubbard, and Sider for contrasting views on the authorship (Simonides or Semonides?) and literary history of this elegy (19–20 W²), part of which appears in *POxy* 3965.26. Masaracchia's suggestion that the "leaves" elegy resembles part of Herodotus' account of Plataea is especially interesting in view of Obbink's hypothesis that that all of *POxy* 3965 may belong to the same poem.

17. Cf. How and Wells 1928: vol. 2.209. Eva Stehle kindly pointed out this example.

18. Note that the hexameter in 7.178.2 includes the word ἀθάνατον, which is twice attested in the new Simonides: fr. 11.15 (partially restored) and 28.

but it seems more likely to come from a Delphi-centered dactylic doublet of the same story.

Other unannounced poetic lines occur in the battle narratives as well. Almost a century ago, Verrall discovered several slightly adjusted hexameters in the speech of an anonymous Spartan messenger requesting that Xerxes make reparations for the death of Leonidas (8.114).[19] Verrall found a similar case in the Plataea *logos*: five near-hexameters in the speech of the Coan woman who pleads with Pausanias to grant her freedom (9.76). Her first words, for example, are: ῏Ω βασιλεῦ Σπάρτης, λῦσαί με τὴν ἱκέτιν αἰχμαλώτου δουλοσύνης, which Verrall "restores" to the hexametric ῏Ω βασιλεῦ Σπάρτης, λῦσαί μ' ἱκέτιν δοριλήπτου | δουλοσύνης.[20]

It is unlikely that all these hexameters and hexameters *manqués* are "accidental." In some cases Herodotus may have composed them himself to create an epic effect,[21] but the preponderance of such lines appearing in dramatic contexts, especially speeches, makes it plausible that they were adapted from epic or elegiac accounts of recent events.[22] In any case, Verrall's findings raise the possibility that these Herodotean speeches are influenced by poetic narratives.

We can conclude three things at this point: first, Herodotus very probably knew the Plataea elegy; second, as a heroic narrative poem, the elegy was likely to have helped shaped memory of the battle, perhaps even for those who witnessed it; third, Herodotus reflects poetic accounts at many points in his battle narratives. Now it is time to see whether, and how, he may have used this particular poem.

Convergences?

First, there are several similarities in general perspective between the Plataea elegy and Herodotus' account. The elegy begins by setting up an analogy between the Greeks who fought at Troy and those who fought at Plataea. In Herodotus' account

---

19. Verrall 1903: 101–2. The speech occurs just after the battle of Salamis; Simonides is supposed to have composed a poem on that battle as well, although the Suda notice is too confused for us to know whether this also was in elegiacs. Cf. Rutherford ("The Text") in this volume on how many Salamis poems are reported, and in what meters.

20. Verrall 1903: 99–101 hypothesizes that these lines were inscribed on a dedication tablet illustrating the scene of the rescue, but offers no parallels to such an elaborately "captioned" early fifth-century relief. I find it doubtful that the anecdote of Pausanias and the Coan woman came specifically from Simonides' account of Plataea (even discounting that the passage is more readily "restored" to hexameters rather than elegiacs), but cf. Shaw, this volume at n. 68. If this were the case, the elegy would have an anecdotal tone quite different from what is attested in our fragments—but of course those fragments preserve only a fraction of the original poem. (Cf. West 1993a: 4 on the possible length of the poem, "hardly less than a hundred lines, perhaps much more.")

21. As with the "dactylic flourishes" with which Roman historians often begin their accounts (cf. Sallust *BJ* 1.1 and 5.1, Livy *Praef.* 1, Tacitus *Ann.* 1.1.1). On this phenomenon, and esp. on Thucydides' almost hexametric prediction (δηλώσει ὅμως μεῖζον γεγενημένος αὐτῶν: 1.21.2) that his nonpoetic account will show the present war to be greater than older (and more poetically described) events, cf. Moles 1993: 103.

22. As West 1993a: 8 notes, the Plataea elegy surely contains direct speech in fr. 14.3]έγω. This is quite different from the "dactylic flourishes" described in the preceding note.

of the Persian Wars, both the narrator and some of the historical actors also assume or assert a close relationship between the events of 480–479 B.C.E. and the epic past. In their crucial expedition to seek Sicilian aid against Xerxes' forces, the Athenians explain to Gelon of Syracuse that they deserve strategic precedence over Sicilian Greeks because of the role the Athenian Menestheus played at Troy; Spartans in the same context warn Gelon that Agamemnon himself would groan if he heard that Sparta was not leading the Greek alliance (Hdt. 7.159, cf. *Il.* 7.125); in speeches before the confrontation at Plataea, Athenians claim their right to a position of honor in the battle line on the basis of earlier Athenian heroic exploits, including those at Troy (Hdt. 9.27).[23] Such examples of historical actors arguing from heroic precedents in Herodotus, however, are not the same as the narrator's own analogical use of the Trojan War, its heroes, and its fame in Simonides' Plataea poem. Closer to the elegy is Herodotus' tendency to draw broad parallels between the two great intercontinental wars, attested in his ironic proemium and elsewhere in the *Histories*.[24]

Moreover, both Herodotus and Simonides present accounts of the battle from a broad perspective, insofar as they describe the actions of Greeks from several cities that participated in the battle. Simonides begins emphatically with Spartans in fr. 11.25, as he narrates their march from the Eurotas to the Isthmus, (probably) Eleusis, and ultimately to Plataea. Other poleis are mentioned as well in the same context: Corinth (35), Megara (Ν]ίσου πόλιν, 37), probably Athens (Παν]δίονος, 41 and perhaps Κεκρο]πος, 42).[25] The fragmentary condition of the papyrus makes it impossible to be certain what is said about them here, yet all three cities are not only included in Herodotus' account of the allies, but also named on the famous Serpent Column inscription, dedicated at Delphi, listing those who fought the Persians (ML 27). It is unlikely that Simonides would mention them in this context if they were merely serving as geographical markers without any relevance to their role in the forthcoming battle. In the case of the Corinthians, we know that elsewhere in the elegy Simonides describes their position in the battle line at Plataea and indicates their brave actions there (frr. 15–16).

These general resemblances—Trojan War parallels and multi-polis perspective—of course do not prove that Herodotus used the Plataea elegy in constructing his account. After all, an inclusive perspective is not implausible in accounts of a battle that really did involve Greeks from many cities. And the analogy with the Greeks

---

23. Cf. also the story of Melampous' demand that Proitos give him a third of his kingdom before he will cure Proitos' maddened daughters (adumbrated in *Od.* 11.281–97 and 15.226–42), which Hdt. 9.34 compares to Teisamenos' demanding Spartan citizenship before he will serve as their seer. For more on the phenomenon of justifying present policy on the basis of "mythical" precedents in Herodotus, see Knox 1979: 11–12.

24. Cf. Boedeker 1988: 42–43 for a brief discussion of Trojan/Persian War parallels in Herodotus. On the analogy cf. also Georges 1994: 61f.

25. For the multi-polis perspective, see further Obbink 1998b and this volume at n. 34; Parsons, this volume before n. 42; Bearzot 1997: 78. Aloni, this volume at nn. 66ff., suggests that the elegy was commissioned by Sparta or specifically by Pausanias; a stronger "Spartan" position is taken by Pavese 1995 and Burzacchini 1995: 23–26. In Boedeker 1995b, I argue that alternatives to a Spartan commission—especially the possibility of a poetic competition—should also be considered. I agree with Aloni about the likelihood of reperformances of the poem, in whole or in part, at symposia in various poleis.

who fought at Troy is not limited to these two accounts: another parallel can be found at Athens, dating from just a few years after Plataea—part A of the "Eion poem" = "Simonides" 40(a) *FGE* (Aeschines *In Ctes.* 183ff.).[26]

ἔκ ποτε τῆσδε πόληος ἅμ' Ἀτρεΐδῃσι Μενεσθεύς
    ἡγεῖτο ζαθέον Τρωικὸν ἐς πεδίον,
ὅν ποθ' Ὅμηρος ἔφη Δαναῶν πύκα θωρηκτάων
    κοσμητῆρα μάχης ἔξοχον ὄντα μολεῖν.
οὕτως οὐδὲν ἀεικὲς Ἀθηναίοισι καλεῖσθαι
    κοσμητὰς πολέμου τ' ἀμφὶ καὶ ἠνορέης.

Once from this city Menestheus with the sons of Atreus
    went as leader to the holy plain of Troy;
Homer once said [*Il.* 2.553–54] that, of the stout-corseleted Danaans
    he was outstanding as marshal in battle.
So it is not unseemly that Athenians be called
    marshals in war and manliness.

This epigram, one of three related poems reportedly inscribed on three herms in the Athenian Agora, with its analogy between the Athenians who besieged the Persians in Thrace and those who fought at Troy, shows that such comparisons were in the air very soon after Plataea, and would have been available to Herodotus from many sources.[27] (In light of this, it is almost surprising that the Trojan analogy does not play an overt role in Aeschylus' *Persians*, produced in 472.)[28] The Plataea elegy, which must date to the immediate aftermath of the battle, indicates that this analogy was made even sooner than we had realized, and suggests that its dissemination may perhaps owe something to Simonides.[29] The phenomenon of Trojan War as a paradigm for Persian War is, moreover, not confined to verbal sources, but is prominent in public monuments as well.[30]

---

26. On the poem, cf. also Plut. *Cimon* 7.6 and Demosth. *Lept.* 112. On the battle, cf. Hdt. 7.107, Thuc. 1.98, Diod. Sic. 11.60.

27. Hall 1989: 102 briefly discusses the Trojan/Persian War analogy as it develops in tragedy at a somewhat later period. For the longevity of the concept, cf. Georges 1994: 61–65.

28. On the general subject of Homeric reminiscences in the *Persians*, see Sideras 1971: 198–200. I thank David Sider for this reference.

29. On the early date of the elegy, cf. Aloni, this volume at n. 64, and Boedeker 1995b; West 1993a: 9 suggests a later date. On the Trojan/Persian War analogy, cf. also Barchiesi in this volume.

30. On the analogy between Greek confrontation with Persians and mythological events, including supernatural interventions, cf. Castriota 1992: 28, commenting that the Marathon painting in the Stoa Poikile, datable to the early 460s, was, like Aeschylus' *Persians*, "exceptional in depicting relatively contemporary events in a medium normally reserved for mythic representations." Cohen 1994 demonstrates a change in representations of Herakles (from bow-bearer to club-bearer) as a result of the Persian Wars and the resulting association of Persians with archery. Whitley 1994: 229 argues that the Marathonomachoi were assimilated to Homeric heroes by the style of their burial; he refers this fact, however, to incipient democratic ideals, not to the impact of their confrontation with the Persians. Antonaccio 1994: 119 notes that the mound in which the Athenians were buried "may in fact have been a reused Bronze Age tumulus" and concludes that this would have been a way for the Athenian state "to elevate the fallen." I examine the question of the "heroic age" analogy in more detail elsewhere in this volume (Boedeker "Heroization").

To return briefly to the "multi-polis" question: the Eion elegy, in contrast to the Plataea poem, obviously focuses on a single polis. The Plataea elegy appears to be unique among extant Persian War poems (including the *Persians*) in including so many allied cities by name. Most epigrams praising participants in the Persian Wars refer to the citizens of a single polis (e.g., 11 *FGE* for Corinthians, 16 *FGE* for Megarians). A few honor the fighters of more than one polis, but they do so collectively without mentioning any city by name: Ἕλληνες (15.1 *FGE*, the inscription on the panhellenic altar of Zeus Eleutherios, dedicated after Plataea: Plut. *Arist*. 19.7), Ἑλλάδος εὐρυχόρου σωτῆρες (17b.1 *FGE*, inscribed on the base of the Serpent Column dedicated at Delphi after Plataea, together with a list of the allied cities: Diod. Sic. 11.33.2). It is conceivable that the lyric poem on those who fell at Thermopylae refers to all Greeks who died there, not only the Lacedaemonians; but there, too, as far as we know, no city is mentioned by name.[31] The Plataea elegy is exceptional: the narrative proper begins with Sparta, which plays a dominant role in fr. 11—but even apart from fr. 11.35–41, frr. 15–16, where the Corinthians are praised, suffice to show that the Lacedaemonians are not alone at Simonides' Plataea.

Second, besides these general resemblances, Herodotus' account recalls Simonides' rather closely in several places; indeed, apart from the "Trojan War" prooemium, nearly every passage in the Plataea elegy has been compared with a passage in Herodotus. As I suggested above, this is in part a circular argument, inasmuch as both Parsons and West used the text of the *Histories* as a guide for the placement and restoration of many papyrus fragments. Most boldly, for example, West's ingenious reconstruction of the badly tattered fr. 14 is based on the prominent role played by the seer Teisamenos in Herodotus 9.33–36 (West 1993a: 7–9). Even so, the points of contact are impressive.

Fragment 11, the longest continuous passage (fragmentary as it is) in the new elegy, describes the march from Sparta to Eleusis, probably includes a passage of omen-taking, and (following Parsons: see above at n. 25) the arrival of Athenian forces at that point; all this follows closely the account in Herodotus 9.19. Quite plausible are West's supplements in fr. 11.39–40 θεῶν τεράε]σσι πεποιθότες and Ἐλευσῖνος γῆς ἐ]ρατὸν πεδίον, although they were suggested by Herodotus' account (9.19.2) describing how the Peloponnesians camped and sacrificed with good omens at Eleusis:

Ἐκ δὴ ὦν τοῦ Ἰσθμοῦ καλλιερησάντων τῶν ἱρῶν ἐπορεύοντο πάντες καὶ ἀπικνέονται ἐς Ἐλευσῖνα· ποιήσαντες δὲ καὶ ἐνθαῦτα ἱρά, ὡς σφι ἐκαλλιέρεε τὸ πρόσω ἐπορεύοντο . . .

After the sacrifices turned out well, they all proceeded from the Isthmus and arrived at Eleusis. They made sacrifices there too, and when these turned out well for them they proceeded further . . .

There is a danger of circularity in all this, but the extant scraps of the elegy do accord remarkably well with the sequence proposed here.

---

31. 531 *PMG*. Cf. Molyneux 1992: 186–87 on the possibility that the Thermopylae poem celebrates all the Hellenes who participated in that battle.

Immediately following, in fr. 11.41, West restores Παν]δίονος. This corresponds to the continuation of Herodotus' account (9.19.2) where the Athenians (descendants of Pandion, although not so called in the Herodotus passage) join the Peloponnesians:

... Ἀθηναῖοι δὲ ἅμα αὐτοῖσι, διαβάντες μὲν ἐκ Σαλαμῖνος, συμμιγέντες δὲ ἐν Ἐλευσῖνι.

... and with them the Athenians, who had come over from Salamis and joined them at Eleusis.

Here, in contrast to Parson's preference (1992a: 37–38), West does not rely on the immediate Herodotean context. Rather, he suggests that at this point the elegy says the Medes were "driven out of the land of Pandion" (fr. 11.41 with app. crit.); West presumably connects this with Herodotus' description of Mardonios' voluntary withdrawal from Attica by way of Decelea (Hdt. 9.13–15), or possibly with the battle against Persian cavalry in which Masistios was killed (fr. 11.43 with app. crit.)—a skirmish located by Herodotus at Erythrae in Boeotia (Hdt. 9.20–23).

West's suggested restoration of line 41, Μηδείους γαίης Παν]δίονος ἐξε[λάσ- α]ντες, while attractive, thus raises a question of literary and historical plausibility. If, as West's Simonides says, the enemy was "driven out" of Attica before the battle of Plataea, we might expect other authors to mention this feat as well, whether based on the event itself or on Simonides' account. Herodotus' silence about such a rout, given his preoccupation with Persian presence in Athens, is surprising.[32] Surprising, too, is the silence of Plutarch, who would have been well motivated to comment on Herodotus' omission of such a deed in his essay on the historian's "malignity." Since Plutarch quotes from the Plataea elegy to defend the Corinthians' role in the battle (*De Herod. malign.* 872d), we can assume he is familiar with the elegy; his failure to note another Herodotean "omission" of Greek bravery thus becomes an argument against the presence of such a report in the elegy. Another argument from silence comes from Aristophanes' *Lysistrata*. Although that comedy highlights other occasions of Spartan-Athenian cooperation, such as Spartan help in expelling the Peisistratids (*Lys.* 1150–56), and even their cooperation during the Persian War (1247–61), it fails to mention the (Spartan-led) rout of Persians from Attica that West would restore to Simonides' text.

At the risk of pressing too far the disparity between Simonides' conjectured ἐξε[λάσα]ντες and Herodotus' description of Mardonios' unemcumbered withdrawal to Boeotia, I concur with Parsons that the poet more likely spoke here of the "descendants of Pandion" joining the Peloponnesians at Eleusis, as Herodotus describes.[33] In any event, reference to the army's activities at Eleusis, if that is indeed

32. In Hdt. 9.3, Mardonios recaptures a virtually deserted Athens in the summer of 479, when the Athenians have already moved to Salamis (9.6).
33. Parsons 1992a: 36–37 notes that ἐξε[λάσα]ντες would fit, although this verb presents a "literal-minded difficulty": Herodotus says the Athenians sailed from Salamis to Eleusis, so "sallied forth" would seem odd. "I can think of no suitable word for 'disembarking'. Perhaps the passive, πόλεως Παν]δίονος ἐξε[λαθέ]ντες?" This reading corresponds with the movements described in Hdt. 9.3 and 6.

what Simonides preserves here, would accord well with the role attributed to Eleusinian Demeter during the battle itself (see below).

Herodotus may also have followed Simonides in reporting the starting lineup of forces on both sides. Such lists are prominent in the *Histories'* account of the battle (e.g. 9.26–28, 31) and arguably important in the elegy as well. In fr. 13.8–10 "Medes and Persians" are mentioned in contrast to "sons of Doros and Herakles." Aloni (this volume, at n. 69), following West (1993a: 7), takes these verses to refer to the battle line in general, with Dorians and particularly Spartans representing the Greek forces, and Medes and Persians the invading army. But as I have suggested elsewhere, they may instead refer to a section of the battle line, part of a catalog of opposing forces. In 9.31, Herodotus says the Lacedaemonians and their Tegean allies were drawn up precisely opposite the Persians. Again in 9.46–48, after describing several notorious shifts of position that would be quite inappropriate to the elegy's encomiastic tone, Herodotus has the Lacedaemonians and Tegeans once again stationed opposite the Persians, with the Medes facing the (also mostly Dorian) forces of Corinth, Potidaia, Orchomenos, and Sikyon—more elaborate than the elegy, but following generally the same pattern.[34] Further, in his interpretation of frr. 15 and 16 (the Simonidean verses quoted by Plutarch), Luppe argues that the elegist is here describing the Corinthians' position in the battle line: μέσσοις (fr. 15.1) would mean "[stationed] in the middle," rather than "[fighting] in the midst" (of the battle at large).[35] Thus Luppe's interpretation supports the notion that the elegy represented the position and actions of some of the specific contingents, rather than simply the two sides in general. Although both accounts probably included a catalog of the battle line, Herodotus' presentation of the Corinthian role at Plataea contrasts sharply with the positive if imprecise picture of Simonides frr. 15–16; I will return to these important differences in the concluding section.

Finally, the presence of supernatural agents in both narratives strengthens the possibility that Herodotus was influenced by the Plataea elegy. Gods and heroes are cited frequently in the elegy—not only in the proemium,[36] but in the central narrative as well: Menelaus and the Dioscuri in fr. 11.30–31 (discussed by Hornblower in this volume), probably Zeus "nodding" (νεύσαντο[ς) in fr. 14.7, possibly another divinity in the same fragment as well (14.9),[37] and Demeter in fr. 17.1.

The chance preservation of the name of Demeter, an Olympian conspicuously rare in Homeric epic, is highly suggestive. Herodotus frequently mentions the shrine

---

34. In Boedeker 1995b I use this catalog, along with the cities mentioned in fr. 11.35–42, to argue against an overly Sparta-centric interpretation of the elegy.

35. Luppe 1994: 21–24. Aloni, this volume at n. 57, also suggests that the Corinthian fragments may be part of a kind of catalog.

36. W² proposes the names of Apollo (partly attested), Athena, and Hera, in the Trojan War context of the proemium, fr. 11.8–10.

37. West 1993a: 8 proposes Ares as the agent who will drive the Persians out of Asia, fr. 14.9. His suggestion is made on the basis of several epigrams that mention Ares in such a context (e.g., 15.1 *FGE*), but as Kurt Raaflaub points out to me, Ares was not associated in cults with Greek victory or Greek freedom from the Persians; cf. Pritchett 1979: 158–61 on the paucity of fifth-century cults of Ares.

of Eleusinian Demeter at Plataea (9.57, 69, 97, 101, and especially 65);[38] in 9.62.2 he describes fighting χρόνον ἐπὶ πολλόν "for a long time" around it, recalling, as Parsons 1992a: 40 and West 1993a: 9 point out, δηρόν["for a long time" at fr. 17. 5 of the elegy, four lines after Demeter's name is mentioned. It would be possible, of course, to read these merely as topographical references, but in describing the intense fighting around Demeter's shrine, Herodotus explicitly allows that in the fighting at Plataea the goddess responded to the Persians who had destroyed her holy place at Eleusis:

> Θῶμα δέ μοι ὅκως παρὰ τῆς Δήμητρος τὸ ἄλσος μαχομένων οὐδὲ εἷς ἐφάνη τῶν Περσέων οὔτε ἐσελθὼν ἐς τὸ τέμενος οὔτε ἐναποθανών, περί τε τὸ ἱρὸν οἱ πλεῖστοι ἐν τῷ βεβήλῳ ἔπεσον. δοκέω δέ, εἴ τι περὶ τῶν θείων πρηγμάτων δοκέειν δεῖ, ἡ θεὸς αὐτή σφεας οὐκ ἐδέκετο ἐμπρήσαντας [τὸ ἱρὸν] τὸ ἐν Ἐλευσῖνι ἀνάκτορον.

> It is a marvel to me that not one of the Persians fighting alongside the grove of Demeter appeared either to have entered the *temenos* or to have died in it, although very many of them fell in the unhallowed ground around the shrine. If it is right to have an opinion in matters of the gods, my opinion is that the goddess herself did not welcome those who had burned her palace at Eleusis. (9.65.2)

Herodotus' opinion that the goddess "did not welcome" those who had destroyed her Eleusinian shrine may cautiously echo the vengeance suggested by ῥύσιον[in Simonides fr. 17.7,[39] six lines after the mention of Demeter's name.

Herodotus' conspicuously guarded editorializing here recalls several well-known passages where he declares himself unwilling to comment on beliefs or practices that pertain to the gods (e.g., 2.3.2, 2.65.2); this is one way that the historian distinguishes his own *logos* from his poetic and local (oral) sources. To be sure, Herodotus frequently overcomes his self-conscious reluctance to talk about divine matters;[40] in any case such a declaration is certainly in part a rhetorical device to add credibility to the narrator's voice. But even acknowledging this, it is likely that his repeated naming of gods in the context of this battle (and others) reflects sources, or genres, in which supernatural actors were at home—as is certainly the case in the Plataea elegy.[41]

Considered cumulatively, such resemblances indicate that Herodotus was familiar with the Simonidean elegy and used it, albeit critically, as one of his sources for the Plataea *logos*. Far more significant, however, are the differences between the elegy and Herodotus' prose account, and it is with these that I will conclude.

---

38. Herodotus also reports Pausanias' prayer to Hera (9.61.3–62.1) at a critical moment, and mentions her temple at several junctures in the campaign (9.52, 69.1).

39. Noted also by Rutherford in this volume, ad fr. 17.

40. Cf. Lateiner 1989: 64–67 for this reluctance and 196–205 for a rich catalog of passages in which divine action comes into play in Herodotus. Gould 1994 provides an excellent general introduction to Herodotus' treatment of religion.

41. Mark Toher suggests to me that Herodotus could have received much information about Plataea from survivors of the battle, and I agree that stories of supernatural intervention may well have come from "eye-witnesses" (cf. the story of the apparition at Marathon, specifically attributed to the hoplite Epizelos the Athenian, Hdt. 6.117). But the verbal echoes of fr. 17 in Hdt. 9.62 and 65 indicate that in this case the elegy itself was a source for Demeter's role at Plataea.

Differences

To say that Herodotus knew the Plataea elegy, even that it can be listed among his sources for the battle, is certainly not to say that the two accounts resemble each other closely. In length and complexity, attitude toward the participants, narrative focus (e.g., Spartan or Athenian)—to cite just a few of the more obvious differences— Herodotus' account differs greatly from what we can see of the elegy. Furthermore, we can assume both that Simonides' poem was known to some in Herodotus' audience, and that the battle itself was one of the more famous events recounted in the *Histories*. This double familiarity would present a challenge to Herodotus: how to establish the worthiness of *his* version? To see how he responded would ideally include a detailed analysis of both accounts in their entirety; the state of the evidence makes this impossible, but fortunately the papyrus fragments allow at least a few points of comparison.

First, Herodotus appears to give a much more complex account of the campaign than Simonides; in particular, as often, he highlights conflicts among the Greek allies. For example, in 9.6–10 it is Athenians and finally a Tegean who have to convince the ever-hesitant Spartans to meet the Persians in Boeotia. The corresponding section of the elegy, in contrast, describes Pausanias' troops marching out heroically to preserve Greek freedom, mindful of their *arete*, accompanied by Menelaus and the Dioscuri (fr. 11.25–34), with no hint of reluctance or delay.

Apparent in this episode as well is the Athenian perspective (reasonably attributed to Athenian sources)[42] that frequently informs Herodotus' narrative (e.g. 9.6–9, 22–23, 46, 60–61.1).[43] As Nyland has recently shown, however, such a perspective is not evenly distributed throughout the Herodotus' account of the battles, but confined to certain circumscribed anecdotes.[44] Equally vivid anecdotes about Pausanias' Hellenic moderation (9.78–79, 82), Amomphoretos' Laconian singlemindedness (9.53–57), and Teisamenos' crucial role (9.33–36) would seem to come from sources closer to Sparta. In the Plataea episode at least, Herodotus evidently does not confine his sympathies or his narrative viewpoint to a single polis.

Whatever their value for the historical record, these varied perspectives must reflect both Herodotus' sources of information and his own interest in the fragile Greek alliance that existed half a century before.[45] Herodotus portrays that alliance as problematic and precarious even in its most glorious days—a perspective not appropriate to a praise-poem, and hardly to be imagined in the flush of victory immediately after Plataea, but highly appropriate to contemporary circumstances in the 430s or 420s. The *Histories* often tell of disagreements among Greek allies, especially

---

42. E.g., How and Wells 1928: vol. 2.308 (ad 9.46), Masaracchia 1978: 182 (ad 9.60).

43. Simonides' poem tends to keep Sparta sharply in focus (e.g., fr. 11.25–36), as mentioned above.

44. Nyland 1992 believes that much of Herodotus' information comes from medizing Greeks.

45. In general, great caution is called for in attributing to Herodotus uncritical acceptance of what his sources tell him. The fact that he writes "I must say what is said, but I don't have to believe it" (7.152.3, cf. 2.123.1, 4.195.2) indicates a higher level of skepticism about such *logoi* than is sometimes attributed to the narrator of the *Histories*. See further Dewald 1987, esp. 150–53; Boedeker 2000.

about whether and where to fight (this happens at Salamis as well as Plataea): his Greeks, unlike Simonides' (as far as we can tell), barely manage to stay together until they can meet the Persians and defeat them.

Another example of Herodotus' more complicated and less eulogistic narrative has already been mentioned. In describing the Corinthians' demeanor and achievements at Plataea (9.69), he provides a less flattering picture than that in the elegy (in contrast to his judgment of their bravery at Salamis, 8.94.4). Whereas Simonides' Corinthians take their position in the midst of the battle line (frr. 15–16 West), Herodotus' Corinthians never seriously engage the enemy, but run off in disorder when they hear of the Greek victory. Herodotus thereby provokes Plutarch's charge in *De Herodoti malignitate* 872d (cf. also *Arist.* 19.7) that he meanly devalues Corinthian heroism in the battle. Plutarch's source here for how the Corinthians "really" acted at Plataea is of course an excerpt from this very elegy,[46] which he accepts as an unbiased report by virtue of its being a historical elegy rather than a lyric poem for performance in Corinth.[47] This passage could be used to argue that the historian was not aware of the elegy, but, like Plutarch, I think it more likely that Herodotus took care to differentiate his own account from the poetic encomium.[48] The Plataea elegy then may have influenced Herodotus' narrative in negative as well as positive ways, by providing a well-known text from which he could differentiate his own version.

One reason for the complex nature of Herodotus' account as compared to Simonides' is of course that the memory of the Persian Wars, and of Plataea in particular, has been filtered through the intervening decades of hostility among the then-allied poleis, above all Athens and Sparta. Plataea itself, long allied with Athens, destroyed by Sparta at the instigation of Thebes during the Peloponnesian War (in 427, cf. Thuc. 3.52–68), is a particularly resonant site in fifth-century history.[49] If, as is likely,[50] Herodotus knew its subsequent history as Simonides could not, this knowledge would make all the more poignant the great victory that was won there, and all the more intelligible the squabbling traditions reflected in Herodotus' account (e.g.,

---

46. By calling on a witness to the Corinthians' bravery in fr. 16.1, Simonides may reflect a difference of opinion about their engagement in the battle even at this early stage.

47. If space permitted, it would be instructive to compare the tone and contents of lyric and elegiac battle-poetry. Even beyond their shared differences from Herodotus, the extant parts of the Plataea elegy and the Thermopylae lyric (531 *PMG*) poems, for example, suggest that there may also be considerable differences between these two forms, linked no doubt to different performance occasions. Plutarch (*De Herod. malign.* 42 872D) assures his reader that as an elegy, the Plataea poem was more historically credible and less biased than would be an ᾆσμα performed locally. Assuming Plutarch is correct, the elegy must also present a different view of Plataea than the song (ὕμνον) that Pindar says he would sing about Plataea *at Sparta* (*Pyth.* 1.77–79). Pindar *Paean* 2, which includes praise and also narrative about the recent past, would also be important for a study of battle-poems with different functions; cf. Rutherford, this volume, at nn. 27 and 40. On the Thermopylae lyric and its possible influence on historiography, see Flower 1999.

48. If this is true, Herodotus resembles Thucydides' reaction against the "mythodic" history of poets and logographers, as I argue in Boedeker 1995b.

49. Cf. Prandi 1988, esp. 43–69 and 93–120. For recent contrasting views on the changing relations among Plataea, Athens, and Sparta, cf. Hennig 1992 and Badian 1993.

50. On the date of completion of the *Histories*, cf. Fornara 1971 and 1981.

the questions of which poleis really engaged in the battle, and which Plataean tombs were really cenotaphs erected years later: Hdt. 9.85.3).

A similar level of detail also exists in stories for which Herodotus could have had little or no historical information, let alone eyewitnesses: in ethnographies (e.g., the patrivorous Issedones, 4.26), reported private conversations (most notoriously, that of Atossa and Darius in bed, 3.134), "historical" events based on mythological paradigms,[51] even the proemium (e.g., Io came down to the shore "on the fifth or sixth day" after the Phoenicians arrived in Argos: 1.3). Such incidental detail is one way that Herodotus invests his account with the verisimilitude and hence authority of a Homer; unlike Simonides he claims no relationship to a Muse.[52] The Plataea elegy, where we have text enough to judge, offers a much more compressed narrative than the *Histories*—for example, in its sweeping description of the march from Sparta. But if West is correct that a prophecy is reported at fr. 14, the poem may at the same time be describing recent events from a grand, almost godlike perspective (cf. West 1993a: 7–9).

Aloni discusses at length the elegy's intended performance context, disagreeing with West's apparent assumption (1993a: 5) that it was composed for a symposium. I agree with Aloni that the Plataea poem was intended for performance at a festival, very likely at Plataea itself (cf. Boedeker 1995b); elsewhere in this volume I argue that this elegy reflects an important stage in the process of assimilating contemporary war dead to immortalized heroes, above all to those who died at Troy, and thus may even have played a role in establishing a hero cult for those who died at Plataea.[53]

Be that as it may, Simonides' elegy has as its explicit aim to offer the combatants undying *kleos*, whereas Herodotus' proemium describes different goals: both to preserve great deeds from fading away and to examine the question of historical responsibility, cause, or blame (*aitiê*).[54] Thus Herodotus is interested in such problems as the empty tombs at Plataea, cover-up attempts of those ashamed because they did not take part in the battle. Herodotus' narrative, aware of the heroic reputation that already existed for the Plataiomachoi in poetry and tomb cult, either justifies that reputation or critiques it where appropriate. His account sees the heroic past, celebrated by Simonides, in the light of the contemporary world, where the fragile alliance that once preserved Greek freedom at Plataea has turned to hostility and overt warfare.

The differences between Herodotus' and Simonides' accounts of Plataea, then, are in part "literary"—a function of their different genres, and in part "historical"— reflecting the battle's varying significance in the light of contemporary circumstances. Simonides' elegy is a praise-poem, composed shortly after the deeds it celebrates,

---

51. Cf. Sourvinou-Inwood 1988 on the story of Periander and his son Lykophron (Hdt. 3.50–53). Yet this story, too, has elaborate details, including reported conversations (3.52). For similar phenomena in Herodotus' Demaratos saga, cf. Boedeker 1987.

52. On Simonides' Muse, cf. Stehle, this volume.

53. On the Plataea elegy and immortalization of Spartans in particular, see Stehle, this volume, adducing Tyrtaeus fr. 12 W. Loraux 1986: 55 maintains that the elegies of Tyrtaeus "inspired" the collective fifth-century Athenian epitaphs, sharing with them eulogy of the dead and encouragement of the living.

54. On *aitiê* in this context, see Nagy 1990: 218, 228.

while Herodotus' far more critical prose account took shape some fifty years later, in a different world, where Plataea had a more poignant meaning.[55] Not for Herodotus the ancient heroes accompanying the Spartan army from the Peloponnese (as in fr. 11.29–32); and not for Simonides the need to persuade the Spartans to march at all (compare Hdt. 9.6–11 with Simon. fr. 11.25–29).

Herodotus, dependent on human sources each with their own perspective, of course differs greatly from the Homeric poet with his omniscient Muse. He also, I propose, has a relationship to his subject matter very different from sources such as Simonides' poem—all the more apparent when both are reporting the "same" deeds. The Plataea elegy provides a precious missing link between epic narrative about the distant past and more critical historiography about the recent past, allowing us thereby to fill some gaps in our understanding of Greek ways to commemorate the heroes of war.

55. This would of course be even more dramatic after the Spartan-Theban destruction of the town in 427, to which Thucydides gives such eloquent (Athenian) witness (3.52–68).

7

SIMON HORNBLOWER

Epic and Epiphanies
Herodotus and the "New Simonides"

My aim in this essay is to measure the gap, if any, between what Herodotus was doing in his *Histories* and what Simonides was doing in his newly published poem. At first sight the two operations look similar because the subject matter is shared: they both describe a factual event, the battle of Plataea in 479 B.C.E. The productions of the two men are not even completely distinguishable by reference to meter, that is, to the specific forms of prose and poetry, because Herodotus, though not writing a poem, breaks into Homeric verse rhythms from time to time, in ways interestingly discussed by Deborah Boedeker in the present volume.[1] This is something even Thucydides does occasionally for special effect and at moments of high emotion.[2] So neither content nor form offers a way of distinguishing between the two genres. One obvious move at this early point would be to discard the notion of genre altogether as inappropriate to the pre-Aristotelian literary world we are dealing with. But that would not be right. In Thucydides (1.21) we have a clear distinction between on the one hand (οὔτε . . . οὔτε) what the poets have hymned about, ὑμνήκασι, and on the other hand what the *logopoioi* have composed, ξυνέθεσαν. (The latter verb does not necessarily imply writing down, although it is too often so taken. That is, Thucydides is talking about genres, not distinguishing between oral and written.)

Where, then, shall we draw the line between epic and history? One appealingly specific criterion has recently been suggested. Denis Feeney, in his exciting *The Gods in Epic*, writes, "The characterful narration of divine action is the irreducible line of demarcation between epic and history."[3] As Feeney concedes, the historians, not just

---

I am grateful, for help of various kinds, to Deborah Boedeker, Denis Feeney, Alan Griffiths, Robert Parker, and Katerina Zacharia.

1. Boedeker, this volume, "Historiography," at nn. 16–22.
2. Dover 1997: 169.
3. Feeney 1991: 261. See also Cameron 1995: 265f. ("particular concentration during the Persian Wars") and n. 21 for the epiphanies in Simonides, treating Boreas and the Dioscuri as proper epiphanies. On epic and historiography, cf. generally van Seters 1997: 18–31.

Herodotus but even Thucydides, contain instances of epiphanies, actual or presumed appearances of the gods in real space and time. Thus Thucydides tells us that the Spartan Brasidas, who has offered a bonanza reward for the capture of a tower on the Lekythos promontory in the territory of Torone, decides, after the tower collapses, that there was a divine hand at work and diverts the money to the building of a sanctuary to Athena (4.116). This gets into the list of epiphanies in Greek historians in that least fanciful of compilations, Pritchett's *Greek State at War*.[4] But Feeney is right to imply that something important is missing here, namely, *characterful* narration. Thucydides does not whisk us up to Olympus and show us Zeus saying to Athena, "All right, dear child, I allow you to destroy the tower at Torone."

I begin with general remarks on history and myth; in the second section, I shall talk specifically about the Persian Wars as a subject for myth; finally, I shall come to epiphanies, which have been detected in the new Simonides, and try to estimate their significance.

History and Myth

To quote Ronald Syme on Roman imperial virtues, "this engaging topic has not gone short of exponents."[5] In Hellenistic antiquity, the relation between the two notions gave rise to arguments of considerable asperity, generally taking their starting point from Homer and involving great names like Eratosthenes, Polybius, and Strabo; the best introduction is Polybius book 24 with Walbank's commentary.[6] But I am concerned with modern perceptions. It is striking how different the topic looks now from the way it looked in, say, 1960, the year of A. E. Wardman's Momigliano-influenced paper in *Historia* titled "Myth in Greek Historiography." The most successful recent line of attack has been to narrow down the concept of myth, in particular by confining the treatment to kinship claims, claims of mythical ξυγγένεια, and the way such claims of kinship affect real decisions reported by hard-nosed historians of the Thucydidean type. Thus Irad Malkin's *Myth and Territory in the Spartan Mediterranean* insists that perceived colonial ties were as important as real ones.[7] The book confines itself to fictions, and fictionalized exaggerations, about real or prehistorical Spartan Heraclid foundations. Again, a new book by C. P. Jones, *Kinship Diplomacy in Graeco-Roman Antiquity*,[8] takes us from Homer to Libanius and is particularly good on the way in which use of kinship claims evolves over time, especially when the Romans come along. The single discovery that released this burst of kinship-related work was surely the publication in 1988 of the late-third-century B.C.E. inscription from Lycian Xanthos reporting the appeal for funds from the little Dorian metropol-

---

4. Pritchett 1979: 11–46; on epiphanies, see also Henrichs in Hornblower and Spawforth 1996: 546 with bibliography there cited; Versnel 1987; Sinos 1993; Burkert 1997: 20f.
5. Syme 1958: 754.
6. Walbank 1979.
7. Malkin 1994.
8. Jones 1999.

itan city of Kytenion (*SEG* 38.1476); Olivier Curty has collected and commented on the kinship inscriptions including the Kytenion text.[9] I think it is above all this general development that has encouraged modern historians of ancient Greece to see myth in a different and more focused way. I leave out the Romans, except to mention Tacitus' wonderfully contemptuous remark about Nero's oratorical allusion to the supposed Roman descent from Troy, "and other more or less fabulous claims" ("aliaque haud procul fabulis": Tac. *Ann.* 12.58). If we now look back to Wardman, we find little about all of this: only the Tereus and Procne episode in Thucydides (2.29), which Wardman cited merely because the scholiast memorably comments that here alone does Thucydides introduce a myth. It is only recently that we have understood this passage properly and grasped that Thucydides is here engaged in polemic against a supposed Thracian/Athenian kinship connection, a connection explicitly asserted in the *Anabasis* of Xenophon.[10]

How does all this bear on the new Simonides? My answer is that it was precisely the pervasiveness of *syngeneia* concepts which made it possible for Greeks to bridge the mythical and historical worlds in so apparently effortless a way (Tacitus being a rather grumpy exception). Hence Simonides in fr. 13 W² passes effortlessly from the Medes and Persians to the sons of Doros and . . . Herakles in the next line. This mention of Dorians takes us, as Parsons plausibly argues,[11] to the battle of Plataea, which Aeschylus (*Pers.* 817) said was won "by the Dorian spear," Δωρίδος λόγχης ὕπο. The Spartan kings were descended from Herakles, so the notion of *syngeneia* transports us from the world of the mythical heroes to real-life events of 479 B.C.E. If we want a specific context, there is the Tegean-Athenian agon at Hdt. 9.26–27 in which the Heraklidai feature on both sides of the argument—until the Athenians, in rather Thucydidean fashion, say, "Enough of all this ancient history."

The Persian Wars

The author of the Demosthenic *Epitaphios* (1391) includes a passage that any student of the New Simonides somehow needs to come to terms with.[12] The author draws a clear distinction between recent episodes, ὑπογυιότερα, like the Persian Wars, which

9. Curty 1995.
10. Parker 1996: 174, citing Xen. *Anab.* 7.12.31, and Jones 1999: 30.
11. In the *editio princeps*, Parsons 1992a: 32.
12. Ps.-Dem. *Epitaphios* paras. 9–10 = 1391 ἃ δὲ τῇ μὲν ἀξίᾳ τῶν ἔργων οὐδέν ἐστι τούτων ἐλάττω, <u>τῷ δ' ὑπογυιώτερ' εἶναι τοῖς χρόνοις οὔπω μεμυθολόγηται,</u> οὐδ' εἰς τὴν ἡρωικὴν ἐπανῆκται τάξιν, ταῦτ' ἤδη λέξω. ἐκεῖνοι τὸν ἐξ ἁπάσης τῆς Ἀσίας στόλον ἐλθόντα δὶς ἠμύναντο καὶ κατὰ γῆν καὶ κατὰ θάλατταν, etc. "I shall mention the following deeds which, though in point of merit they are in no way inferior to the former, still, *through being more recent, have not yet been mythologized* or even elevated to heroic rank. Those men singlehanded twice repulsed by land and sea the expedition assembled out of the whole of Asia," etc.
On this passage see Otis 1964: 6 (from a chapter titled "The Obsolescence of Epic"); also Thomas 1989: 221 (at 210 and n. 57 she takes the speech to be authentically Demosthenic, a point that makes no difference for my purposes).

(the speaker says) have "not yet been mythologized," and the subject matter of myth proper. This seems odd at first blush. The Persian Wars tradition has been much studied in the years since 1961, the date of Habicht's pioneering study on false documents about the Persian Wars,[13] itself prompted by the discovery and publication of the so-called Themistocles decree (ML 23). There is no doubt that the facts about and the importance of the Persian Wars, a run of successes down to the battle of the Eurymedon in perhaps 467, were distorted and inflated by image-makers, above all at Athens; this led to the promotion to what could nontechnically be called cult-status of individuals like Miltiades. Athens was certainly the main center of the manufacture of the Persian Wars tradition; but one interesting aspect of the lionization of the individual victors deserves to be brought out more clearly than it usually is. Athens, even before Ephialtes' changes of the 460s, was a jealous and in some sense a democratic place; there were limits to how far human beings could be exalted there. The possibilities were much greater once you left Athens and went elsewhere, above all to Delphi. There we find Miltiades astonishingly commemorated in a statue group as virtually one of the eponymous heroes of Athens, on the evidence of the periegete Pausanias (10.10.1). We should note another feature of the Persian Wars tradition: the special prominence accorded in postclassical times to Athens' ally Plataea, with its Hellenistic cult of Homonoia of the Greeks.[14] Now, the Oxyrhynchus papyri date as physical objects and copies from the Roman imperial period; it may be no chance that the part of the poem we have is concerned with, precisely, the battle of Plataea. That is, the new Simonides itself confirms the direction taken in later centuries by the Persian Wars tradition.

Simonides, in ways I shall discuss later, gave extravagant prominence to the Spartan commander Pausanias the regent, and by introducing Achilles into his poem generally suggested (as Peter Parsons observed in the *editio princeps*)[15] a comparison between Persian Wars and Trojan, and between the fame, the *kleos*, of both groups. This analogy was perhaps picked up by Herodotus in his proem, in which Helen of Troy features as the last and most fully described of the female abductions from which the historian jumps forward to the Persian Wars. I say it was "perhaps" picked up because there must have been much praise-poetry between Simonides and Herodotus, and in such a situation we should be careful about talking of innovation and influence. Thucydides seems to have reacted against Herodotus, dismissing the Persian Wars as insignificant by comparison with the Peloponnesian.[16] But as Habicht 1961 showed, the Persian Wars tradition was back on course in the fourth century B.C.E., which was indeed the period of its greatest exuberance.

How then could Ps.-Demosthenes, to return to him, speak as he did? I suggest the answer is to be found by looking at the historical realities. According to the myth,

---

13. Habicht 1961.
14. Étienne and Piérart 1975; Boedeker, this volume, "Heroization."
15. Parsons 1992a: 32. For the equation between Achilles and Pausanias, see Lloyd-Jones 1994; see also Boedeker, this volume, "Heroization," at n. 59, citing other (less plausible) views.
16. Thuc. 1.23.1. But compare the interesting remark about Thermopylae at 4.36.3, which suggests a rather different and more conventional attitude; see my commentary (Hornblower 1996: 191).

Persia had been spectacularly defeated and humiliated in 490 and again in 480/479, a humiliation symbolized by the rags in which Aeschylus' *Persians* has Xerxes return. The reality was rather different. Herodotus is obliquely and uneasily aware of another and opposite sort of defeat in the middle of the century, the so-called Egyptian disaster of the mid-450s. The usual name of this episode, "Egyptian," can disguise from us the fact that it was a defeat on a huge scale inflicted on Athenians, Samians (ML 34), and others by those very same Persians whose weakness and effeminacy became such a *topos*, in ways explored by modern students of literary orientalism. Thucydides reported the disaster bluntly in his *Pentekontaetia*; but it is there in Herodotus too, in a couple of very significant proleptic mentions, at 3.12 and 7.7, discussing Achaimenes son of Darius. Herodotus is extremely tactful about how he mentions the Egyptian revolt and its suppression, alluding specifically only to the death of Achaimenes, that is, to the initial successes of the anti-Persian forces; but Herodotus' hearers needed no reminding how the military position was totally reversed by Megabyzos son of Zopyros. A good deal has been written about Herodotus' handling of Egyptians as "the other," his fascination with Egyptian religion, and so on. Not enough stress has been laid, in my view, on what Egypt would have meant in the third quarter of the fifth century to Athenians and Samians, many of whose families would have lost a member in that awful debacle.

So much, very briefly, for the mid-fifth century. Thucydides too was conscious that the image of the Persians as a military joke was far from the truth; in one of his latest datable passages, at the end of 2.65, he shows awareness that it was actually Persia that finished off the Peloponnesian War when the two Greek powers looked like merely fighting each other to a standstill. The fourth century was different, the period of notorious Persian reliance on Greek hoplites to recover rebellious Egypt. But even in this period, the period of Demosthenes, we should not be too quick to disparage Persian military effectiveness.[17] If, then, we return to Herodotus and Simonides, one possible difference, with all due caution about the flavor of the whole poem of which we have may just have a fragment, is that Herodotus displayed—as Simonides did not (and perhaps given his dates, whatever exactly they were,[18] could not) display—some awareness of the Persian reality as evidenced by the Egyptian disaster in particular; and also some awareness more generally of a tension between the real and the constructed Persia.[19] My point is not that Herodotus was a historian and therefore was subtle enough to have a subtext, whereas Simonides as a straight celebratory poet was not so subtle; on the contrary, Simonides, whom Parsons describes as a poet of "great scope and range,"[20] may for all we know have been perfectly capable of uttering what Vergilian scholars call Two Voices or even Further Voices; that is, there are veiled allusions underneath the obvious ones. My point has more simply to do with chronology; if we assume for crude biographical reasons that Simonides'

---

17. See Hornblower in Lewis et al. 1994: 47f.
18. I agree with Parsons 1992a: 6 that a date for the poem fairly soon after the Persian Wars is implied by the honorific treatment of Pausanias, who was subsequently disgraced.
19. For this see Pelling 1997.
20. Parsons in Hornblower and Spawforth 1996: 1409.

knowledge went no further than at latest the Eurymedon battle (about 466), it would not be surprising that for him the myth of the epically defeated Persian was still intact. If it is really true that we should not read "Kekrops" at fr. 11.42 W^2, that would eliminate Athens, the main factory of later Persian War propaganda, and that would be surprising indeed. But we still have to explain the apparent reference in the immediately preceding line to Pandion. West wants to have Simonides say that the Spartans drove the Persians out of the land of Pandion, that is, Attica; but Boedeker defends Parsons's original supposition that Pandion, if not Kekrops, hints at the arrival of the Athenians.[21] However that all may be, Herodotus wrote for or declaimed to a more bruised generation. The Persian Wars tradition was potent, but in the end Ps.-Demosthenes, though he accepts the merit of the Persian War victors, was in a way right: the mythologizing of the Persian Wars was not a straightforward matter until Alexander swept the Persian empire away altogether. In a way, the Persian Wars never really ended, or rather they kept breaking out again.

Epiphanies

Two have been detected in the New Simonides, one of the Dioscuri and one of Zetes and Kalais, the children of Boreas.[22] The main Simonidean evidence for Boreas is the fragmentary word καλαι—and perhaps a description of Oreithyia's hair, both at fr. 3 W^2 = fr. 20, which seems to have been part of the elegy on the battle of Artemisium; there is also perhaps fr. 4 W^2 (not, however, attributed to the Plataea poem). For the Dioscuri we have the statement in the main Plataea section (fr. 11.30 W^2) that the Spartans left the Eurotas and the city of Sparta in the company of the horse-taming hero sons of Zeus, the Tyndarids, and of Menelaus.

So we have, perhaps, the magnificent picture of the Dioscuri riding out with the Spartan army, an epiphany indeed, comparable to their appearance as stars at the battle of Aegospotami, as celebrated in epigram at Delphi (ML 95 with Plut. *Lys.* 12.1); or at the battle of lake Regillus when the Spartans lent them to the Romans, as immortalized in one of Macaulay's *Lays*. But in what sense did the Dioscuri really accompany the Spartan army? As Pritchett says,[23] the Herodotean reference[24] to the Dioscuri regularly following the Spartan army may really be a way of saying that their statues or images were carried: statues could be regarded as epiphanies of the god.[25] The better view is that Herodotus is talking about images.[26]

---

21. Boedeker, this volume, "Historiography," at n. 33. In favor of the reading "Kekrops," see also Obbink, this volume, at n. 34.

22. On Boreas and Kalais, see A. H. Griffiths in Hornblower and Spawforth 1996: 253, with a very ingenious and attractive suggestion about the Boreas cult at Athens; and on the Dioscuri, Parker ibid. 484.

23. Pritchett 1979: 14f.; see the economical note by Parsons, 1992a: 35.

24. Above all Hdt. 5.75.

25. See Austin 1964: 89f., note on Verg. *Aen.* 2.178 "numenque reducant" for the way *deus* is sometimes used in Latin of a statue in which the god is thought to dwell. See also the excellent discussion of Versnel 1987: 46f. and now Harrison 2000: 83 n. 52.

26. Parker 1989: 147 ("in effigy, we presume").

But there is a problem about the relation between Simonides and the relevant Herodotus passage. Parsons rightly observes that Herodotus there says that when only one king went out on campaign (as was supposed to be the rule after the late-sixth-century debacle there described, a botched intervention at Athens) only one of the Dioscuri, or Tyndaridai, as they are called there and by Simonides, went out. One king, one Dioscurus: that seems fair enough. But what of Plataea in 479? Parsons (1992a: xx) says: "Both brothers [i.e., both Dioscuri] accompany the army . . . On this expedition there was indeed only one king, Pleistarchos, Hdt. 9.10.2; but the Tyndarid rule was broken (or Herodotus, or Simonides, got it wrong)." With diffidence, I wonder if it is quite right to assume, as Parsons here does, that the under-age Pleistarchos was on the expedition at all. The Greek is ἐγίνετο μέν νυν ἡ ἡγεμονίη Πλειστάρχου τοῦ Λεωνίδεω, but, Herodotus immediately goes on, Pleistarchos was a παῖς and Pausanias was his cousin and guardian (Hdt. 9.10.2).[27] The Greek surely means "by custom or prescriptive right the actual king *would have* had the command": in other words, Herodotus is not saying Pleistarchos was actually on the campaign; he is saying he would have been if he had been old enough. (Parsons's formulation further down the page is that "the actual commander" was Pausanias, but here too he seems to suggest, by quoting the words "hegemony of Pleistarchos," that Pleistarchos was physically present, though he stops short of saying so in so many words.)

Three other points should be noted. First, the king from the other line, Leotychidas, was away commanding the fleet (8.131)—and he should not be forgotten when we are distributing Dioscuri. After all, the Dioscuri were peculiarly associated with naval activity; see above all *Homeric Hymn* 33, but there is other evidence as well. There is, however, a complication about Leotychidas' command; David Lewis once pointed out that no other proper Spartan king ever commands a fleet.[28] Lewis continued, "I have sometimes wondered whether the nauarchy may not owe its origin to some kind of tabu against the king going to sea and whether Leotychidas' appointment on this occasion does not almost imply that he is not considered a proper king"; Lewis was here referring to the dubious way in which Kleomenes got Demaratus deposed. This is fascinating, but the same Herodotean chapter (8.131) that describes Leotychidas as "general and nauarch" also gives his complete royal genealogy back to Hyllos and Herakles and ends with a ringing sentence calling him a king of the other house, τὴν ἑτέρην οἰκίην. So Herodotus, at least, seems to want us to treat him as a proper king, whatever may have been thought in some quarters.

Second, we are told (Hdt. 9.10, end of chapter) that Pausanias did choose a coadjutant, namely, Euryanax son of Dorieus, a man of his own house; the principle of collegiality was thus semi-maintained—at least at the outset, though notoriously Pausanias as we shall see arrogated to himself all the glory.

Third, Pleistarchos is not mentioned again in book 9, which does suggest he was not on the campaign. So, if I am right, there was not even one king at Plataea. Did this

---

27. Macan 1908: 608 and Grene 1987: 615 take the Greek, rightly I think, to mean "by custom or prescriptive right the actual king *would have* had the command" (that is Macan; Grene has "the leadership indeed belonged to Pleistarchos").
28. Lewis 1977: 45.

mean the Spartans took no Dioscuri with them to Plataea, or did it mean they took both Dioscuri, or just one? A nice point. Insofar as Herodotus' remark about the usual practice (n. 24 above) suggests a one-one correlation between kings and Dioscuri, the answer ought to be: no king, no Dioscuri, unless Pausanias was allowed one on behalf of the absent Pleistarchos; but a regent is not a king and kings are what Herodotus is talking about in book 5. Pausanias surely cannot have had both Dioscuri with him, because Leotychidas and the fleet were presumably entitled to one of them. So my answer is that there were no images of the Dioscuri at Plataea. It therefore ought to follow logically, and now it will be seen why I have made such a meal of this apparently trivial point, that Simonides' mention of the Dioscuri may refer to an actual epiphany, not to the merely routine and physical carting round of a statue or of a couple of portable statues or jars; although what Simonides seems to be describing is the routine start of a campaign rather than a special crisis at which a divine apparition might be appropriate. The bracketing with Menelaus might be thought to strengthen that conclusion, but I hesitate to use that argument because I suppose an image of Menelaus is not unthinkable. Perhaps they even took with them the bones of Menelaus, who knows? As Moses Finley once observed about the Spartans, "I am frankly unable to visualize these people."[29]

The Dioscuri, I conclude, were manifest at Plataea in the aniconic sense that they were manifest with the fleet at Aegospotami, accompanying Lysander, who like Pausanias was not a king. I stress in all this that words like "ought" and "logically" may be absurdly out of place. I agree with Parsons that we must reckon with error on the part of Herodotus or his sources, or inconsistency on the part of the real-life Spartans; after all, Herodotus' various statements about what the kings could or could not do together and singly are famously hard to reconcile. And I doubt if a poet like Simonides will have worried too much about, or expected his audience to notice, delicate points of Spartan *Staatsrecht*—always assuming that he knew about them, composing as he was at a date when our source for them, namely Herodotus' history, did not yet exist. But if we are being strict, we must leave the statues of the Dioscuri out of account. Leotychidas, that is, the fleet, may have had an image or statue. The army, that is, Pausanias and the forces at Plataea, did not. It therefore seems more likely that Simonides had a proper, by which I mean aniconic, epiphany (a useful distinction, though a crude one, and slightly misleading and modern in that a Spartan soldier would no doubt have regarded the images of the Dioscuri as a proper presence). If so, Herodotus ignored this detail of the poem. This on Feeney's criterion would put the poet in a different category from Herodotus, in whose Persian War narrative there is (with one spectacular exception I shall be coming to) not a great deal in the epiphany department,[30] if we ignore the outsize hoplite who appeared to Epizelos at Marathon on Epizelos' own account, and one or two other doubtful items gathered by Pritchett.[31]

29. Finley 1975: 171.
30. Herodotean epiphanies: 6.117 (Epizelos); 6.127 (Laphanes the Arcadian); 8.122 (Aiginetan aristeia); 6.105ff. (Pan).
31. Pritchett 1979: 23–26.

If we restrict ourselves to Herodotean epiphanies of the Dioscuri, gods who are after all rather prone to epiphany,[32] there are just two, apart from the statement we are concerned with, to the effect that they followed the Spartan army. The first is in book 6, and is ignored by Pritchett, no doubt because it is not a military epiphany. It is the statement that among the suitors of Agariste of Sikyon was one Laphanes son of Euphorion from Azania in Arcadia, and that this Euphorion, according to the Arcadian story or tradition, entertained the Dioscuri. This may, I suppose, be just a vivid way of saying that Euphorion conducted rites of *theoxenia* for the Dioscuri in some recognized capacity; but the formulation is interesting as showing that at least in Arcadia a real epiphany of the Dioscuri was thinkable as late as the early sixth century. The other is said to be a military epiphany of the Dioscuri, but it strikes me as pretty roundabout evidence; it is the dedication by the Aiginetans of three stars as their *aristeia* from the battle of Salamis. It is a modern conjecture that two of these stars represent the Dioscuri (admittedly a frequent iconographic association) while the third is held, in an ingenious but somewhat arbitrary conjecture, to represent Apollo Delphinios. Neither of these passages exactly brings the Dioscuri to the center of Herodotean action. If we ask about Herodotean epiphanies more generally, the best by far is Philippides' (auditory rather than visual)[33] experience of a real god, namely Pan, before the battle of Marathon, and Pan's rebuke, which Herodotus says led to institution of a Pan cult at Athens. This is much more of an epiphany than Athena at Thucydides' Torone, but still (it might be insisted) not quite an epiphany that diverts or forwards the main action in a Homeric or Vergilian manner, like Phoebus Apollo abandoning Hector in *Iliad* 22. However, we might speculate whether Pan's Arcadian origins are relevant politically to a narrative in which Athens and Sparta are already shown as moving towards their secular fifth-century opposition; after all, there is good evidence for Arcadian/Spartan hostility in and after 480 B.C.E. Alternatively, we can look at Herodotus' Pan epiphany in quite a different way and say that it is there for aetiological reasons, the setting up of the cult. Similarly, Boreas is there because Herodotus says (7.189) that the Athenians built a temple to him by the Ilissus. In rather a similar way, some of Herodotus' best stories are there partly to explain proverbs, such as "drinking wine Scythian style"; "Hippoclides doesn't care"; "remember Gelon" (6.84.3; 6.129.4; cp. 7.158 3 with Macan).

Since Pan is important for the argument, I must examine the passage a little more closely. It may be objected that the chapter begins with a distancing device, "as Philippides said, and as he told the Athenians." One could add that what follows is in *oratio obliqua*, which John Gould and others take to be a way of expressing distance from or reserve towards his subject matter;[34] and that the following chapter (6.106) repeats that all this was what Philippides said he had seen (ὅτε περ οἱ ἔφη καὶ τὸν Πᾶνα φανῆναι). But the situation is not quite so simple. During chapter 105, Pan is

---

32. Versnel 1987: 44.
33. Versnel 1987: 49f. (with a very good general discusssion of the Pan epiphany). See also now Harrison 2000: 82f., though given his general position I am not sure why he calls this the most "notorious" case of a divine epiphany in Herodotus.
34. Gould in Hornblower 1994: 96.

said to promise future help, and at the end of the chapter we are told that when things had "settled well" for the Athenians (κατασταντων σφι εὖ τῶν πραγμάτων, "when the crisis was over")[35] they decided/believed that it was true, πιστεύσαντες εἶναι ἀληθέα, and set up the cult. At a minimum this means Athenians at large, not just Philippides, thought a real epiphany had occurred, though, as Alan Griffiths points out to me, the word πιστεύσαντες implies that other views were possible. But perhaps we can go further. It has been suggested, for instance by Garland,[36] that Pan's help took the form of a panic (Pan-ic) attack inflicted on the Persians in the battle. If this is right, and is at back of κατασταντων . . ., we have, so to speak, two epiphanies (if we are going to use that rather elusive word), one private, one public. The public one, the battle panic, was held to confirm the private one. Rather like seeing a flying saucer, you need confirmation. Unfortunately there is a difference of opinion among the historians of Greek religion. Borgeaud[37] does not believe that Pan sent a panic in the battle, because panics happen to armies in quiet states rather than on the battlefield. Garland does believe that Pan produced battle panics, and Parker is noncommittal but cautiously seems to accept the possibility ("Perhaps he sent his own 'panic' fear against their enemies"). And there is a fourth-century bronze plaque, knowledge of which I owe to Alan Griffiths, with a head of Pan which may show that *battle* panic was associated with Pan by about 350 B.C.E.[38]

The weakness of the idea of the "second [i.e., battle-panic] epiphany" is that it is a lot to get out of the vague and coy κατασταντων . . . .. Also, it is not exactly what is said to have happened in the battle (6.112). There the Persians see the Athenians advancing at a run, δρόμῳ, and think the *Athenians* are mad. If the Persians themselves went out of their minds (i.e., they panicked), Herodotus does not say so, though it is reasonable to suppose that they were pretty scared by the unexpected sight. But one still might want to say that the Persians, perhaps in the previous night, may have felt some restless panic of the type Borgeaud believes constituted the essence of "panic," and that some rumor of this reached the Athenians.

The strength of the idea is that it makes elegant sense of the data: before the battle Pan promises help, after the battle the Athenians decide that Pan did help them. How else does Pan help you in (or before) a battle except by inflicting panic on your enemies? A "Simonides" epigram[39] interestingly links Miltiades, victor of Marathon, with the new Pan cult. Page thinks it is roughly contemporary, though as usual refuses Simonidean authorship. So what with that, Herodotus, and the archeological evidence discussed by Parker, it is tempting to think that the Athenians believed that something Pan-related happened in the battle. It remains true that Herodotus does not commit himself on the veracity of what I have called the private epiphany, but he goes further than just attributing it to the say-so of Philippides. I continue to find this a slightly bothersome item, in that it looks like a poetic epiphany, and moreover may

---

35. Parker 1996: 164.
36. Garland 1992: 51–54.
37. Borgeaud 1988: 136.
38. For the bronze plaque, see Fleischmann (catalog) 1994: 72, no. 28.
39. *FGE* pp. 194f. (Simonides no. V).

have "forwarded the action" (as I put it above) in that it affected the course of a decisive battle.

If we leave aside Pan, and I am not absolutely saying we should, then indeed Simonides may be visualizing the Dioscuri at a different and more epic, that is, personified, level from any of their appearances in Herodotus, depending on the form the Dioscuri actually took in Simonides' poem, a question I have just tried to settle. But unless the twins did something dramatic in some lost bit of the poem, there is just not room for them to do or say anything exciting in the part of the poem we are concerned with, because it goes straight on to mention Menelaus and then passes on to Pausanias the regent. In any case (see above), the context of their mention is a routine departure of the army.

As for Kalais/Zetes, the only relevant Herodotean passage is at 7.189. Boreas, son-in-law of the Athenians (he married Oreithyia, daughter of Erechtheus), helped the Athenians before the battle of Artemisium, that is, the Persian fleet was damaged by the north wind (an odd passage because actually the wind was an east wind, the *Hellespontias* or *apeliotes*). This is unsatisfying for connoisseurs of epiphanies, though it is included in Pritchett's list of military epiphanies; but as Parsons says,[40] Simonides both wrote an elegy about Artemisium and described Boreas' abduction of Oreithyia, so the relevant fragment (fr. 3 W^2) "may then belong to the corresponding episode in an Artemisum Elegy of Simonides."

Yet, so far I have been accepting that the epiphany knife can cleanly separate the two slices of raw meat, that is, epic and history. Put as strongly as Feeney does, the point is hard to quarrel with that there are no Homeric councils of the gods in Herodotus or Thucydides, whereas they would have not have been absolutely unthinkable in Simonides. But let us put a weaker case, and ask just how consistently and ferociously Thucydides maintains the rationalism and secularity for which he is so famous, and how far this sets him apart from epic. One can approach the point from opposite directions. The first way is by insisting on the way the very best epic, namely Homer, actually avoids the magical and the outré (I think of Jasper Griffin's demonstration of this point in his article on the "Epic Cycle and the Uniqueness of Homer.")[41] The second way is via Thucydides and his narrative registers. In the great plague description in book 2, Thucydides is the clinician in a white coat with a stethoscope round his neck, but in the next book (3.87), he informs us in the same breath both that there was a recurrence of the plague and that there was a large number of earthquakes just then. He is too artful to say *propter hoc*, but the juxtaposition leaps from the page, and recalls the curious chapter at the end of the *Archeology* (1.23) which includes portents such as earthquakes, alongside the more logically linked exiles and sudden deaths, as concomitants of the great war. There is a nice parallel in Edward Hyde, Earl of Clarendon, whose knowledge of Thucydides was good, and owed in part to his friend Thomas Hobbes. He describes the death of Oliver Cromwell near the end of the great *History of the Rebellion* and speaks in the same breath[42] of a terrific storm

40. Parsons 1992a: 41.
41. Griffin 1977.
42. Clarendon 1988: 91.

that "accompanied" (nice choice of word!) the death of the great man. Like Thucydides, Clarendon is too sophisticated to do more than tell us the two facts—the death; the storm—and then move on. Historiography, like epic, had its moods and registers, and we should not talk of Thucydides or Herodotus as if their handling was even throughout the two-volume Oxford Classical Text extent of each of them. Generic crossover can be a very arresting device, and we should reckon with the possibility that Herodotus' Pan may be just such a deliberate and daring crossover, a real epic feature in a real historian.

Finally, there is Simonides' mention of Menelaus.[43] There is no problem about the stress on this family in a general sort of way, just half a century after the Spartans had got hold of the bones of Menelaus' nephew Orestes, a few years after Kleomenes had insisted on his Achaian credentials on the Athenian acropolis (Hdt. 5.72), and very soon after Syagros in Sicily had protested that for Sparta to hand over the hegemony to the upstart Gelon would make Agamemnon groan in his grave. Robin Osborne has in any case observed recently[44] that the dedications to Helen found twenty years ago at the Menelaon[45] go back to the seventh century, and thus show that the "bones of Orestes" policy was no new departure, rather a shift of emphasis, although strictly the dedications to Menelaus himself as opposed to Helen do not, contrary to what Osborne seems to imply, antedate 500 B.C.E. or at earliest the sixth century. Nor, for what it is worth, do they postdate 500 B.C.E.; more on that below, where I shall suggest that the word "strictly" is after all out of place. The Agamemnon motif in Spartan history ran and ran, thus that unromantic and ugly little figure Agesillaos sacrificed at Aulis where Agamemnon had sacrificed.[46] Richard Buxton has some good remarks on this topic; he brushes aside the apparent inconsistency between all this and the strident Dorianism of the Herakleia project of the 420s. As Buxton well puts it: "Myths function like shoes: you step into them if they fit. Old shoes, like traditions that are (or seem) ancient, are usually the ones you feel most comfortable with. But, just now and then, a new occasion may require the use of something more appropriate."[47] The only particular problem some have felt is why Menelaus rather than Agememnon should feature in Simonides, thus Parsons in the *editio princeps*: "By the fifth century, it is normally assumed, Agamemnon had taken his i.e. Menelaus' place." Lloyd-Jones has, however, shown that the pairing of Menelaus and the Dioscuri was entirely appropriate.[48] In any case we may invoke Buxton's point: a fortiori, if the whole Achaian theme can be dropped and picked up again, so too, within that theme, Menelaus and Agamemnon can be stressed at dif-

43. Menelaus: Hdt. 1.65 (Orestes' bones); "Kleomenes on the Acropolis": Hdt. 5.72; Syagros: Hdt. 7.159 with Griffiths 1976: 23f.
44. Osborne 1996: 289.
45. Cult of Helen and Menelaus: *SEG* 26.457 (dedication to Helen, bronze aryballos ca. 675–650 B.C.E.; Menelaus is mentioned, but only in terms of his relationship to Helen, as Hall 1995: 602 points out.); 458, (bronze meat-hook, sixth cent. B.C.E.); and 459 (dedication to Menelaus, limestone stele, ca. 500 B.C.E.). For a possible sixth-century dedication to Menelaus on a bronze phiale see *SEG* 35. 321 and Hall 1995: 602.
46. Xen. *Hell.* 3.4.3. See also Shaw, this volume, n. 84.
47. Buxton 1994: 196.
48. For Menelaus and the Dioscuri, see Lloyd-Jones 1994: 1–3 at 3.

ferent times. That is, talk of mythical X "taking the place" of mythical Y may be too absolute. If we insist on an answer, I suggest that Agamemnon may have been more suitable, because of the Aulis sacrifice, for an expedition where eastern overseas conquest was envisaged, as by Agesilaos. For domestic protection and more local campaigning, Menelaus and the Dioscuri were more suitable. (Ian Rutherford suggests that Menelaus and the Dioscuri go together because of shared interest in Helen;[49] but that still leaves the problem, why are they there at Plataea?) We should remember how bad is our evidence for this sort of thing in the fifth century because of Thucydidean selectivity: it is significant that we jump straight from Herodotus to Xenophon before we find Agamemnon again. After all, the Menelaon was still an active sanctuary in the third century (Polyb. 5.18–22), and there is every reason to suppose that he was important at Sparta for the whole half millennium before then.

Some concluding remarks: presence or absence of epiphanies looks at first sight like a valuable way of distinguishing epic from history, except that we soon find that "epiphany" is rather a baggy concept. Thus Henrichs on "epiphany" in the new *Oxford Classical Dictionary* says that the god "reveals his presence or manifests his power,"[50] and Versnel, after a review of the different ways in which gods might manifest themselves, concludes that "the term *epiphaneia* denotes two things: the personal appearance of a god and his miraculous deeds."[51] The noun ἐπιφάνεια is postclassical; it is used in the Lindian Chronicle in about 100 B.C.E. (*FGrHist* 532, an occurrence omitted by LSJ even in the new supplement); after that, we find it in Dionysius of Halicarnassus and Diodorus. It covers everything from a display of divine power in a general sort of way and without any actual vision being involved, through episodes like Apollo's personal rebuke to Diomedes in *Iliad* 5, down to the use of "epiphany" for what may happen in temple medicine during incubation. In particular, we remember that at lowest, "epiphanies" include episodes like Thucydides' collapsing tower at Torone where someone—in this case Brasidas—merely thinks a divine hand was at work.

To go back to our epic/history distinction, we have to frame it as "presence or absence of epiphanies, but not every epiphany: only really colorful and, as Feeney says, characterful or characterized ones of the kind we get in epic." Hence an obvious risk of a circle or a platitude: it is epic-type epiphanies that will enable us to spot an epic and to distinguish epic from history. Applying this criterion, we will certainly end up, after all, putting Herodotus on one side of the divide and *perhaps* Simonides on the other. So we should not get too excited about Simonides writing history before Herodotus. But with each of these writers a doubt remains. The Herodotean doubt arises from the epiphany of Pan, which is not quite like the others in his work and much more like what poets do. The Simonidean doubt arises from a simpler cause, our ignorance about whether the poet went on elsewhere in the poem to do anything with the Dioscuri and Menelaus after he had introduced them.

49. Rutherford, this volume, at n. 65.
50. Henrichs in Hornblower and Spawforth 1996: 546.
51. Versnel 1987: 52.

8

DEBORAH BOEDEKER

Paths to Heroization at Plataea

In a speech written a century after the event, Isocrates extravagantly suggests of the Athenians who fought in the Persian War:

> I even think that one of the gods, admiring their excellence, brought about the war so that men of such natures would not remain unknown or end their lives without fame (ἀκλεῶς τὸν βίον τελευτήσαιεν), but would be found worthy of the same things that happened to those who are descended from gods and are called *hemitheoi* (τοῖς ἐκ τῶν θεῶν γεγονόσι καὶ καλουμένοις ἡμιθέοις). The bodies of those men the gods gave over to the constraints of nature, but the memory of their excellence they made undying (τῆς δ' ἀρετῆς ἀθάνατον τὴν μνήμην ἐποίησαν).[1]

Not only Isocrates' gods but the Greeks themselves kept alive the memory of those who fought the Persians—and not only by remembering their deeds. Regular offerings and perhaps even a festival suggest that those who fell at Plataea were honored with a kind of "hero cult" already by their contemporaries.[2] This is remarkable, since before the Persian War era, contemporary Greek war dead did not collectively receive cultic honors.[3] The Athenian tyrannicides Harmodios and Aristogeiton, to be sure, were honored with statues in the Athenian Agora as well as graves and sacrifices in the Kerameikos, but the tributes paid these far-from-anonymous saviors are quite

---

An earlier version of this paper, titled "The New Simonides and Heroization at Plataia," was published in *Archaic Greece: New Approaches and New Evidence,* ed. Nick Fisher and Hans van Wees (Cardiff 1998): 231–49; this substantially revised version is printed here by kind permission of the University Press of Wales.

1. *Panegyrikos* 84. The passage is discussed in Loraux 1986: 41.

2. At some point the Athenians who died at Marathon began receiving annual offerings as well, but our evidence for this dates only from the second century B.C.E. See below at n. 64.

3. Welwei 1991: 54ff., writing before the publication of *POxy* 3965, maintains that those who fell in the Persian War battles did not receive hero cult, but only commemorative rituals. Flashar 1996: 73 follows Welwei, emphasizing Dem. *Epitaphios* 8ff., on which see below at n. 65. Boehringer 1996: 50 maintains that annual offerings are enough to indicate that there was a hero cult for the Plataiomachoi. This lack of consensus largely reflects differing definitions about what constitutes "hero cult"; see further below.

different from offerings to the collective war dead.[4] Herodotus' Solon could tell Croesus that what Tellos of Athens achieved—prosperity, surviving descendants, death on the battlefield, and public burial—constitute the greatest human happiness; his list, however, is silent about heroic honors (Hdt. 1.30).

Herodotus does report several cults established for Greek war dead in the period of conflicts with Persia. Of these, one involves a group of warriors: some Phocaeans, who had emigrated to Sardinia to escape Persian rule at home, became embroiled with Etruscans and Carthaginians and were stoned to death by their Etruscan captors. After a dramatic omen, in which all who passed by their burial site were paralyzed, the Etruscans consulted the Delphic oracle and were told to institute an elaborate festival, which, Herodotus reports, they still kept in his day (Hdt. 1.163–67). That tale itself, purporting to explain an Etruscan festival as hero cult for a group of mistreated Greeks, has raised historical eyebrows.[5] Plausible or not, according to Herodotus the Phocaean heroization came about in response to a mysterious sign, and the festival was authorized by Delphi. Both these features occur as well in Herodotus' account of the heroization of Onesilos of Cyprus, who was killed in battle against the Persians; like the Phocaeans, Onesilos' cult was celebrated by his enemies, who were told by the oracle to sacrifice to him as a hero ('Ονησίλῳ δὲ θύειν ὡς ἥρωι, Hdt. 5.114). Not so with the Plataiomachoi: to the extent that they were honored, they were honored by their own, without omen and without Delphic authorization.

Public burial and regularly repeated offerings can be placed along a single axis of honors paid to collective war dead, but they are separated from one another by a significant gap. That gap seems to have been bridged in the Persian War era at Plataea—and perhaps a little later in Athens, in response to new perceptions of the relationship between citizen-defender and community.[6] Even if it corresponds to a shift in civic identity or ideology, the move from honorable burial (such as Solon's Tellos enjoyed) to hero-like offerings perpetuated by a community is a significant, even startling, change in practice. Simonides' Plataea elegy, I will argue, helps answer the question of how a shift to hero-like honors could be motivated, assimilated, and understood. I will first briefly review the evidence for a cult of the fallen at Plataea, which is historiographical and archaeological and comes from outside the elegy. Then, by analyzing the unusual double nature of Achilles within the proem, I will try to show how Simonides opens the way for an "immortalization" of the Plataiomachoi that is broader than Homeric *kleos*. Finally, I will consider the ways that Simonides' Plataiomachoi are comparable to Achilles and the Danaan *hemitheoi* who fought at Troy, to show how the analogy between them was constructed for the audience of the elegy.

4. On the cult of the Tyrannicides, cf. Arist. *Ath. Pol.* 58.1, "Demosth." 19.280. For discussion see Fornara 1970, Kearns 1989: 55, Taylor 1991: 5–8, Boehringer 1996: 50.

5. Fontenrose 1968: 98, cited in Boehringer 1996: 44. Asheri 1988: 360, commenting on Hdt. 1.167.2, however, notes that there was a treasury of the Agyllans at Delphi and believes the story may be substantially historical.

6. For differing views on the controversial topic of "heroization" of Athenian war-dead in the fifth century, see Loraux 1986 and Welwei 1991.

Heroization at Plataea?

First, there are the tombs. Like most Greek war dead of this period, those who died at Plataea were buried in the place where they fell—although it was unusual for Greeks of so many cities to be buried at a single battle site.[7] As at Marathon, where the Athenians, their slaves, and their Plataean allies had separate burial mounds,[8] so too at Plataea the dead were buried in separate tombs, city by city, according to Herodotus—distinct tombs for Athenians, Tegeans, Megarians,[9] and Phliasians, with two for Spartiates (differentiated according to age-grade) and another for their helots (Hdt. 9.85.1–2).[10] In another passage, Herodotus says there were 159 Greek dead from the cities of Sparta, Athens, and Tegea (9.70.5),[11] but in later accounts the numbers were far grander. Plutarch reports that 1,360 Greeks fell (*Arist.* 19.4); Diodorus Siculus says there were more than ten thousand (11.33.1), making the number of casualties better suit the importance of this battle in later Hellenic tradition.[12] Whatever the numbers, in Herodotus' account burial *in situ* at Plataea becomes an important issue for civic self-representation: Aigina and other poleis are said to have erected cenotaphs at Plataea some years after the battle, ἐπαισχυνομένους τῇ ἀπεστοῖ τῆς μάχης ("ashamed of their absence from the fight," Hdt. 9.85.3).[13]

Second, there are the regularly repeated offerings to the dead. Thucydides attributes to the Plataeans a speech (dated to 427) in which they try to convince the Spartans not to destroy their city, reminding them how every year they have brought gifts of garments, first fruits, and other offerings to the tombs of "your fathers who were killed by the Persians and are buried in our land" (Thuc. 3.58.4).[14] The annual offerings appear to have been reinstituted after Sparta allowed the Plataeans to return to their city four decades after its destruction, if we can rely on Isocrates' *Plataikos*.

---

7. See Pritchett 1985: 94–106 with references and passim, on varying practices in this regard; the Athenian "ancestral custom" of bringing the war dead home for burial was fairly unusual, and probably began shortly after the Persian Wars.

8. Paus. 1.32.3, cf. 10.20.2. Cf. Welwei 1979, Hammond 1992, and Mersch 1995 for questions about the location of these tombs.

9. (Other?) Megarians who fell in the Persian Wars enjoyed a heroon in Megara itself, according to Paus. 1.43.2; on the interpretation of this passage see Welwei 1991: 54–55.

10. Perhaps related to the funeral and tomb cult is a ceremony of which the Plataeans remind the Spartans in a defensive speech in Thucydides, dated to 429: Pausanias presided at a bull sacrifice to Zeus Eleutherios ("Zeus of Freedom") in the Plataean agora, and administered an oath guaranteeing that the allies would uphold forever the independence of Plataea (2.71).

11. N. Fisher plausibly suggests to me that the helot dead mentioned in Hdt. 9.85 are ignored in this low figure.

12. Conversely, the number of Persians killed at Marathon increased dramatically in the retelling; cf. Flashar 1996: 72 f.

13. Unsurprisingly, this passage is contested by Plutarch, *De Herod. malign.* 872F–873A, who maintains that no one else ever charged fellow-Greeks with betraying the cause by being absent from the battle.

14. It might be assumed from this speech that *only* Spartans received these gifts, but the point should not be pressed. Given their desperate circumstances, Thucydides' Plataeans could plausibly be downplaying their special relationship to Athens, passing over in silence any rites connected with the current arch-enemy of their Spartan judges. See also next note.

This speech, supposedly delivered about 373 by Plataeans asking Athens to restore their city after it was destroyed by Thebes, again mentions Plataean tomb cult on behalf of those who shared dangers (συγκινδυνεύσαντες) in the fight for freedom (14.61).[15]

Third, there is a panhellenic festival. In addition to their prestigious burial and yearly offerings, Plutarch writes that the Plataiomachoi were honored by an annual festival called the Eleutheria, culminating in a bull sacrifice at the site of the funeral pyre and a libation poured by the archon of Plataea to those who died fighting for "the freedom of the Greeks" (*Arist.* 21). Every four years the Eleutheria was held on a grander scale, including athletic contests. According to Plutarch, the original celebration was proposed by the Athenian Aristides soon after the battle.[16]

Such an event would have had precedents not only in the funeral games held for sixth-century aristocrats, but also in regularly repeated festivals commemorating earlier battles, notably the Spartan Parparonia and Gymnopaidia.[17] Possible evidence for a fifth-century Eleutheria is provided by three bronze prize vessels, dating from roughly 480 to 440 and inscribed Ἀθεναῖοι · ἆθλα ἐπὶ τοῖς ἐν τῶι πολέμοι ("The Athenians [gave these] prizes for those [who died] in the war").[18] Eugene Vanderpool, the first to discuss the vessels as a group, believed they were prizes awarded at the official funeral games for war dead celebrated in Athens, beginning shortly after the battle of Plataea (according to Diod. Sic. 11.33.3).[19] Pierre Amandry, however, comparing all inscriptions attested on prize vessels, claimed that in no other example does the name of the prizegivers appear in the nominative. Therefore, in Amandry's view, the inscription "the Athenians [gave these] prizes" indicates that the vessels were not awarded for games held in Athens itself; he proposed that they may have been awarded either for a fifth-century version of the Eleutheria at Plataea or for the Herakleia at Marathon, expanded to a panhellenic festival in honor of the Marathonomachoi.[20] In addition to the literary testimonia for the festival and this

15. The identity of the συγκινδυνεύσαντες so honored is not specified, but since the speech is written for an Athenian audience, it seems likely that Athenian graves were among those tended by the Plataeans.

16. The festival is mentioned also in Diod. Sic. 11.29.1–2 (with a different story about its origin), Strabo 9.2.31, Paus. 9.2.5. See Étienne and Piérart 1975: 63–67 for a succinct review of the evidence.

17. See Roller 1981: 1–7 for epigraphic and literary evidence of archaic funerary games; also Parker 1989: 149–50.

18. See Vanderpool 1969 and Amandry 1971: 612–25 on the three vessels. Vanderpool (2–3) dates the two lebetes to "around or shortly after 480 B.C." and "a trifle later"; the hydria to "the second half of the fifth century B.C."; Amandry (612), dates the three vessels to roughly 480, 465, and 450; the editors of *IG* I³ 523–25, to 480–70?, 460–50?, and 450–40?. Étienne and Piérart 1975: 55 note in a different context that ἐπί with the dative is regularly used of honors offered to heroes or to the dead, citing literary parallels. So too Nagy 1990: 121.

19. Vanderpool 1969: 4–5; accepted, e.g., by Roller 1981: 7; Pritchett 1985: 107. Osborne 1993: 23 appears to accept this context as well. Parker 1996: 132 n. 36 disagrees with Amandry's attribution of the bronze vessels "to an (unattested) funerary context away from the city itself," although without discussing Amandry's argument about the formulation of the inscription. Loraux 1986: 30 accepts Amandry's conclusions.

20. Amandry 1971: 620–25, citing Vanderpool 1942 on the expanded Herakleia. Contra Stupperich 1977 (notes): 41 n. 5, although this argument is directed mostly against a Marathonian provenance. The editors of *IG* I³ 523–25 likewise disagree with Amandry's argument that the vases were not awarded in Athens, and support Vanderpool 1969 in attributing them to the Athenian *agon epitaphios*.

possible fifth-century evidence, several inscriptions from the second century c.e. suggest that Athens and Sparta competed in a formal debate for leadership of the games each time they were held.[21]

In 1975, Roland Étienne and Marcel Piérart published an influential article in which they argue that the Eleutheria was not established until well into the fourth century. In contrast to the Plataean tomb cult attested in Thucydides, there is no clear evidence for the Eleutheria festival until the third century.[22] They conclude that the games were most likely founded when Alexander restored the city walls of Plataea in 338, influenced by a myth of panhellenism retrojected to the time of the Persian Wars and especially the battle of Plataea.[23]

Étienne and Piérart's conclusion, reasonable as it is and convincing as it has been to many scholars, is based essentially on silence.[24] One fifth-century source where we might expect to hear about the festival (an important but not a decisive part of their argument) is the speech of Thucydides' Plataeans mentioned above, where they plead with the Spartans for their city's survival in the Peloponnesian War (3.58.4). But this speech does not provide a good argument from silence: in the circumstances, it would be unwise for the Plataeans to mention anything connected with Athenian patronage, as our evidence suggests may have been the case with the festival.[25] To be sure, Greeks in the fourth century and later had their own reasons for celebrating the freedom of Hellenes, but it is not in itself improbable that Plutarch's Eleutheria was an expanded revival of an earlier festival.[26]

Honored tombs, annual offerings, possibly a fifth-century (proto-)Eleutheria festival: what do such practices indicate about the status of those who receive them? Recent assessments of hero cult suggest that it may be more useful to think of a continuum of honors paid to the dead in the archaic and classical periods, rather than defining absolute categories such as "ordinary dead" and "hero" (a term that classical sources avoid for the collective dead of the Persian Wars).[27] Regularly repeated festi-

---

21. Robertson 1986.

22. A fact that Amandry took into account as well; see 1971: 621: Plutarch must be describing a later revival of the festival.

23. Étienne and Piérart 1975: 65–75. On this revival of Persian War ideology and its expression in "false documents," see Habicht 1961.

24. See especially Schachter 1994: 125–43, who lays out the ancient evidence with great clarity (although he does not discuss Amandry's view of the prize vessels), and substantially agrees with the chronology proposed by Étienne and Piérart; see also Pritchett 1985: 119–20 with notes. In connection with the "New Simonides," some scholars continue to assume the existence of a fifth-century Eleutheria festival, e.g., Haslam 1993: 135; Aloni, this volume at n. 62; Pavese 1995: 22, 24.

25. On the Thucydides passage, see n. 14 above, and Étienne and Piérart 1975: 66–67. On Athenian patronage or co-sponsorship, see above at nn. 18–21.

26. I note, too, that the expanded Herakleia festival at Marathon, which would offer a parallel of sorts to a fifth-century contest in honor of the fallen at Plataea, likewise leaves no trace in the literary record, although it is supported by plausible (not definitive) epigraphic evidence. Cf. Vanderpool 1942. Bearzot 1997: 78 suggests that there may have been a fifth-century predecessor to the Eleutheria; see also Boedeker 1995b: 222.

27. E.g., Seaford 1994: 114–17; Parker 1996: 33–39. Antonaccio 1995 analyzes the archaeological evidence for archaic hero cult. For example, in the *Panegyrikos* passage cited at the beginning of this chaper, Isocrates does not call the Greeks who fought the Persians "heroes"; "Demosth." 60.9 says explicitly that they have not yet attained τὴν ἡρωϊκὴν . . . τάξιν (but see below at nn. 66 f.).

vals and offerings, nevertheless, signal that individuals or groups so honored were close to the "heroic" end of this continuum—they were treated as "somehow immortalized dead mortals," in Snodgrass's deliberately loose formulation.[28] The Plataeans' speech in Thucydides (cited above at n. 14) further encourages this view of the Plataiomachoi, by referring to the Spartans buried there as if they were still alive, about to be abandoned in the territory of their old enemies the Thebans (3.58.5). As Simon Hornblower comments: "The dead Spartans of the battle of Plataea are here virtually conjured back to life: what will they think about being left in hostile terrain among their murderers . . . ?"[29]

The fragments of the Plataea elegy cannot prove that the dead of Plataea were honored as heroes in the fifth century. But in view of Thucydides' testimony of their tomb cult, Herodotus' picture of their prestigious burial spot, and the possible evidence for a fifth-century festival complete with games, the new Simonides fragments offer further evidence as to how the (implicit) heroization of contemporaries *en masse* was facilitated or justified.

Bridging the Gap

The Plataea elegy shows what model was used for the delicate matter of elevating a group of contemporaries to a new status: the Trojan War heroes, celebrated in poetry and, some of them, "immortalized" in cult. I do not mean that the Homeric epics, or the funerary practices described in them, provided the primary motives or patterns for hero cults as they developed in the Greek world.[30] On the contrary, the growth of Greek hero cults was a complex process intertwined with contemporary political and ideological developments; archaic funerals no doubt helped to shape epic descriptions of funerals at least as much as the reverse.[31] My argument rests rather on the relationship between the two groups of Greek warriors mentioned in Simonides' poem, which posits the Danaans who fought at Troy as predecessors of the allied Greeks who fought at Plataea.

The analogy begins in what appears to be the proem of the elegy. The poet recalls the defeat of Troy, then states that "undying fame" (ἀθάνατον κλέος) was poured on the Danaans by the man who received the true story from the Muses (fr. 11.15–18)—a reference to Homeric epic. Now the poet bids farewell to Achilles, son of Thetis, and calls on his own Muse to provide ordered beauty (κ[όσμον) for his song,[32] so that

---

28. Snodgrass 1988: 20–21. Similar criteria for "heroization" are set by Boehringer 1996, esp. 51.

29. Hornblower 1991a, ad 3.58.5.

30. Cf. Farnell 1921, esp. 284–342; this view has been developed more recently by Coldstream 1976 and Rupp 1988 (cited by Antonaccio), against whose views see now the discussion of Iron Age "heroic" graves by Antonaccio 1995: 221–43.

31. See Whitley 1988, Boedeker 1993, Seaford 1994, esp. 180–86 with references and Antonaccio (preceding note).

32. Capra and Curti 1995: 31–2 argue for τόνδ[ε μελ]ίφρονα κ[όλλοπα χο]ρδῆς instead of West's τόνδ[ε μελ]ίφρονα κ[όσμον ἀο]ιδῆς (fr. 11.19): the poet asks the Muses not to grant *kosmos* to his song, but to regulate the key of his lyre, at this point of transition between epic and historical poetry.

"[fame] undying" ([κλέος] ἀθάνατον)[33] will come to the brave men who went out from Sparta to save Greek freedom (fr. 11.19–28, as restored by West). Thus this very song is to provide a way for the Spartans and others[34] who fought at Plataea to achieve the kind of deathlessness that Homeric epic provided for the Greeks at Troy.

The "Eion poem" (XL *FGE*), discussed elsewhere in this volume,[35] also draws an analogy between the Trojan and Persian Wars: it compares the Athenians who successfully besieged Persians at the Thracian city of Eion to the Athenian leader Menestheus at Troy, who was praised by Homer as κοσμητῆρα μάχης ἔξοχον "outstanding marshaller of battle" (*Il.* 2.553–54). The Eion poem was composed after that city was captured in 476, while the Plataea elegy, with its unproblematic mention of Pausanias and relatively panhellenic spirit, can best be ascribed to the period immediately after the battle in 479.[36] If this dating is correct, the new elegy provides our earliest extant example of an analogy drawn between the Trojan and Persian Wars.[37]

The Plataea elegy differs from the Eion poem, however, in significant ways. It mentions Greeks from several cities instead of only one; it presents the speaker as key to the undying fame of those he praises, just as his wise predecessor, thanks to the Muses, was responsible for the immortal *kleos* of the heroes at Troy.[38] Most significant for my argument here, the Eion poem commemorates valor explicitly so that it may inspire future readers to equivalent efforts:

> μᾶλλόν τις τάδ' ἰδὼν καὶ ἐπεσσομένων ἐθελήσει
> ἀμφὶ περὶ ξυνοῖς πράγμασι δῆριν ἔχειν

> seeing these (memorials), someone of those to come will be more willing
> to engage in strife for the common good.

(XL C.3–4 *FGE*)

The Plataea elegy, in contrast, explicitly means to *establish* the fame of its subjects. Thus the speaker calls the Muse to help him arrange his song "so that someone in the future will recall" the men who marched out of Sparta (fr. 11.21–25).

---

33. ἀθάνατον is attested, κλέος is supplemented by West (fr. 11.28).

34. Spartans are predominant in the fragments we have, esp. fr. 11.25–34; Athenians may be mentioned in fr. 11.41, and Corinthians are subjects of praise in the verses of this poem cited by Plutarch, *De Herod. malig.* 872D–E. On "panhellenism" in the Plataea elegy, see Aloni 1994, Boedeker 1995b, Pavese 1995.

35. This volume, Boedeker "Historiography" at nn. 26–30, Rutherford at n. 45.

36. The Spartan regent came under suspicion and was recalled to Sparta probably by mid-477, according to the careful calculation of Loomis 1990, and ended up starving to death rather than leaving his asylum in a Spartan temple: Thuc. 1.134. Along with Aloni and others, I think it likely that the funeral at Plataea was the occasion when Simonides' elegy was first performed, although my argument here does not depend on that connection. On the date of the Plataea elegy, see Aloni, this volume after n. 56; Boedeker 1995b; Bearzot 1997.

37. Whitley 1994: 213 suggests, however, that already in 490 the cremation burial of the Marathonomachoi—in a mound, with stelae—was modeled after Homeric burials. See also Flashar 1996.

38. The Eion poem's silence about its maker corresponds to its mode of presentation: the speaker's role is emphasized in praise-poems that were meant for performance, such as victory odes and the Plataea elegy, but not in those designated for inscription and reading. On the speaker's position in the Plataea elegy, see Stehle, this volume.

The speaker of the Plataea elegy, as we have seen, hopes to provide the same kind of ἀθάνατον κλέος to his contemporaries that the earlier poet gave to the Danaans (assuming the restoration of κλέος "fame" in fr. 11.28 is correct). Such a close parallel between contemporary hoplites and heroes of the Trojan War, however familiar to readers of Herodotus,[39] would have been a bold stroke for a poet in 479. An epinician ode, of course, may propose a Trojan-era hero as parallel to a contemporary athletic victor, as Aias is parallel to Timodemos of Acharnai in Pindar's *Nemean* 2.14–15— although, as Burnett points out, this is attested less frequently than modern readers might expect.[40] Gregory Nagy describes this resemblance as ideological: the contemporary athlete's struggle to win in the Games is denoted in the same terms (e.g., πόνος and ἄεθλος) that apply in poetry to the life-and-death efforts of heroes of old.[41] But the Plataea elegy sets forth an even closer resemblance, if indeed it explicitly aspires to provide for contemporary Greek warriors the same kind of "undying fame" as that granted to their predecessors, also warriors, at Troy.

This immortal fame is in part the *kleos* bestowed by poetry that will be reperformed, but I propose that in the Plataea elegy it suggests something more as well. The fame of both groups of Greek warriors, those at Troy and those at Plataea, is described not as ἄφθιτον "unfading" as in Homeric diction, but ἀθάνατον "undying" (fr. 11.15 and 28);[42] I propose that "undying" here applies to the subjects of *kleos* as well as the *kleos* itself—that is, the Danaans have become not only famous but deathless, and the speaker hopes that the Plataiomachoi too will share this fate.

My reason for proposing this rests largely on two passages in the proemium, where the speaker evidently addresses Achilles, referring to him as son of Thetis (an important feature to which I shall return). A vocative is very likely in fr. 10.5:

> κούρης εἰν]αλίης ἀγλαόφη[με πάϊ
>
> glorious [son] of the sea-dwelling [girl]

and virtually certain in fr. 11.19–20:

> ἀλλὰ σὺ μὲ]ν νῦν χαῖρε, θεᾶς ἐρικυ[δέος υἱέ
> κούρης εἰν]αλίου Νηρέος . . .
>
> [but] fare you well now, famous [son] of the goddess
> [girl] of sea-dwelling Nereus . . .

---

39. E.g., Hdt. 7.159 and 161.3: Spartan and Athenian speakers tell Gelon of Syracuse that their cities' roles in the Trojan War explain why they should supersede him as leaders of the Greek alliance. Hdt. 9.27.4 reports another (weak) argument based on Athenian prowess at Troy.

40. Burnett 1985: 79–80 suggests that the epinician poets did not use Trojan War heroes very often because the Homeric epics had rationalized them too thoroughly: "the fame of these warriors had become finite and natural; one admired them for their achievements and strength, but not as vessels in which a supernatural force had been conveyed to the surface of the earth . . . An awesome moment that strained rational belief was thus the deepest requirement for an epinician myth; a more superficial but equally essential one was that the fiction should show some structural or imagistic congruity with the occasion of victory."

41. Nagy 1990: 151, cf. also 138–40. On πόνος and ἄεθλος see also Loraux 1982b.

42. Stehle, this volume at nn. 44f., raises the possibility that ἀθάνατον κλέος may be a conscious elegiac variant of the epic formula.

Familiar as are invocations of gods in Homeric Hymns and other praise-poems (see this volume, Obbink at nn. 15–17 and Aloni at nn. 27–30), invocations of long-dead mortal men or women are very unusual in archaic epos.[43] Rarely, the narrator of epic apostrophizes a character. In the *Odyssey* this occurs only in a common formulaic line introducing a speech by Eumaios, and is frequently[44] attributed to the metrical usefulness of the vocative form of his name: "Responding you said to him/her, Eumaios the swineherd."[45] In *Iliad* 16, Patroclus is similarly addressed by the narrator: "Groaning deeply you said to him, Patroclus the horseman" (*Il.* 16.20; cf. 16.744 and 843). Even more striking than these examples are the seven apostrophes to Patroclus in the space of 260 lines (the last five of them concentrated within a hundred lines) describing his final attack on the Trojans and the moment of his death.[46]

Direct address to a character at a critical moment is perhaps the most extraordinary trope of all those the epic performer uses to make vivid to his audience the story he is recreating. The pathos of the line ἔνθ' ἄρα τοι Πάτροκλε φάνη βιότοιο τελευτή ("So there, Patroclus, the end of your life appeared," *Il.* 16.787) was noted already by ancient commentators.[47] Egbert Bakker would go further, arguing that for poet and audience "Patroklos literally *is* there, and the poet's addressing him creates, as well as presupposes, a maximum of presence in the epic performance. The apostrophe marks the point where the reenactment that is the essence of epic storytelling reaches its climax and where the participatory involvement of the poet, and thereby of the audience, is greatest."[48]

But even though Achilles' death is also described in the Plataea elegy, the addresses to him are of a different nature. Fragment 10.5 is too fragmentary to encourage much conjecture about its context, but in fr. 11.19–20 the vocative is used not within a narrative, as is the case with Patroclus in the *Iliad* passages, but in the transition between one narrative and another. Achilles at this point is not a character whose actions are being described or even lamented, as he is in Homeric epic (or as Patroclus is in the passages cited above); rather, he is an addressee being honored by the poetic performance. The apostrophes to Achilles frame the poet's account of what happened at Troy, including the death of Achilles himself.

In his illuminating general article on the new fragments, M. L. West asks why Achilles receives so much attention in the proemium, and suggests, "Possibly the poem happened to be composed at the time of some festival or ritual in Achilles' hon-

---

43. In epinician, the victorious athlete can be praised in the second person, but of course that addressee is (ideally) alive and present at the performance of the song in his honor. See Nagy 1990: 150 with bibliography.

44. But weakly, in the judgement of Bakker 1993: 23.

45. *Od.* 14.55, 165, 360, 442, 507; 16.60, 135, 464; 17.274, 311, 380, 512, 579; variants in *Od.* 15.325 and 22.194. See Heubeck and Hoekstra 1989: 195–96, ad 14.55.

46. Apostrophes to Patroclus: 16.584, 693, 744, 754, 787, 812, 843; 744 and 843 introduce speeches. Menelaus is apostrophized seven times in the *Iliad*. On the pathetic quality of Iliadic apostrophes see Janko 1992, ad 13.602–3, with Parry 1972 and Block 1982. More recently, Kahane 1994: 110–13 argues on the basis of metrical positioning for the "sympathetic" nature of apostrophes to Eumaios, Patroclus, and Menelaus.

47. See the scholia on this passage, as noted by Heubeck and Hoekstra (n. 45 above).

48. Bakker 1993: 23.

our, and Simonides took his cue from that."[49] Hugh Lloyd-Jones, however, maintains that Achilles is integrally connected to the elegy's subject matter: he provides a model for the Greeks who fought at Plataea.[50] Most important for my argument, however, is the fact that the hero of Troy is not just *mentioned* in the Plataea poem, but *invoked*:

> ἀλλὰ σὺ μὲ]ν νῦν χαῖρε, θεᾶς ἐρικυ[δέος υἱέ
> κούρης εἰν]αλίου Νηρέος· αὐτὰρ ἐγώ . . .

Obbink shows that the formula χαῖρε . . . αὐτὰρ ἐγώ occurs in passages where the speaker concludes his address to a god and turns toward another story—marking a transition from hymn to epic or from proemium to *nomos* within a poetic performance.[51] In the Plataea elegy, correspondingly, the formula marks the change in focus from the old Trojan War heroes to the recent battle of Greeks against Persians.[52]

In fr. 11.19–20, the address to Achilles is followed immediately by the speaker's address to his "many-named Muse." Obbink shows that such a double invocation is not unusual in "early didactic, encomiastic, and paraenetic forms of rhapsodic composition," above all in archaic hymns. For example, Obbink continues, in the *Works and Days* Hesiod addresses Perses as well as the Muses, and Pindar in *Pythian* 1 calls upon his patron Hieron as well as the Muse and other gods.[53] But I propose that the invocation of Achilles in the Plataea elegy is also, in an important way, different from the practice Obbink describes. For although Achilles is invoked as if he were a living, attentive presence, like the brother in the *Works and Days* or the laudandus in *Pythian* 1, in all probability his death is described in the same poem—and described to Achilles himself.

Remarkably, in the proem Simonides devotes more time to the death of one warrior (at least fr. 11.1–8) as to the conquest and sack of Troy (fr. 11.9–14).[54] Following West's plausible supplements (now bolstered by Barchiesi's convincing argument that Horace adapted the passage), someone—probably Achilles himself—is killed by Apollo's hand at Troy:

> παῖ[σε] σ . [. . . σὺ δ' ἤριπες, ὡς ὅτε πεύκην
> ἢ πίτυν ἐν βήσ[σαις οὔρεος οἰοπόλου
> ὑλοτόμοι τάμ[νωσι
> πολλὸν δ' † ἤρῶς[
>]ος λαὸν[
> Πατρ]όκλου σα[
> οὐ δή τίς σ' ἐδ]άμασσεν ἐφ[ημέριος βροτὸς αὐτός,
> ἀλλ' ὑπ' Ἀπόλλ]ωνος χειρὶ [τυπεὶς ἐδάμης.

---

49. West 1993a: 5.
50. Lloyd-Jones 1994: 1; Capra and Curti 1995: 30 further discuss Achilles' role in the proemium.
51. Obbink, this volume, at n. 13, citing *Hymn. Hom. Apollo* 545–46. See also Capra and Curti 1995: 30 on a very similar pattern in epinician; they also point out that the invocation itself has a wider range of uses.
52. See Obbink, this volume, after n. 25.
53. Obbink, this volume, at nn. 15–16.
54. Pace Rutherford, this volume, after n. 25.

> str[uck you ... and you fell, as when a larch]
>   or pine-tree in the [lonely mountain] glades
> is felled by woodcutters ...
>   and much ...
> [A great grief seized] the war-host; [much they honored you,]
>   [and with Patr]oclus' [ashes mingled yours.]
> [It was no ordinary mortal] laid you low,
>   ['twas by Apoll]o's hand [that you were struck.]

(fr. 11.1–8; translation West 1993a: 168)

Achilles in the Plataea elegy thus has a double status: he dies, as befits an epic hero, but he is addressed as if alive, as befits a hero of cult. The latter conclusion finds strong support in Christiane Sourvinou-Inwood's study of addresses to the dead on archaic and classical grave monuments and in literary contexts, which shows that before the fourth century χαῖρε or χαίρετε is not used as a form of address to the ordinary dead, but is restricted to the living and occasionally applied to heroized or divinized dead, by analogy with salutation to gods and heroes.[55] The narrator's χαῖρε to the "dead" Achilles in the Plataea elegy belongs to the same heroizing sphere.

Further, Achilles is both times invoked not by name or patronymic, but as son of his sea-goddess mother. In Homeric tradition, significantly, Thetis helped preside at her son's burial and funeral games, which was the locus of his immortalization in cult.[56] Moreover, as Capra and Curti point out, this genealogy emphasizes Achilles' status as *hemitheos*, son of one divine parent, and indeed as representative par excellence of the entire γενεὴ ἡμιθέων (fr. 11.15) who received undying fame from Homer.[57] His representative role for the Greeks at Troy supports the hypothesis that Achilles serves here as paradigm for the collective Greeks at Plataea,[58] rather than for a single figure such as Pausanias, as Lloyd-Jones and Shaw propose, or Leonidas, as argued by Pavese.[59]

Achilles' dead-but-alive status brings to mind a passage in Tyrtaeus (12.31–32 W):

> οὐδέ ποτε κλέος ἐσθλὸν ἀπόλλυται οὐδ' ὄνομ' αὐτοῦ,
>   ἀλλ' ὑπὸ γῆς περ ἐὼν γίγνεται ἀθάνατος

> Never does his noble fame perish nor his name,
>   but even though he is under the earth he becomes deathless.

In a similar vein, Simonides' famous lyric on the dead of Thermopylae counts the ways in which the Three Hundred differ from ordinary dead, including: "Their tomb

---

55. Sourvinou-Inwood 1995: 180–216.

56. *Od.* 24.73–92. See Pavese 1995: 9–10 for further testimonia on Thetis' role; and esp. Nagy 1979: 172, 175 on Achilles' funeral/immortalization.

57. Capra and Curti 1995: 30 also point out that in the *Iliad* only Achilles receives the epithet ὠκύμορος "swift-fated," which is applied to the ἡμιθέων γενεή in Simon. fr. 11.18.

58. Capra and Curti 1995: 30 note that Simonides clearly emphasizes the collective nature of the expedition to Plataea. Thus I concur with Aloni, this volume at n. 48: "Achilles does not serve as the heroic paradigm for a particular warrior; he is the model for all those who are mourned and praised." On Achilles' importance in the elegy see also Fantuzzi, this volume.

59. Lloyd-Jones 1994: 1; Shaw, this volume at nn. 79f.; Pavese 1995: 20–24, followed by Burzacchini 1995: 24–25.

is an altar, instead of laments is remembrance, sorrow for them is praise" (531.3 *PMG*). The Plataea elegy, as Stehle suggests, may recall the promise of "immortality" expressed in Tyrtaeus' elegy, although (as Stehle herself points out) ordinary Spartan war dead did not receive hero cult.[60]

The idea that those who die in battle enjoy a special status becomes familiar in classical Athens as well, as Nicole Loraux and others have demonstrated at length, perhaps influenced by Tyrtaeus' Spartan themes.[61] Indeed, it is often assumed that the Athenians who fell at Marathon began receiving cultic honors right after that battle. If this is the case, hero cult for Greeks who died fighting Persians would predate the battle of Plataea by more than ten years—yet we have no literary or epigraphic evidence for a hero cult at Marathon before an ephebic inscription dating to 122/121 B.C.E. (*IG* II² 1006.26f.; cf. Paus. 1.32.4).[62] Further indication that Athenians treated their war dead as "immortals" comes in a funeral speech allegedly given a few decades after the battle of Plataea: according to Plutarch's source, the late fifth-century biographer Stesimbrotos, Pericles asserted that those who fell in the Samian War (439 B.C.E.) became ἀθάνατοι like the gods, who are not visible but are judged to be immortal ταῖς τιμαῖς ἃς ἔχουσιν καὶ τοῖς ἀγαθοῖς ἃ παρέχουσιν ("because of the honors they possess and the good things they provide").[63]

This strong statement, attributing to the dead not only honor but active dispensation of benefits, may appear to be contradicted by the *Epitaphios* attributed to Demosthenes a century later, where the speaker has been understood to declare that the Athenians who fell against the Persians had not yet reached "heroic rank."[64] But this is not exactly what the text says. The speaker rather declares that the great deeds of early Athenians (e.g., those who fought the Amazons or rescued the Heraklids) have been recorded by poets and historians; in contrast, the equally worthy deeds (ἔργα) of those who fought in the Persian Wars "have not yet been mythologized or raised to heroic [epic?] rank" (οὔπω μεμυθολόγηται οὐδ' εἰς τὴν ἡρωϊκὴν ἐπανῆκται

---

60. Cf. Fuqua 1981: 221–25 and Stehle at nn. 52–57. Of course we should not exaggerate Spartan honors for warriors: as Parker 1989: 146 reminds us, "it was the Athenians and not the Spartans who honoured their war-dead with elaborate public rites." Parker nevertheless concludes (148), "Such heroisation for patriotic service is perhaps something distinctively Spartan, at least in its extent."

61. The Tyrtaeus elegy is quoted by Plato (*Laws* 629a–630b), showing that it was known in Athens by the early fourth century, admittedly long after the Persian Wars. Pritchett 1985: 94–260, esp. 174–75 on Plataea, discusses evidence for the burial of war-dead; see also Stupperich 1977: 62–70, on "Gefallenenbestattung und Heroisierung." Loraux 1986: 55 believes that Tyrtaeus' elegies inspired fifth-century Athenian epitaphs, as well as some themes of funeral orations. Sourvinou-Inwood 1995: 191–94 makes a strong case on semantic grounds (the use of χαίρετε: cf. above at n. 55) for the special status of the Athenian war dead.

62. The latter emphasized by Parker 1996: 137 n. 57. But see Vanderpool 1942: 334–36 on epigraphic evidence for an expansion of the Herakleia at Marathon, perhaps in recognition of the fallen. Shapiro 1991: 645 suggests that heroic honors offered to the fallen at Marathon may be a way to make up for the lack of an aristocratic individual burial.

63. Plut. *Per.* 8.9, citing Stesimbrotos (*FGrH* 107 F 9). This passage is among those discussed by Loraux 1986: 39–41 and Parker 1996: 135–36 in their treatments of the "immortality" of Athenian war dead. Parker notes that the Stesimbrotos passage, "if pressed, shows that the patriotic dead were believed still—note the present tense—to 'confer benefits.'"

64. Flashar 1996: 73. Vandiver 1991: 65 understands the passage correctly.

τάξιν, 60.9). "Heroic status" here applies not to the men but to their deeds: clearly, Ps.-Demosthenes is considering praise in literature rather than treatment in cult.

But the larger question is not so much one of semantics (indeed, whatever honors the collective war dead may have received, no classical author speaks of them as "heroes")[65] as of practices and attitudes. Did the dead receive regular cult, were they considered "immortal" not only in their fame but even in being able to interact with the living—as indicated by Pericles' speech here or by the speech of Thucydides' desperate Plataeans (3.58.4, discussed above at nn. 13 and 28)? The answer to these questions appears to be a qualified "yes."

This brings us back to the double status of Achilles in the Plataea elegy. I have argued that Simonides' invocation of Achilles, together with the second-person narrative of his death, is strikingly different from the typical practice of Homeric epic vis-à-vis a narrative hero. In Homeric epic, Achilles serves precisely as the death-bound—rather than undying—hero par excellence; even in the *Odyssey,* where his shade makes several appearances, there is no reference to his enjoying a special kind of afterlife.[66] In the sphere of religious practice, by contrast, as Shaw richly demonstrates in this volume, Achilles was honored with hero cults in many places: from Sigeion near Troy to sites around the Black Sea to a number of places in mainland Greece, including several in Laconia.[67] Even if these cults originated in the late archaic period as a result of the spread of the Homeric poems (which I think is unlikely), it is all but certain that for the audience of the Plataea elegy Achilles was a powerful figure in cult as well as in song. Simonides' proem draws on both aspects of his heroism.

Is it possible that such a double heroic status applies to the Plataiomachoi as well? With his Muse's help the poet hopes to make their *kleos* undying (fr. 11.28), but what about their immortality in cult? Nothing in our fragments indicates that the poet addressed this issue directly, and it is unlikely that he did. Archaic and classical texts that deal with the heroization of the war dead tend to be very circumspect;[68] Simonides probably treated the ontological status of the Plataiomachoi with typical reticence. It seems unlikely that the poet would venture on his own authority to attribute to contemporaries the kind of immortality enjoyed by the famous heroes of cult. Individuals or groups in this period—and in connection with the Persian conflicts—could indeed be "officially" designated as recipients of hero cult, but probably only when so authorized by a prestigious oracle on the basis of a remarkable sign.[69] Simonides can *suggest* that the Plataiomachoi have become heroes (probably offerings made annually to the fallen can suggest the same thing), but to declare this

65. Boehringer 1996: 50; Welwei 1991: 61, specifically on the Plataiomachoi.
66. See Nagy 1979 and Schein 1984 for detailed analyses of the mortality of the Homeric Achilles. Nagy 1979: 184 and passim analyzes the different kinds of immortality associated with epic and hero cult.
67. See Farnell 1921: 285–89 and references p. 409; on public laments for Achilles, see also Seaford 1994: 139 n. 151. Hommel 1980 revives the argument (contra Farnell) that Achilles was essentially a god; Hooker 1988 provides a counter-argument, whereas West 1993a: 5 writes that in cult, Achilles is sometimes venerated as a "hero," sometimes a "god."
68. Loraux 1986: 38–41 discusses this question with regard to classical Athens, concluding that the Athenian war dead were considered and treated as heroes in the annual public funeral ceremonies.
69. See above at n. 5.

explicitly, on his own authority, would be going too far. As David Boehringer has recently summarized the problem:

> The hesitation of ancient sources in the classical period is not astonishing, if one keeps in mind that there were no models for this heroization. In no case do we hear that the cults were sanctioned by Delphi. It is a matter of newly-introduced practices of the political community. Probably for this reason, fifth- and fourth-century authors did not explicitly understand them as hero-cults. (1996: 50; my translation.)

At the same time, the new Simonides fragments give us a clearer idea of where models could be found when it became appropriate for Greek city-states to honor their war dead more highly than before.

The new Simonides gives us a glimpse of how the heroes of Homeric poetry were used as predecessors of the Greeks who fell at Plataea to help effect the transformation of dead contemporaries into heroes of cult as well as song. This is done in part by adopting heroic poetry's perspective on its own immortalizing power: as the Danaans received undying *kleos* from Homer, so Simonides hopes to confer it upon the Plataiomachoi (fr. 11.15–7, 23–28). But as I have argued, by apostrophizing the son of Thetis, the poet is suggesting even more: Simonides evokes Achilles' immortal nature as a figure of cult, in addition to the mortality that so strongly characterizes him in the *Iliad*. Moreover, I believe that the elegy develops the resemblance between Danaans and Plataiomachoi beyond the sphere of *kleos*, by providing a broad basis on which men of the present day can be compared to the *hemitheoi* of the past. It remains to show how the analogies are developed.

Points of Comparison

It would be natural to assume that the comparison between the heroes of Troy and Plataea rests upon the fact that both battles were panhellenic efforts against a barbarian, Asiatic force.[70] The elegy does mention Greeks from a number of cities, which could reflect the panhellenic nature of the expedition to Troy. The "Greek vs. barbarian" theme, however, is almost as subdued in the elegy's extant fragments as it is in the *Iliad*, although Simonides may imply some sense of a Greek "cause" at Plataea. For example, if West's *exempli gratia* restoration of fr. 11.25–26

> ἀνδρῶ]ν, οἳ Σπάρτ[ηι τε καὶ Ἑλλάδι δούλιον ἦμ]αρ
> ἔσχον] ἀμυνόμ[ενοι μή τιν' ἰδεῖν φανερ]ῶ[ς

is correct, Simonides' Plataea narrative begins with the Spartans leaving their city to "ward off the day of slavery from Sparta and Greece."[71] A second possible "Greek vs.

---

70. E.g., Bearzot 1997: 76. Castriota 1992 shows that later fifth-century monuments posit this resemblance; conversely, Kierdorf 1966: 15 suggests that experiences of the Persian War (burning of temples) serve as a paradigm for the herald's report of the destruction of Troy in Aeschylus, *Agamemnon* 527 (cf. *Persae* 811).

71. Parsons 1992a: 34 suggests restoring fr. 11.25 as either οἳ Σπάρτ[ης ὥρμησαν καρτερὸν ἄλκ]αρ or οἳ Σπάρτ[ηι - - - δούλιον ἦμαρ. The phrase δούλιον ἦμαρ is of course Homeric. In the *Iliad*, however, it is used of the "day of slavery" that *Trojans* will face if they lose the war (6.463); if Simonides used the same phrase

Persian" reference appears in fr. 13.8–10, where the "sons of Doros and Herakles"[72] are drawn up against "Medes and Persians." Even these readings, though, would convey a far more subdued sense of Hellenic identity than is found in the "Greek vs. barbarian" dichotomy that developed a few decades later, particularly in Athenian tragedy.[73]

What the elegy does focus on repeatedly are close relations between mortals and immortals, a feature shared by both groups of Greeks. Achilles appears in connection with his divine mother Thetis and her father Nereus, probably with Apollo as his honorific killer as well. The destruction of Troy may be aided by Hera and Athena,[74] and more probably involves the chariot of Justice:

> Παλλὰς δ' ἐγγὺ]ς ἐοῦσα πε[ρικλεὲς ἄ]στ[υ καθεῖλεν,
> σὺν δ' ῞Ηρη, Πρ]ιάμου παισὶ χ[αλεπτ]όμ[εναι
> εἵνεκ' Ἀλεξά]νδροιο κακόφρ[ονο]ς, ὡς τὸν [ἀλιτρόν
> ἀλλὰ χρόνω]ι θείης ἅρμα καθεῖλε Δίκ[ης.

(fr. 11.9–12)

For the Plataiomachoi our meager fragments attest a remarkable number of gods and cult heroes.[75] Several local heroes of the Trojan War era, "wide-ruling Menelaus" and the "horse-taming sons of Zeus, the Tyndarid heroes," apparently accompany the army departing from Sparta (fr. 11.30–31):[76]

> οἳ μὲν ἄρ' Εὐ]ρώταν κα[ὶ Σπάρτη]ς ἄστυ λιπόντ[ες
> ὥρμησαν] Ζηνὸς παισὶ σὺν ἱπποδάμοις
> Τυνδαρίδα]ις ἥρωσι καὶ εὐρυβίηι Μενελάω[ι

(fr. 11.29–31)

In addition, Simonides' brief account of the march to Plataea (fr. 11.36–41) is characterized by the names of local heroes as well: Pelops, Nisos (of Megara), Pandion (of Athens). Demeter would inevitably be linked with the ἐ]ρατὸν πεδίον of fr. 11.40 if, as is likely, this plain refers to Eleusis, and her name is clearly attested in fr. 17.1.[77] The Greeks at Plataea, like those at Troy, apparently enjoy Olympian support as well. As West proposes, it must be Zeus who is "nodding" approval, while (much less certainly) another god "will drive" the enemy out of Asia (. . . ἐξ Ἀ]σίη]ς ἐλάσει νεύσαντο[ς . . ., fr. 14.7).[78] Fragments 15–16 mention the Corinthians' hero Glaukos

---

here, he changed its application to the Greek side. (The formula is also attested in *Od.* 14.340 and 17.323, but without referring to slavery as a result of large-scale war.) The same phrase is attested on Persian War monuments, including Simonides XXa *FGE*, *CEG* 2, *IG* I³ 503, 26 ML; see Raaflaub 1985: 29–30, 32–33.

72. This phrase, however, may indicate not all the Plataiomachoi but only Spartans and some other Peloponnesians; see Boedeker 1995b: 224–25.

73. See Hall 1989 and, more generally, Georges 1994.

74. If West's *exempli gratia* restoration of fr. 11.9–10 is correct "[Pallas Athena] being [near seized the famous cita]del, [together with Hera, ang]ry with the sons of [Pr]iam": cf. West 1993a: 6.

75. As mentioned by West 1993a: 7.

76. On the importance of Menelaus and the Dioscuri at Sparta, see Parker 1989: 147–48, 152–53. Lloyd-Jones 1994: 3 cites an oracle that similarly pairs Spartan Menelaus and the Dioscuri.

77. For Demeter in the Plataea tradition, see Boedeker, this volume, "Historiography," at nn. 37–38.

78. West 1993a: 8 suggests Ares as the subject of ἐλάσει.

and their great deity Helios, evoked as witness of their bravery. The Greeks at Plataea, then, set out in the company of Trojan-era heroes; Zeus and Helios (and perhaps other gods) attend to their deeds. Such associations strongly reinforce the Plataio-machoi's resemblance to those who fought at Troy.

Isocrates, as we have seen, proposes that the gods themselves were concerned to immortalize the valor and fame of those who fought the Persians, just as they did for their own sons who had fought at Troy (*Panegyrikos* 84).[79] Like Ps.-Demosthenes, however, Isocrates does not speak of cult for the Greeks who fell in the Persian Wars. Nevertheless, the hero-like cult status of some fifth-century war dead is attested in fifth-century sources (Thucydides for the Plataiomachoi and, indirectly, Stesimbrotos for Athenian war dead a generation later), and finds possible archaeo-logical support as well.[80]

In the Plataea poem, I have argued that Achilles is presented as doubly immor-tal—on the one hand, he like all the Danaans has undying *kleos*, thanks to the wise poet and the Muses; on the other, Achilles can still be invoked as a living presence even while his death is narrated. For the Danaans' counterparts at Plataea the poet hopes to offer undying *kleos* as well; he attributes to them divine, even Olympian, patrons, and describes them marching out in company with immortalized heroes of old. The Plataea elegy thus deftly sets up relationships between the two groups of Greek war-riors that help us understand how, in the early fifth century, contemporaries fallen in battle might be perceived as worthy of both song and cult, even immediately after their death. Without explicitly calling them "heroes," Simonides' tentative but highly suggestive analogies open up the possibility that the immortality enjoyed by Achilles and the other *hemitheoi* at Troy may apply as well to their successors in his own day—those buried in the glorious tombs at Plataea.

79. Divine favor is an aspect of heroization about which recent discussions have had rather little to say, and which probably does not apply to all instances. Cf. the sensible reconstruction of Parker 1996: 136–37 of the process in which Athenian war dead were heroized.
80. See above at nn. 18–20.

9

P.-J. SHAW

Lords of Hellas, Old Men of the Sea

The Occasion of Simonides' Elegy on Plataea

When the Oxyrhynchus fragments of Simonides' elegy on the battle of Plataea were published in 1992, they evoked a rich response in scholarly debate, and by no means the least of the questions posed by the poem was that of the occasion of its performance. Several suggestions have been put forward, but none is so conclusive as to have gained unanimous acceptance, and the debate continues. The proem to the elegy contains an invocation to the son of the sea-nymph, almost certainly to be identified as Achilles.[1] Boedeker shows that in this context Achilles is treated not only as the epic hero who is mortal, but also as the semi-divine recipient of *cult*, addressed as though alive.[2] Ewen Bowie has argued that the genre of narrative elegy, of which this poem is an example, was appropriate for performance at a public occasion. If the choice of Achilles as subject of the invocation were understood, that occasion might become obvious; conversely, if it were known for *what* occasion the elegy was composed, it might be possible to explain Achilles' presence in the proem; but as yet neither has been clearly established.[3] West suggested that the elegy may have been performed at

An earlier version of this paper was read at the Annual Meeting of Graduate Students in Ancient History at St. Hilda's College, Oxford, on March 21, 1998. On that occasion, valuable questions were asked, and comments made, by Robert Parker, Christy Constantakopoulou, and Louis Rawlings. I am especially grateful to Professor Parker for allowing me to attend the mini-conference at New College, Oxford in November 1997, in the course of which I gained much from conversations with Ewen Bowie, and with Ian Rutherford who later, and most generously, brought this paper to the attention of the editors. I am also very grateful to Deborah Boedeker for her tactful and judicious suggestions, and to the anonymous readers for Oxford University Press who gave valuable advice. I am indebted to Nick Fisher for countless cheerful and constructive criticisms. For the flaws that remain in the paper I take sole responsibility. What I owe my husband, Dr. Stephen Shaw, for his patience, sagacity, and unwavering support, I cannot begin to calculate.

1. Parsons 1992a: 4–50.
2. Boedeker 1995b: 224 and this volume, "Heroization," at nn. 50–55; see also this volume, Obbink at n. 24 and Clay. Callinus fr. 1.19 W promises that the brave warrior will, if he survives, become ἄξιος ἡμιθέων.
3. Bowie 1986: 13–35, esp. 27–34 for the performance of elegy at panhellenic public occasions; Boedeker, this volume, "Heroization," at nn. 49–59. Schachter 1998: 25 includes the choice of Achilles as one of four features that must be understood before a plausible context for the poem can be established. I am grateful to Deborah Boedeker for drawing my attention to Schachter's article.

some festival of Achilles, but the evidence for such occasions is scarce;[4] certainly, before 1992 no one would have connected Achilles specifically with the battle of Plataea or with the Plataiomachoi, and his presence here, particularly as a *cultic* figure, has taken scholars by surprise. It is likely that Simonides, in composing the poem, whether for contest or commission, had powerful people to consider, one or more of whom may be mentioned in it; and it is not unreasonable to suppose that it was they, or one of them, for whom Achilles was especially significant, perhaps as a cultic hero, and who therefore may have influenced Simonides' choice.[5] Thus Achilles' presence in the proem may be explained as much by virtue of his cultic as of his epic identity, and this cultic identity may point to an occasion for the performance and, perhaps, to influences that were brought to bear on its composition.

Although Simonides assimilates the victory of Plataea to that of Troy, the latter victory was gained under the leadership of Agamemnon, not Achilles. Furthermore, Plataea was a panhellenic victory whereas, as Thucydides remarks, the term *Hellene* itself was scarcely used by Homer. However, Thucydides goes on to identify the first Hellenes as, simply, "the followers of Achilles," one of three elements in his Homeric contingent, of which the others were Achaeans and Myrmidons.[6] Put like this, it becomes understandable that, in an account of Panhellenic victory, the Hellenes should honor and invoke him. In this essay, it is Achilles' role as leader of the Hellenes, as well as his cultic identity, that I use as a key to the occasion for Simonides' elegy. I consider first the (attested) cults and toponyms of Achilles, and I then compare this distribution with the line-up of personalities present in what has survived of the elegy to try to discern what relationship, if any, exists between them. In the course of this analysis, I note that cults of a major deity of the Hellenes, one peculiarly associated with their origins, have a high profile in this pattern; I also note that a little-known network connected with this same Hellenic deity is thrown into interesting relief. I propose, on the strength of these observations, a panhellenic occasion for the performance of the Plataea elegy, and I conclude by suggesting who may be responsible for Achilles' presence in the proem, and why.

The distribution, through the Greek world, of cults of Achilles and of toponyms derived from his rare name, could not be described as random (Map 1). Cults are manifest, albeit sparsely, through early written reference and archaeology, though since most of the rituals and toponyms west of the Euxine Sea are attested in late sources such as Pausanias (hereafter referred to as "the Periegete"), their antiquity is

---

4. West 1993a: 5. Cults of Achilles have been discussed by Farnell 1921: 286–87; Hommel 1980; Hooker 1988: 1–7; Dowden 1989: ch. 3; Hedreen 1991. These studies pre-date the publication of the Plataea fragment. Lloyd-Jones 1994: 1 has insisted that, in this context, the poet specifically relates Achilles to the Plataiomachoi.

5. Aloni, this volume at nn. 69–73, argues for the importance of Pausanias to the poem.

6. Thuc. 1.3.2–3; *Il.* 2.681–85; cf. Strabo C370. This usage may have been obscured by the convention whereby the word Ἕλληνες can be translated as either "Hellenes" or "Greeks," terms which then become interchangeable. Arist. *Meteor.* 352–52b; Apollod. 1.7.3; *Marm. Par. FGrH* 239 A6; Polyhist. *FGrH* 273 F106; Dion. Hal. 4.25.3. Cf. Isoc. *Panegyr.* 50. Homer (*Il.* 2.527) uses Πανέλληνας at the Locrian entry. Rutherford, this volume at n. 25, argues that Achilles' war was panhellenic; Aloni, this volume at n. 37, adduces Simonides' reference to Homer as indicative of the panhellenic nature of the Plataea poem. Recent discussions: Hall 1997: 46; Fowler 1998: 10.

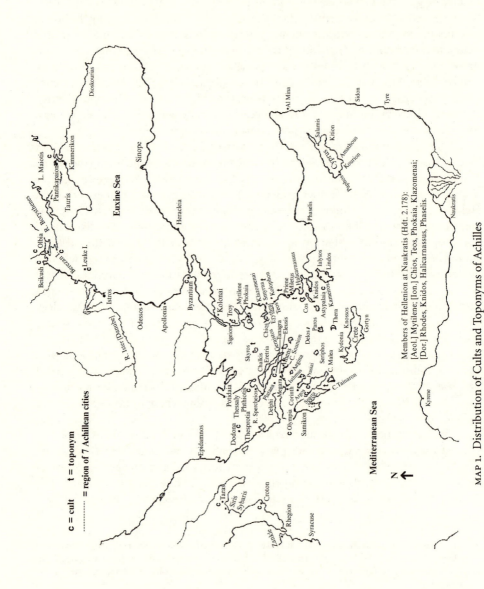

MAP 1. Distribution of Cults and Toponyms of Achilles
(Derived from the work of K. Dowden, 1989.)

c = cult   t = toponym

- - - - - = region of 7 Achillean cities

Members of Hellenion at Naukratis (Hdt. 2.178):
[Aeol.] Mytilene; [Ion.] Chios, Teos, Phokaia, Klazomenai;
[Dor.] Rhodes, Knidos, Halicarnassus, Phaselis.

hard to establish. Achilles' Homeric contingent has an east Thessalian character, but the evidence there for cult is sparse: Hellenistic coins, and a late account from Philostratus of a Thessalian sacrifice and annual pilgrimage to Achilles' tomb, which stood in Mytilenian territory near Sigeion on the Hellespont.[7] Mytilene was the sole Aeolian member of a Hellenic organization that existed in Herodotus' day—the Helleneion at Naukratis (Map 1).[8] In the *Odyssey*, Agamemnon describes Achilles' funeral at Sigeion, an image that may also be found in *POxy* 3876, which Garner would attribute to Stesichorus. Philostratus' hymn distinguishes Achilles' mortal remains, which lay at Troy, from the divine element he received from his mother, which was held by Pontos—that is, the Euxine Sea.[9]

Achilles was thus a cultic hero on the Hellespont, the site of his tomb, but the "eye" of his cult was located on the north shore of the Euxine; an epithet applied to him there in the Hellenistic era was Ποντάρχης.[10] Herodotus includes the region as part of Scythia, and Alcaeus calls Achilles the lord of Scythia ('Αχίλλευς ὁ τὰς Σκυθίκας μέδεις); the Royal Scythians inhabited part of the district and, unlike other Scythians, worshipped Poseidon.[11] There is evidence, from the late sixth century onward, for cult of Achilles centered on the Milesian colony of Olbia, and for *divine* cult there from the first century c.e.; Herodotus refers to the *dromos* of Achilles, possibly the spit of land south-east of Olbia near the river Borysthenes, and games were held in his honor perhaps as early as the fourth century b.c.e.[12] Other evidence is

7. British Museum Catalogue *Thessaly*: pl. VII.1 (cf. p. 6) for coins of Larissa Kremaste; Philostr. *Her.* 53.8–18. Sigeion: Hdt. 5.94; Arrian *Anab.* 1.12. Strabo (C596) says that Ilians sacrifice to Achilles, Antilochus, Patroclus, and Aias, but not to Herakles. Libations offered at Ilion: Hdt. 7.43. On the friendly relations existing between Thessalians and Peisistratids: Hdt. 5.62. Hegesistratos' nickname *Thessalos*: Thuc 1.20; Arist. *Ath. pol.* 17.3–4. According to Plato (*Hipp.* 228B–C), performance of Homeric epic at the Panathenaia was instituted by the Peisistratid Hipparchus.

8. Naukratis Hellenion: Hdt. 2.178; Hall 1997: 49–50. Pausanias (3.3.8) states that Achilles' spear was dedicated in the sanctuary of Athene at Phaselis, another member of the Hellenion.

9. *Od.* 24.35–94; *POxy* 3876 frr. 61–62, 64–65, 67; Garner 1993: 154–55. Anderson 1986: 241ff. and n. 109 sees in Philostratus' account of funeral rites for Achilles (*Her.* 187, 207f.) a possible compound between those of Theseus and those of his native Lemnos. Achilles was patron hero of Caracalla, who performed funeral rites for him at his tomb (Dio Cass. 78.16.7); these included the hoplitodromos, which was also run at Plataea (Philostr. *Gymn.* 7f.); Anderson 1986: 249. Cf. n. 52 below. Nagy 1979: 338–47 discusses Achilles and *pontos*. Pindar (*Isth.* 8.34, also *Nem.* 3.35) calls Thetis ποντίαν θεόν (cf. n. 53 for Ποσειδῶν Πόντιος). Rumpel 1883: 386; Slatkin 1991: 70–77.

10. Diehl 1954: 1–18 on Achilles as Ποντάρχης; *CIG* 2.2080; Dzikowski 1939: 84ff. Nagy 1979: 120 argues that Achilles was a cultic hero not of Delphi but of the Hellespont; see also Garner 1993: 162–63. No cult of Achilles is attested at Delphi, only that of Neoptolemos, itself instituted because it was necessary to honor an Aiakid there (Pind. *Nem.* 7.44), which implies that Achilles was *not* honored there in the same way. Schachter 1998: 26, 28 makes similar observations.

11. Alcaeus fr. 354 (Z.31) = Page 1968: 89, no. 166; Rohde 1925: ch. 4 n. 3; Dzikowski 1939: 91. On Royal Scythian worship of Poseidon: Hdt. 4.59. See Hedreen 1991: 324 for the Scythian distribution of Achilles' cult. Antonaccio 1995: 145.

12. *Dromos* of Achilles: Hdt. 4.55, 76; Plin. *HN* 4.95. Grove of Achilles: Strabo C307; Dio Chrys. 36.9.14, 14.5. Borysthenites called themselves 'Ολβιοπολῖτες (Hdt. 4.18). Games at Olbia: *SIG* 3.730; Rohde 1925: 66, ch. 14.2 nn. 99, 102. Hedreen 1991: n. 5 surveys Euxine sites. Dowden 1989: 54–60, 213–15 deals with cults and toponyms.

scattered from the eastern end of the Black Sea, at Milesian Pantikapaion,[13] to the western, opposite the Ister delta where an island commonly identified as Leuke, the "White Island," has yielded dedications, the earliest from the late sixth century. These include a fifth-century inscription on an Attic lekythos: Γλαῦκός με ἀνέθηκεν Ἀχιλλῆι Λευκῆ μεδέοντι παί{ε}ς Ποσιδήο ("Glaukos son of Posideios dedicated me to Achilles lord of Leuke"), as well as dedications from mariners.[14] A fourth-century inscription assures the Hellenes that the inhabitants are looking after the island—which implies that the place had Hellenic significance.[15] Herodotus states that the Borysthenites came from Miletus, which he says was founded by the Aeolian Neleids; to Neleus was also attributed the establishment of the Milesian cult of Poseidon. No cult of Achilles is attested at Miletus itself, and the city suffered years of *stasis* before the ejections of Aristagoras and Histiaeus and the Persian destruction, so the cults and the Milesian colonies on the Euxine may belong to a refugee population.[16]

When Histiaeus was expelled, he fled first to Mytilene, and thence to Byzantium, whose founder set up an altar and bath of Achilles; a late source names the founder "Byzas," but Justin transmits Pompeius Trogus' statement that the city was founded by Pausanias, victor of Plataea.[17] At the Kodrid city of Erythrai, Achilles was included in a cult of Thetis, though the evidence for this is post-fifth century; and on the island of Astypalaia he was honored (says Cicero) as a god.[18] At Tanagra, there was a shrine of Achilles, according to Plutarch, who also says that the Epirotes claimed Aiakid ancestry and worshipped Achilles—often called Aiakid by Homer; there was also a cult of Zeus "Hellanios" near Dodona.[19] The chief Aiakid stronghold was Aegina, whose population, before it was settled by Dorian Argives from Epidauros, worshipped Zeus Panhellenios, and were once called Myrmidons.[20]

---

13. Pantikapaion and Achilleion: Strabo C493–94.

14. *SEG* 30.869. Sailors recounted seeing Achilles, as did Leonymos of Croton: Paus. 3.19.11–13; Arr. *Peripl. M. Eux.* 23, 32ff.; Philostr. *Her.* 55.2–3, 56.2–4, 6–9; Konon *FGrH* 26 F1.xviii ap. Phot. 186 s.v. Αὐτολέων ἢ Στησίχορος; Amm. Marc. 22.8.41. In the *Aethiopis*, Thetis (on Leuke) mourns Achilles as he is mourned in Simonides' elegy (Proc. *Chrest.* 20). Cf. Pind. *Nem.* 4.49–50, for Timasarchos of Aegina at Adresteia in Sikyon: ἐν δ' Εὐξείνῳ πελάγει φαεννὰν Ἀχιλεύς νᾶσον· and *Ol.* 2.78–80, at Akragas, for Theron: Ἀχιλλέα τ' ἔνεικ', ἐπεὶ Ζηνὸς ἦτορ ǀ λιταῖς ἔπεισε, μάτηρ; also Eur. *IT* 434f.; Rohde 1925: 64–65; Edwards 1985: 221.

15. Latyschev 1916²: no. 325.

16. Milesian Borysthenes: Hdt. 4.78. Miletus and *Neileus*: Hdt. 9.97; Ephoros *FGrH* 70 F183 ap. Ath. 523E. Miletus and *Neleus*: Arist. fr. 556 (Rose); Polyb. 16.12.2 (that N. *re*-founded Miletus). Parian reordering, and Athenian settlement, of Miletus: Hdt. 5.29 and 97. Aristagoras: Hdt. 5.30–38, 49–51, 97; Histiaeus: Hdt. 6.1ff.

17. Hdt. 6.5. Byzantium: Hesych. *FGrH* 390 F1.16; Iust. *Epit. Hist. Philipp. Pomp. Trog.* 9.1.3: "haec [sc. Byzantium] namque urbs condita primo a Pausania, rege Spartanorum, et per septem annos possessa fuit." Cf. n. 46 below.

18. Erythrai: *SIG* 3.1014; founded by the Kodrid Neleus, Hellan. *FGrH* 323a F11 ap. Harpokr. s.v. Ἐρυθραῖοι. Graf 1985: 351 discusses Erythrai, and its cults of Enyalios and Hecate, both of whom are connected with Achilles in Roman Sparta; cf. n. 32 below. Astypalaia: Cic. *De natura deorum* 3.45 and *CIG Ins. Mar. Aeg.* 3.182. In myth, Phoenix's daughter Astypalaia bore the Argonaut Ankaios to Poseidon: Ap. Rhod. *Arg.* 1.188, 2.865–67 and Schol. 2.866.

19. Tanagra: Plut. *Mor.* 299C–300A; Rhianos *POxy* 2463. On the probable shrine of Achilles outside the Delion Gate: Roller 1974: 155. Plut. *Pyrrh.* 1.2: Ἀχιλλεὺς ἐν Ἠπείρῳ τιμὰς ἰσοθέους ἔσχεν, and 26.6 for Pyrrhus as an Aiakid.

20. Myrmidons: Pind. *Nem.* 3.13 and Schol; Strabo C375; Ap. Rhod. *Arg.* 4.1766–72. Panhellenic Zeus: Paus. 2.29.6–30.3. Epidaurian settlers: Paus. 2.29.5.

At the Isthmian sanctuary of Poseidon, the Periegete describes an altar to the Sea, and to the Nereids, daughters of the Old Man of the Sea, one of whom was Thetis; he claims to have seen several similar altars on his travels through Hellas and, near the shores, precincts dedicated to the Nereids, where Achilles was also honored.[21] He mentions a shrine and festival of Achilles on the east Peloponnesian coast at Prasiai, or Brasiai, where Ino first came ashore, and the name "Prasiai" is probably derived from Prax, Neoptolemus' descendant, who made a shrine for Achilles beside the Eurotas on the route north from Sparta. Ephebes in Roman Sparta sacrificed to Achilles before fighting the mock battle on the Platanista island, although Prax's shrine itself was, by then, permanently closed.[22] The statement of the scholiast to Apollonius of Rhodes, that Laconian perioikoi honored Achilles ὡς θεόν, could be a reference to these rituals. A propos of this perioikic cult, the Astypalaian example, and the divine cult at Olbia, it may be significant that Achilles' position in the proem to the Plataea elegy is one usually occupied by a divinity, as West has observed.[23] The Periegete provides the sole record of a lament by women at a μνῆμα of Achilles at Olympia; a similar lament was performed at Croton, an Achaean colony; and at Taras, Aristotle records a cult of the Aiakidai and a temple of Achilles, at a place once named "Sigeion" by its Trojan population![24]

Achillean toponyms occur at Priene, which was founded by the Neileid Aipytos, and at the once-Aeolian Smyrna. A spring at Miletus was called Achilleion,[25] and harbors were named Achilleion on Skyros, scene of Achilles' cross-dressing draft-dodging, and at the Achaean Helots' stronghold, Cape Tainaron, site of an asylum sanctuary of Poseidon.[26] Tainaron, haunt of the Minyan Euphemos, is joined to the

---

21. Paus. 2.1.8; cf. nn. 27 and 28 below.

22. Prasiai (Brasiai): Paus. 3.24.5; Philochoros *FGrH* 328 F204. The Heraklids received divine honors only at Attic Prasiai. Prax's shrine: Paus. 3.20.8. An unidentified Archaic sanctuary was uncovered in about the right place, early last century: Dickins 1906–7: 169–73; Antonaccio 1995: 183. Brasidas, whose name surely shares a root with Brasiai, was assimilated to Achilles by Plato (*Symp.* 221C). *Platanista* mock-battle: Paus. 3.14.8–10. The cult of Thetis was allegedly introduced to Sparta by a Messenian woman named Kleo: Paus. 3.14.4.

23. Schol. Ap. Rhod. *Arg.* 4.814 (Merkel); cf. *PMG* 558. West 1993a: 5. Cf. nn. 12 and 18 above.

24. Olympia: Paus. 6.23.3; Nagy 1979: 114. Croton: Schol. Lyk. *Alex.* 857: ἡ Θέτις ἀνέθηκε κῆπον τῇ Ἥρα ἐν Κρότωνι—'Οπλοσμία δὲ Ἥρα—ἔνθα καὶ αἱ γυναῖκες πενθοῦσι τὸν Ἀχιλλέα, πενθικὰ ἱμάτια φοροῦσαι.; Strabo C262; Diod. Sic. 8.17. Taras: Arist. *Mir.* 840a106ff.: ἔστι δὲ καὶ Ἀχιλλέως νεὼς παρ' αὐτοῖς, and ὑπὸ τῶν Τρώων τῶν κατασχόντων αὐτὴν Σίγειον ὠνομάσθαι. On the relationship between hero cult and public laments, see Seaford 1994: 139–41.

25. Priene: Xen. *Hell.* 3.2.17, 4.8.17; Strabo C633, C636. Priene controlled the Panionion, and sanctuary of Heliconian Poseidon: Hdt. 1.148. (cf. *Il.* 2.575, 8.203, 20.404); Paus. 7.24.4–5. Smyrna: Steph. Byz. *Ethn.* s.v. *Achilleion*; Hdt. 1.149. See also Paus. 9.29.4 on Smyrna. According to Mimnermus, Smyrna was taken from the Aeolians by Milesian Kolophon: Αἴπυ < > τε Πύλον Νηλήϊον ἄστυ λιπόντες | ἱμερτὴν Ἀσίην νηυσὶν ἀφικόμεθα, | ἐς δ' ἐρατὴν Κολοφῶνα βίην ὑπέροπλον ἔχοντες | ἑζόμεθ' ἀργαλέης ὕβριος ἡγεμόνες· | κεῖθεν †διαστήεντος ἀπορνύμενοι ποταμοῖο | θεῶν βουλῇ, Σμύρνην εἵλομεν Αἰολίδα. Mimn. fr. 9 W ap. Strabo C634; Anth. Lyr. Graec. 1.i.50–57. Miletus: Aristoboulos *FGrH* 139 F6 ap. Ath. 243D; Hedreen 1991: 323; Hall 1997: 51–52.

26. Achilles' sojourn on Skyros: *Kypria* ap. Proc. *Chrest.* 1. His coming to harbor there: Lesch. Mit. *Il. Mikr.* 5 ap. Eust. ΣΒ *T.* 326: ἔστι δὲ ἐν τῇ Εὐβοίᾳ νῆσος λιμένας ἔχουσα Ἀχίλλειον καὶ Κρήσιον. He appears as a ghost to Neoptolemus: *Il. Mikr.* 1. Crawley 1893: 243–45. Tainaron: Paus. 3.25.4–6. Hades could be reached from Tainaron. *Ostraka* of the later fifth and early fourth centuries B.C.E. found at Olbia attest to the importance of Ἑρμῆς Ψυχοπομπός there. Cf. Diod. Sic. 1.96, Plut. *Mor.* 758B; Lebedev 1996: 269–72.

Mani peninsula by an isthmus; from there, up the west coast of the peninsula and round the Messenian gulf, were strung the seven cities with which Agamemnon hoped to lure Achilles back into the fray.[27] Agamemnon encourages Achilles by pointing out that the cities are πᾶσαι δ' ἐγγὺς ἁλός ("all near the sea"), and that the men who live in them σε δωτίνῃσι θεὸν ὡς τιμήσουσι ("shall honor you with gifts as though you were a god"). At one of them, the still-beautiful Kardamyli, the Periegete records a precinct of the Nereids beside the sea—perhaps of the kind where Achilles was also honored, in the manner he described while at the Isthmus of Corinth.[28]

Though motley, this collection displays some marked characteristics. First, Achilles has a strong affinity with water: the shore, islands, straits, isthmuses, springs, harbors, sailors, his epithet Ποντάρχης, deities of the sea. Second, Poseidon, the sea deity par excellence, was also the great god of the Aeolians—and the distribution of Achillean cult is predominantly Aeolian. Third, by contrast, there are no indications of Achilles as a cultic hero in the traditional Aiakid territories of Aegina, Salamis, Attica; however, Pindar rarely passes up the opportunity to mention Achilles in epinicia for Aiginetans. Fourth, most of the Achillean cult sites and toponyms are associated with people regarded, from Herodotus' time onward, as marginalized: ex-Milesians; Achaean colonists at Croton; the ejected Partheniai of Taras; Achaean Helots; Neleids, driven from the Peloponnese; at Olympia, perhaps Triphylian Minyai, whose cities were destroyed in Herodotus' lifetime;[29] Laconian perioikoi, possibly Minyai again, at Prasiai, and whoever had worshipped at Prax's shrine.

How does this distribution resonate with the population of Simonides' elegy and the Plataiomachoi of Herodotus' version? On the face of it, hardly at all. Achilles is a cult-hero mainly for, first, those who did not fight in the battle, such as Milesians and Erythraeans, Eleans who turned up too late, and most of the Achaeans; second, those whose names were omitted from the Serpent Column at Delphi and the Plataean Zeus at Olympia, such as the few Achaeans who were part of the force, that is, the two hundred Paleans and the men from the Achaean colony of Croton;[30] and third, Thessalians and some Scythians (Amyrgian), who were, at least in the Herodotean account, the enemy.[31] But of the others, the following may be said.

27. Pind. *Pyth.* 4.43–45, 174–75, and 4.176 for Neleus' son Periklymenos from Pylos. The seven cities : Καρδαμύλην Ἐνόπην τε καὶ Ἱρὴν ποιήεσσαν | Φηράς τε ζαθέας ἠδ' Ἄνθειαν βαθύλειμον | καλήν τ' Αἴπειαν καὶ Πήδασον ἀμπελόεσσαν· | πᾶσαι δ'ἐγγὺς ἁλός, νέαται Πύλου ἠμαθόεντος· (*Il.* 9.150–53 and 9.292–95). See Seaford 1994: 196.

28. Kardamyli and Enope: Paus. 3.26.7–8. Line 3 of fr. 10 W² of the elegy includes the letters].θωνη.., for which West suggested Μηθώνη (W²: 118 10 n. 3). Could this be Μοθώνη, once named Πήδασος, one of the "seven cities," which the Lacedaemonians awarded to Naupliote refugees? Paus. 4.24.4, 35.1–2; Strabo (C359) uses the form Μηθώνη. See Rutherford, this volume, at n. 47.

29. Hdt. 4.149 on Triphylian Minyai.

30. Inscription on column: *SIG* 31+ = Tod 1933: vol. I, 19 = ML 27(19). Paleans: Hdt. 9.28, 31. Croton: Hdt. 8.47; Seriphos (Hdt. 8.46, 48) was also omitted. Zeus dedicated at Olympia after Plataea: Paus. 5.23.1–2.

31. Locrians fought for Mardonios at Plataea (Hdt. 9.31). Diodorus (11.3.2) includes Perrhaebians, Magnetans, Achaeans of Phthia, Locrians, and Thessalians amongst Hellenes ranged beside Persians at the outset of Xerxes' campaign. Simonides had friends at Pharsalos and Crannon (Cic. *De or.* 2.86.352–53; Quintil. 11.2.11–16); he composed for Thessalians (Theocr. 16.34–47); he also composed for Anaxilas of Rhegion, whose origins were Messenian (Thuc. 6.4–5; cf. Hdt. 6.23, 7.164). Garner 1993: 163 argues for a Locrian link with Achilles. Could the political map have altered radically between Simonides' time and that

Pandion: Eleusinian Demeter is crucial in the campaigns of Salamis, Plataea, and Mykale. It was the Aeolian Eumolpos, son of Poseidon, who was responsible for the introduction of the mysteries from Thrace, not Pandion, but the Periegete alludes to the tradition that Pandion's son Lykos brought "the initiations of the great goddesses to higher eminence" among the Messenians, and that, like Neleus, he came as a fugitive to one of the "seven cities"—Arene.[32]

Nisos: Megara is more promising, for it colonized Byzantium, but Nisos himself, Pandion's son, did not remain at Megara; his affinity lies with Athens where he was buried. Before Plataea, Megarian and Athenian envoys had gone to Sparta together to persuade the Ephors to dispatch a force; and three hundred Athenians went to the relief of the hard-pressed Megarians during the battle. However, an advance guard of Lacedaemonians was attacked at Megara by Mardonios.[33] Megara *did* boast the tomb of Iphigeneia, worshipped by the Taurian Scythians.[34]

Ephyra was named for a daughter of Ocean, and this toponym occurs in Epirus, in Thessaly, as a κώμη near the river Sellëeis in northern Elis, and another, also on a R. Sellëeis, west of Corinth. Simonides draws a distinction between the men of Ephyra, on the one hand, and Corinth, which he styles the capital of *Glaukos*, on the other. This is interesting, because the Homeric Glaukos, son of Aeolid Sisyphus, hailed not from Corinth but from Ephyra, as his great-grandson the Lycian Glaukos relates when he identifies himself to Diomedes. Corinth itself is assigned by Homer to Agamemnon, and by Hesiod to Aias. The Corinthians claimed that the Isthmian Games were instituted by Sisyphus for the drowned Melikertes, son of the seagoddess Leukothea or Ino.[35] At Potniai, Glaukos kept mares that devoured him,

---

of Herodotus? Members of both Lacedaemonian royal houses were involved in intrigue with Thessalians: Pausanias' half-uncle Kleomenes just before Marathon, and Leotykhidas not long after Mykale (Hdt. 6.74, 72). Cf. Rutherford, this volume, at n. 29, where he refers to Bearzot's argument for a Thessalian slant to the elegy.

32. Hdt. 8.65; 9.64; 9.101. Entrance to Ploutos at Eleusis: Paus. 1.38.5. The *Homeric Hymn to Demeter* 25, 52–59 concerns Pandion, rather than Athens, and sets Hecate at Eleusis; she was worshipped in Neleid Ionian cities, including Erythrai, and Kolophon, where nocturnal sacrifice was offered to her of a black bitch puppy; the Periegete includes this in his account of the only other nocturnal puppy sacrifice known to him, made to Enyalios by the boys of Roman Sparta who are to fight the mock-battle on Platanista, before which they sacrifice to Achilles. Paus. 3.14.8–10, 3.20.8; Plut. *Mor.* 277B, 280C, 290D. Graf 1985: 257–59. Cf. n. 22 above. In the Hesiodic Catalog 71 (also Paus. 1.43.1) Iphigeneia becomes Hecate through the agency of Artemis. As Rutherford, this volume at n. 70, observes, Hecate prophesies for the Abderites (Pind. *Paean* 2.77) rather as the seer does for the Spartiates in this elegy (fr. 14 W²). Her prophecy also concerns a river. The Periegete (2.30.2) states that Hecate was the goddess most honored by the Aeginetans. Lykos: Paus. 4.1.6–7, 6.6; 1.19.4–5.

33. Alternative founder of Megara: Megareus of Onchestos, son of Poseidon (Hellan. *FGrH* 4 F78 ap. Steph. Byz. *Ethn.* s.v. Νίσαιαι; Paus. 1.39.4–6). Schachter 1998: 27 argues that *Eleusinian* Pandion was by now just an eponymous Attic hero, and that Simonides refers here to *Megarian* Pandion. Megarians claimed that Megara received its name from Dorian sanctuaries or chambers (μέγαρα) of Demeter.

34. Iphigeneia: Hdt. 4.103.2; cf. Lucian *Tox.* 6.

35. Paus. 2.1.1, citing Eumelos. Strabo C338, and bk. 7 fr.16d (ap. Eust. at *Il.* 2.659) where he was said to have known of nine "Ephyras." Elean Ephyra: *Il.* 2.659, 15.531; Hippias of Elis *FGrH* 6 F12 ap. Schol. Pind. *Nem.* 7.53. Thessalian Ephyra: Pind. *Pyth.* 10.55 (for Hippokleas of Thessaly); Pindar begins by linking Lacedaemon and Thessaly, both ruled by Heraklids. Strabo C442, and bk. 7 frr. 15a–16 (ap. Eust. at *Il.* 2.750) where he identifies the bellicose Ἔφυροι of *Il.* 13.301 as Perrhaebian. Glaukos to Diomedes: *Il.* 6.145–211,

whereupon he became the Taraxippos that terrified horses at the Isthmian Games. The Corinthians are much more prominent in this poem than in Herodotus' account of Plataea, as Plutarch notes indignantly; they formed part of the section that faced Mardonios' contingent of Medes, and were perhaps the strongest allies of the Lacedaemonians at this period. Simonides' patrons may have included a Corinthian family, the Oligaithidai, for whom Pindar later composed *Olympian* 13.[36]

If West is right to propose μάν]τιος ἀντιθέου at fr. 11W² 1.22, the seer is likely to be the Klytiad Elean, Teisamenos, who had by disingenuous means secured Spartiate status, and also prophesied for the Spartiates at Tanagra, where the victorious commander was Pausanias' brother, Nikomedes.[37] Tradition persistently connects the Klytiad ancestor, Aeolian Melampous, with Neleus and Thessaly, but Melampous' roots lay in Triphylia, populated by Minyai, Epeians, and Eleans. Triphylian Pylos is probably the city of Neleus. Achilles was at some period mourned at Olympia, but it is hard to assess the nature of Elean identity before the Persian wars; Achilles' μνῆμα at Olympia may have been the work of Pisatans or Achaeans who, at different times, had been responsible for the Olympic festival.[38]

Just as Ephyra is distinguished from Glaukos' capital, so—in this elegy—are the sons of Doros from those of Herakles (from whom Neoptolemus' children, including Prax's parent, claimed descent through their mother), the men of Sparta from the men of the Eurotas, and Sparta itself from what, in the fragment, is supplemented as "Hellas." While a late author like the scholiast to Apollonius of Rhodes may have identified all Laconians who were not actually from Sparta as perioikoi, we cannot with confidence employ this term as a political classification in a late archaic context; Laconian perioikoi who honored Achilles ὡς θεὸν could have been, for Simonides, simply "from the Eurotas."

The Tyndaridai are heroes of the Spartiate army; like Achilles, they too assisted mariners.[39] Herodotus relates how the Lacedaemonians were moved to receive the

---

including (at 1.146): οἵη περ φύλλων γενεή, τοίη δὲ καὶ ἀνδρῶν, cf. Simonides fr. 19.1 W². Arist. *Rhet.* 1363a 14. Corinth, and Agamemnon: *Il.* 2.570, 576; and Aias: Hes. *Cat.* 68. 55–62 (Berlin *Pap.* 10560); cf. n. 58 below. Lycian Glaukos killed by Aias over Achilles' body: Q. Smyrn. 3.278ff. Sisyphus: Hes. *Cat.* 4 ap. Plut. *Mor.* 747; Schol. Pind. *Pyth.* 4.263; Paus. 2.3.10–4.3. Melikertes: Paus. 2.1.3; Philostr. *Her.* 20.24. See Rutherford, this volume, at n. 73.

36. Taraxippos: Verg. *Georg.* 3.268; Paus. 6.20.19. The Periegete (9.8.1) describes a ritual at Potniai, of dropping piglets into a chasm, which reappeared a year later at the Aiakid Dodona. The companions to the Πέρσαι in Aeschylus' *tetralogia* were Γλαύκος Ποτνιεύς, Φινεύς, Προμηθεύς (hypothesis to Πέρσαι). Phineus was aided by the Boreads (Ap. Rhod. *Arg.* 1.211, 1.298, 2.240), Prometheus knew Thetis' secret; these subjects recall the content of the Plataea poem. Corinthians at Plataea: Plut. *Mor.* 872D. Oligiaithidai: *SLG* 339–40. Cf. below, nn. 50, 74, 76.

37. Thuc. 1.107. The Periegete (4.14.8) states that when the Messenians poured libations to their hero Aristomenes they called him "son of Nikomedes," but according to most other Hellenes his father was "Pyrrhos."

38. The Klytiads appear to have been honored at Chiot Kardamyla (Graf 1985: 35–37). The games were reordered in Olympiad 77 (conventionally 472 B.C.E.; Paus. 5.9.3). The temple of Zeus was built with the spoils from a war with the Pisatans, and the victory tithe for Tanagra, set up on the pediment by the Lacedaemonians, provides a terminus ante quem for its construction (Paus. 5.10.2–3). See Strabo (C357) for Achaean control of the games.

39. Cf. n. 14 above.

Minyan grandchildren of the Argonauts who had fled from Lemnos, precisely because of their descent from the Tyndaridai.[40] Menelaus may represent Amompharetos and the Pitanate *lochos* (whose very existence Thucydides denied); in *Trojan Women*, Euripides styles Menelaus "king of Pitana"; another Pitana was one of the twelve Aeolian cities.[41]

The entire host is led by the only named historical figure: Pausanias, the son of Kleombrotos, who himself may have received an honorific epithet in the poem. Of Plataea, Herodotus wrote νίκην ἀναιρέεται καλλίστην ἀπασέων τῶν ἡμεῖς ἴδμεν Παυσανίης ὁ Κλεομβρότου τοῦ Ἀναξανδρίδεω ("the fairest victory yet known . . . won by Pausanias, son of Kleombrotos son of Anaxandridas"), and put words like these into the mouth of the Aeginetan Lampon, son of Pytheas.[42] Similar language characterizes the distich, attributed to Simonides, that Pausanias wanted inscribed on the Serpent Column, where he is styled Ἑλλήνων ἀρχηγὸς, and the yet more grandiloquent title Pausanias gave himself on the bronze krater dedicated to Poseidon on the Bosphoros: ἄρχων Ἑλλάδος εὐρυχόρου. The epithet εὐρύχορος was also used of Hellas by the Homeric Achilles' mentor, Phoenix.[43] A krater six times as large was set up near Olbia by another Scythian lord, Ariantes.[44] Pausanias called himself ὁ ἡγεμὼν τῆς Σπάρτης in a letter to Xerxes, but never, as Lazenby notes, ὁ ἡγεμὼν τῶν Λακεδαιμονίων[45] Thus he styled himself leader of what are probably two distinct elements in Simonides' elegy, Sparta and Hellas.

Pausanias' own career took him, first, past the site of Achilles' shrine by the Eurotas, en route for the Isthmus, which his father Kleombrotos had fortified the pre-

---

40. Hdt. 4.145; Ap. Rhod. *Arg.* 4.1761–62.

41. Eur. *Tro.* 1112: μηδὲ πόλιν Πιτάνας χαλκόπυλόν τε θεάν. Callimachus (*Hymn* 3.172–73) sets Artemis at Pitana: ἢ Πιτάνης (καὶ γὰρ Πιτάνη σέθεν), which the Scholiast (172a) defined as πόλις Λακεδαιμονίας. When Pindar (*Ol.* 6.28) praises the Iamid Hagesias of Syracuse, he asks the winning mule-car to bring his song πρός Πιτάνάν δὲ παρ' Εὐρώτα πόρον ("to Pitana by the ford of the Eurotas"); cf. Hdt. 3.55 on the Lacedaemonian Archias, son of Samios, who lived ἐν Πιτάνῃ. Plutarch (*Mor.* 601B) implies that, in his time, Laconian Pitana was still important in its own right. Hornblower, this volume at nn. 44–46, comments on the relatively low profile of Menelaus in fifth-century Spartan traditions; is it a coincidence that the Pitanate had also been edited out of the version of Plataea that reached Thucydides?

42. Hdt. 9.63–64. Lampon: Hdt. 9.78: ὦ παῖ Κλεομβρότου, ἔργον ἔργασταί τοι ὑπερφυὲς μέγαθός τε καὶ κάλλος, καί τοι θεὸς παρέδωκε ῥυσάμενον τὴν Ἑλλάδα κλέος καταθέσθαι μέγιστον Ἑλλήνων τῶν ἡμεῖς ἴδμεν ("Son of Kleombrotos, you have done a deed of surpassing greatness and glory; by heaven's favor you have saved Hellas, and thereby won greater renown than any Greek known to men"). Pindar composed *Nemean* 5 for the Aeginetan boy pankratiast Pytheas, son of Lampon, son of Kleonikos (*Nem.* 5.4), and *Isthmian* 6 and 5 for his brother Phylakidas, perhaps a few years before Plataea.

43. Thuc. 1.132.2: Ἑλλήνων ἀρχηγὸς ἐπεὶ στρατὸν ὤλεσε Μήδων | Παυσανίας Φοίβῳ μνῆμ' ἀνέθηκε τόδε ("When as captain of the Hellenes he had destroyed the Persian host, Pausanias dedicated this memorial to Phoebus"), originally in Doric and the first person (*AP* 6.197); see Parsons 1992a: 36. Krater: Nymphis *FGrH* 432 F9 ap. Ath. 536B; I am grateful to an anonymous reader for Oxford University Press for pointing out that Nymphis was from *Pontic* Heracleia. Εὐρύχορος used by Phoenix: *Il.* 9.478–80. Simonides and Pausanias: Plato *Epist.* 2.311A; Plut. *Mor.* 105A. Rutherford, this volume, at nn. 28 and 39–40; Schachter 1998: 28.

44. Ariantes: Hdt. 4.81.2–5.

45. Lazenby 1975: 235. Arist. *Pol.* 1301b20, 1307a2, 1333b34 on Pausanias' attempt to establish sole monarchy and overthrow the Ephorate.

vious year. Here, the Hellenes being mustered, he performed the *diabateria* before advancing via Eleusis to Plataea and the battle. Sometime later, after the campaign in Cyprus, he set himself up at Byzantium, which is probably when he inscribed the krater to Poseidon.[46] The Spartiates recalled him, in authoritative manner, but he acquitted himself and returned to Byzantium, taking a trireme not from the Spartans' naval base at Gytheion but from the Euboian Dryopian settlement of Hermione—an action that has puzzled historians.[47] When Herodotus gazettes the contingents who, under Kleombrotos, fortified the Isthmus, he records that Dryopians also inhabited a region of Laconia round Asine, near Kardamyli, one of the "seven cities."[48] Pausanias moved to Kolonai, whose legendary king Kyknos was, according to one tradition, killed by Achilles; he was recalled a second time, and for good, after which he became involved in some way with Helots at Tainaron. A notorious violation of Poseidon's asylum there was perpetrated by Ephors, who dragged from it some Helot, or Laconian, suppliants, thereby bringing *agos* upon Sparta; this, together with the Spartiates' violation of the sanctuary sought by Pausanias in the temple of Athene Chalkioikos, outside which he died, prompted the Athenians' tit-for-tat demand on the eve of the Peloponnesian War that Sparta expel these curses.[49]

Does anything connect these two catalogs? First, there is, in the elegy, a palpable Aeolian presence from the Isthmus westward, echoing the Aeolian pattern of Achillean cult-sites. Given Simonides' allusion to the sons of Doros, it is surprising to find Corinth personified in its Aeolian hero Glaukos, son of Sisyphus, rather than the Dorian Aletes. Thucydides remarks that Corinth had been Aeolian until the Dorians came (whenever that was).[50]

Second, just as Achilles inhabits the water margins, so the sea divinities—Ocean, Nereus (the Old Man of the Sea, who may, in Simonides' elegy on Artemisium, have received the epithet ἀγλαόφημος, as Achilles does in the Plataea fragment),[51] their

46. While there, he may have killed a Byzantine girl, Kleonike, and afterward sought purification at the shrine of Eurynome at Triphylian Phigalia: Plut. *Kim.* 6; Paus. 3.17.8; cf. n. 17 above. Phigalia: Paus. 8.39.5–42.12. Where the river Neda flowed nearest to Phigalia, boys cut their hair to the river—a distinctly Achillean gesture! At nearby Lykosoura there was a river named "Plataniston." Recent excavations at Phigalia have uncovered quantities of piglet bones (cf. n. 36), and lamps suggesting a nocturnal ritual: Tomlinson 1995–96: 12.

47. Thuc. 1.128.3. The Periegete states (2.35.5; 3.14.5) that the Spartan cult of Demeter Χθονία originated at Hermione; there he also records a short-cut to Hades, a stadium where the Tyndaridai raced, a sanctuary of Poseidon, and a temple of Aphrodite Ποντία (Paus. 2.34.6–35.11). Dryopians in southern Euboia: Hdt. 1.54. Links between Messenia and (Dryopian) Hermione and Asine: *IG* iv.4.619, 2–4, 6–9 (συγγενεία, φιλία); Theopompos *FGrH* 115 F383 ap. Strabo C373; Paus. 4.8.3, 27.8, 34.9.

48. Hdt. 8.73.

49. Pausanias then moved to Kolonai (Thuc. 1.131.1). Achilles and Kyknos: *Kypria* ap. Proc. *Chrest.* 1. Helots and Tainaron: Thuc. 1.132.4; 1.128.1.

50. Thuc. 4.42. Cf. nn. 35–36 above. Aletes is son of Hippotas and thus connected with Aeolus: Ap. Rhod. *Arg.* 4.819–20; Konon *FGrH* 26 F1.xxvi ap. Phot. 186 s.v. Κάρνος ἢ Κόδρος. In *POxy* 3876 fr. 62.5, a relation of Aeolus son of Hippotades may be placing the shroud on the corpse: Garner 1993: 161. Schachter 1998: 29 argues that the elegy was composed at the behest of Pausanias, the Spartiates, and the Dorians to win the hearts and minds of Asian Greeks; if that were so, why did not Simonides refer to the *Dorian* heroes of Corinth and Megara? Cf. n. 33 above.

51. Simonides fr. 3.13 W^2, fr. 10.5 W^2; West 1993: 3–4. The Old Man of the Sea is identified as Nereus in the *Iliad* (18.140f.) and at Gytheion (Paus. 3.21.9).

daughters Ephyra and Thetis, and Ino/Leukothea—are all pieces in this puzzle, with Poseidon himself most prominent of all. Though often displaced as principal deity by others, Poseidon was especially worshipped in the following ways: by all Hellenes as Hippios and as Isthmios at the Isthmus; at Triphylian Samikon, where Telemachus found the Pylians sacrificing black bulls to him (the prescribed sacrificial victim also at the Eleutheria festival, which was instituted to commemorate the victory of Plataea, and has been discussed as a possible context for this elegy);[52] and widely in Laconia. In Sparta he was worshipped as Hippokourios and Asphalios, but also as the family god Genethlios, and as Domatitas, whose sanctuary stood by the Dioscuri "Starters," near the house of Menelaus;[53] and as Tainarios, whose sanctuary stood near the Hellenion, where the defense plans against Xerxes (or those for Menelaus' punitive expedition to Troy) were drawn up.[54]

Third, these cults of Poseidon in Sparta give entry to an elusive network, which leads back to Achilles and, perhaps, Pausanias. Two places, connected in the comparison between the Achillean cultic map and the personalities mentioned in Simonides' elegy, command attention precisely because on the one hand they are otherwise regarded as insignificant but, on the other, they are also related to each other in a separate respect: Prasiai and Hermione were members of the Kalaurian Amphictyony, of which Strabo provides the only surviving record.[55] The other members were Nauplia, later resettled at Methone, once called Pedasos, one of the seven Achillean cities; Athens, with its strong Neleid connection;[56] Minyan Orchomenos; Epidauros, of which more in a moment; and Aegina, with its erstwhile Myrmidons and cult of Zeus Panhellenios.[57] Prasiai and Nauplia must once have been independent, though by Strabo's time their dues were paid by Sparta and Argos respectively. Margalit Finkelberg has made the important observation that, while, in the Homeric *Catalog*

52. Himer. 3.10. Hdt. 9.81; Plut. *Thes.* 25; Strabo C380, C343; *Od.* 3.1. Poseidon was worshipped at Onchestos (*Il.* 2.506, cf. Hom. Hymn 3.230, also 4.186–87; Pind. *Isth.* 1.32–33 and 4.19), and as Ἑλικώνιος (*Il.* 8.203, 20.404; *Hom. Hymn* 22.3) at the Panionion (Hdt. 1.148). Pausanias presided at the sacrifice of a bull to Zeus Eleutherios in the Plataean agora (Thuc. 2.71); cf. n. 9 on the hoplitodromos at Plataea and Caracalla's games for Achilles. Eleutheria: Boedeker, this volume, "Heroization," at nn. 16–26.

53. The priestess of Poseidon Domatitas was also Priestess of Karneios Oiketas, possibly a pre-Dorian cult; this priesthood was hereditary, suggesting considerable antiquity. Paus. 3.14.2; cf. 3.15.7; Aristid. 1, p. 29. The sanctuary of P. Domatitas stood next to the Dioscuri Starters at one end of the Dromos, near Menelaus' house (Paus. 3.14.7), and that of Poseidon surnamed Genethlios next to the heroon of Kleodaios (Neoptolemus' father-in law) and Olbios (Paus. 3.15.10). The Pohoidia were also held in Poseidon's honor at Laconian Helos, an Achaean town, and possibly at Thouria, in the region of the seven Achillean cities. Fifth-century Attic drama reflects a strong link between Poseidon and Helots; a fragment of Eupolis' *Helots* alludes to τέμενος Ποτειδᾶ ποντίω (Eup. fr. 149 KA; cf. *Hom. Hymn* 22.3); Schumacher 1993: 72. Pindar (*Isth.* 8.34) calls Thetis ποντίαν θεόν; cf. n. 9 above. Whether "Helot" refers to an ethnic group or the servile class is beyond the scope of this paper to discuss.

54. Paus. 3.13.3–6; *IG* v.131. Paus. 3.12.5 and *CIG* 1374. Xen. *Hell.* 4.7.4 for Lacedaemonians' paean and sacrifice to Poseidon.

55. Strabo C374.

56. Ποσειδῶν Καλαυρεάτης appears in a fifth-century Athenian schedule of accounts, *CIA* 1.273. Cf. n. 28 above; also Farnell 1907: 80 n. 4.

57. And its Phoibaion Lake. At Sparta there was a Phoibaion where boys sacrificed before the Platanista battle (Paus. 2.30.7; cf. 3.14.9).

of Ships, Diomedes' contingent includes Troizen, Epidauros, Aegina, and Hermione, in the Hesiodic *Catalog of Women* it is Aias who has the usufruct, so to speak, of these cities, and also of Corinth and Megara.[58]

It is possible that the cult of Kalauria was that of Poseidon Geraistios. Strabo remarks that, among the Hellenes, reverence for the god at this sanctuary was so deep-rooted that when Demosthenes sought asylum there, even the Macedonian Archias was not prepared to violate it. The majority of Kalaurian members inhabited the eastern Argolid, whose population at the time of Plataea included Macedonians.[59] Schumacher draws attention to the probable link between this Amphictyony and other cults and asylum sanctuaries of Poseidon Geraistios (Map 2).[60] The eponymous sanctuary stood on the southern tip of Euboia—whence Dryopians had come to Hermione. Here, at Geraistos, Nestor, Menelaus, and their companions took refuge from a storm and sacrificed bulls to Poseidon.[61]

Discussing the myth of three brothers, Geraistos, Kalauros, and Tainaros, sons of Zeus, Schumacher noted the distribution of festivals and month, clan, and personal names derived from Geraistos. These include games held on Euboia, probably by Pindar's time; kourotrophic nymphs in Crete and Arkadia;[62] a clan at Troizen, and a festival held there in "Geraistios," a month name also found on Kalauria and, according to Thucydides, in Sparta—suggesting the existence of a festival of considerable importance and antiquity. Poseidon Tainarios and a hero named Tainaros were also honored in Sparta, and Hellenistic inscriptions mention the festival of Tainaria in which races were run on the beach at Tainaron. All three brothers were reconnected in Sparta once Sparta assumed responsibility for Prasiai's Kalaurian membership. These sanctuaries of Poseidon enjoyed the status of ἄβατον and ἄσυλον, as did those on Tenos, at Samikon, and at the Isthmus, while for the festivals at Samikon and at the Isthmus the truce known as ἐκεχειρία was declared.[63] Tainaron, Malea, Sounion, and the Geraistian refuges are listed as sacred to Poseidon by Euripides, in *Cyclops*,

58. Hes. *Cat.* 68.55–62 (Berlin *Pap.* 10560). Finkelberg 1988: 32, 35–36. Cf. n. 35 above. Fowler 1998: 9 conjectures, from the fact that the Aeolid stemma is so detailed, that Hesiod was an Aeolid.

59. Strabo C374; Hdt. 8.43.

60. The storm off the south Euboian Cape Kaphereus was caused by Nauplios, son of Poseidon and Amymone, to avenge the death of his son Palamedes. Eur. *Tro.* 90 and *Hel.* 1122; Strabo C368.

61. Schumacher 1993: 62–87; *Od.* 3.174. In the fourth century c.e., Libanius (*Or.* 1.16) crossed the sea and landed at Geraistos, in conscious imitation of Nestor.

62. Pind. *Ol.* 13.112 and Schol. *Ol.* 13.159b (Drachmann). For καρύστονικος on Athenian casualty list: ML 48.27; cf. Hdt. 9.105 for the best Athenian warrior at Mykale, Hermolykos son of Euthynos, killed in war with Karystos ca. 472–469 B.C.E., and buried at Geraistos (Thuc. 1.98.3). Does καρύστονικος mean "victor at the Geraistian Games" or "victorious in war against Karystos"? Strabo (C416) refers to the Achaeans of Pontos as colonists from Orchomenos, and mentions another Orchomenos in the vicinity of Karystos. "Geraistian" kourotrophic nymphs in Crete and Arkadia (near Gortyn?): *Etym. Mag.* s.v. Γεραίστου: χωρίον τῆς Ἀρκαδίας παρὰ τὸ γέρας ὅτι τιμιόν ἐστι διὰ τὸ ἐκεῖ τὸν Δία σπαργανωθῆναι.

63. Ath. 639C for month name at Troizen; and at Sparta, Thuc. 4.119. Schumacher 1993: 76 suggests that the Kalaurian Poseidon may have been the "Poliouchos" worshipped at Troizen; the title "Poliouchos" may also once have belonged to Athene Chalkioikos, in whose sanctuary Pausanias was a suppliant (for all the good it did him). The territory of Triphylian Makistia was also called Platanista; the toponym is a recurrent feature in this survey—there is even a village called Platanistos near Geraistos. Pylians: *Od.* 3.4. ἐκεχειρία: Schumacher 1993: 71 and 72ff. for Tainaron, Kalauria, and Geraistos.

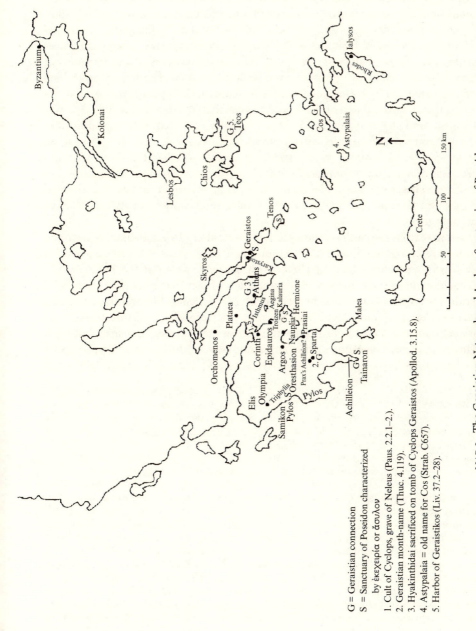

MAP 2. The Geraistian Network and Asylum Sanctuaries of Poseidon.
(Derived from the work of R. Schumacher, 1993.)

G = Geraistian connection
S = Sanctuary of Poseidon characterized
    by ἐκεχειρία or ἄσυλον
1. Cult of Cyclops, grave of Neleus (Paus. 2.2.1–2.).
2. Geraistian month-name (Thuc. 4.119).
3. Hyakinthidai sacrificed on tomb of Cyclops Geraistos (Apollod. 3.15.8).
4. Astypalaia = old name for Cos (Strab. C657).
5. Harbor of Geraistikos (Liv. 37.2–28).

and Geraistos himself is identified as the Cyclops, on whose grave in Athens the Hyakinthidai were ritually slaughtered; the Periegete says the Cyclopes were worshipped at the Isthmus, where Neleus also lay buried.[64] Unger argued that the Isthmian festival had originated with that of Geraistos. Γεραίστιος appears in a fragment of Sappho; it is too tiny to be informative, but Sappho was from Aeolian Lesbos, conquered by Achilles, according to tradition. The scholiast to Euripides' *Orestes* (at *Or.* 990) recounts how Lesbos was the kingdom of Oinomaos, whose charioteer Myrtilos was killed by Pelops at Geraistos.[65] The name Geraistos is not common, but there was an unusually high proportion of Geraistian personal names on Cos, which had been colonized by Megara and the Kalaurian member Epidauros.[66] And Cos is interesting for two other reasons: Strabo says that the old name for Cos was Astypalaia, and the Astypalaians honored Achilles as a divine hero;[67] and after Plataea, Pausanias was swift to assist a suppliant, a woman from Cos, whose father, Hegetorides, was Pausanias' *xenos*. Boedeker doubts whether the Coan woman's speech was drawn from Simonides' elegy.[68] Since the Geraistian network, a number of Achillean sites, and scenes of Pausanias' independent action coincide several times, this may be a genuine connection—perhaps an Amphictyony or a network of *xenia*. I can only guess.[69]

It is time to lay the cards on the table. Sometime after Plataea, Pausanias inscribed a bronze krater to Poseidon thus: "This monument of his prowess is dedicated to lord Poseidon by Pausanias, ruler of Hellas with its wide spaces, at the Euxine sea, a Lacedaemonian by birth, the son of Kleombrotos, of the ancient race of Herakles."[70] Poseidon was bound up with the origins of the Hellenes. Plutarch says that the ancient Hellenes sacrificed to him as "Patrigeneios," regarding moisture as their primary substance;[71] Poseidon of Family and House was honored in Sparta; Poseidon as Πατήρ at Eleusis; Poseidon's priest at Hermione was called πατήρ τῆς πόλεως.[72]

---

64. Eur. *Cycl.* 290–95. Paus. 2.2.1–2. Hyakinthidai: Apollod. 3.15.8; cf. Phanodemos *FGrH* 325 FF3–4. For oracular verse whereby Poseidon exchanged Delos for Kalauria with Leto, and Delphi for Tainaron with Apollo: Ephoros *FGrH* 70 F150 ap. Strabo C374; similarly Briareus allotted Acrocorinth to Apollo and the Isthmus to Poseidon.

65. Unger 1877: 34–40. Sappho fr. 96.33 LP.

66. Schumacher 1993: 66. Fraser and Matthews 1987: 107.

67. Strabo C657. The Homeric Coans were led by the sons of Thessalos: *Il.* 2.677–79.

68. Hdt. 9.76. Boedeker, this volume, "Historiography," at nn. 21–22. Cf. Griffiths 1976: 23 on Syagros' speech, and the conjecture of West 1993a: 3 on the λόγος about the Athenian prayer to Boreas. Did Simonides' elegy refer to the Coan woman's supplication, or Alexander of Macedon's nocturnal visit (Hdt. 9.46)? Coans were among the forces of Artemisia of Halicarnassus, a Troizenian colony (Hdt. 7.99).

69. Maps: Dowden 1989: 48; Schumacher 1993: 64. Tausend 1992: 57ff. argues that most amphictyonies were ethnic rather than political, economic, or military in character. See Fowler 1998: 12–13.

70. μνᾶμ' ἀρετᾶς ἀνέθηκε Ποσειδάωνι ἄνακτι | Παυσανίας ἄρχων Ἑλλάδος εὐρυχόρου | πόντου ἐπ' Εὐξείνου, Λακεδαιμόνιος γένος, υἱὸς | Κλεομβρότου, ἀρχαίας Ἡρακλέος γενεᾶς (Ath. 536B).

71. Plut. *Mor.* 730E: οἱ δ' ἀφ' Ἕλληνος τοῦ παλαιοῦ καὶ πατρογενείῳ Ποσειδῶνι θύουσιν, ἐκ τῆς ὑγρᾶς τὸν ἄνθρωπον οὐσίας φῦναι δόξαντες, ὡς καὶ Σύροι ("Those descended from Hellen of old have also sacrificed to 'patriarchal Poseidon,' believing as the Syrians do that man developed from the moist element"). I can think of at least one Milesian who held this view!

72. Paus. 2.38.4; *CIG* 1223; Paus. 2.34.10. Heliconian Poseidon was worshipped at the Panionion, but also at Helice and at Sinope. Neileus established the cult of Poseidon at Miletus. Poseidon also appears on coins of Caracalla: Farnell 1921: 83 n. 57; cf. nn. 9 and 11 above.

The incidence of Poseidon and sea deities, Achilles' habitat on the water-margins, the Geraistian network (?), and Simonides' attention to the Isthmus and a Corinth identified by its Aeolian hero, Glaukos the Taraxippos, all suggest a Poseidonian context. Since the character of both victory and elegy appears strongly panhellenic, then, as Rutherford suggests in this volume, a panhellenic occasion would be a plausible setting.[73] Put the two together and you get the Isthmian Games. Herodotus records that after Plataea, the third victory tithe, a nine-and-a-half-foot bronze Poseidon, was set up at the Isthmus; this was perhaps at the Isthmian Games of the following year, 478 B.C.E. Luppe wonders whether Simonides' phrase οἶ⟨ον⟩ κάλλιστον μάρτυν ἔθεντο πόνων, χρυσοῦ τιμήεντος ἐν αἰθέρι· was to be taken as referring literally to gold, such as captured weapons. It could refer to gold adornment of this statue, or to a golden funerary urn, such as may have crowned Achilles' burial mound on the Hellespont, if Garner's conjecture on *POxy* 3876 fr. 67b. 4–5 is anywhere near the mark.[74] Pindar's eighth Isthmian Ode, composed for an Aeginetan victor that year, included a scene of mourning for Achilles.[75] In Simonides' proem, Achilles' fall is likened to that of a pine, ancient symbol of Poseidon and sacred to him at the Isthmus, where, according to the Periegete, there stood a row of these trees; Callimachus uses the old name of Ephyra as site of the games in a verse about the pine wreath for Isthmian victors; and drowned Melikertes is mourned on a bed of pine boughs, in a verse by Euphorion.[76] The altar to the Nereids at the Isthmus was near the shore; a precinct may once have existed there, such as those the Periegete saw elsewhere in Hellas, where they were honored, and perhaps Achilles with them.

There is more to the Isthmus than this, though, for it is also the panhellenic mustering point, especially in the military sense. The site may have been merely convenient, but strategic convenience does not preclude political significance. The Hellenes held council there twice before Thermopylae, and after Leonidas' death they regrouped there under Pausanias' father Kleombrotos and fortified it; it was there, too, that they cast votes on Poseidon's altar for the prize of valor after Salamis.[77] The

73. Rutherford, this volume at nn. 37–40, argues for Delphi. See this volume, Barchiesi at n. 19, Aloni at nn. 37–40. If victory and elegy *are* panhellenic, this would militate against the suggestion made by Schachter 1998: 28–29 of a ritual at Achilleion on the Hellespont as the occasion of performance.

74. Bronze Poseidon at the Isthmus: Hdt. 9.81. Luppe 1994: 22–24; Rutherford, this volume at nn. 40 and 78; Garner 1993: 162, and 159 where he emphasizes that Achilles' funeral was beside the sea. Plutarch's statement (*Mor.* 872E) that the elegy was not designed for performance *in Corinth* is intended to support Simonides' veracity in his allusion here to Corinthian prowess, i.e., it was not a matter of "compliment" but a matter of "fact." Cf. nn. 35–36 above; this volume, Aloni at nn. 57–58, Rutherford after n. 25.

75. Pind. *Isth.* 8, esp. l. 34: ποντίαν θεόν referring to Thetis (cf. nn. 9 and 53), and ll. 57–60: ἀλλά οἱ παρά τε πυρὰν τάφον θ᾽ Ἑλικώνιαι παρθένοι | στάν, ἐπὶ θρῆνόν τε πολύφαμον ἔχεαν. | ἔδοξ᾽ ἦρα καὶ ἀθανάτοις | ἐσλόν γε φῶτα καὶ φθίμενον ὕμνοις θεᾶν διδόμεν, in which the Heliconian Muses mourn Achilles, and the Immortals approve his committal, *though dead*, to the hymns of goddesses.

76. Call. fr. 59 Pfeiffer. Collect. Alex. *Euph.* 84. Barchiesi 1995: 34–36 and this volume, discusses the assimilation of Achilles to a pine in other sources: Hor. *Carm.* 4.6.10; Catull. 64.105–9. Cf. Ael. *Var. hist.* 12.61; Ap. Rhod. *Arg.* 1679–86. Herodotus (6.37) relates how Croesus warned the Lampsakenes that if they did not release Miltiades, σφεας πίτυος τρόπον . . . ἐκτρίψειν; by which he meant that, just as the pine, alone of all trees, puts out no shoots once it is felled, they too would be wiped out.

77. Hdt. 7.172–75; 8.71–72; 8.123. Thuc. 2.10–11; Diod. Sic. 11.3.3.

hegemony of Hellas passed to the Athenians not long afterward, but in the fourth century Philip, Alexander, and Demetrios Poliorketes each proclaimed himself leader of Hellas, and each did so at the Isthmian Games. When T. Quinctius Flamininus in 196 B.C.E., and Nero in 67 C.E., proclaimed the liberation of the Hellenes, they also did so at the Isthmian Games.[78]

The Isthmian Games may have been the occasion of the Plataea elegy, but why should Achilles, whom scholars have never before had reason to associate with the Persian Wars, be invoked in the proem? What influence can be detected here? I conclude this essay with a suggestion. Outside the Euxine Sea, the incidence of cults and toponyms of Achilles is most pronounced in Laconian territory. Even Homer, whom Simonides recruits as a trustworthy witness, hints at *divine* honors for Achilles in the context of the "seven cities" in south-west Laconia. In Sparta itself, however, Achilles was never an important figure in the way that, for example, the Dioscuri were. They and Menelaus go with the army to Plataea, but Achilles does not. Arch-warrior he may be, but he is not leader of Sparta. In what survives of this elegy, pride of place goes to the army from Sparta and the Eurotas—the contingent heading the lists on the victory dedications—and it is led, as is the whole force of the Plataiomachoi, by Pausanias son of Kleombrotos.[79] He is leader of Sparta; but, just as his Laconian contingent is host to the majority of Achillean sites, so his curriculum vitae also corresponds more closely with the Achillean map than does that of any other presence in the poem. Perhaps his own family observed a cult of Achilles. More importantly, Pausanias at Plataea is what Achilles was at Troy: leader, or in his own words ἀρχηγὸς, of the Hellenes; and his phrase on Poseidon's krater, Παυσανίας ἄρχων Ἑλλάδος εὐρυχόρου | πόντου ἐπ' Εὐξείνου, is redolent of Achilles the *cult* hero.[80]

From their hegemony, individual and collective, of the Hellenes, Pausanias and the Lacedaemonians were soon to be dislodged by the Athenians, and the focus and nature of that hegemony was to alter until the time of Philip. Indeed, it was from one of the Achillean sites, Skyros, that—shortly after Plataea—the Athenian Cimon would recover the bones of an alternative hero, Theseus.[81] Pausanias would himself become marginalized, die an unpleasant death, be reviled in Athenian tradition and, for a time, in that of Sparta. But from Simonides, to whom he was no stranger, he

---

78. Plut. *Alex.* 14.1; cf. Justin. 11.3.1–2, and Diod. Sic. 17.4.1. Plut. *Dem.* 25.3; *Flam.* 10.3ff., 12.8. Livy 33.38 lists those who benefited from T. Quinctius: Macedonian *Orestai*, Magnesians, Perrhaebians, and Dolopians were declared free; Thessalians were declared free and received Phthiotic Achaea; Phocis and Locris were annexed to the Aetolians, and Pharsalos and Leukas restored to them; Corinth, Triphylia, and Heraia were restored to the Achaeans; although Eumenes received Oreus and Eretria, they and Karystos were declared free; Lychnidus and Parthini were awarded to Pleuratus. Cf. n. 31. Sueton. *Nero* 24.2, cf. 37.3. Poseidon Isthmios was on coins struck by Nero.

79. Aloni, this volume, at nn. 63–66; Rutherford, this volume, at nn. 25–26 and 31; Schachter 1998: 28–29 all refer to "Spartan" prominence in the poem; cf. Aesch. *Pers.* 816–17; Pind. *Pyth.* 1.77.

80. Rutherford, this volume at n. 47, suggests that the proem might open with a reference to a descendant of Achilles; could this be his "descendant" qua leader of the Hellenes? Schachter 1998: 28–29 also stresses this cultic resonance when he argues for Achilleion as the scene of performance.

81. This action of Cimon's is notably absent from Thucydides' account; it is recorded by Plutarch (*Thes.* 36) and the Periegete (3.3.7). I am grateful to Dr. Louis Rawlings of Cardiff University for pointing out to me its chronological and political relevance to the subject discussed here.

received lavish acknowledgment in the poem, and his army with him, so presumably at the time of its composition neither had yet been displaced from their prestigious position.[82] Several scholars have suggested that Pausanias is the dominant influence on Simonides' composition. I suggest that it is on account of Pausanias *as current leader of Hellas* that Achilles, the original leader of Hellas, is invoked in the proem of this elegy. The fact that the Plataiomachoi are treated collectively by Simonides, even though the hero is singular, has been taken to preclude the possibility that Achilles acts as paradigm for an individual; but while Achilles, as representative and commander of all Hellenes, reconciles the singularity of the hero invoked, with the panhellenic plurality of the Plataiomachoi he may also, and simultaneously, be identified with the present leader, Pausanias.[83] If Agesilaos, eighty years later, could consciously imitate Agamemnon,[84] why should not Pausanias have done the same with Achilles, or Simonides have done it for him?

Provided Achilles be allowed his identity as leader of the original Hellenes, then a panhellenic celebration of the victory gained under Pausanias' command at Plataea—particularly if it took place at the Isthmus, where the Hellenes mustered and deliberated in time of crisis, where they acknowledged a leader, where they worshipped Poseidon, god of their genesis, and dedicated to him a victory tithe, and where Thetis and her sisters adorned his sanctuary, and may once have been honored, with Achilles, in a precinct by the shore—would be just the sort of place you might expect to hear an invocation to Achilles, the first lord of Hellas and scion of the Old Man of the Sea.

82. Boedeker, this volume, "Heroization," at n. 36.

83. Capra and Curti 1995: 30 stress the collectivity of the Plataiomachoi. Boedeker, this volume, "Heroization" at n. 59, argues that Achilles "serves here as paradigm for the collective Greeks at Plataea, rather than for a single figure"; similarly Aloni, this volume at n. 48. Both Lloyd-Jones 1994: 1 and Pavese 1995: 20–24 see Achilles as paradigm for an individual; Lloyd-Jones and now Schachter 1998: 29–30 suggest Pausanias; Pavese's choice of Leonidas is weakened by the necessity of postulating his presence in some earlier, unknown section of the poem.

84. The Boeotian League, incensed by Agesilaos' act, intervened to stop him. Before sailing for Ephesus, Agesilaos assembled his fleet at Geraistos (Xen. *Hell.* 3.4.4 and *Ag.*1.8; Plut. *Ag.* 6.4). Procopius (*De bell.* 8.22.27–29) mentions a ship built of stones for Artemis Bolosia at Geraistos; it bore an inscription in hexameters stating that it was dedicated by Agamemnon (who *is* associated here with a force of Hellenes): Νῆά με λαϊνέην ἱδρύσατο τῆδ' Ἀγαμέμνων Ἑλλήνων στρατιῆς σῆμα πλοϊζομένης. Schumacher 1993: 77. See also Hornblower, this volume, at n. 46.

10

JENNY STRAUSS CLAY

The New Simonides and Homer's *Hemitheoi*

The proem to Simonides' recently discovered "Battle of Platea" elegy is addressed to the hero Achilles.[1] How long it was and whether it dealt with the hero's birth and other exploits remains unclear. Fragment 10 surely deals with Achilles, but its precise contents are obscure. The beginning lines of the far more extensive fr. 11 apparently describe the hero's death in an epic simile adapted from Homer.[2] The damaged lines that follow (9–14) provide a brief summary of the end of the Trojan War, the destruction of Troy, and the return of the Greeks:

]σεοῦσα πε[ρικλεὲς ἄ]στ[υ καθεῖλεν,
   Πρ]ιάμου παισὶ χ[   ]ομ[10
εἵνεκ' Ἀλεξά]νδροιο κακόφρ[ονο]ς, ὡς τὸν[
   ]ι θείης ἅρμα καθεῖλε Δίκ[ης.
τοὶ δὲ πόλι]ν πέρσαντες ἀοίδιμον [οἴκαδ' ἵ]κοντο
   φέρτατοι ἡρ]ώων ἀγέμαχοι Δαναοί[³

Before breaking off, Simonides credits Homer with the heroes' renown:

οἷσιν ἐπ' ἀθά]νατον κέχυται κλέος ἀν[δρὸς] ἕκητι   15
   ὃς παρ' ἰοπ]λοκάμων δέξατο Πιερίδ[ων
πᾶσαν ἀλη]θείην, καὶ ἐπώνυμον ὁπ[λοτέρ]οισιν
   ποίησ' ἡμ]ιθέων ὠκύμορον γενεή[ν.

At first glance, the claims on Homer's behalf seem exaggerated. As Aloni notes, the incidents alluded to—the death of Achilles, the fall and sack of Troy, and the returns of the heroes—are actually not recounted in Homer.[4] Yet Simonides may well have

---

An earlier version of this paper appeared in Deborah Boedeker and David Sider (eds.), *The New Simonides, Arethusa* 29.2 (1996): 243–45, and is used here by kind permission of the Johns Hopkins University Press.

1. First published in Parsons 1992a ; cf. W² 118–22.
2. See the discussion of Barchiesi, this volume.
3. I omit some of the more speculative supplements included in W².
4. Aloni, this volume, at n. 31; on differences from Homer, see Stehle, this volume.

ascribed an *Iliou Persis* to Homer. To be sure, by exaggerating Homer's accomplishment, Simonides can rhetorically magnify his own. As Homer granted immortal fame to the heroes, so too will Simonides to the Plataean heroes he celebrates.

Lloyd-Jones has observed that the diction of these lines is peculiarly evocative of the epic, both in the choice of ἀοίδιμος, a Homeric *hapax*, which occurs when Helen tells Hector that Zeus set an evil destiny upon herself and Paris, to make them ἀοίδιμοι for men to come (*Il.* 6. 357–58), as well as the epithet ὠκύμορος, which in four of its five occurrences is used by Thetis of her son.[5] For Simonides, not just Achilles but the whole race of the heroes is ὠκύμορος. As he says in his *Threnoi* (523 *PMG*):

> †οὐδὲ γὰρ οἳ πρότερόν ποτ᾽ ἐπέλοντο,
> θεῶν δ᾽ ἐξ ἀνάκτων ἐγένονθ᾽ υἷες ἡμίθεοι,
> ἄπονον οὐδ᾽ ἄφθιτον οὐδ᾽ ἀκίνδυνον βίον
> ἐς γῆρας ἐξίκοντο τελέσαντες.†

> Not even those who once lived before us,
> the demigods, sons born from our lords, the gods,
> brought to completion a life without toil or decline or danger,
> and arrived at old age.

In addition to the many verbal echoes of Homer that have already been observed by others, fr. 11 as a whole contains another, I believe more precise, allusion. The two passages are linked not only by the similarity of their contents, but also by the term ἡμίθεος, a *hapax* in Homer and surprisingly rare elsewhere. Hesiod uses it almost as the *terminus technicus* to refer to his fourth race, the race of heroes who fought at Thebes and at Troy: ἀνδρῶν ἡρώων θεῖον γένος, οἳ καλέονται | ἡμίθεοι, προτέρη γενεῇ κατ᾽ ἀπείρονα γαῖαν (*Works and Days* 159–60).[6] Similarly, the Hesiodic *Catalog of Women* closely links the suitors of Helen and the Trojan War with Zeus' plan to destroy the ψυχὰς ἡμιθέων (fr. 204.100 Merkelbach-West).[7] In Alcaeus 42.13 Voigt, Achilles is called one of the *hemitheoi*, as is one of Alcman's Hippocoontids in the Louvre Partheneion (3.7 Calame). Callinus' praise of the brave warrior implies that, if he survives, he will be ἄξιος ἡμιθέων (1.19 W); he becomes the equal of those legendary heroes of the past. Whenever the term is used in these passages, it suggests a retrospective vision, looking back at the legendary past from the vantage of the present. But the comprehensive vision of the Trojan War with which Simonides brings his proem to a close most closely resembles Homer's similarly synoptic view at the beginning of the twelfth book of the *Iliad*.

In *Iliad* 12, Homer momentarily pulls back from the immediate action on the battlefield to distance himself from the heroes who fought before Troy. From that unique vantage, those who participated in the Trojan War belong to an earlier generation and to a different world, the ἡμιθέων γένος ἀνδρῶν. As he begins his narrative of the

---

5. Lloyd-Jones 1994: 2–3.
6. Capra and Curti 1995: 28–29 argue that ἐπώνυμον in line 17 does not mean "famous" but retains its usual sense. They translate: "The short-lived race, which takes its name from the half-gods," and supply a verb of singing (e.g., ἄεισε) at the beginning of line 14.
7. For a recent discussion of this controversial fragment, see Koenen 1994: 26–34.

assault on the Achaean wall, Homer looks forward to a future time when it will have disappeared (12.10–16):

> ὄφρα μὲν ῞Εκτωρ ζωὸς ἔην καὶ μήνι' Ἀχιλλεὺς   10
> καὶ Πριάμοιο ἄνακτος ἀπόρθητος πόλις ἔπλεν,
> τόφρα δὲ καὶ μέγα τεῖχος Ἀχαιῶν ἔμπεδον ἦεν.
> αὐτὰρ ἐπεὶ κατὰ μὲν Τρώων θάνον ὅσσοι ἄριστοι,
> πολλοὶ δ' Ἀργείων οἱ μὲν δάμεν, οἱ δὲ λίποντο,
> πέρθετο δὲ Πριάμοιο πόλις δεκάτῳ ἐνιαυτῷ,   15
> Ἀργεῖοι δ' ἐν νηυσὶ φίλην ἐς πατρίδ' ἔβησαν . . . .

> While Hector lived and Achilles raged,
> and the city of lord Priam remained unsacked,
> so long too the great wall of the Achaeans stood firm.
> But when all the best of the Trojans died,
> and many of the Argives perished, but others survived,
> the city of Priam was sacked in the tenth year,
> and the Argives went on ships to their own country . . . .

At that point the gods in concert will destroy the wall, κάππεσον ἐν κονίῃσι καὶ ἡμιθέων γένος ἀνδρῶν (12.23). In characterizing Homer's accomplishment as making a name among men to come for the ἡμιθέων ὠκύμορον γενεήν, Simonides likewise distances himself from the heroes of Troy and, above all, Achilles. In the next line, the poet will salute Achilles as paradigmatic demigod (θεᾶς ἐρικυ[δέος υἱέ] 19) and take his leave of the hero, before turning to the task at hand. In echoing the Homeric passage and in using the expression ἡμίθεοι, Simonides both links and dissociates himself with Homer and his subject matter. Troy and the race of the ἡμίθεοι, celebrated by his illustrious predecessor may be dead and gone, but Simonides will grant the same immortal κλέος to his contemporaries.

11

SARAH MACE

Utopian and Erotic Fusion in a New Elegy by Simonides

Only such sensational finds as have come to light with the publication of *POxy* 3956 could have overshadowed yet another treasure from the same papyrus: a beautiful and unusual new sympotic elegy by Simonides, now 22 W². We owe the recovery of this poem to the efforts of Peter Parsons, who worked out the relationships between a small fragment of the new papyrus (3965, fr. 27) and three separate scraps of anonymous elegiac verse published by Lobel in 1954 (*POxy* 2327).[1] To accompany his reconstruction, Parsons also provided a wealth of parallels and suggested a variety of interpretations (Parsons 1992a: 24, 45–49). M. L. West, for his part, edited the elegy along with the other new fragments in *IEG* II² and suggested generous supplements for its many lacunae; West also published an interpretation of the poem.[2] The following examination of the language and themes of Simonides 22 builds on these solid foundations, but leads to some conclusions that are more specific than Parsons's and different from West's.

The remains of the elegy consist of twenty-one mostly fragmentary verses. Both beginning and end of the poem are lost, but luckily the best preserved portion contains its core: the speaker's wish to travel to an idyllic island.[3]

An earlier version of this paper appeared in *ZPE* 113 (1996): 233–47, and is used here by kind permission of the editors of *ZPE*. I would like to thank Alan Cameron for first calling my attention to the new Simonides; David Sider and Deborah Boedeker encouraged me and advised me in the first phase of composition. I am especially grateful to Ludwig Koenen, whose critical acumen and scholarly expertise helped improve the *ZPE* article immensely. My colleague Scott Scullion kindly read the penultimate version of that piece and the new Postscript and suggested some apt refinements.

1. For the details see n. 3. Lobel, who "assembled" the fragments of 3965 and "left a transcript and some notes toward a commentary" (Parsons 1992a: 4–5) saw the relationship between 3965 fr. 27 and 2327 frr. 3 and 4. The insight that "fr. 4 must combine with frr. 1–2 col. ii" as being "two parallel strips" belongs to Parsons (1992a: 4–7, 24, 45, 46–49). He frames his invaluable proposal most modestly: "the combination of 2327 fr. 4 with frr. 1–2 ii produces sense enough to seem plausible" (1992a: 49).

2. West 1993a. References to Simonides' elegies in this paper follow the numeration in W². When this paper was first written (March 1996), to my knowledge there was only one other published discussion devoted to Simonides 22, namely, Hunter 1993a; see further n. 80. See now Rutherford, Yatromanolakis, Hunter, and others in this volume.

3. *POxy* 2327 fr. 3 (22.1–7) = Adesp. eleg. 29 W¹; *POxy* 2327 fr. 4 (22.8–14, center section) = Adesp. eleg. 31 W¹; *POxy* 2327 fr.2(a) col. ii + (b) (22.8–21, left section) = Adesp. eleg. 30 W¹; 3965 fr. 27 (22.6–15, right sec-

Simonides 22 W²

```
[                    ]⸱οιϲι θαλάϲϲηϲ
    [                ]⸱ουϲα πόρον·
    [               ]μενοϲ ἔνθα περαναⱶ
        [                              ]                    4
[                        ]οιμι κέλευθο[ν
    [                ]ν κόϲμ[ο]ν ἰο[ϲτ]εφάνων
    [            ] ἕδοϲ πολύδενδρον ἱκο[ίμην
    ε̣ [⸱⸱⸱⸱⸱]ἐϋαγ[έ]α νῆϲον, ἄγαλμα β[ίου·          8
κα[ί κεν] Ἐχεκ[ρατί]δην ξανθότρ[ιχα
    ὀφ[⸱⸱⸱⸱⸱⸱⸱⸱⸱ ]⸱ν χεῖρα λάβοιμ[ι
ὄφρα νέο[ν] χ[αρίε]ντοϲ ἀπὸ χροὸϲ ἄν[θοϲ
    λείβοι δ’ ἐκ βλ[εφάρ]ων ἱμερόεντα [πόθον·      12
καί κεν ἐγ[ὼ(ν) ]⸱δοϲ ἐν ἄνθε[ϲι(ν)
    κεκλιμένοϲ λευκ[ο]ῖϲ φαρκίδαϲ ἐκ⸱[
χαίτη[ιϲι]ν χαρίε[ντ]α νεοβλαϲτ[
    ⸱[⸱⸱⸱⸱⸱⸱⸱ ]⸱εὐανθέα πλε[        ϲτέφανον    16
μο[⸱⸱⸱⸱⸱ ]δ’ ἱμερόεντα λιγὺν⸱[
    ἀρτι[επέα] νωμῶν γλῶϲϲαν ἀ[
[                                        ]
    τῶνδε⸱[                                         20
εὐκομπ[
```

Language and Themes

Travel (1–5 [+ 6?])

Perhaps as many as twenty verses into the poem, but more likely nearer the beginning,[4] three fragmentary line-endings refer to a voyage by sea: 1 θαλάϲϲηϲ;[5] 2 πόρον;[6]

---

tion). In both papyri variants and additions were made by the original hand, though in 3965 still others were made by a second hand (Lobel 1954: 67; Parsons 1992a: 5). Parsons's observation (1992a: 47) that "such interlinear variants may preserve corruptions just as much as corrections" is quite to the point. In the case of this poem, at least, the readings of *both* papyri seem superior to the variants. The correction in 1 (-οιϲι to -οιο) perhaps (?) regularizes a transferred epithet (see n. 5 below); in 7 the *v.l.* πολύυμνον in 2327 is less apposite than πολύδενδρον (see n. 30 below); for λειβ- rather than λειπ- in 12, see n. 46 below; for εὐκομπ[rather than εὔπομπ[in 21, see below at n. 75.

4. West 1993a: 12 estimates that "less than twenty lines" stood between this poem and Simon. fr. 21. Parsons, likewise: "ten to twenty verses might be lost in between" (Parsons 1992a: 49; cf. 7, 33). Since both beginning and end of the elegy are lacking, Simonides 22 was at least 21+ verses long and could have been 41+; indications of a thematic frame in the extant text suggest that the lower number is more nearly correct. Parsons 1992a: 49 wonders whether Simon. fr. 28 (3, first line) with its "reference to a symposium, desire and perhaps old age" should be joined with 22. I agree with West (loc. cit.) that these fragments come from different poems; although the two share some themes, the development of each appears to be independent. Cf. Hunter 1993a: 12 and Rutherford, this volume, at n. 98. For the suggestion that this fragment and others "fell within the compass" of one of the historical elegies, see Obbink, this volume, at nn. 66ff.

5. Unless Parsons's supplement is along the right lines, we need a "transferable" adjective that could have plausibly modified both θαλάϲϲηϲ and an appropriate dative plural.

6. -ουϲ ἄπορον is possible (Parsons 1992a: 49) but ἔνθα implies arrival. For more on πόροϲ, see n. 13 below.

and 3 ἔνθα περανα[.⁷ No part of 4 is preserved (a pentameter), but in the next verse the speaker expresses a wish to take a journey in his own person:]οιμι κέλευθο[ν.⁸

It might seem self-evident that 1–4 are part of the speaker's wish and that 5ff. are resumptive; Lobel paraphrased 3: "Having finished my journey?" (Lobel 1954: 75). κέλευθος, however, could be indefinite ("a journey") and thus initiate a new phase of the discourse. In this case, 22.1–4 would contain a description of a voyage other than the poet's own; Simonides presumably identified the other traveller and (with ἔνθα) stated his destination.⁹ West, too, believes that 1–4 are separate from the speaker's wish ("Simonides will hardly have spent seven lines getting from his embarkation to the mention of his destination"). He suggests that 1–4 refer to a journey to be undertaken by Simonides' addressee(s) and interprets the poem as a propemptikon (West 1993a: 13).¹⁰ One must wonder, though, whether the link between the voyage described in 1–4 and the speaker's own was quite so arbitrary.¹¹ Should not this first voyage be more directly relevant to the speaker's wish—paradigmatic in some way?

Since the speaker refers in 5ff. to an imaginary journey to a utopian island (see below, "General Parallels"), any number of voyages from myth and heroic legend could have served as a paradigm for the poet's own.¹² One possibility is a voyage of adventure to a fabulous landscape like Herakles' trips to the far west, perhaps, or a journey involving the Argonauts.¹³ A portion of Stesichorus' account of a voyage to the island of the Hesperides in the *Geryoneis* resembles Simonides 22.1–8 at points (Stes. *SLG* S8.1–4; Erythia and an infant Erytion? *SLG* ad loc.; cf. *PMGF* I):¹⁴

> διὰ] κ[ύ]μαθ' ἁλὸς βαθέας ἀφίκον-
> το θ]εῶν περικαλλέ[αν ν]ᾶσον
> τ]όθι Ἑσπερίδες π[αγχρ]ύσεα δώ-
> μα]τ' ἔχοντι·

---

7. "Apparently περάναις for which περήνας would be expected" (Lobel 1954: 75).
8. West's supplement must be substantially if not literally correct. Hunter 1993a: 13 suggests ἐθέλ]οιμι κέλευθο[ν (cf. Theocr. 7.61–2); for problems with interpreting Simonides 22 via Theocr. 7.61–71, see n. 80 below.
9.]μενος and περάναις (3) suggest a masculine subject.
10. Cf. Simonides' propemptikon for Hieron of Syracuse (580 *PMG*). West's proposal depends in part on reading the variant εὐπομπ[at 21 (see n. 75, and my discussion at n. 80 below).
11. Cf. West 1993a: 12: "Simonides *turned aside for a few moments* to describe the voyage he personally would like to make." (My emphasis.)
12. For heroic and mythic content in elegy, cf., e.g., Call. 6 (Thebes), Mimn. 19 (Niobe) and 21 (Ismene) with West 1974: 14 and n. 22. For the idea of a "mainly mythological" *Lyde* of Antimachus, see West 1974: 18. Most relevant to the present context are: Mimn. 11, 11a (the Argonaut voyage, see next note, end) and 12 (the sun's cup, see below with n. 15).
13. For πόρος of ocean crossings in the context of fantastic journeys, cf., e.g., πόρον Ὠκεανοῖο (Hes. *Thgn.* 292, Herakles' return with Geryon's cattle πέρην κλυτοῦ Ὠκεανοῖο [294]); παρ' Ὠκεανοῦ πατρὸς ἄςβεστον πόρον (Aesch. *PV* 531, the distant home of the Oceanid Chorus). For Colchis described in fabulous terms cf. Mimn. 11a (with 11 and Strab. 1.2.40).
14. Both texts include: "voyage" (θαλάσσης . . . πόρον . . . περαναί and κέλευθο[ν Simon. 22.1–5; διὰ] κ[ύ]μαθ' ἁλὸς βαθέας Stes. S8.1); "arrival" (ἱκο[ίμην Simon. 22.7; ἀφίκοντο Stes. S8.1–2); an idyllic island destination (εὐαγ[έ]α νῆςον Simon. 22.8; περικαλλέ[αν ν]ᾶςον Stes. S8.2) and at least one feature singled out by a relative adverb of place (ἔνθα Simon. 22.3; τ]όθι Stes. S8.3).

Another possibility for the paradigmatic voyage of 1–4 is a subject that was already popular with the poets: Helios' daily trek from the east to the western Hesperides (with a requisite allusion to his return journey in his famous cup). Once again, Stesichorus' version recalls the opening verses of Simonides fr. 22 W²: ὄφρα δι' ὠκεανοῖο περάσας | ἀφίκοιτο, sc. Helios (Stes. 185.2–3 *PMG*; S17.2–4 *PMGF*); despite a troubled text, Aeschylus' may as well.[15] The most likely hypothesis, however, is that 1–4 contain an account of some individual who was translated to an idyllic existence after death. Tradition associates several heroes with this fate (e.g., Menelaus, Achilles, Peleus, Diomedes, Cadmus), but the possibilities are by no means limited to these (cf. Parsons 1992a: 49):[16] an Attic skolion proclaims that Harmodius joined Achilles and Diomedes on the Islands of the Blest (894 *PMG*); a late fifth-century hydria by the Meidias painter portrays Attic heroes in the garden of the Hesperides;[17]philosophers and poets, too, might join the ranks of the blessed dead.[18]

Verse 6 should also perhaps be referred to the poet's journey. One possibility is "[the sea], glory of the violet-crowned [Nereids]" (Parsons 1992a: 45). Theognis 250 (ἀγλαὰ Μουσάων δῶρα ἰοστεφάνων) suggests, on the other hand, that the individuals described in 6 as ἰο[cτ]εφάνων are the Muses (cf. Bacchylides 5.3; *AP* 13.28.12).[19] κόcμ[ο]ν could then refer to the poet's art (Lobel in Parsons 1992a: 45; West 1993a: 13). West neatly supplements 5–6 as follows (West 1993a: 12):

πρήcc]οιμι κέλευθο[ν,

φόρτον ἄγων Μουcέω]ν κόcμ[ο]ν ἰοc[τ]εφάνων

This proposal has much to recommend it: there are good parallels for κόcμοc in the sense of "song" (Parsons 1992a: 32; West 1993a: 13; esp. Simon. fr. 11.23 W²; add Pind. *Ol.* 11.14: κόcμον . . . ἀδυμελῆ κελαδήcω) and *Pyth.* 3.72–76 contains a similar idea about poetic "freight";[20] the idea also suits the transition from journey (5) to destination (7ff.); finally, a reference to poetry would anticipate the (re?)introduction of the theme at 17ff. Still, given the fragmentary nature of the text, we should not dis-

15. Fr. 69.2–4 Radt: δέπαc ἐν τῷ διαβάλλει πολὺν οἰδματόεντα †φέρει δρόμου πόρον οὕθειc† (περίδρομον Sidgwick [vel sim.], cυθεὶc "ingeniose M. Schmidt, Conington, Ellis, sed, si πόρον sanum est, contra metrum Ionicum," Radt). If Simonides did not treat the subject of the Sun's cup, he would be in the minority! We owe to Athenaeus (11.469c–470d) a rich collection of passages from all genres alluding to this cup, often in the context of its loan to (or appropriation by) Herakles during his raid of Geryon's cattle.

16. For the idea that the entire race of heroes is translated to the Islands of the Blest in Hesiod, see Koenen 1994: 5 with n. 12.

17. Burn 1987: 15–25.

18. Cf. "Speusippus" 1(a).2 *FGE* (of Plato's soul): ἀθάνατον τάξιν ἔχει μακάρων; cf. 1(b).2 ἰcόθεον τάξιν. For philosophers and poets together, cf. διατριβαὶ δὲ φιλοcόφων καὶ θέατρα ποιητῶν (Ps.-Plat. *Axi.* 371d). For poets alone, Parsons 1992a: 49 cites Aristoph. *Frogs* 85 where Agathon is said to have gone εἰc μακάρων εὐωχίαν and Dioscorides 18.8 *HE* (*AP* 7.407) where the μακάρων ἱερὸν ἄλcοc is mentioned in connection with Sappho's fate. Cf. also the Orphic Katabasis (n. 49 below, end) where poets are mentioned in the company of other virtuous men in Hades (103–6) and *AP* VII 12 (of Erinna beyond Acheron): ἔχειν δὲ χοροὺc ἄμμιγα Πιερίcιν.

19. Cf. also Pind. *Isthm.* 7.23: ἰόπλοκοc of the Muses.

20. Pindar speaks of a hypothetical ocean voyage (εἰ κατέβαν 72; ἐξικόμαν κε βαθὺν πόντον περάcαιc 76) which would take him to Hieron with a freight of celebratory poetry. Cf. *Nem.* 5.2–3: Pindar's instructions to his "sweet song" to board any available vessel to carry its message of victory from Aigina.

miss the other alternative out of hand: that κόϲμ[ο]ν is the speaker's first reference to his destination (cf. ἄγαλμα in 8). The "violet-crowned" ones in verse 6 would then be the inhabitants of the utopian island. These could still be Muses (Parsons 1992a: 45; for Muses in utopian settings see on Eur. *Bacch.* 402–26, below at nn. 71–73); otherwise Simonides' island could have been the "glory of the Nymphs" (Parsons 1992a: 45) or, perhaps, the "glory of the violet-crowned Hesperides."

The Island Destination (7–18)

After expressing his wish to travel at 5, Simonides turns next to describe his desired destination with ἱκο[ίμην at 7.[21] Not only the cumulative effect of the details in the opening description (7–8), but virtually all the features of the poet's imaginary island have ties to traditional representations of utopias in early Greek poetry.[22]

Descriptions of utopian locales in Greek poetry are conservative: poets used the same well-defined group of features to describe such various places as Elysium, the Islands of the Blest, the Hesperides' island, and Olympus.[23] Prose writers, too, such as the early historians, Herodotus, and Plato, employ the poetic language and *topoi*.[24]

---

21. Hunter 1993a: 13 suggests ἵκο[ιτο, but]οιμι (5) and the movement from travel to destination in 5–7 leaves little doubt about West's supplement; cf. also λάβοιμ[ι (10).

22. Taken together, the features of Simonides' island are consistent with the Islands of the Blest or Elysium (Parsons 1992a: 46, 49; West 1993a: 12), but could imply any one of a number of idyllic abodes. It may or may not be relevant that Simonides spoke in an unknown context of Atlas holding heaven on his shoulders, a detail associated with the western island of the Hesperides (556 *PMG*; cf. Hes. *Thgn.* 517–19; Eur. *Hippol.* 742–47). Simonides also referred to the long-lived Hyperboreans (570 *PMG*) and to the marriage of Achilles and Medea in the Elysian plain (558 *PMG*).

A comprehensive review of the scholarship on representations of utopias in classical poetry goes beyond the scope of this article; a selective survey follows with some attention to sources of additional bibliography. Baldry 1952, Gatz 1967, Ferguson 1975, Lincoln 1980, Edwards 1985 (with bibl. at n. 1), Davies 1987 (with bibl. at introductory note), Gelinne 1988 (with bibl. at n. 3), Lloyd-Jones 1985 (= Lloyd-Jones 1990: 80–105 with Addendum, 105–9), Romm 1994. For "utopianism" in the late fifth and early fourth centuries and in Xenophon, see Dillery 1995: 41–54, 63–95.

23. The most familiar Greek utopias are found in Hesiod: the golden race (*WD* 109–20; cf. Alcmaeonis 7 *PEG*) and the Islands of the Blest (*WD* 166–173; see further *RE* 14.1 [1930]: 628–32, s.v. μακάρων νῆϲοι). For related material in Hesiod, cf. *WD* 43–46, 90–95, 225–37; fr. 1.6–13 and fr. 204.95ff. with West 1969: 132–36, West 1985: 119–21, and Koenen 1994. Homer gives us Elysium (*Od.* 4.563–68; see further *RE* 5.2 [1905] 2470–76, s.v. *Elysion*), Olympus (*Od.* 6.42–46; cf. Pind. fr. 143 and Bacch. fr. 23, p. 106 S.-M.), and several idyllic islands in the *Odyssey*, e.g., Ogygia, Scheria; cf. also the land of the Cyclopes. Pindar describes both the Island of the Blest (*Ol.* 2.56–80; cf. Pind. fr. 129) and the land of the Hyperboreans (*Pyth.* 10.29–46; see further *RE* 9.1 [1916]: 258–79, s.v. *Hyperboreer*). For the Hesperides' island, cf. Hes. *Thgn.* 215–16, 274–75, 517–18; Stes. S8 *SLG* (cited in "Travel" above); Eur. *Hippol.* 742–51 (see "General Parallels"); also Adesp. 1023 *PMG* and Ibyc. S182 4–8 *SLG*; see further West *Thgn.* ad 215 and 275; *RE* 8.1 (1913): 1243–48, s.v. *Hesperiden*. Utopian concepts also appear in prayers for blessings (e.g., Aesch. *Eum.* 902ff. and *Suppl.* 625ff.; cf. Call. h. Art. 121–35) and in unspecified idyllic landscapes, e.g., Adesp. 926(a) *PMG* and Ibycus 286 *PMG*; they are also the basis of Sophocles' idealized portrait of Colonos at *OC* 668–93 (see further n. 72 below). Finally, an Orphic Katabasis (n. 49 below, end) describes an abode reserved for the blessed dead at 130–35.

24. E.g., Pherekyd. 3 F 16 *FGrH* (the Hesperides' island); 3 F 84 (the Islands of the Blest), Theop. 115 F 75 (with Flower 1994: App. 1, Romm 1994: 67, and Dillery 1995: 45–48). Hdt. 3.17ff. and 114 (Aithiopians); 4.32–35 (Hyperboreans). Plato, e.g., *Rep.* 363a–d (see n. 39 below), 614e; *Phaedr.* 247a–b, 248b; *Gorg.* 523aff. (with Dodds's notes ad loc.); *Symp.* 179e–180b; *Statesman* 268d–275b. Cf. also Ps.-Plat. *Axi.* 371c–d. For further references and discussion, see Baldry 1952: 84, 87 and Dillery 1995: 41–54 and passim.

Utopian commonplaces were even common enough to be fertile subject matter for fantasy and parody. Mock utopias were a favorite among the writers of Old Comedy, and in the *Frogs*, in particular, Aristophanes exploits traditional utopian concepts and diction in his seriocomic portrayal of the blessed afterlife of initiates.[25] Lucian's parody of life on the Island of the Blest in the *True History* (2.4–29) is particularly instructive in that he selects the most distinctive utopian *topoi* for distortion and exaggeration.[26]

The defining features of Greek literary utopias are easily summarized.[27] Such places are regularly portrayed as removed from ordinary existence, either in time or by geography (at the ends of or underneath the earth). Climate is always central: springlike conditions prevail, particularly sunshine and fair breezes; there is a complementary exemption from inclement weather, such as clouds, rain, and winter storms. Luxuriant plant growth is a constant: trees and flowers flourish and the earth produces her crops spontaneously. The inhabitants, accordingly, enjoy an abundant livelihood and a life of ease. The most far-reaching improvements on the ordinary human lot are health, strength, and youth (exemption from disease, debility, and old age); in some cases, inhabitants derive the ultimate benefit: immortality.

ἕδος πολύδενδρον (7).   Simonides first refers to his distant[28] island destination as ἕδος (7). This noun (along with ἕδρα) is frequently used of idyllic locales in archaic and classical poetry, applied most often to the "abode" or "habitation" of the gods (e.g., θεῶν ἕδος, αἰπὺν Ὄλυμπον, *Il.* 5.367, etc.; θεῶν ἕδος αἰπὺν ... οὐρανόν, Sol. 13.21–22). Pindar actually restricts his use of ἕδος to "dwelling place, abode of gods and heroes" (e.g., ὁ δὲ χάλκεος ἀσφαλὲς αἰὲν ἕδος μένει οὐρανός, *Nem.* 6.3–4; Slater, s.v.).[29] Furthermore, when used of utopian locales, ἕδος regularly stands in apposition to another noun (cf. examples cited above with Hom. *Il.* 5.868). Simonides' ἕδος apparently stands in apposition to νῆσον (8) or, perhaps, to another noun lost from the beginning of 7, 6, or 5 (e.g., ἀκτήν, ἄλσος or κῆπον).

Simonides' idyllic island is also "rich in trees": πολύδενδρον (7).[30] Poets regularly

25. Cf. also Aristoph. *Clouds* and *Birds*, passim. Other comic references appear at Athen. 6.267e–270a, for which (and others), see Baldry 1952: 84, 86, 87.

26. Cf. also Crates 351 SH (Diog. Laert. 6.85), a clever utopian parody on a wallet (πήρη). The fantastic traveller's tale of Iamboulos (Diod. Sic. 2.55–60) exploits nearly every utopian theme: a "fortunate island" (νῆσον εὐδαίμονα 2.55.4) in distant reaches where the traveller "will live blessedly" (μακαρίως ζήσεσθαι 2.55.4); temperate atmosphere; crops growing spontaneously and superabundantly; inhabitants dwelling in meadows, free of disease, living long and enjoying easy deaths (57.4–5). See Ferguson 1975: 124–29.

27. Poets typically enumerate utopian features in catalogs that follow the form: liabilities absent, ἀλλά, assets present. Expressions with α-privative (negated or not as the context requires) are frequent; the eternal quality of the features mentioned is frequently emphasized (αἰεί; οὔτε ποτέ; ἤματα πάντα). See Davies 1987.

28. The journey itself (5) implies geographical remove, as at Stes. S8.1–2 *SLG*. Cf. δίχ' ἀνθρώπων βίοτον καὶ ... ἐν πείρασι γαίης (Hes. *WD* 167–68, Islands of the Blest); τὴν νῆσον ... τηλόθ' ἐοῦσαν (*Od.* 5.55, Ogygia); ἑκὰς ἀνδρῶν ἀλφηστάων (*Od.* 6.8, Scheria).

29. Cf. LSJ s.v. ἕδος 2. For ἕδρα/ἕδραι in the same sense, cf., e.g., εὔκυκλον ἕδραν (Pind. *Nem.* 4.66, Olympus); χρυσέαις ἐν ἕδραις (*Pyth.* 3.94, Olympus); ἐν ἕδραις ἐνθάδε (Aristoph. *Frogs* 324).

30. πολύυμνον (*l.v.* 2327) lacks the pointedness of πολύδενδρον in this utopian context, pace Parsons 1992a: 45: "Neither epithet informative in itself." Cf. also εὔδενδρον ... τέμενος (Simon. 507 *PMG*).

feature trees as part of the abundant plant life characteristic of Greek utopias,[31] often noting that they are remarkable in some respect (size, lushness, or produce).[32] The trees on Simonides' island are especially numerous (πολυ-); further, πολυ- compounds appear elsewhere, on occasion, to emphasize the superabundance of flora in utopian contexts (e.g., πολύκαρπον, a garland, Aristoph. *Frogs* 328; πολυρρόδους, meadows, ibid. 448).

εὐαγ[έ]α νῆϲον (8).   In verse 8, Simonides specifies that his imaginary destination is an island, a typical utopian setting, and describes it as "bright," εὐαγ[έ]α (West in Parsons 1992a: 47).[33] Once again, Greek literary utopias of all kinds are traditionally bathed in bright light. This feature is particularly pronounced in underworld settings where there is preternatural illumination (e.g., τοῖϲι λάμπει μὲν μένοϲ ἀελίου, Pind. fr. 129.1; ἅλιον ἔχοντεϲ, *Ol.* 2.62; φῶϲ κάλλιϲτον, ὥϲπερ ἐνθάδε, Aristoph. *Frogs* 155; ἥλιοϲ καὶ φέγγοϲ, ibid. 454–55; ἀπαλαῖϲ ἡλίου ἀκτῖϲιν, Ps.-Plat. *Axi.* 371d).[34] In open-air settings, like Simonides' island, bright sunshine goes hand in hand with the exemption from inclement weather (e.g., μάλ᾽ αἴθρη | πέπταται ἀνέφελοϲ, λευκὴ δ᾽ ἐπιδέδρομεν αἴγλη, *Od.* 6.44–45, Olympus; cf. 4.566, the Elysian plain).

ἄγαλμα (8).   Simonides' introductory description of the island culminates in verse 8 with ἄγαλμα (in apposition to νῆϲον). West's ἄγαλμα β[ίου makes good sense. Translation to a utopian island, with all that it entails, might well be described as the crowning "glory" or "delight" of human life, whether construed as a mark of divine favor (like Menelaus' prophesied destiny in *Od.* 4) or as a reward for virtue (as in some eschatological passages). In sum, through a few but well chosen details in 7–8 (implied geographical remove, island setting, ἕδοϲ, prolific plant life and bright

31. E.g., νῆϲοϲ δενδρήεϲϲα (Ogygia, *Od.* 1.51); φέροντά τε δένδρεα καρπόν (Hesperides' island, Hes. *Thgn.* 216; cf. Pherekydes 3 F 16 *FGrH*). Lucian says, hyperbolically, that *every* kind of flower and plant flourishes on the Island of the Blest: ἡ δὲ χώρα πᾶϲι μὲν ἄνθεϲιν, πᾶϲι δὲ φυτοῖϲ ἡμέροιϲ τε καὶ ϲκιεροῖϲ τέθηλεν (*Ver. hist.* 2.13). Cf. Parsons 1992a: 46.
32. E.g., ἔνθα δὲ δένδρεα μακρὰ πεφύκαϲι τηλεθόωντα (Scheria, *Od.* 7.114); ὕλη δὲ ϲπέοϲ ἀμφὶ πεφύκει τηλεθόωντα (Ogygia, *Od.* 5.63). Trees in Pindar's descriptions of the abode of the blessed dead are particularly striking: ἀγλαῶν δενδρέων (*Ol.* 2.73) and χρυϲοκάρποιϲιν . . . ⟨δενδρέοιϲ⟩ (fr. 129.5). In his invented land of the Meropes, Theopompus features δένδρα τὸ μέγαθοϲ πλατάνου μεγάληϲ (115 F 75c *FGrH*).
33. The adjective that modifies νῆϲον spans 2327 fr. 2(a) col. ii and fr. 4: ευα [ ]α. At least two letters are needed to fill the gap. West 1993a: 13 (cf. 22.8 W²) ultimately printed εὐαέα, suggesting a "corruption . . . to εὐαγέα" under the influence of εὐαγέωϲ δ᾽ ἀνδρῶν ἐϲ] which he supplies at the beginning of 7. The hypothetical nature of this corruption notwithstanding, εὐαέα would be apposite in the context. Pleasant winds, typically Zephyros, appear in a whole array of Greek utopias, e.g., *Od.* 4.567–68 (Elysian plain) and 7.118–19 (Scheria); cf. [Bacchylides] *Epigr.* 2.2 S.-M (1 *FGE*) where Zephyros is the "most fecund" (πιοτάτῳ) of winds. Lucian draws attention to Zephyros as a standard utopian feature with a typical gesture of parody: this is the *only* wind that blows on the Island of the Blest: εἷϲ ἄνεμοϲ πνεῖ παρ᾽ αὐτοῖϲ ὁ Ζέφυροϲ (*Ver. hist.* 2.12). Cf. also ἔνθα μακάρων νᾶϲον ὠκεανίδεϲ αὖραι περιπνέοιϲιν (Pind. *Ol.* 2.70–72).
34. Cf. Koenen 1994: 30 n. 69. Nilsson repeatedly emphasizes the contrast between light and dark as the essential opposition between a utopian afterlife and Hades, e.g., "einerseits das lichte Land der Inseln der Seligen . . . andererseits die dumpfe und modrige Welt der wesens- und bewusstseinslosen Schatten" (Nilsson 1967: 329; cf. 324–29 passim).

light), Simonides has painted his desired island destination in the colors of a traditional literary utopia.[35]

Flowers (13–14) and Garland (15–16). When Simonides proceeds to describe his activities on the island in 9ff., new details are also consistent with the utopian setting. In 13–14 he speaks of "reclining" (κεκλιμένος) in "flowers" or in some flowery place (ἐν ἄνθε[ ), and one need not seek far to find flowers as a feature of utopia.[36] Pindar adorns his eschatological paradise in *Ol.* 2 with gleaming "flowers of gold" (72) and elsewhere locates the blessed dead in "meadows of purple roses" (φοινικορόδοις . . . λειμώνεσσι, fr. 129.3); he even uses the metaphor of blooming flowers to describe the unalloyed bliss of the inhabitants (παρὰ δέ σφισιν εὐανθὴς ἅπας τέθαλεν ὄλβος 129.7). Flowers abound in Aristophanes' description of the blessed underworld abode in the *Frogs* (351/2, 373–74a, 441–42, 448–49; stage-properties, perhaps?) and Lucian provides the touchstone of parody: not only does his blessed island bloom with every kind of flower (n. 31 above), but also visitors are bound with shackles of flowers, pass through a λειμὼν εὐανθής, sit on flowery couches, and adorn themselves with flowers delivered by nightingales (*Ver. hist.* 2.5–6, 13–14).

Next the poet refers to "weaving" (πλε[κ- or πλε[ξ-) what is certainly a "garland" (Lobel 1954: 75; Parsons 1992a: 45). This garland is "lovely" (χαρίε[ντ]α 15), made (appropriately) "of beautiful flowers" (εὐανθέα 16) and is (or is associated with something else that is) "freshly bloomed" (νεοβλαστ[15).[37] When added to the speaker's reference to his reclining posture, the garland completes the suggestion of a sympotic scene.[38] Although the trappings of symposia provide the sole setting for much occasional archaic verse, they are also a traditional complement to utopian landscapes. Pindar's blessed dead sport garlands (*Ol.* 2.74), as do both his Hyperboreans (*Pyth.* 10.40) and Aristophanes' blessed initiates (*Frogs* 329–330/1); Plato criticizes "Musaeus and his son" for portraying the blessed afterlife as consisting of the merely frivolous pleasures of the symposium;[39] Lucian makes the symposium central.[40] On the other

35. The description in 7–8 would suggest all the additional advantages that tradition attaches to such places. Cf. Dover 1993: 60 on Aristophanes' description of the abode of the blessed initiates in the *Frogs*: "It is to be presumed that the paradise enjoyed by the initiates is exempt from toil, fatigue, pain, sickness, sorrow, and fear."

36. Greek utopias are often set in flowery meadows, e.g., λειμῶνες μαλακοί (Ogygia, *Od.* 5.72); Pind. fr. 129.3; Aristoph. *Frogs* 326, 373–74a, 448–49; Diod. Sic. 2.57.1 (Iamboulos' island) and λειμῶνάς τ(ε) ἱερούς (Orpheus DK B.20.6 [= 4{A 67}.6, Colli 1977: 1.182–85]; cf. Dover 1993: 60). For the erotic associations of such settings, see n. 41 below.

37. Cf. Simon. 27.4 W²: στεφάνους] εὐανθέας. See Parsons 1992a: 46 for other possibilities in 15–16. The alliteration of the palatals κ (14) and χ (11 and 15) is striking.

38. For more sympotic "scraps" from 3965 see Parsons 1992a: 7 and West 1993a: 10 n. 20.

39. Μουσαῖος . . . καὶ ὁ υἱὸς αὐτοῦ . . . [τοὺς δικαίους] εἰς "Αιδου . . . ἀγαγόντες τῷ λόγῳ καὶ κατακλίναντες καὶ συμπόσιον τῶν ὁσίων κατασκευάσαντες ἐστεφανωμένους ποιοῦσι τὸν ἅπαντα χρόνον ἤδη διάγειν μεθύοντας, ἡγησάμενοι κάλλιστον ἀρετῆς μισθὸν μέθην αἰώνιον (*Rep.* 363c–d).

40. καὶ μὴν καὶ βοὴ σύμμικτος ἠκούετο ἄθρους . . . οἵα γένοιτ' ἂν ἐν συμποσίῳ, τῶν μὲν αὐλούντων, τῶν δὲ ἐπᾳδόντων, ἐνίων δὲ κροτούντων πρὸς αὐλὸν ἢ κιθάραν (*Ver. hist.* 2.5; cf. 14ff.). Cf. Parsons 1992a: 49. For idealized banqueting in the afterlife in Roman funerary art (often with the inclusion of music or Muses), cf. Cumont 1942 [1966]: 291–97, 371–79.

hand, this suggestion of a symposium among the flowers in Simonides 22 W^2 sets the scene for a quite different aspect of the poet's fantasy: erotic love.[41]

Eros (9–14). At verse 9 the poet introduces into his imaginary scene a male[42] companion with attractive blond hair (ξανθότρ[ιχα),[43] whom he presents in 10–12 as the object of his admiration and desire. Verse 10 contains the idea of desired physical contact (χεῖρα λάβοιμ[ι),[44] followed by conventional erotic language focusing on skin and eyes in 11–12. The most reasonably secure supplements of the whole piece give us a "youthful bloom"[45] emanating "from lovely skin" and the dripping of "desirable longing from the lids."[46] Although the poet's recumbent posture is apparently a convivial rather than sexual pose, the passage is unmistakably erotic in tenor, reminiscent in some respects of the seduction scene in the Cologne Epode: παρθένον δ' ἐν ἄνθε[cιν | τηλ]εθάεccι λαβὼν | ἔκλινα (Archil. 196a.42–44).[47]

Although not typically included in traditional catalogues of utopian assets, erotic love is at least implicit from the beginning: Menelaus will spend eternity in the Elysian plain in the company of Helen (*Od.* 4.569) and Herakles lives ageless and immortal on Olympus with Hebe as his wife (Hes. *Th.* 950–55; fr. 25.26–29; fr. 229.6–13).[48] From the fifth century onward, references to eros in utopian settings are increasingly pointed. In Empedocles' revisionist account of the Golden Age, "Zeus was not king, nor Kronos, nor Poseidon, but Cypris was queen" (DK B 128) and the comic poet

41. For the persistent association in the Greek literary tradition of flowery landscapes (meadows in particular) with erotic love, see Bremer 1975: 268–80; Slings 1978: 38. Simonides' flowers bridge the utopian and erotic themes quite concretely: ἄν[θος (11) refers to the desirable young blooming beauty of his companion (see further n. 45); χαρίε[ντ]α (15), of the garland, picks up the phrase χ[αρίε]ντος ἀπὸ χροὸς (11), of the boy.

42. The sex of the companion is confirmed by the strong likelihood of "Echecratidas" in 9 (see below, "Fantasy and Reality") and type of erotic language. For attention, e.g., to the eyes in homoerotic contexts, cf. Alc. 59(a) *PMG*; Ibyc. 287.1–4 *PMG*; Pind. fr. 123.2–9. Cf. also Simon. 27.5 W^2: π]αῖδ' ἐρατόν.

43. For ξανθός of hair, see Irwin 1974: 57 with n. 55, 91 with nn. 30–31, 135; Parsons 1992a: 45.

44. Parsons notes (1992a: 45, with parallels) that the hand-clasp has a variety of connotations—"pledge," "reassurance," "welcome," and "courtship"; the context plainly implies the last.

45. Simonides' νεο[υ] . . . ἄν[θος (11) may be a variation of the familiar ἥβης ἄνθος, i.e. a general reference to youth's "bloom"; cf. LSJ s.v. ἄνθος (A) II. From the earliest period ἄνθος was used in this way of either sex, e.g., κουρήιον ἄνθος ἔχουcαι (*Hymn. Hom. Cer.* 108, the daughters of Keleus; cf. Richardson 1974: nn. ad 108, 279); ἄνθος δ' ἀπερρύηκε παρθενήιον (Archil. 196a.27 W^2); παῖς καλὸν ἄνθον ἔχων (Theogn. 994); νηπία ἐοῦς' ἔθανον καὶ οὐ λά[β]ον ἄνθος ἔτ' ἥβας (Friedländer 1948: #32). Simonides' χ[αρίε]ντος ἀπὸ χροὸς may, however, indicate that ἄνθος refers more specifically to the downy skin of a prepubescent boy. Solon 27.5–6 W^2, e.g., marks the third stage of life by the growth of facial hair and loss of the skin's "bloom" (γένειον . . . | λαχνοῦται, χροιῆς ἄνθος ἀμειβομένης); cf. Griffith 1983 ad A. *Pr.* 23 and 7. On the development of ἄνθος/ἀνθέω from the literal sense of "upward physical growth," see Aitchison 1963: 271–78. The loss of the verb at the end of verse 11 hinders a definitive interpretation.

46. Cf. τῶν καὶ ἀπὸ βλεφάρων ἔρος εἴβετο δερκομενάων | λυσιμελής (Hes. *Thgn.* 910–11, the Charites). West's λείβοι must be right: λείβει 2327 is superior to the variant λείπει in point of sense, and the emendation brings the mood in line with the other finite verbs in the text; cf. also Lobel 1954: 75 and Parsons 1992a: 47. For the image of liquid desire, see Davies 1983: 496–97 and Cyrino 1995: 48–51, 63–64, 81–84, 138.

47. Cited also by Parsons 1992a: 48. Consider Simonides' focus on the body of the beloved: hair (9), hand (10), skin (11), and eyes (12).

48. Hebe is a symbol of Herakles' eternal youth as well as his divine consort. For early passages that combine utopian *topoi* with the "meadow of love," see Bremer 1975.

Philetairos gives musicians the special privilege of erotic pleasures after death (τούτοιc ἐν ῞Αιδου γὰρ μόνοιc ἐξουcία | ἀφροδιciάζειν ἐcτίν, fr. 17.2–3 KA).⁴⁹ The most explicit conjunctions of eros and a utopian afterlife come from the Roman tradition. Tibullus claims that Venus herself will escort him to the Elysian plain where lovers continue to sport at the bidding of Amor (Tib. 1.3.57–58; 63–66); Roman funerary monuments often juxtapose images of an idyllic afterlife with Erotes.⁵⁰ Still, the most original aspect of Simonides 22 is not so much that it is an unusually early conjunction of utopian and erotic themes; rather that Simonides developed the erotic scene by exploiting another poetic tradition not elsewhere associated with utopian *topoi*.

Wrinkles (14).   No single word in the fragment carries more weight for the interpretation of the poem as a whole than φαρκίδαc in 14.⁵¹ Parsons and West both correctly seek to complete the lacunose verse-end with the idea of banishing or "driving away" these wrinkles; similarly, L. Koenen suggests, for example, ἐκ π[άλι δύc or ἐκ τ[ότε δύc.⁵²

The concept of shedding or banishing old age is perfectly consistent with the poet's utopian fantasy. Exemption from old age is *de rigueur* in the utopian tradition

---

49. Cf. Dover 1993: 60 on the life of the blessed initiates in the *Frogs*: "We may surely take sexual activity for granted." For the appearance of abstract erotic forces in a utopian escape-wish by Euripides, see below, "General Parallels"; cf. also Dioscorides' wish that Anacreon may have the wherewithal in the underworld to enjoy drinking, dancing, and "embracing golden Eurypyle" (βεβληκὼc χρυσέην χεῖρac ἐπ᾽ Εὐρυπύλην, *AP* VII 31.9–10). Lucian describes the sex life of his utopian islanders, but largely as a parody of ethnographic writing (περὶ δὲ cυνουcίαc καὶ ἀφροδιcίων οὕτω φρονοῦcιν κ.τ.λ., *Ver. hist.* 2.19). An Orphic Katabasis includes (34–36) the curious feature of Erotes inflicting tortures on the wicked in the afterlife (Merkelbach 1951; Lloyd-Jones 1978 (app. crit. ad v. 35), "Nodum sollerter solvit C. W. Macleod: . . . etiam post mortem vitia vitiosos torquere, libidines ergo libidinosos."

50. Cumont 1942 (1966): 291–97, 336. Cf. esp. the bas-relief with Herakles reclining in an idyllic garden in the company of winged Erotes, Muses, and an old man (291–92 with Pl. XXV, 1). Elsewhere we find a young man reclining with winged Erotes and a female musician (296–97 with Pl. XXV, 2), a married couple with Erotes (296–97), and Erotes at a funerary banquet (336). For another view of the significance of this iconography, see Nock 1972: 894: "Erotes in later art and poetry . . . have no erotic suggestion whatsoever—no more than the Cupids on the columns of the Harvard Memorial Church." A few examples, however, seem unequivocal, e.g., Cumont 1949: 256–57: a painting depicting a female votary of Sabazius being introduced into the banquet of the blessed with "divertissements" of "une saveur érotique très accusée"; cf. also epitaphs from Anatolia containing "le souhait d'obtenir encore dans l'autre vie les plaisirs amoureux" (257; cf. 302). Particularly arresting is a tomb that sports the following inscription: Γέρμηc ἐξ ῾Ιερῆc Τελεcίcτρατοc ἐν | Μακάρων νήcοιc κεῖμαι· ἔτι τῶνδε χρέοc ποθέω, where τῶνδε refers to erotic decoration on the tomb, including "Une scène érotique, dont l'acteur masculin fait preuve d'une virilité démesurée" (Cumont 1940: 5–7).

51. For the rare φαρκίδαc, see Parsons 1992a: 45. Hunter 1993a: 13 explains why the apparently anomalous short iota is no cause for concern. Hunter suggests further that φαρκίδαc may be "an otherwise unattested word for food of some kind, like the 'beans' of Theocritus 7.66." For specific objections to Hunter's "feasting" hypothesis and use of Theocr. 7 as a parallel, see n. 80 below. See also Rutherford, this volume, at n. 92.

52. Per litteras. Cf. τὸ γῆρac ἐκδύμι (Aristoph. *Peace* 336); τὸ δ᾽ ἐκδύοιμι (sc. γῆρac, Call. fr. 1.35 Pf.); πολιὸν δὲ γῆρac ἐκδύc (Bergk⁴: ἐκάc P; *Anacreont.* 53.7 West). Perhaps the idea is that of "smoothing out" the wrinkles. Cf. Phoenix's characterization of a (hypothetical) rejuvenation as θεὸc . . . | γῆρας ἀποξύσας (*Il.* 9.445–46), where Leaf notes that Aristotle uses γῆρας (*HA* v. 15.6) for "the slough or cast-off skin of a serpent."

everywhere from Hesiod's golden race (οὐδέ τι δειλόν | γῆρας ἐπῆν [*WD* 113–14]) to Pindar's Hyperboreans (οὔτε γῆρας οὐλόμενον κέκραται | ἱερᾷ γενεᾷ [*Pyth*. 10. 41–42]). The Chorus of blessed dead at Aristoph. *Frogs* 345 refer specifically to the corollary of rejuvenation: γόνυ πάλλεται γερόντων.[53] On the other hand, the speaker's express desire to be rejuvenated reveals the most telling fact about him, namely that he is advanced in age. (For more on the poetic *topos* of advancing age, see Hunter, this volume, at nn. 22ff.) The essence of the erotic scene, therefore, is an aging lover's desire for a young beloved, a situation that, in turn, participates in one of the most familiar themes of Greek erotic lyric and elegy: old age as an impediment to eros. Typically, an aging speaker laments that his years place a barrier between him and the object of his desire. In Anacreon 358 *PMG*, for example, the speaker describes how an attractive young girl (νήνι 3) rejects him, heaping scorn on his white hair (τὴν μὲν ἐμὴν κόμην, λευκὴ γάρ, καταμέμφεται 6–7).[54] Simonides' unique twist to this theme of an aging lover's frustrated desire is to introduce the erotic situation in the context of a utopian fantasy—an imaginary setting where, de facto, the impediment of old age will no longer exist (see further, "General Parallels" and "Conclusion," below).

Before φαρκίδας, the papyrus shows λευκ[ ] : "spacing depends . . . on the precise ranging of the two strips" (Parsons 1992a: 48). Although West favors λευκ[ά]c, "white wrinkles" is, at best, a peculiar phrase. A reference to complexion is unlikely since λευκός (aut sim.), while used regularly of women, is pejorative for males (Irwin 1974: 129–35). A reference to a white beard, that is, in the vicinity of the wrinkles, seems far-fetched.[55] Maybe the phrase is meant to recall the familiar γῆρας πολιόν?[56] A sec-

---

53. Parsons's skepticism about the link between exemption from old age and rejuvenation is misplaced ("I have found no evidence that the Blest were rejuvenated," 1992a: 49); he does concede that "the idea itself seems natural enough." For a *magical* rejuvenation in Simonides, cf. 548 *PMG* (Jason by Medea). Theopompus takes the idea of utopian rejuvenation to its absurd extreme. In the land of the Meropes, if someone eats the fruit of trees that grow near the "river of pleasure," he not only sheds old age, but races backwards through all the phases of life until he disappears: τὸ μὲν γὰρ γῆρας ἀπορρίψας ἐπὶ τὴν ἀκμὴν ὑποστρέφει, εἶτα ἐπὶ τὴν τῶν μειρακίων ἡλικίαν ἀναχωρεῖ, εἶτα παῖς γίνεται, εἶτα βρέφος, καὶ ἐπὶ τούτοις ἐξαναλώθη (115 F 75c *FGrH*). Cf. Dillery 1995: 46–48.

54. The poet turns this melancholy situation into a triumph of revenge by leveling the charge of lesbianism at the girl (cf. Mace 1993: 347–49). Examples of poems based on the theme of frustrated desire in old age are easily multiplied: Ibyc. 287 *PMG* (an aged speaker expresses horror at the advent of a fresh love); *Anacreont*. 51 (a speaker urges a girl not to flee because of his white hair: white lilies among roses make garlands attractive!); the unkind Anac. 394(b) *PMG* (μνᾶται δηῦτε φαλακρὸς Ἄλεξις, where "bald" presumably implies that Alexis was wooing at an advanced age; see Mace 1993: 349–50; cf. *Anacreont*. 7 [female scorn for baldness]); Anac. 379(a) and (b) *PMG* (an injunction for Eros to fly past an individual with a gray beard); Pind. fr. 123.1 S.-M. (an aging speaker's concern for καιρός in the pursuit of young men; see further "General Parallels" below); Palladas *AP* 11.54 (female scorn for the speaker's white hair with his profession of indifference and solace found in wine). For Anac. 395.1–2 *PMG* (and in general) see Giangrande 1968: 100–3, 108–19. For eros and old age in Anacreon, the anacreontic poems, and elsewhere, see also Rosenmeyer 1992, esp. 57–61, 138–39; also 53–54 and 60 on *Anacreont*. 52A, and 178–80 on the possible relationship among Palladas *AP* 11.54, *Anacreont*. 7, and Theocr. 7.120–21. For references to gray hair in these poems and others, see nn. 56–58 below.

55. Odysseus' rejuvenation, e.g., entails a reference to the darkening, specifically, of his beard: κυάνεαι δ' ἐγένοντο γενειάδες ἀμφὶ γένειον (*Od*. 16.176; cf. Irwin 1974: 90–91).

56. Irwin 1974: 194 n. 91 gives more than a dozen citations from Homer to Aristophanes for γῆρας πολιόν; cf. also *Anacreont*. 53.7 West; λευκὸν γῆρας apparently only once: Soph. *Ai.* 625 (Irwin 1974: 195).

ond option is λευκ[α]ῖc, to be taken with χαίτη[ιc ι]ν in the next verse. A reference to hair color often signals the contrast between youth and age in early lyric and elegy, particularly in erotic contexts.[58] Simonides could have identified his young beloved in 9 as ξανθότρ[ιχα precisely in anticipation of a reference to his own white hair.[59] Still, this proposal would entail a fairly radical hyperbaton and, more to the point, would violate the logic of the fantasy: an individual who is otherwise shedding the tokens of age (such as wrinkles) should not be referring to his white hair as a fact of the present. In the end, Parsons's λευκ[ο]ῖc (with ἄνθε[c ι(ν)) may be the least dramatic of the three suggestions, but yields the most plausible sense and syntax.[59]

Poetry (17–18).   The final feature of the speaker's imaginary utopian existence is the practice of his own poetic calling: ἄρτι [επέα] νωμῶν γλῶccαν (18).[60] Like other sympotic elements, musical performances of all kinds suit the utopian milieu: Pindar's Hyperboreans enjoy maiden choruses, lyres, and auloi (*Pyth.* 10.37–39; Μοῖcα δ' οὐκ ἀποδαμεῖ, 37) and Aristophanes' initiates refer to the "breath of auloi" (*Frogs* 154, 313; cf. Pind. fr. 129.7).[61] At the same time, Simonides also links this reference to poetry to the erotic theme through a verbal echo: ἱμερόεντα λιγύν (17) picks up ἱμερόεντα (12), associated with the boy's desirable eyes; suggested in 17 is a mellifluous seductive sound, perhaps of the aulos.[62] Finally, Simonides' reference to his poetic craft may also serve a transitional function, linking the themes of the fantasy directly to the *hic et nunc* of the poem's performance. On the principle that the skill of the poet redounds to the greater glory of the honorand, the speaker's claim to eloquence would be a suitable prelude to the section of direct encomium to which he may have turned next (see below, "Fantasy and Reality").

57. For Anac. 358 and 379 *PMG*, see next note; λεῦκαι δ' ἐγένο]ντο τρίχεc ἐκ μελαίναν (Sappho fr. 58.13–14); πολιοὶ μὲν ἡμὶν ἤδη κρόταφοι κάρη τε λευκόν (Anac. 395.1–2 *PMG*; see n. 54 above); εὖτέ μοι λευκαὶ μελαίνηc' ἀναμεμείξονται τρίχεc (Anac. 420 *PMG*, probably an erotic context); μή με φύγηc ὁρῶcα τὰν πολιὰν ἔθειραν (*Anacreont.* 51.1–2; see n. 54 above); ἀλλ' ἐγὼ εἰ λευκὰc φορέω τρίχαc, εἴτε μελαίναc, οὐκ ἀλέγω (Palladas *AP* 11.54.3–4; see n. 54 above). Cf. τρίχαc γέρων (acc. spec., *Anacreont.* 39.4). Cf. also Irwin 1974: 194–96 and Rosenmeyer 1992: 58–59.
58. As in Anac. 358 *PMG*, where χρυcοκόμηc (2) of Eros (and thus associated with the love-object) anticipates the rejected speaker's reference to his white hair at 6–7; Anac. 379 *PMG* speaks of a gray-bearded man and Eros with wings of shining gold (χρυcοφαέννων [χρυcοφαείνων, Fick]). Cf. also Anac. 418 *PMG*: κλῦθι μεο γέροντοc εὐέθειρα χρυcόπεπλε κοῦρα.
59. See Parsons 1992a: 48 for lore on white flowers.
60. Lobel 1954: 76 first suggested ἄρτι [επέα], but with reservations about the traces. Parsons and West endorse the supplement, the former citing ἀρτιεπὴc γλῶccα (of the poet) at Pind. *Isthm.* 5.46–47 (48). West's ἀ]πὸ cτόματοc 18 fin. seems unlikely: as his parallels imply, a reference to the actual utterance seems needed to support the prepositional phrase: τέρεν φθέγγετ' ἀπὸ cτόματοc (Theogn. 266); ψεῦδοc . . . ἐξέλθη . . . ἀπὸ cτόματοc (609–10). Cf. also Simon. 585.1–2 *PMG*: ἀπὸ cτόματοc ἱεῖcα φωνάν.
61. Music is central to Lucian's parody both in general (individual performances and choruses) and by virtue of the presence of such luminaries as Homer, Anacreon, and Stesichorus (*Ver. hist.* 2.15). Muses appear in Sophocles' idyllic Colonos (*OC* 691–92); for singing Hesperides at Eur. *Hippol.* 742–43 and an idyllic Pieria, seat of the Muses, at Eur. *Bacch.* 409–11, see below, "General Parallels." See also Rutherford, this volume, at n. 94.
62. λιγύc "may describe the singer, the instrument, the voice or the song" (Parsons 1992a: 48); West favors the last in this context. Theogn. 241–43 uses λιγυ- of both voice and aulos. For the aulos in elegiac performance, see West 1974: 5–14 passim.

General Parallels

The hypothesis that Simonides 22 W^2 contains an original, perhaps unique fusion of utopian and erotic themes can be supported by a brief survey of two groups of potential parallels: poems based on the theme of rejuvenation and those framed as utopian escape-wishes.

Rejuvenation.   Alcman 26 *PMG* is a first-person wish for rejuvenation based on the speaker's fantasy of being transformed into a bird:[63]

> οὔ μ' ἔτι, παρcενικαὶ μελιγάρυεc ἱαρόφωνοι,
> γυῖα φέρην δύναται· βάλε δὴ βάλε κηρύλοc εἴην,
> ὅc τ' ἐπὶ κύματοc ἄνθοc ἅμ' ἀλκυόνεccι ποτήται
> νηδεὲc ἦτορ ἔχων, ἁλιπόρφυροc ἱαρὸc ὄρνιc.

In the prologue to the *Aetia*, Callimachus also bases a rejuvenation fantasy on a metamorphosis, in his case into a cicada (fr. 1.32–36 Pfeiffer):[64]

> ἐγ]ὼ δ' εἴην οὑλ[α]χύc, ὁ πτερόειc,
> ἆ πάντωc, ἵνα γῆραc ἵνα δρόcον ἢν μὲν ἀείδω
> πρώκιον ἐκ δίηc ἠέροc εἶδαρ ἔδων,
> αὖθι τὸ δ' ἐκδύοιμι, τό μοι βάροc ὅccον ἔπεcτι
> τριγλώχιν ὀλοῷ νῆcοc ἐπ' Ἐγκελάδῳ.

These two wishes for rejuvenation would appear to have more in common with one another than either has with Simonides 22 W^2. By contrast with Simonides' utopian fantasy, both Alcman and Callimachus employ the motif of transformation. Whereas the underlying motivation of Simonides' rejuvenation wish is desire, the other two are motivated explicitly by feelings of decrepitude, and the wished-for transformations are designed to remove the debilities of old age.[65] Although poetry is just one of several elements in the sympotic milieu of Simonides' fantasy, it is central to the wishes of Alcman and Callimachus.[66] Finally, even the discursive style of Simonides 22 may be contrasted with the urgent and emotional tone of the other two.[67]

Anacreontea 53 West, though not a wish, also focuses on the theme of rejuvenation: the aging speaker describes how the sight of a company of young men inspires in him a feeling of youthfulness, an eagerness to dance and a kind of Bacchic frenzy (1–8; 9–14 add the element of wine):

63. Cf. Antigon. Caryst. *Mir.* xxiii (27), ad Alc. 26.
64. West has already proposed that the passage is relevant to Simonides 22: "Is the Cyrenaean elegist recalling the Cean?" (West 1993a: 14); cf. Hunter 1993a: 12 n. 2.
65. Alcman complains about the weakness of his limbs (1–2) and old age weighs as heavily upon Callimachus as Sicily does upon Enkelados. Alcman's *kerylos* would enjoy the power of free flight; life as a tiny winged cicada would restore Callimachus to agility and mobility.
66. Alcman wants to restore waning artistic powers and Callimachus desires to become a creature that is, above all, a singer.
67. Alcman employs repetition (βάλε δὴ βάλε, 26.2) and Callimachus combines repetition (ἵνα γῆραc ἵνα δρόcον, 33) with asyndeton (32), interjection (33) and anacolouthon (33–35). Cf. Fehling 1969: 176, 303.

ὅτ' ἐγὼ 'c νέων ὅμιλον
ἐcορῶ, πάρεcτιν ἥβα.
τότε δή, τότ' ἐc χορείην
ὁ γέρων ἐγὼ πτεροῦμαι,
παραμαίνομαι, κυβηβῶ.
παράδοc· θέλω cτέφεcθαι·
πολιὸν δὲ γῆραc ἐκδύc
νέοc ἐν νέοιc χορεύcω.

This poem features neither a magical transformation nor translation to an idyllic locale; instead the speaker's rejuvenation is akin to the altered psychological state of an ecstatic devotee of Dionysus (5; cf. 9, 14). Though it may be said that *Anacreontea* 53 shares an erotic element with Simonides 22 W², this speaker's desire for the young men of verse 1 remains only implicit; desire would, in any case, have to be interpreted as one of several *sources* of his feeling of rejuvenation rather than the underlying *motive* for the wish as in Simonides 22.[68]

Utopian Escape-wishes.   Turning now to the utopian theme, several well-known choral passages by Euripides contain first-person fantasies about escaping some undesirable situation by fleeing to an idyllic locale.[69] Even though none of the fantasies involves old age, two passages invite comparison with Simonides 22 on the basis of other shared themes.

At Eur. *Hipp.* 732–51, the Chorus wish to be transformed into birds so that they might wing their way west, ultimately to "the apple-sown shore of the singing Hesperides" (cited also by Parsons 1992a: 46). Euripides portrays the Hesperides' island as the garden of the gods, situated Ζηνὸc παρὰ κοίταιc (749), where Zeus and Hera celebrated their marriage (Barrett 1964: 305). Although this utopian escape-wish shares erotic overtones with Simonides 22, it ultimately leaves an entirely different impression. Euripides' passage is highly stylized, populated by divinities and riddled with mythical allusions, some of them obscure.[70] Simonides features neither gods nor figures of myth in his fantasy, but instead uses simple language to paint a naturalistic scene with an emphasis on the human element: the beloved boy, and poetry performed by himself.

---

68. See also Rosenmeyer 1992: 60–61. A curious inversion of a rejuvenation wish appears at Euripides' *Her.* 637–54. The Chorus begin by praising youth and (in verses that apparently inspired Callimachus) excoriating old age as "a burden heavier than the crags of Aitna" (637–40). Then, rather than fantasizing about fleeing old age themselves, they wish to banish *it*: under the sea, from the habitations of men, and, finally, away through the aither borne on its *own* wings: ἀλλὰ κατ' αἰθέρ' αἰεὶ πτεροῖcι φορείcθω (653–54).

69. On Euripidean escape lyrics in general, see Barrett 1964 ad *Hippol.* 732–34 and 1290–93. (See also now Eur. *Phoen.* 163–67 and 234–38 with Mastronarde 1994, nn. ad loc.)

70. The Chorus imagine themselves borne over the "water of Eridanos" (737), "a purely fabulous stream of the far west" (Barrett 1964 ad loc.), where Phaethon's female kin mourn him with amber tears (i.e., in tree form, 738–41); the garden itself is guarded by the Old Man of the Sea where Atlas holds up the vault of heaven (744–47); there is mention of the divine marriage and the Hesperides themselves and their music; the place flows with "ambrosial" (i.e., immortal) springs and the gods themselves are present to enjoy the bounty of "the divine earth, giver of *olbos*" (750–51).

The utopian escape-wish at *Bacchae* 402–16 yields a similar contrast. Here the Asiatic maenads fantasize about exchanging their persecution in Thebes for three idyllic destinations where they might worship Dionysus in peace: Cyprus, Egypt, and Pieria.[71] Here the erotic element is even more pronounced: Cyprus is "the island of Aphrodite" and home of the Erotes (402–5) and Pieria, as well as being "seat of Muses" (μούϲειοϲ ἕδρα), is the dwelling place of the Charites and Pothos (409–15). The thematic correspondences between this passage and Simonides 22 (desired travel to a utopian locale, eros, and music) again reveal the essential difference. In this Euripidean utopia, too, music and eros are stylized, appearing in the form of divinities and abstractions.[72] Absent again is the humanizing focus and, with it, the particularity and poignancy of Simonides' development of the theme of the aging lover.[73]

A third poetic treatment of the theme of utopian escape comes from the Latin tradition: Horace, *Epode* 16. In an apocalyptic vision of the fall of Rome as a result of civil war (1–14), Horace exhorts the Roman people to abandon the city for some idyllic locale ("arva, beata I petamus arva, divites et insulas," 41–42). Then, after a (more or less) traditional description of this desired utopian destination (43–62), Horace finally proclaims: "piis secunda vate me datur fuga" (67). Save for the common theme of utopian escape, the contrast between Simonides 22 and *Epode* 16 is stark. Nothing in Simonides' personal occasional poem anticipates Horace's application of the theme to contemporary politics nor his authoritative delivery of pronouncements to fellow citizens as poet-*vates*. (For more on Simonides and Horace, see Sider and Barchiesi, this volume; for an expanded interpretation of this passage, see Harrison, this volume, at nn. 37ff.)

Of the poets who did handle the themes of rejuvenation and utopian escape, it would appear that Simonides alone chose to exploit the connection between the two.

Fantasy and Reality

Transition to the Here and Now ([19? +] 20–21 [+ 22f.?]).   The final tattered verses of Simonides 22 yield only scanty clues (two words in all), which may nevertheless provide some hint as to the direction in which this complex of utopian, sympotic, and erotic themes was ultimately heading.[74] τῶνδε in 20 is conceivably part of a forward-

---

71. Cyprus here represents the eastern boundary of the known world and Pieria is a northern extreme (see Dodds 1960 ad loc.). On the text of 406, see Diggle 1994. Koenen, who at one time (1976: 140 n. 44) had endorsed Meineke's ⟨χθόνα⟩ θ' ἂν ἑκατόϲτομοι I βαρβάρου ποταμοῦ ῥοαὶ I καρπίζουϲιν ἄνομβροι (406–08; Πάφον, codd.), now prefers Diggle's text (but {θ} ἂν instead of ⟨τ⟩ἂν; per litt.).

72. For other examples of abstract erotic forces in utopian settings, cf. Sophocles' description of an idyllic Colonos at *OC* 668–93 (esp. ἁ χρυϲάνιοϲ Ἀφροδίτα, 691–92); also Emped. DK B 128 (see above at n. 49).

73. A third utopian escape-wish appears at Eur. *Hel.* 1478–86. The Chorus wish to take wing and fly to a utopian Libya situated at the southern extreme of the known world, marked by an ideal climate and abundant produce. Specifically they wish to exchange ὄμβρον . . . χειμέριον (1481) for ἄβροχα πεδία καρποφόρα τε (1485). The "picturesque" predominates here with no other thematic overlap with Simonides 22.

74. "20–21 on a detached fragment (fr. 2[b] of 2327) which Lobel thought 'located here by both cross and vertical fibres.' Note that the overlap of cross fibres is very small, so that the horizontal alignment is not necessarily reliable" (Parsons 1992a: 48). Cf. Hunter 1993a: 13 with n. 10. It makes no difference to the argument even if a substantial number of verses intervened between 18 and 20.

looking transition: a reference to the men (or things) of "here and now." One could hardly fail to associate εὔκομπ[in 21[75] with the idea of ennobling poetry. The word may have marked a transition to the subject of encomium.[76] To be sure, these details are hardly secure or informative enough to answer questions concerning the aim, audience, and occasion of this sympotic elegy definitively. A suggestion of Parsons, however, makes it possible to pursue all these questions in considerably greater depth.

Echecratidas.　Parsons has made the important observation that in 9 one may read the proper name Ἐχεκ[ρατί]δην (Parsons 1992a: 47). There are two known Thessalians of this name, the earlier of whom has a confirmed connection to Simonides. Echecratidas (1) was the father of Antiochos, one of Simonides' patrons; Echecratidas (2) was a Thessalian king and father of an Orestes mentioned by Thucydides as an exile in 457/456.[77]

Tempting as it might be to introduce Echecratidas (1) into this poem, the dramatic fiction makes the identification improbable: Simonides would hardly have expressed a poetic wish to take a journey to a timeless idyllic landscape so that he could enjoy erotic pleasures with his patron's aged (or, worse, dead) father. In fact, West's identification of the individual in verse 9 with Echecratidas (1) is the point at which his interpretation of the fantasy goes badly awry (cf. Hunter 1993a: 14 n. 12). West suggests that the poet greets his old friend Echecratidas with a hand-clasp at verse 10 and then turns to the object of his desire, "an unspecified couching companion" (West 1993a: 13); at verse 13 he offers: ἐγ[ὼ μετὰ πα]ιδός. The paleographical problem of the supplement notwithstanding,[78] there is no indication that more than one other person joins the speaker in this idyllic landscape; nor is there any hint that the desired physical contact in 10 is merely "friendly" by contrast with the erotic tenor of the following verses. If anything is certain about this poem, it is that the blond mentioned in 9 and the individual on whom the speaker focuses erotic attention at 10–12 are one and the same.[79] West does, in fact, take this point into account with an alternative scenario: παιδός could refer to a *rejuvenated* Echecratidas (ibid.; cf.

---

75. Verse 21 εὔκομπ[suprascr. π, i.e., εὔπομπ[: perhaps another reading that is preferable to a variant (see n. 3). West 1993a: 13 favors εὔπομπ[and, in keeping with his interpretation of the poem as a propemptikon, detects a wish for a fair journey: "perhaps εὔπομπ[ος predicatively of a god (e.g., Poseidon), with optative verb" (see above at nn. 10–11; see also further below). If εὔπομπ[is correct, I would suggest instead a reference to a "following" breeze that would waft the speaker to his utopian island—in other words, a conclusion to the fantasy by way of ring composition.

76. For κόμπος as the epinician "vaunt," cf. Pind. *Nem.* 8.49; *Isthm.* 1.43 and 5.24; also *Pyth.* 10.4. For related εὐ-compounds in encomiastic poetry, cf., e.g., φρενὸς εὐκλέας ὀιστοὺς (*Ol.* 2.90); λύτρον εὔδοξον . . . καμάτων (*Isthm.* 8.1).

77. For Echecratidas (1) see Parsons 1992a: 47 (esp. Theocr. 16.34 and schol. [= Simon. 528 *PMG*]) and West 1993a: 12 and 13 with nn. 28 and 29. For Echecratidas (2) see Parsons 1992a: 47.

78. Haslam 1993: 135, in an otherwise highly favorable review of *IEG* II², singled out this supplement as one of the few that "stretch the evidence to or beyond the breaking point." For the difficulty of filling the gap in a way that suits the traces, see Parsons 1992a: 48.

79. Cf. Haslam 1993: 134: "this is a romantically homo-erotic piece in which it seems that the aged poet envisions . . . reclining on flowers in the sensual company of the lovely Echekratides." Parsons also thinks that Echecratidas is the love-object (46, 49, and passim) and contributes the (queried) suggestion that this older Echecratidas is young "in the poet's memory" (Parsons 1992a: 47).

Parsons, quoted at n. 81 below). Still, this leaves us with a hypothesis that is nearly as awkward: that the poet is celebrating the past adolescent homoerotic allure of a man presumably best known to his audience as head of the family and father of the adult Antiochus.

Of the two individuals identified by Parsons, the more suitable candidate for a part in Simonides 22 is Echecratidas (2). This solution is hardly satisfactory, though, for the obvious reason that it involves rejecting evidence that connects Echecratidas (1) directly with the poet. We need not, however, retreat from the question at this impasse, since there is a third possibility that is open to none of the objections of the other two. Antiochus might well have named a son after his father. This hypothetical Echecratidas (3), grandson of the known Echecratidas (1), would not only have been the son of Simonides' patron, but presumably also of a suitable age to receive a homo-erotic compliment. As it turns out, we have an excellent parallel for the situation in Pindar's encomium for Theoxenos of Tenedos (fr. 123). Here, too, a poet in the guise of an aging admirer celebrates the desirability of a patron's young relative: a brother of Aristagoras for whom Pindar wrote *Nem.* 11 (see further below).

Aim, Audience, and Occasion. On the evidence available to us, obviously we cannot, in the end, conclusively identify the Echecratidas of this poem. Still, an occasional sympotic elegy that focused on *any* named individual must have had some point for its original audience. We must, therefore, return to the dramatic fiction for hints as to what that point might have been.

The poet's wish to travel to an idyllic island in order to shed old age and consort with the desirable young Echecratidas is manifestly the centerpiece of the elegy. West's view that the poem is a propemptikon is unsatisfactory for relegating the central utopian wish to a mere πάρεργον and, accordingly, the prominently featured Echecratidas to a secondary role (see above at n. 11).[80] Moreover, by either of West's hypotheses, Simonides' fantasy involves meeting a friend in the hereafter who has pre-deceased him.[81] If the elegy were a tribute to a dead family member, it would, in effect, be a lament or consolation, which it is surely not;[82] the specter of death, if present at

---

80. Hunter 1993a pursues the idea of the propemptikon and proposes two alternative interpretations on the basis of Theocr. 7.61–71: "*either* a wish for X's [the addressee's] safe journey to the island and a description of the party X will hold on arrival (vv. 1–12), followed by the corresponding party which the poet will hold (vv. 13 ff.); *or* a wish for X's safe journey to the island (vv. 1–8), followed by the celebratory party which the poet will hold (vv. 9 ff.)." The primary objection is—as has been argued here throughout—that the island is no real destination, but an imaginary utopian locale. Moreover, correspondences between Simon. 22 and Theocr. 7.61–71 are no more (and perhaps a little less) than what one would find in any two sympotic passages: a flowery garland (Theocr. 7.64), reclining posture (66) and music (71ff.). The differences are more marked: Theocritus' fireside setting (66); Lycidas' herdsman companions (71) and the speaker's toast of his beloved (65; 69–70). Even Hunter muses on the question "whether the similarity between the two passages . . . is fortuitous."

81. West 1993a: 13: "Echekratidas . . . is dead now, but Simonides recalls him as an old and dear friend." Cf. Parsons's "extreme view" (1992a: 49): "The aged Simonides longs to escape . . . to meet again the dead Echecratidas in all his desirable youth."

82. Consider, by contrast, the pathos of a real Simonidean consolation: cῆμα καταφθιμένοιο Μεγακλέος εὖτ' ἂν ἴδωμαι, | οἰκτίρω cε τάλαν Καλλία, οἶ' ἔπαθεc (fr. 91; cf. West 1974: 21). Simonides' lament for

all, hangs only vaguely over the speaker whose advanced age is the basis of his wish to become young again.[83] Nor does the elegy contain any element that could be construed as paraenetic.[84]

We are left with the conclusion that Simonides 22 is, as it appears, an erotic poem. But, as the dramatic fiction implies, the elegy is not erotic in the most straightforward sense (i.e., written with intent to woo). By expressing his wish to consort with Echecratidas, Simonides celebrates the young man's desirability. Yet by casting the scene in the form of a fantasy and emphasizing his own advanced age, he implicitly renders the issue of any erotic relations between them moot.[85] Instead, he has made Echecratidas the object of encomium with an erotic theme and at the same time offered him a compliment that is a masterpiece of delicacy to which no one could object. Pindar, too, in a homoerotic encomium for his patron's relative, distances himself delicately from the role of suitor. He stresses his own advanced age and the importance of καιρός in erotic pursuit, disparages *other* men who could resist Theoxenos' flashing eyes (fr. 123.2–9), and hints finally that his own admiration is part and parcel of a general appreciation of the beauty of boys (εὖτ' ἂν ἴδω παίδων νεόγυιον ἐς ἥβην [11–12]).[86]

The occasion for which Simonides composed this elegy was presumably a private (rather than public or festival) gathering at which the recitation of erotic and encomiastic poetry would have been equally at home.[87] A convivial setting appears

Antiochus includes a reference to the grief of his bereaved mother (528 *PMG*; cf. West 1993a: 13). (For a revised interpretation of 528, see my Postscript to this chapter. For a different view, see Yatromanolakis.) Even the two words of Simonides 23 W² speak more to the topic of consolation than the remains of 22 in their entirety (ἀμύντορα δυσφροσυνάων, of wine). Nor does the fragment resemble any other early extant consolation poetry, e.g., Archil. 11–13; Theogn. 355–60; Pind. *Nem*. 8.44–51, *Isthm*. 3/4.34–42; and the poems classified by West 1993a: 16 as "praise of a dead friend."

83. Since Simonides presumably composed this work to be performed in propria persona, even a loose verisimilitude would suggest that he regarded himself as relatively advanced in age at the time. Still, this does not necessarily help to date the elegy. Since perceptions of what constitutes old age are relative (and poetic license is always a consideration), Simonides (?b. Ol. 56 [556/552, Suda Σ 439]) might have referred to himself as old when in what we would consider early middle age. Cf. West 1993a: 16.: "Simonides already feels old, but that need not exclude a date as early as the 490s." For discussion of this issue and a collection of interesting examples, see Cameron 1995: 175–81.

84. Consider, by contrast, the overtly paraenetic posture of Simon. 20 W² (esp. ἀλλὰ σὺ ταῦτα μαθών . . . φράζεο δὲ . . . [11–13]); Simon. 19 W² (instruction in the proper understanding of a Homeric dictum); 21 contains the didactic *topoi* of δίκη, ὕβρις, and (possibly) αἰδώς.

85. Simonides' erotic encomium is, therefore, in effect a *recusatio*. The Suda entry (s.v. Σιμωνίδης Λεωπρεποῦς) catalogs the poet's literary output as: historical elegies/lyrics, θρῆνοι, ἐγκώμια, ἐπιγράμματα, παιᾶνες, καὶ τραγῳδίαι καὶ ἄλλα (cf. *IEG* II²: 114). Fr. 22 W² is not an epigram in the sense that the word is applied to the collection transmitted under Simonides' name; nor, as just argued, is it in any sense a θρῆνος. If it corresponds to any category in the Suda entry, it is to the "encomia." Campbell 1991: 331 glosses these ἐγκώμια as "epinicians," but cf. the Suda entry for Pindar: ὀλυμπιονίκας, πυθιονίκας, . . . ἐγκώμια. For more on the Suda entry, see this volume, Parsons at nn. 23–27, Rutherford at nn. 3ff., and Obbink at nn. 36ff.

86. Despite this poetic disclaimer, the biographers had their way with Pindar, recording that he died ἀνακεκλιμένον εἰς τὰ τοῦ ἐρωμένου Θεοξένου αὐτοῦ γόνατα (Suda, s.v.); see Groningen 1960: 51–83, esp. 76–78; Bowra 1964: 274–77.

87. See West 1974: 10–21 (11–12 on the "civilian symposium"; 13–14 on elegiac performance) and Herington 1985: 36–38 with Appendix V.A: "Testimonia on Elegiac Performance."

to be reflected in elements of Simonides' fantasy: his reclining posture (14), garland (15–16), and poetic performance (17–18). We should probably imagine a party hosted by Antiochus (father of the honorand) with Echecratidas himself present in the company of family members and a circle of intimates to appreciate the compliment.

Conclusion

Simonides based his homoerotic encomium for Echecratidas on an apparently unique fusion of the themes of utopian escape and the trials of the aging lover. The effect of this unusual meeting of ideas is powerful. Descriptions of utopias in Greek poetry, from Homer and Hesiod on, speak to the human yearning to be exempt from the liabilities of the mortal lot, particularly old age and death. Equally compelling is the predicament of unrequited desire, not least when old age offers the impediment. Simonides forges a link between the erotic and utopian themes (and thus the poetic traditions associated with them) through the idea of rejuvenation. The result is that, in the context of this occasional erotic encomium, Simonides' twofold wish-fulfilling fantasy offers to the imagination—if only for a moment—the attainment of two supremely desirable goals.[88] It cannot help but exercise a doubly powerful appeal.

POSTSCRIPT

In the following chapter, Dimitrios Yatromanolakis proposes a new reconstruction of Simon. 22 W². Yatromanolakis believes that this poem may be a *threnos* and that its speaker could be a woman who "expresses her wish to travel across the sea, and her longing to meet her dead husband [again], even in the afterlife" (at nn. 43–44). Endorsing Parsons's supplement Ἐχεκ[ρατί]δην in verse 9, Yatromanolakis further proposes that the female speaker might be Echecratidas' wife Dyseris, mother of Simonides' patron Antiochus. Dyseris' *threnos* (to be performed in propria persona or by proxy) is addressed either to her husband Echecratidas or (as Yatromanolakis thinks is more likely in view of other evidence, for which see below), to Antiochus, with Echecratidas' son either eliciting a mention of his father or being named himself by a patronymic. Yatromanolakis is guarded about insisting on any interpretation of such a difficult and fragmentary text as being definitive (at nn. 3, 24, 63), but nevertheless maintains that "an attempt to recover the song's content is clearly desirable" (at n. 3). I heartily agree with both points, but would add that, even in the case of so fragmentary a text as this, it *is* possible to determine which reconstructions are more plausible than others.

    Two of Yatromanolakis's propositions are not open to question. It is well attested that Simonides enjoyed a reputation in antiquity for his threnodic poetry

---

88. Elsewhere, by contrast, Simonides treats old age and mortality in a more direct and uncompromising fashion, e.g., 520, 641 *PMG*, and 19, 20, 21.5 ff. W². At 20.12f., Simonides' advice is to accept the inevitable with an admixture of endurance and hedonism: ψυχῇ τῶν ἀγαθῶν τλῆθι χαριζόμενος.

(Yatromanolakis after n. 20). Also, a scholion on Theocritus (16.36–37, pp. 327f. Wendel = 529 *PMG*) apparently reliably records that Simonides wrote *threnoi* and epinicia for his Thessalian patrons Antiochus, Aleuas, and the Scopadai (ἐπινικίους ἔγραψε καὶ θρήνους). It does not, incidentally, seem to belie the scholion that Theocritus himself does not mention *threnoi*, but only varied lyric productions (αἰόλα φωνέων | βάρβιτον ἐς πολύχορδον 16.44–45) and epinicia (τιμᾶς δὲ καὶ ὠκέες ἔλλαχον ἵπποι κ.τ.λ. 16.46f.). Yatromanolakis's problematic proposition, however, involves the evidence he adduces for the "the tradition that Simonides composed a *threnos* for Dyseris' son Antiochus" (Yatromanolakis 1998: 5, modified in this volume [at n. 22] to "the testimonia that Simonides probably composed a threnodic piece for Dyseris' son Antiochus.").

Citing the beginning of an oration by Aelius Aristides in honor of a dead pupil (Εἰς Ἐτεωνέα ἐπικήδειος), Yatromanolakis (at n. 19) reports that Aristides

> juxtaposes Dyseris' name with that of Simonides, and stresses the great grief she felt over her dead Antiochus: ποῖος ταῦτα Σιμωνίδης θρηνήσει, . . . ποία δὲ Δύσηρις Θετταλὴ τοσοῦτο πένθος ἐπένθησεν ἐπ' Ἀντιόχῳ τελευτήσαντι; (528 *PMG*)

It seems essential, however, to reproduce the words in the ellipsis to do justice to the passage:

> ποῖος ταῦτα Σιμωνίδης θρηνήσει, τίς Πίνδαρος ποῖον μέλος ἢ λόγον τοιοῦτον ἐξευρών; τίς χορὸς (Στησίχορος coni. Taylor) ἄξιον φθέγξεται τοιούτου πάθους; ποία δὲ Δύσηρις Θετταλὴ τοσοῦτο πένθος ἐπένθησεν ἐπ' Ἀντιόχωι τελευτήσαντι;

First, Aristides' interposition of Pindar and a "chorus" between Simonides and Dyseris interrupts any strict juxtaposition of the two (Taylor's Στησίχορος, also treated with skepticism by Wilamowitz [see Yatromanolakis n. 19], seems unlikely). More to the point, the continuation of the passage (following 528 *PMG*) explains Aristides' otherwise mysterious transition from futures (θρηνήσει, φθέγξεται) to an aorist (ἐπένθησεν). Aristides is in fact citing Dyseris' grief at Antiochus' death as a paradigm for the grief of Eteoneus' mother (as punctuated by Dindorf): ποία δὲ Δύσηρις Θετταλὴ τοσοῦτο πένθος ἐπένθησεν ἐπ' Ἀντιόχωι τελευτήσαντι, ὅσον νῦν μητρὶ τῇ τούτου πένθος πρόκειται; Evidently Aristides' rhetorical strategy in this eulogy was to list a series of paradigmatic figures who reflect his desire to honor the dead boy with the services of, first, an exemplary threnodist (e.g., Simonides), second, an exemplary melic poet as encomiast (e.g., Pindar), and third, some ideal chorus to make a suitable public demonstration of grief. Aristides then singles out Dyseris as a paradigmatic *mater dolorosa*. This hardly justifies Yatromanolakis's conclusion in the earlier version of his study that "according to the testimony quoted above, [Dyseris] delivered a lament, composed by Simonides, on the death of her son Antiochus" (Yatromanolakis 1998: 9, modified somewhat in this volume before n. 47) nor his reference to "the song of mourning to which Aristides alludes" (n. 28). On the contrary, it seems clear that whereas Aristides refers to Simonides, Pindar, and the chorus as those who could best give eulogy an artistic form (as he would aspire to do himself), he introduces Dyseris as a grieving parent, parallel to Eteoneus' mother.

The next question to consider is whether the speaker of Simon. 22 W^2 is at all likely to be a woman. Yatromanolakis argues that "as long as we do not have any supplementary papyrus scrap of the same fragment which would provide traces for the gender of the speaking voice we cannot be certain in this respect" (at n. 15). I would contend that the poem contains other cues that indicate with reasonable certainty that its speaker is a man.

In general, it would be unusual for Simonides and for most male archaic lyricists to have written a poem in a woman's voice. Adducing "examples of a female voice as the poetic persona in male poetry" (n. 22), Yatromanolakis cites no more than five instances, none of which belong to Simonides, and one of which (unless the language is figurative) is spoken by a mare (Thgn. 257–60). One might also recall that Simonides' own most memorable female voice—Danaë—is not the speaker of 543 *PMG*, but quoted directly by the poetic "I": (εἶπεν 7). Thus, the burden of proof would seem to lie with one who would propose a female speaker for Simon. 22 W². On the other hand, there appear to be positive indications that the speaker of the poem is male (see my n. 9). Mainly, verses 9ff. contain recognizably male homoerotic *topoi* (see my n. 42). Even if one concedes for the moment that the language is not necessarily homoerotic, but generically erotic, it seems eccentric to attribute this diction to an individual of Dyseris' profile: a mature if not old woman, addressing an older spouse (much less a son). Yatromanolakis himself writes of verse 12, "It remains an open question whether [the verse] could be exclusively taken as alluding to a conjugal relationship" (n. 28; cf. also my section on "Eros" at nn. 42–50). Next, Yatromanolakis's examples of occurrences of ἱμερόεις (cf. Simon. 22.12, 17) elsewhere "in lamentatory context" (n. 35) do not make for compelling evidence that the word is more at home in a *threnos* than in an erotic poem: when the adjective modifies γόος (*Od.* 10.398) it has its typical connotation (which it shares with other words of the same root) of the "desire/desirability" of poetic productions (cf. LSJ s.vv.); the second example modifies κόλπος ([Moschos] 4.56–58) which is an erotic not lamentatory substantive in any case. When ἱμερόεντα modifies πόθον (aut sim.) in Simon. 22.12, its erotic connotations speak for themselves. When the adjective recurs in 17 with λιγύν, even though the substantive does not survive here either, the verse is clearly concerned with the aesthetics of a poet-singer's voice (the *mourner*) rather than "the feelings of longing that the dead would reciprocate to the loved *persona loquens* who imagines visiting him" (i.e., the *mourned one*; Yatromanolakis at n. 35; see also my n. 62). One final problem with Yatromanolakis's hypothesis that the speaker of the poem is a woman also involves the allusion to poetic activity in verses 17–18. This statement, which would apply most naturally to the speaker, is grammatically masculine (νωμῶν γλῶσσαν 18). On Yatromanolakis's view, the poetic "I," Dyseris, would have to be casting her *addressee*, rather than herself, in the role of poet.

At this point it is worth adding a word or two about genre. Among Yatromanolakis's objections to interpreting the poem as a homoerotic encomium is that "there appears to be no reference or allusion to pederastic poems by Simonides" (n. 6). The manifestly erotic language of the fragment aside, it seems forced to argue that we need to be told explicitly that an archaic lyric poet wrote homoerotic poetry in order to assume that he did so. It seems more likely that posterity's emphasis on the pathos of Simonidean *threnoi* overshadowed discussion of his other genres. On the other hand, Yatromanolakis's hypothesis that the poem is threnodic becomes problematic when one considers that, if it is a *threnos*, on Yatromanolakis's own showing it differs dramatically in character from known Simonidean *threnoi* (see his details and bibliography at nn. 55–58; see also my n. 82 [with discussion in the text] and n. 85).

Finally, Yatromanolakis objects to the reconstruction of the poem as a homo-erotic encomium for an adolescent because it "leads to the 'creation' of an entirely new Echecratidas (for whose existence there is no evidence)" (n. 13). As it turns out, there *is* an historically attested Echecratidas who has a good claim to be Echecratidas son of Antiochus (my "created" Echecratidas [3]). As Yatromanolakis points out (n. 13), John Molyneux has suggested that Echecratidas, father of the Orestes mentioned at Thuc. 1.111.1 (my Echecratidas [2]), could also be the elder Echecratidas' grandson (my Echecratidas [3]) (see Molyneux 1992: 127 with n. 78). Yatromanolakis rejects the link as "not confirmed by any evidence" (n. 13), but it makes little sense to ignore the fact that Orestes' father has the same name, place of origin, status, and conjectural date as the Echecratidas whose existence is suggested by the internal logic of Simon. 22 W^2.

Although I am obviously not convinced by Yatromanolakis's proposed recon-struction of the poem, I am indebted to him for prompting me to reconsider my own interpretation. Moreover, Yatromanolakis calls attention to the possible identification between Echecratidas (2) and Echecratidas (3)—a step I did not take myself. As for details, Yatromanolakis strengthens my argument for the existence of an early poetic tradition of rejuvenation in the underworld by adding the "general context of the Aristophanic line" (n. 5) and makes a praiseworthy proposal for verse 14: ἐκτ[ανύσας (n. 12), supported by the compelling parallel at *AP* 11.408.2, οὐδὲ παρειάων ἐκτανύσεις ῥυτίδας.

Nigel Nicholson, in a recently published study, kindly shown me in advance by the author, focuses on Pindar, but makes a substantial contribution to the interpre-tation of Simon. 22 W^2 by supplying some independent support for the view that the poem is a homoerotic encomium of a young Echecratidas, son of Antiochus.[89] Nicholson argues that Pindar uses the metaphor of "poet as pederast" in order to evoke "an earlier mode of poetic production where poets addressed their words to youths," with the poet taking a stance that "deflects attention away from the real cir-cumstances of Pindar's poetic production, obscuring the poet's status as a μισθωτός, a wage-earner." Although there are difficulties inherent in "combin[ing] a pederastic poetic persona with an adult patron," Pindar's regular strategy for meeting the chal-lenge is to interpose a "third term" between himself and the patron: "either a differ-ent, youthful addressee, a memory of the patron when he was young, or a mythical analog." Nicholson then relates Pindar's use of a pederastic *persona* directly to Simon. 22 W^2, offering the poem (and Ibykos' "Polykrates Ode," 282 *PMG*) as evidence that a poet's employment of a pederastic stance "to disguise the new relations of produc-tion in the late archaic period was not Pindar's invention, but was developed by his predecessors in the sixth century as the close relationship between poet and patron first began to dissolve."

Although Nicholson explicitly shrinks from stating whether he thinks that the Echecratidas of Simon. 22 W^2 is more likely to be Antiochus' adolescent son or aged

---

89. Nicholson 1999/2000.

father (remembered or imagined by Simonides as an *eromenos*), his characterization of Pindar's pederastic strategy points toward the latter view. When Pindar adopts a pederastic *persona*, he tends to cast *either* a younger version of his patron in the role of *eromenos* (by evoking his youthful victories) *or* a patron's younger relative. There is no example, on the other hand, of Pindar's casting a patron's *father* in a mediating role. Moreover, Nicholson concedes that if the addressee of Simon. 22 W^2 is Antiochos' father, the "tone is considerably more aggressive than that of Pindar's odes," by which I believe he means that the poet would be adopting an overly intimate tone toward his patron's elderly relative.

Ultimately, Nicholson's discussion of Pindar's practice favors the hypothesis that a young Echecratidas plays *eromenos* to Simonides' pederastic persona. Nicholson, too, seems to come to this conclusion instinctively. He writes at one point, for example, that Simonides' poem "has become an object of exchange in a three-way relation: the patron commissioned it from Simonides, and Simonides addressed it to a younger member of the patron's family." In the end, it is a striking endorsement both of Nicholson's and my arguments that his description of Pindar's procedure in the "epinicians addressed to victors in the youth contests" closely resembles my recon-struction of the occasion of Simon. 22 W^2. Of Pindar, Nicholson writes, "The father or head of the clan pays the poet, but remains in the background while the youth receives the praise." As I originally reconstructed the occasion of Simonides' poem, "We should . . . imagine a party hosted by Antiochus (father of the honorand) with Echecratidas himself present in the company of family members and a circle of inti-mates to appreciate the compliment."

12

DIMITRIOS YATROMANOLAKIS

To Sing or to Mourn?

A Reappraisal of Simonides 22 W²

Simonides fr. eleg. 22 W², admirably edited by Peter Parsons in 1992,[1] has recently kindled the interest of scholars as to the reconstruction of its content and context. No doubt, the new fragment "intrigues and tantalizes";[2] all the more since the text as it has come down to us is badly preserved, and only broadly comprehensible. An attempt to recover the song's content is clearly desirable, but, as is the case with other aspects of archaic Greek literature and culture, we should be attentive to the polyvalence of its fragmentation.[3] I shall here address the issue from a different vantage point and propose a new view of how this fragment may be "read."

In the first edition of the fragment, Parsons, while admitting that "the content is very conjectural" (1992a: 7), proceeded to offer a tentative overall interpretation of the new poem: the aged Simonides longs to travel across the sea to the Island of the Blest (ll. 1–8), there to see once more the dead Echecratidas—the father of a Thessalian patron of Simonides (ll. 9 ff.; see Simon. 528 *PMG*),[4] join him in a sym-

---

An earlier version of this paper appeared in *ZPE* 120 (1998): 1–11, and is used here by kind permission of the editors of *ZPE*. I should like to thank R. A. Coles and J. R. Rea of the Ashmolean Museum, Oxford, for letting me examine the original papyri several times. I am also grateful to S. Mace for very kindly allowing me to read her paper in advance of the 1996 publication. At different stages A. M. Bowie, R. A. Coles, N. Gonis, P. Roilos, and I. C. Rutherford offered advice, which improved the proposed reconstruction in many ways. I would also like to express my gratitude to G. Nagy, D. Obbink, and C. Sourvinou-Inwood, who discussed thoroughly with me the views propounded here and made incisive suggestions. Finally, I owe a special debt to P. J. Parsons for his insightful suggestions, unstinting interest, and encouragement.

1. In joining *POxy* 3965 fr. 27 with *POxy* 2327 frr. 2(a) col. ii, 2(b), 3, and 4 (a link partly proposed earlier by E. Lobel), Parsons ingeniously suggested that the combination of 2327 fr. 4 with frr. 1–2 col. ii of the same papyrus is plausible because of the satisfactory sense it produces (Parsons 1992a: 46–49).

2. Hunter, this volume, before n. 1.

3. I discuss this aspect of archaic cultural fragments in a forthcoming book on Sappho (Yatromanolakis forthcoming).

4. For Echecratidas, see below at nn. 15–26.

posium, and recover his lost youth (ll. 13ff.).[5] According to this reconstruction, the whole fragment is about longing for the kind of rejuvenation that could be attained in the Island of the Blest.[6] West saw the fragment from the same perspective (1993a: 12–14), but modified Parsons's interpretation at certain points: the fragment is addressed to Echecratidas' living son Antiochus (or to other members of that noble Thessalian house), and belongs to the "genre" of *propemptikon* (cf. εὔπομπ[in line 21).[7]

As far as I know, there are two other contributions to the interpretation of the fragment in question,[8] those recently made by R. Hunter (1996) and S. Mace (reprinted, with revisions, in this volume). Hunter takes as his starting point Theocr. 7.61–71, where the αἰπόλος Lycidas sings a *propemptikon* for Ageanax's voyage to Mytilene and describes the rustic festivity that he will hold on Ageanax's safe arrival

---

5. On the notion of rejuvenation, Parsons is cautious (Parsons 1992a: 49, referring to Davies 1987: 265ff. and Hes. *WD* 113f.): "I have found no evidence that the Blest were rejuvenated; the idea itself seems natural enough, given that conditions in Elysium parallel those of the Golden Age, where old age had no place." Mace, this volume at n. 53, adduces Aristoph. *Frogs* 345 (γόνυ πάλλεται γερόντων) as evidence for the concept of rejuvenation (of the blessed dead); the general context of the Aristophanic line quoted suggests this idea (see ll. 346f. ἀποσείονται δὲ λύπας χρονίους τ' ἐτῶν παλαιῶν ἐνιαυτούς). The fact that Simonides referred in his poetry to a rejuvenation of Jason by Medea (548 *PMG* Φερεκύδης δὲ καὶ Σιμωνίδης φασὶν ὡς ἡ Μήδεια ἀνεψήσασα τὸν Ἰάσονα νέον ποιήσειε) has little bearing on our issue. For the motif of rejuvenation by skin-sloughing, see Henderson 1987, comment on *Lys.* 670–71.

6. The fragment does not explicitly refer, but only, perhaps, alludes, to the Island (or Isles) of the Blest. Although these isles were imagined to be very fertile (see, e.g., Hes. *WD* 170ff. καὶ τοὶ μὲν ναίουσιν . . . | ἐν μακάρων νήσοισι . . . | ὄλβιοι ἥρωες, τοῖσιν μελιηδέα καρπόν | τρὶς ἔτεος θάλλοντα φέρει ζείδωρος ἄρουρα), other real or utopian islands can have been so (for utopias in Greek literature, including the Isles of the Blest, see Mace at n. 23). The word εὐαέα in l. 8 is very much to the point in the context of the Isles of the Blest (εὐαγέα would perhaps be even more apposite in such a context; see Mace at n. 34: "this feature is particularly pronounced in underworld settings where there is preternatural illumination"); so also is the description of the flowery place where the man is reclining (cf. the parallels adduced by Mace, after n. 35). For all that, if we accept that Echecratidas, whose name has been reconstructed in our fragment (safely, as far as I can see), is the Thessalian ruler and father of Antiochus, "there is no obvious island on which his hand might be shaken-unless indeed on the Island of the Blest" (Parsons 1992a: 47). In my view, though Echecratidas could be argued to be a totally different person, not connected with the historical person at all (cf. P. Maas's view about Ibyc. S151 *PMGF*, that the Polycrates who appears in l. 47 has nothing to do with the famous tyrant of Samos, but is just a young man, homonymous with the tyrant [Maas 1922: 578; reported also by Wilamowitz 1922: 511]; thus the aforementioned fragment should be classified in the genre of παιδικά or παίδεια), it would be difficult to accept such a coincidence, in view of the existence of this name in the tradition about the life of Simonides (see below). As to Percy's contention that Simonides may have written pederastic verses (1996: 169), it is worth noting that, in contrast to other poets, there appears to be no reference or allusion to pederastic poems by Simonides (note that in Apul. *Apol.* 9 Helm, which is not mentioned by Percy, "Cius" may refer to Bacchylides: see Helm's app. crit., and Snell-Maehler's app. crit. on Bacchylides' ἐρωτικά [p. 91]; cf. also Hunink's comments on Apul. *Apol.* 9.6 [1997: vol. II, 40]). In Simon. 27.5 W², the context can only be extremely conjectural; even the reconstruction of l. 5 (π]αῖδ' ἐρατὸν σ[) is questionable.

7. According to West, the frame of the Elysian visit is a voyage to be undertaken by Antiochus: "from wishing his noble Thessalian patron godspeed, Simonides turned aside for a few moments to describe the voyage he personally would like to make" (West 1993a: 13).

8. For a concise review of the scholarship written so far on this fragment, with further suggestive remarks, see Rutherford in this volume. More recently, Brillante (2000) seems to believe he has found the "correct" interpretation of the fragment.

at the island.[9] As Hunter construes the fragment,[10] there are two alternatives that this may accommodate: "*either* a wish for X's safe journey to the island and a description of the party X will hold on arrival, followed by the corresponding party which the poet will hold (vv. 13ff.); *or* a wish for X's safe journey to the island (vv. 1–8), followed by the celebratory party which the poet will hold (vv. 9ff.)."[11] Thus, according to Hunter, the poetic persona refers to a journey that is going to be undertaken by another person, and imagines the party (or rather the two parties) that will be held in the future.

In his *editio princeps*, Parsons considered three possibilities for the nature of the journey described in the fragment: it "might be (a) real; (b) escapist, on the pattern of Eur. *Hipp.* 732ff., where the chorus long to fly away to the Island of the Hesperides; (c) post mortem, as Posidippus SH 705.22" (1992a: 46). While Hunter argues for the first possibility, the second one is further explored by Mace. She sees in lines 7ff. a description of a utopian landscape, which the poetic persona wishes to reach in order to consort with a male companion, who is the object of his admiration and desire. In Mace's view, the fragment is *unique* in its fusion of utopian and erotic themes: the speaker expresses his imaginary wish to travel to an idyllic island, where he will be rejuvenated,[12] and attain physical contact with the young Echecratidas. She also contends, however, that the Echecratidas of 22 W^2 cannot be identified with the father of Antiochus, but with a hypothetical Echecratidas, son of Antiochus, who was so named after his grandfather;[13] the fragment is thus an erotic encomium of Echecratidas' desirability, and its occasion was possibly one of those private gatherings at which erotic and encomiastic poetry was frequently recited and sung.[14]

9. Cf. also Hunter 1996: 26.

10. Among others, the following two textual suggestions are put forward: ἱκο[ίμην in l. 7 to be changed to ἵκο[ιτο, and, perhaps (p. 14 n. 11), λάβοιμ[ι in l. 10 to λάβοι μ[.

11. It seems that Hunter's interpretation may not take fully into consideration ll. 9–12, where, according to himself, some kind of amorous coloring occurs (1993a: 14 n. 12); it is not clear how X, as soon as he reaches the island of his destination, is involved in "amatory" handholding (λάβοι in l. 10) with a male figure called, perhaps, Echecratidas (or, alternatively, how the poet, as his party starts, leads off (λάβοιμι in l. 10) with the expression of his love interest in that lad), unless we assume that the fragment is a kind of *propemptikon* for Echecratidas who is away, and whom the poetic "I" is waiting for to come to his island.

12. If l. 14 in any way supports the theory of rejuvenation (see n. 5 above and n. 28, and discussion at n. 36 below), then, in addition to those supplements proposed by Parsons and West, see Koenen's ἐκ π[άλι δύς or ἐκ τ[ότε δύς (in Mace at n. 52); I would be inclined to propose ἐκτ[ανύσας, which would also fit that context (cf. Lucian *AP* 11.408.2 οὐδὲ παρειάων ἐκτανύσεις ῥυτίδας, which is a striking parallel). Bernsdorff 1996 has made the same suggestion independently.

13. Although Mace's argument that the island mentioned in l. 8 might be a utopian locale is perhaps plausible, it forces her to suppose that the poetic persona wishes to have an "erotic" encounter with a young Echecratidas (the known Echecratidas, the father of Antiochus, would have perhaps been elderly during Simonides' sojourn in Thessaly [see below, n. 26]), and hence leads to the "creation" of an entirely new Echecratidas (for whose existence there is no evidence), the grandson of the known Echecratidas. I should mention that, although it has been proposed that the Echecratidas mentioned by Thuc. 1.111.1, ruler of the Thessalians and father of Orestes (whom the Athenians tried to restore from exile in 457 B.C.E.) could be the grandson of Echecratidas, the father of Antiochus (see Molyneux 1992: 127 and n. 78), this link is not confirmed by any evidence either.

14. I.e., "a party hosted by Antiochus (father of the honorand) with Echekratidas himself present in the company of family members and a circle of intimates to appreciate the compliment" (Mace after n. 87).

In what follows, I suggest a new line of interpretation of this fragmentary text. Despite the fact that the proposed reconstruction provides a probable occasional and performative context and takes into account some indirectly attested evidence about Simonides' songs of mourning, it should be considered tentative, given the state of the papyrus.

What is the evidence that in fr. 22 W^2 the person speaking is male? As far as I can see, none. The speaking subject could well be a young or an old man, but could just as plausibly be a *woman*. As long as we do not have any supplementary papyrus scrap of the same fragment that would provide traces for the gender of the speaking voice we cannot be certain in this respect.[15] Is there any textual evidence that could lead us to a tentative identification of this voice? Parsons supplements line 9 as follows: κα[ί κεν] Ἐχεκ[ρατί]δην. However conjectural this may be, it is indeed very difficult to think of another supplement that would fit both the space in the papyrus and the internal structure of the line in general; besides, the name "Echecratidas" is somehow connected with the literary life of Simonides. According to the Schol. Theocr. 16.34–35 Wendel (= Simon. 528 *PMG*), "Antiochus was the son of Echecratidas and Dyseris, as Simonides says." The name of Echecratidas' wife, Dyseris,[16] possibly[17] appears again in an epigram from the Palatine Anthology (6.136) attributed to Anacreon (6 *FGE*). But, most importantly, Aelius Aristides, shortly after 161 c.e.,[18] in the proem of an oration he delivered to honor the death of one of his students (31.2 Keil = Simon. 528 *PMG*), juxtaposes Dyseris' name with that of Simonides,[19] and stresses the great grief she felt over her dead Antiochus: ποῖος ταῦτα Σιμωνίδης θρηνήσει, . . . ποία δὲ Δύσηρις Θετταλὴ τοσοῦτο πένθος ἐπένθησεν ἐπ᾽ Ἀντιόχῳ τελευτήσαντι, ὅσον νῦν μητρὶ τῇ τούτου πένθος πρόκειται; ("What Simonides will mourn these?. . . What Dyseris of Thessaly grieved so mournfully over her dead Antiochus, as much as the mother of this youth now has?"). And we know from another scholion on Theocritus (16.44 Wendel = Simon. 529 *PMG*) that Simonides "composed epinician odes and

---

15. There is no way either to confirm or reject the hypothesis that our fragment constitutes part of a long piece whose beginning might have been 21 W^2, so that the general idea that permeated the whole song could, in broad outline, be: "I can never be a cautious wallflower. Even now, in old age, I long for love and wine. Hasten the day, when I recover my youth in the symposium of the Blest." (Parsons 1992a: 49; cf. p. 7 of his edition). For an estimation of the number of lines that stood between Simon. 22 W^2 and 21 W^2, see the references in Mace, n. 4.

16. We know almost nothing about her (apart from the passages quoted here, see Hippocrates *Epid.* 5.25); for Dyseris' doubtful identification with the sister of the Thessalian noble Scopas (famous mainly from Simonides' songs about the whole family of Scopadai), and, consequently, the identification of Antiochus with the son of Scopas' sister who was one of the victims in the mass destruction of the Scopadai (in a collapse of a banqueting hall; Simon. 510 and 521 *PMG*), see Molyneux 1992: 125f. There is some evidence for a probable relation between the Scopadai and the Echecratidai (through marriage?): see Molyneux 1992: 122, 128–29, and 134ff.

17. Cf. Molyneux 1992: 127.

18. See Behr 1981: 393 (notes to orat. XXXI).

19. Aelius Aristides also mentions—in the same context—Pindar and a chorus (see Keil's app. crit.: "τίς χορός] Στησίχορος ci. Taylor ad Lysiam p. 686; Stesichorum naenias (θρήνους) non composuisse monet Wil."; for Stesichorus' laments, the evidence [in Cannatà Fera 1990: 17–18] is equivocal). However, it should be stressed that there is no evidence for Pindar's connection with the Echecratidai, nor, moreover, that he wrote laments for any of them. As a consequence, Gow's comment on Theocr. 16.34–39 ("the inference that his death was the subject of a θρῆνος by Simonides or Pindar is plausible") appears inaccurate.

dirges for the aforementioned distinguished Thessalians [sc. Antiochus, Aleuas, and the Scopadai[20]]" (. . .τοῖς προειρημένοις ἐνδόξοις ἀνδράσι τῶν Θεσσαλῶν ἐπινικίους ἔγραψε καὶ θρήνους).

From several testimonies about Simonides, it appears that for a long time after his death he was widely renowned for his threnodic poetry. Catullus begs for a little word of comfort "more lugubrious than the tears of Simonides" (38.8), reflecting the celebrity of Simonides' threnodic poetry in antiquity (see also Hor. *Carm.* 2.1.37–38). Moreover, Quintilian (10.1.64) speaks of Simonides' "praecipua . . . virtus," which "lies in the power to excite pity, so much so that some prefer him in this respect to all writers of the genre"[21] (cf. Dion. Hal. *Imit.* 6.205 U.-R.).

Who is the speaking subject in our fragment? I am inclined to believe that, in view of the testimonia that Simonides probably composed a threnodic piece for Dyseris' son Antiochus, and since the Cean poet was well known for his threnodic poetry, the text preserved in *POxy* 2327 (frr. 2(a) col. ii + 2(b) + 3 + 4) and 3965 (fr. 27) may be part of a threnodic song sung by a woman[22] or quoted by Simonides in the context of a broader threnodic composition.[23] Thus our fragment, which refers to someone's desire to undertake a journey (apparently imaginary) in order to reach Echecratidas on an island not at any rate connected with his historical background, may, with some plausibility, be (or refer to) a threnodic piece sung by Dyseris[24]—not, as far as its fragmentary nature allows us to see, for her son Antiochus,[25] but for her husband Echecratidas, as Parsons's likely supplement Ἐχεκ[ρατί]δην in l. 9 suggests.[26] The relationships between the poet and the family of his patron Antiochus

20. Cf. Molyneux 1992: 118, 121, and n. 37.

21. The translation is by Campbell (1991: 359 [test. 41]). On the "pathetic" style of Simonides' poetry, see Nisbet and Hubbard on Hor. *Carm.* 2.1.38, and Rosenmeyer 1991: 5–6.

22. For examples of a female voice as the poetic persona in male poetry, see Alc. fr. 10 V., Theogn. 257–60, 579–82, 861–64 W, and, perhaps, Anacr. fr. 385 *PMG*.

23. In view of Danae's lament composed by Simonides (543 *PMG*), where Danae is an intradiegetic speaker within the poetic narrative, we should consider the possibility that fr. 22 W², as reconstructed here, is part of Dyseris' threnodic song as being narrated by Simonides. Thus, the speaking subject can be Dyseris, her song being embedded in a more extensive song in honor of Antiochus.

24. See n. 23. That the singing of lament is mostly—but not exclusively—associated with women is evident not only in Greek tradition, but also in most traditions the world over. See, very selectively, Cavanagh and Mee 1995: 46–47; Ahlberg 1971, esp. 77–83; Alexiou 1974: 212 n. 107 and passim; Kurtz 1984: 315–18, 321–28; Shapiro 1991: 634–37, 646–47, 650–51; Alexiou 1991: 263–66; Seremetakis 1991; Finnegan 1970: 147–66; Huntington and Metcalf 1991: 54–55; Knudsen 1988: 79–97; Kligman 1988: 153–55 and 150–214 passim; Johnson 1988: 135–62. For "male tears" in Greek archaic and classical literature, see Segal 1993: 63–67 and bibliography cited at the endnotes of p. 248.

25. But see n. 28 below.

26. The evidence for the history of Thessaly of the sixth and fifth centuries is very meager, and historians usually confine themselves to assumptions and conjectures (see, apart from the bibliography cited by Molyneux 1992: ch. 6, *CAH²*: vol. III, part 3, 294ff., Carlier 1984: 412–17, Hornblower 1991b: 80–81, and Helly 1995: 104–7 [on the Echecratidai]). For an approximate dating of Simonides' Thessalian period, with a discussion of the most important earlier views, see Molyneux 1992: 132–38 (for his view on L. A. Stella's revised dating of Simonides [ca. 532–450, in contrast to the traditional dating ca. 556–468], see passim, but esp. 339–45). After scrutinizing all the existing evidence about Antiochus' *tageia*, Molyneux argues that Antiochus' "whole period of office must be placed somewhere between 510 and 498" (1992: 135). In default of sufficient evidence for most of the Thessalian rulers, it would be venturesome and, perhaps, pointless to give here an approximate date for Echecratidas' death (note, however, that if this song is in fact addressed to Antiochus [see below, at n. 28], his death can be placed around 500 B.C.E.).

(i.e., the Echecratidai) are adequately attested,[27] and the hypothesis of a threnodic song composed by Simonides for the wife of Echecratidas seems a tempting one to follow. It is true that the song of mourning that Aelius Aristides attributes to Dyseris was delivered for her son Antiochus and not for her husband Echecratidas, and this fact may create some resistance to the idea put forward above. However, we should perhaps allow that our fragment may have been a threnodic song for Antiochus, the son, but that it may also have contained references to his dead father; in that case, Dyseris, in the song about the loss of her son, expresses her desire to see Echecratidas, and arguably, her wish that Antiochus have a safe journey to that εὐσεβῶν χῶρον (Pind. fr. 129 Maehler) and join his father.[28] Here I give a reconstructed form of the text under consideration. There follow brief notes mainly on the adopted *exempli gratia* supplements (ll. 9–10) which are different from those supplied by West in *IEG*[2] (and/or Parsons), and on some difficulties that arise from West's text. At the end, I consider some interesting implications that ensue from construing the fragment in the manner proposed here. It should be stated that my main aim is not to provide the reader with a different text for Simon. 22 W[2], but rather to offer a new approach towards the understanding of this fragment of song.

$$].οιο \; θαλάσσης$$
$$]ρουσα \; πόρον·$$
$$]μενος \; ἔνθα \; περανα[$$
$$]$$
$$]οιμι \; κελευθο[\qquad \qquad 5$$
$$]ν \; κόσμ[ο]ν \; ἰο[στ]εφάνων$$
$$]ἔδος \; πολύδενδρον \; ἱκο[ίμην$$
$$εσ[....] \; εὐαέα^{29} \; νῆσον, \; ἄγαλμα \; β[^{30}$$
$$κα[ί \; κεν] \; Ἐχεκ[ρατί]δην \; ξανθότρ[ιχα \; κεῖνον \; ἰδοῦσα$$
$$ὀφ[θαλμοῖσι \; φίλ]ον \; χεῖρα \; λάβοιμ[ι \; πάλιν \qquad \qquad 10$$
$$οφρα.ε.[.] \; χ[αρίε]ντος \; ἀπὸ \; χροὸς \; αν[$$
$$λείβει \; δ' \; ἐκ \; βλ[εφάρ]ων \; ἱμερόεντα \; [$$
$$καί \; κεν \; επ[-⏑⏑]υδος \; ἐν \; ἄνθε[σι(ν) \; ἡδέσιν \; εἴη$$

27. See also Molyneux 1992: 127–29. For Simonides' connections with other Thessalian patrons, see Molyneux 1992: 117–45, who discusses much of the previous bibliography.
28. It remains an open question whether l. 12 could be exclusively taken as alluding to a conjugal relationship. If λείβει δ' ἐκ βλ[εφάρων] ἱμερόεντα[could be used to express affectionate, not sensual, feelings, and φαρκίδας in l. 14 was governed by a verb (or a verbal expression) meaning "to avoid" (i.e., "X, dying in his youth, avoided seeing wrinkles on his face, that is, he did not experience that sign of aging"), then the reconstructed threnodic song could refer to the deceased Antiochus only (Echecratides might be a patronymic), and be identified with the song of mourning to which Aristides alludes. I owe much of this idea to Christiane Sourvinou-Inwood. Additionally, Gregory Nagy has drawn my attention to the information given by Roussel, that the name "Alcmeonides" was both a personal name and a patronymic (Roussel 1976: 62). Although this is an attractive possibility, in what follows I constantly use the name "Echecratidas" as referring to the husband of Dyseris in order to avoid confusion, and thus I consider only the alternative view that Echecratidas might here be evoked in the context of Dyseris' mourning for Antiochus.
29. εὐαγ[έ]α also is possible (see n. 6, and comment on l. 8 below).
30. Or κ[.

κεκλιμένος λευκὰς³¹ φαρκίδας ἐκ.[

χαίτη[ισι]ν χαρίε[ντ]α νεοβλαστ[15

   .[. . . . . . .] εὐανθέα πλε[ξάμενος στέφανον

μο[   ] δ' ἱμερόεντα λιγὺν .[

   ἀρτι[   ] νωμῶν γλῶσσαν α[

[   ]

   τῶνδε .[20

εὐπομπ[

Lines 2–3. The ending -ρουσα, which West takes to refer to a ship (see his app. crit. "navis? fort. φέ]ρουσα"), might instead lend support to the proposed presence of a woman's voice in the fragment (and constitute the only textual reference to her?). However, note that the following word could be either πόρον or ἄπορον (the latter, perhaps, would reflect the obstacles that one would encounter in finding a way to meet the deceased man, an idea that would be at home in a threnodic song). As]μενος ἔνθα περανα[stands in l. 3, it could be reconstructed in many different ways; a likely restoration seems hardly possible, since the semantic function of ἔνθα is here vague, and]μενος might even constitute the last part of the genitive of a noun.

Line 5. Tentatively, I consider that here the reconstructed female voice is posing a "rhetorical" question, such as πῶς κεν ῥηΐδίην τάχα νῦν εὕρ]οιμι κέλευθο[ν,³² expressing her grief. This kind of question is very often found in ritual laments (Alexiou 1974: 161–65).³³ Besides, such a construction might justify the use of the potential optative, since this mood can denote wish, after the interrogative πῶς or τίς (especially in tragedy, see Kühner-Gerth I, 235). All the same, it should be pointed out that in all other cases in the fragment where a potential optative is used, the notion of "wish" is not obligatory, since one might suggest that the whole fragment in a way constitutes the apodosis of an implied conditional clause that may have been expressed in some form earlier in the poem (for example, εἰ + opt. -ἄν + opt., "remote future"): that is to say, that there could possibly be a sentence like "If I were to manage to reach him in the place he has now gone, I would . . .," mainly followed by images of, and thoughts about, an imaginary trip to that island (the mood arguably remaining the same in the narrative that follows).

Line 8. I adopt Parsons's emendation of εὐαγ[.]α into εὐαέα (see, however, Haslam 1993: 135: "I do not see why εὐαγέα should not stand").

Lines 9–10. I have changed West's [ἰδ]ών (l. 10) into [. . .ἰδοῦσα] (l. 9). The ὀφ[θαλμοῖσι] in l. 10 seems almost certain. Dr. Revel Coles confirms that the traces

---

31. Or λευκ[ο]ῖς, cf. Parsons 1992a: 48, Hunter 1993a: 13, and Mace at n. 55.

32. Cf. ῥηΐδίη (sc. οἶμος) in Hes. *WD* 292.

33. Such a threnodic ἀναφώνησις seems to have occurred in a poem by Simonides himself, some phrases of which have been preserved in a commentary on Simonides edited in Lobel 1959 (*POxy* 2434 frr. 1 (a) + (b) + 2 = Simon. 608.1 (a) +(b) + 2 *PMG*): see l. 28 τίς ἄμφατις ἔσται (and cf. l. 17 in both Page's *PMG* and Campbell's edition [1991]).

after omicron in *POxy* 2327, fr. 2(a) col. ii.3 support the decipherment of a dotted phi. For the ending -ον in φίλ]ον, cf. Parsons 1992a: 47: "]ον or]ων." West's tentative πάλιν after λάβοιμ̣[ι (μ is the best candidate here) may not raise any important objections.

Lines 11–12. The decipherment of the beginning of l. 11 is uncertain. ὄφρα or ὄφρ᾽ α-? Or neither of these (see Parsons 1992a: 47 "φρ likely, although only their feet remain")? νέο[ν] is a mere conjecture ("after α, 'parts of uprights suggesting ν or π', then perhaps the base and the end of the cross-bar of ε, but I do not think other rounded letters excluded, then to the right of a damaged patch a trace in the form of a small λ, 'prima facie χ'," Parsons 1992a: 47). Even χ[αρίε]ντος may be considered somewhat doubtful (in view of χαρίε[ντ]α in l. 15?, cf. however ἱμερόεντα in ll. 12 and 17). The construction and the general meaning of ll. 11–12 are also vague (note that *POxy* 2327 fr. 2(a) col. ii provides the variant reading λείπει for the beginning of the line). West's emendation λείβοι in l. 12 is not supported by anything in the text (why not λείβη?). A conjectural supplement such as ἄν[θος] is taken as the subject of l. 11, but in l. 12 the subject changes abruptly (West translates: "so that his lovely skin's young bloom [should breathe on me], | and he'd distil sweet longing from his eyes" [1993b: 171]). Apart from this retrospective transition, which may not be unparalleled,[34] it should be noted that the epithet ἱμερόεις[35] could here allude to the feelings of longing that the dead would reciprocate to the loved *persona loquens* who imagines visiting him.

Line 13. ἐν ἄνθε[σι(ν) ἡδέσιν εἴη replaces West's ἐν ἄνθε[σιν ἁβρὰ πάθοιμι (for ἄνθε[σι(ν) ἡδέσιν cf. *Cypr.* fr. 4.4–5 Bernabé = Davies [note that Bernabé differs from Davies in the punctuation of these two lines]). The letter after **KAIKENE** can be either Π or Γ (ἔπ[ειτα?, which occurs in early elegiac and iambic poetry). Generally, it is hard to fill in the gaps of the line and, especially, to find a supplement for]υδος (see Parsons 1992a: 48, for his attractive suggestion ὁ φροῦδος, which would fit a threnodic context). West's μετὰ πα]ιδός seems improbable, mainly in view of the unexpected difficulties it creates for the general meaning of the line (see the interpretation offered by West 1993a: 13: "μετὰ πα]ιδός: Echecratidas? Perhaps rather an unspecified couching-companion," and cf. the objections raised by Hunter 1993a: 14 n. 12 and Haslam 1993: 135). Moreover, as far as the traces in both papyrus fragments (*POxy* 2327 fr. 4.6 and 3965 fr. 27.8) are concerned, I find it very difficult to read iota before ΔOC (cf. Parsons 1992a: 45: "rather flattened top and stem of upsilon"). Besides, see Parsons's estimation of the number of letters missing: κενε.[. . . . .].δος.

Line 14. A difficult line, since its end, which could help us to understand the exact function of φαρκίδας, is lost. For the poor "literary" attestation of that word, see

---

34. It seems to me that West's reconstruction here presupposes that either such an abrupt change of subject is acceptable, or that there is a synecdochic relation between ἀπὸ χροὸς ἄνθος and Echecratidas. But could we postulate—or adhere to—either of these ideas in restoring the fragmentary ll. 11–12?

35. For ἱμερόεις in lamentary context, see, e.g., the Homeric πᾶσιν δ᾽ ἱμερόεις ὑπέδυ γόος (*Od.* 10.398), and [Moschus] *Megara* 4.56–58: . . . τὰ δέ οἱ θαλερώτερα δάκρυα μήλων | κόλπον ἐς ἱμερόεντα κατὰ βλεφάρων ἐχέοντο | μνησαμένη τέκνων τε καὶ ὧν μετέπειτα τοκήων.

Parsons 1992a: 45–46. Note that φ is not entirely certain: in *POxy* 2327 fr. 4.7 the trace of the top of the upright could not exclude a letter such as ψ (in 3965 fr. 27.9 there is only a "short horizontal trace at mid-level" [Parsons 1992a: 45]). Hunter speculates that φαρκίδας may not mean "wrinkles," but rather be an unattested word "for food of some kind" (1993a: 13). Nevertheless, if the appropriate meaning of φαρκίδας is "wrinkles" here, then it might in context mean that the man [is sloughing off or covering?] his wrinkles by weaving and wearing wreaths over his head.[36] After ἐκ.[all is uncertain.

Lines 20–21.   Does εὔπομπ[suggest a wish that the dead man may have a safe journey to his new home in the afterlife? Be that as it may, it is not easy to decide whether these two lines, which have been preserved in a detached fragment (= *POxy* 2327 fr. 2[b]) that Lobel joined with *POxy* 2327 fr. 2(a) col. ii on the basis of the fibers, belong to that fragment (see Parsons's warning, 1992a: 48).

If 22 W² is a part of a woman's threnodic song,[37] then the proposed reconstruction may be an approximation to the truth. Among the analogies in motifs and expression that this fragment could have with songs of mourning preserved in Greek literature and beyond,[38] the general theme of the longing that a living person feels to see and even touch a dead loved one seems the most striking one to be discussed here. This thematic motif seems to occur first in Homer (*Il.* 23.62ff.): Achilles meets his loved friend Patroclus *in his dream*, and the first thought that comes to his mind is to embrace him (97ff.).[39] In the *Odyssey* (20.61–65, 79–81), Penelope's wish to die to see Odysseus in the afterworld is most telling: Ἄρτεμι ... αἴθε μοι ἤδη | ἰὸν ἐνὶ στήθεσσι βαλοῦσ' ἐκ θυμὸν ἕλοιο | αὐτίκα νῦν, ἢ ἔπειτά μ' ἀναρπάξασα θύελλα | οἴχοιτο προφέρουσα κατ' ἠερόεντα κέλευθα, | ἐν προχοῇς δὲ βάλοι ἀψορρόου Ὠκεανοῖο. | ... ὡς ἔμ' ἀϊστώσειαν Ὀλύμπια δώματ' ἔχοντες, | ἠέ μ' ἐυπλόκαμος βάλοι Ἄρτεμις, ὄφρ' Ὀδυσῆα | ὀσσομένη καὶ γαῖαν ὕπο στυγερὴν ἀφικοίμην ("Artemis ... would that now you would fix your arrow in my breast and take away my life in this very hour; or else that a storm wind might catch me up and bear me from here over the murky ways, and cast me away at the mouth of backward-flowing Okeanos. ... Would that in such a manner those who have dwellings on Olympus would blot me from sight, or that fair-tressed Artemis would smite me, so that I might even pass beneath the hateful earth to see Odysseus").[40] In Greek tragedy the motif

36. In such a case, the supplements considered in n. 12 would turn out to be unimaginative.

37. This also suggests an established context of performance.

38. One of them is the woman's reference to the hands of the dead; cf., e.g., Eur. *Tr.* 1178f., where Hecuba mourns over the dead body of Astyanax.

39. Cf. the remarks of Edwards (1986: 91, n. 18) on the purpose of the episode of Patroclus' ghost in Book 23 of the *Iliad*: "Perhaps present in his [sc. the poet's] mind (at least subconsciously) are the themes of fruitless reunion with a loved one after death (cf. Anticleia, Elpenor), the prediction to a living man of his own death ..., and perhaps even the hero's visit to the underworld to reclaim a lost friend (Heracles, Theseus, Orpheus, Gilgamesh)."

40. This is an adapted version of Murray and Dimock's translation (1995: 284–87). To my mind, there is no compelling reason why ὀσσομένη in l. 81 should not be taken literally in this context. Following LSJ⁹, J. Russo (among others) is inclined to take its meaning as equivalent to that of ὀσσόμενος ... ἐνὶ φρεσί, used

occurs with some further ramifications. In Euripides' *Alcestis*, after the burial of Alcestis, Admetus and the Chorus sing a lament on their way back home. ζηλῶ φθιμένους, Admetus declares, κείνων ἔραμαι, | κεῖν' ἐπιθυμῶ δώματα ναίειν ("I envy the dead, I long for their state, I yearn to dwell in those halls below": 866–67), and after the reiteration of many cries of grief by Admetus in the first strophe, the Chorus concludes: τὸ μήποτ' εἰσιδεῖν φιλίας ἀλόχου | πρόσωπον σ' ἔσαντα λυπρόν ("No more to see your dead wife face to face is painful": 876–77).[41] Finally, in the first anti-strophe Admetus exclaims: τί μ' ἐκώλυσας ῥῖψαι τύμβου | τάφρον ἐς κοίλην καὶ μετ' ἐκείνης | τῆς μέγ' ἀρίστης κεῖσθαι φθίμενον; ("Why did you keep me from throwing myself into the open grave and lying there dead with her, the best of women?": 897–99). This extreme longing to be united with the dead reappears in Euripides' *Supplices*, where Evadne leaps into the flaming tomb of her husband Kapaneus.[42] Generally, the few examples given here for the aforementioned motif, while by no means representative of the number of cases where this occurs, are probably enough to provide a literary context within which our fragment could be considered.

According to the reconstruction proposed here, the woman who may constitute the speaking subject in our fragment expresses her wish to travel across the sea,[43] and her longing to meet her dead husband[44] [again], even in the afterlife, which is imag-ined as a fertile and beautiful island, perhaps the Island of the Blest or Elysium (Parsons 1992a: 49).[45] Possibly in the context of her mourning for Antiochus,[46] she

---

of Telemachus (in a very different context) at *Od.* 1.115; according to Russo, "Penelope wishes to die with an image of Odysseus in her mind's eye" (1992: 113). However, in an earlier insightful article, Russo himself has construed ll. 80–81 as "her fervent wish to be dead so she can meet Odysseus under earth" (1982: 7 n. 9). It seems questionable whether the former meaning should be opted for here, all the more since the par-ticiple is dependent on a verb of motion (ἀφικοίμην), and can, therefore, be viewed as assuming the func-tion of a final participle; cf., e.g., Eur. *Supp.* 120 τούτους θανόντας ἦλθον ἐξαιτῶν πόλιν, and Collard 1975, comment on Eur. *Supp.* 63–64.

41. Note that σ' ἔσαντα in l. 877 is an emendation by Wilamowitz (the MSS have ἄντα). The *Alcestis* trans-lations are from Kovacs 1994.

42. See also Euripides' *Protesilaos*, where Laodameia makes a statue of her dead husband Protesilaos and hides it into her room, but when her father Akastos finds out the truth and orders the statue to be burnt, she throws herself into the blaze (see further Webster 1967: 97–98).

43. For a detailed analysis of the first six lines of the fragment, see Mace at nn. 4–20. Mace speculates that in ll. 1–4 the speaker refers to a paradigmatic voyage undertaken most probably by a hero, who, according to tradition (Mace at n. 16), "was translated to an idyllic existence after death" (e.g., Menelaus, Achilles, Peleus). Mace's proposal depends on her remark (at n. 9) that "κέλευθος . . . could be indefinite ('a jour-ney') and, thus, initiate a new phase of the discourse" (cf. also West 1993a: 13, who suspects that ll. 1–3 "are not part of the Elysian visit—Simonides will hardly have spent seven lines getting from his embarkation to the mention of his destination—but of its frame: a voyage to be undertaken by Antiochus, or whoever the poem was addressed to"). Since this part of the poem is highly fragmentary, any argument that could be advanced about it is destined to be mere conjecture. In my view, we should take ll. 1–6 as simply refer-ring to the speaker's imaginary journey (in this context ἰο[στ]εφάνων probably refers to the Nereids (or the Oceanid Nymphs) ("the sea, the glory of the Nereids", Parsons 1992a: 45); the meaning then would be ". . . through the glory of the Nereids (their dwelling) I would arrive at an abode rich in trees, that airy island . . ." [?]).

44. However, cf. n. 28 above.

45. For a concise history of Elysium and the Isles of the Blest (including the White Island) with further bibliography, see Sourvinou-Inwood 1997; see also Sourvinou-Inwood 1995: 32–56.

46. See above at nn. 21–28.

describes an imaginary visit there, her encounter with handsome Echecratidas, his possible involvement in a banqueting scene. There is reason to believe that this woman may be identified with Dyseris, the wife of the Thessalian ruler Echecratidas, since, as Aristides' passage quoted above suggests, her πένθος for her son Antiochus was probably expressed by her in Simonidean verses; the connections of Simonides with several ruling families in Thessaly are adequately attested,[47] and indeed he is known to have composed laments for some of them (see Schol. Theocr. 16.44, quoted above). Finally, as regards the "symposiastic" scene in the afterworld, two main observations will suffice: first, nowhere in the fragment is there any indication that what is described in ll. 13 ff. should be identified with a proper (archaic or classical) male symposion: it would be safer if we took it as an imaginary banqueting scene. Second, even if the fragment referred to a proper symposion in the underworld, this would not be unparalleled: banquet scenes in afterlife[48] are frequently depicted on the so-called *Totenmahl* reliefs.[49] The male "symposiasts" recline on their *kline*, while their female consorts sit beside them or stand.[50] In the νεκρόδειπνα (or *Totenmahle*) the *kline* is presented more as a symposion couch (and not as a deathbed).[51] A man who is possibly a hero is shown feasting;[52] and even a cupbearer may appear.[53] Although it has been suggested that these reliefs depict the ordinary dead, it is more likely that they are heroes: in this case, the image of the symposion could articulate the notion of heroization, an image of the hero, and thus function as an image of blessed afterlife. To conclude, there is nothing unlikely in the banqueting scene described in our fragment being metaphorically accommodated in a threnodic song. This image is in accordance with the more general consolatory theme of a blessed afterlife, which would be expected to occur in the genre of threnodic poetry.[54]

What are the main corollaries if Simon. 22 W^2 is indeed a threnodic song? For a start, it is the first example of a rather personal threnodic poem composed by Simonides.[55] From the fragmentary threnodic compositions generally attributed to the poet (frr. 520–25 *PMG*), we can know only very little about the style of Simonidean threnodic songs.[56] In this fragment there is no ecstatic manifestation of grief such as that found in laments in Greek tragedy, but the fragment seems also to be devoid of the reflective, consolatory, and gnomic mood which characterizes the fragments of

---

47. See n. 27.

48. For some "symposiastic" scenes in blessed underworld settings, see Mace at n. 49.

49. See, generally, Fritze 1896, Thönges-Stringaris 1965, Dentzer 1982: 11–13 and ch. 7, Garland 1985: 70–71, Murray 1988: 243–47 (who mainly adopts the arguments propounded by Dentzer), and Larson 1995: 43–50. For banquets of the dead in Greek and Egyptian literature, see Vermeule 1979: 72–74.

50. For the position of the body of both sexes in the depiction of such sympotic scenes, see Dentzer 1982: 347–50.

51. Boardman 1990: 128.

52. Drink is usually stressed more than food, see Vermeule 1979: 57–58.

53. See Boardman 1990: 128.

54. Cf. Nagy 1979: 171–72.

55. See, however, n. 33.

56. For Simonides' laments, see Reiner 1938: 72–82, Harvey 1955: 168ff., Alexiou 1974: 103–5 and 132, and Cannatà Fera 1990: 23–27. I intend to discuss in detail elsewhere the fragments that have come down to us under the title Σιμωνίδου Θρήνων and those that have conventionally been considered as Simonidean *threnoi*.

Pindar's *threnoi* that have survived.[57] It is a refined and restrained song of mourning, though perhaps indicative of that passion for which Simonides' threnodic songs were famous in antiquity. The reconstructed female speaking subject arguably longs to meet Echecratidas in the afterworld, see his face, touch his hands—in general, show him her feelings, thus evoking his mutual emotions.[58] She probably likes to know that her dear Echecratidas does not feel grieved in the afterworld, that he entertains himself by reclining, weaving wreaths, and singing. So far as the fragment permits us to see, she is not dwelling on recollections of the past, but rather pondering the nature of the island where the man is now living. In her threnodic song she transforms her wish to an imaginary reality, and carefully draws, with her song, pictures of fantasy that appear true.

Second, the song reconstructed above has been composed in elegiac meter. This may support the existence of a genre of threnodic elegy: the ἔλεγος in the sense of "sung lament" that the ancients attributed to it may now be more closely associated with the elegiac meter, since the proposed reconstruction suggests that around the end of the sixth or the beginning of the fifth century, if not earlier, threnodic songs were composed in this meter. Furthermore, Pausanias' testimony[59] about the Arcadian Echembrotos, whose mournful songs (*elegeia*), accompanied by the aulos, were known in antiquity, should possibly be taken as more authoritative, and not utterly dismissed as "worthless as evidence for the nature of early elegy."[60] As Alexiou and West, among others, have maintained,[61] this and some further evidence suggest

---

57. See Alexiou 1974: 103–4 (cf. also Cannatà Fera 1990: 30–31).

58. If we assume that in l. 12 there was a reference to ἱμερόεις πόθος. But it is doubtful whether πόθον should be taken as the only possible supplement after ἱμερόεντα.

59. Paus. 10.7.4–6 (3.101 Rocha-Pereira) τῆς δὲ τεσσαρακοστῆς ὀλυμπιάδος καὶ ὀγδόης . . . ταύτης ἔτει τρίτῳ ἆθλα ἔθεσαν οἱ Ἀμφικτύονες κιθαρῳδίας . . ., προσέθεσαν δὲ καὶ αὐλῳδίας ἀγώνισμα καὶ αὐλῶν· ἀνηγορεύθησαν δὲ νικῶντες . . ., καὶ αὐλῳδὸς Ἀρκὰς Ἐχέμβροτος . . .· [. . .] δευτέρᾳ δὲ πυθιάδι . . . αὐλῳδίαν τε (<τό>τε Dindorf) κατέλυσαν, καταγνόντες οὐκ εἶναι τὸ ἄκουσμα εὔφημον· ἡ γὰρ αὐλῳδία μέλη τε ἦν αὐλῶν τὰ σκυθρωπότατα καὶ ἐλεγεῖα {θρῆνοι} προσᾳδόμενα τοῖς αὐλοῖς. μαρτυρεῖ δέ μοι καὶ τοῦ Ἐχεμβρότου τὸ ἀνάθημα.

60. Bowie 1986: 23. On the general contention of Bowie's article that there is no compelling evidence for the existence of threnodic elegy in the archaic period, see the important note by Lewis (1987), where he draws attention to two sixth-century epigraphical texts whose first person is an anonymous mourner who expresses feelings about the dead. Lewis concludes: "I cannot help thinking . . . that the existence on stone of two sixth-century texts of lamentation goes some way to breaking down the dividing-line between the funerary epigram and a hypothetical threnodic elegy and offers more support for the existence of the latter than Bowie is prepared to allow." For a recent, concise discussion of threnodic elegy, see Gentili 1988: 32–34. Note that Fowler (1987: 87–88) holds that Echembrotos' and Sakadas' ἔλεγοι (or ἐλεγεῖα) were probably "fairly stylized formal laments sung to the aulos at musical contests," and that although these laments may not have been originally composed in the elegiac meter, they were regularly composed in this meter by the fifth century. For the view that the association of the words ἔλεγος and ἐλεγεῖον cannot be shown to be of any significance for the origin of elegy, see, more recently, Fowler 1987: 86–88, and Lambin 1988 (who proposes that the word ἐλεγεῖον comes from the form *ἑλικεῖον (or *ἑλικήιον), which can be associated with such words as ἕλιγμα, ἑλίκη, ἕλιξ, ἑλίττω, etc., and is "l'équivalent du latin *versus* (cf. *vertere*), une 'ligne qui tourne [dans l' écriture βουστροφηδόν]'" [76]). For a discussion of the terms ἐλεγεῖον, ἐλεγεία, and ἔλεγος, and the circumstances of performing threnodic elegies, see Bartol 1993: 18–30 and 53–54 (the latter partly based on Bowie's views).

61. Alexiou 1974: 104, and West 1974: 4–5 (see also West 1992: 337).

that, at an early stage, a kind of threnodic elegy had existed, and that "elegoi were pre-sumably performed at funerals."[62] As a consequence of that, the elegiac lament of Euripides' *Andromache* may have its origin in those sung laments that the tradition ascribes to the early Greeks.[63]

It might be objected that Simon. 22 W^2 is preserved in so mutilated a state that no clue can be found to its content. However, the possibility at least remains open that this fragment was part of a threnodic song composed by an author renowned for his capacity to excite passion through his *threnoi*.

POSTSCRIPT

In the Postscript to her "Utopian and Erotic Fusion in a New Elegy of Simonides (22 West^2)" in this volume, Sarah Mace objects to the reconstruction I proposed in *ZPE* 120 (1998), 1–11 (reprinted, with revisions, in this volume). I am most grateful to the editors for giving me the opportunity to take the dialogue further.[64]

Simon. 22 W^2 has come down to us in so mutilated a state that scholarly opti-mism as to plausible (or "more plausible")[65] reconstructions may be at present mis-leading. Fragments *adesp. eleg.* 29, 30, and 31 in West's first edition of *Iambi et Elegi Graeci*,[66] in conjunction with suggestions made by him both in the critical apparatus of his 1972 edition, and in his *Studies in Greek Elegy and Iambus* (West 1974: 168), attest to the risks that a reconstruction of such a fragmentary text may involve. The origins of the scholarly reception of Simon. 22 W^2 go back to Merkelbach and Barigazzi;[67] but West's 'reading' has proved influential in constructing the outline of the frag-ment's possible content:

> There [fr. 29 W^1], after remains suggesting a sea crossing (image for emotional dis-turbance?), we see the poet wishing to arrive at a certain distant goal. Something that in different texts might be either]δενδρον or]υμνον [that is, now 22.7 W^2] must be a celebrated grove, and it does not seem far-fetched to think of the metaphorical grove of Venus described in the anonymous hexameters quoted [by Hippolytus, *Ref.*

---

62. West 1974: 13. Bowie 1986: 22–27 has argued against this view. Some of his arguments may be open to question in the light of my reconstruction of Simon. 22 W^2 (but whatever the case might be, I would not agree with his view that μαρτυρεῖ δέ μοι . . . in the passage by Pausanias quoted above explains Pausanias' characterization of αὐλῳδία [Bowie 1986: 23]).

63. Based mainly on the passage by Pausanias quoted and this Euripidean lament composed in elegiac meter, Page (1936; followed by Bowra 1938: 86–88 = Bowra 1953: 104–7), held that laments in elegiac form were probably composed in the archaic period, but the existing evidence supported only a hypothesis which connected the elegiac lament of Andromache (*Andr.* 103–16) with a kind of lamentatory elegy that flourished in the northern Peloponnese in the seventh and sixth centuries and was represented by poets such as Echembrotos and Sakadas. Such a connection may not seem necessary, if my main argument about Simon. 22 W^2 is accepted.

64. I here reply only to Mace's Postscript that appears in this volume; a full critique of Mace's article will not be undertaken here. I would like to thank Sumi Furiya, Albert Henrichs, and Christiane Sourvinou-Inwood for their comments on this Postscript.

65. Mace p. 203.

66. That is, the three fragments of *POxy* 2327 that now constitute parts of the new fragment 22 W^2.

67. Merkelbach 1956: 88 ("fr. 2 col. II beschreibt ein Fest"), and Barigazzi 1963: 65ff.

5.8; see West 1974: 134]. In the succeeding column someone appears to be being praised for beauty of appearance and voice ... in the context of a symposium.[68]

Had there been preserved at the time more words or lines of the new fragment 22, the whole image might have appeared different.[69] As Peter Parsons has most subtly put it, there is "beyond the ravages of time, and the dangers of transmission, the larger problem of reconstructing a picture from glimpses."[70]

In her Postscript, Mace holds that there are two objections[71] to the reconstruction of fr. 22 W² I have suggested: first, that the evidence I adduce for a threnodic song that Simonides composed for Dyseris' son Antiochus appears to her invalid;[72] and second, that my suggestion that the speaking subject in the fragment may be female is vulnerable. Both objections can be shown to be false.

The connection between Simonides and Dyseris in Aelius Aristides' Εἰς Ἐτεωνέα ἐπικήδειος (31. 2 Keil), that Mace apparently credits to me, has been suggested by many scholars over the last two centuries at least.[73] Let us examine the passage in more detail:

ποῖος ταῦτα Σιμωνίδης θρηνήσει, τίς Πίνδαρος ποῖον μέλος ἢ λόγον τοιοῦτον ἐξευρών· τίς χορὸς ἄξιον φθέγξεται τοιούτου πάθους· ποία δὲ Δύσηρις Θετταλὴ τοσοῦτο πένθος ἐπένθησεν ἐπ' Ἀντιόχῳ τελευτήσαντι, ὅσον νῦν μητρὶ τῇ τούτου πένθος πρόκειται· (ed. Keil)

Mace first points out that there occurs no *strict* juxtaposition between Simonides and Dyseris; no one has suggested that there does. Similarly, her remark that "the continuation of the passage (following *PMG* 527) explains Aristides' otherwise myster-

---

68. West 1974: 168.

69. Barigazzi 1963 offers a rather different reconstruction. Note also that in the more recent history of "reconstructive" reception of fr. 22 W², "before the name of Echecratidas was restored (i.e., before *POxy* 3965, fr. 27 was added at the left), it seemed that these might actually be the Islands of the Blessed, and]δην might be Peleides, which would suit the emphasis on Achilles in the other fragments very well" (Rutherford, this volume, n. 88).

70. Parsons, this volume, at n. 40.

71. She also makes two minor points (pp. 205–6) in response to my nn. 6 and 13. First, it is of course true that many archaic lyric and elegiac poets wrote pederastic poetry and that we do not need to be explicitly told that a poet did so in order to speculate that he may. However, my point remains that we cannot assume that all of them necessarily did so. Second, Mace, based on my n. 13, now takes K. J. Beloch's (not, as she thinks, J. H. Molyneux's) proposed identification of "Echecratidas (2)" and "Echecratidas (3)" as offering support to her argument about a young Echecratidas, hypothetical son of Antiochus. But there have been other equally conjectural proposals; see, e.g., Müller 1858: 280 n. 3 for a different identification. Given how little is known about Thessalian rulers of the sixth and fifth centuries, little, if anything, can be built upon such conjectures.

72. It is noteworthy that Mace, while attempting to refute the evidence I adduce, does not feel it necessary to provide evidence to support her hypothesis for the existence of a Simonidean homoerotic encomium for a (historically unattested) young son of Antiochus characterized by what she calls "an apparently unique fusion of the themes of utopian escape and the trials of the aging lover" (before n. 88; cf. her view that "of the poets who did handle the themes of rejuvenation and utopian escape, it would appear that Simonides alone chose to exploit the connection between the two" [sic], after n. 73).

73. The references are numerous; see, e.g., Schneidewin 1835: Simon. fr. 48 Εἰς Ἀντίοχον Λαρισσαῖον, Bergk 1882: Simon. fr. 34 Εἰς Ἀντίοχον, Flach 1883–84: 629, Bowra 1961: 323, Cannatà Fera 1990: 26–27, Molyneux 1992: 127, West 1993a: 13, and Rutherford, this volume.

ious transition from futures (θρηνήσει, φθέγξεται) to an aorist (ἐπένθησεν)" (p. 204), does not affect the connection between Simonides and Dyseris. The transition from futures to an aorist would not be mysterious at all: Aristides now refers to a specific example of πένθος made in the past by the Thessalian Dyseris, paralleling in what follows the grief Dyseris expressed at the loss of her son with the sorrow Eteoneus' mother is presently facing.

The most problematic point in Mace's argument against the connection between Simonides and Dyseris, is that "evidently Aristides' rhetorical strategy in this eulogy was to list a series of paradigmatic figures," that is, the threnodist Simonides, the encomiastic poet Pindar, an ideal chorus, and a paradigmatic *mater dolorosa*, Dyseris (Mace, p. 204). Of Dyseris, the newly created paradigmatic *mater dolorosa*, we unfortunately know almost nothing (see my n. 16); references to her name throughout Greek literature are exceptionally few. Moreover, to say that Dyseris was considered (at least by Aristides) a paradigmatic *mater dolorosa* is to neglect the actual means through which she could achieve such a status. How can a historical figure like Dyseris, who perhaps did not play a particularly leading role in Thessaly, become famous in antiquity? The answer is partly given by Theocritus 16.42–47: Antiochus and other Thessalian rulers would have lain unremembered (ἄμναστοι) had Simonides not immortalized them in song. Cf. the scholion on Theocritus 16. 34–35, which also says that "[Antiochus' and Aleuas'] wealth would have contributed nothing to their present fame, had they not been celebrated in song by Simonides." Interestingly, the same scholion gives Simonides as the only source of information about Antiochus' parentage, while for Aleuas it refers to all the information collected by Euphorion: τὰ δὲ περὶ Ἀλεύαν τὸν Σίμου πάντα ἀνείλεκται Εὐφορίων. ὁ δὲ Ἀντίοχος Ἐχεκρατίδου καὶ Δυσήριδος υἱὸς ἦν, ὡς φησι Σιμωνίδης. The scholiast's primary source for Antiochus' family is Simonides. It is also noteworthy that Schol. Theocr. 16. 36–37 again cites Simonides as a source for Scopas' parentage, but this time he is explicit about the genre of the composition in which the information is given: Κραννὼν δὲ πόλις Θεσσαλίας, ὅθεν Σκόπας ὁ Κραννώνιος Κρέοντος καὶ Ἐχεκρατείας υἱός. καὶ Σιμωνίδης ἐν Θρήνοις ("Crannon is a city of Thessaly, whence came Scopas the Crannonian, son of Creon and Echecrateia. Simonides too mentions that in his *Threnoi*").

In a *threnos* for Scopas, Simonides referred to Scopas' parents; in another composition, he mentioned the names of Antiochus' parents. In addition, Schol. Theocr. 16.44 reports that Simonides composed epinician odes and *dirges* for the Thessalian rulers Antiochus, Aleuas, and the Scopadai. As Theocr. 16.42–47, cited above, suggests, the basic source for Dyseris' mourning for Antiochus must have been Simonides: Aelius Aristides displays strong familiarity with Simonides' poetry,[74] and his *Or.* 31.2 testifies further to the fact that in antiquity Simonides was renowned for his threnodic poems. Aristides' aim in the proem of his funeral speech for Eteoneus (31.1–2) is to acknowledge the need for mourning (and praise), and to exemplify his statement (31.1 Keil) that, "if mourning (θρῆνοι) had not yet become a custom of mankind, it

---

74. References to Simonides' name or poems attributed to him include the following: *Or.* 3.97, 3.140f., 3.151, 28.59–61 and 63–67, 32.24, 50.36.

would now have rightly been instituted on account of him [Eteoneus]."[75] There follow references to Simonides, Pindar, and a chorus. As far as the chorus[76] is concerned, Aristides wonders, even if rhetorically, whether its members would be able to sing worthily of Eteoneus' death.[77] The last example Aristides cites is more specific: Dyseris of Thessaly (not just Dyseris) and her mourning for Antiochus, to be compared to the present mourning of Eteoneus' mother. That Dyseris and her mourning should be connected with the poetry of Simonides is suggested by the following: first, no connection between Pindar and the Echecratidai is attested (nor is there evidence that he composed *threnoi* for any of them); second, Simonides must have composed a threnodic song for Antiochus' death (cf. above); and third, Dyseris, who was mentioned in one of Simonides' compositions, now appears in the context of a discussion about his threnodic poetry. To conclude, Simonides must have made Dyseris' mourning for her son known to all those familiar with his poetry.

In my original reconstruction, I suggested that Simon. fr. 22 W^2 may constitute part of a threnodic song delivered for Antiochus, but that it may also have contained references to his dead father. The scholiast on Theocr. 16.34–35 attests that in Simonides' poetry Echecratidas and Dyseris appeared as the parents of Antiochus. I would here like to extend my argument further: in view of Danae's lament composed by Simonides (543 *PMG*), where Danae is an intradiegetic speaker within the poetic narrative, we should consider the possibility that fr. 22 W^2, as reconstructed in this chapter, constitutes part of Dyseris' threnodic song as being narrated by Simonides. Thus, the speaking subject is Dyseris, her song being embedded in a more extensive song in honor of Antiochus.

Let us now consider another aspect of Aristides' passage. Why was the specific example of Dyseris' mourning singled out and employed at the beginning of the funeral speech for Eteoneus? Can any analogies between Antiochus' and Eteoneus' death be traced? Although it cannot be shown that Aristides, well versed as he was in Simonides' poetry, may be here alluding to parallel structures between Dyseris' song of mourning and his funeral oration, there occur a few indications that might point to this direction. First, in Aristides' speech particular emphasis is placed on the great mourning of Eteoneus' mother, and on her role in Eteoneus' life.[78] Second, Eteoneus died young; Antiochus, despite his (alleged?) marriage with the Milesian hetaira Thargelia,[79] may have died at a young age.[80] More interestingly, there might be another analogy between the funeral oration for Eteoneus and the mourning for

75. All the translations of passages from Aristides' oration in this Postscript are by Behr 1981: 154–57.
76. Mace speaks for "some ideal chorus"; for a more precise understanding of choruses in Aristides, cf. *Or.* 18.7 ποῖαι συναυλίαι καὶ συνῳδίαι χορῶν ... ἀρκέσουσιν ἀνοιμῶξαι πόλιν. I wonder whether Aristides' reference to ἡλικιωτῶν χοροί later in the speech (31.11) has some relevance to the present passage. I would refrain from adopting Taylor's conjecture Στησίχορος in *Or.* 31.2, since it is not supported by any extratextual or intratextual indications. Cannatà Fera's arguments in support of this conjecture are not conclusive either (cf. n. 19 above).
77. Note the wording τίς χορὸς ἄξιον φθέγξεται τοιούτου πάθους.
78. *Or.* 31.2, 3, 4, 6, 8, 9, 11–12.
79. See Molyneux 1992: 127–28. For Thargelia, see, recently, Gera 1997: 179–83.
80. Molyneux 1992: 128, and Gera 1997: 182.

Antiochus. While at the beginning of his speech Aristides states that, apart from mourning, praise for the dead is evidently needed, toward the middle of the speech (11–13) his praise for Eteoneus takes the form of proper mourning, to the extent that he imagines himself assuming the role of a weeping actor in a tragedy (14). Praise has clearly been turned into lamentation, but now consolation in the form of praise is duly introduced: ὥσπερ ἐν τραγῳδίᾳ τινὶ ὡς ἀληθῶς μεταξὺ τῶν ὀδυρμῶν δοκῶ μοι κατακούειν φωνῆς ἀπὸ μηχανῆς θεοῦ τινος μεταβάλλοντος τὸν θρῆνον εἰς εὐφημίαν ("as it was truly in some tragedy, in the midst of my lamentation, I seem to hear the voice of some god on the theatrical machine, who changes my mourning into words of praise"). The *deus ex machina* discloses that the young Eteoneus has gone neither to Cocytus nor to Acheron, but has become an ageless hero, and, for this reason, the journey he goes on is not to be pitied (15). Because of his admirable life, Eteoneus is now "blessed and envied by all" (18), and his good reputation will be living among the people. Aristides himself holds that "it would be proper to sing of him even in the drinking songs, like Harmodius, and to say, 'You did not die'" (19). Aristides does not quote the whole song for Harmodius, but we know that, after the initial address (φίλταθ' Ἁρμόδι', οὔ τί που τέθνηκας, *PMG* 894. 1), there was a reference in the song to Harmodius being in the Isles of the Blest, among famous heroes. Pindar, in his *Threnoi* (fr. 129 Maehler), had described such a blessed afterlife locale (cf. *Ol.* 2. 56–80);[81] Simonides may have also referred to such a setting, as fr. 22 W² suggests. What would be interesting for us here is that, if my reconstruction of fr. 22 W² is in the right direction, the Simonidean threnodic song may have shared another similarity with Aristides' oration.

The other objection that Mace raises in her critique is equally problematic, not only in terms of the individual remarks she makes, but also in terms of the approach to archaic lyric fragments she advocates. Her first, and main, point here is that "it would be *unusual* for Simonides and for most male archaic lyricists to have written a poem in a woman's voice" (p. 205; my emphasis).[82] This is a priori destined to be a highly subjective thesis, since, *in the fragmentary corpus of archaic lyricists that has survived*, there occur certain examples of a poetic persona with a female voice. Given the number of preserved archaic lyric fragments, how many instances would we need to argue that such an idea is plausible?[83] Mace further oddly remarks that none of the examples I cite belong to Simonides (*sic*), and that "the burden of proof would seem to lie with those who would propose a female speaker for Simon. fr. 22 W²." She also restates her (equivocal) points that the ending]μενος and the supplemented περάνα[ς in line 3 appear to be positive indications for a male subject in the poem,[84] and that in lines 9ff. there occur "recognizably male homoerotic *topoi*" (p. 205).

---

81. Aristides, in his funeral oration for Eteoneus, mentions a threnodic song by Pindar (31.12 = fr. 136a Maehler).

82. Cf. also her argument that the allusion to poetic activity in ll. 17–18 "would apply *most naturally* to the speaker" (p. 204; my emphasis).

83. As David Sider points out to me, the following instances in later Greek literature may also be of some relevance: Asclepiades 19 *HE*, and Philodemus *Epigrams* 25, 26, 36 Sider. For a concise discussion of the early examples I cite in n. 22, see Sider 1997: 26 n. 6.

84. See, however, my comments on l. 3.

Moreover, Mace contends that the occurrence of ἱμερόεις, especially in terms of the conjectural supplement πόθον, defines the general context of the fragment. However, ἱμερόεις here does not modify πόθον; also for the notion of ἱμερόεις γόος she discusses, see Kokolakis's thorough study (1987). All in all, Mace's arguments against a female speaking-subject in the fragment do not make for a persuasive case. Finally, her last remark about a "dramatic" difference in character between the reconstructed threnodic song and preserved fragments of Simonidean *threnoi* is obviously based on modern views about the purported style of Simonides' (and Pindar's!) fragmentary laments that have survived (cf. my n. 33, p. 218, and, especially, Parsons's discussion of "Styles" in this volume, after n. 43).

13

THOMAS K. HUBBARD

"New Simonides" or Old Semonides?

Second Thoughts on POxy 3965 fr. 26

In an earlier publication I had argued on a number of grounds for a late sixth-century date for the iambic poet Semonides of Amorgos, and observed that this dating would make it possible for the disputed elegy on the "leaves and lives of men" (previously identified as either Semonides, fr. 29 D, or Simonides, fr. 8 W[1]) to be a reply to Mimnermus, fr. 2 W, as it seems to be, and still be written by Semonides, as suggested by its close parallels in theme, tone, and wording to the iambic fr. 1 W of Semonides.[1] The new Simonides papyrus (*POxy* 3965), which appeared very soon after the writing (and somewhat before the publication) of the earlier article, clearly necessitates a reconsideration of the authorship question, since *POxy* 3965 fr. 26 of the papyrus contains the remains of what had been vv. 6–13 of that elegy and demonstrates that they were in fact part of a longer elegy than what is quoted in Stobaeus 4.34.28. Although some controversy has arisen concerning the unity of the poem (which West now divides into frr. 19 and 20 W[2]),[2] it seems quickly to have become a matter of established consensus that the authorship controversy has been resolved, since the same papyrus contains other fragments which are unquestionably from works of Simonides.[3]

The purpose of my present contribution is to suggest that this consensus may be premature. What the new papyrus does prove is that Simonides of Ceos produced a wide range of elegiac poetry, including both historical narratives (such as the Plataea and Artemisium poems) and traditional sympotic elegy (such as the poem on the

An earlier version of this paper appeared in Deborah Boedeker and David Sider (eds.), *The New Simonides*, *Arethusa* 29.2 (1996): 255–62, and is used here by kind permission of the Johns Hopkins University Press. The author expresses his thanks to D. Sider, D. Obbink, D. G. Martinez, and E. F. Cook for discussing various aspects of this problem with him. They are in no way responsible for the conclusions of this essay.

1. Hubbard 1994: 191–93.

2. See Parsons 1992a: 43 and West 1993a: 10–11, although West speculates that fr. 19 W[2] might indeed have been part of the same poem, following rather than preceding fr. 20 W[2]. The unitarian thesis is ably maintained by Obbink and Sider in this volume.

3. West 1993a: 10 is quite categorical; Parsons 1992a: 43 deems the question resolved only for fr. 20 W[2], but inclines to Simonidean authorship of fr. 19 W[2] too.

voyage to the happy island = fr. 22 W^2). Advocates of Simonidean authorship of the "leaves" poem thus need no longer resort to the problematic hypothesis that this poem was originally one of the Simonidean funeral epigrams, as Fraenkel once proposed.[4] However, the papyrus really adds little to the attribution debate beyond this.

We must bear in mind that ancient tradition, with only two exceptions, uniformly records the iambic poet's name not as "Semonides," but "Simonides." The late grammarian Choeroboscus (ap. *Et. Magn.* 713.17) distinguishes the two names, identifying "Semonides" as an iambic poet, "Simonides" as a melic poet, and the spelling Semonides appears to be confirmed by the Herculaneum papyrus of Philodemus' *Poetics* (*PHerc* 1074, 20 N = *Tract. tert.*, fr. f, col. III [Sbordone]). Modern scholars have for the sake of avoiding confusion adopted this distinction in spelling, but the preponderance of references to "Simonides" of Amorgos suggests that this was probably the name (or at least a name) by which even the Alexandrians knew him. The possibilities for confusion in attribution of works to these two poets are manifold, and it was likely even a conundrum for Alexandrian editors, who often had to make highly arbitrary decisions about where to place a given text. While the iambic poems could easily enough be assigned to "Simonides" of Amorgos and the melic poems to Simonides of Ceos, the issue becomes much murkier with regard to elegiacs. References to historical events or personages connected with the Cean's life might be of some help. But the iambic poet's date was apparently unknown to the Alexandrians,[5] and I have suggested that it was probably much closer to the other Simonides' time than usually recognized, in which case this too could be suspect as a ground for distinguishing them.

The Suda tells us with some specificity that the Amorgine "Simonides," in addition to his iambs, wrote two books of elegy and an *Archaeology of the Samians.*[6] To be sure, the Suda's titles are not always reliable. But since Semonides' ties with Samos seem well grounded,[7] the *Archaeology*, presumably in elegiacs,[8] must indeed be his

---

4. Fränkel 1962: 237 n.14. His view was tentatively endorsed by Davison 1955: 129–30 and Lloyd-Jones 1975: 97.

5. For a survey of the chronographic evidence, which bases his date on nothing but a false synchronism with Archilochus, see Hubbard 1994: 175–81.

6. The Suda entry, s.v. Σιμωνίδης (σ 446 Adler), states ἔγραψεν ἐλεγείαν ἐν βιβλίοις β', ἰάμβους. Under the entry for Simmias of Rhodes (σ 431 Adler) we are given further information which must have been from the original entry for Semonides: ἔγραψε κατά τινας πρῶτος ἰάμβους, καὶ ἄλλα διάφορα, Ἀρχαιολογίαν τε τῶν Σαμίων. No one doubts that the second half of Simmias' entry must indeed have been displaced from the Semonides entry, since neither the archaic date given here nor the Samian/Amorgine nationality nor the status as "first iambographer" can possibly apply to the Hellenistic Simmias of Rhodes, but they do correspond to information we find elsewhere concerning Semonides. For a fuller discussion of this entry, see my remarks in Hubbard 1994: 179–80.

7. The Suda entry on Simmias of Rhodes (see n. 6 above) suggests that Semonides led Samian settlers of Amorgos: ἦν δὲ τὸ ἐξαρχῆς Σάμιος· ἐν δὲ τῷ ἀποικισμῷ τῆς Ἀμοργοῦ ἐστάλη καὶ αὐτὸς ἡγεμὼν ὑπὸ Σαμίων. Proclus (ap. Phot. *Bibl.* 239, 319b28–31 [Henry]), who has a time-reckoning scheme quite distinct from the Suda's, confirms that some sources regard Semonides as Samian: Σιμωνίδης ὁ Ἀμόργιος ἢ, ὡς ἔνιοι, Σάμιος. That Amorgos was indeed partially settled from Samos is firmly established; see Ruppel 1927: 313–15; Shipley 1987: 51, 118. So far as we know, Simonides of Ceos had no connections with Samos at all.

8. On this poem and its place within a well-developed tradition of political/historical elegy (of which the *Battle of Plataea* is a splendid example), see Bowie 1986: 31. This seems to be precisely the kind of poetic

and not the other Simonides'. It is unlikely that this longer work would have been his only venture in elegiac composition; the parallel cases of Archilochus and Solon show that it was common for the same poet to write both iambic and elegiac verse. That we do not have any other Simonidean elegies extant should not trouble us. How much true Simonidean elegy did we have prior to the new discoveries?

Given that the shorter elegiac poems of both Semonides and Simonides are unlikely to have been assembled as collections within their own lifetimes, and that their names and possibly even their floruits were either scarcely or not at all distinguishable, the attribution of any single sympotic elegy with no apparent political references must be regarded as uncertain. Even if we assume that the new papyrus and the earlier *POxy* 2327 were copies of the canonical Alexandrian edition of Simonides of Ceos, it is not safe to take for granted the accuracy of the Alexandrian attributions of individual poems, particularly in the case of shorter, nonhistorical elegies.

However, it is also not safe to take for granted that our papyri actually were copies of the Alexandrian edition. Parsons raises the possibility of an anthology, only to dismiss it.[9] But little notice has been given to a potentially significant anomaly in our papyri, which is their grouping together of two very different elegiac forms—lengthy historical narrative and shorter sympotic pieces.[10] However fallible the Alexandrians were in matters of authorship and attribution, they were quite careful and deliberate in the classification of works by genre and even subgenre, and had elaborate taxonomies for grouping the works of a given poet into different books: witness the multiple subgenres into which the choral lyric of Pindar and Bacchylides was divided, or the classification of Sappho's lyrics into eight books based on metrical forms, with a ninth book wholly of epithalamia.[11] Even elegy may have been subject to such subclassification, as suggested by the book division of the Theognid corpus: the overtly pederastic poems were segregated into a much shorter second book, though formally no different from the other elegies.[12] Accordingly, one is entitled to wonder whether it is really credible that the Alexandrians would have grouped poems like the *Plataea* and *Artemisium* in the same book as shorter sympotic poems. Indeed, the special

---

work Polycrates might be expected to commission, again suggesting a late sixth-century date for Semonides.

9. Parsons 1992a: 5–6.

10. It seems fairly clear that the papyri contain at least two other sympotic elegies (frr. 21–22 W^2), and possibly scraps of several others (frr. 27–33 W^2). See Parsons 1992a: 7, West 1993a: 11–14, Hunter 1993a: 11–14. For a different view, see Obbink in this volume.

11. For Pindar's book divisions, see *Vita Ambrosiana* (p. 3, 6–9 Drachmann); for Bacchylides, in addition to the familiar *Epinicia* and *Dithyrambs*, see Stob. 3.11.19 for *Hyporchemata* and 4.44.16 for *Prosodia*, Plut. *De mus.* 1136f. for *Partheneia*, Athen. 15.667c for *Erotika*. On Sappho, see the discussion of Page 1955: 112–19, who demonstrates on the basis of fr. 103 LP that the book lengths varied greatly, from 1320 lines in book I to around 130 lines in book VIII. Adhering to organizational principles apparently took precedence over uniformity in size for the Alexandrian editors. For the arbitrariness and artificiality of the Alexandrian generic subcategories, see Harvey 1955: 157–75.

12. The antiquity of this book division has been a matter of controversy. Although the division and title are clearly marked in the one manuscript (A) which contains 1231–1389, Carrière 1948: 89–93 and West 1974: 43–45 argue, not implausibly, that the second book was the result of a Byzantine bowdlerization of the Theognid collection. However, in favor of the book's antiquity, see Harrison 1902: 259–60 and Young 1961: xi.

notice which the *Artemisium* poem receives in the Suda entry for Simonides implies that it was of a sufficient scale to be circulated as a book in its own right; our fragments suggest a comparable length for the *Battle of Plataea*. What we have may rather be an excerpted one-volume compilation of Simonidean elegy, taking samples out of the various books available,[13] possibly even including some of what may actually have belonged to the Amorgine "Simonides." If our present collection is not in fact the work of Alexandrian scholarship in its prime, the possibilities for confused attribution are even greater.

It may at this point be worthwhile to review the positive grounds for retaining this poem as the work of Semonides. The parallels with Semonides' iambic fr. 1 W are simply too close to deny.[14] In both poems we have all men given over to vain hope:

> πάρεστι γὰρ ἐλπὶς ἑκάστωι | ἀνδρῶν (Simon. fr. 19.4–5 W²)

> ἐλπὶς δὲ πάντας κἀπιπειθείη τρέφει (Semon. fr. 1.6 W)

In both we see overinflated youthful ambitions come to naught:

> θνητῶν δ' ὄφρα τις ἄνθος ἔχει πολυήρατον ἥβης,
>   κοῦφον ἔχων θυμὸν ἀτέλεστα νοεῖ (Simon. fr. 20.5–6 W²)

> νέωτα δ' οὐδεὶς ὅστις οὐ δοκεῖ βροτῶν
> Πλούτωι τε κἀγαθοῖσιν ἵξεσθαι φίλος (Semon. fr. 1.9–10 W)

In both, men aim at the impossible (Simon. fr. 20.6 W² ἀτέλεστα νοεῖ; Semon. fr. 1.7 W ἄπρηκτον ὁρμαίνοντας); in both, men know nothing (Simon. fr. 20.9 W² οὐδὲ ἴσασιν; Semon. fr. 1.4 W οὐδὲν εἰδότες). In both poems, men fail to anticipate old age and death (first term) and disease (second term):

> οὔτε γὰρ ἐλπίδ' ἔχει γηρασέμεν οὔτε θανεῖσθαι,
>   οὐδ' ὑγιὴς ὅταν ἦι, φρόντιδ' ἔχει καμάτου (Simon. fr. 20.7–8 W²)

> φθάνει δὲ τὸν μὲν γῆρας ἄζηλον λαβὸν
> πρὶν τέρμ' ἵκηται, τοὺς δὲ δύστηνοι βροτῶν
> φθείρουσι νοῦσοι (Semon. fr. 1.11–13 W)

In both poems, men's *nous* is deficient (Simon. fr. 20.9 W² νήπιοι, οἷς ταύτηι κεῖται νόος; Semon. fr. 1.3 W νόος δ' οὐκ ἐπ' ἀνθρώποισιν), because they do not recognize the brevity of their life (Simon. fr. 20.9–10 W² οὐδὲ ἴσασιν | ὡς χρόνος ἔσθ' ἥβης καὶ βιότοι' ὀλίγος; Semon. fr. 1.3–4 W ἀλλ' ἐπήμεροι | ἃ δὴ βοτὰ ζόουσιν, οὐδὲν εἰδότες |

---

13. It is clear that such excerpted anthologies existed, even long before the date of this papyrus. See Turner 1987: 60 for a third-century B.C.E. anthology of lyric passages from Euripides, and Turner 1987: 82 for a second-century B.C.E. anthology of epigrams.

14. A number of scholars (including names such as Wilamowitz, Maas, Schmid, Jaeger, Schadewaldt) have defended Semonidean attribution on these grounds: see the bibliography on the question in Babut 1971: 23 n.36 and Lloyd-Jones 1975: 97. It may be worthy of note that this poem is preserved in the same chapter of Stobaeus (4.34) as the disputed elegy. Stobaeus is our principal source for the work of Semonides, and quotes him as often (at least five times: frr. 1–4, 7 W) as Simonides of Ceos (frr. 521–24 *PMG*, fr. 88 W²). At least one other Stobaean fragment is of disputed authorship (Simon. fr. 525 *PMG* = Semon. fr. 42W); see Wilamowitz 1913: 153 n.2.

ὅκως ἕκαστον ἐκτελευτήσει θεός). Moreover, both poems seem to respond to the negative and pessimistic reflections on the brevity of human life and joy by exhortations not to dwell on our impending evils, but to let our soul take pleasure in the present goods available to us:

ἀλλὰ σὺ ταῦτα μαθὼν βιότου ποτὶ τέρμα
ψυχῆι τῶν ἀγαθῶν τλῆθι χαριζόμενος (Simon. fr. 20.11–12 W²)

εἰ δ' ἐμοὶ πιθοίατο,
οὐκ ἂν κακῶν ἐρῶιμεν, οὐδ' ἐπ' ἄλγεσιν
κακοῖς ἔχοντες θυμὸν αἰκιζοίμεθα (Semon. fr. 1.22–24 W).

The elegiac poem puts the encouragement in a more positive form than the iambic text, but the ultimate message seems to be the same. This exhortation to present sympotic enjoyment may be fleshed out in the fragmentary lines that follow in the papyrus, with their mention of song (fr. 20.14 W² Ὁμηρ[ος), banquets (fr. 20.17 W² θαλίηισι), and perhaps garlands (fr. 20.18 W² ἐϋστρέπτων), but it is also possible that these lines begin another poem.[15]

There is no intertextual polemic apparent between these two texts of the sort we see with the Homeric citation of fr. 19.1–4 W² as a response to Mimnermus' use of the same allusion in his poem on naive youth and impending old age (fr. 2 W).[16] Indeed, it is difficult to imagine how a poet of the Cean Simonides' originality and intellectual subtlety would have allowed himself to copy so closely the poem of an earlier iambographer. But it is quite conceivable for the Amorgine Semonides to have recast, with a few changes in emphasis, one of his own elegiac poems into one in iambic form (or vice versa),[17] without the least concern over originality.

The close parallels with Semonides, fr. 1 W, and Mimnermus, fr. 2 W, may help resolve two significant structural questions that have arisen concerning the poem. The first problem is whether the five lines which manuscript S of Stobaeus (but not M and A) place before fr. 20.5–12 W² should indeed be considered part of the same poem, or isolated as a separate fragment (fr. 19 W²), since the papyrus shows no sign of them. The themes of youth, vain hope, and ignorance of mortality are common to all four texts, and the evident allusion to Mimnermus in the commonplace Homeric

15. As restored by West, fr. 20.13–15 W² would refer to Homer as an example of poetic immortality. But this restoration is highly conjectural; Parsons 1992a: 44 doubts that πανδαμά[τωρ can be the correct reading of v. 15, because the third letter is unlikely to be nu. A Pandora search reveals that West's λήθην] γλώσσης is also without parallel in Greek texts of the classical period: tongues do not elsewhere remember or forget. If fr. 20.13–15 W² continue the poem with a lesson about the permanence of the poet's reputation, who is the σύ of v. 12 and how is this lesson supposed to apply to him? Surely the unspecified σύ is a generic Everyman, not someone who is being exhorted to obtain fame by writing poetry like Homer. Parsons is just as likely to be correct in speculating that the passage could refer to Homer *not* escaping something (slander?) or even that the passage does not refer to Homer at all (reading ὃ μὴ ν[όμιμον).

16. On this poem as a reply to Mimnermus, see my more detailed discussion in Hubbard 1994: 192–93.

17. I suspect that the elegiac poem must have come first, since its frame of reference and direct model appear to be Mimnermus' elegiac fr. 2 W. The iambic poem drops the polemical reference to Mimnermus' poem at the beginning and instead elaborates the theme of the gods' inscrutable will. Its ending is laconic and cryptic, leaving only implied the exhortation to present enjoyment which is developed more openly by the elegiac text.

quote "which few have taken to heart, although receiving it into their ears" strongly suggests that fr. 19 W² was indeed the polemical opening to a longer meditation on these themes, such as we find in fr. 20 W². Fragment 20 W² is just as replete with verbal echoes of Mimnermus' poem as fr. 19 W².[18] But whereas Mimnermus ends in a state of complete negation and despair, fr. 20 W² responds with a more positive exhortation, as we have observed.

If we do accept that frr. 19 and 20.5ff. W² are part of the same poem, written in response to Mimnermus, we must admit that they were divided by at least four (and possibly more) intervening lines (= fr. 20.1–4 W²), of which we have only a few letters, suggesting that something "abides . . . for a brief time." I believe that the content of Semonides fr. 1 W and Mimnermus fr. 2 W gives us a clue to the probable nature of these intervening lines. Both parallel texts contain in their middle section a catalog of the ills that may beset men (Semon. fr. 1.11–22 W; Mimn. fr. 2.5–15 W): old age, death, heartbreak, loss of wealth, lack of children, disease, war, shipwreck, suicide. What is it that "abides . . . for a brief time"? One is at first tempted to suppose youth (on the analogy with Mimn. fr. 2.7–8 W μίνυνθα δὲ γίνεται ἥβης | καρπός), but this idea is already expressed in fr. 20.10 W² and would be redundant here. More likely the phrase has to do with wealth and prosperity (thus comparable to Mimn. fr. 2.11–12 W). It is hard to know what other misfortunes and disappointments may have been listed in these lines, but it is understandable why Stobaeus would have left this catalog section out in favor of the beginning, with its familiar Homeric citation, and the important excerpt which all three Stobaeus manuscripts contain. This scenario seems more likely than to suppose that the excerptor attached similar lines from another poem: the thought of fr. 19 W² does not really seem complete by itself.

With the discovery of an important new literary papyrus, there is often in the rush of scholarly excitement a tendency to conclude that old controversies have been settled or that the new discovery may be of greater importance for some questions than it actually is. Without in any way downplaying the significance of the *Plataea* poem or what this papyrus adds to our knowledge of Simonidean elegy and its variety, I would submit that the authorship question concerning the "leaves" poem is still far from settled. Indeed, if this poem is not the work of Simonides of Ceos, it may be the case that much else in our papyrus also is not. While fr. 22 W² can be regarded as securely Simonidean, assuming that the restoration Ἐχεκ[ρατί]δην is correct,[19] any other fragment of sympotic elegy might equally well be considered the work of Semonides of Amorgos.

---

18. These include v. 3 τυτ]θὸν ἐπὶ χρό[νον (= Mimn. fr. 2.3 W πήχυιον ἐπὶ χρόνον), v. 5 ἄνθος ἥβης (= Mimn. fr. 2.3 W ἄνθεσιν ἥβης), v. 7 οὔτε . . . γηρασέμεν οὔτε θανεῖσθαι (= Mimn. fr. 2.6–7 W ἡ μὲν ἔχουσα τέλος γήραος ἀργαλέου, | ἡ δ' ἑτέρη θανάτοιο), v. 9 οὐδὲ ἴσασιν . . . (= Mimn. fr. 2.4–5 W εἰδότες οὔτε . . . | οὔτ' . . .), v. 10 ὡς χρόνος ἔσθ' ἥβης καὶ βιότοι' ὀλίγος (= Mimn. fr. 2.7–8 W μίνυνθα δὲ γίνεται ἥβης | καρπός).

19. For Simonides' connections with the Echecratidae, a family of Thessalian princes, see fr. 528 *PMG*, and the discussion of Molyneux 1992: 127–29; Scopas' mother was named Echecrateia (fr. 529 *PMG*), suggesting the family's close connection with the Scopadae. See Mace and Yatromanolakis, this volume.

14

MARCO FANTUZZI

Heroes, Descendants of *Hemitheoi*

The Proemium of Theocritus 17 and Simonides 11 W²

The eulogy to Ptolemy by Theocritus (*Id.* 17) starts with a comparison between Ptolemy II, the laudandus of whom Theocritus sets about singing, and two well-known and frequent themes of poetry, namely Zeus and the heroes of the ancient epic:

> ἐκ Διὸς ἀρχώμεσθα καὶ ἐς Δία λήγετε Μοῖσαι,
> ἀθανάτων τὸν ἄριστον, ἐπὴν † ἀείδωμεν ἀοιδαῖς·
> ἀνδρῶν δ' αὖ Πτολεμαῖος ἐνὶ πρώτοισι λεγέσθω
> καὶ πύματος καὶ μέσσος· ὃ γὰρ προφερέστατος ἀνδρῶν.
> ἥρωες, τοὶ πρόσθεν ἀφ' ἡμιθέων ἐγένοντο,
> ῥέξαντες καλὰ ἔργα σοφῶν ἐκύρησαν ἀοιδῶν·
> αὐτὰρ ἐγὼ Πτολεμαῖον ἐπιστάμενος καλὰ εἰπεῖν
> ὑμνήσαιμ'· ὕμνοι δὲ καὶ ἀθανάτων γέρας αὐτῶν.

> (*Id.* 17.1–8)

As Zeus is the greatest among gods, Ptolemy is the greatest among men; the ancient heroes had already found skilled singers for their deeds in their past. Theocritus, therefore, who knows how to celebrate the glory of his characters as skill-fully as the ancient bards, wants to dedicate his hymn to his contemporary hero, who deserves to be sung of more than he has been before.

At the end of the poem we again find these same three themes of song, where the real emphasis is again put on Ptolemy, who is even more clearly equated to the demigods:

> χαῖρε, ἄναξ Πτολεμαῖε· σέθεν δ' ἐγὼ ἶσα καὶ ἄλλων
> μνάσομαι ἡμιθέων, δοκέω δ' ἔπος οὐκ ἀπόβλητον
> φξέγξομαι ἐσσομένοις· ἀρετήν γε μὲν ἐκ Διὸς αἰτεῦ.

> (*Id.* 17.135–37)[1]

An Italian version of this paper, with slight additions, was published in *Prometheus* 24.1 (1998): 97–110.

1. The complex allusive play of the closure, that contaminates epilogues of *Homeric Hymns*—especially *Hymn. Hom.* 15 and 20: δίδου δ' ἀρετήν τε καὶ ὄλβον; 2, 4, 6, 10, 19, 25, 28, 29, 30, 33: χαῖρε (or χαίρετε) . . .

The last words in the last line are in fact said about Zeus, as was anticipated in the first line, but the promise for a new song concerns only Ptolemy, subject of the song who is "equal to the other demigods."[2]

In l. 5, Theocritus specifies the ἥρωες sung by the bards for their deeds (primarily, the Greek warriors who had fought in Troy)[3] as those "who in the past descended from the demigods" (τοὶ πρόσθεν ἀφ' ἡμιθέων ἐγένοντο). This surely serves an important function in Theocritus' context. As soon as the proem is finished, the eulogy starts precisely with a presentation not only of the divine status of Ptolemy II's parents, Ptolemy I and Berenice, but also with a strong emphasis on his descent from the demigod Herakles: Aphrodite had prevented Berenice's descent to Acheron after her death and let her share divine status (45–50), while Ptolemy I Soter, like Alexander, had been presented with immortality (15f.)[4] and had received a throne in the resi-

---

αὐτὰρ ἐγὼ καὶ σεῖο (or αὐτὰρ ἐγὼ ὑμέων τε) καὶ ἄλλης μνήσομ' ἀοιδῆς; 31: χαῖρε ἄναξ . . . ἐκ σέο δ' ἀρξά- μενος κλήσω μερόπων γένος ἀνδρῶν, ἡμιθέων ὧν ἔργα θεοὶ θνητοῖσιν ἔδειξαν; 32: σέο δ' ἀρχόμενος κλέα φωτῶν ᾄσομαι ἡμιθέων ὧν κλείουσ' ἔργματ' ἀοιδοί, has already been brought to light by Perrotta 1978 [1926]:182.

The conclusion of *Id.* 17 together with *Id.* 1.145 χαίρετ'· ἐγὼ δ' ὕμμιν καὶ ἐς ὕστερον ἅδιον ᾀσῶ show that Theocritus interpreted the hymnodic formulaic close χαῖρε . . . αὐτὰρ ἐγὼ καὶ σεῖο καὶ ἄλλης μνήσομ' ἀοιδῆς as a promise of a future song to the god. In fact the hymnodic line can be interpreted either in this way (in the light of *Hymn. Hom. Apoll.* 177f. αὐτὰρ ἐγὼν οὐ λήξω ἑκήβολον Ἀπόλλωνα Ι ὑμνέων), or as an announcement of the new (ἄλλη) epic recitation that was going to follow the hymnodic preamble, in the light of *Hymn. Hom. Aphr.* 293, 9.9, and 18.11 σεῦ δ' ἀρξάμενος μεταβήσομαι ἄλλον ἐς ὕμνον. Very helpful on this matter is Richardson 1974: 324f.; cf. also Fröhder 1994: 57–59.

2. I prefer to understand l. 135 in this way (Theocritus will sing of Ptolemy, who is by nature a subject equal to demigods celebrated by the *aoidoi* of the past, and who also will become equal to them through the poetry of Theocritus), taking into consideration what Theocritus maintains in the preamble of the song, and passages like Eur. *El.* 994–97 χαῖρε, σεβίζω σ' ἴσα καὶ μάκαρας, κ.τ.λ. Cf. also below n. 4, on μακάρεσσι . . . ὁμότιμος . . . ἀθανάτοις of ll. 15f. (the interpretation by A. S. F. Gow seems to be different: "of thee no less than of other demigods will I make mention"). In my opinion, we are allowed to suppose that Theocritus' strategy was to interpret the status of Ptolemy through the existential category of the heroes as ex-mortals destined to divinization, though he sometimes appears to present Ptolemy as endowed with a greater degree of divinity than the heroes: cf. Griffiths 1979: 72, and below n. 25 (see, however, Sanchez-Wildberger 1955: 32 and Nikitinski 1996: 62 for two other views).

3. With ἥρως Greek culture indicated two different figures: on one hand, the protagonists of the epic poems, most of them mortal; on the other, the human beings that became objects of a religious cult after death, which they were considered to survive thanks to some form of immortality (this latter religious-cultic figure is documented for us only from the post-Homeric period). However, already in Hesiod's age the status of the immortal in a blessed place on the borders of the world, and sometimes also real forms of cult, were attributed not only to the religious heroes, but also to some epic heroes, among them—but not only— Achilles (see Hes. *WD* 161–73). Achilles was certainly considered immortal as early as the end of *Aethiopis*, see *PEG* p. 69 (cf. Edwards 1985; Boedeker, "Heroization," this volume, at n. 67). Simonides also shared the belief about the immortality of Achilles in the Elysian fields, as we know from 558 *PMG* (preceded possibly by Stesich. *POxy* 3876.37–77 = *PMGF* pp. 315–25, cf. Garner 1993, and certainly by Ibyc. 291 *PMGF*; followed by Pind. *Ol.* 2.28–80). This cultic worship of the traditional mortal epic hero Achilles (on which see esp. Shaw, this volume) may have allowed Simonides to apostrophize him through the hymnodic form which would appear to have been reserved to gods: cf. West 1993a: 5, Boedeker, "Heroization"; differently Aloni, this volume, at nn. 29–30.

4. The expression μακάρεσσι . . . ὁμότιμος . . . ἀθανάτοις has been explained by most modern scholars only from a formal point of view, after the Homeric *hapax* of *Il.* 15.186, where Poseidon is called ὁμότιμος to Zeus, or after the Ptolemaic court-title ὁμότιμοι τοῖς συγγενέσι, attested, e.g., in *PTebt* 254. In ll. 15ff., however, Theocritus might have intended to hint closely at a precise cultic qualification of the first Ptolemies,

dence of Zeus (17–19). Both Ptolemy I and Alexander are defined by Theocritus as "sons of the sons" of Herakles (23), as both of them had as πρόγονος the καρτερὸς Ἡρακλείδης (26): either Hyllus or one of the mythical founders of the Macedonian dynasty (like Perdicca or Caranus, who were believed to be Hyllus' descendants). Both Ptolemy and Alexander, therefore, ἀριθμεῦνται ἐς ἔσχατον Ἡρακλῆα (27), Herakles being the most famous demigod of Greek religion.[5]

The introduction of the heroes as "descendants of demigods in the past" makes them comparable to the laudandus, the contemporary hero who is going to be presented both as a son of divinized ex-mortals and as an ἀπόγονος from a ἡμίθεος. At one and the same time, therefore, Theocritus is able to compare himself to the bards of the heroes and to compare Ptolemy, first among men, to Zeus, first among gods. Moreover, since the demigod from whom Ptolemy descended was Herakles, the peculiar definition of the heroes in l. 5 could lead the reader to think also of Zeus, Herakles' father, and give a more pregnant sense to the first line of the poem. Theocritus started with the mention of the first among gods in accordance with poetic traditions (2; see n. 22 below), but perhaps the initial ἐκ Διὸς ἀρχώμεσθα implied at the same time that Ptolemy also "originated" from Zeus, either because gods generally and Ptolemy II in particular were under Zeus' protection, as Theocritus himself affirms further below (ll. 73–76, see also Call. *Hymn* 1.79), following the Hesiodic maxim ἐκ δὲ Διὸς βασιλῆες of *Theogony* 96, or because Ptolemy I and II are finally Zeus' descendants by blood, through Herakles the demigod, "son of Zeus," as Theocritus himself emphatically reminds us in l. 33, sealing the presentation of Ptolemy's ancestry (12–33).

The fact is that until a few years ago the definition of the heroes as "sons of the demigods," without parallel in the tradition,[6] seemed rather odd[7] because it is contrary to the common equivalence heroes = demigods, or heroes = sons of one divine and one human parent,[8] which Theocritus himself accepted elsewere in accordance with the tradition: in the conclusion of our poem (ll. 135f. ἄλλων | μνάσομαι ἡμιθέων), in 18.18 (where the hero Menelaus is called ἡμίθεος), and in 22.29 (where the Argonauts are called θεῶν φίλα τέκνα). We can credit the Hellenistic age as much as we want with an experimental taste for *l'art-pour-l'art*, but we can hardly believe

---

who as early as 280 B.C.E. were worshipped by the Nesiotai with ἰσόθεοι τιμαί (*SIG* 390 = *IG* XII.7.506, 25ff.; cf. Fraser 1961). On the important difference between the status of ἰσόθεος and the status of god tout court, cf. Habicht 1970: 195–200 and 212, Badian 1996: 11–26.

5. The stress on the descent of Ptolemy II from Herakles has several parallels. Most meaningful is the inscription *OGIS* 54.1–6, where Ptolemy calls himself at the same time son of the θεοὶ ἀδελφοί and ἀπόγονος of Herakles (and of Dionysus): βασιλεὺς μέγας Πτολεμαῖος, υἱὸς βασιλέως Πτολεμαίου καὶ βασιλίσσης Ἀρσινόης θεῶν Ἀδελφῶν, τῶν βασιλέως Πτολεμαίου καὶ βασιλίσσης Βερενίκης θεῶν Σωτήρων, ἀπόγονος τὰ μὲν ἀπὸ πατρὸς Ἡρακλέους τοῦ Διός, τὰ δὲ ἀπὸ μητρὸς Διονύσου τοῦ Διός, κ.τ.λ. A similar genealogy is ascribed to Ptolemy IV in Satyrus *FGrH* 631 F 1. On these and other analogous testimonies, cf. Weber 1993: 213ff., Huttner 1997: 124–45.

6. It was pointed out as problematic by Gow 1952 ad loc., Meincke 1965: 93, Griffiths 1979: 72, Vox 1997: 263 n.3.

7. Lévêque 1991: 305 called it "curieuse." The correct consideration that "auch in Id. 17.5 ἥρωες sind nicht von ἡμίθεοι abgegrenzt, sondern bilden in ihrer Einheit Väter-Söhne dieselbe Rasse" (Nikitinski 1996: 62) does not reduce the variance of Theocritus' definition with the tradition.

8. See Hes. *WD* 159f. (with schol. ad loc.), Simon. 523 *PMG*, Pind. *Pyth.* 4.12f., Plat. *Rep.* 391d, Apoll. Rhod. 1.548 and 4.1773, Polyb. 3.47.8.

that Theocritus could introduce the very common concept of the epic hero in such an anomalous way just to fit the needs of his own context.

I suggest that the origin of Theocritus' qualification of the epic heroes can now be traced back to the elegy by Simonides for the Greeks fallen at Plataea (11 W²). In this poem, the fact that the warriors who fought the Trojan War gained glory through the poetry of Homer is presented by Simonides in the following way: ἐπώνυμον ὁπ[λοτέρ]οισιν Ι ποίησ'⁹ (sc. Homer) ἡμιθέων ὠκύμορον γενεή[ν· (11.17–18). This last phrase of Simonides could have been the model for Theocritus' description of the Homeric heroes: τοὶ . . . ἀφ' ἡμιθέων ἐγένοντο . . . σοφῶν ἐκύρησαν ἀοιδῶν, over-interpreting ἡμιθέων . . . γενεή as "progeny of demigods."

From a merely lexical point of view, the meaning "progeny" is possible for γενεή in every age, and at least in the archaic age even more so than for γένος.¹⁰ "Progeny," moreover, would be more than plausible in the context of the first part of the Simonidean elegy, which concerns Achilles. Lines 17–18 deal with the heroes fighting at Troy, not specifically with Achilles, but the attribute ὠκύμορος, which is itself pri-marily intended to juxtapose the short life of the Greek warriors with the perpetuity of their glory (cf. 11.15 W²), might also focus somehow more specifically on Achilles, the ὠκύμορος hero par excellence, to whose death Simonides had just devoted ten lines.¹¹ Now, not only was Achilles himself a demigod, as the son of the goddess Thetis and the mortal Peleus, but he was also a descendant of demigods, since he had Zeus as an ancestor via his grandfather Aeacus, son of Zeus. In fact, however, at least in the *Iliad*, Achilles is always and only in touch with his mother, while Zeus never appears to remember that he is the ancestor of Achilles; moreover, Simonides calls Achilles θεᾶς ἐρικυ[δέος υἱέ Ι κούρης εἰν]αλίου Νηρέος in 11.19–20 W² (see also 10.5). At one point in the *Iliad*, though, during the boast over the body of the defeated Asteropeus, who was a demigod as the grandson of the river god Axius, and therefore in a situ-ation where emphasizing superhumanity even in comparison with other demigods was advisable, Achilles boasted about his descent from Aeacus the son of Zeus, and called himself one of the "children of Zeus":

> χαλεπόν τοι ἐρισθενέος Κρονίωνος
> παισὶν ἐριζέμεναι ποταμοῖο περ ἐκγεγαῶτι.
> φῆσθα σὺ μὲν ποταμοῦ γένος ἔμμεναι εὐρὺ ῥέοντος,
> αὐτὰρ ἐγὼ γενεὴν μεγάλου Διὸς εὔχομαι εἶναι.
> τίκτέ μ' ἀνὴρ πολλοῖσιν ἀνάσσων Μυρμιδόνεσσι

9. ποίησ' is the way both Parsons and West restore the main verb. Capra and Curti 1995: 30 propose ἄεισ', in accord with their different interpretation of ἐπώνυμος; see below n. 14.

10. As remarked most recently by Most 1997b: 111f., there are some passages in the archaic epos where γένος and γενεή almost overlap, but "the language of epic is also capable of making a clear distinction between the two terms. Only γένος can be applied to what we would call a biological species so as to distinguish it implicitly from other species. . . . Only in much later texts . . . can γενεή be used in this meaning. . . . In early epic, on the other hand, a γενεή is a subset of γένος; the term distinguishes from one another members of two subgroups who all belong to the same γένος, but who differ from one another by being born earlier or later and hence belong to different generations."

11. The contextual influence of Achilles on the epithet which, surely, Simonides uses for the whole race of the heroes ought not to be underestimated: as remarked by Poltera 1997: 260, this adjective was "une gén-eralisation pudiquement évitée par Homère" in connection with the other heroes at Troy.

Πηλεὺς Αἰακίδης· ὃ δ᾽ ἄρ᾽ Αἰακὸς ἐκ Διὸς ἦεν.

(21.184–89)

This very status of Achilles as a twofold demigod might fit Theocritus' eulogistic aims very well, because this was exactly the status of Ptolemy that the poet was going to sing of, as we can see from the following lines (13–33): Ptolemy was both a demigod, as the son of the divinized Ptolemy Soter, and a descendant of the demigod Herakles, Διὸς υἱός (33).

My saying that γενεή *could* mean "progeny" in ancient Greek, and that this meaning was not absurd in the context of Simonides' elegy, does not imply that I suppose Simonides to have used the term in this meaning. Quite the opposite. By calling the Homeric heroes (ἐπώνυμος) ἡμιθέων γενεή, Simonides intended most probably to follow in a more or less direct way the tradition of *Iliad* 12.23 κάππεσον ἐν κονίηισι καὶ ἡμιθέων γένος ἀνδρῶν (which, as the only passage of Homer where the word ἡμίθεος appears, can be supposed to be the model of Simonides)[12] or of Hes. *WD* 159f. ἀνδρῶν ἡρώων θεῖον γένος οἳ καλέονται ἡμίθεοι—a tradition which Simonides had followed in another fragment, 523 *PMG*: † οὐδὲ γὰρ οἳ πρότερόν ποτ᾽ ἐπέλοντο, θεῶν δ᾽ ἐξ ἀνάκτων ἐγένονθ᾽ υἷες ἡμίθεοι.[13] Therefore "race of demigods" proves to be the meaning of Simonides' ἡμιθέων γενεή, beyond any reasonable doubt. My intention is merely to suggest a possible episode in the later fate of Simonides' text. I am not proposing that Theocritus was making a mistake in interpreting the Simonidean phrase, or that he stretched its meaning unawares. Still, it is by no means unusual for a Hellenistic poet to exploit the form of a previous author's phrase, and even to stretch its meaning a bit to fit his own context—just a bit, because, as I mentioned above, the interpretation of γενεή as "progeny" is not inadmissable from a lexical point of view, and this meaning is plausible rather than absurd for Simonides' context.[14]

---

12. Cf. Clay's conclusion, this volume: "In echoing the Homeric passage and in using the expression ἡμίθεοι, Simonides both links and dissociates himself with Homer and his subject matter. Troy and the race of the ἡμίθεοι, celebrated by his illustrious predecessor may be dead and gone, but Simonides will grant the same immortal κλέος to his contemporaries."

13. Compare later Asclep. *AP* 9.64.7f. = *HE* 1024f. μακάρων γένος ἔργα τε μολπαῖς ǀ καὶ γένος ἀρχαίων ἔγραφες (sc. Hesiod) ἡμιθέων.

14. The possible imitation of Simonides by Theocritus neither helps to settle the matter of the interpretation of ἐπώνυμος—"famous" (predicative of γενεή) or "named after" (attributive of γενεή)—in Simon. 11.16–17 W², nor consequently allows us to decide on the restorations of the verbal form at the beginning of l. 18 (ποίησ᾽, with ἐπώνυμος predicative, or ἄεισ᾽, with ἐπώνυμος attributive: see above n. 9).

The interpretation ἐπώνυμος = "famous" was proposed by Parsons 1992a: 31 on the grounds of the very likely imitation of this Simonidean passage in Theocr. 16.44–46 θεῖος ἀοιδὸς ὁ Κήιος . . . ἐν ἀνδράσι θῆκ᾽ ὀνομαστοὺς ὁπλοτέροις, though ἐπώνυμος is nowhere surely attested with the meaning "famous" (but cf. Lloyd-Jones 1994: 2; see also Sourvinou-Inwood [personal communication, cited by Rutherford 1996: 180], according to whom ἐπώνυμος would contrast the race of the heroes with the men of the third generation, who were νώνυμοι in Hes. *WD* 154). The second interpretation was proposed by Capra and Curti 1995: 29f.: ἐπώνυμος ἡμιθέων γενεή would hint at Hes. *WD* 159f. ἡρώων θεῖον γένος, distinguishing the fourth race of the heroes from the first three, which were called after the name of a metal; cf. Burzacchini 1995: 31 for a sensible criticism of this interpretation).

Simonides had already spoken of the κλέος gained by the Iliadic heroes by means of Homeric poetry (see 11.15 f.). Therefore it is not necessary for Theocritus to have been thinking of the Simonidean ἐπώνυμος

The reasons that might have motivated Theocritus to focus his attention on this Simonidean phrase, and more generally to show his allusive intentions towards Simonides' elegy for the fallen at Plataea, are several. ἡμιθέων . . . γενεή occurred in a passage of the elegy that mentioned the Greek heroes fighting at Troy, and Achilles as well, but they were rapidly dismissed by Simonides in order to go on with the real subject of the poem, a human and contemporary subject expressly juxtaposed to the heroic themes (see above all 11.25–28). One of the elements more strikingly emphasized in reference to these heroes was that they had gained immortal glory by means of Homer (14–18); therefore Simonides most probably wished to present himself as the new *aoidos* who was going to provide the contemporary Greeks who had defeated the Persians with new κλέος ἀθάνατον (28). It is a fact that Theocritus 17 deals with the same concepts that had been stated by Simonides, and with characters who have the same roles: there is a juxtaposition between past heroic themes of poetry, and human and contemporary subjects; there is the statement that the Greek heroes fallen at Troy had gained κλέος, and furthermore, that they had gained it by means of epic poetry. Moreover, through his allusion to this passage of the elegy for the warriors of Plataea, Theocritus himself could implicitly adopt in respect of Simonides (plus the epic *aoidoi*) the same stance that Simonides had had towards Homer. He would be referring to Simonides, who had compared himself with Homer, in order to compare his poem's ability to provide the κλέος; not only to the ability to glorify the ancient epos, but also to the ability of Simonides himself to glorify his subjects. The hypothesis that Theocritus' allusion to the Simonidean poem carries this further implication appears even more probable if we consider that in such a way the proem of the eulogy for Ptolemy would simply propose an implicit comparison between Theocritus and the same two poets, Simonides and Homer, whom in his other encomiastic poem (for Hiero; cf. 16.34–57) Theocritus had explicitly and emphatically pointed to as capable of providing human achievements with κλέος, and had explicitly compared with himself.[15]

It is well known that this other Theocritean eulogy, for Hiero, owes much to the Plataea poem;[16] possibly even the structure of Theocr. 16 as a whole resembles that of Simonides' poem.[17] As far as Theocr. 17 is concerned, the comparison between the poet's uncertainty of how to begin the poem, faced with many themes on the worth of the laudandus, and the woodcutter's uncertainty of which tree to cut first in the wood (ll. 9–12), could also be derived from an adaptation of the comparison that is found in *POxy* 2327 fr. 5 παῖ[σέ] ο.[| ἢ πίτυν ἐν βήσ[σαις | ὑλοτόμοι τάμ[νωσι,

---

"famous" γενεή, when he hinted at the glory conquered by the ἥρωες through the ancient *aoidoi*. Likewise, nothing forbids (or compels) supposing that Theocritus intended ἐπώνυμος in the meaning suggested by Capra and Curti, and that he overinterpreted Simonides' lines as "descent from demigods, which is called after them."

15. Cf. Parsons 1992a: 31 and Parsons 1992b: 10–12.

16. On Theocr. 16 and the New Simonides cf. Parsons 1992b, Barchiesi in this volume, Hunter 1996: 90–109, Rutherford, this volume, at nn. 58–59.

17. See Rutherford, this volume, at nn. 58–59: "The structure of Theocritus, *Id.* 16 as a whole resembles that of the Plataea poem, with an earlier section discussing earlier praise-poetry (Simonides and the Thessalians), and a later hinting at the possibilities of contemporary praise (Hiero's military exploits), thus replicating what Simonides does for himself vis-à-vis Homer."

namely, the start of what we have of Simonides' elegy in West's reconstruction.[18] Theocritus might have been driven to exploit the imitation of this simile while speaking of the choice of the theme by the semantic ambiguity of the concept of ὕλη ("wood," but also "subject"), which clearly underlay Simonides' text, though it is not expressed in the surviving fragments.[19]

I should also add that the first part of the eulogy of Ptolemy possibly adopted as its model the first part of Simonides' elegy in honor of the victory of the Greeks at Plataea.[20] We cannot be completely sure that *POxy* 2327 fr. 5 is the beginning of Simonides' elegy. At any rate it is sure that the elegy included a short hymn to Achilles and to the Greeks who died fighting against the Trojans, then went on to bid farewell to Achilles as theme of the song (19f.), and to pass on to the celebration of the glory of the contemporary Greeks who had fought against the Persians. The structure of the Simonidean poem most probably goes back to the normal procedure of the archaic *aoidoi*, who used to begin their recitations of pieces from the heroic epos with a proemium devoted to a god, such as are most of the "Homeric" hymns of short or medium length that we have, and then went on to recite the epic: Simonides "compressed in miniature" a hymn (the hymn to Achilles) and an epos (the story of the second Persian war).[21] In my opinion, through the relationship between Zeus and the Muses or celebratory poetry,[22] between ancient heroes and ancient *aoidoi*, between Ptolemy and Theocritus, which ends with the final choice of Ptolemy as the theme of the song, Theocritus continues Simonides' attempt at miniaturizing, and concentrates the short hymnodic proem of the model in an even shorter priamel of only six lines.

In fact Simonides' starting section had been short, but not at all irrelevant for the structure, and it was most probably assigned with a specific function—one that the shorter *Homeric Hymns* had fulfilled as preambles for the rhapsodic performances[23]—contextualizing the poem to its first performance. In the case of Simonides' elegy this might have been a local festivity for the divinized hero Achilles, or a celebration of Leonidas as a new Achilles, or of the fallen at Plataea as the new heroes dead for their fatherland, commissioned either by the Spartan Pausanias, or

---

18. West, *IEG*² considers this papyrus scrap to be the beginning of his fr. 11, and prints it before *POxy* 2327 frr. 6 + 27 etc. In his reconstruction the simile would have pictured the fall of Achilles or of Patroclus, and would be part of the proem here as well as in Theocr. 17. According to other scholars, the scrap should be collocated at a different point of the narrative, and the simile would refer to the death of some Greeks fallen at Troy. For a review of the problem, and a very important Horace parallel that would favor West's interpretation, cf. Barchiesi, this volume.

19. A hypothesis suggested to me by M. L. West during the meeting of the Oxford Philological Society, where the first draft of this paper was presented, on Halloween of 1997.

20. Full discussions of the features and limits of the encomiastic nature and intent of Simonides' elegy in Aloni 1994: 9–22 and Boedeker 1995: 217–22.

21. Cf. Parsons 1992b: 12 and above all Aloni 1994: 13–15. On the possible variance of the divine subject of the epic proemia with Simonides' hymn to a mortal hero, cf. Aloni, this volume, at nn. 30–32 (but see above n. 3).

22. For Zeus as a common theme of the proemia of the *aoidoi*, see, e.g., Pind. *Nem.* 2.1–3. The initial joint mention of both the Muses and the proems from Zeus hints in all probability at the beginning of Hesiod's *Theogony* and *Works and Days*, as well as the proem of Aratus' *Phaenomena*: Cf. Fantuzzi 2000.

23. Cf. Aloni 1990.

for some more panhellenic memorial day.[24] We cannot ascertain whether a Hellenistic poet such as Theocritus could fully grasp the pragmatic function that that preamble had fulfilled for Simonides. At any rate, if, as I believe, Theocritus' eulogy was conceived for performance during a specific celebration in honor of Ptolemy, this occasion did not match with the Achilles theme—especially if he really wanted to show his new hero Ptolemy endowed with a superior level of divinity than the ancient epic heroes.[25]

So, with one of the acts of formal adaptation/appropriation that are typical of the Hellenistic re-use of the archaic lyric poetry,[26] Theocritus not only reduces further the size, but also transforms the function of Simonides' proem: the mini-hymn to Achilles that Simonides had stopped in order to pass on to the real subject matter of his eulogy becomes a short list of some possible, famous themes of poetry celebrated by the ancient aoidoi in their performances of heroic epic and in their introductory προοίμια (see n. 22)—a short list that Theocritus promptly interrupts in order to pass on to the real subject of his eulogy.

If my hypothesis about Theocritus' allusive strategy is correct, we might suppose an allusion to Simonides also in the αὐτὰρ ἐγώ through which Theocritus introduces his preference for the human laudandus Ptolemy rather than for Zeus as subject of the song (17.7). The opposition between the personal choice of the theme and other possible themes sung by other poets obviously had been often expressed through phrases including ἐγώ (see for instance Alcm. 1.77 *PMG*), but the specific phrase αὐτὰρ ἐγώ had achieved some kind of metapoetic specialization as it came to begin the formulaic last line of many *Homeric Hymns*, namely the line through which, soon after bidding χαῖρε "farewell" to the god, the poet drew the audience's attention to the transition from the hymnodic prelude on a divine matter to the heroic matter of the following recitation of epic: αὐτὰρ ἐγὼ καὶ σεῖο (or αὐτὰρ ἐγὼν ὑμέων) καὶ ἄλλης μνήσομ' ἀοιδῆς (see above, n. 1). Nevertheless, in the *Homeric Hymns* this last line had pointed out the transition from the song for a god to the song for heroes, as is made explicit in the epilogues of the *Hymns to Helios* (31: χαῖρε ἄναξ . . . ἐκ σέο δ' ἀρξά-μενος κλήσω μερόπων γένος ἀνδρῶν ἡμιθέων ὧν ἔργα θεοὶ θνητοῖσιν ἔδειξαν), and to *Selene* (32: χαῖρε ἄνασσα θεά . . . σέο δ' ἀρχόμενος κλέα φωτῶν ᾄσομαι ἡμιθέων ὧν κλείουσ' ἔργματ' ἀοιδοὶ Μουσάων θεράποντες ἀπὸ στομάτων ἐροέντων).

24. For these hypotheses cf., respectively, West 1993a: 5; Pavese 1995: 22f.; Aloni 1994: 20 n.34, 1997: 25–27; Parsons 1992a: 3 and Boedeker 1995b: 223f. (with different arguments).

25. "Why be a mere Achilles when you can join the Olympians?": cf. Griffiths 1979: 76. Callimachus appears to have thought of Arsinoe's divinization in analogous terms: cf. Meillier 1979: 219. Lines 55–57 certainly exploit the mythological paradigm of Achilles born of the goddess Thetis to be a warrior as gallant as Peleus, analogous to Ptolemy II born of the divinized Berenice to be a warrior like Ptolemy I. At any rate the parallelism between Achilles and Ptolemy II is not emphasized as unique, because Diomedes is also mentioned along with Achilles (53f.). After all, as a matter of fact, Ptolemy II was anything but a brilliant warrior: possibly the comparison between him and the martial epic heroes is intentionally scanty, and might also entail some hint of irony: cf. Effe 1995: 116f. Theocritus also leaves implicit for the reader the parallelism between Berenice and Thetis which 55–57 could involve, but did not actually exploit (cf. the different intention of Call. fr. 228, where the altar consecrated to Arsinoe, about which we know from the diegesis, was most probably connected with Thetis' altars of l. 15).

26. Cf. Fantuzzi 1993: 37ff.

Different is the structural value of the αὐτὰρ ἐγώ in Simon. 11.19ff.: ἀλλὰ σὺ μὲ]ν νῦν χαῖρε, θεᾶς ἐρικυ[δέος υἱὲ | κούρης εἰν]αλίου Νηρέος· αὐτὰρ ἐγώ [| κικλήσκω] σ’ ἐπίκουρον ἐμοί, π[ολυώνυμ]ε Μοῦσα, | εἴ περ γ’ ἀν]θρώπων εὐχομένω[ν μέλεαι, κ.τ.λ. Here, too, αὐτὰρ ἐγώ is coupled with the farewell to the hero (/god?) Achilles celebrated in the preceding short hymn, but here after the conclusion of the song about the god, no new song for traditional epic heroes follows; instead, the Muse is invoked to help the poet sing about ἄνδρες (25), though these "men" benefit from some kind of heroization by the poet himself.[27] The hymnodic transition between mythologic subject matter and heroic subject matter gains a new function in Simonides' new encomiastic context, so as to mark the transition between Achilles, the introductory theme, heroic (divine?) subject matter, and the contemporaneous Greeks, victors over the Persians, the real subject matter of the song. The result is that the phrase αὐτὰρ ἐγώ had a much stronger force in Simonides. We cannot be sure that with αὐτὰρ ἐγώ Simonides implied any opposition to the hymnodic tradition where this phrase had been used for a different transition. Ancient readers, however, could at least read it as a statement of the choice of human subject matter, marking not only the end of the heroic-divine theme just treated (Achilles), but also the total suppression of any performance of heroic epos that might be expected following χαῖρε . . . αὐτὰρ ἐγώ at the end of a hymnodic prelude. It seems much more probable that Simonides had this intention—or that fr. 11.19–25 can be read in this way— if one considers that a *praeteritio* of this kind would be in line with the eulogistic tradition that has its most explicit representative in the poem by Ibycus in honor of Polycrates, S151 *PMGF*.[28]

The innovative re-use of the hymnodic αὐτὰρ ἐγώ that was the basis of Simonides' text appears to find its immediate continuation in Empedocles 21 B 35 DK,[29] where it is probably used to introduce the internal transition from a part of a more narrative-mythological nature to more specifical wisdom poetry.[30] In Theocritus I would see another probable example of the adoption of αὐτὰρ ἐγώ with the value attested to us for the first time in Simonides—namely as the *praeteritio* of epic-heroic themes that signals the transition from a preliminary part of the poem,

---

27. See Boedeker, this volume, "Heroization," passim.

28. *Praeteritio* is the best term to synthesize the attitude of Ibycus in the proem of this encomium, where he hints at Iliadic themes such as Agamemnon or the Greek heroes at Troy, who were famous for their handsomeness, but defines them as more suitable subjects for the Muses and their omniscience, and instead passes on to declare his own preference for a human laudandus and his intention to provide him with the same glory as the epic characters. I would not rule out that, together with the obvious precedent *Il.* 2.484–93, these lines of Ibycus, or better the encomiastic topos exemplified by Ibycus, were the models of Theocr. 16.1–4 αἰεὶ τοῦτο Διὸς κούραις μέλει, αἰὲν ἀοιδοῖς, | ὑμνεῖν ἀθανάτους, ὑμνεῖν ἀγαθῶν κλέα ἀνδρῶν. | Μοῖσαι μὲν θεαὶ ἐντί, θεοὺς θεαὶ ἀείδοντι· | ἄμμες δὲ βροτοὶ οἴδε, βροτοὺς βροτοὶ ἀείδωμεν.

29. αὐτὰρ ἐγὼ παλίνορσος ἐλεύσομαι ἐς πόρον ὕμνων, | τὸν πρότερον κατέλεξα, λόγου λόγον ἐξο- χετεύων | κεῖνον· ἐπεὶ νεῖκος μὲν ἐνέρτατον ἵκετο βένθος | δίνης κ.τ.λ.

30. Cf. Obbink, this volume, at n. 27: "Although the fragment as quoted by Simplicius contains no direct address, we may assume that the formula αὐτὰρ ἐγώ indicates, just as in the new Simonides fragment, the rhapsode's transition from one section of his poem to another. We may conclude further that the type of discourse and the form of address contained in the preceding passage were distinctly different, more mythological, and less specifically didactic."

and leads to the real and proper theme of the song itself, a human, though heroized, laudandus.[31]

After all, Simonides' poem had been an eulogy dedicated to human and contemporaneous protagonists, who were "heroized" at least through the parallelism with Achilles (one of the epic heroes who became immortal after his death, according to a tradition certainly known to Simonides, cf. n. 3 above).[32] Moreover, Simonides' poem was written in elegiac distichs, and not in a lyric metre as were the other kinds of encomiastic poetry known to us from the archaic tradition. In fact, both the content and the form of the poem for the dead in Plataea had good chances to be precedents of obvious importance for a Hellenistic poet intending to write an encomium in hexameters for a contemporaneous subject who was to be deified, like his parents, after his death, and is most emphatically compared to the heroes of epos.

31. According to Rutherford, this volume, n. 59, Theocritus would exploit the Simonidean expression as a model also in his other encomium (16.66), referring it to the "vulgar" patron who only cares about gaining more money, and opposing him to his own superior addressee, Hiero II. Incidentally, Theocritus' farewell refusal of the "vulgar" patron (χαιρέτω, v. 64) also possibly echoed Simonides' farewell to Achilles (ἀλλὰ σὺ μὲ]ν νῦν χαῖρε, v. 19)—but this may be a casual coincidence.

Something similar to the stylistic pose of Simonides—and also a possible modified imitation of the Simonidean (-Theocritean) αὐτὰρ ἐγώ—may occur at the end of another famous Hellenistic proem, Apoll. Rhod. 1.18–22: νῆα μὲν οὖν οἱ πρόσθεν ἔτι κλείουσιν ἀοιδοί Ι Ἄργον Ἀθηναίης καμέειν ὑποθημοσύνῃσι· Ι νῦν δ' ἂν ἐγὼ γενεήν τε καὶ οὔνομα μυθησαίμην Ι ἡρώων, δολιχῆς τε πόρους ἁλός, ὅσσα τ' ἔρεξαν Ι πλαζόμενοι· Μοῦσαι δ' ὑποφήτορες εἶεν ἀοιδῆς.

32. This kind of parallelism fitted probably well the encomiastic ideology of Simonides, who at least once had directly equalized one of his *laudandi* with the ancient heroes Herakles and Polydeuces, far beyond the paradigmatic comparisons typical of the epinician poetry: see 509 *PMG*, apud Lucian. *Pro Imag.* 19 ἀλλὰ πῶς ἐπήνεσε ποιητὴς εὐδόκιμος τὸν Γλαῦκον; οὐδὲ Πολυδεύκεος βίαν φήσας ἀνατείνασθαι ἂν αὐτῷ ἐναντίας τὰς χεῖρας οὐδὲ σιδάρεον Ἀλκμάνας τέκος. ὁρᾷς ὁποίοις αὐτὸν θεοῖς εἴκασε; μᾶλλον δὲ καὶ αὐτῶν ἐκείνων ἀμείνω ἀπέφαινεν. καὶ οὔτε αὐτὸς ὁ Γλαῦκος ἠγανάκτησεν τοῖς ἐφόροις τῶν ἀθλητῶν θεοῖς ἀντεπαινούμενος, κ.τ.λ. This exaggeration possibly involves some ironic slant, which would not be extraneous to the serious-comic character of some Simonidean hyperboles, but may also be the result of Lucian's rereading.

15

RICHARD HUNTER

The Poet Unleaved

Simonides and Callimachus

Simonides 22 W^2 intrigues and tantalizes. Peter Parsons, to whom we owe this combination of *POxy* 2327 and 3965,[1] tentatively interpreted both the journey described in the wretched tatters of the first verses and the "party" that occupies the main bulk of the fragment as a fantasy, perhaps of rejuvenation in the next life: "The extreme view would be this: The aged Simonides longs to escape (now, or after death), carrying his poetry, across the sea to the place of many trees, the Island of the Blest (Elysium), there to meet again the dead Echecratidas in all his desirable youth; they will join in the symposium; the wrinkled Simonides too will recover his youth."[2] In a full and careful discussion of the fragment, Sarah Mace argues that the journey was not a post-mortem fantasy, but a utopian one—the aging poet desires to consort with a handsome boy on a make-believe island from where, as in all utopias, old age is banished.[3] On her view, the poem is an encomium of a young patron, or a patron's son, and the utopian eroticism makes it clear that *in the real world* the poet is not in fact a potential suitor (he is far too old); for such erotic encomium Mace helpfully compares Pindar's famous verses on the melting beauty of Theoxenos (fr. 123 Maehler). More recently, Dimitrios Yatromanolakis has seen in the fragments a female lament for Echecratidas or his son.[4]

The relation between 22 W^2 and the other elegiac remains has also evoked some interest. Potentially the most fruitful suggestion, noted by both Dirk Obbink and

---

The title of this essay alludes in part to a memorable modern use of the idea that "human generations are as leaves," in Gerard Manley Hopkins's "Spring and Fall."

1. Parsons 1992a: 46–47.

2. Parsons 1992a: 49. In Hunter 1993a I proposed a different reconstruction on the basis of similarities with the propemptikon for Ageanax sung by "Lykidas" in Theocritus 7. For the sake of simplicity, I shall here adopt the broad outlines of the Parsons-Mace reconstruction, though the question of the relation of the poetic voice to the journey of the opening verses has not gone away; that Theocritus 7 echoes Simonides still seems to me probable, on any reconstruction of the latter.

3. Mace, this volume.

4. Yatromanolakis, this volume.

David Sider in the APA panel and in this volume, is that some or all of the "leaves" and "erotic" fragments (19–22 W²) in fact belong to the Plataea poem, perhaps as a personal *sphragis* to an otherwise "public" poem. In Obbink's words, "As in fr. 11 W² [i.e., the main Plataea fragment], the poet . . . lays claim to his unique authorship of the poem, and secures it against tampering and rhapsodic expansion at the end, by means of a ranked comparison with Homer."[5] If something along these lines is correct, then it is likely that the immortal *kleos* of the heroes of the Trojan War and of the Plataean campaign stood in some kind of contrast to the aging body of the poet. Simonides was one of the conventional *makrobioi* of antiquity, "[poets] who lived to a ripe old age,"[6] and it is indeed themes of immortality and aging that are the most striking shared element running through these fragments; this, rather than the relation between these fragments and the Plataea poem, is the thread which I wish to pursue here.

In the *sphragis* that closes his *Persai*, probably composed towards the end of the fifth century, Timotheus of Miletus claims to have been the object of *momos*, "blame," from the young rulers of Sparta on the grounds that he "dishonors the older Muse with new songs":

> ἀλλ' ὦ χρυσεοκίθαριν ἀέ-
> ξων μοῦσαν νεοτευχῆ,
> ἐμοῖς ἔλθ' ἐπίκουρος ὕμ-
> νοις, ἰήιε Παιάν·   205
> ὁ γάρ μ' εὐγενέτας μακραί-
> ων Σπάρτας μέγας ἀγεμὼν
> βρύων ἄνθεσιν ἥβας
> δονεῖ λαὸς ἐπιφλέγων
> ἐλᾶι τ' αἴθοπι μώμωι,   210
> ὅτι παλαιοτέραν νέοις
> ὕμνοις μοῦσαν ἀτιμῶ·
> ἐγὼ δ' οὔτε νέον τιν' οὔ-
> τε γεραὸν οὔτ' ἰσήβαν
> εἴργω τῶνδ' ἑκὰς ὕμνων·   215
> τοὺς δὲ μουσοπαλαιολύ-
> μας, τούτους δ' ἀπερύκω,
> λωβητῆρας ἀοιδᾶν,
> κηρύκων λιγυμακροφώ-
> νων τείνοντας ἰυγάς.   220
> πρῶτος ποικιλόμουσος Ὀρ-
> φεὺς χέλυν ἐτέκνωσεν
> υἱὸς Καλλιόπας ⟨
>   ⟩ Πιερίαθεν·
> Τέρπανδρος δ' ἐπὶ τῶι δέκα   225

---

5. Obbink, this volume, at n. 71.

6. The standard list includes Homer, Hesiod, Anacreon, Simonides, Sophocles, and Stesichorus, cf. Cic. *De sen.* 22–23, Val. Max. 9.12.8, Lucian *Macrob.* 26; cf. further below after n. 33. Simonides celebrates the fact that he is eighty years old in an epigram (28 *FGE*).

ζεῦξε μοῦσαν ἐν ὠιδαῖς·
Λέσβος δ' Αἰολία νιν Ἀν-
τίσσαι γείνατο κλεινόν·
νῦν δὲ Τιμόθεος μέτροις
ῥυθμοῖς τ' ἐνδεκακρουμάτοις   230
κίθαριν ἐξανατέλλει,
θησαυρὸν πολύυμνον οἴ-
ξας Μουσᾶν θαλαμευτόν.

You who foster the new-fashioned muse of the golden cithara, come, healer Paian, as helper to my songs; for Sparta's great leader, well-born, long-lived, the populace riotous with the flowers of youth, buffets me, blazing hostility, and hounds me with fiery censure on the grounds that I dishonor the older muse with my new songs; but I keep neither young man nor old man nor those in their prime away from these songs of mine; it is the corrupters of the old muse that I fend off, debauchers of songs, uttering the loud shrieks of shrill far-calling criers. Orpheus, Calliope's son, he of the intricate muse, was the first to beget the tortoise-shell lyre in Pieria; after him Terpander yoked his muse in ten songs; Aeolian Lesbos bore him to give glory to Antissa; and now Timotheus brings to new life the cithara with eleven-stringed measures and rhythms, opening the Muses' chambered treasure with its abundance of song.

(791.202–33 *PMG*, trans. Campbell [adapted])

Timotheus' response to "criticism," a programmatic strategy that Callimachus was to make famous, is that no one of (Timotheus') musical taste is prohibited access to his poetry (v. 215), "neither young man nor old man nor those in their prime," and he fashions himself as the heir to the greatest lyric poets of tradition, Orpheus and Terpander, who are here brilliantly appropriated for Timotheus' own musical project.[7] Timotheus perhaps says nothing explicit about his own age in this passage,[8] but though old poets can sing "new" songs (cf. *Od.* 1.351–2), the equivocation with *neos*, both "new" and "young" (cf. 203, 211, 213), and the rhetoric of his argument at least distance him from conservatism; his contempt for those of different musical tastes (216–20) is reminiscent of the impatience of the trendily modern "Weaker Argument" and the newly educated Pheidippides in Aristophanes' *Clouds*. This relation between the age of the poet—his *neotes*, whether that be understood in purely chronological terms or in terms of the relationship he constructs towards poetic tradition—and the novelty of his songs was to have a long life in Greek and Roman poetry. When at the opening of *Odes* 3.1 Horace seems to echo Timotheos (215 εἴργω—*arceo*), his new songs, "carmina non prius audita," are sung "uirginibus puerisque." The "old" relation is put to a new use.

It is Callimachus, the "fantastically" old man who sings new songs, who most fully teases out these themes:

ἔλλετε Βασκανίης ὀλοὸν γένος· αὖθι δὲ τέχνηι
κρίνετε,] μὴ σχοίνωι Περσίδι τὴν σοφίην·

---

7. Cf. Hunter 1996: 146–47.
8. ἰσήβαν (v. 214) seems more likely to mean "in the prime of life" than "equal in age to myself."

μηδ' ἀπ' ἐμεῦ διφᾶτε μέγα ψοφέουσαν ἀοιδήν
    τίκτεσθαι· βροντᾶν οὐκ ἐμόν, ἀλλὰ Διός.   20
καὶ γὰρ ὅτε πρώτιστον ἐμοῖς ἐπὶ δέλτον ἔθηκα
    γούνασιν, Ἀπόλλων εἶπεν ὅ μοι Λύκιος·
". . . . . . ἀοιδέ, τὸ μὲν θύος ὅττι πάχιστον
    θρέψαι, τὴ]ν Μοῦσαν δ' ὠγαθὲ λεπταλέην·
πρὸς δέ σὲ] καὶ τόδ' ἄνωγα, τὰ μὴ πατέουσιν ἅμαξαι   25
    τὰ στείβειν, ἑτέρων ἴχνια μὴ καθ' ὁμά
δίφρον ἐλ]ᾶν μηδ' οἶμον ἀνὰ πλατύν, ἀλλὰ κελεύθους
    ἀτρίπτο]υς, εἰ καὶ στεινοτέρην ἐλάσεις."
τῶι πιθόμη]ν· ἐνὶ τοῖς γὰρ ἀείδομεν οἳ λιγὺν ἦχον
    τέττιγος, θ]όρυβον δ' οὐκ ἐφίλησαν ὄνων.   30
θηρὶ μὲν οὐατόεντι πανείκελον ὀγκήσαιτο
    ἄλλο]ς, ἐγὼ δ' εἴην οὑλαχύς, ὁ πτερόεις,
ἆ πάντως, ἵνα γῆρας ἵνα δρόσον ἣν μὲν ἀείδω
    πρώκιον ἐκ δίης ἠέρος εἶδαρ ἔδων,
αὖθι τὸ δ' ἐκδύοιμι, τό μοι βάρος ὅσσον ἔπεστι   35
    τριγλώχιν ὀλοῶι νῆσος ἐπ' Ἐγκελάδωι.
. . . . Μοῦσαι γὰρ ὅσους ἴδον ὄθματι παῖδας
    μὴ λοξῶι, πολιοὺς οὐκ ἀπέθεντο φίλους.

Begone, you baneful race of Jealousy! hereafter <judge> poetry by art, not by the Persian chain, and do not look to me for a song loudly resounding. It is not mine to thunder; that belongs to Zeus. For, when I first placed a tablet on my knees, Lycian Apollo said to me: ". . . poet, feed the victim to be as fat as possible but, my friend, keep the Muse slender. This too I bid you: tread a path that carriages do not trample; do not <drive your chariot> upon the common tracks of others, nor along a wide road, but on <unworn> paths, though your course be more narrow." <I obeyed>, for we sing among those who love the clear voice of <the cicada> and not the noise of asses. Let <others> bray just like the long-eared brute, but let me be the dainty, the winged one. Oh yes indeed! that I may sing living on dew-drops, free sustenance from the divine air; that I may then shed old age, which weighs upon me like the three-cornered island upon deadly Enceladus. . . . for if the Muses have not looked askance at one in his childhood, they do not cast him from their friendship when he is grey.

(Callimachus fr. 1.17–38, trans. Trypanis [adapted])[9]

In place of the braying ass, traditionally a very un-Apolline animal,[10] Callimachus chooses for himself the model of the cicada, beloved of the Muses because its only concern is song (Plato *Phaedrus* 259b–d). Against the heavy weight of "ass poetry" is set the fragile lightness of the winged cicada with its pure sound. An Aristotelian treatise on sounds classifies the song of the cicada as *liguros* "clear, high" and *leptos* "thin" (*On things heard* 803b19),[11] and (to anticipate somewhat) we may

9. I print Massimilla's text, and have kept papyrological marks to a minimum.
10. Cf. Ambühl 1995.
11. Good discussion of such descriptions of sound in Asper 1997: 177ff.

note that the "[song] clear and full of desire" (ἱμερόεντα λιγύν) which probably belongs to the voice of the poet at v. 17 of the Simonides fragment would well suit a "young" or rejuvenated singer. The cicada is, however, also a vulnerable creature resembling an old man,[12] and one which can so easily be crushed by those who do not appreciate its special beauty. In one respect, however, Callimachus must confess to a likeness to the ass, the quintessential beast of burden. However "light" his song, the poet bears a heavy burden (βάρος),[13] that of old age, which cannot be sloughed off. It crushes him as Sicily crushes the giant who rebelled against Zeus, and his only consolation—although no small one—is that the Muses do not abandon their favorites, unlike the dawn-goddess Eos who abandoned Tithonus (*Homeric Hymn to Aphrodite* 218–38). Still in old age the poet is able to write as he would wish: vv. 37f. rework famous verses from the prologue of Hesiod's *Theogony* (81–84) both to demonstrate the continued poetic power which is the blessing of the Muses[14] and, on any reconstruction of the relationship between "Reply" and "Dream," to prepare for the "Hesiodic" scene that is to follow.

The poet's wish for rejuvenation seems to have been granted in that he proceeded to dream that he really was young again[15] and was transported to meet the Muses on Helicon. Callimachus here replays Hesiodic experience in two related ways. Although in the proem to the *Theogony* Hesiod himself gives no indication of how old he was when confronted on the mountainside by the Muses, it is a reasonable guess that the Hellenistic age constructed Hesiod's encounter with the Muses as an experience of his youth—the boy sent out "once upon a time" (*Theog.* 22) to look after the lambs[16]— as also were the corresponding encounter between the Muses and the young Archilochus[17] and the young Aeschylus' dream of Dionysus.[18] The Hesiodic text itself encourages such a construction by representing the meeting with the Muses as some-

---

12. Cf. *Iliad* 3.148–53, Wimmel 1960: 111f. For a discussion of the time at which "old age" sets in cf. Cameron 1995: 174–84.

13. The opposition that is evoked here is sharpened by the fact that βαρύς is the standard term for "deep" sounds, the opposite of ὀξύς, cf. [Arist.], *On things heard* 803a8, LSJ s.v. βαρύς III 1. The loud "thundering" (cf. Asper 1997: 196–98) that Callimachus rejects (v. 20) prepares for this opposition. Callimachus here may not merely be playing with a conventional piety (together with the familiar assimilation of Homer to "Zeus"), but he may also have an eye on Aristophanes' *Clouds*, where not only does Pheidippides dismiss Aeschylus as ψόφου πλέων "full of bombast" (1366f.), but thunder is explicitly denied to Zeus by the impious Socrates and the buffoonish Strepsiades (374ff.); by implication, the Telchines are aligned with such tasteless creatures.

14. Note the elaborate *uariatio*: Διὸς κοῦραι μεγάλοιο—Μοῦσαι, γεινόμενον—παῖδας. Callimachus' ὄθματι . . . μὴ λόξωι perhaps picks up Hesiod's πάντες ἐς αὐτὸν ὁρῶσι διακρίνοντα θέμιστας | ἰθείηισι δίκηισιν.

15. Cf. Lynn 1995: 147f., Andrews 1998: 14–17.

16. "Ascraeo . . . seni" at Verg. *Ecl.* 6.70 does not, I think, argue against this hypothesis, cf. below at n. 33. Note the virtuoso combination of Homer, Hesiod, and Callimachus at Quintus Smyrnaeus 12.308–10 ὑμεῖς γὰρ πᾶσάν μοι ἐνὶ φρεσὶ θήκατ' ἀοιδήν, | πρίν μοι ἔτ' ἀμφὶ παρειὰ κατασκίδνασθαι ἴουλον | Σμύρνης ἐν δαπέδοισι περικλυτὰ μῆλα νέμοντι κ.τ.λ. I do not know the evidence upon which McKay 1959: 4 bases his claim that "It is taken for granted by the ancients that Hesiod [became a poet] at a venerable age."

17. *SEG* 15.517, inscribed about the middle of the third century in the "Archilocheion" at Paros, cf. Kambylis 1963, below at n. 24.

18. When he was a boy, Aeschylus fell asleep while guarding grapes in the countryside, and Dionysus appeared to him and told him to write tragedy (Pausanias 1.21.2 = Aesch. Test. 111 *TrGF*).

thing that happened in the past, "once upon a time" (*Theog.* 22); Hesiod recalls what the Muses then said to him, as Callimachus recalls the youthful instructions he received from Apollo. Secondly, Callimachus seems to evoke a tradition, attested explicitly only in later antiquity, that Hesiod was in fact rejuvenated and thus lived twice, a tradition that may, as Ruth Scodel demonstrated,[19] also be important for the choral song on old age in Euripides' *Heracles Furens* (637–700), to which Callimachus makes explicit allusion (vv. 35–36 ~ *HF* 638–40) and which is important for this whole section of Callimachus' prologue.[20] As the Euripidean chorus asserts that it will never cease to "mingle the Graces with the Muses" (*HF* 673–75), so at the very head of his poem Callimachus does just this, for the Muses are introduced in the "Dream" and are central to the whole structure of books 1 and 2, whereas the first *aition* of book 1 is the Parian ritual in honor of the Graces (frr. 5–9 Massimilla). Whether or not the legend of Hesiod's double life was known to Euripides (and Simonides?), it is clear that the Callimachean dream was merely one of a number of poetic strategies by which Hellenistic and Roman poets represented the great tradition ("passing on") to which they felt themselves heir;[21] the metempsychosis of Homer into Ennius (Ennius, *Annales* frr. 3–10 Skutsch) is, along with dream experience, perhaps the best known such strategy. If, however, Callimachus' rejuvenation takes the form of a dream experience in which he reaches into the distant past to relive the experience of Hesiod, this may prompt us to ask about the nature of the "old age" which oppresses him. When interpreting this literally, we must always allow for humorous exaggeration. The Telchines have accused him of behaving like a child, though he is a grown man, and so he exaggerates just how old he is as part of the demonstration of the absurdity of their criticisms.[22] Whatever view is taken of how old Callimachus actually was when he composed the "Reply," it seems clear that there is more at stake here than just encroaching senility.

The approach or arrival of the weakness of old age seems to have been a familiar poetic *topos* (cf. Alcman 26 *PMG* [= 90 Calame], Eur. *HF* 637–700), which suggests that it may not be correct to read it at a simple, literal level; it is rather a recognizable poetic code, even when the poet is in fact (and is known to be) old. For Callimachus, the best contemporary witness to the code is the so-called "Seal" of Poseidippos (705 *SH*), in which the poet from Pella invokes the Muses to join him in singing[23] "hateful old age" and, perhaps under the influence of the (?)newly-founded Archilocheion on Paros, wishes to become a second Archilochus, as Callimachus was a "second Hesiod," with honors and a cult decreed by Apollo.[24] While his poetry will find immortal *kleos*, he himself will find his own kind of eternity:

---

19. Scodel 1980.
20. Cf. Basta Donzelli 1991, Livrea 1997.
21. See the excellent discussion of Bing 1988a: 56–71.
22. Cf., e.g., Lynn 1995: 180 n.17. On the charge of being a "child" cf. Asper 1997: 149–50.
23. With ϲυναείϲατε for the transmitted ϲυναειϲαδε, rather than Friedrich's ϲυναείρατε, particularly in view of v. 21. The text is very uncertain, however.
24. I follow Lloyd-Jones 1963: 88; the Delphic decree that Lloyd-Jones discusses was also a very striking example of divine favor to a poet, and must have struck a particular chord with an initiate, if that indeed is what Poseidippos was.

μηδέ τις οὖν χεύαι δάκρυον. αὐτὰρ ἐγὼ
γήραι μυστικὸν οἶμον ἐπὶ Ῥαδάμανθυν ἱκοίμην
δήμωι καὶ λαῶι παντὶ ποθεινὸς ἐών,
ἀσκίπων ἐν ποσσὶ καὶ ὀρθοεπὴς ἀν' ὅμιλον
καὶ λείπων τέκνοις δῶμα καὶ ὄλβον ἐμόν.

Let no one shed a tear, but in old age may I travel the mystic path to Rhadamanthys, missed by the citizens and all the people, needing no staff to walk and speaking clearly to the multitude, leaving house and prosperity to my children.

(Poseidippos, 705.21–5 *SH*)

What in Callimachus is a wish for rejuvenation is in Poseidippos a wish for good health up until death in old age,[25] followed by a journey "on the mystic path to Rhadamanthys." Whether we interpret this as meaning that Poseidippos was merely initiated into the "mysteries of the Muses" or that he was actually an initiate of a Dionysiac or "Orphic" cult,[26] the language has a history of particular relevance in the present context. Poseidippos prays to remain *orthoepes*, "speaking properly," to the end of his life, whereas the voice of Simonides 22 W[2] imagines such fluency (ἀρτιεπέα νωμῶν γλῶσσαν, with West's very probable supplement) to be the result of new-found strength;[27] the prayer for bodily health to the last, being ἀσκίπων ἐν ποσσί, finds many parallels throughout Greek literature, but it looks here like a reworking of Hesiod's description of men of the Golden Age, "when there was no terrible old age, but ever undiminished in feet and hands they took pleasure in feasts, free of all ills" (*WD* 114f.). Whereas, therefore, Callimachus uses Hesiod to console himself with the Muses' protection of their favorites and his own piety, Poseidippos prays for public honors from his own people[28] and continued good health until old age, followed by the certain reward of the just initiate. Not for Poseidippos the impossible wish of becoming young again (cf. v. 25); his "immortality" will be more certain and more long-lasting. "Old age," however "hateful" at the opening of the poem, seems itself now almost a mark of poetic distinction. This is, as we shall see, by no means an isolated third-century example.[29]

As for Callimachus, the wish to rid himself of the burden of old age, like the cicada, arises from Apollo's poetic program: cicada poetics is the poetics of the "slender Muse" and the narrow path. The sequence of thought suggests that the old age which crushes the poet is at one level what we have learned to call "the burden of the past," that consciousness of tradition of Hesiod, Pindar, Euripides, Aristophanes, and the other great figures of the past whose voices well up through Callimachus' verses, a consciousness that hems our every move with qualification, deferral, and doubt, and that, like old age, restricts the freedom of action we associate with "the light one, the winged one." In Plato's myth, cicadas were the first poets, free to sing and honor the

25. For the poetic heritage of such a wish cf. Mimnermus fr. 6 W[2], on which see below after n. 45.
26. Cf. Rossi 1996: 65, Burkert 1998: 394f. For the former view see Asper 1997: 86, with bibliography.
27. Rossi 1996: 62 rather understands ὀρθοεπής as "speaking just things."
28. The model here is not merely Archilochus, but possibly also Philitas of Cos, cf. Hollis 1996, Hardie 1997.
29. The larger questions about the relation between "the Seal" and Callimachus' "Reply" will not be considered here.

Muses as they liked, with no constraining tradition of song behind them. It is Callimachus who, for us, makes the decisive move in understanding "rejuvenation" in terms of the literary tradition, thus completing the triangle of related ideas—the weight of years, the weight of tradition, and the hope for immortality. Tradition is figured in terms of human aging. Callimachus *is* old and weary, crushed by the immobilizing sense of the years that have preceded. When the Telchines tell Callimachus "to grow up," what they mean is that he should adopt a poetics sanctioned by time and archaic practice (cf. *Iambos* 13), together with the moral seriousness that attends it. Callimachus rejects both the poetics and the *gravitas* in his extraordinary wish to start all over again.

The link which both Callimachus and Poseidippos forge between "old age" and poetic success is familiar in the Hellenistic period. Very like Poseidippos' *Seal* is the surviving part of an anonymous poem on the death of the Alexandrian poet Philikos of Corcyra, presumably composed near in time to his death (mid-third century B.C.E.):[30]

> ἔρχεο δὴ μακάριστος ὁδοιπόρος, ἔρχεο καλοὺς
> χώρους εὐσεβέων ὀψόμενος, Φίλικε,
> ἐκ κισσηρεφέος κεφαλῆς εὔυμνα κυλίων
> ῥήματα, καὶ νήσους κώμασον εἰς μακάρων,
> εὖ μὲν γῆρας ἰδὼν εὐέστιον Ἀλκινόοιο
> Φαίηκος, ζώειν ἀνδρὸς ἐπισταμένου·
> Ἀλκινόου τις ἐὼν ἐξ αἵματος ⟨   ⟩
>   ]ο Δημοδόκου

> Go on your way, blessed wayfarer, go on your path, Philikos, to see the fair land of the god-fearing dead. Your head crowned with ivy, rolling forth your lines of lovely song, go in revel [*komos*] to the Islands of the Blessed. Happy, that you saw the festive old age of an Alcinous, the Phaeacian, a man who knew how to live. Born of Alcinous' line . . . Demodocus
>
> (980 *SH*, trans. Page [adapted])

Having lived to the same ripe old age as his countryman King Alcinous, who welcomed Odysseus at his court,[31] Philikos is to pass in *komos* to the Isles of the Blessed, still "rolling forth" his lovely poems. This *komos* is particularly appropriate to a (dramatic) poet who was a priest of Dionysus (Ath. 5.198b–c), but it may also be worth asking whether the epigram evokes the blessed afterlife that an initiate of Dionysiac mysteries may expect. As such, Philikos will experience the happiness for which Poseidippos can only pray; his ability to take an active and productive part in a *komos* bears witness to the fact that, at the end, he was in fact ἀσκίπων ἐν ποσσὶ καὶ ὀρθοεπὴς ἀν' ὅμιλον. Be that as it may, and however common the idea of a perpetu-

---

30. For discussion cf. Gabathuler 1937: 66–67, Fraser 1972: I 608–9, II 859, *FGE* 460f. David Sider has made the interesting suggestion that Philikos composed this epitaph for himself; cf. below on Meleager's epitaphs for himself.

31. Scheria was standardly identified in antiquity with Corcyra.

ation in the afterlife of the habitual practices (real or constructed) of the present life,[32] the link between poetic glory and old age is not merely the conventional one that a long life is a sign of divine favor. Rather, it is to be associated also with the presentation of poets and other sages of the archaic and classical past as "old" as well as "of old" (οἱ πάλαι ποιηταί).[33]

The "old man" who appears in the programmatic dream of Herodas 8 is, fairly certainly, Hipponax himself; in *Iambus* 1.58, Callimachus presents Thales as an old man; Anacreon is commonly "old"'(ὁ πρέσβυς, ὁ γέρων) in the rich tradition of fictitious epitaphs about him and throughout the *Anacreontea*,[34] and Alcaeus of Messene designates both Hesiod and Hipponax as ὁ πρέσβυς.[35] Much of the impetus comes, of course, from these poets' own poetry and/or the legends about these *makrobioi*: "Hesiodic old age" was proverbial,[36] and surviving fragments of Anacreon's poetry make much play with his advanced years (cf. 395, 418 *PMG*). Nevertheless, it is hardly surprising (or new) that great age was invested with symbolic meaning also. Thus Dioscorides praises his older contemporary Machon as both τι τέχνης | ἄξιον ἀρχαίης λείψανον, "a remnant worthy of the ancient art" (i.e., Old Comedy), and as ὁ πρέσβυς.[37] Machon may well have enjoyed a long life, but it is the interplay between his age and the nature of his art that is central to the rhetoric of the epigram. More striking still is one of the epitaphs which Meleager composed for himself:

ἀτρέμας, ὦ ξένε, βαῖνε· παρ' εὐσεβέσιν ὁ πρέσβυς
    εὕδει κοιμηθεὶς ὕπνον ὀφειλόμενον
Εὐκράτεω Μελέαγρος, ὁ τὸν γλυκύδακρυν Ἔρωτα
    καὶ Μούσας ἱλαραῖς συστολίσας χάρισιν·
ὃν θεόπαις ἥνδρωσε Τύρος Γαδάρων θ' ἱερὰ χθών,
    Κῶς δ' ἐρατὴ Μερόπων πρέσβυν ἐγηροτρόφει.
ἀλλ' εἰ μὲν Σύρος ἐσσί, σαλάμ· εἰ δ' οὖν σύ γε Φοίνιξ,
    ναίδιος· εἰ δ' Ἕλλην, χαῖρε· τὸ δ' αὐτὸ φράσον.

Go quietly by, stranger; among the god-fearing ones the old man sleeps the sleep which is due to all, Meleager son of Eucrates, who outfitted Eros, he of sweetness and tears, and the Muses with merry graces. Heavenborn Tyre and the sacred land of Gadara brought him to manhood, and Cos, the lovely land of the Meropes, nursed his old age. If you are a Syrian, Salaam!, if a Phoenician, Naidios!, if a Greek, Chaire!, and say the same yourself.

(*AP* 7.419 = *HE* 4000–7)

32. Cf., e.g., Antipater, *AP* 7.27 (= *HE* 260–269) on Anacreon, εἴης ἐν μακάρεσσιν, Ἀνάκρεον, εὖχος Ἰώνων, | μήτ' ἐρατῶν κώμων ἄνδιχα κ.τ.λ.

33. Cf. Theocritus *Epigr.* 21.1 on Archilochus (ὁ πάλαι ποιητής), Dioscorides *AP* 7.411.6 (= *HE* 1596) on Aeschylus (ἀρχαίων ... τις ἡμιθέων), Bing 1988a: 56f., 1988b.

34. Cf. Antipater, *AP* 7.27.10 (= *HE* 269); Leonidas, *APl* 306.1 (= *HE* 2152), 307.1 (= *HE* 2514); "Simonides," *AP* 7.24.9 (= *HE* 3322); Ovid, *AA* 3.30 "uinosi Teia Musa senis."

35. *AP* 7.55.6, 7.536.1 (= *HE* 75, 76).

36. Cf. Scodel 1980, above at n. 19.

37. *AP* 7.708 (= *HE* 1617–22).

Meleager makes play with his advanced years at death also in two of the three other epitaphs that he composed for himself,[38] but in the present poem he evokes a familiar rhetoric by which the epitaph will be read one day in the (distant) future by a passer-by and Meleager will long have become ὁ πρέσβυς in two senses, both "old when he died" and "an old/revered poet." Meleager thus foresees, and to some extent constructs, his own passage into the pantheon of "great poets of the past."[39] This is the symbolic language that Callimachus actualizes when he implies that the Telchines want him to "act his age." For Callimachus, however, the poetry of *techne* must not follow the patterns of the past, but must enact a radical break with the past; it must, in other words, be *neos*, that is, both "young" and "new." It is a very Callimachean irony that such poetry is produced by a man whose "decades of years are not few" (fr. 1.6) and is sanctioned by the example of one of the "oldest" of past poets, namely Hesiod. Here, as elsewhere, it is the Telchines who misunderstand the poetry *both* of the past *and* the present.

This association of age and *sophia* is neither new nor surprising, and finds its close counterpart in contemporary iconography. "In the Greek imagination, all great intellectuals were old.... There exists no portrait of a truly young poet, and certainly not of a young philosopher."[40] From the very earliest representations, Homer is depicted as (sometimes very) "old,"[41] but great age, as an almost inevitable characteristic of representations of great poets and thinkers of the past, seems to be a development of the third century.[42] Of particular interest for Hellenistic poetry is a wretchedly preserved set of statues of poets and philosophers from the exedra of the Sarapeion at Memphis: if Hesiod is correctly identified in this group, then he was represented as a very old man indeed.[43] However that may be, it is clear that, in the third century, the doubleness of "age" was expressed in the language of both plastic art and poetry.

In seeking to trace the history of these ideas in archaic and classical poetry, we may begin again with the same stasimon of Euripides' *Heracles*. Under the present dispensation, men, not even good men, can live, or more specifically "be young," twice (*HF* 655–72); for some fortunate men the consolation for this is the *kleos* conferred by poetry. Bacchylides 3.88–92 (a poet who brings us very close to Simonides) expresses this conventional thought with neat economy:

> ἀνδρὶ δ' οὐ θέμις, πολιὸν παρέντα
> γῆρας, θάλειαν αὖτις ἀγκομίσσαι

---

38. *AP* 7.417, 418 (= *HE* 3984–93, 3994–99); the odd one out is at *AP* 7.421 (= *HE* 4008–21). On these poems cf. Gutzwiller 1998.

39. Our almost complete ignorance of Tellen makes it difficult to draw conclusions from his designation as πρέσβυς at Leonidas, *AP* 7.719.1 (= *HE* 2001).

40. Zanker 1995: 22. For much information on ideas about old age cf. Falkner and Luce 1989.

41. Cf. Zanker 1995, ch. 4 (166–71 for Hellenistic images of Homer); Schefold 1997. Homer remains, of course, an old man in the sixth-century ekphrastic epigrams of Christodorus, *AP* 2.322, 325.

42. Cf. Zanker 1995: 68–75.

43. Cf. Lauer and Picard 1955, Ridgway 1990: 131f. For "Hesiod" cf. Lauer and Picard, figs. 47, 48, 51. The date of the individual sculptures and of the group as a whole remains disputed (early third or early second century?).

ἥβαν. ἀρετᾶς γε μὲν οὐ μινύθει
βροτῶν ἅμα σώματι φέγγος, ἀλλὰ
Μοῦσά νιν τρέφει.

It is not permitted to a man to dismiss grey old age and recover again the bloom of youth. The light of *arete* does not, however, fade with men's bodies, but the Muse nurtures it.

(Bacchyl. 3.88–92)

It is presumably some version of this sequence that lies concealed in the tatters of Simonides 20.13 ff. W² on the immortality that Homer has conferred. For poets, moreover, there is, as the Euripidean chorus implies, a further consolation in the joy of singing that is itself a perpetuating of life, perhaps even, through the grace of the Muses, a rejuvenation. More ambiguous is the relationship between this rhetoric and *eros*. In different contexts, old age may be figured as bringing some release from the disturbing passions of *eros* (so, most famously, Sophocles and Cephalus at Plato *Republic* 1.329b–d) or rejection by the objects of desire (Mimnermus 1 W), but in any case *eros* is intimately connected with the self-presentation of the poet as old. The apparently erotic content of 22 W², set in the world of the imagination rather than the real present, may in fact be a way of trying to buy *eros* off, rather as Ibycus seems (?ironically) to wish the passion away:

Ἔρος αὖτέ με κυανέοισιν ὑπὸ
    βλεφάροις τακέρ' ὄμμασι δερκόμενος
κηλήμασι παντοδαποῖς ἐς ἄπει-
    ρα δίκτυα Κύπριδος ἐσβάλλει·
ἦ μὰν τρομέω νιν ἐπερχόμενον,
ὥστε φερέζυγος ἵππος ἀεθλοφόρος ποτὲ γήραι
ἀέκων σὺν ὄχεσφι θοοῖς ἐς ἅμιλλαν ἔβα.

Once more with melting looks from under his dark brows Eros draws me into the boundless nets of Kypris with enticements of every kind. Ah, I tremble at his attack, as a yoke-horse, a prize-winner but now in old age, enters the contest with the swift chariot unwillingly.

(Ibycus, 287 *PMG*)

So, too, the opening poem of Horace's fourth book of *Odes*, in which "the aging poet" resists the renewed call to Venus' arms and that may begin with an echo of this poem of Ibycus, might owe a debt to Simonides, in view of the Greek poet's great importance for *Odes* 4.[44]

Simonides frr. 19–20 deal with the aging of man, the brevity of youth, and the immortality that Homer conferred; they allude also, as many scholars have noted, to Mimnermus' famous lines (fr. 2) on aging and our likeness to leaves; there is, in other words, an overt engagement in these fragments with the poetic tradition. Stobaeus

---

44. Cf. Barchiesi 1996; Harrison, this volume.

has in fact preserved a number of fragments of Mimnermus' *Nanno* on the curse of old age (frr. 1–5), which suggest a "classic" status for this poet on this subject (as, for example, Sappho was in matters of *eros*): subsequent treatments may therefore call Mimnermus to mind, however fleeting the verbal echo.[45] In one other case, at least, we know that Mimnermus was early associated with this theme: his wish (or that of a character in his poetry?) to die at age sixty "free of disease and grievous cares" (fr. 6) was explicitly corrected by Solon (fr. 20) to a wish to die at age eighty.

Simonides 21 W^2 also concerns the aging process, in this case a physical/sexual awakening, a transition, perhaps, from *eromenos* to potential *erastes*, from *pais* to *neos* (cf., e.g., Theognis 1319–20). Although the language of *hybris* and *dike* is the standard language of *eros*, it is also very much the moral language of Hesiod's *Works and Days*.[46] Hesiod was, as we have seen, granted two lives, though how early the legend starts—and, in particular, whether it was available to Simonides—we cannot say. Be that as it may, Hesiod is par excellence the poet of aging, for the *Works and Days* deals with the aging of all mankind; the poet himself lives in an age of aging (174ff.), when babies will eventually be born with grey hair, an age that will end up with no respect for *dike*, and no *aidos*, but *hybris* everywhere. The Hesiod of *Works and Days*, who speaks to Perses as an older advisor to an errant younger brother, seems important for these fragments of Simonides. The tone is didactic (ἀλλὰ σὺ ταῦτα μαθών κ.τ.λ., 20.11 W^2), the rejection of optimistic fantasy seems Hesiodic, and in particular 20.9 W^2, however formulaic, finds its closest parallel in *WD* 40, νήπιοι, οὐδὲ ἴσασιν ὅσωι πλέον ἥμισυ παντὸς κ.τ.λ. The later poet speaks to the *nepioi*, the "young" as well as foolish, with the authority of age, though the message is in many ways non-Hesiodic. The young never imagine that life will change, that they will grow old, but the poet, with the special *sophia* granted by tradition and his hopes for immortal *kleos*, he knows (note the pointed ἀνήρ . . . ἀνδρῶν at the end of successive verses, marking Homer's knowledge of the human condition, 19.1 W^2); but—and it is a big "but"— the poet also grows literally old, and all the *sophia* in the world does not prevent him from wishing to escape this mortality. Indeed, his very consciousness, his awareness of the truths of the tradition, what Callimachus, as we saw, fashioned as "the burden of the past," makes him already "old" and adds a new burden—unlike other men, *he* cannot live carefree. Here is a very non-Hesiodic irony. It is the succession of poets— Homer, Hesiod, Mimnermus—that has taught Simonides that men, and poets, are like the succession of leaves; an allusion to Mimnermus' allusion to Homer makes the point clear enough—poetic tradition and immortality merely emphasize the mortality of the poet's own body.[47] Perhaps, then, it was from Simonides that Callimachus drew some of his inspiration for the conception of "literary tradition" as a kind of

---

45. Mimnermus' use of Tithonus as an example of the miseries of old age (fr. 4) may be relevant to Callimachus' evocation of this figure. Cf. Crane 1986: 269–78.

46. So too αἰδώς (v. 9), but the supplement is uncertain at best.

47. Simonides' allusion to Homer "through" Mimnermus is an early example of what critics of Hellenistic and Roman poetry call "double allusion" or "window reference," cf., e.g., McKeown 1987: 37–45. No device could be better suited to demonstrate the weight and depth of tradition.

aging; in any event, it is within this nexus of ideas that the famous Horatian passage on the successive generations of words (*Ars Poetica* 60–72) is to be placed.[48]

Much—too much—of this argument has been based on (unspoken) assumptions about the internal relationship of 19–22 W². Papyri, however, invite supplements of more than one kind and, as we grow old, the temptation to see patterns within the broken fragments becomes a mechanism of survival. Simonides, who knew all about consolation, would certainly have understood that.

48. Cf. Sider, this volume.

16

ALESSANDRO BARCHIESI

Simonides and Horace on the Death of Achilles

This essay is a speculative attempt[1] to link the recent Simonides with Horace, at many removes from "direct evidence": it is based on other people's papyrological insight, and on a literary critical reasoning. In his initial publication, Parsons 1992a: 28 recorded West's proposal to locate *POxy* 2327 fr. 5 immediately before 2327 fr. 6, which in turn overlaps with *POxy* 3965 fr. 1, these three fragments laid out with two others to form Simon. 11 W^2. Parsons observes, first, that 2327 fr. 5 clearly speaks of the death of a hero, fr. 6 of the death of someone who dies at the hand of Apollo; second, that the physical evidence of the papyrus is compatible with but does not provide absolute proof of the relationship mentioned above between the two pieces; and third, that nonetheless other contexts can be imagined for fr. 5, even within the elegy on Plataea,

An earlier version of this paper appeared in Deborah Boedeker and David Sider (eds.), *The New Simonides*, *Arethusa* 29.2 (1996): 167–92, and is used here by kind permission of the Johns Hopkins University Press. For their comments on this article I am grateful to Tom Hubbard, Richard Hunter, R. G. M. Nisbet, R. Merkelbach, and the editors; and to Peter Parsons for first stirring my interest in the new Simonides. I also thank Antonio Aloni for letting me see his article (1994) in advance of publication. [The original version of this chapter was translated by David Sider, who gratefully acknowledges the assistance of John Van Sickle.]

1. For more, see Barchiesi 1996. That longer paper is deliberately extreme in putting a pressure for Simonidean influence on Horace; its plausibility depends of course on how far one is ready to accept a survival and influence of Simonidean poetry in antiquity (in favor, for different epochs, see Rutherford, Boedeker, "Historiography," and Harrison in this volume), but also on broader assumptions about poetic memory in Horace. There are at least three important issues at stake, which are, I think, worth pursuing. First, "Simonides" in the first century b.c.e. is both an author and a cultural icon, that is, he is represented by texts but also by ideas and imaginings about his personality and life choices (see, in addition to the bibliography in my 1996 paper, Farrell 1997: 373–83). Second, the centrality of Pindaric influence in the late Horace, demonstrated by explicit Horatian pointers, and supported by the survival and modern fame of the four books of epinicia, can have the effect of outshining important influences by lyric authors whose work has disappeared. Third, Horace uses literary allusion to such a degree of density that individual models can be absorbed and merge in clusters or genealogies, without creating a staccato effect in the memory of the well-read recipient. On the complexity of Horatian memory see also Harrison in this volume and the thorough and nuanced reappraisal in Cavarzere 1996.

to which certainly belongs fr. 11.6–45 W². The "heroic death" which is compared to a tree cut down by woodcutters could be that of one of the combatants in Plataea[2] rather than that of Achilles, as it would have to be if West's collocation for fr. 5 is accepted.

West's proposal, which provides my starting point, seems to me undeniably the best so far advanced, for two reasons: first, fr. 5 ends one column and fr. 6 begins another;[3] second, the use of a simile which so clearly alludes to Homer (as I shall show below) presupposes strong epic coloring. If the simile appeared in the "hymn," or proem, to Achilles (and not in a battle narrative), the Homeric effect is very much in accord with some other allusions already observed in the same context; for example, the ways in which ὠκύμορος and ἀοίδιμος are used, as shown by Lloyd-Jones 1994: 1–3.[4] The hymn to Achilles would appear even more enriched if we could see it as a sort of hymn to Homer as well. On the other hand, I find no sign that Simonides in any fragment of the Plataea battle elegy, even when displaying epic coloring,[5] went so far as to employ that most Homeric of epic features, the extended simile. (See Stehle in this volume for other divergences from Homeric style.)

I would like, therefore, to point out a consequence of the consecutive collocation of *POxy* 2327 frr. 5 + 6, one which remains valid even if we do not accept West's supplements for vv. 1–3. That is, even if all these restorations prove to miss the mark, the following sequence can still be safely reconstructed. First, *someone strikes a blow*: Apollo against Achilles, to judge from 11.7–8 W². Second, *The warrior falls like . . .* (an unspecified kind of tree?) *or like a pine cut by woodsmen in the glades.*

This is sufficient to make us think that this fragment, in the position assigned it by West, was the model for Horace *Carm.* 4.6.9–12.

> Dive, quem proles Niobea magnae
> vindicem linguae Tityosque raptor
> sensit et Troiae prope victor altae
>   Phthius Achilles,
> ceteris maior, tibi miles impar,
> filius quamvis Thetidis marinae
> Dardanas turris quateret tremenda
>   cuspide pugnax.
> *ille, mordaci velut icta ferro*
> *pinus aut* impulsa cupressus Euro
> *procidit late* posuitque collum in
>   pulvere Teucro.

2. Parsons, followed by Lloyd-Jones 1994: 1, suggests Masistios or Mardonios. According to Herodotus (for what the comparison is worth), Mardonios was struck down while fighting on a white horse (9.63), and Masistios, thrown from his wounded horse, was dispatched with great difficulty by a blow to his eye, the only part of his body left uncovered by his armor (9.22).

3. Parsons 1992a. Barigazzi 1963: 70 had already tentatively raised the possibility of placing the simile among the fragments on the battle, but, knowing only *POxy* 2327, he desisted.

4. On the former epithet in Homer see especially Slatkin 1991: 36–38.

5. Cf. West 1993a: 9 (with an emphasis different from mine and in a different context): "The initial hymn to Achilles struck an epic note . . . there is even an epic simile. . . . There is no change of register as we move into the main narrative."

> ille non inclusus equo Minervae
> sacra mentito male feriatos
> Troas et laetam Priami choreis
>   falleret aulam

(*Odes* 4.6.1–16)

As in Simonides, the comparison describes the blow and the unforeseen fall of Achilles. And as in Simonides the comparison is twofold, one part being a pine tree cut down by axes. The sonorous combination "mordaci . . . icta" recalls the *figura* etymologica ὑλοτόμοι . . . τάμνωσι. I see no reason to think that we are dealing with a *locus communis* here. On the one hand, the two poets apply the same image to the same moment in the Trojan cycle, and the various accounts of the death of Achilles do not seem to offer many alternative sources. And, on the other hand, the similes of the type "fall like a tree" can be divided into two categories: typical deaths in Homeric battle scenes;[6] and, in later poetry, the downfalls of various strange types. Thus, Apollonios speaks in this way of the Giants, the Spartoi, and Talos; Catullus of the Minotaur; and Vergil of a boxer and, metaphorically, of the fall of an entire city.[7]

It is clear that both Simonides and Horace, taking their Homeric originals for granted, can quite similarly refer to the image of a hero's death in battle. This time, however, the hero is the greatest of all, not least because of his height. Note, with Kiessling-Heinze, how "procidit late . . . in pulvere" alludes to *Od.* 24.39–40, where among the shades Achilles hears the story of his death from Agamemnon. If Horace, as I believe, is here making use of both Simonides and *Odyssey* 24, it is interesting to note that the Homeric model was already present in Simonides himself. For if it is true that Simon. 116 W^2 speaks of the urn in which were united the ashes of Achilles and Patroclus (so West), it is clear that Simonides too was looking to *Odyssey* 24, which is the most detailed Homeric text on the death of Achilles. And the very fact that Simonides made a Homeric allusion reinforces Simonides' following programmatic declaration that it was Homer who had made memorable the short-lived heroes.[8] Horace continues and extends this intertextual linkage.

---

6. *Il.* 13.389–92 = 16.482–84 is the closest parallel to Simonides, and seems to be West's principal guide in his reconstruction:

> ἤριπε δ' ὡς ὅτε τις δρῦς ἤριπεν ἢ ἀχερωΐς
> ἠὲ πίτυς βλωθρή, τήν τ' οὔρεσι τέκτονες ἄνδρες
> ἐξέταμον πελέκεσσι νεήκεσι νήϊον εἶναι·

Note that the second simile describes the death of a major warrior (Sarpedon), an episode that more than superficially seems to anticipate Achilles' fate. Among other Homeric models, note *Il.* 17.53ff. for the role of the wind as a destructive agent, which anticipates Eurus in Horace.

7. Cf., e.g., Ap. Rhod. 1.1003ff., 3.1374ff., 4.1682ff. (where in one simile are combined the actions of the wind and of woodcutters); Catull. 64.105ff. (see below, n. 9); Verg. *Aen.* 2.626ff., 5.448ff. The *locus classicus* for the comparisons along these lines is now Nisbet 1987.

8. The allusion works on so many levels that its density calls to mind the intertextuality we are accustomed to attribute to Alexandrian poetry. First, In *Od.* 24, Agamemnon tells Achilles of his future fame (83–84, 93–94), after having recounted his death in a manner designed to complete the fame ordained by the *Iliad*. Simonides first implicitly recalls this passage in his narration, then he declares explicitly that Homer has immortalized the names of the heroes and he continues, in his own fashion, Agamemnon's discourse on

R. G. M. Nisbet (per litteras) adds that the use of *late* in Catullus 64.109 is also pertinent in that it seems to be echoed by Horace. Compare his "ille ... velut ... pinus ... procidit late" with "nam velut ... pinum ... illa prona cadit late" (Catull. 64.105–9). It is worth noting that Horace employs the fall of the Catullan Minotaur to recall the Homeric model ἐν στροφάλιγγι κονίης | κεῖσο μέγας μεγαλωστί (*Od.* 24.39–40), as though the echo of the Minotaur served to introduce a divergent, less sympathetic, point of view,[9] whereas the Roman poet chooses to look at Achilles' death with a sense of liberation from a threat that is altogether alien to the Greek models here summarized from Homer, Simonides, and (see below) Pindar.

In both Simonides and Horace, the Homeric simile receives a new justification. The tree-felling imagery must be rooted in Thetis' anticipated lament: she had remembered (Hom. *Il.* 18.56–57) the boy growing up like "a young shoot ... a tree on a mountain slope." At the risk of sounding too rationalistic, I would note that tradition has it that Achilles was not struck at the throat or the breast—as is usually the case with Homeric warriors who fall to the ground "like a tree"—but at the heel[10] or ankle. Achilles' fall is modelled on that of a tall pine not only because of its height,[11] but also because his body was felled by a blow to the base, just like a tall trunk assailed almost at its root by the woodcutters.[12]

---

untimely death and the perpetuation of Achilles' name. If, then, as seems probable given the hymnic structure, Achilles was regularly cited in the second person, Simonides found a surprising way to recreate the grammatical situation of *Od.* 24, not otherwise reproducible, i.e., Simonides picks up from Agamemnon his second-person address to Achilles about his death and funeral (with its effects of the type "the flames consumed you ... we gathered your white bones"). On the other hand, this adherence to the model could also produce (in the best tradition of intertextuality) some deviation: on the basis of the reconstruction so far advanced, it seems probable that Simonides attributed the death of Achilles to Apollo alone, with a resulting amplification of the Homeric tradition in which Paris is always seen as Achilles' murderer. (On different accounts of the event see conveniently Gantz 1993: 625–28.)

9. Catull. 64 is pertinent also because the human victims sacrificed to the Minotaur (64.80) are later recalled at the sacrifice of Polyxena (362–370), while the image of Achilles becomes ever more disquieting. The mortal blow by Apollo is foreshadowed by his absence from the marriage that will lead to Achilles' birth (209–302).

10. Stesichorus had earlier (if one accepts the reconstruction of Garner 1993: 159) made mention of a blow to the heel or ankle (σφυρός, *POxy* 3876 fr. 43.ii.8). In another direction, R. G. M. Nisbet has pointed out to me that "mordaci ... icta" is comparable to the bite of a serpent (Ov. *Trist.* 5.4.12 "ictus ab angue"; note also the use of *mordax* for arrows poisoned with snake venom, Ov. *Pont.* 3.3.106) and that the location of the blow is comparable to the typical bite of a serpent (Ov. *Met.* 10.10 "occidit in talum serpentis dente recepto"). For the imagery cf. Eur. *Hyps.* fr. 60.72 with Bond ad loc.

11. Which need not exclude other motivations: Herodotus 6.37 is evidence for the idiomatic phrase "destroy like a πίτυς" = "destroy utterly," since this tree, once cut down, is incapable of regrowth. Horace employs the reverse image of the resilience of the Romans: *Carm.* 4.4.57 "duris ut ilex tonsa [v.l. tunsa] bipennibus," which is based on Pind. *Paean* 4.263–69; cf. Lefkowitz 1991: 159. We do not know what other tree Simonides mentioned, but for Horace's choice of the cypress we may imagine that the tree is appropriate for reasons either realistic (height, lack of solidity), symbolic (funerary associations), or mythological (the cypress was "invented" by the divine protagonist of the Horatian ode; cf. Ov. *Met.* 10.107 "nunc arbor, puer ante deo dilectus ab illo").

12. In a less rationalistic vein, the duplicity of the agents mentioned in the model, the woodcutters and the wind, with their distinct traditions in epic similes, seems to suggest a hesitation on the part of the poet concerning the mysterious and inexplicable nature of the divine intervention that brought about the end of Achilles' life. I owe this observation to Richard Hunter.

The context in Horace *Carm.* 4.6.1–20, as has been noted by the commentators, takes its direction, by and large, from Pindar *Paean* 6,[13] where Apollo kills Achilles, although Pindar's sober description of the fatal blow, θρασεῖ φόνῳ πεδάσαις (v. 86), cannot have been the inspiration for Horace's simile. His description of Achilles as *filius . . . Thetidis marinae* (v. 6) is usually compared to Pindar *Paean* 6.83f. κυανοπλόκοιο παῖδα ποντίας Θέτιος, but the elegy on Plataea now offers us two other parallel periphrases: 10.5 W² κούρης εἰναλίης ἀγλαόφημε πάι and 11.19–20 θεᾶς ἐρικυδέος υἱέ | κούρης εἰναλίου Νηρέος.[14] It may be that these and other similarities[15] directed Horace's memory from Pindar to Simonides—both poets being important models for the fourth book of the *Odes*. To Simonides' function as a model in some of the lyrics of the Fourth Book—cf. 4.9.5–7 "non . . . Pindaricae latent Ceaeque . . . camenae"—I return elsewhere;[16] for now, let me merely point out how Simonides' *Plataea* and Horace's *Carm.* 4.6. have in common (more so than Pindar) the use of myth in a patriotic context.

Horace orients his poetry towards the *Carmen Saeculare*. He thus finds himself in a situation which is neither usual for him (a poet who has unexpectedly been honored as a public author in a public inscription);[17] nor does it have strong support from Greek precedents. The elegiac production of Simonides is important because it offers a rare precedent (apart from epic, epinician, or threnody, but in rapport with all three) of a poet who sings themes of collective importance that are based on public patronage.[18] Simonides exalts, in a sort of hymnic proem, the heroism of Achilles, who contributed to the Greek victory over the Trojans; he then sings, as an updated Homer, of the battle against the Persians for the survival of Greece. The panhellenic tone[19] anticipates Herodotus' linkage of the siege of Troy and the Persian invasion:

13. Cf. Fraenkel 1957: 400–7.

14. Cf. Rutherford in this volume on fr. 11.19 W².

15. For research on Pindar and Simonides in context see Rutherford and Mace. One may hope for results that also involve Horace, given that the "dialogue" between Pindar and Simonides brings up poetic themes and programs that will be important for Horatian lyric; cf. *Carm.* 4.9.5–7 (quoted in my text); Barchiesi 1996.

16. For now one may simply note that *Carm.* 4.7 has been at the center of speculation about Horace as imitator of Simonides (or Semonides!). Cf. Cataudella 1927–28: 229–32, Oates 1932: 76–90. Further links are necessitated by the new Simonides fragments 19–29 W²; cf. Parsons 1992a: 43, West 1993a: 10–11 ("Lives, leaves"), and Sider in this volume. And Theocritus 16, an important model for *Carm.* 4.8 and 4.9, can now be reevaluated (thanks to Parsons 1992b: 10–12) in terms of its allusions to Simonides (keeping in mind the methodological lesson of Merkelbach 1952). I discuss Hor. *Carm.* 4.6, 4.7, 4.8, and 4.9 at greater length in Barchiesi 1996.

17. See below, n. 22. "Vatis Horati" (*Carm.* 4.6.44) comes as a complete surprise because Horace had already defined himself as *vates* in the last verse of *Epod.* 16, with a vastly different significance and context. The (anachronistic) role of *chorodidaskalos* which Horace assumes in *Carm.* 4.6 is compatible with the Pindaric influence, but also of course with the Simonidean.

18. On the commission and genre of Simonides' *Plataea*, see Aloni, Boedeker, "Historiography," etc. in this volume.

19. "Panhellenic" need not imply a reference to a particular commission (on the performance context, see the important discussions by Boedeker, "Historiography," Aloni, etc. in this volume): here I am thinking of Horace's *regard éloigné*. Naturally, however, the "civil" Horace of this period is interested in the development of a language that celebrates anti-Persian unity. His use of *Medus* at *Carm. Saec.* 54 to indicate the Parthian danger is a good example of what I mean, as are the "Sea-battle at Salamis" staged by Augustus

Greece versus Asia, and Achilles as forerunner of the fighters at Plataea.[20] The intervention of Apollo, the only one capable of stopping him, is recorded *ad majorem gloriam* of the hero. Horace is about to sing of the rebirth of Troy, which Apollo had made possible[21] by killing Achilles, the man who would have put to the sword the entire race (Hor. *Carm.* 6.4.16–20); a victorious Achilles would have meant no Aeneas, no Rome, no Augustus (21–24). The agreement and opposition between the two contexts show how neatly Horace has extracted an image from a hymn to Achilles killed by Apollo and transferred it to a song for Apollo the killer of Achilles.[22]

---

in 2 B.C.E. and the other Augustan revivals of Athenian figural propaganda; cf., e.g., Hardie 1986, index s.v. Persians; Schneider 1986; Spawforth 1994. These kinds of Augustan cultural propaganda do much to explain the function that Simonidean celebratory elegy plays in the lyrics of Horace's fourth book of *Odes*.

20. Simonides is therefore a pioneer in the process of painting the Trojans as barbarians, which emerges in the course of fifth-century Athenian cultural history. (But see Boedeker, "Heroization," at nn. 70–73.) Cf. the observations of Cole 1992: 53–54 and n. 6, writing on Bacchylides without knowledge of the new Simonides papyri.

21. The link between Horace and the text of Simonides is stronger if in 11.10 W² we read Πριάμου παισὶ χαριζόμεναι, as is argued by Parsons 1992a: 28 and Luppe 1993: 3f., rather than χαλεπτόμεναι (West 1993a: 6); cf. Luppe's rendering: "Apollo tötete Achilleus den Troern zu Gefallen."

22. *Carm.* 4.6 ends with a reference to the role of public singer assumed by Horace for the *Carmen Saeculare*: "vatis Horati" (44). It would be interesting to understand better the poetic persona assumed by Simonides in his *Plataea*. West's reconstruction (1993a: 7–9) speaks at length on the prophetic activities of Teisamenos, the divine *mantis* who foresaw the course of the battle and who affirmed the gods' agreement to a Spartan victory. Perhaps Simonides was somehow suggesting a contrast between the seer Teisamenos, guarantor of the future, and the singer Simonides, guarantor of the memory of this action. ("As a *vates*, Horace is the mouthpiece of the god both of poetry and of prophecy, pronouncing incantatory verses, fabricating the *carmina* that themselves fabricate the Roman secular present and guarantee its future," Putnam 1986: 123). In West's reconstruction, Teisamenos not only predicts the victorious strategy but also prophesies long-lasting future memory of the Greek victory (14.5–6 W²). There is a notable similarity to the language used by Simonides for his own function as singer who guarantees the memory of this action (11.20–28 W²). On the persona of the performer of the elegy, see further Stehle in this volume.

17

STEPHEN HARRISON

Simonides and Horace

Introduction: History of the Issue

The intertextual relationship of Simonides and Horace has been much illuminated by the publication of the new Simonides fragments. The cautious judgement of Nisbet and Hubbard in their 1970 survey of the sources of the *Odes* in volume I of their classic commentary ("an occasional aphorism comes from Simonides") marked an advance on some earlier treatments that ignored Simonides' influence on Horace entirely; their volume II (1978) moved further, positing more Simonidean echoes, and this can now be supplemented by proposals of more extensive allusions.[1]

In this context, the 1932 dissertation of W. J. Oates, *The Influence of Simonides of Ceos upon Horace*, deserves much credit, as post-1992 publications on the topic of Horace and Simonides have acknowledged.[2] Oates's dissertation began from the fact that two fragments of Simonides are plainly echoed in well-known lines from Horace's second Roman ode: 524 *PMG* ὁ δ' αὖ θάνατος κίχε καὶ τὸν φυγόμαχον is famously behind "mors et fugacem persequitur virum" (*Odes* 3.2.14), while 582 *PMG* ἔστι καὶ σιγᾶς ἀκίνδυνον γέρας underlies the enigmatic "est et fideli tuta silentio I merces" (3.2.25–26). Though I would not accept all Oates's arguments, his central idea that these two fragments derive from a single poem, which he labels the "Ode on Civic

---

I am most grateful to Robert Parker for inviting me to give a paper on this topic at a colloquium on the New Simonides in Oxford in November 1997, to Dirk Obbink for kind bibliographical aid, to Richard Hunter for the point in n. 11, and to Alessandro Barchiesi and (especially) Robin Nisbet for helpful criticism.

1. It seems particularly odd that Simonides is not mentioned in Fraenkel 1957, but he is not mentioned in the chapter on Horace and the Greek lyric poets in Wilamowitz 1913, which was influential on Fraenkel (see Fraenkel 1964 [1948]: 570). On a possible echo of the career of Simonides in that of Horace cf. Nisbet and Hubbard 1978: 203; Feeney 1993: 43 recognizes the importance of Simonides for Horace, but has no space to pursue the topic.

2. Oates 1932; cf. Gigante 1994, a brief but useful survey, and the excellent Barchiesi essay in this volume, a revised translation of Barchiesi 1995, and Barchiesi 1996.

Virtue," seems attractive:[3] as Oates himself points out (p. 41), there is some evidence for Simonides' fame as a poet of civic virtue in antiquity, above all a passage of Ammianus (14.6.7 = 15 *PMG*): "For as the lyric poet Simonides teaches, it is fitting for him who is to live happily in accordance with perfect reason to have above all a country which is renowned."[4] That a Horatian ode might use a single poem of a Greek lyric poet as a substantive model is surely unproblematic since Fraenkel's famous demonstration of the reworking of Pindar's first *Pythian* in *Odes* 3.4, or since Pasquali's account of the close use of an Alcaean sympotic lyric (338 LP) in *Odes* 1.9.[5] This leaves open the notion that the line which immediately precedes "mors et fugacem persequitur virum," and to which it is closely linked, the famous 3.2.13 "dulce et decorum est pro patria mori," might itself be linked with Simonides. This line is commonly related to Tyrtaeus 10.1–2 W:

> τεθνάμεναι γὰρ καλὸν ἐνὶ προμάχοισι πεσόντα
> ἄνδρ᾽ ἀγαθὸν περὶ ᾗ πατρίδι μαρνάμενον,

but these lines notoriously give no model for the problematic *dulce*.[6] Could this have come from Simonides' lost poem on civic virtue? Death is sweet because of the individual's devotion to the fatherland,[7] a point that such a poem might possibly have made.

Oates also treats possible Simonidean echoes in *Odes* 1.28, the Archytas ode, relating it with Wilamowitz to the sepulchral epigram in the Greek Anthology (*AP* 7.77) ascribed to Simonides (85 *FGE*): "This is the savior of Simonides of Ceos, who even in death returned thanks to the living."[8] This refers to a well-known story that Simonides buried a corpse he found by the sea; the ghost of the corpse then appeared to him and told him not to sail on a voyage that he had previously planned, in order to avoid shipwreck.[9] Here I would be more skeptical, as Nisbet and Hubbard are in their commentary: the resemblances between this story and the Archytas ode are tenuous, and the Horatian text has no obvious allusion to Simonides. But Oates is more successful with *Odes* 4.7, the famous "Diffugere nives," where he plausibly argues that the conjunction of nature imagery with reflection on mortality reflects several Simonidean sources.

Nisbet and Hubbard's cautious view of the importance of Simonides for Horace in the first volume of their commentary, already cited, is (as are some of their other

---

3. And was found so by contemporary reviewers: Wilkinson 1933, Helm 1933.

4. "ut enim Simonides lyricus docet, beate perfecta ratione victuro ante alia patriam esse convenit gloriosam."

5. *Odes* 3.4 and Pindar *Pythian* 1: Fraenkel 1957: 273–85. *Odes* 1.9 and Alcaeus 338 LP: Pasquali 1920: 75–86, Nisbet and Hubbard 1970: 116. Of course, Horatian poems also use glancing single references to earlier Greek poems—see especially Cavarzere 1996.

6. Which Professor Nisbet once proposed to remove by emendation to "dulci decorum est pro patria mori," where it is much easier with *patria*; for another view cf. Harrison 1993.

7. Cf. Harrison 1993, adducing Achilles Tatius 3.22.1 and Cicero *Off.* 1.57.

8. οὗτος ὁ τοῦ Κείοιο Σιμωνίδεω ἐστὶ σαωτήρ | ὃς καὶ τεθνηὼς ζῶντ᾽ ἀπέδωκε χάριν. Cf. Oates 1932: 56–75, following Wilamowitz 1893 [1935].

9. Cf. Nisbet and Hubbard 1970: 319.

cautious views) relaxed in their second volume. There they suggest that the final stanza of *Odes* 2.20 has possible Simonidean coloring (21–24):[10]

> absint inani funere neniae
> luctusque turpes et querimoniae:
>   compesce clamorem ac sepulchri
>   mitte supervacuos honores.

They compare Simonides 531.1–3 *PMG*, from the remains of the lyric lament for those who died at Thermopylae:

> τῶν ἐν Θερμοπύλαις θανόντων
> εὐκλεὴς μὲν ἁ τύχα, καλὸς δ᾽ ὁ πότμος,
> βωμὸς δ᾽ ὁ τάφος, πρὸ γόων δὲ μνᾶστις, ὁ δ᾽ οἶκτος ἔπαινος.

They rightly note that the resemblance is general, with both contexts merely stressing that great fame, though one could point out that *Odes* 2.20.21 "neniae" alludes quite precisely to the lyric genre of θρῆνοι to which 531 *PMG* is usually assigned, and for which Simonides was particularly famed (see below).[11] This could make a quite specific point: the poet Horace is not only like the Spartans at Thermopylae in needing no tomb because of fame, he outdoes them—he does not even need the poetry of Simonides in which that need for a tomb is denied (he has, after all, the poetry of Horace).

Nisbet and Hubbard on the same passage also point out that scholars have long held[12] that the next two lines of this same Simonidean fragment are also imitated by Horace at *Odes* 3.30.1–5:

> Exegi monumentum aere perennius
> regalique situ pyramidum altius,
> quod non imber edax, non Aquilo impotens
> possit diruere, aut innumerabilis
> annorum series et fuga temporum.

The echo of 531.4–5 *PMG* is indeed clear:

> ἐντάφιον δὲ τοιοῦτον οὔτ᾽ εὐρὼς
> οὔθ᾽ ὁ πανδαμάτωρ ἀμαυρώσει χρόνος.

In fact, the Simonidean intertext points to some ambiguities in Horace, as Tony Woodman has reminded us: ἐντάφιον "shroud," with its reference to burial, reminds us that *monumentum* can mean "tomb" as well as the more general "memorial" or "monument," while εὐρὼς suggests that *situ* means "rot" as well as "site" or "structure."[13] But this is not the end of the Simonidean coloring here: in line 3, though the theme of the lack of damage through wind and rain can be traced to a Pindaric con-

---

10. Nisbet and Hubbard 1978: 336–37.
11. I owe this point to Richard Hunter.
12. Professor Nisbet points out that this allusion is noted as early as Mitscherlich 1800: II 297.
13. Cf. Woodman 1974:1 18; for the senses of *situs* see *OLD* s.v. Professor Nisbet suggests to me the nicely ambiguous translation "Pyramids in the regal mold."

text,[14] the metaphor of *edax* and the tooth of time has also been long connected with a fragment of Simonidean epigram (88 W²), ὅ τοι Χρόνος ὀξὺς ὀδόντας, | καὶ πάντα ψήχει καὶ τὰ βιαιότατα.[15] We should also note that both 2.20 and 3.30 are the last poems in their book, and the latter the last in the first collection of *Odes*: when Horatian lyric turns to thoughts about the immortality of poetry, it seems to turn to imitation of Simonides. We will see below that the other final poem of the first collection, *Odes* 1.38, may also have Simonidean coloring.

These previously known echoes of Simonides in contexts of poetic immortality may be neatly linked with Alessandro Barchiesi's work on the presence of Simonides in the fourth book of *Odes*, which brings the new fragments effectively into play.[16] In his shorter piece (this volume) Barchiesi makes an excellent case that Horace *Odes* 4.6 echoes the Achilles proem to the Plataea elegy; in his longer *Classical Antiquity* piece, he expands this to include arguments for echoes of Simonides in *Odes* 4.7 (following Oates), 4.8, and 4.9: indeed, he sees the four poems as a Simonidean group in the fourth book, and Simonides as a crucial influence for the two central features in *Odes* 4—its concern with the praise of political and military achievement, and its concern with the power of poetry to commemorate and perpetuate. This second theme has an evident link with the Simonidean echoes already seen in *Odes* 2.20 and 3.30: once again the idea of lasting poetic commemoration is linked with Simonides. While I myself would wish to give higher place to Pindar and the epinician tradition in *Odes* 4, and to see the concern for commemoration as owing at least as much to Pindar as to Simonides, Barchiesi's arguments are presented with typical creativity and intelligence; particularly interesting is the way in which he connects Simonides' famous role in the history of mnemonic technique (see below) with his concern for poetic memory and commemoration.[17]

Thus far bibliographical survey, with some comments. In what remains I want to discuss three points: first, the general reception of Simonides in Rome, and how this might affect Horatian imitation; second, the possible reverberations in Horace and other Roman poets of the lyric poem on Salamis and the elegy on the battle of Artemisium, 3 W², revealed for us in the new fragments; and third, the possible imitations by Horace of the new sympotic fragment, 22 W².

Simonides at Rome: Memory Man, Man of Sorrow

The Roman tradition about Simonides has two main elements. First, he is famously mentioned by Cicero as the inventor of a mnemonic system (*De or.* 2.352–53). This achievement is subsequently noted by other Roman writers, no doubt getting their information from Cicero (Quintilian 11.2.11–13, Tacitus *Ann.* 11.14.2). Second, he is

---

14. Pindar *Pyth.* 6.10–14, cited already by Orelli and Baiter 1850: 515, clearly also alluded to by the Horatian passage.
15. Found already in Müller 1900: II 338.
16. Barchiesi, this volume and 1996.
17. Barchiesi 1996: 20–21.

considered the poetic specialist in lamentation.[18] The key passages here include two from Horace, and are worth consideration:

> paulum quid lubet allocutionis,
> maestius lacrimis Simonideis.
>
> (Catullus 38.7–8)

Here, with some irony and hyperbole, Catullus asks his poetic friend Cornificius for verses to console him in the manner of Simonides;[19] "allocutionis" and "lacrimis" indicate Simonides' fame for moving but uplifting poetry of lamentation. This is made more specific in the much later judgment of Quintilian (10.1.64):

> Simonides, tenuis alioqui, sermone proprio et iucunditate quadam commendari potest, praecipua tamen eius in commovenda miseratione virtus, ut quidam in hac eum parte omnibus eiusdem operis auctoribus praeferant.

"Eiusdem operis" here would seem to refer to lyric poetry, since in Quintilian Simonides is treated as the last figure in a survey of Greek lyric poets (10.1.61–64) that also includes Pindar, Stesichorus, and Alcaeus, a list which like Quintilian's comments on Pindar is taken from Horace (from *Odes* 4.9, see below).[20] The allusion must consequently be to Simonides' lyric *threnoi*, which seem to have been especially popular, to judge from the number of fragments usually assigned to them in the modern editions of Simonides.[21] Such has also been the usual interpretation of the first of Horace's two explicit mentions of Simonides—*Odes* 2.1.37–40:

> sed ne relictis, Musa procax, iocis
> Ceae retractes munera neniae,
>   mecum Dionaeo sub antro
>   quaere modos leviore plectro.

Here Horace directs his playful erotic lyric away from the theme of civil war and lamentation to lighter themes. Nisbet and Hubbard regard "Ceae . . . neniae" as simply indicating Simonidean pathos, but the specific color of *nenia*, "funeral dirge," might argue (as at 2.20.21, see above) that it was a translation of Κήιοι θρῆνοι "Cean dirges": Horace is warning himself off a particular species of lyric poetry rather than a general literary mode. But the context is also suggestive. In the previous stanza the poem has been strongly lamenting the casualties of sea-battles (33–36):

> qui gurges aut quae flumina lugubris
> ignara belli? quod mare Dauniae
>   non decoloravere caedes?
>   quae caret ora cruore nostro?

18. This is stressed by Gigante 1994: 56–57, to which this section is indebted.
19. For the comic interpretation, rightly refuting the effusions of nineteenth-century romanticism, cf. Copley 1956.
20. Quintilian 10.1.61 explicitly alludes to Horace's judgement of Pindar's inimitability in *Odes* 4.2 ("Horatius eum merito nemini credit imitabilem") and uses the same image of a mighty river for Pindaric style ("velut quodam eloquentiae flumine"; cf. *Odes* 4.2.5 "monte decurrens velut amnis"). On Quintilian's use of *Odes* 4.9 see n. 25 below.
21. Fr. 520–31 *PMG* are all thought to come from *threnoi*.

Given that the staining of water with blood is a feature particularly associated with the battle of Salamis (Aeschylus *Persians* 420, Herodotus 8.77, Timotheus *Persians* [791 *PMG*] 31ff.), it is tempting to take this as an allusion to Simonides' lyric poem on the battle of Salamis, the existence of which (as Martin West has noted)[22] is confirmed by the publication of the new fragments. The battle of Actium with its Orientalizing aspect could be easily assimilated to the Greek wars against Persia and their naval victories, but this is far from the context of this ode, discussing Pollio's tragic history of the civil wars, which seems not to have got as far as 31 B.C.E.[23] In this context, very different from that of *Odes* 1.37 (for which see below), the implication of a reference to a poem celebrating Salamis might be that imitating Simonides can be inappropriate politically as well as poetically: Horace's *Odes* are not dirges, and the lamentation for the tragic and inglorious dead of the civil wars before Actium, commonly presented in Augustan discourse as an era of pointless disaster from which Rome is rescued by the great man,[24] is very different from celebrating glorious triumph against a barbarian enemy as Simonides had done over the Persians, and from the later appropriation of that celebration for Actium. Thus there are two reasons to avoid the Simonidean model here.

Finally, this reception of Simonides as a serious poet continues in the later of the two Horatian allusions, *Odes* 4.9.5–12:

> non, si priores Maeonius tenet
> sedes Homerus, Pindaricae latent
>   Ceaeque et Alcaei minaces
>   Stesichorive graves Camenae:
> nec, si quid olim lusit Anacreon,
> delevit aetas: spirat adhuc amor
>   viventque commissi calores
>   Aeoliae fidibus puellae.

Here Simonides (though Bacchylides might also lurk in the toponym *Ceae*)[25] is firmly framed with the lofty Pindar, Alcaeus, and Stesichorus in the serious stanza as opposed to the more frivolous Anacreon and Sappho in the lighter stanza. In fact, the only possible exception to this Roman picture of Simonides as the poet of lamentation is a disputed passage in the *Apologia* of Apuleius, of 158–59 C.E., where Apuleius

---

22. West 1993a: 2.

23. For the particular assimilation of Actium to Salamis cf. Galinsky 1996: 203. There is no hard evidence that Pollio's *Historiae* extended beyond Philippi, though the stress of Horace's ode on naval battles might suggest the campaigns of the mid-30s against Sextus Pompeius, and Actium would have been highly problematic. For discussion and bibliography cf. Nisbet and Hubbard 1978: 8–10, Henderson 1996: 63 n.10.

24. E.g., *Odes* 1.2.25–52, 4.15.4–20, Vergil *Georg.* 1.498–514, *Aen.* 1.286–96.

25. So Fraenkel 1957: 424. It seems more than coincidental that the four lyric poets chosen for discussion by Quintilian 10.1.61–4, Pindar, Stesichorus, Alcaeus, and Simonides, are the same four listed in *Odes* 4.9.6–8; if this is so, then Quintilian clearly interpreted "Ceae . . . Camenae" as referring to Simonides. Dion. Hal. *De imit.* 420–21 (a reference I owe to Professor Nisbet) perhaps suggests that these four were grouped together already in the Hellenistic period, though Dion. Hal. *Comp. Verb.* 173 conversely groups Simonides with Sappho and Anacreon.

is defending himself against a charge of writing homoerotic poetry to the sons of friends by citing examples of great and serious writers who did the same (*Apol.* 9.6):

> Fecere tamen et alii alia, etsi vos ignoratis: apud Graecos Teius quidam et Lacedaemonius et Cius cum aliis innumeris . . .

"Teius" is clearly Anacreon, "Lacedaemonius" probably Alcman; but with "Cius," which like "Ceus" refers to a native of Ceos,[26] there are two problems. First, "Cius" is a conjecture for the MSS "civis," admittedly an easy and probable conjecture; but there is also the issue of who is meant here if "Cius" is right.[27] Since there were two great poets of Ceos, Simonides and Bacchylides, either could be meant, assuming that Bacchylides like Simonides wrote erotic poetry.[28] If it were Simonides, and he is the more famous of the two and the more likely to be referred to as "the Cean poet," as at Horace *Odes* 2.1.38 (above), then Apuleius is clearly using his general Roman reputation as a poet of tragic and dignified themes: even the great poet of lamentation occasionally let himself go in erotic trifles. Given that the context refers specifically to homoerotic poetry addressed to the sons of friends, and that the new Simonidean 22 W[2] can be argued to do precisely that in its apparent treatment of Echecratidas (see below), this passage could even conceivably allude to 22 W[2] itself.

Naval Echoes: Salamis and Artemisium

Here I make three brief points. First, on Salamis. I have already noted that the new fragments seem to confirm that the Suda was right in claiming that Simonides wrote a lyric poem to celebrate the Greek victory at Salamis;[29] this might have further implications for Horace, since the existence of such a poem by Simonides is surely in some degree relevant to the interpretation of the Horatian ode on Actium, *Odes* 1.37. We have already seen that the final part of *Odes* 2.1 might possibly have some coloring from the Simonidean account of Salamis; and though 1.37 begins famously from a poem of Alcaeus,[30] its narrative of naval victory may well look back to Simonides on Salamis. In particular, the use of the Homericizing simile of the hawk and dove in lines 17–20 might well owe more to Simonides, who famously includes a Homericizing simile in the new Plataea elegy, than to Alcaeus, for whom such a simile is not firmly attested.[31] Second, on Artemisium: the very fact that a great Greek poet wrote a triumph elegy on a famous naval battle may have consequences in Roman poetry beyond Horace: here one thinks of Propertius 4.6, the Actium elegy, which has resemblances to the Callimachean hymn but may also look back to an older

---

26. *Ceus* is closer to the Greek form, though *Cius* is often found in MSS: for the evidence cf. *TLL Onomasticon* 2.289.16ff.

27. See Hunink 1997: II 40.

28. For discussion see Hunink 1997: II 40.

29. Suda IV.361.9ff. Adler; cf. West 1993a: 2.

30. Alcaeus 332 LP: cf. Nisbet and Hubbard 1970: 411.

31. Unless inc. auct. Lesb. 10 LP is Alcaean. For the epic coloring of *Odes* 1.37.17–20 cf. Nisbet and Hubbard 1970: 415–16, for the Simonidean epic simile in the Plataea elegy fr. 11.1–4 W[2].

elegiac tradition.[32] Sadly, the exiguous remains of the Artemisium elegy in the new fragments (1–4 W[2]) offer no parallel between the two poems apart from the poet's claim of divine intervention in both battles, itself a frequent topic in such contexts. Third, if Martin West's reconstruction of 3 on Artemisium is correct and the Old Man of the Sea appeared to give a prophecy, which seems more likely than not,[33] then this scene too may have had some reverberations in Horace's *Odes*. In *Odes* 1.15 we find a narrative of the voyage of Paris and Helen from Sparta to Troy, a voyage in which they are interrupted by a calm in which Nereus, the Old Man of the Sea, prophesies the coming destruction of Troy as a consequence of their actions, a prophecy that then takes up the rest of the poem (1.15.1–5):

> Pastor cum traheret per freta navibus
> Idaeis Helenen perfidus hospitam,
> ingrato celeris obruit otio
>   ventos, ut caneret fera
> Nereus fata: ". . . ."

Porphyrio in late antiquity famously comments that this imitates a poem of Bacchylides in which it was Cassandra who prophesied to the guilty couple, a prophecy well attested elsewhere.[34] In other versions the prophecy takes place before Paris leaves Troy;[35] Horace's change of location for the prophecy to the voyage itself might explain why Nereus replaces Cassandra, but this might also be explained by an allusion to Simonides. This formal resemblance is matched by a probable resemblance of theme: Nereus' prophecy in Horace foretells in detail the coming of the just vengeance of the Greeks and the merited fall of Troy, and the hypothetical prophecy of Nereus in Simonides would surely have made a very similar prediction of a future battle in which Greeks justifiably conquer Asians. There are of course major contextual differences (Nereus appears to the offenders in Horace, but to the "innocent" party, the Athenians, at Artemisium; the taking of Troy is not a sea-battle; and Artemisium does not involve the sack of a city), but the potential similarities are certainly worth consideration, and may explain an otherwise puzzling feature of Horace's version.

The Islands of the Blest: Escape, Symposium, Closure?

Here I turn to the splendid fragment 22 W[2], in which the poet seems to imagine a voyage to the Islands of the Blest and a symposium with an erotic partner amid flowers. The Isles of the Blest, as Peter Parsons points out in his original Oxyrhynchus publication,[36] are a literary *topos* since Hesiod *WD* 170–73, but here I would wish to agree

---

32. On the Callimachean coloring of Propertius 4.6 cf. Cairns 1984, though I disagree with his notions of the poem's choral performance.
33. West 1993a: 3–4.
34. Nisbet and Hubbard 1970: 188–89.
35. Ibid.
36. Parsons 1992a: 46.

with Sarah Mace in positing a connection between the utopianism of the Simonidean fragment and that of Horace's sixteenth *Epode*.[37] There the poet urges his fellow citizens to abandon Rome, riven by civil war, and sail to the Islands of the Blest with their miraculous peace and fertility (*Epod.* 16.41–56):

> nos manet Oceanus circumvagus: arva, beata
>   petamus arva, divites et insulas,
> reddit ubi Cererem tellus inarata quotannis
>   et imputata floret usque vinea.
> germinat et nunquam fallentis termes olivae,
>   suamque pulla ficus ornat arborem,
> mella cava manant ex ilice, montibus altis
>   levis crepante lympha desilit pede.

What this text shares with the Simonidean fragment is the idea of utopian escape to the paradisiacal Islands of the Blest; Mace (after n. 73) notes the parallel of utopian escape, but does not explicitly point out that the islands are involved in both cases, surely the strongest link between the two passages. In both cases the islands provide a refuge, in Horace from civil war, in Simonides (we may conjecture from 22.14 W^2) from old age. As Parsons notes, the wish of the chorus at Euripides *Hipp.* 732ff. to escape from their dreadful situation to the Islands of the Hesperides is similar, and those islands are indeed presented as fertile, but the Islands of the Hesperides are not those of the Blest, and the Horatian poem might look back more naturally to Simonidean elegy than to tragedy.[38] In Horace the flight is presented as a fantastic and improbable solution to a real and inevitable problem; we might guess that the same was true of Simonides, who cannot truly escape the misery of old age just as Horace cannot truly escape the civil discord of Rome. This would add support to those who hold that the Simonidean passage talks about a fantastic journey of rejuvenation envisaged as happening during the poet's lifetime, rather than about what will happen after the poet's death.[39] As Mace notes, the contrast between the two uses of the theme is stark:[40] more explicitly, Horace adapts the whimsical erotic fantasy of Simonides to a grim political situation of civil war.

The picture of the poet at the end of 22 W^2 is a classic sympotic pose: the poet seems to be reclining in the flowery meadows of the islands with a male erotic partner, possibly Echecratidas, wearing a garland and singing. While most of this is again a common *topos*, I would like to end by exploring possible connections with another poem of Horace, 1.38, the brief last poem of the first book of *Odes*:

> Persicos odi, puer, apparatus:
>   displicent nexae philyrae coronae;
> mitte sectari, rosa quo locorum
>   sera moretur.

---

37. See Mace, this volume, after n. 73.

38. *Epode* 16 has in any case some Greek elegiac color: it presents the poet as taking a bouleutic role appropriate to an archaic elegiac poet (Fraenkel 1957: 48), and its meter is very close to the elegiac couplet.

39. Here I agree with West 1993a and Mace.

40. Mace, this volume, after n. 73.

> simplici myrto nihil allabores
> sedulus curo: neque te ministrum
> dedecet myrtus neque me sub arta
>   vite bibentem.

Here too the poet is reclining sympotically in an outside location ("arta sub vite" surely suggests a terrace under the shade of a trained vine) in the company of an attractive male. There is much talk of garlands, and the poem in my view has an irresistible homoerotic color, as David West has recently argued; the fact that the poet is so concerned about his wine-pourer's garland surely suggests this, as does the fact that it is made of myrtle, the plant of Venus.[41] The poem is also surely symbolic: in its final position it is overwhelmingly tempting to take it as talking about poetry, like the other three final odes of Horace's four books.[42] The preference for simple living becomes a Callimachean preference for small-scale poetry, and the poet's drinking stands metapoetically for the writing of sympotic poetry.[43]

The possible echoes here of the Simonidean fragment (outdoor symposium, poetry, attractive young man) are so far vague and perhaps coincidental. But as noted in the discussions of *Odes* 2.20 and 3.30 above, Simonidean imitation tends to occur at the end of Horatian lyric books, and the two poems might also share a closural function. There has been much debate about whether 20–22 W^2 are a single poem. Horatian parallels might seem to suggest that 22 is from a poem separate from 20 and 21, the close of a shortish piece and perhaps even of a book: the wish for a journey to an eternal rest, the reference to old age, and the metapoetical allusion to singing are all elements that might conceivably suggest a closing sequence.[44] Some support for this comes from another closural poem in Horace's *Odes*: 2.20, the famous poetic swan, whose last stanza has already been seen as comparable to a fragment of Simonides (see above). Here I quote the first two stanzas:

> Non usitata nec tenui ferar
> penna biformis per liquidum aethera
>   vates, nec in terris morabor
>   longius, invidiaque maior
> urbis relinquam. Non ego pauperum
> sanguis parentum, non ego quem vocas,
>   dilecte Maecenas, obibo
>   nec stygia cohibebor unda.

Though the symposium and erotic elements are both absent here, the idea of the poet cheating his mortality by continuing to sing as the consequence of a fantastic jour-

---

41. D. West 1995: 190–94.

42. So Pasquali 1920: 324, Fraenkel 1957: 298, Cody 1976: 87–89 (too enthusiastic), attacked by Nisbet 1995: 421–23 (too conservative).

43. Simple living = Callimachean poetry: Mette 1961. Drinking = symposiastic poetry: *Epistles* 1.19.8–11 (surely a reference to sympotic odes).

44. For the thematic grammar of poetic closure in ancient works, including metapoetical elements and the notion of departure, cf. Fowler 1989 and Roberts, Dunn, and Fowler 1997: 304; for old age in a concluding sphragis cf. the Seal of Posidippus (705.5 *SH*).

ney is clearly shared with Simonides: Horace as swan flies as far as the Hyperboreans, 14–16 "visam … | … Hyperboreosque campos," presumably singing all the way. The fact that Horace here in this closural fantasy alludes to his patron Maecenas may also point to the probable allusion to the prince Echecratidas in 22 W[2]: personally, I would agree with Mace in seeing erotic color here and regarding Echecratidas the younger as the most likely candidate,[45] but whichever Echecratidas is meant and whether or not he is treated erotically, that he is mentioned at all surely constitutes some form of compliment to a patron, often a feature of book closure in Hellenistic and Roman poetry books.[46]

Conclusion

Our knowledge of the intertextual relationship of Simonides and Horace is thus materially increased by the publication of the new Simonidean fragments. As often, the hermeneutic benefit is mutual: Simonides allows us to interpret Horace more fully, while Horace suggests strategies of interpretation for Simonides. Of course, much of this is highly conjectural, but such considerations cannot fail to enrich a reading of either author.

45. Mace, after n. 79; her parallel with Pindar's treatment of Theoxenos of Tenedos (fr. 125 Snell) seems a good one. For a different interpretation, see Yatromanolakis, this volume.
46. Cf., e.g., *Odes* 4.15 (Augustus), Vergil *Ecl.* 10.70–74 (Gallus), *Georg.* 4.559–62 (Augustus), Callimachus *Aetia* fr. 112.2,8 (Ptolemaic royal family).

18

DAVID SIDER

"As Is the Generation of Leaves" in Homer, Simonides, Horace, and Stobaeus

Stobaeus 4.34.28 (Σιμωνίδου) comprises frr. 19 (MS S) + 20.5–12 (MSS SMA) W² (i.e. MS S presents **X** + **Y** as one continuous passage).

19 W² Stobaeus

> ἓν δὲ τὸ κάλλιστον Χῖος ἔειπεν ἀνήρ·
> "οἵη περ φύλλων γενεή, τοίη δὲ καὶ ἀνδρῶν."
> παῦροί μιν θνητῶν οὔασι δεξάμενοι
> στέρνοις ἐγκατέθεντο· πάρεστι γὰρ ἐλπὶς ἑκάστῳ
> 5 ἀνδρῶν ἥ τε νέων στήθεσι ἐμφύεται.   **X**

20 W² *POxy* 3965 fr. 26; Stobaeus

>]ειθ
>]ντ[. . .] . [
> τυτ]θὸν ἐπὶ χρό[νον
> . . . . . .] . . [. . . . .]ω παρμεν. [
> 5 θνητῶ‚ιν δ' ὄ‚ιφρα τις‚ ἄνθος ἔχει πολυήρατον ἥβης,
> κοῦφο‚ιν ἔχων θυμ‚ιὸν πόλλ' ἀτέλεσ‚ιτα νοεῖ·
> οὔ‚ιτε γὰρ ἐλπίδ' ἔχ‚ιει γηρασέμεν ‚ιοὔτε θανεῖσθαι,
> οὐδ' ὑγιὴς ὅτιαν ἦ φ‚ιροντίδ' ἔχει κ‚ιαμάτου.
> νή‚ιπιοι οἷς ταύι‚τη‚ι κεῖται νόος ο‚ιὐδὲ ἴσασιν   **Y**
> 10 ὡς χρό‚ινος ἔ‚ισθ' ἥβης καὶ βιότοι' ὀλι‚ίγος
> θνη‚ιτοῖς· ἀλλὰ ‚ισὺ‚ι ταῦτα μαθὼν βιότου ποτὶ τέρμα
> ψυχῇ τῶν‚ι ἀγαθῶν τλῆθι χα‚ιριζόμενος
> −‿‿] φράζευ δὲ παλα[ιοτέρου λόγον ἀνδρός·
> ἢ λήθην] γλώσσης ἔκφυγ' Ὅμηρ[ος −‿

An earlier version of this paper appeared in Deborah Boedeker and David Sider (eds.), *The New Simonides. Arethusa* 29.2 (1996): 263–82, and is used here by kind permission of the Johns Hopkins University Press.

15   . . . . . (.)]πα . δαμα[
            . . . . (.)]ω ψυδρῆς ε[
         . . . . . (.)] ἐν θαλίηισι [
            . . .]ι ἐϋστρέπτων [
20   . . . .]ων ἔνθα καὶ [ἔνθα
            .] . . [ ] . [

(Unattributed readings are owed to West)

19 1 τι Hecker   2 = *Il.* 6.146 (τοιήδε S)   3 μὴν Hermann

20 3 τυτθόν e.g. Parsons   4 ὀπίσ]ω e.g. Parsons   fin. ο[vel ε[5 εχε[ι *Π*   ἔχη Stob.
πολυηράτου Wil.   8 οὐδ᾿ Stob.   οὔθ᾿ Hartung   9 νηπίοισι vel νηπίοις Stob. (correxerat
Camerarius)   10 βιοτοι᾿ *Π* (coniecerat Cam.)   βιότου Stob.   13 vel παλα[ιγενέος West
παλα[ιοτέρων Parsons   14 ἔκφυγ᾿ Ὅμηρος Parsons   ῥῆμα δὲ πᾶν] . . . ἔκφυγ᾿ ὃ μὴ
ν[όμιμον Parsons   15 ὕ]παρ e.g. Parsons   πανδαμάτωρ West, sed ν non legendum   18
ων sscr. ·οι[

Translation:

19 The man from Chios said one thing best: "As is the generation of leaves, so is the
generation of men." Few men hearing this take it to heart. For in each man there is
hope which grows in the heart of the young.

20 . . . for a short time . . . abide . . . As long as a mortal has the desirable bloom of
youth with a light spirit he thinks many unaccomplished deeds. For he has no expectation that he will grow old or die, nor when healthy does he think about illness. Fools
are they whose thoughts are thus! Nor do they know that the time of youth and life
is short for mortals. But you, learning this at the end of your life, endure, delighting
in good things in your soul . . . Consider [the account of the man of] old. Homer
escaped [the forgetting of his words] . . . false . . . in feasts . . . well-plaited . . . here and
[there] . . .

Stobaeus

Glaukos, asked his identity on the battlefield by Diomedes, responds with one of
Homer's most famous similes:

Τυδείδη μεγάθυμε τίη γενεὴν ἐρεείνεις;
οἵη περ φύλλων γενεή, τοίη δὲ καὶ ἀνδρῶν.
φύλλα τὰ μέν τ᾿ ἄνεμος χαμάδις χέει, ἄλλα δὲ ὕλη
τηλεθόωσα φύει, ἔαρος δ᾿ ἐπιγίγνεται ὥρη·
ὣς ἀνδρῶν γενεὴ ἡ μὲν φύει, ἡ δ᾿ ἀπολήγει.

(*Il.* 6.145–49)

Great-hearted son of Tydeus, why do you ask of my birth?
Just as is the generation of leaves, so also is that of men.
Some leaves the wind spills to the ground, but others the

burgeoning wood grows anew, and the springtime comes again.
Thus one generation of men grows, another passes away.

Poets have alluded to this simile from the very beginning. The first to do so may in
fact be Homer himself. Later in the *Iliad*, Apollo tells Poseidon that he will not fight
with him for the sake of mortals:

> δειλῶν, οἳ φύλλοισιν ἐοικότες ἄλλοτε μέν τε
> ζαφλεγέες τελέθουσιν, ἀρούρης καρπὸν ἔδοντες
> ἄλλοτε δὲ φθινύθουσιν ἀκήριοι.

(Il. 21.464–66)

> wretched, who like leaves at one time burgeon in their
> glory, enjoying the fruit of the land, but at a later time
> lifelessly pass away.

This later passage surely echoes the earlier. As Richardson notes, there is a nice contrast between book 6, where Diomedes says that he would not fight Glaukos if he is a
god, and book 21, where Apollo refuses to fight another god for the sake of mortals.[1]

Later classical authors who clearly allude to this simile are Mimnermus,
Simonides, Pindar, Bacchylides, Aristophanes, Vergil, and Horace.[2] We shall look
more closely at these echoes in due course, but the author we must look at first is
Simonides, whose poem containing a citation of *Il.* 6.146,[3] known to us from its inclusion in Stobaeus' *omnium-gatherum*, now appears as one of the two literary passages
that allow us firmly to identify him as the author of *POxy* 3965 (and hence *POxy* 2327
as well). The overlap between Stobaeus and the papyrus does more, however, than
merely establish Simonidean authorship; it also has a surprise.

---

1. Richardson 1993: 93, who also notes that Plutarch *Mor.* 104e–f quotes the two passages together.
Richardson is here following Leaf 1900–1902 ("an obvious reminiscence," ad 21.464ff.), who, however,
thought the latter passage was composed by a poet other than that of the Diomedes-Glaukos passage; but
this generation of Leafish criticism has largely passed away. Fränkel 1921: 41 n. 1 considers both *Iliad* passages exempla of a common *Typus*. Cf. also Griffith 1975: 76f., Weber 1955: 60–62. For ancient treatments of
the simile in this passage, cf. Maftei 1976: 20–21.
2. The word "allude" comprehends actual citation as well as more oblique ways of recalling an earlier
poem. Cf. Pasquali 1968: 275, Conte 1986: 24f., Hinds 1998 passim. The Greeks themselves had a surprisingly rich repertory of terms to describe the various ways a later writer made use of an earlier one; e.g.,
παρατίθεσθαι (straightforward quotation; e.g., Simon. fr. 19 W²), μεταποιεῖν (see Solon fr. 20.3, cited
below), μεταγράφειν (see Appendix, A, below), παρῳδία, παραδιόρθωσις, παραποίησις, κ.τ.λ.; cf. T. W.
Allen 1934: 76f. for the vocabulary and passim for examples.
3. That Simonides quotes Homer was doubted by Davison 1955, who applies his admirable acumen to
argue that (i) since the line in question is gnomic, and (ii) since Homer uses γενεή both before and after
the simile to mean "birth, pedigree," and within the simile to mean "generation," Homer therefore bor-
rowed (and "misused") the simile from elsewhere, and that Simonides may not be referring to Homer as
the Man from Chios. Even if we grant that Greeks would have even noticed that γενεή was used in two
senses, this is a perverse conclusion: would anyone reading Simonides think that he was referring to anything other than this famous passage? It is, furthermore, now disproved by Simon. fr. 20.14 W² Ὅμηρ[.
Furthermore, as Lardinois 1997:218 points out, the word in the explanatory text (l. 145) that leads to the
word in the gnome may work as much by suggestion as by pure synonymy. See further Fantuzzi in this volume, n. 14.

Before the publication of the papyrus in 1992, we possessed, or thought that we did, a continuous 13–line elegiac poem which seemed to be nearly complete. Only the fact that its first line is the pentameter reveals that the beginning is lacking,[4] but most people seemed content to imagine that only one hexameter line was missing.[5] Stobaeus' line 13 was reasonably taken to end the poem. (Stobaeus' line numbers, which long were traditional, will be cited in the form Stob. 13; otherwise line numbers are those of frr. 19 and 20 in West's new ordering of the fragments.)

The papyrus, however, puts Stobaeus' selection in a new setting that demands that we rethink this whole question of the origin of Stob. 1–13. More precisely, Stob. 6–13 is preceded in *POxy* 3965 by traces of four lines which are inconsistent with Stob. 2–5 (and with Camerarius' "v. 1"; see above, n. 5), and is followed by traces of eight lines that allow for the possibility that Simonides' poem did not end at Stob. 13. What then is the relationship between Stob. 1–5 (which West in his second edition now calls fr. 19 and which I shall refer to as **X**) and Stob. 6–13 (which now equal vv. 5–12 of fr.20 W^2 and which I shall call **Y**)? Did Simonides' poem end with **Y**, or does what follows in the papyrus continue the poem? What does the new material surrounding **Y** (if we conclude that it is all part of the same poem) tell us about the larger context from which Stobaeus selected his verses?

We begin, however, with a brief argument for what I have so far taken for granted, namely that Simonides of Ceos is the author of the poem that quotes Homer's simile on the generation of leaves, for although we are now using the poem to establish

4. The δέ can be inceptive; cf. Denniston 1954: 172f. Athenaios 602b-c (text in West *IEG* s.v. Dionysius Chalcus) says that Apollo (in a Delphic oracle, 327 PW) and the elegies of Dionysios Chalkous occasionally begin with the pentameter; cf. Smith 1901: 183f., Korzeniewski 1968: 39f. Surely, though, if Simonides had done so, he would have been named alongside or instead of the far less famous Dionysios. It should be noted, however, that if the papyrus had confirmed that the poem did in fact begin with a pentameter, we could trot out as comparanda some few other verses where Simonides (or "Simonides" in the epigrams) toys with traditional metrics: (i) *Epigram* 1 *FGE* breaks the name Ἀριστογείτων between hexameter and pentameter; (ii) *Epigram* 52 adds an iambic trimeter to an elegiac distich; (iii) *Elegy* 92 W^2 comprises a hexameter followed by a trochaic tetrameter containing the same words as the hexameter in a different order; *Epigram* 44 contained (in a way no longer recoverable) a hyperbaton of syllables (cf. Page ad loc. for the details). Because of these quirky verses I am tempted to claim for Simonides *Adespota elegiaca* 20 W^2 ἡμεῖς δ' εἰς Ἕλλης πόντον ἀπεπλέομεν, where the word *Hellespont* is broken by the pentameter's midline caesura into its original form, Helle's pontos. (Bergk attributed the line, which is anonymous in Aphthonios, to Callimachus, who has the similarly formed pentameter ἱερά, νῦν δὲ Διοσκουρίδεω γενεή (fr. 384a Pf.) Aside from (iii), which seems to have a humorous intent, these deviations involve proper names, which is not the case with the leaves poem.

Note too that Stobaeus begins his citation of Mimnermus 5 W with a pentameter, where we know from another citation that at least three lines preceded, which Stobaeus, who will even occasionally alter his text in order for it to have a more general character, omitted probably because they contained a first person singular; cf. Hense 1916: 2584 and Campbell 1984: 55. Similarly, Stobaeus begins his quotation of Archil. fr. 193 W with the shorter epode line. (Nobody automatically thinks that a passage ascribed to an unknown tragedy by Stobaeus begins with the original line 1 of the play, but there is a subconscious tendency to do so with a self-contained passage from an elegiac or iambic poet.)

5. A substitute for which was supplied by Joachim Camerarius: οὐδὲν ἐν ἀνθρώποισι μένει χρῆμ' ἔμπεδον αἰεί. Note that his μένει . . . αἰεί, and hence the thought of the entire line, is vindicated by the papyrus's attestation of some form of παραμένειν. Note too that this line and the two conjectures of Camerarius 1550: 81f. in the apparatus were finally correctly credited to him by West 1972: 114. Earlier editors had credited them to Ursinus 1568: 167. (I thank Fred Schreiber for locating these early editions for me.)

that Simonides is the author of the papyri, many recent scholars have argued for placing the poem among the works of Semonides of Amorgos.[6] This is not an altogether
unreasonable assumption, for the Amorgine is in fact called Σιμωνίδης in all our
manuscript sources but Choeroboscus ap. *Etym. Gen. et Magn.* 713.17, who distinguishes between the iambographer Σημωνίδης and the lyric poet Σιμωνίδης.[7] And
one source, the Suda s.v. Σιμωνίδης says of the Amorgine that ἔγραψε ἐλεγείαν ἐν
βιβλίοις β', so that any elegy ascribed simply to Simonides could, prima facie, be by
either poet, especially since iotacism obviously plays a role in medieval manuscripts.[8]
Given this state of affairs, it remains just barely possible, as is argued by T. K. Hubbard
in this volume, that the Oxyrhynchus papyrus contains a poem falsely ascribed to
Simonides by the Alexandrian editor, and that the poem can still be safely listed
among those of Semonides. There are, it should be noted, no elegiac verses which can
be surely ascribed to the Amorgine, although if he did write a history of Samos, it was
likely to have been written in elegaics. (See the introduction to this volume.) There
is, nonetheless, little reason to doubt the bona fides of the Alexandrian editor who
produced the book that is the archetype for both *POxy* 2327 and *POxy* 3965. Our starting point, accordingly, will be that at least **Y** was written by Simonides of Ceos. As we
proceed, furthermore, it will be seen how comfortably the poem sits with Simonides'
poetic practice elsewhere, especially his frequent allusion to other poets.

What, though, of **X** (Stob.1–5), which the papyrus now shows not to have immediately preceded **Y**, as it does in Stobaeus? Or rather, as it does in one manuscript of
Stobaeus, for the new publication alerts us to a hitherto minor and neglected point
of manuscript transmission: Of the three Stobaean manuscripts reported to contain
this poem (**X** + **Y**), only one, S, representing the best family, contains all thirteen lines;
the other two, M and A, from the lesser family, omit the first five lines.[9] Not much

6. First Bergk, followed by, among others, Diehl and Wilamowitz, who says simply "An der Identität des
Verfassers lässt schon die innere Übereinstimmung keinen Zweifel. . . . Und die Form ist des Keers
unwürdig" (Wilamowitz 1913: 273 n. 3). Others have rejected the attribution to Semonides without being
willing to grant it to Simonides; e.g., Fränkel 1962: 237 n. 14, who suggests that the poem comes from a grave
epigram which like many another was attributed to the poet of Ceos. For a brief review of the controversy,
cf. Lloyd-Jones 1975: 97 (who tends to agree with Fränkel), West 1974: 179f. All arguments up until the present have been based on subjective criteria of style, which are all the more unreliable given the small sam-
pling of elegy on which to base a judgment. Davison 1955: 130 was properly cautious when he said that
scholars should not deny the poem to Simonides "until we are much better informed than we are at present about the style of Simonides' elegies." Oates's (1932: 84–90) marshalling of the external evidence
demonstrates that Simonidean authorship should never have been doubted.

7. Text in the testimony to Semonides in West *IEG*. It should be pointed out, however, that a first-century
B.C.E. papyrus of Philodemus refers to the iambographer as Σημωνίδης: *De poet.* Tr.C, *PHerc* 1074 fr. f, col.
III.5 ed. Sbordone. An error of ioticism, although not totally impossible, is nonetheless unlikely, as in his
survey of scribal errors in the Herculaneum papyri Crönert 1903 nowhere records alteration of iota and
eta. When, moreover, Philodemus refers to the Kean the papyri have Σιμ-. This strongly suggests that
Choeroboscus' distinction is a real one, and that in the pre-ioticist texts available to the Alexandrians (and
to Philodemus) the two authors were easily and correctly kept distinct.

8. Cf. Severyns 1938: 118; although *LGPN* 1–3 records several epigraphic instances of the name Σημωνίδης.
(An unmistakable error on Stobaeus' part occurs when he ascribes Simon. 582 *PMG* to Athenodorus; 3.33.5;
cf. Hense 1916: 2566.)

9. S: Vindob. cod. philos. et philol. gr. lxvii, saec. xi ineuntis. **M**: Escurial. LXXXX (Σ II 14), cod. Mendozae,
saec. xii ineuntis. **A**: Paris. cod. gr. 1984 saec. xiv. Cf. Wachsmuth 1884: vol. I, pp. xxx–xxxi; Hense 1916:
2550–54; Lello-Finuoli 1967. For a stemma, see *IEG* I.x.

could have been made of this earlier because S and MA often diverge from each other (M and A rarely do). In particular, they frequently differ in their lemmata (with either S or MA lacking the proper heading). And either S or MA occasionally lacks passages found in the other. (A third frequent type of divergence, when their selections are found in a different order, does not concern us here.) Given this state of the manuscripts, it was thus not only safe but also reasonable for editors to follow S and print its reading as one poem, or at any rate a continuous selection, from Simonides—as did all editors until West in his second edition.

What, then, is the relationship between **X** and **Y**? Several possibilities suggest themselves. The first, and most obvious, is that **X** and **Y** derive from the same poem of Simonides and were excerpted in this order, each selection originally having had its own heading, or lemma. The first heading would be the one we have, Σιμωνίδου, "by Simonides." The second, in accord with Stobaeus' usual practice, would have been ἐν τῷ αὐτῷ, "in the same (work)."[10] That is, according to this reconstruction, the exemplar for SMA had (i) Σιμωνίδου followed by **X**; and (ii) ἐν τῷ αὐτῷ followed by **Y**. Thereafter, in the MA family the eye of the scribe would have jumped from the first lemma to the text following the next lemma; whereas in S the second heading dropped out, with the result that two passages were run together as one.

Each of the steps I have outlined has parallels and near parallels elsewhere in Stobaeus. For example, Stob. 4.8.4, where, after the lemma Εὐριπίδου Ἠλέκτρα, SMA offer two unknown verses (= Eur. fr. 850 N^2). If, as is likely, these two lines are also Euripidean (as are the three previous selections and the two following), this would be another passage in Stobaeus (this time in the common exemplar for SMA) where the scribe jumped from a lemma to the text following the next lemma. Or consider Stob. 4.10.20–21, where in SMA the one lemma τοῦ αὐτοῦ (sc. Εὐριπίδου) Ἀνδρομάχης is followed by two verses from the *Andromache* (764f.) plus two unknown iambic verses (= Adesp. 537 *TrGF*). Here we have a parallel for two distinct texts run together under one heading after the second lemma (perhaps Εὐριπίδου—Hense suspects that the lines come from Euripides' *Andromeda*) was lost.[11]

---

10. It will be useful to have before us the standard types of lemmata found in Stobaeus (and in similar collections). The author's name appears in the genitive (far less often in the nominative), either alone or accompanied by the work (or type of work = book; e.g., Προσωδίων), which is given (i) in the dative (with or without ἐν), (ii) in the genitive (with or without ἐκ/ἐξ), or (iii) (least often) in the nominative. When two or more successive selections are from a different work of the same author, the second (and any following) lemma either repeats the author's name or is τοῦ αὐτοῦ, along with the name of the work (e.g., τοῦ αὐτοῦ Δικτύι). It should also be noted that even when S and MA agree on the author and work they do not always agree on the details of identification as given above; Hense 1916: 2565–67.

11. In looking for typical errors of the sort we seem to have in the Simonides passage, I have, for reasons of time, limited myself to the poetic passages in book 4. A wider search could well turn up even more interesting parallels. Cf. also 4.4.3–4, 7.8–9, 8.10–13, 9.4–5, 13.1–2. For a survey of typical scribal errors in Stobaeus (similar to Douglas Young's surveys of the MSS of Pindar and Aeschylus, and hence not helpful for this article), see Hernández Muñoz 1989. As in the *Greek Anthology*, errors of attribution arise and multiply as passages are copied from one anthology to another; for Euripides, cf. Zuntz 1972: 44–46, Guerrini 1970–71, Luppe 1988. Note also that Bowra 1958: 231–40 (following Wil.) argues that Stob. 1.5.12 Εὐριπίδου Πηλεῖ (620 N^2), a lyric prayer to the Fates, was in fact written by Simonides. Page, however, disagrees: see 1018 *PMG*.

But for a closer parallel to the state of the manuscripts in the Simonides selection(s), consider the way S and MA diverge in quoting from a text we can control: Bacchylides.

Stob. 4.34 (περὶ τοῦ βίου, ὅτι βραχὺς καὶ εὐτελὴς καὶ φροντίδων
        ἀνάμεστος)[12]

23   Σόλωνος (SMA)
        οὐδὲ μάκαρ οὐδεὶς πέλεται βροτός, ἀλλὰ πονηνοὶ
        πάντες ὅσους θνητοὺς ἥλιος καθορᾷ.

24   Βακχυλίδου Προσοδίων (MA)
        πάντεσσι θνατοῖσι δαίμων ἐπέταξε πόνους ἄλλοισιν
        ἄλλους. (SMA) [fr. 13 Sn.]

25   Τοῦ αὐτοῦ (SMA) Ἐπινίκων (MA)
        οὐ γάρ τις ἐπιχθονίων πάντα γ᾽ εὐδαίμων ἔφυ. (SMA) [5.54]

26   Ἐν ταὐτῷ (MA)
        θνατοῖσι μὴ φῦναι φέριστον, μηδ᾽ ἀελίου προσιδεῖν φέγγος
        [5.160],
        ὄλβιος δ᾽ οὐδεὶς βροτῶν πάντα χρόνον [fr. 54] (SMA)[13]

That is, manuscript S, by omitting the lemma for selection 24, runs it together quite impossibly with the previous selection, an elegiac couplet of Solon (14 W); and, more interestingly for our purposes, it identifies Solon as the author of 25; finally, S runs together Bacchylides 5.54 and 5.160 under one heading as if they were continuous. (MA keep the two verses distinct.) And S and MA together add to 5.160 another (probably Bacchylidean) tag as though it followed immediately, which, as the papyrus of Bacchylides shows, it most definitely does not. Clearly another heading before ὄλβιος κ.τ.λ., probably τοῦ αὐτοῦ, was missing in the exemplar of SMA.

These selections from Bacchylides also raise the possibility that **X** and **Y** may come from two separate poems of Simonides. The second lemma, that is, could have been τοῦ αὐτοῦ. Perhaps we can discount this possibility on the grounds that it is unlikely that Stobaeus would have collated selections from two poems, each of which mentioned Homer and the shortness of human life (cf. fr. 20.14 W² Ὅμηρ[ος]). (Below we shall briefly consider the relationship between frr. 19 + 20 W² and fr. 11 W².)

---

12. Each chapter in Stobaeus gathers passages illustrative of a particular *topos*. Some others from book 4 are: περὶ ναυτιλίας καὶ ναυαγίου (17), περὶ δεσποτῶν καὶ δούλων (19), γαμικὰ ἀγγέλματα (23), περὶ τῶν παρ᾽ ἀξίαν εὐτυχούντων (43).

13. Somewhat similar is Stob. 4.1.2–3, where, although in SMA the lemma Εὐριπίδου Φαέθοντι is followed by six verses, the fragmentary codex Claromontanus, containing the beginnings of the last three of these lines, shows that they were not preceded by the first three. Cf. Diggle 1970: 33f., 60f. Similarly, Menander *Kybernetai* 301 Kock, assigned to Menander by Stob. 3.22.19 (S, om. MA), lost the last four of its eleven lines (the seven remaining now = Menander *Kybernetai* fr. 218 K–A) when the papyrus of the *Dyskolos* showed that they belonged there (= vv. 284–87). A similar question, as yet unresolved by a papyrus find, concerns the sixteen lines that Stob. 4.53.6–7 assigns to Menander's *Hypobolimaios*: is it one fragment (fr. 481 Kock) or two, and if from two are they from the same play (frr. 416a + b Sandbach) or from different ones (frr. 373 and 871 K–A)? Cf. Zuntz 1956, Gomme and Sandbach 1973: 707f.

On Stobaeus as a source of Presocratic passages, see now Laks 1997: 240–62 and Mansfeld and Runia 1997: 196–271.

Moreover, since both **X** and **Y** seem to have been written in response to Mimnermus (see below), it would be neater to imagine that they came from but one poem. This same consideration also rules out any suggestion that (although possible in terms of the mechanical errors found in the manuscripts of Stobaeus) **X** was written by a poet other than Simonides.

There is a third possible relationship between **X** and **Y**; that they come from the same poem, but in reverse order, as has been suggested by West.[14] This cannot be disproved, for in some few places elsewhere, where we can control the text, Stobaeus does indeed invert the order. At 4.29.36–37, for example, he quotes Eur. *El.* 550f. immediately before 369f. and at 4.6.1–2 he quotes *Il.* 2.204f. before 196f.[15] West bases his argument in large part on his own reconstruction of the lines following **Y**, which suggest to him that **X** would better follow than precede. But it is surely risky, if not methodologically questionable, to derive a sense of how the poem (whose overall length we do not know) might have gone on the basis of one extract, and then on the basis of the two extracts to decide that their position should be altered; all the more risky since Stobaeus more often keeps to the correct order.

We conclude, therefore, that Simonides 19 and 20 W² derive, in this order, from but one poem of Simonides. Stobaeus, as he did with the Bacchylides excerpts and elsewhere, extracted from a longer poem only those lines illustrative of his current rubric. As Hense 1916: 2584 has shown, he also omits or even alters personal names in the vocative or first-person references in order to enhance the general or gnomic nature of the selection. Our Simonides extracts, for example, appear under the rubric περὶ τοῦ βίου, ὅτι βραχὺς καὶ εὐτελὴς καὶ φροντίδων ἀνάμεστος, which may be loosely translated as "life is solitary, poor, nasty, brutish, and short." Stobaeus omitted, it seems, a passage in which something is said to "abide" (20.4, παρμεν.[, which can only come from παραμένω). The previous line, which is reasonably restored τυτ]θὸν ἐπὶ χρό[νον, may be part of a contrasting thought or, if part of the same clause, may have been negated. That is, while one may say that something remains for a short time (using μένω), παραμένω, which means "last a long time," sits ill with the phrase "for a short time." Moreover, it is hard to see why Stobaeus would omit this couplet if it too spoke of things lasting but a short time. One reason could be that it is something other than human life—his rubric—that does not last long. Thus Stobaeus has done more than select, he has, no doubt unintentionally, produced in effect a new poem—and not a bad one—on the shortness of human life. Only the fact

---

14. West 1993a: 10f., who credits Parsons 1992a: 43 with having first put forward this idea, although all the latter says is, "It is tempting to think that MA represent the original extract, S a secondary conflation of two extracts on similar themes," without specifying where he thinks **X** came from. More tersely on p. 6, Parsons says "the new context shows that lines 1–5 of the [Stobaean] quotation did not originally belong." Gigante 1994: 61 agrees with West.

15. Similarly, *Il.* 21.463–66 and 17.466f. are quoted out of order at 4.34.46f. Diggle 1970 (see above, n. 13) reconstructs Euripides' *Phaethon* so that Stob. 4.1.3 precedes 4.1.2. (Although he discusses the readings of Stobaeus' text in detail, Diggle does not justify having inverted Stobaeus' order.) There are also cases of Stobaeus' quoting Theognis out of manuscript order, but the Theognidean corpus, clearly not a continuous work, invites this kind of disruption. Furthermore, Stobaeus' source for Theognis probably contained the separate poems in another order; cf. Groningen 1966: 443–45.

that it begins with the pentameter line could have signaled its incompleteness (see above).

In other words, Simonides' reference to the shortness of human life was probably set in a larger context where it was contrasted with something else that *does* last. The contrast begins with φράζευ δέ, "but consider" (20.13), and must carry over at least to the next line which says that Homer escaped something having to do with γλῶσσα, his words. West's reconstruction of v. 14, ἢ λήθην] γλώσσης ἔκφυγ᾿ Ὁμηρ[ος, is not compelling, and his restoration of πανδαμάτωρ for the next line, attractive as it is for his and my understanding of the overall sense, cannot stand up to close scrutiny of the papyrus.[16] Nonetheless, what little we can read does suggest that Homer, that is, his poetry, provides the desired contrast with ephemeral human life. We can probably go further and suggest that Simonides, not satisfied with granting this power to Homer alone, claimed, implicitly or explicitly, some of this for himself; that is, his poems too will continue to be sung during festive occasions (20.17).

Mimnermus

Whether or not this self-comparison with Homer is itself embedded in a larger context (see below), it should not be forgotten that Simonides succeeds another poet who recalls the generation of leaves simile: Mimnermus 2 W:

> ἡμεῖς δ᾿, οἷά τε φύλλα φύει πολυάνθεμος ὥρη
>   ἔαρος, ὅτ᾿ αἶψ᾿ αὐγῆς αὔξεται ἠελίου,
> τοῖς ἴκελοι πήχυιον ἐπὶ χρόνον ἄνθεσιν ἥβης
>   τερπόμεθα, πρὸς θεῶν εἰδότες οὔτε κακὸν
> οὔτ᾿ ἀγαθόν· Κῆρες δὲ παρεστήκασι μέλαιναι,
>   ἡ μὲν ἔχουσα τέλος γήραος ἀργαλέου,
> ἡ δ᾿ ἑτέρη θανάτοιο· μίνυνθα δὲ γίνεται ἥβης
>   καρπός, ὅσον τ᾿ ἐπὶ γῆν κίδναται ἠέλιος.
> αὐτὰρ ἐπὴν δὴ τοῦτο τέλος παραμείψεται ὥρης,
>   αὐτίκα δὴ τεθνάναι βέλτιον ἢ βίοτος.
> πολλὰ γὰρ ἐν θυμῷ κακὰ γίνεται· ἄλλοτε οἶκος
>   τρυχοῦται, πενίης δ᾿ ἔργ᾿ ὀδυνηρὰ πέλει·
> ἄλλος δ᾿ αὖ παίδων ἐπιδεύεται, ὧν τε μάλιστα
>   ἱμείρων κατὰ γῆς ἔρχεται εἰς Ἀίδην·
> ἄλλος νοῦσον ἔχει θυμοφθόρον· οὐδέ τίς ἐστιν
>   ἀνθρώπων ᾧ Ζεὺς μὴ κακὰ πολλὰ διδοῖ.

Just as the flowery season of spring gives birth to leaves as soon it grows in the rays of the sun, so we, like them, delight for a short time in the bloom of youth, knowing

---

16. This was first pointed out by Haslam 1993: 135. Cf. West's translation of these lines: "Ponder the [saying of a man] of old—for Homer's tongue's escaped [oblivion;] all conquering Time has spared him, never dimmed his name, and never found his testimony] false . . . in festivity . . . well-turned [arguments (?)]" (West 1993b: 171). Apart from πανδαμάτωρ being ruled out by the tracings, I doubt that Simonides would have repeated the adjective with χρόνος; cf. Simonides 531.5 *PMG*, printed below. (Bacchylides 13.205 also has πανδαμάτωρ χρόνος; Homer limits the adjective to ὕπνος.)

nothing, neither good nor ill, from the gods. But black Cares stand alongside, one holding forth an end of painful old age, the other that of death. The fruit of youth is brief, the length of one day's sun spreading itself over the earth. But the moment youth passes, right then death is better than life, because many evils fall to our spirits: One household may be consumed and the pains of poverty befall its land. Another man is without heirs; desiring them more than anything he passes to Hades. Another has an illness that eats at his spirit. There is nobody to whom Zeus does not give many ills.

Since this passage is transmitted by Stobaeus, indeed in 4.34, the same chapter on the worthlessness of human life to include the Simonides poem, it may well be that it too has been wrenched from a larger, and no longer recoverable, context.[17] More sure, however, is the likelihood that Simonides alludes to this poem as he does to Homer.[18] This was argued by Hubbard 1994 (who, however, argues for Semonidean authorship), in part because "Semonides' [*sic*] παῦροί μιν θνητῶν οὔασι δεξάμενοι | στέρνοις ἐγκατέθεντο (lines 3–4) clearly implies that the Homeric line he has just quoted is a tag frequently heard and bandied about, but seldom understood in its full implications" (p. 192). That Simonides responds to Mimnermus now receives further support from *POxy* 3965's [τυτ]θὸν ἐπὶ χρό[νον], which recalls Mimnermus' πήχυιον ἐπὶ χρόνον.

Mimnermus, and indeed everybody who compares men to leaves, rings changes on the Homeric model. Where Glaukos dispassionately describes the passing away of one generation to make room for the next, Mimnermus rather gloomily focuses on the withering and death half of the simile: not even the memory of youth can bring joy to an old man; rather, even youth is spoiled, at least in retrospect, because of its brief span and its nescience of what is to come. "Nothing lasts," while not explicitly stated by Mimnermus, is easily inferred. Simonides' use of the verb παραμένειν is far more easily seen as response to Mimnermus' than to Homer's use of the simile.[19] And

17. With Mimnermus cf. Job 14: 7–14, [Moschos] 3.99–104. West 1992 in his app. crit. suggests that this passage "paullo post [Mimnermi] fr. 12 locare possis," but this latter poem on the daily voyage of the sun does not seem to me to fit well with fr. 2. Far closer in thought and language are frr. 1 (τίς δὲ βίος) and 3–7. The differences between Homer and Mimnermus that are detailed below lead Allen 1993: 41 to doubt whether Mimnermus intends a Homeric allusion; similarly Fowler 1987: 32f., Lardinois 1995: 234–36. I disagree with Allen and Fowler but without further argument, since for my purposes it will be enough to show that Simonides thought that Mimnermus was alluding to Homer (which may in fact be taken as an argument that this is indeed what Mimnermus was doing). Ably arguing that Mimnermus here and elsewhere was indeed alluding to Homer is D'Ippolito 1993. In particular, he calls attention (p. 296) to the fact that the two Keres mentioned on vv. 5ff. are modeled on the διχθαδίας Κῆρας of Achilles (Il. 9.411; see below, n. 19), with the important difference that Mimnermus does not want to be cut down in the flower of his youth but only after it is complete and the fun is over. D'Ippolito calls this kind of variation a *trascodificazione* (p. 294), but Simonides might have called it a banalization.

18. When it could be argued that it was Semonides rather than Simonides who wrote the poem, the possibility existed that Mimnermus wrote afterwards and in response to the former; so, e.g., Babut 1971. See further Hubbard in this volume, Allen 1993: 41f.

19. Although of course all but explicit in Homer is that the ὕλη, the "stock" of mankind endures, a point well brought out by Morpurgo 1927, whose article, although it gives short shrift to Simonides, offers a use-

Homer, as was suggested above, provides a counter-example to Mimnermus in that poetry (Homer's if not Mimnermus') can not only itself last, it can provide a kind of immortality to its heroes. Mimnermus' poem having no heroes, there is nothing for the poet to record for later ages. Simonides' version thus rejects Mimnermus and returns to Homer for a more positive message.

Nor would this be the only time Simonides alludes to Mimnermus, as Mimn. 1 W τίς δὲ βίος, τί δὲ τερπνὸν, ἄτερ χρυσῆς 'Αφροδίτης; clearly lies behind Simonides 584 PMG τίς γὰρ ἀδονᾶς ἄτερ θνατῶν βίος ποθεινὸς ἢ ποία τυραννίς; τᾶσδε ἄτερ οὐδὲ θεῶν ζηλωτὸς αἰών. Since Athenaeus, who cites this passage, gives full credit to Simonides for the thought, there was presumably no overt mention of Mimnermus in this poems, but the allusion, which seems obvious to us, may have escaped Athenaeus' notice.[20] It should also be noted that Simonides clearly echoes and often openly names other predecessors:[21] (i) Pittacus in 542 PMG; note especially 11ff. οὐδέ μοι ἐμμελέως τὸ Πιττάκειον | νέμεται, καίτοι σοφοῦ παρὰ φωτὸς εἰρημένον· χαλεπὸν φάτ᾽ ἐσθλὸν ἔμμεναι; (ii) Stesichorus and Homer are named in Simonides' Europa (564 PMG). Verses 1–3 are a variation of Stesichorus' The Funeral Games of Pelias (cf. Stes. 179 PMG); v. 4 οὕτω γὰρ "Ομηρος ἠδὲ Στασίχορος ἄεισε λαοῖς; (iii) Hesiod WD 289–92 on the difficulty of obtaining arete is alluded to in 579 PMG ἔστι τις λόγος | τὰν 'Αρετὰν ναίειν δυσαμβάτοισ᾽ ἐπὶ πέτραις, κ.τ.λ.; (iv) Kleoboulos' infamous Midas epigram comes in for criticism in 581 PMG τίς κεν αἰνήσειε νόῳ πίσυνος Λίνδου ναέταν Κλεόβουλον . . . μωροῦ | φωτὸς ἄδε βουλά; (v) Schol. Pind. Ol. 13.31 καὶ Αἴσων, οὗ μέμνηται Σ., where μνήσεται must mean "names."[22]

There can be no doubt, therefore, that in his own poem (frr. 19–20 W²) Simonides sets Homer against Mimnermus, aligning himself with the former. This pugnacious poet of intertextuality[23] disagrees with Mimnermus' use of only half of the leaves simile (there is no replacement of leaves in Mimnermus), arguing that there are indeed things that endure: there are, for example, and in direct contradiction to Mimnermus, delights for the soul even when one is old. And, as the scrappy reference

---

ful brief survey of the generation-of-leaves topos. On Mimnermus, see also Griffith 1975 and Garner 1990: 3–8, who notes that vv. 5–7 allude to the passage where Achilles speaks of his double fate (9.410f.):

μήτηρ γάρ τέ μέ φησι θεὰ Θέτις ἀργυρόπεζα
διχθαδίας κῆρας φερέμεν θανάτοιο τέλοσδε.

20. And we should note in this context that Simonides is credited with having twice compared Homer and Hesiod: (i) Gnom. Vat. 514 Sternbach = T 47(j) Campbell Ἡσίοδον μὲν αἱ Μοῦσαι, "Ομηρον δὲ αἱ Χάριτες ἐτέκνωσαν, and (ii) App. Vat. 217 Sternbach = T 47(k) Campbell Σιμωνίδης τὸν Ἡσίοδον κηπουρὸν ἔλεγε, τὸν δὲ "Ομηρον στεφανηπλόκον, τὸν μὲν ὡς φυτεύσαντα τὰς περὶ θεῶν καὶ ἡρώων μυθολογίας, τὸν δὲ ὡς ἐξ αὐτῶν συμπλέξαντα τὸν 'Ιλιάδος καὶ 'Οδυσσείας στέφανον. These are most likely the usual biographical falsehoods laid bare for us by Lefkowitz 1981 (pp. 49–56 on Simonides), but hiding behind them may be a passage in Simonides' poetry where his two predecessors were more artfully set alongside one another.

21. And in 89 W² he names himself (for his mnemonic powers).

22. Fr. 215 Bergk. Since Aison is otherwise unknown, Bergk would read Κιναίσων, i.e., Κιναίθων for καὶ Αἴσων, but the precise name is irrelevant for my immediate purpose; cf. Poltera 1997:578.

23. For discussion of intertextuality in classical poetry, cf. Conte 1986: 23–31, Bonanno 1990: 11–40. Weber 1955: 65 also uses Simonides' habit of citing others as evidence to suggest that he was the author of the leaves elegy.

after **Y** to Homer and feasts allows us to infer, one of these delights may be listening to the accounts of heroes, Homer's account and perhaps Simonides' as well. The retelling of these stories, in turn, grants to Diomedes, Glaukos, and others an enduring glory beyond their own mortal lives. As Sarpedon says to Glaukos, through their battle prowess they attain a near divine status as their glory is proclaimed during feasts in Lycia (ἕδρη τε κρέασίν τε ἰδὲ πλείοις δεπάεσσιν, *Il.* 12.311; cf. Simon. fr. 20.17 ἐν θαλίῃσι). Sarpedon, it is true, says nothing here about the glory of heroes continuing after death, but Helen does, using the same adjective ἀοίδιμος which Simonides does at fr. 11.13.[24] Cf. also Simon. 531 *PMG*:

> τῶν ἐν Θερμοπύλαις θανόντων
> εὐκλεὴς μὲν ἁ τύχα, καλὸς δ' ὁ πότμος,
> βωμὸς δ' ὁ τάφος, πρὸ γόων δὲ μνᾶστις, ὁ δ'
>   οἶκτος ἔπαινος·
> ἐντάφιον δὲ τοιοῦτον εὐρὼς
> οὔθ' ὁ πανδαμάτωρ ἀμαυρώσει χρόνος.

Moreover, by quoting rather than paraphrasing a line from the generation of leaves simile, Simonides illustrates not only that the glory of heroes endures but also that the poetry that details their bravery does as well. Or, more to the point, the immortality of heroes is entailed in the immortality of the poems narrating their deeds. Men's *doxa* does not die with them; rather, it ἔσχατον δύεται κατὰ γᾶς (Simon. 594 *PMG*).[25]

Horace

Simonides and Mimnermus were followed by others who allude to and ring changes on Homer's simile; most can be dealt with briefly in the appendix, but the papyrus now shows us that Horace's use of this simile is more complex and interesting than we could have known from Stobaeus' citation alone. In addition to *Ode* 4.7 (*Diffugere nives*), which subtly brings to mind both the change of seasons implied in Homer's simile and man's ignorance of the future as found in Simonides,[26] Horace's *Ars Poetica* quite overtly echoes Homer's leaf simile. Placed within the relevant context, it is as follows:

> et nova fictaque nuper habebunt verba fidem, si
> Graeco fonte cadent parce detorta. quid autem

---

24. Cf. Lloyd-Jones 1994: 1.

25. On this frequently discussed *topos*, see now Suarez de la Torre 1998.

26. Cf. Cataudella 1927–28, who compares *Ol.* 4.7.19f. "cuncta manus avidas fugient heredis amico quae dederis animo" with the last line of Stobaeus' selection; Oates 1932: 76–90. Oates's survey of Simonides' influence on Horace remains essential, but see also Bonanno 1990 passim (see her index), Gigante 1994, Barchiesi 1996 and in this volume, Harrison in this volume. Among earlier works, cf. Arnold 1891: 101f., Christ 1941: 40–45. Furthermore, in addition to the individual passages discussed by these authors, Horace's practice of beginning poems with "mottoes" taken from earlier poets may also reflect Simonidean influence, although it can also be found in Theocritus 29 and Catullus 56; cf. Norden 1909: 371, Conte 1986: 25.

Caecilio Plautoque dabit Romanus ademptum
Vergilio Varioque? ego cur, acquirere pauca
si possum, invideor, cum lingua Catonis et Enni
sermonem patrium ditaverit et nova rerum
nomina protulerit? licuit semperque licebit
signatum praesente nota producere nomen.
Ut silvae foliis pronos[27] *mutantur in annos,*
prima cadunt: ita verborum vetus interit aetas,
et iuvenum ritu florent modo nata vigentque.
debemur morti nos nostraque.

(vv. 52–63)

mortalia facta peribunt,
nedum sermonum stet honos et gratia vivax.
multa renascentur quae iam cecidere, cadentque
quae nunc sunt in honore vocabula, si volet usus,
quem penes arbitrium est et ius et norma loquendi.

(vv. 68–72)

Brink 1971: 147, as well as other commentators, has compared Horace directly to Homer, adducing Simonides, Mimnermus, and others solely as parallels. Note, though, that Horace uses the simile to compare the generation of leaves, not, as Homer does, to that of men, but, rather, to the age/generation of words. A closer rendering of Homer would not of course be appropriate to the context of the *Ars Poetica*; whereas words, especially the words allowed or disallowed to the poet, are the particular subject of this didactic poem. Horace, it appears, wants the poet to be able to say something new while maintaining the good taste appropriate to art. A prudent use of new words, drawn from a *Graecus fons*, should be permitted, just as it was to his predecessors Caecilius, Plautus, Cato, and Ennius. The old, in other words, supplies the new.

Now, in illustration comes our simile, which quite clearly derives from a Greek *fons*, but which, equally clearly, is employed to make a different point. For it is not merely the "stock" of mankind that lasts through the generations, but also the living and mutating *usus* of language (v. 72): the older generation of words passes away like that of leaves; newer words take their place like the young of humans. Thus, Horace's complex simile, which interjects a comparison with leaves into that of leaves and men, differs from Homer's original. It thus not only describes, it also illustrates Horace's general point in this passage about the prudent modification of Greek examples.

But Horace's adaptation of Homer to the realm of poetry, as we now see in the papyrus, is not altogether new. Simonides too contrasted the generation of leaves with, it seems, the permanence of poetry. But, as Horace goes on immediately to say, "we and all that we have owe a debt to death," "debemur morti nos nostraque" (v. 63). In *his* adaptation of the leaves simile, Horace thus presents us with an oblique criticism of Simonides' adaptation; and he signals this by directly translating a phrase

---

27. Brink 1971: 149 does not convince me that *pronos* is corrupt. It appears, rather, to be an extension of the word's application to heavenly markers of passing time such as the sun (or day) or season-marking constellations like Orion (*OLD* s.v. 5b). The years, that is, fall to earth like leaves.

from an epigram that he knew under Simonides' name: θανάτῳ πάντες ὀφειλόμεθα.[28] As Brink 1971: 150 points out, of the several possible parallels for "owing" something to death, only Simonides has the first person plural—to which Horace adds "nostraque" in an "adroit zeugma," which "extends the comparison from man to his works" (Brink 1971: 150). Horace thus signals both his debt to and his difference from Simonides. "Nedum sermonum stet honos et gratia vivax" (*AP* 69): no poem is immortal. And, more to Horace's immediate point, his application of Simonides' application of Homer's simile of leaves fits perfectly into Horace's context as he exemplifies his teachings about the way a Latin author should use his Greek predecessors.[29] A further but not unwelcome complication: Since Simonides, as we have seen, in alluding to the line from Homer, criticizes Mimnermos for *his* allusion to the generation of leaves simile, Horace would thus be setting himself in the family of poets who trace their family tree back to Homer. To put this another way, Horace all but declares that he himself, Simonides, and the Latin poets he names in this passage (and doubtless others as well) cannot be understood fully unless one recognizes the precise poetic tradition in which they have placed themselves.

Simonides

One final question: what kind of poem did Simonides write? If there was not much more than we have in frr. 19–20, West may be correct to regard it as a sympotic elegy. But the similarities between the leaves poem and *Elegy* 11, the Plataea elegy, namely, the references both to man's mortality and the immortality granted by Homer to the heroes who had died in battle, allow for the possibility that the passage containing the leaves simile, which makes this same point, also was part of this battle elegy. Despite the excellent arguments for public performance brought forward by Aloni (1994 and in this volume) and by Boedeker (1995b and "Heroization" in this volume), perhaps we should not absolutely rule out the possibility of sympotic performance. Just as frr. 10–11 have presented us with a new mix of genres (see Obbink in this volume, esp. at n. 27), we should allow, at least at this early stage of our understanding of the new material, that a long poem performed either in private or in public could praise warriors and their poets, and then (after who knows what else) pass on to criticism of poets who have failed to understand the value of this kind of poetry (namely,

---

28. "Simonides" *Epigram* 79 *FGE*; *AP* 10.105 Σιμωνίδου, Pl ἄδηλον. Page may be right in denying authorship to Simonides, but all that is necessary for my purpose is that Horace saw the epigram under his name either in a *Sylloge Simonidea* (there may have been more than one) or in Meleager's *Stephanos*; cf. Page 1981: 119–23; Cameron 19931–2, 270–72. (The collection of epigrams ascribed to Simonides contains what may be a four-line excerpt from one of his battle elegies: *Epigram* 19(a) *FGE*.)

    Similarly, Wilamowitz 1893, modified by Oates 1932: 63f., argues for an influence on Horace *Odes* 1.28 of "Simonides" *Epigram* 67 *FGE*.

29. One further, unrelated, Simonidean allusion in the *Ars*: "ut pictura poesis" (361); cf. Plut. *Mor.* 346f. (= T 47(b) Campbell). Less certain: in his survey of the various genres of Greek poetry, Horace categorizes the epinicia by contest, "et pugilem victorem et equuum certamine primum" (84), which is how the Alexandrians arranged those of Simonides, unlike the two other famous writers of epinicia, Pindar and Bacchylides. I owe this observation to Alessandro Barchiesi. See further, Obbink, this volume at n. 40.

Mimnermus). And if Homer could insert the leaves simile into a battle narrative, so too (as Deborah Boedeker observes) could Simonides, who clearly puts himself forward as Homer *redivivus*. Furthermore, if frr. 19–20 belong to the Plataea poem, Theocritus' allusion to Simonides' alluding in fr. 11 to Homer would be echoed by Horace's allusion to this same poem of Simonides, again where he alludes to Homer on the immortality granted by poetry.[30] Horace's allusion to and use of his predecessors accordingly becomes all the more complex.

We have seen that Simonides actually names writers with whom he disagrees, Pittacus and Kleoboulos (and perhaps Hesiod). It does not seem unreasonable that here he not only names but also addresses Mimnermus, and that the second-person address of fr. 20.11–13 was clearly directed to him. Simonides would thus be closely following Solon, who also took Mimnermus to task for having prayed for death at age 60 (fr. 6 W). Rather, Solon says, addressing him by his patronymic in the second person (or so it seems; the text is not entirely secure: fr. 20.3–4 W),

> καὶ μεταποίησον Λιγιαστάδη, ὧδε δ' ἄειδε·
> "ὀγδωκονταέτη μοῖρα κίχοι θανάτου."[31]

Conceivably West is correct to supply Mimnermus' own words (ἑξηκονταέτη μοῖρα κίχοι θανάτου) in Solon's poem, which would make the parallel with Simon. frr. 19–20 even closer.[32] Simonides goes further than Solon, however, in criticizing not only Mimnermus' poems concerning old age and death,[33] but also his very understanding of the nature and power of poetry, which has the power to transcend the mortality which so dejects Mimnermus, and hence to be a source of joy for those warriors and poets whose fame will outlive them.

APPENDIX

In addition to the passages in Homer, Mimnermus, Simonides, and Horace given in the course of this article, passages by the following poets also allude to Homer's

---

30. Theocr. 16.42–47 and Simon. 11.l1–14 W[2]; cf. Parsons 1992b: 10–13, Lloyd-Jones 1994: 2, Clay, Barchiesi, and Hunter in this volume, and Barchiesi 1996.

31. As Gerber 1997: 109 notes, Solon (too) may be addressing a Mimnermus who is no longer living. On the relationship in general between Solon's poem and Mimnermus', cf. Tuomi 1986, esp. 20–25, where he points out that a future indicative after κἂν νῦν (the reading of the MSS, which should be kept) is more modal than temporal and hence says nothing about the historical relationship between Mimnermus and Solon.

32. Note also Sappho fr. 137, where Sappho addresses Alcaeus about his hesitancy to speak of a shameful action. Aristotle quotes the fragment, prefacing it with Alcaeus' own words in such a way that it seems possible that Sappho incorporated his verses into her own poem. Page 1955: 107–9 considers only the possibilities that Alcaeus' poem, known to Sappho's audience, was altogether distinct from Sappho's poem, i.e., that Sappho would expect her audience to recall his lines; or that the words given Alcaeus were composed by Sappho as part of a poem in the form of a dialogue. In any case, we have one poet addressing and criticizing another, but not, perhaps, on the subject of the other's poetry.

Euenos thrice in his elegies addresss a Simonides who may well be our poet (West 1993a: 13f.), but these short passages do not allow us to see how the particular Simonides addressed is in any way relevant to the point being made (Euenos frr. 8a–c W = Theogn. 467–96, 667–82, 1341–50). See Rutherford in this volume at n. 87.

33. On Simonides' own old age, see Mace and Hunter in this volume.

simile. The accompanying bibliographical notes make no claim to be comprehensive. For references to this simile in prose, see Cribiore 1994.

A "Mousaios." According to Clem. *Strom.* 6.738, Homer "rewrites" (μεταγράφει) the following verses of Mousaios:

> ὡς δ' αὔτως καὶ φύλλα φύει ζείδωρος ἄρουρα·
> ἄλλα μὲν ἐν μελίῃσιν ἀποφθίνει, ἄλλα δὲ φύει·
> ὡς δὲ καὶ ἀνθρώπων γενεὴ καὶ φῦλον ἑλίσσει.
>
> (B 5 DK = A 2 Colli)

The rewriting of course goes the other way; cf. West 1983: 39–44.

B Pindar (i). *POxy* 32 (1967) 2622.12–13 = fr. 346 Sn.-M.

> αὐ]τίκα νιν φθιμένων [ψυχαί Lobel
>]τρέφεται καὶ ὅσ' ἐν πόντῳ [

Lloyd-Jones 1967: 206–29, esp. 215 (1990: ch. 11), following Lobel, argues that this fragment of Pindar, set in the Underworld, like the passages of Bacchylides (below, D) and Vergil (G), compared souls to leaves.

C Pindar (ii). *Ol.* 12.13–16.

> υἱὲ Φιλάνορος, ἤτοι καὶ τεά κεν
> ἐνδομάχας ἅτ' ἀλέκτωρ συγγόνῳ παρ' ἑστίᾳ
> ἀκλεὴς τιμὰ κατεφυλλορόησεν ποδῶν,
> εἰ μὴ στάσις ἀντιάνειρα Κνωσίας σ' ἄμερσε πάτρας.

Cf. Nisetich 1977: 235–64, esp. 259f.

D Bacchylides 5.63–67.

> ἔνθα δυστάνων βροτῶν
> ψυχὰς ἐδάη (sc. Ἡρακλῆς) παρὰ Κωκυτοῦ ῥεέθροις,
>   οἷά τε φύλλ' ἄνεμος
> Ἴδας ἀνὰ μηλοβότους
> πρῶνας ἀργηστὰς δονεῖ.

While maintaining Homer's comparison of souls to leaves, Bacchylides cleverly changes the emphasis from the impermanence of living leaves to the weightlessness and passivity of dead leaves buffeted by the wind. Cf. Lefkowitz 1969: 45–96, who notes that "Bacchylides' specific designation of the locale of his simile as 'sheep-nourishing hills of Ida' further brings to mind the scene of the *Iliad* and the beginnings in the mountains's quiet pastures of the Trojan War's destruction" (66).

E Empedocles B 17.3 DK.

> δοιὴ δὲ θνητῶν γένεσις, δοιὴ δ' ἀπόλειψις.

Cf. Obbink 1993: 85.

F Aristophanes *Birds* 685.

> ἄνδρες ἀμαυρόβιοι, φύλλων γενεᾷ προσόμοιοι.

This line begins an anapestic prelude within a choral ode whose structure Obbink (this volume, n. 15) compares to that of Simon. fr. 11 W².

G Vergil *Aeneid* 6.309f.

> quam multa in silvis autumni frigore primo
> lapsa cadunt folia.

As a reference to dead souls, this cannot help but recall Homer's simile, but Vergil assimilates it to the usually distinct image of the *multitude* of leaves, which is not a part of Glaukos' simile; cf., e.g., *Il.* 2.468 μυρίοι, ὅσσα τε φύλλα καὶ ἄνθεα γίγνεται ὥρῃ. Ap. Rhod. 4.216f. ἢ ὅσα φύλλα χαμᾶζε περικλαδέος πέσεν ὕλης | φυλλοχόῳ ἐνὶ μηνί.

Bibliography

TEXTS

Lobel, E., ed. 1954. "2327: Early Elegiacs." *The Oxyrhynchus Papyri* 22: 67–76.
———, ed. 1959a. "2434. Commentary on Lyric Verses. (?Simonides)." *The Oxyrhynchus Papyri* 24: 95–101.
———, ed. 1959b. "2431." *The Oxyrhynchus Papyri* 25: 87–91.
Lobel, E., et al., eds. 1948. "2225." *The Oxyrhynchus Papyri* 19: 68–69.
Parsons, P. J. 1992a. "3965: Simonides, Elegies." *The Oxyrhynchus Papyri* 59: 4–50.
　　Review: W. Luppe, *Gnomon* 68 (1996): 193–96.
West, M. L. 1972. *Iambi et Elegi Graeci*. Vol. II. Oxford.
———. 1992. *Iambi et Elegi Graeci*. 2d ed. Vol. II. Oxford.
　　Reviews: M. W. Haslam, *BMCR* 4 (1993): 131–35; J. H. Molyneux, *CR* 44 (1994): 201; G.Burzacchini, *Gnomon* 69 (1997): 193–98; S. R. Slings, *Mnemmosyne* 48 (1995): 466–69.

BOOKS AND ARTICLES

Adkins, A. 1972. "Truth, ΚΟΣΜΟΣ, and ΑΡΕΤΗ in the Homeric Poems." *CQ* 22: 5–18.
Ahlberg, G. 1971. *Prothesis and Ekphora in Greek Geometric Art*. Göteborg.
Aitchison, J. M. 1963. "Homeric ἄνθος." *Glotta* 41: 271–78.
Alexiou, M. 1974. *The Ritual Lament in Greek Tradition*. Cambridge.
———. 1991. "Literature and Popular Tradition." In D. Holton (ed.), *Literature and Society in Renaissance Crete*, 239–274. Cambridge.
Allen, A. 1993. *The Fragments of Mimnermus: Text and Commentary*. Palingenesia 44. Stuttgart.
Allen, T. W. 1934. "Theognis." *PBA* 20: 71–89.
Aloni, A. 1981. *Le muse di Archiloco: Ricerche sullo stile archilocheo*. Copenhagen.
———. 1990 (1992). "Proemio e funzione proemiale nella poesia greca arcaica." In *Lirica Greca e Latina: Atti del Convegno di Studi Polacco-Italiano, Poznan 2–5 maggio 1990 = AION* (Fil-Let) 12: 99–130.
———. 1994. "L'Elegia di Simonide dedicata alla battaglia di Platea (Sim. frr.10–18 W^2) e l'occasione della sua performance." *ZPE* 102: 9–22.
Amandry, P. 1971. "Collection Paul Canellopoulos (I)." *BCH* 95: 585–626.
Ambühl, A. 1995. "Callimachus and the Arcadian Asses: The Aitia Prologue and a Lemma in the London Scholion." *ZPE* 105: 209–13.

Anderson, G. 1986. *Philostratus*. London.

Anderson, R. D., P. J. Parsons, and R. G. M. Nisbet. 1979. "Elegiacs by Gallus from Qasr Ibrîm." *JRS* 69: 125–55.

Andrews, N. 1998. "Philosophical Satire in the *Aitia* Prologue." In M. A. Harder, R. F. Regtuit, and G. C. Wakker (eds.), *Genre in Hellenistic Poetry*, 1–19. Groningen.

Antonaccio, C. M. 1995. *An Archaeology of Ancestors. Tomb Cult and Hero Cult in Early Greece*. Lanham, Md.

Arnold, T. 1891. *Die griechische Studien des Horaz*. Halle a. S.

Asheri, D. 1988. *Erodoto, le Storie. Libro I: La Lidia e la Persia*. Milan.

Asper, M. 1997. *Onomata Allotria: Zur Genese, Struktur und Funktion poetologischer Metaphern bei Kallimachos*. Stuttgart.

Austin, N. 1967. "Idyll 16: Theocritus and Simonides." *TAPA* 98: 1–21. Repr. in B. Effe (ed.), *Theokrit und die griechische Bukolik*, 105–25. Darmstadt 1986.

Austin, R. G. 1964. *P. Vergili Maronis Aeneidos Liber Secundus*. Oxford.

Babut, D. 1971. "Sémonide et Mimnerme." *REG* 84: 17–43.

Badian, E. 1993. "Plataea between Athens and Sparta: In Search of Lost History." In E. Badian, *From Plataea to Potidaea: Studies in the History and Historiography of the Pentecontaetia*, 109–123. Baltimore.

———. 1996. "Alexander the Great Between Two Thrones and Heaven." In A. Small (ed.), *Subject and Ruler: The Cult of the Ruling Power in Classical Antiquity. Papers Presented at a Conference Held in the University of Alberta on April 13–15, 1994*, 11–26. Ann Arbor.

Bakker, E. 1993. "Discourse and Performance in Homeric Poetry." *CA* 12: 1–25.

Baldry, H. C. 1952. "Who Invented the Golden Age?" *CQ* 2: 83–92.

Barbantani, S. 1997. *L'elegia encomiastica in età ellenistica*. Diss. Milan.

Barchiesi, A. 1995. "Simonide e Orazio sulla morte di Achille." *ZPE* 107: 33–38. [An English version appears in this volume.]

———. 1996. "Poetry, Praise, and Patronage: Simonides in Book 4 of Horace's Odes." *CA* 15: 5–47.

Barigazzi, A. 1963. "Nuovi frammenti delle elegie di Simonide (*Ox. Pap.* 2327)." *MH* 20: 61–76.

Barrett, W. S. 1954. "Bacchylides, Asine and Apollo Pythaios." *Hermes* 82: 425–29.

———. 1964. *Euripides: Hippolytos*. Oxford.

———. 1978. "The Oligaithidai and Their Victories (Pindar, *Olympian* 13; SLG 339, 340)." In R. D. Dawe, J. Diggle, and P. E. Easterling (eds.), *Dionysiaca: Nine Studies in Greek Poetry Present to Sir Denys Page on his Seventieth Birthday*, 1–20. Cambridge.

Bartol, K. 1993. *Greek Elegy and Iambus: Studies in Ancient Literary Sources*. Poznań.

———. 1999a. "Between Loyalty and Treachery: *P.Oxy.* 2327 fr. 1 + 2(a) col. 1 = Simonides 21 West²—Some Reconsiderations." *ZPE* 126: 26–28.

———. 1999b. *Jambi i Elegia*. Vol. I of *Lyrika Grecka: Wybór Tekstów i Komentarz*, ed. J. Danielowicz. 2 vols. Warsaw.

Basta Donzelli, G. 1991. "La seconda giovinezza di Callimaco (fr. 1, 32 ss. Pf.)." In *Studi di filologia classica in onore di Giusto Monaco*, 387–94. Palermo.

Bearzot, C. 1997. "P.Oxy. 3985: Considerazioni sulla data e sull'ispirazione dell'elegia di Simonide per la battaglia di Platea." In B. Kramer et al. (eds.), *Akten der 21. internationalen Papyrologenkongresses Berlin 13.–19.8.1995*, 1: 71–79. Stuttgart.

Becker, O. 1937. *Das Bild des Weges*. Hermes Einzelschriften 4. Berlin.

Behr, C. A. 1981. *P. Aelius Aristides: The Complete Works*. Vol. II: *Orat. XVII–LIII*. Leiden.

Bengtson, H. 1951. "Themistokles und die delphische Amphiktyonie." *Eranos* 49: 85–92.

Bérard, C. 1982. "Récupérer la mort du prince: héroïsation et formation de la cité." In Gnoli and Vernant 1982: 89–105.

Bergk, T. 1882. *Poetae Lyrici Graeci*⁴. Vol. III. Leipzig.

Bernabé, A. 1987. *Poetarum Epicorum Graecorum. Testimonia et Fragmenta.* Pars I. Leipzig.

Bernsdorff, H. 1996. "Zu Simonides Fr. 22 West²." *ZPE* 114: 24–26.

Billot, M.-F. 1989–90. "Apollo Pythéen et l'Argolide archaïque: histoire et mythes." *Archaiognosia* 6: 35–100.

Bing, P. 1988a. *The Well-Read Muse: Present and Past in Callimachus and the Hellenistic Poets.* Hypomnemata 90. Göttingen.

———. 1988b. "Theocritus' Epigrams on the Statues of Ancient Poets." *A&A* 34: 117–23.

Block, E. 1982. "The Narrator Speaks: Apostrophe in Homer and Vergil." *TAPA* 112: 7–22.

Blome, P. 1984. "Lefkandi und Homer." *WJ* 10: 9–22.

Boardman, J. 1976. "The Kleophrades Painter at Troy." *AK* 19: 3–18.

———. 1990. "*Symposion* Furniture." In Murray 1990: 122–31.

Boedeker, D. 1987. "The Two Faces of Demaratus." In D. Boedeker (ed.), *Herodotus and the Invention of History = Arethusa* 20: 185–201.

———. 1988. "Protesilaos and the End of Herodotus' *Histories.*" *CA* 7: 30–48.

———. 1993. "Hero Cult and Politics: The Bones of Orestes." In Dougherty and Kurke 1993: 164–77.

———. 1995a. "Heroizing History: Simonides' Elegy on Plataea." In J. Papademetriou (ed.), *Proceedings of the First Annual Conference (May 1994) of the Hellenic Society for Humanistic Studies,* 121–135. Athens.

———. 1995b. "Simonides on Plataea: Narrative Elegy, Mythodic History." *ZPE* 107: 217–29.

———. 2000. "Herodotus' Genres." In Depew and Obbink 2000.

Boedeker, D., and D. Sider (eds.). 1996. *The New Simonides = Arethusa* 29: 2.

Boegehold, A. 1965. "The Salamis Epigram." *GRBS* 6: 179–86.

Boehringer, D. 1996. "Heroisierung historischer Persönlichkeiten." In Flashar, Gehrke, and Heinrich 1996: 37–61.

Bonanno, M. G. 1990. *L'allusione necessaria: Ricerche intertestuali sulla poesia greca e latina.* Rome.

Borgeaud, P. 1988. *The Cult of Pan in Ancient Greece.* Chicago.

Bousquet, J. 1992. "Les inscriptions gréco-lydiennes." In H. Metzger (ed.), *Fouilles de Xanthos* 9: 147–96. Paris.

Bowie, E. L. 1986. "Early Greek Elegy, Symposium and Public Festival." *JHS* 106: 13–35.

———. 1990. "*Miles Ludens?* The Problem of Martial Exhortation in Early Greek Elegy." In Murray 1990: 221–29.

———. 1993. "Lies, Fiction and Slander in Early Greek Poetry." In C. Gill and T. P. Wiseman (eds.), *Lies and Fiction in the Ancient World,* 1–37. Austin.

Bowra, C. M. 1934. "Simonides in the *Theognidea.*" *CR* 48: 2–4.

———. 1938. "The Epigram on the Fallen of Coronea." *CQ* 32: 80–88. Repr. in C. M. Bowra, *Problems in Greek Poetry.* Oxford 1953: 93–107.

———. 1958. "A Prayer to the Fates." *CQ* 52: 231–40.

———. 1961. *Greek Lyric Poetry: From Alcman to Simonides².* Oxford.

———. 1964. *Pindar.* Oxford.

Bremer, J. M. 1975. "The Meadow of Love and Two Passages in Euripides' *Hippolytus.*" *Mnemosyne* 28: 268–80.

Bremmer, J. (ed.). 1987. *Interpretations of Greek Mythology.* London.

Brillante, C. 2000. "Simonide, fr. eleg. 22 West²." *QUCC* n.s. 64: 29–38.

Brink, C. O. 1971. *Horace on Poetry: The "Ars Poetica."* Cambridge.

Broadhead, H. D. 1960. *The Persae of Aeschylus.* Cambridge.

Bundy, E. L. 1972. "The 'Quarrel Between Kallimachos and Apollonios,' Part 1: The Epilogue of Kallimachos's Hymn to Apollo." *CSCA* 5: 39–94.

Burkert, W. 1985. *Greek Religion.* Trans. by J. Raffan. Cambridge, Mass.

———. 1997. "From Epiphany to Cult Statue." In A. B. Lloyd (ed.), *What Is a God? Studies in the Nature of Greek Divinity.* London: 15–34.

———. 1998. "Die neuen orphischen Texte: Fragmente, Varianten, 'Sitz im Leben.'" In W. Burkert et al. (eds.), *Fragmentsammlungen philosophischer Texte der Antike—Le raccolte dei frammenti di filosofi antichi.* Aporemata 3. Göttingen: 387–400.

Burn, L. 1987. *The Meidias Painter.* Oxford.

Burnett, A. P. 1985. *The Art of Bacchylides.* Cambridge, Mass.

Burzacchini, G. 1995. "Note al nuovo Simonide." *Eikasmos* 6: 21–38.

———. 1997. Review of W². *Gnomon* 69: 193–98.

Buxton, R. 1994. *Imaginary Greece.* Cambridge.

Cairns, F. 1984. "Propertius and the Battle of Actium (4.6)." In T. Woodman and D. West (eds.), *Poetry and Politics in the Age of Augustus,* 129–168. Cambridge.

Calabi Limentani, I. (ed.). 1964. *Plutarchi Vita Aristidis.* Florence.

Calame, C. 1987. "Spartan Genealogies." In Bremmer 1987: 153–86.

———. 1995 [1986]. *The Craft of Poetic Speech in Ancient Greece.* Ithaca, N.Y.

Camerarius, J. 1550. *Libellus Scholasticus utilis et valde bonus quo continentur Theognidis . . . Simonidis . . . etc.* Basel.

Cameron, Alan. 1993. *The Greek Anthology: From Meleager to Planudes.* Oxford.

———. 1995. *Callimachus and His Critics.* Princeton.

Campbell, D. A. 1984. "Stobaeus and Early Greek Lyric Poetry." In D. Gerber (ed.), *Greek Poetry and Philosophy: Studies in Honour of Leonard Woodbury,* 51–57. Chico, Calif.

———. 1991. *Greek Lyric III.* Loeb edition. Cambridge, Mass.

Cannatà Fera, M. 1990. *Pindarus: Threnorum Fragmenta.* Rome.

Capra, A., and M. Curti. 1995. "Semidei Simonidei: Note sull'elegia di Simonide per la battaglia di Platea." *ZPE* 107: 27–32.

Carlier, P. 1977. "La vie politique à Sparte sous le Règne de Cleomène 1er." *Ktema* 2: 65–84.

———. 1984. *La royauté en Grèce avant Alexandre.* Strasbourg.

Carrière, J. 1948. *Théognis de Mégare: Étude sur le recueil élégiaque attribué à ce poète.* Paris.

Carson, A. 1988. "Simonides Negative." *Arethusa* 21: 147–57.

———. 1992. "How Not to Read a Poem: Unmixing Simonides from Protagoras." *CP* 87: 110–30.

Castriota, D. 1992. *Myth, Ethos, and Actuality: Official Art in Fifth-century B.C. Athens.* Madison, Wis.

Cataudella, Q. 1927–28. "L'elegia di Semonide e l'ode di Orazio IV.7." *Bollettino di Fil. Class.* 34: 229–32. Repr. in Q. Cataudella, *Intorno ai lirici greci,* 16–20. Rome 1972.

Catling, H. W. 1982. "Excavations and Study at the Menelaion, Sparta, 1978–81." Λακωνικαί Σπουδαί 6: 28–43.

———. 1983. "Study at the Menelaion, 1982–3." Λακωνικαί Σπουδαί 7: 23–31.

Cavanagh, W., and C. Mee. 1995. "Mourning before and after the Dark Age." in C. Morris (ed.), *Klados: Essays in Honour of J. N. Coldstream.* London: 45–61.

Cavarzere, A. 1996. *Sul limitare: Il "motto" e la poesia di Orazio.* Bologna.

Choremis, A. K. 1977. "Γεραιστὸς (Καστρι) Καρυστίας." *Archaiologikon Deltikon* 28. Chron.: 305–6.

Christ, G. 1941. *Simonidesstudien.* Freiburg.

Clarendon, Edward, Earl of. 1888. *History of the Rebellion and Civil Wars in England.* Ed. W. Dunn Macray. Vol. VI. Oxford.

Cody, J. V. 1976. *Horace and Callimachean Aesthetics.* Collection Latomus 147. Brussels.

Cohen, B. 1994. "From Bowman to Clubman: Herakles and Olympia." *Art Bulletin* 76: 695–715.

Coldstream, J. N. 1976. "Hero-Cults in the Age of Homer." *JHS* 96: 8–17.

Cole, T. 1992. *Pindar's Feasts or the Music of Power.* Rome.

Coles, R., and D. Obbink. 1998. "Oxyrhynchus: A City and Its Texts." at http://www.csad.ox.ac.uk/POxy/ (Oct. 1, 1998).

Collard, C. 1975. *Euripides: Suppplices*. Edited with Introduction and Commentary. Groningen.

Colli, G. 1977. *La sapienza greca*. Vol. I. Milan.

Conte, G. B. 1986. *The Rhetoric of Imitation: Genre and Poetic Memory in Virgil and Other Latin Poets*. Ithaca, N.Y.

Copley, F. O. 1956. "Catullus, c. 38." *TAPA* 87: 125–29.

Cougny, E. (ed.). 1890. *Epigrammatum Anthologia Palatina cum Planudeis et Appendice Nova*. Vol. III. Paris.

Crane, G. 1986. "Tithonus and the Prologue to Callimachus' *Aetia*." *ZPE* 66: 269–78.

Crawley, A. E. 1893. "Achilles at Skyros." *CR* 7: 243–45.

Cribiore, R. 1994. "A Homeric Writing Exercise and Reading Homer in School." *Tyche* 9: 1–8.

Crönert, W. 1903. *Memoria Graeca Herculanensis*. Leipzig. Repr. Hildesheim 1963.

Cuffari, G. 1983. *I riferimenti poetici di Imerio*. Palermo.

Cummer, W. 1978. "The Sanctuary of Poseidon at Tainaron, Lakonia." *AM* 93: 35–43.

Cumont, F. 1940. "Une pierre tombale érotique de Rome." *L'Antiquité Classique* 9: 5–11.

———. 1942 [1966]. *Recherches sur le symbolisme funéraire des Romains*. Paris.

———. 1949. *Lux Perpetua*. Paris.

Cunliffe, R. J. 1963. *A Lexicon of the Homeric Dialect²*. Norman, Okla.

Curty, O. 1995. *Les parentés légendaires entre cités grecques*. Paris.

Cyrino, M. S. 1995. *In Pandora's Jar: Lovesickness in Early Greek Poetry*. Lanham, Md.

Danielewicz, J. 1994. "Nowo odkryte elegie Simonidesa." *Meander* 49: 211–18.

Davies, M. 1983. "Alcman 59ᴬ P." *Hermes* 111: 496–97.

———. 1987. "Description by Negation: History of a Thought-Pattern in Ancient Accounts of Blissful Life." *Prometheus* 13: 265–84.

———. 1988. *Epicorum Graecorum Fragmenta*. Göttingen.

Davison, J. A. 1955. "Quotation and Allusions in Early Greek Literature." *Eranos* 53: 125–40.

Day, J. 1989. "Rituals in Stone." *JHS* 109: 16–28.

———. 2000. "Epigram and Reader: Generic Force as (Re-)Activation of Ritual." In Depew and Obbink 2000: 37–57.

Denniston, J. D. 1954. *The Greek Particle²*. Oxford.

Dentzer, J.-M. 1982. *Le motif du banquet couché dans le Proche-Orient et le monde grec du VIIème au IVème siècle avant J.-C.* Paris.

Depew, M., and D. Obbink (eds.). 2000. *Matrices of Genre: Authors, Canons, and Society*. Cambridge, Mass.

De Selincourt, E., and H. Darbishire (eds.). 1947. *William Wordsworth: Poetical Works*. Vol. IV. Oxford.

Dewald, C. 1987. "Narrative Surface and Authorial Voice in Herodotus' *Histories*." *Arethusa* 20: 147–70.

Dickins, G. 1906–7a. "The *Hieron* of Athena Chalkioikos." *ABSA* 13: 138–39.

———. 1906–7b. "A Sanctuary on the Megalopolis Road." *ABSA* 13: 169–73.

Diehl, E. 1925. *Anthologia Lyrica Graeca*. Vol. II. Leipzig.

———. 1954. "Pontarches." *RE* 22: 1–18.

Diggle, J. 1970. *Euripides: Phaethon*. Cambridge.

———. 1994. *Euripidis Fabulae*. Vol. III. Oxford.

Dillery, J. 1995. *Xenophon and the History of His Times*. London.

D'Ippolito, G. 1993. "Compattezza e novità nella poesia di Mimnermo (auto- e intertestualità." In R. Pretagostini (ed.), *Tradizione e innovazione nella cultura greca da Omero all'età ellenistica: Scritti in onore di Bruno Gentili*. Vol. 1: 285–300. Rome.

Dodds, E. R. 1960. *Euripides: Bacchae²*. Oxford.

———. 1959. *Plato: Gorgias*. Oxford.

Dougherty, C. and L. Kurke, eds. *Cultural Poetics in Archaic Greece: Cult, Performance, Politics*. Cambridge.

Dover, K. J. 1993. *Aristophanes. Frogs.* Oxford.

———. 1997. *The Evolution of Greek Prose Style.* Oxford.

Dowden, K. 1989. *Death and the Maiden.* London.

Drews, R. 1976. "The Earliest Greek Settlements on the Black Sea." *JHS* 96: 18–31.

Ducat, J. 1990. *Les hilotes. BCH* Suppl. 20. Paris.

Dzikowski, N. 1939. "The Olbian Inscription *CIG* 2080 Rediscovered." *JHS* 59: 84–91.

Edwards, A. T. 1985. "Achilles in the Underworld: *Iliad, Odyssey* and *Aethiopis.*" *GRBS* 26: 215–27.

Edwards, M. E. 1991. "Being and Seeming: Empedocles' Reply." *Hermes* 119: 282–93.

Edwards, M. W. 1986. "The Conventions of a Homeric Funeral." In J. H. Betts et al. (eds.), *Studies in Honour of T. B. L. Webster.* Vol. I: 84–92. Bristol.

Effe, B. 1995. "Alexandrinische Herrscherlob." In B. Effe and G. Binder (eds.), *Affirmation und Kritik: Zur politischen Funktion von Kunst und Literatur im Altertum.* Trier: 107–23.

Ervin, M. 1959. "Geraistai Nymphai Genethlai and the Hill of the Nymphs: A Problem of Athenian Mythology and Topography." Πλάτων 11: 146–59.

Étienne, R., and M. Piérart. 1975. "Un décret du koinon des hellénes à Platées en l'honneur de Glaucon, fils d' Étéoclès, d'Athènes." *BCH* 99: 51–75.

Falkner, T. M., and J. de Luce (eds.). 1989. *Old Age in Greek and Latin Literature.* Albany.

Fantuzzi, M. 1993. "Il sistema letterario della poesia alessandrina nel III sec. a. C." In G. Cambiano, L. Canfora, and D. Lanza (eds.), *Lo spazio letterario della Grecia antica.* Vol. I.2: 31–73. Rome.

———. 2000. "Theocritus and the Demythologizing of Poetry." In Depew and Obbink 2000: 135–51.

Farnell, L. R. 1907. *Cults of the Greek States.* Vol. IV. Oxford.

———. 1921. *Greek Hero Cults and Ideas of Immortality.* Oxford.

Farrell, J. 1997. "The Phenomenology of Memory in Roman Culture." *CJ* 92: 373–83.

Feeney, D. C. 1991. *The Gods in Epic.* Oxford.

———. 1993. "Horace and the Greek Lyric Poets." In N. Rudd (ed.), *Horace 2000: A Celebration,* 41–63. London.

Fehling, D. 1969. *Die Wiederholungsfiguren und ihr Gebrauch bei den Griechen vor Gorgias.* Berlin.

Ferguson, J. 1975. *Utopias of the Classical World.* London.

Finkelberg, M. 1988. "Ajax's Entry in the Hesiodic Catalogue of Women." *CQ* 38: 31–41.

Finley, M. I. 1975. *The Use and Abuse of History.* London.

Finnegan, R. 1970. *Oral Literature in Africa.* Oxford.

Flach, H. 1883–84. *Geschichte der griechischen Lyrik.* Tübingen.

Flashar, M. 1996. "Die Sieger von Marathon: Zwischen Mythisierung und Vorbildlichkeit." In Flashar, Gehrke, and Heinrich 1996: 63–85.

Flashar, M., H.-J. Gehrke, and E. Heinrich (eds.). 1996. *Retrospektive: Konzepte von Vergangenheit in der griechisch-römischen Antike.* Munich.

Fleischman (Catalog). 1994. *A Passion for Antiquities: Ancient Art from the Collection of Barbara and Lawrence Fleischman.* Malibu.

Flower, M. A. 1994. *Theopompus of Chios: History and Rhetoric in the Fourth Century* B.C. Oxford.

———. 1999. "Simonides, Ephorus, and Herodotus on the Battle of Thermopylae." *CQ* 48: 365–80.

Fontenrose, J. 1968. "The Hero as Athlete." *CSCA* 1: 73–104.

Fornara, C. W. 1970. "The Cult of Harmodios and Aristogeiton." *Philologus* 114: 154–80.

———. 1971. "Evidence for the Date of Herodotus' Publication." *JHS* 91: 25–34.

———. 1981. "Herodotus' Knowledge of the Archidamian War." *Hermes* 109: 149–56.

Fowler, D. P. 1989. "First Thoughts on Closure: Problems and Prospects." *MD* 22: 75–122.

Fowler, R. L. 1987. *The Nature of Early Greek Poetry: Three Preliminary Studies.* Toronto.

———. 1998. "Genealogical Thinking, Hesiod's *Catalogue*, and the Creation of the Hellenes." *PCPS* 44: 1–19.

Fraenkel, E. 1957. *Horace.* Oxford.

———. 1964 [1948]. "The Latin Studies of Hermann and Wilamowitz." In E. Fraenkel, *Kleine Beiträge zur klassischen Literatur.* Vol. II: 563–76. Rome. [First publ. *JRS* 38: 28–34.]

Fränkel, H. 1921. *Die homerischen Gleichnisse.* Göttingen.

———. 1962. *Dichtung und Philosophie des frühen Griechentums²*. [1st ed. 1951.] Munich.

———. 1973 [1951]. *Early Greek Poetry and Philosophy.* Trans. by M. Hadas and J. Willis. New York.

Fraser, P. M. 1961. "The Foundation-Date of the Alexandrian Ptolemaieia." *HThR* 54: 141–45.

———. 1972. *Ptolemaic Alexandria.* 3 vols. Oxford.

Fraser, P. M., and Matthews, E. 1987. *A Lexicon of Greek Personal Names.* Vol. I: *The Aegean Islands, Cyprus, Cyrenaica.* Oxford.

French, A. 1987. *Sixth Century Athens: The Sources.* Sydney.

Friedländer, P., with the collaboration of H. B. Hoffleit. 1948 [1987]. *Epigrammata: Greek Inscriptions in Verse from the Beginnings to the Persian Wars.* Berkeley.

Fritze, H. von. 1896. "Zu den griechischen Totenmahlreliefs." *AM* 21: 347–66.

Fröhder, D. 1994. *Die dichterische Form der homerischen Hymnen.* Spudasmata 53. Hildesheim.

Frost, F. J. 1980. *Plutarch's* Themistocles: *An Historical Commentary.* Princeton.

Funghi, M. S., and G. Messeri Savorelli. 1992. "Lo 'scriba di Pindaro' e le biblioteche di Ossirinco." *SCO* 42: 43–62.

Fuqua, C. 1981. "Tyrtaeus and the Cult of Heroes." *GRBS* 22: 215–26.

Gabathuler, M. 1937. *Hellenistische Epigramme auf Dichter.* St. Gallen.

Gale, M. 1994. *Myth and Poetry in Lucretius.* Cambridge.

Galinsky, G.K. 1996. *Augustan Culture.* Princeton.

Gallavotti, C. 1973–74. "Il proemio di Empedocle." *Helikon* 13/14: 7–34.

Gantz, T. 1993. *Early Greek Myth.* Baltimore.

Garland, R. 1985. *The Greek Way of Death.* Ithaca, N.Y.

———. 1992. *Introducing New Gods.* London.

Garner, R. 1990. *From Homer to Tragedy: The Art of Allusion in Greek Poetry.* London.

———. 1993. "Achilles in Locri: P. Oxy. 3876 frr. 37–77." *ZPE* 96: 153–65.

Gatz, B. 1967. *Weltalter, goldene Zeit und sinnverwandte Vorstellungen.* Spudasmata 16. Hildesheim.

Gelinne, M. 1988. "Les Champs Élysées et les Îles des Bienheureux chez Homère, Hésiode et Pindare." *Les études classiques* 56: 225–40.

Gentili, B. 1968. "Epigramma ed elegia." In *L'épigramme Grecque.* Entretiens Hardt 14: 39–81.

———. 1985. *Poesia e pubblico nella Grecia antica da Omero al V secolo.* Rome.

———. 1988. *Poetry and Its Public in Ancient Greece: From Homer to the Fifth Century.* Trans. by T. Cole. Baltimore.

Georges, P. 1994. *Barbarian Asia and the Greek Experience: From the Archaic Period to the Age of Xenophon.* Baltimore.

Gera, D. 1997. *Warrior Women: The Anonymous "Tractatus de mulieribus."* Mnemosyne Suppl. 162. Leiden.

Gerber, D.E. 1991. "Early Greek Elegy and Iambus 1921–1989." *Lustrum* 33: 7–225.

———. 1994. "Greek Lyric Poetry since 1920. Part II: From Alcman to Fragmenta Adespota." *Lustrum* 36: 7–188.

——— (ed.). 1997. *A Companion to the Greek Lyric Poets.* Mnemosyne Suppl. 173. Leiden.

Giangrande, G. 1968. "Sympotic Literature and Epigram." In *L'Épigramme grecque.* Entretiens Hardt 14: 93–177.

Gigante, M. 1993. "Attendendo Posidippo." *SIFC* 11: 5–11.

———. 1994. "Orazio tra Simonide e Posidippo." *Atti dell' Accademia delle Scienze di Torino: Supplemento al Vol. 128, Classe di Scienze Morali, Storiche e Filologiche*, 55–71.

Gill, C., and T. P. Wiseman (eds.). 1993. *Lies and Fiction in the Ancient World*. Austin.

Gnoli, P., and J.-P. Vernant (eds.). 1982. *La mort, les morts dans les sociétés anciennes*. Cambridge.

Goldhill, S. 1988. "A Footnote in the History of Greek Epitaphs: Simonides 146 Bergk." *Phoenix* 42: 189–97.

Gomme, A. W., and F. H. Sandbach. 1973. *Menander: A Commentary*. Oxford.

Goodwin, W. W. 1890. *Syntax of the Moods and Tenses of the Greek Verb*. Boston.

Gould, J. 1973. "Hiketia." *JHS* 93: 74–103.

———. 1994. "Religion in Herodotus." In Hornblower 1994: 91–106.

Gow, A. S. F. 1952. *Theocritus²*. 2 vols. Cambridge.

Graf, F. 1985. *Nordionische Kulte: Religionsgeschichtliche und epigraphische Untersuchungen zu den Kulten von Chios, Erythrai, Klazomenai und Phokaia*. Bibliotheca Helvetica Romana 21. Rome.

Grene, D. 1987. *Herodotus: The History*. Chicago.

Griffin, J. 1977. "The Epic Cycle and the Uniqueness of Homer." *JHS* 97: 39–53.

Griffith, M. 1975. "Man and the Leaves: A Study of Mimnermos Fr. 2." *CSCA* 8: 73–88.

———. 1983. *Aeschylus: Prometheus Bound*. Cambridge.

Griffiths, A. 1976. "What Syagros Said: Herodotus 7.159." *LCM* 1: 23–24.

———. 1989. "Was Kleomenes Mad?" In Powell 1989: 51–78.

Griffiths, F. T. 1979. *Theocritus at Court*. Mnemosyne Suppl. 55. Leiden.

Groningen, B. A. van. 1960. *Pindare au banquet*. Leiden.

———. 1966. *Theognis: Le premier livre*. Amsterdam.

Guerrini, R. 1970–71. "I frammenti degli Eraclidi di Euripide." *SCO* 19–20: 15–31.

Gutzwiller, K. 1998. "Meleager: From Menippean to Epigrammatist." In M. A. Harder, R. F. Regtuit, and G. C. Wakker (eds.), *Genre in Hellenistic Poetry*, 81–93. Groningen.

Habicht, C. 1961. "Falsche Urkunden zur Geschichte Athens im Zeitalter der Perserkriege." *Hermes* 89: 1–35.

———. 1970. *Gottmenschentum und griechische Städte²*. Munich.

———. 1985. *Pausanias' Guide to Ancient Greece*. Berkeley.

Hall, E. 1989. *Inventing the Barbarian*. Oxford.

Hall, J. M. 1995. "Approaches to Ethnicity in the Early Iron Age of Greece." In N. Spencer (ed.), *Time, Tradition and Society in Greek Archaeology: Bridging the Great Divide*, 6–17. London.

———. 1997. *Ethnic Identity in Greek Antiquity*. Cambridge.

Hammond, N. G. L. 1992. "Plataea's Relations with Thebes, Sparta, and Athens." *JHS* 112: 147–50.

Hardie, A. 1997. "Philitas and the Plane Tree." *ZPE* 119: 21–36.

Hardie, P. 1986. *Virgil's Aeneid: Cosmos and Imperium*. Oxford.

Harrison, E. 1902. *Studies in Theognis*. Cambridge.

Harrison, S. J. 1993. "*Dulce et decorum*: Horace *Odes* 3.2.13." *RM* 116: 91–93.

Harrison, T. 2000. *Divinity and History: The Religion of Herodotus*. Oxford.

Harvey, A. E. 1955. "The Classification of Greek Lyric Poetry." *CQ* 5: 157–75.

———. 1994. "The Contribution of Papyrology to the Study of Greek Literature: Archaic and Hellenistic Poetry." In *Proceedings of the 20th International Congress of Papyrologists, Copenhagen, 23–29 August, 1992*, 98–105. Copenhagen.

Haslam, M. W. 1993. Review of W². *BMCR* 4: 131–35.

Hedreen, G. 1991. "The Cult of Achilles in the Euxine." *Hesperia* 60: 313–30.

Helly, B. 1995. *L'état thessalien: Aleuas le Roux, les tétrades et les tagoi*. Lyon.

Helm, R. 1933. Review of Oates 1932. *PhW* 888–91.

Henderson, Jeffrey. 1987. *Aristophanes' Lysistrata*. Edited with Introduction and Commentary. Oxford.

Henderson, John. 1996. "Polishing off the Politics: Horace's Ode to Pollio, 2.1." *MD* 37: 59–136. [Revised in J. Henderson, *Fighting for Rome*, 108–159. Cambridge 1998.]

Hennig, D. 1992. "Herodot 6, 108: Athen und Plataiai." *Chiron* 22: 13–24.

Henry, W. B. 1998. "Simonides, *PMG* 541." *ZPE* 121: 303–4.

Hense, O. 1916. "Johannes Stobaios (18)." *RE* 9: 2549–86.

Herington, J. 1985. *Poetry into Drama*. Berkeley.

———. 1991. "The Poem of Herodotus." *Arion* ser. 3.1: 5–16.

Herman, G. 1987. *Ritualised Friendship and the Greek City*. Cambridge.

Hernández Muñoz, F. 1989. "Tipologia de las faltas en las citas euripideas de los manuscritos de Estobaeo." *CFC* 23: 131–55.

Heubeck, A., and A. Hoekstra. 1989. *A Commentary on Homer's Odyssey*. Vol. II: *Books IX–XVI*. Oxford.

Hiller, E. 1886. "Die antiken Verzeichnisse der pindarischen Dichtungen." *Hermes* 21: 257–71.

Hind, J. G. F. 1983–84. "Greek and Barbarian Peoples on the Shore of the Black Sea." *AR* 30: 71–97.

———. 1993. "Archaeology of the Greek and Barbarian Peoples Around the Black Sea." *AR* 39: 82–112.

Hinds, S. 1998. *Allusion and Intertext: Dynamics of Appropriation in Roman Poetry*. Cambridge.

Hollis, A. S. 1996. "Heroic Honours for Philetas?" *ZPE* 110: 56–62.

Hommel, H. 1980. *Der Gott Achilleus*. Sitzungsberichte der Heidelberger Akademie der Wissenschaften, Philosophisch-historische Klasse. Heidelberg.

Hooker, J. T. 1988. "The Cults of Achilles." *RM* 131: 1–7.

Hornblower, S. 1991a. *A Commentary on Thucydides*. Vol. I: *Books I–III*. Oxford.

———. 1991b. *The Greek World 479–323 B.C.* Revised ed. London.

———. 1992. "The Religious Dimension to the Peloponnesian War." *HSCP* 94: 169–97.

——— (ed.). 1994. *Greek Historiography*. Oxford.

———. 1996. *A Commentary on Thucydides*. Vol. II: *Books IV–V.24*. Oxford.

Hornblower, S., and A. Spawforth (eds.). 1996. *The Oxford Classical Dictionary*[3]. Oxford.

How, W. W., and J. Wells. 1928. *A Commentary on Herodotus*. 2 vols. [Reprint, with corrections, of 1912 edition.] Oxford.

Howie, J. G. 1998. "Thucydides and Pindar: The *Archaeology* and *Nemean 7*." *Papers of the Leeds International Seminar* 10: 75–130.

Hubbard, T. K. 1994. "Elemental Psychology and the Date of Semonides of Amorgos." *AJP* 115: 175–97.

Hunink, V. 1997. *Apuleius of Madaura: Pro Se De Magia*. 2 vols. Amsterdam.

Hunter, R. 1993a. "One Party or Two? Simonides 22 West[2]." *ZPE* 99: 11–14.

———. 1993b. *The Argonautica of Apollonius: Literary Studies*. Cambridge.

———. 1996. *Theocritus and the Archaeology of Greek Poetry*. Cambridge.

Huntington, R., and P. Metcalf. 1991. *Celebrations of Death: The Anthropology of Mortuary Ritual*. Cambridge.

Huttner, U. 1997. *Die Politische Rolle der Heraklesgestalt im griechischen Herrschertum*. Stuttgart.

Huxley, G. 1969. *Greek Epic Poetry*. Cambridge, Mass.

Irwin, E. 1974. *Colour Terms in Greek Poetry*. Toronto.

Isager, S. 1999. "The Pride of Halicarnassos: Editio Princeps of an Inscription from Salmakis." *ZPE* 123: 1–23.

Jaeger, W. 1959. "The Greek Ideas of Immortality." *HThRev* 52: 135–47.

———. 1966 [1932]. "Tyrtaeus on True Arete." In W. Jaeger, *Five Essays*, 101–42. Trans. by A. M. Fiske. Montreal.

Janko, R. 1981. "The Structure of the Homeric Hymns: A Study in Genre." *Hermes* 109: 9–24.

———. 1992. *The Iliad: A Commentary.* Vol. IV: *Books 13–16.* Cambridge.

———. 2000. *Philodemus: On Poems I.* Oxford.

Jebb, R. 1914. *Sophocles: The Plays and Fragments.* Vol. I: *The Oedipus Tyrannus.* Cambridge.

Jeffery, L. H. 1961. *The Local Scripts of Archaic Greece.* Oxford.

Johnson, E. L. 1988. "Grieving for the Dead, Grieving for the Living: Funeral Laments of Hakka Women." In J. L. Watson and E. S. Rawski (eds.), *Death Ritual in Late Imperial and Modern China*, 135–62. Berkeley.

Jones, C. P. 1996. "ἔθνος and γένος in Herodotos." *CQ* 46: 315–20.

———. 1999. *Kinship Diplomacy in the Ancient World.* Cambridge, Mass.

Jost, M. 1985. *Sanctuaires et cultes d'Arcadie.* Paris.

Kahane, A. 1994. *The Interpretation of Order: A Study in the Poetics of Homeric Repetition.* Oxford.

Kambylis, A. 1963. "Zur 'Dichterweihe' des Archilochos." *Hermes* 91: 129–50.

Kearns, E. 1989. *The Heroes of Attica.* BICS Suppl. 57. London.

Kelly, F. 1976. *Audacht Morainn.* Dublin.

Kelly, T. 1966. "The Calaurian Amphictyony." *AJA* 70: 113–21.

———. 1967. "The Argive Destruction of Asine." *Historia* 16: 422–31.

Kennell, N. M. 1996. *The Gymnasium of Virtue: Education and Culture in Ancient Sparta.* Chapel Hill.

Kierdorf, W. 1966. *Erlebnis und Darstellung der Perserkriege.* Hypomnemata 16. Göttingen.

Kiessling, A., and R. Heinze (eds.). 1958–59. *Q. Horatius Flaccus.* 3 vols. Berlin.

Kligman, G. 1988. *The Wedding of the Dead: Ritual, Poetics, and Popular Culture in Transylvania.* Berkeley.

Klos, Herbert. 1947. *Der Einfluss der archaischen Poesie auf das Werk des Herodotos.* Diss. Vienna.

Knox, B. M. W. 1979. "Myth and Attic Tragedy." In B. M. W. Knox, *Word and Action: Essays on the Ancient Theater*, 3–24. Baltimore.

Knudsen, A. 1988. "Men Killed for Women's Songs." *Culture and History* 3: 79–97.

Koenen, L. 1976. "Egyptian Influence in Tibullus." *ICS* 1: 127–59.

———. 1994. "Greece, the Near East, and Egypt: Cyclic Destruction in Hesiod and the *Catalogue of Women*." *TAPA* 124: 1–34.

Kokolakis, M. M. 1987. "'Ἱμερόεις γόος.' Ἀπὸ τὸν Ὅμηρο στὴν τραγικὴ καθαργή." In Φίλια Ἔπη εἰς Γεώργιον Ε. Μυλωνᾶν, 215–44. Athens.

Koller, H. 1956. "Das kitharodische Prooimion: Eine formgeschichtliche Untersuchung." *Philologus* 100: 159–206.

Korzeniewski, D. 1968. *Griechische Metrik.* Darmstadt.

Kovacs, D. 1994. *Euripides.* Vol. I. Loeb edition. Cambridge, Mass.

Kranz, W. 1961. "Sphragis: Ichform und Namensiegel als Eingangs- und Schlußmotiv antiker Dichtung." *RM* 104: 3–46, 97–124. Repr. in W. Kranz, *Studien zur antiken Literatur und ihrem Fortwirken*, 27–78. Heidelberg 1967.

Krischer, T. 1965. "Herodots Prooimion." *Hermes* 93: 159–67.

Kurke, L. 1991. *The Traffic in Praise.* Ithaca, N.Y.

Kurtz, D. C. 1984. "Vases for the Dead: An Attic Selection, 750–400 B.C." in H. A. G. Brijder (ed.), *Ancient Greek and Related Pottery*, 314–28. Amsterdam.

Kurtz, D. C., and J. Boardman. 1986. "Booners." *Greek Vases in the J. Paul Getty Museum* 3: 35–70.

Laks, A. 1997. "Du témoignage comme fragment." In Most 1997a: 237–72.

Lambin, G. 1988. "Ἔλεγος et ἐλεγεῖον." *RPh* 62: 69–77.

Lardinois, A. P. M. H. 1995. "Wisdom in Context: The Use of Gnomic Statements in Archaic Greek Poetry." Diss. Princeton.

———. 1997. "Modern Paroemiology and the Use of Gnomai in Homer's *Iliad*." *CP* 92: 213–34.

Laroche, D. 1989. "Nouvelles observations sur l'offrande de Platées." *BCH* 113: 183–98.

Larson, J. 1995. *Greek Heroine Cults*. Madison.

Lateiner, D. 1989. *The Historical Method of Herodotus*. Toronto.

Latyschev, V. V. 1916. *Inscriptiones Antiquae Orae Septemtrionalis Ponti Euxini*[2]. Petrograd.

Lauer, J.-Ph., and C. Picard. 1955. *Les statues ptolémaïques du Serapieion de Memphis*. Paris.

Lazenby, J. F. 1975. "Pausanias, Son of Kleombrotos." *Hermes* 103: 235–51.

———. 1988. "Aischylos and Salamis." *Hermes* 116: 168–85.

———. 1993. *The Defence of Greece*. Warminster.

Leaf, W. 1900–1902. *The Iliad*. 2 vols. London.

Lebedev, A. 1996. "Pharnabazos, the Diviner of Hermes: Two Ostraka with Curse Letters from Olbia." *ZPE* 112: 268–72.

Lefkowitz, M. 1969. "Bacchylides Ode 5: Imitation and Originality." *HSCP* 73: 45–96.

———. 1981. *The Lives of the Greek Poets*. Baltimore.

———. 1991. *First-Person Fictions: Pindar's Poetic "I."* Oxford.

Lehnus, L. 1989. *Bibliografia Callimachea*. Genova.

Lello-Finuoli, A. L. di. 1967. "Il Florilegio Laurenziano." *QUCC* 4: 139–73.

Lerat, L. 1946. "Geraistos et les Geraistai." *RA* 25: 196–203.

Lévêque, P. 1991. "Le blond Ptolémé, les héros et les dieux." In *Mélanges É. Bernand*, 303–7. Paris.

Lewis, D. M. 1977. *Sparta and Persia*. Leiden.

———. 1987. "Bowie on Elegy: A Footnote." *JHS* 107: 188.

Lewis, D. M., J. Boardman, S. Hornblower and M. Ostwald (eds.). 1994. *Cambridge Ancient History*. Vol. VI: *The Fourth Century B.C.* Cambridge.

Lincoln, B. 1980. "On the Imagery of Paradise." *Indogermanische Forschungen* 85: 151–64.

Linders, T., and G. Nordquist (eds.). 1987. *Gifts to the Gods*. Boreas 15. Uppsala.

Livrea, E. 1997. "*Callimachus senex, Cercidas senex* ed i loro critici." *ZPE* 119: 37–42.

Lloyd-Jones, H. 1963. "The Seal of Posidippus." *JHS* 83: 75–99. Repr. in Lloyd-Jones 1990: 158–95.

———. 1975. *Females of the Species: Semonides on Women*. Ridge Park, N.J.

———. 1978. "Iterum de 'Catabasi Orphica'." *Kyklos: Griechisches und Byzantinisches Rudolf Keydell zum neunzigsten Geburtstag*. Berlin: 1978: 88–100 (with P. J. Parsons). Repr. in Lloyd-Jones 1990: 333–42.

———. 1985. "Pindar and the Afterlife." In *Pindare*. Entretiens Hardt 17.245–83. Repr. in Lloyd-Jones 1990: 80–105, Addendum 105–9.

———. 1990. *Greek Comedy, Hellenistic Literature, Greek Religion, and Miscellanea: The Academic Papers of Sir Hugh Lloyd-Jones*. Oxford.

———. 1994. "Notes on the New Simonides." *ZPE* 101: 1–3.

Lobel, E. 1925. Σαπφοῦς Μέλη. Oxford.

———. 1954. "2327: Early Elegiacs." *The Oxyrhynchus Papyri* 22: 67–76.

———. 1981. "Simonides." In *Papyri Greek and Egyptian, Edited by Various Hands, in Honour of E. G. Turner on the Occasion of his Seventieth Birthday*, 21–23. London.

Loomis, W. T. 1990. "Pausanias, Byzantion and the Formation of the Delian League. A Chronological Note." *Historia* 39: 487–92.

Loraux, N. 1982a. "Mourir devant Troie, tomber pour Athènes: De la gloire du héros à l'idée de la cité." In Gnoli and Vernant 1982: 27–43.

———. 1982b. "Ponos. Sur quelques difficultés de la peine comme nom du travail." *Annali del seminario di studi del mondo classico, Napoli: Archeologia e storia antica* 4: 171–92.

———. 1986 [1981]. *The Invention of Athens: The Funeral Oration in the Classical City*. Cambridge, Mass.

Lüders, H. 1959. *Varuna*. Vol. II. Göttingen.

Luppe, W. 1988. "Zu einer Stobaios-Stelle aus Euripides." *Hermes* 116: 504–5.

———. 1993. "Zum neuesten Simonides: P.Oxy. 3965 Fr. 1/2327 Fr. 6." *ZPE* 99: 1–9.

————. 1994. "Die Korinther in der Schlacht von Plataiai bei Simonides nach Plutarch (Simon. Fr. 15 und 16 W²; *P.Oxy.* 3965 Fr. 5)." *Arch. f. Pap.* 40: 21–24.

Luria, A. R. 1975. *The Mind of a Mnemonist.* Trans. by L. Solotaroff. Harmondsworth.

Lynn, J. K. 1995. "Narrators and Narration in Callimachus." Diss. Columbia.

Maas, P. 1922. Review of *Oxyrhynchus Papyri*, Vol. 115. *PhW* 42: 577–84.

Macan, R. W. 1908. *Herodotus: The Seventh, Eighth and Ninth Books.* Vol. I, part 2. London.

Mace, S. 1993. "Amour, Encore! The Development of δηὖτε in Archaic Lyric." *GRBS* 34: 335–64.

Maftei, M. 1976. *Antike Diskussionen über die Episode von Glaukos und Diomedes im VI. Buch der Ilias.* Beiträge zur klass. Philologie 74. Meisenheim.

Malkin, I. 1994. *Myth and Territory in the Spartan Mediterranean.* Cambridge.

Mansfeld, J. and D. Runia. 1997. *Aëtiana: The Method and Intellectual Context of a Doxographer.* Vol. I: *The Sources.* Leiden.

Marinatos, N., and Hägg, R. (eds.). 1993. *Greek Sanctuaries: New Approaches.* London.

Marincola, J. 1996. "Introduction." In *Herodotus: The Histories*, trans. by A. de Sélincourt. Penguin edition. London.

Masaracchia, A. (ed.). 1978. *La sconfitta dei Persiani: Libro IX delle Storie.* Milan.

Mastronarde, D. J. 1994. *Euripides: Phoenissae.* Cambridge.

Matthews, V. J. 1974. *Panyassis of Halikarnassos.* Mnemosyne Suppl. 33. Leiden.

Mazzarino, S. 1966. *Il pensiero storico classico.* Bari.

McKay, K. J. 1959. "Hesiod's Rejuvenation." *CQ* 9: 1–5.

McKeown, J. 1987. *Ovid: Amores.* Vol. I. Liverpool.

McNamee, K. 1981. *Abbreviations in Greek Literary Papyri and Ostraca.* BASP Suppl. 3. Chico, Calif.

————. 1992. *Sigla and Select Marginalia in Greek Literary Papyri.* Papyrologica Bruxellensia 26. Brussels.

Meiggs, R., and D. Lewis. 1969. *A Selection of Greek Historical Inscriptions to the End of the Fifth Century B.C.* Oxford.

Meillier, C. 1979. *Callimaque et son temps.* Lille.

Meincke, W. 1965. *Untersuchungen zu den enkomiastischen Gedichten Theokrits.* Diss. Kiel.

Merkelbach, R. 1951. "Eine orphische Unterweltsbeschreibung auf Papyrus." *MH* 8: 1–11.

————. 1952. "Bettelgedichte (Theokrit, Simonides und Walther von der Vogelweide)." *RM* 95: 312–27.

————. 1956. "Literarische Texte unter Ausschluss der Christlichen." *Arch. f. Pap.* 16. 82–129

Mersch, A. 1995. "Archäologischer Kommentar zu den 'Gräbern der Athener und Plataier' in der Marathonia." *Klio* 77: 55–64.

Mette, H. J. 1961. "*Genus tenue* und *mensa tenuis* bei Horaz." *MH* 18: 136–39.

Miller, A. W. 1986. *From Delos to Delphi: A Literary Study of the Homeric Hymn to Apollo.* Mnemosyne Suppl. 93. Leiden.

Minnen, P. van, and K. A. Worp. 1993. "The Greek and Latin Literary Texts from Hermopolis." *GRBS* 34: 151–86.

Mitscherlich, C. W. 1800. *Q. Horati Flacci Opera.* 2 vols. Leipzig.

Moles, J. L. 1993. "Truth and Untruth in Herodotus and Thucydides." In Gill and Wiseman 1993: 88–121.

Molyneux, J. H. 1992. *Simonides: A Historical Study.* Wauconda, Ill.

Morpurgo, A. 1927. "Οἴη περ φύλλων . . . (Iliade, vi)." *A&R* 8: 81–87.

Most, G. W. 1994. "Simonides' Ode to Scopas in Contexts." In I. J. F. de Jong and J. P. Sullivan (eds.), *Modern Critical Theory and Classical Literature.* Mnemosyne Suppl. 130. Leiden: 127–52.

———— (ed.). 1997a. *Collecting Fragments—Fragmente Sammeln.* Aporemata 1. Göttingen.

————. 1997b. "Hesiod's Myth of the Five (or Three or Four) Races." *PCPS* 43: 104–27.

Murray, A. T., and G. E. Dimock. 1995. *Homer: The Odyssey Books 13–24*. Loeb edition. Cambridge, Mass.

Murray, O. 1988. "Death and the Symposion." *A.I.O.N. (sez. di archeologia e storia antica)* 10: 239–57.

——— (ed.). 1990. *Sympotica: A Symposium on the* Symposion. Oxford.

Müller, K. O. 1858. *A History of the Literature of Ancient Greece*. Trans. G. C. Lewis and J. W. Donaldson. Vol. I. London.

Müller, L. 1900. *Q. Horatius Flaccus: Oden und Epoden*. 2 vols. Leipzig.

Nagy, G. 1976. "The Name Achilles: Etymology and Epic." In A. M. Davies and W. Meid (eds.), *Studies in Greek, Italic, and Indo-European Linguistics Offered to L. R. Palmer*, 209–37. Innsbruck.

———. 1979. *The Best of the Achaeans: Concepts of the Hero in Archaic Greek Poetry*. Baltimore.

———. 1987. "Herodotus the *Logios*." *Arethusa* 20: 175–84.

———. 1989. "Early Greek Views of Poets and Poetry." In G. Kennedy (ed.), *Cambridge History of Literary Criticism*, Vol. I: 1–77. Cambridge.

———. 1990. *Pindar's Homer: The Lyric Possession of an Epic Past*. Baltimore.

———. 1996. *Poetry as Perfomance: Homer and Beyond*. Cambridge.

Nicholson, N. 1999/2000. "Pederastic Poets and Adult Patrons: Maintaining Authority in Late Archaic Lyric." *CW* 93: 235–59.

Nikitinski, O. 1996. *Kallimachos-Studien*. Frankfurt a. M.

Nilsson, M. P. 1951. *Cults, Myths, Oracles and Politics in Ancient Greece*. Lund.

———. 1967. *Geschichte der griechischen Religion*³. Vol. I. Munich.

Nisbet, R. G. M. 1987. "The Oak and the Axe: Symbolism in Seneca, *Hercules Oetaeus* 1618ff." In M. Whitby et al. (eds.), *Homo Viator: Classical Essays for J. Bramble*, 243–251. Bristol.

———. 1995. *Collected Papers on Latin Literature*. Oxford.

Nisbet, R.G.M., and M. Hubbard. 1970. *A Commentary on Horace, Odes I*. Oxford.

———. 1978. *A Commentary on Horace, Odes II*. Oxford.

Nisetich, F. J. 1977. "The Leaves of Triumph and Mortality: Transformation of a Traditional Image in Pindar's *Olympian* 12." *TAPA* 107: 235–64.

Nock, A. D. 1972. *Essays on Religion and the Ancient World*. Vol. II. Oxford.

Norden, E. 1909. *Einleitung in die Altertumswissenschaft*. Vol. I. Berlin.

Nyland, R. 1992. "Herodotos' Sources for the Plataiai Campaign." *L'antiquité classique* 61: 80–97.

Oates, W. J. 1932. *The Influence of Simonides of Ceos upon Horace*. Princeton. Repr. New York 1971.

Obbink, D. 1993. "The Addressees of Empedocles." *MD* 31: 51–98.

———. 1996. "The Hymnic Structure of the New Simonides." *Arethusa* 29.2: 193–203.

———. 1998a. Images of *POxy* vol. 59. At http: //www.csad.ox.ac.uk/POxy/ (Oct. 1, 1998).

———. 1998b. "Athenians at Plataea." At http: //www.csad.ox.ac.uk/POxy/ (Oct. 1, 1998).

———. Forthcoming. "Readers and Intellectuals at Oxyrhynchus." In A. K. Bowman et al. (eds.), *Oxyrhynchus: A City and Its Texts*. London.

O'Hara, J. J. 1998. "Venus or the Muse as 'Ally' (Lucr. 1.24, Simon. Frag. eleg. 11.20–22 W)." *CP* 93: 69–74.

Orelli, J. G., and J. G. Baiter. 1850. *Q. Horatius Flaccus*. 2 vols. Tours.

Osborne, R. 1993. "Competitive Festivals and the Polis: A Context for Dramatic Festivals at Athens." In A. H. Sommerstein et al. (eds.), *Tragedy, Comedy, and the Polis*, 21–38. Bari.

———. 1996. *Greece in the Making*. London.

Otis, B. 1964. *Vergil, a Study in Civilized Poetry*. Oxford.

Padel, R. 1974. "Imagery of the Elsewhere. Two Choral Odes of Euripides." *CQ* 24: 227–41.

Page, D. L. 1936. "The Elegiacs in Euripides' *Andromache*." In *Greek Poetry and Life: Essays presented to Gilbert Murray*, 206–30. Oxford.

———. 1955. *Sappho and Alcaeus: An Introduction to the Study of Ancient Lesbian Poetry.* Oxford.

———. 1968. *Lyrica Graeca Selecta.* Oxford.

———. 1981. *Further Greek Epigrams.* Cambridge.

Palmer, L. 1963. *The Interpretation of Mycenaean Greek Texts.* Oxford.

Papachatzis, N.D. 1976. "Ποσειδῶν Ταινάριος." *Archaiologike Ephemeris:* 102–25.

Parker, R. 1983. *Miasma: Pollution and Purification in Early Greek Religion.* Oxford.

———. 1989. "Spartan Religion." In Powell 1989: 142–72.

———. 1996. *Athenian Religion: A History.* Oxford.

Parry, A. 1972. "Language and Characterization in Homer." *HSCP* 76: 1–22.

Parsons, P. 1992a. "3965: Simonides, Elegies." *The Oxyrhynchus Papyri* 59: 4–50.

———. 1992b. "Poesia ellenistica: Testi e contesti." *Aev. Ant.* 5: 9–19.

———. 1994. "Summing Up." In *Proceedings of the 20th International Congress of Papyrologists, Copenhagen, 23–29 August, 1992,* 122. Copenhagen.

Pasquali, G. 1920. *Orazio lirico.* Florence.

———. 1968. *Pagine stravaganti.* Vol. II. Florence.

Pavese, C.O. 1995. "Elegia di Simonide agli Spartiati per Platea." *ZPE* 107: 1–26.

Pelling, C. 1997. "East Is East and West Is West—Or Are They? National Stereotypes in Herodotus." *Histos* 1.

Percy, W. A., III. 1996. *Pederasty and Pedagogy in Archaic Greece.* Urbana.

Perrotta, G. 1978 [1926]. "La chiusa del *Tolomeo.*" In G. Perrotta, *Poesia ellenistica: Scritti minori,* Vol. II: 180–86. Rome.

Pfeiffer, R. (ed.). 1949. *Callimachus.* 2 vols. Oxford.

———. 1968. *History of Classical Scholarship: From the Beginnings to the End of the Hellenistic Age.* Oxford.

Podlecki, A. J. 1968. "Simonides: 480." *Historia* 17: 257–75.

Poltera, O. 1997. *Le langage de Simonide.* Bern.

———. 1998. "Von Seleukos zu Simonides und Zurück: Simon. PMG 540." *MH* 55: 129–30.

Poralla, P. 1985 [1913]. *Prosopographie der Lakedaimonier bis auf die Zeit Alexanders des Grossen².* Ed. A. Bradford. Chicago.

Powell, A. (ed.). 1989. *Classical Sparta: Techniques behind Her Success.* London.

——— (ed.). 1995. *The Greek World.* London.

Powell, J. E. 1938. *A Lexicon to Herodotus².* Cambridge.

Powell, J. U. 1925. *Collectanea Alexandrina.* Oxford.

Prandi, L. 1988. *Plataea: Momenti e problemi della storia di una polis.* Padova.

Prato, C. (ed.). 1968. *Tyrtaeus: Fragmenta.* Rome.

Pritchett, W. K. 1979. *The Greek State at War.* Part 3. Berkeley.

———. 1985. *The Greek State at War.* Part 4. Berkeley.

Putnam, M. C. J. 1986. *Artifices of Eternity: Horace's Fourth Book of Odes.* Ithaca, N.Y.

Raaflaub, K. 1985. *Die Entdeckung der Freiheit: Zur historischen Semantik und Gesellschafts-geschichte eines politischen Grundbegriffes der Griechen.* Munich.

Race, W. H. 1987. "P. Oxy. 2438 and the Order of Pindar's Works." *RM* 130: 407–10.

Raubitschek, A. E. 1968. "Das Denkmal-Epigramm." In *L'épigramme grecque.* Entretiens Hardt 14: 3–36. Repr. in A. E. Raubitschek, *The School of Hellas,* 245–65. New York 1991.

Reiner, E. 1938. *Die rituelle Totenklage der Griechen.* Stuttgart.

Richardson, N. J. 1974. *The Homeric Hymn to Demeter.* Oxford.

———. 1993. *The Iliad: A Commentary.* Vol. VI: *Books 21–24.* Cambridge.

Richter, G. M. A. 1965. *The Portraits of the Greeks.* London. Revised and Abridged by R. R. R. Smith: Ithaca, N.Y., 1984.

Ridgway, B. S. 1990. *Hellenistic Sculpture.* Madison, Wis.

Robert, L. 1948. "Épigrammes relatives à des gouverneurs." In L. Robert, *Hellenica* 4: 35–114. Paris.

Roberts, D. H., F. M. Dunn, and D. P. Fowler (eds.). 1997. *Classical Closure.* Princeton.

Robertson, N. 1986. "A Point of Precedence at Plataia: The Dispute between Athens and Sparta over Leading the Procession." *Hesperia* 55: 88–106.

Rohde, E. 1925. *Psyche: The Cult of Souls and Belief in Immortality among the Ancient Greeks.* Trans. by W. B. Hillis. London.

Roller, D. W. 1974. "A New Map of Tanagra." *AJA* 78: 152–56.

Roller, L. E. 1981. "Funeral Games for Historical Persons." *Stadion* 7: 1–18.

Romm, J. 1994. *The Edges of the Earth in Ancient Thought.* Princeton.

Rosenmeyer, P. A. 1991. "Simonides' Danae Fragment Reconsidered." *Arethusa* 24: 5–29.

———. 1992. *The Poetics of Imitation: Anacreon and the Anacreontic Tradition.* Cambridge.

Rosenmeyer, T. G. 1982. "History or Poetry? The Example of Herodotus." *Clio* 11: 239–59.

Rösler, W. 1990. "Mnemosyne in the Symposion." In Murray 1990: 230–37.

Rossi, Laura E. 1996. "Il testamento di Posidippo e le laminette auree di Pella." *ZPE* 112: 59–65.

Roussel, D. 1976. *Tribu et cité: Études sur les groupes sociaux dans les cités grecques aux époques archaïque et classique.* Paris.

Rubin, D. C. 1995. *Memory in Oral Traditions.* New York.

Rumpel, I. 1883. *Lexicon Pindaricum.* Leipzig.

Rupp, E. 1988. "The 'Royal' Tombs at Salamis (Cyprus): Ideological Messages of Power and Authority." *Journal of Mediterrenean Archaeology* 1: 111–39.

Ruppel, W. 1927. "Zur Verfassung und Verwaltung der amorginischen Städte." *Klio* 21: 313–39.

Russo, J. 1982. "Interview and Aftermath: Dream, Fantasy, and Intuition in *Odyssey* 19 and 20." *AJP* 103: 4–18.

———. 1992. *A Commentary on Homer's Odyssey.* Vol. III: *Books XVII–XXIV.* Oxford.

Rutherford, I. C. 1990. "Paeans by Simonides." *HSCP* 93: 169–209.

———. 1996. "The New Simonides: Towards a Commentary." In *The New Simonides, Arethusa* 29.2: 167–92.

———. 1997. "For the Aeginetans to Aiakos a Prosodion: An Unnoticed Title at Pindar *Paean* 6, 123 and Its Significance for the Poem." *ZPE* 118: 1–21.

———. 2001. *Pindar's Paeans: A Reading of the Fragments with a Survey of the Genre.* Oxford.

———. Forthcoming. "An Ally for My Song Or What Simonides' Plataea-Poem May Have Meant to Timotheus."

Salapata, G. 1997. "Hero Warriors from Korinth and Lakonia." *Hesperia* 66: 245–60.

Sanchez-Wildberger, M. 1955. *Theokrit-Interpretationen.* Diss. Zurich.

Sbardella, L. 2000. "Achille e gli eroi di Platea: Simonide, frr. 10–11 W^2." ZPE 129: 1–11.

Sbordone, F. 1976. *Ricerche sui papiri Ercolanesi.* Vol. II. Naples.

Schachter, A. 1994. *Cults of Boiotia.* Vol. III. London.

———. 1998. "Simonides' Elegy on Plataia: The Occasion of Its Performance." *ZPE* 123: 25–30.

Schefold, K. 1997. *Die Bildnisse der antiken Dichter, Redner und Denker^2.* Basel.

Schein, S. L. 1984. *The Mortal Hero: An Introduction to Homer's Iliad.* Berkeley.

Schneider, R. M. 1986. *Bunte Barbaren.* Worms.

Schneidewin, F. G. 1835. *Simonidis Cei Carminum Reliquiae.* Brunswick.

Schumacher, R. 1993. "Three Related Sanctuaries of Poseidon." In Marinatos and Hägg 1993: 62–87.

Scodel, R. 1980. "Hesiod Redivivus." *GRBS* 21: 301–20.

Seaford, R. 1994. *Reciprocity and Ritual: Homer and Tragedy in the Developing City State.* Oxford.

Sedley, D. 1989. "The Proems of Empedocles and Lucretius." *GRBS* 30: 269–96.

Segal, C. P. 1985. "Messages to the Underworld: An Analysis of Poetic Immortality in Pindar." *AJP* 106: 199–212.

————. 1993. *Euripides and the Poetics of Sorrow: Art, Gender, and Commemoration in Alcestis, Hippolytus, and Hecuba.* Durham, N.C.

Seremetakis, N. C. 1991. *The Last Word: Women, Death and Divination in Inner Mani.* Chicago.

Seters, J. van. 1983. *In Search of History: Historiography in the Ancient World and the Origins of Biblical History.* New Haven, Conn.

Severyns, A. 1938. *Recherches sur la Chrestomathie de Proclos.* Vol. I. Paris.

Shapiro, H. A. 1991. "The Iconography of Mourning in Athenian Art." *AJA* 95: 629–56.

Shipley, G. 1987. *A History of Samos, 800–188 B.C.* Oxford.

Sider, D. 1982. "Empedocles' *Persika.*" *Ancient Philosophy* 2: 76–78.

————. 1997. *The Epigrams of Philodemos.* New York.

Sideras, A. 1971. *Aeschylus Homericus.* Hypomnemata 31. Göttingen.

Simon, E. 1967. "Boreas und Oreithyia auf dem silbernen Rhyten in Triest." *A&A* 13: 101–26.

Sinn, U. 1993. "Greek Sanctuaries as Places of Refuge." In Marinatos and Hägg 1993: 88–109.

Sinos, R. H. 1993. "Divine Selection: Epiphany and Politics in Ancient Greece." In Dougherty and Kurke 1993: 73–91.

Slater, W. J. 1969. *Lexicon to Pindar.* Berlin.

————. 1976. "Symposion at Sea." *HSCP* 80: 161–70.

Slatkin, L. 1991. *The Power of Thetis.* Berkeley.

Slings, S. R. 1978. "Anacreon's Two Meadows." *ZPE* 30: 38.

Smith, K. F. 1901. "Some Irregular Forms of the Elegiac Distich." *AJP* 22: 165–94.

Snell, B. 1969. *Tyrtaios und die Sprache des Epos.* Hypomnemata 22. Göttingen.

Snodgrass, A. M. 1988. "The Archaeology of the Hero." in *La parola, l'immagine, la tomba: Atti del Colloquio Internazionale di Capri = AION (Arch.-Storia ant.)* 10: 19–26.

Sourvinou-Inwood, C. 1988. "'Myth' and History: On Herodotus III.48 and 50–53." *Opuscula Atheniensia* 17: 167–82.

————. 1995. *"Reading" Greek Death.* Oxford.

————. 1997. "Elysion." In H. Cancik and H. Schneider (eds.), *Der Neue Pauly,* Vol. III: 1004–5. Stuttgart.

Spawforth, A. 1994. "The Persian Wars Tradition and the Roman Empire." In Hornblower 1994: 233–47.

Spencer, N. (ed.). 1995. *Time, Tradition and Society in Greek Archaeology: Bridging the Great Divide.* London.

Stehle, E. 1997. *Performance and Gender in Ancient Greece.* Princeton.

Stella, L. A. 1946. "Studi Simonidei." *RFIC* 24: 1–24.

Stupperich, R. 1977. *Staatsbegräbnis und Privatgrabmal im klassischen Athen.* Diss. Münster.

Suárez de la Torre, E. "El adjetivo ἐπώνυμος en la elegía por la batalla de la Platea de Simónides (fr. 11.17 West²)." *Lexis* 16: 29–32.

Syme, R. 1958. *Tacitus.* Oxford.

Tarkow, T. A. 1983. "Tyrtaeus 9 D: The Role of Poetry in the New Sparta." *AC* 52: 48–69.

Tausend, K. 1992. *Amphiktyonie und Symmachie.* Historia Einzelschriften 73. Stuttgart.

Taylor, M. 1991. *The Tyrant Slayers².* Salem, N.Y.

Thomas, R. 1989. *Oral Tradition and Written Record in Classical Athens.* Cambridge.

Thönges-Stringaris, R. 1965. "Das griechische Totenmahl." *AM* 80: 1–99.

Tod, M. N. 1933. *Greek Historical Inscriptions.* Vol. I. Oxford.

Tomlinson, R. A. 1995–96. "Archaeology in Greece: Arkadia." *AR* 42: 12.

Trevett, J. 1990. "History in Demosthenes 59." *CQ* 40: 407–20.

Tuomi, R. 1986. καὶ νῦν: Solons Gedicht an Mimnermos im Lichte der Tradition. Turku.

Turner, E. G. 1987. *Greek Manuscripts of the Ancient World².* Rev. P. J. Parsons. BICS Suppl. 46. London.

Unger, G. F. 1877. "Die Isthmientag und die Hyakinthien." *Philologus* 37: 34–40.

Ursinus, F. 1568. *Carmina novem illustrium feminarum . . . et lyricorum . . . .* Antwerp.

Vanderpool, E. 1942. "An Inscribed Stele from Marathon." *Hesperia* 11: 329–37.

———. 1969. "Three Prize Vases." *Archaiologikon Deltikon* 24: 1–5.

Vandiver, E. 1991. *Heroes in Herodotus: The Interaction of Myth and History.* Frankfurt a. M.

Verdin, Herman. 1977. "Les remarques critiques d'Hérodote et de Thucydide sur la poésie en tant que source historique." In *Historiographia Antiqua* (Festschrift W. Peremans). Symbolae Facultatis Litterarum et Philosophiae Lovaniensis, ser. A. Vol. VI: 53–76. Leuven.

Vermeule, E. 1979. *Aspects of Death in Early Greek Art and Poetry.* Berkeley.

Verrall, A. W. 1903. "Two Unpublished Inscriptions from Herodotus." *CR* 17: 98–102.

Versnel, H. 1987. "What Did Ancient Man See When He Saw a God? Some Reflections on Greco-Roman Epiphany." In D. van der Plas (ed.), *Effigies Dei,* 42–55. Leiden.

Vetta, M. (ed.) 1983. *Poesia e simposio nella Grecia antica: Guida storica e critica.* Rome.

———. 1992. "Il simposio: La monodia e il giambo." In *Lo spazio letterario della Grecia antica.* Vol. I: *La produzione e la circolazione del testo,* Pt. 1, *La polis,* 177–218. Rome.

Vian, F. 1944. "Les Géants de la Mer." *RA* 22: 97–117.

Vox, O. 1997. *Carmi di Teocrito e dei poeti bucolici minori.* Turin.

Wachsmuth, C., and O. Hense. 1884–1912. *Ioannis Stobaei Anthologium.* 5 vols. Berlin.

Waern, I. 1951. Γῆς Ὀστέα: *The Kenning in Pre-Christian Greek Poetry.* Uppsala.

Wagner, H. 1970. "Studies in the Origin of Early Celtic Civilisation, I: Old Irish FIR 'Truth, Oath.'" *Zeitschrift für celtische Philologie* 31: 14.

Walbank, F. 1979. *A Historical Commentary on Polybius.* Vol. III. Oxford.

Wardman, A.E. 1959. "Tactics and the Tradition of the Persian Wars." *Historia* 8: 49–60.

———. 1960. "Myth in Greek Historiography." *Historia* 9: 403–13.

Waterhouse, H., and R. Hope-Simpson. 1960. "Prehistoric Laconia: Part 1." *ABSA* 55: 67–107.

———. 1961. "Prehistoric Laconia. Part 2." *ABSA* 56: 114 -75.

Watkins, C. 1979. "Is Tre Fir Flathemen: Marginalia to the Audacht Morainn." *Eriu* 30: 181–98. Repr. in C. Watkins, *Selected Writing.* Innsbruck 1994: 626–43.

———. 1995. *How To Kill a Dragon: Aspects of Indo-European Poetics.* Oxford.

Weber, G. 1993. *Dichtung und höfische Gesellschaft: Die Rezeption von Zeitgeschichte am Hof der ersten drei Ptolemäer.* Stuttgart.

Weber, O. von. 1955. *Die Beziehungen zwischen Homer und den älteren griechischen Lyrikern.* Diss. Bonn.

Webster, T. B. L. 1967. *The Tragedies of Euripides.* London.

Wees, H. van. 1992. *Status Warriors: War, Violence and Society in Homer and History.* Amsterdam.

Welwei, K.-W. 1979. "Das sogenannte Grab der Plataier im Vranatal bei Marathon." *Historia* 28: 101–6.

———. 1991. "Heroenkult und Gefallenenehrung im antiken Griechenland." In G. Binder and B. Effe (eds.), *Tod und Jenseits im Altertum.* Bochumer Altertumswissenschaftliches Colloquium 6: 50–70. Trier.

West, D. 1995. *Horace Odes I: Carpe Diem.* Oxford.

West, M. L. 1966. *Hesiod Theogony.* Oxford.

———. 1969. "Hesiodea." *CQ* 11: 132–36.

———. 1974. *Studies in Greek Elegy and Iambus.* Berlin.

———. 1978. *Works and Days.* Oxford.

———. 1985. *The Hesiodic Catalogue of Women.* Oxford.

———. 1992. *Ancient Greek Music.* Oxford.

———. 1993a. "Simonides Redivivus." *ZPE* 98: 1–14.

———. 1993b (trans.). *Greek Lyric Poetry.* Oxford.

West, W. C. 1977. "Hellenic Homonoia and the New Decree of Plataea." *GRBS* 18: 307–19.

Westlake, H. D. 1977. "Thucydides on Pausanias and Themistocles: A Written Source?" *CQ* 27: 95–100.

Whitley, J. 1988. "Early States and Hero Cults: A Re-appraisal." *JHS* 108: 173–82.

———. 1994. "The Monuments that Stood before Marathon: Tomb Cult and Hero Cult in Archaic Attica." *AJA* 98: 213–30.

Wickersham, J. 1994. *Hegemony in Greek Historians.* Baltimore.

Wide, S. 1893. *Lakonische Kulte.* Darmstadt. Repr. Stuttgart 1973.

Wilamowitz-Moellendorf, U. 1893 [1935]. "De Tribus Carminibus Latinis Commentatio." *Index Schol. Hib.* Göttingen 1893/94. Repr. in U. Wilamowitz-Moellendorf, *Kleine Schriften.* Vol. II: 249–74.

———. 1913. *Sappho und Simonides.* Berlin. Repr. Berlin 1966.

———. 1922. *Pindaros.* Berlin.

Wilkinson, L. P. 1933. Review of Oates 1932, *CR* 47: 87–88.

Wimmel, W. 1960. *Kallimachos in Rom.* Stuttgart.

Woodman, T. 1974. "*Exegi Monumentum*: Horace *Odes* 3.30." in T. Woodman and D. West (eds.), *Quality and Pleasure in Latin Poetry,* 115–28. Cambridge.

Wordsworth, W. 1989. *Shorter Poems, 1807–1820.* Ed. C. H. Ketcham. Ithaca, N.Y.

Wright, M. R. 1981. *Empedocles: The Extant Fragments.* New Haven.

Yates, F. A. 1966. *The Art of Memory.* Chicago.

Yatromanolakis, D. 1998. "Simonides fr. eleg. 22 W^2: To Sing or To mourn?" *ZPE* 120: 1–11.

———. Forthcoming. *Sappho in the Making: Images of Sappho in Greek and Roman Antiquity.*

Young, D. 1961. *Theognis.* Leipzig.

Zanker, P. 1995. *The Mask of Socrates: The Image of the Intellectual in Antiquity.* Berkeley.

Zuntz, G. 1956. "Interpretation of a Menander Fragment (Fr. 416 Koerte = 481 Kock)." *PBA* 42: 209–46.

———. 1971. *Persephone: Three Essays on Religion and Thought in Magna Graecia.* Oxford.

———. 1972. "Is the Heraclidae Mutilated? In G. Zuntz, *Opuscula Selecta: Classica, Hellenistica, Christiana,* 43–53. Manchester. (Originally publ. *CQ* 41 [1947]: 46–52.)

Index Locorum

Note: Fragment numbers for Archilochus, Callinus, Mimnermus, Simonides, Solon, and Tyrtaeus are those of W² unless otherwise noted. Passing references, especially those given in footnotes, are not indexed here. Numbers in italics refer to ancient sources; numbers in Roman type refer to pages in this volume.

Aelius Aristides
  31.2, 204, 211, 221–24 (see also Simonides fr. *528 PMG*)

Aeschylus
  Agamemnon 398, 44
  Myrmidons, 5
  Persians 395ff., 37; *817*, 39, 102, 137
  Fr. 69.2–4, 188 n.15
  Vita Aeschyli 8, 79

Alcman
  26 PMG, 197

Ammianus
  14.6.7, 262

Anacreon
  6 FGE, 211
  358 PMG, 195

Anacreontea
  53 West, 197f.

Anonymous
  980 SH, 249

Apollonius Rhodius
  1.18–22, 241 n.31
  4.216f., 288
  Scholia to: *1.211–15*, 14, 35; *1.583–4a*, 13, 36

Apuleius
  Apology 9.6, 266f.

Aratus *Phaenomena*
  16–18, 71

Archilochus
  1, 95
  13, 90
  15, 109
  196a.42–44, 193

Aristophanes
  Birds 676–736, 70 n.15; *685*, 288
  Clouds 1357–58, 40
  Frogs, passim, 191f., 195
  Lysistrata 1150–56, 1247–61, 128
  Peace 698ff., 57 n.17
  Scholia to: *Peace 736ff.*, 38

Athenaeus
  536B, 178 n.70

Bacchylides
  3.88–92, 251f.
  5.63–67, 287
  13.22, 44

Callimachus
  Aetia 1.17–38, 244–54 passim; *1.32–36*, 197
  Fr. 64, 57

Callinus
  1.19, 183
  6, 5

Catullus
  38.8, 212, 265
  64.105–9, 258

Choerilus
  2 PEG/SH 317, 119

Cicero
  De Oratore 2.352–53, 264

Demosthenes
  Epitaphios 1391, 137, 159

Diodorus Siculus
  11.33, 150, 151

"Eion poem"
  38, 42, 126–27, 154f.

Empedocles
  B 17.3, 287
  B 35, 72–73, 240
  B 128, 193
  B 131, 70–71

Euripides
  Alcestis 886–87, 876–77, 897–99, 217
  Andromache 91–93, 90 n.15; *103–116*, 90, 220 n.63
  Bacchae 402–16, 199; *403ff.*, 52
  Hercules Furens 637–700, 247, 251
  Hippolytus 732ff., 53, 198, 210, 269

Ion 1299, 109
Iphigenia in Tauris 217, 44
Scholia to: *Orestes 990*, 178

Herodotus
  1.30, 149; *1.163–67*, 149
  5.75, 46; *5.114*, 149
  6.105f., 143f.; *6.108*, 47
  7.159, 125; *7.163f.*, 15; *7.178.2*,
    123; *7.189*, 35, 110, 123, 145;
    7.228.3, 47
  8.8, 15, 36; *8.96.2*, 37; *8.131*,
    141
  9.6–10, 131; *9.19*, 47, 87, 88,
    127–28; *9.20*, 122; *9.22–23*,
    47; *9.23–25*, 122; *9.26–27*,
    137; *9.27*, 125; *9.31*, 129;
    9.33–36, 88, 127; *9.36*, 21,
    88; *9.41*, 122; *9.46–48*, 129;
    9.57, 23; *9.62*, 130; *9.63–64*,
    173; *9.65*, 130; *9.69*, 132;
    9.78, 173 n.42; *9.70*, 150;
    9.76, 122, 124; *9.85*, 102, 133,
    150

Hesiod
  Theogony 70 n.15; 22, 246f.;
    81–84, 246; *815*, 109
  Works and Days 10, 70; *27*, 70;
    159f., 183, 236; *654–59*, 97

Himerius
  Or. 47, 37

Homer
  Iliad 2.468, 288; *2.484–93*, 71;
    2.553f., 154
  6.145–49, 273f.; *6.146*, 24;
    6.357–58, 183; *6.358*, 108
  9.150–53, 292–95, 170
  12.10–16, 183f.; *12.23*, 184, 236;
    12.243, 122
  15.653, 47
  16.20, *744*, *787*, *843*, 156 and
    n.46; *16.849f.*, 68
  18.56f., 258
  21.184–89, 235f.; *21.464–66*,
    274
  22.369ff., 122
  23.19–20, 44; *23.62ff.*, 216;
    23.179–80, 44

  Odyssey 5.239, 114
  6.44–45, 191
  8.489, 111
  9.19–20, 115
  12.183, 46, 110
  20.61–65, *79–81*, 216
  24.36–94, 95; *24.36–97*, 86,
    112; *24.39–40*, 257f.

  Scholia to: *Il. 7.76*, 17

Homeric Hymns
  Apollo 172f., 70 n.16; *545*, 94;
    545f., 69
  Hymn 6, 70 n.16

Horace
  Epode 16, 52, 199, 269
  Odes 1.15, 268; *1.38*, 269f.
    2.1.37–40, 265; *2.20*, 270f.
    3.2, 261; *3.30.1–5*, 263
    4.1, 252; *4.6*, 256–60; *4.7*,
    51, 283f.; *4.9*, 266

Ibycus
  287 PMG, 252

Isocrates
  Panegyrikos 84, 148, 163
  Plataikos 150–51

Isyllus 36

"Longinus"
  On the Sublime 13.3, 122

Lucian
  Pro imaginibus 19, 241 n.32
  Vera historia 2.4–29, 190;
    2.5–6, *13–14*, 192; *2.19*, 194
    n.49

Lucillius
  AP 11.408.2, 61

Lucretius 71
  1.24, 46

Meiggs-Lewis inscriptions
    (ML)
  23, 138; *34*, 139; *95*, 140

Meleager
  AP 7.419, 250f.

Mimnermus
  1, 282
  2, 230f., 252, 280f.
  6, 253
  13, 92

Mousaios
  B 5 DK, 287

Papyri Oxyrhynchi
  2327, 7–29 passim, 33, 34, 35,
    59, 65–66, 69, 74–75 n.37,
    81, 82 n.70, 185, 237f.,
    255f.
  2430, 33, 59, 66
  2431, 66
  2432, 66

2433, 66
2434, 66
2623, 59, 66
2624, 66
3876, 167, 179
3965, 7–29 passim, 33, 35, 59,
    65f.

Parmenides
  B 8.52, 46

Pausanias
  2.1.8, 169
  3.24.5, 169
  9.29.4, 92
  10.10.1, 138; *10.7.4–6*, 219 n.59

Philetairos
  17.2–3 KA, 193f.

Pindar
  Isthmian 8, 179 n.75
  Nemean 2.14f., 155
  Olympian 2, 192; *12.13–16*,
    287; *13.96–97*, 45 n.61, 109,
    113
  Paean 2, 41, 48, 132 n.47; *6*,
    259
  Pythian 1, 70; *1.77*, 39, 41, 132
    n.47
  Fr. 77, 48 with n.69; *125*, 201;
    129, 192; *272*, 15; *346*, 287
  Vita Pindari Ambrosiana 15, 37

Plato
  Republic 363c–d, 192 n.39

Plutarch
  Aristides 19, 150; *20*, 100; *21*,
    102, 151
  *De Herodoti Malignitate 36 p.
    869c*, 37; *42 p. 872*, 22–23,
    80, 100f., 128, 132
  Pericles 8.9, 159
  Themistocles 15.4, 15–16

Poseidippos
  705.21–25 SH, 247f.

Quintilian
  10.1.64, 212, 265

SEG
  30.869, 168
  38.1476, 137

Semonides
  1, 229–30
  29 D, 226

Simonides (and "Simonides")
Frr. 1–4, 36–37, 89
1–22, 13–29
3, 35–36, 78, 123, 140, 145, 174
    n.51
4, 140
5–7, 37
7, 35
8–9, 37–38
10, 43, 259
10–18 (see below, Simon.
    Plataea poem)
11, 43–47, 60–61, 67–184 pas-
    sim, 232–41 passim, 256
12, 47
13, 47, 103
14, 48, 92
15–16, 48–49, 80
17, 49
18, 49
19–20, 50–51, 60, 82, 84,
    229–31, 279, 285f.
19–21, 5
19–22, 242–54 passim
21, 5, 46, 84
21–22, 51–53, 64
22, 82, 84, 185–231, 267–69,
    271
23, 202 n.82
23–92, 53–54
26, 226–31 passim
34, 34, 53, 81–82
70, 46
86, 37, 47
87, 49
88, 264
89, 46, 50, 84
116, 257

6 FGE, 47
8 FGE, 98–99
9 FGE, 49, 99
11 FGE, 48
15 FGE, 47, 99
16 FGE, 87, 103
17a FGE, 41, 99
17b FGE, 127
19 FGE, 37
20 FGE, 87
40 FGE (see above, "Eion
    poem")
64 FGE, 49

74 FGE, 49
79 FGE, 285 n.28

506 PMG, 76
508 PMG, 76
510 PMG, 54
511 PMG, 76
512 PMG, 76
513 PMG, 76
514 PMG, 77
515 PMG, 63 and n.47, 77
519 PMG, 76, 78
520–25 PMG, 218
523 PMG, 183, 236
524 PMG, 261
528 PMG, 52, 201–2 n.82, 204,
    208, 211, 222f.
529 PMG, 204, 211, 222
531 PMG, 46, 63–64, 118, 127,
    158f., 263, 283
532 PMG, 78
533 PMG, 35, 78
534 PMG, 35, 78
535 PMG, 37
537 PMG, 33
540 PMG, 33
541 PMG, 66
542 PMG, 63, 64, 282
543 PMG, 64, 223
556 PMG, 189 n.22
557 PMG, 29
558 PMG, 42, 189 n.22
564 PMG, 282
570 PMG, 189 n.22
571 PMG, 38
572 PMG, 48
579 PMG, 282
581 PMG, 282
582 PMG, 261
584 PMG, 282
594 PMG, 283

Plataea poem 38–42, 54, 59,
    65–184 passim
Sea-Battle of Artemisium [?],
    34–37, 59, 78, 89, 267f.
Sylloge Simonidea, 33
Threnoi, 33

Solon
1, 111
20, 253, 286

Stesichorus
Geryoneis 8.1–4 SLG, 187f.

Stobaeus
4.34.28, 24, 60, 62, 226–31
    passim, 272f.; *4.34*, 278

Suda
s.v. *Simonides*, 33–34, 35, 57,
    74–75, 276

Tacitus
Ann. 12.58, 137

Theocritus
7.61ff., 52, 209f.
16, 45, 57, 61, 87, 222
17, 232–41 passim
Scholia on: *16.34–35* (see
    Simonides fr. 528 *PMG*);
    16.36–37 (see Simonides fr.
    529 *PMG*)

Theognis (and *Theognidea*)
250, 188
1345–50, 51

Thucydides
1.21, 135; *1.21–22*, 120; *1.23*, 145;
    1.132, 41, 173 n.43
2.29, 137; *2.71*, 150 n.10;
    3.58, 150, 152f.; *3.87*, 145
4.116, 136

Tibullus
1.3, 194

Timotheus
Persai 41, 50, 83 n.72; *202ff.*,
    46, 243f.

Tyrtaeus
2, 4–5, 92
4, 4–5
10.1–2, 262
12, 116–18

Vergil
Aeneid 6.309f., 288

General Index

Achilles 38, 40–44, 67f., 71f., 86f., 93f., 98, 112, 155–58, 160, ch. 9 passim, 235, 238–40, ch. 16 passim
Actium, battle of 266f.
addressees in poetry 69-71, 77, 93f., 104, 155–57, 160f.
Aeschylus 4, 44, 123
Agamemnon 146f.
Alexandrian editions 33f., 57, 66, 74f., 77, 228, 276
Anacreon 267
Antiochus, son of Dyseris 203f., 212f., 217f., 222–24
ἀοίδιμος 108, 183, 256
Apion 34, 74 n.37
Apuleius 266
Archilochus 89, 228, 246
Aristides 223
Artemisium poem 35–37
asyndeton 51
ἀθάνατος 116, 123 n.18, 155
Athenian role in poem 45, 47, 61, ch. 6 passim
αὐτὰρ ἐγώ 44f., ch. 3 passim, 93f., 110f., 157, 233 n.1, 239f.

Bacchylides 251f., 266–68
Boreas 36, 123, 143
burial of soldiers 149f.

Callimachus ch. 15 passim
Callinus 4f., 89
Catullus 265
χαῖρε in poetry 44f., 77, 93f., 157f., 232f.
Choerilus 119
Choeroboscus 227, 276
cicada, sound of 245f.
Clarendon, Earl of 145f.
Corinthian role in poem 48f., 63, 80, 101, 125, 132, 172; see also Ephyra
coronis 53, 81

Croesus 149

Delphic Amphictyonies 41
Demeter 47, 49, 129f., 162, 171
"Democritus" epigram 37
Demosthenic Epitaphios 137–39
Dike 87
Dioscuri 46, 54, 140–43, 145, 172f.
dithyramb 78
donkey 53
Dyseris 52, 204, 211, 218, 221f.

Echecratidas 51f., 200f., 201–3, 206, 211–13, 217ff.
Echembrotos 219
Eion epigram 42, 126f., 154
elegy 38 n.22, 78f., 88–92, 219f.
   historic 4f., 89f.
   sympotic 50f., 88, 201–3
Eleutheria festival 40, 151f.
Empedocles 70–73
encomium 196, 202f., 210f.
Ephyra 48f., 171
Epicurus 46
ἐπίκουρος 45f., 63, 71, 107–10, 113
epinician 75–77, 96
epiphany 140–47
eros 193f.
escapism 52f.
Eteoneus 223f.
Euenos 51, 286 n.32
Euphorion 143

garlands 192
γενεή 235f., 274 n.3
Geraistos 176–78
Glaukos 171f.

Harmodios and Aristogeiton 148
Helios 188

hemitheoi 148f., chs. 10, 14 passim
Herakles 234, 236
hero cult 117f., chs. 8–9 passim, 233 n.3
Herodotus 48, 88, 101, chs.6–7 passim
Hesiod 70, 246f., 250, 253
Hiero 45, 237
Himerius 37
Hipponax 250
Histiaeus 168
Homer 72, 94f., 182–84
Homeric Hymns 92, 111f.
Horace 199, 244, chs. 16–17 passim, 283–85
hymn 73f., 84

Ibycus 252
immortality, conveyed by poetry 252; *see also*
    ἀθάνατος, κλέος
inscriptions 97-99
Ion of Chios 89f.
Isles of the Blest 249, 268f.
Isocrates 148, 150, 163
Isthmian Games 179f.

Jagger, Mick, compared to Simonides 56
John, Elton, compared to Simonides 67

Kalais and Zetes 36, 123, 140, 145
Kalauria 176
Kekrops 47, 61, 74, 140
kenning 49
κλέος 72, 87, 94, 96f., 114–17, 133, 153–55, 237,
    247f.
κόσμος ἐπέων 110f., 188f.
Kytenion 137

lagoon 53
leaves, similes involving 253, ch. 18 passim
Leotychidas 141f.
Lucretius 46, 71

marginal signs 34, 81, 82 n.70; *see also* coronis,
    paragraphos
Masistios 122
Megara 125, 171
Megistias 47
Meleager 250f.
Menelaus 146f.
metrical passages in prose 123f.
Mimnermus 4f., 42, 83f., 92, 230f., 252f., 280–83,
    285f.
Mousaios 287
Muses 45f., 114
myth and history 136f.

naumachia 35f., 79
Nicanor 74 n.37
Nisos 171

old age ch. 15 passim, 269, 281f., 286
Oreithyia 36

Oxyrhynchus 59, 66

Pan 143–45
Panathenaia 37
Pandion 47, 102, 128, 171
panhellenism 100
Panyassis 4f., 89
paragraphos 81
patronage 57, 62-64
Pausanias, regent of Sparta 41, 100, 138, 141f., 173f.,
    178–81
Pausanias the Periegete 165, 168f.
Philikos 249
Pindar 37 n.18, 57, 75 n.38, 96
Pittacus 63f., 282
Plataea 38, 141f.
Plataea elegy:
    commissioning/origin 38f., 63, 100f.
    contents/extent 33f., 38, 86–88, 242f.
    date 139 n.18
    form/structure 42–44, 50, 60f., 65–67, 74, 91f.,
        123 n.16, 237–39
    genre 41, ch.3 passim, 120, 133
    language 39, 61f.
    meter 41f., 67, 118
    occasion/performance 40f., 66f., 84, chs. 4 and
        5 passim, 133, 179f.
    persona/performer ch. 5 passim, 155
    proem 41f., 73, 92–102, 153f., 256
Pleistarchos 141f.
Polycrates 240
Poseidippos 69 n.14, 247–49
Poseidon 175–79
Priscian 35
propemptikon 52, 187, 201, 209
Propertius 267
Ptolemy I 233f.
Ptolemy II 232f.

recusatio 51
rejuvenation 52, 195, 197f., 209 n.5, 246, 252,
    269

Salamis poem 37f., 82, 267
Scopas 63; *see also* Pittacus
Semonides 42, 62, 89, ch. 13 passim, 275f., 281
Serpent column 41, 125, 127, 170
simile, Homeric 273f.
Simonides:
    life 56f., 62f., 104
    mercenary nature 45, 56f., 63, 77
    mnemonics 58, 84, 264
    writings 4, 33–36, 57f., 64, 66, 74–79, 202 n.85,
        204, 212, 218, 222
    See also Plataea elegy
Skyllias 36
Solon 4f., 97, 228, 286
Spartan role in the poem 39, 46f., 63, 87, 102–4,
    116–19, 125, 127
sphragis 50, 74, 83, 243

Stobaeus 272–80
stomachs 53

Teisamenos 47f., 61, 88, 113, 172
Tellos 149
Themistocles 40
Theocritus 45, 57, 66, 87, 209f., ch. 14 passim, 286
theoxenia 143
Thersander 123
Thetis 29, 71f., 155
threnody 90f., 98, 105, 203–5, 212, 216–19, 222–24, 265
Thucydides 137, 139
Timotheus 41, 46, 243f.

Trojan War, as paradigm 126f.
Tyndarids, *see* Dioscuri
Tyrtaeus 4f., 42, 89, 92, 107, 117–18, 190

utopia 187–90, 198f.

Wordsworth, W., as source of Parsons's title 55, 64
wrinkles 52, 194f., 216

Xenophanes 42

youth 252f.

Zephyrus 37